Power & Society

AN INTRODUCTION TO THE SOCIAL SCIENCES

Thirteenth Edition

Brigid Callahan Harrison
Montclair State University

WADSWORTH
CENGAGE Learning·

Australia · Brazil · Japan · Korea · Mexico · Singapore · Spain · United Kingdom · United States

WADSWORTH
CENGAGE Learning·

Power & Society: An Introduction to the Social Sciences, Thirteenth Edition
Brigid Callahan Harrison

Publisher: Suzanne Jeans

Executive Editor: Carolyn Merrill

Development Editor: Jennifer Jacobson, Ohlinger Publishing Services

Assistant Editor: Patrick Roach

Editorial Assistant: Eireann Aspell

Media Editor: Laura Hildebrand

Brand Manager: Lydia LeStar

Market Development Manager: Kyle Zimmerman

Sr. Rights Acquisitions Specialist: Jennifer Meyer Dare

Manufacturing Planner: Fola Orekoya

Art and Design Direction, Production Management, and Composition: PreMediaGlobal

Cover Image: © Laurent Renault/ iStockphoto, © Hanquan Chen/iStockphoto, © Marilyn Nieves/iStockphoto, © Jon Schulte/ iStockphoto, © Valeriy Evlakhov/iStockphoto

For product information and technology assistance, contact us at **Cengage Learning Customer & Sales Support, 1-800-354-9706**

For permission to use material from this text or product, submit all requests online at **www.cengage.com/permissions**
Further permissions questions can be emailed to **permissionrequest@cengage.com.**

Library of Congress Control Number: 2012954712

ISBN-13: 978-1-133-60441-9

ISBN-10: 1-133-60441-2

Wadsworth
20 Channel Center Street
Boston, MA 02210
USA

Cengage Learning is a leading provider of customized learning solutions with office locations around the globe, including Singapore, the United Kingdom, Australia, Mexico, Brazil and Japan. Locate your local office at **international.cengage.com/region**

Cengage Learning products are represented in Canada by Nelson Education, Ltd.

For your course and learning solutions, visit **www.cengage.com**

Purchase any of our products at your local college store or at our preferred online store **www.cengagebrain.com**

Instructors: Please visit **login.cengage.com** and log in to access instructor-specific resources.

Printed in the United States of America
1 2 3 4 5 6 7 17 16 15 14 13

BRIEF CONTENTS

CONTENTS

CHAPTER 3   Power and Ideology   43

PART 2   Power and the Social Sciences   71

CHAPTER 4   Power and Culture: An Anthropologist's View   72

PART 3   The Uses of Power   289

CHAPTER 10   Power, Race, and Gender   290

CHAPTER 11   Poverty and Powerlessness   329

CHAPTER 12   Power, Violence, and Crime   351

CHAPTER 13   Power and the Global Community   383

Power & Society: An Introduction to the Social Sciences is designed as a basic text for introductory, interdisciplinary social science courses. It is written specifically for first- and second-year students at community colleges and at four-year colleges and universities that offer a basic studies program. *Power and Society* introduces students to central concepts in anthropology, psychology, sociology, political science, economics, and history. But more important, the text focuses these disciplinary perspectives on a central integrative theme—the nature and uses of power in society. In this way, students are made aware of the interdependence of the social sciences. Compartmentalization is avoided, and students are shown how each social science discipline contributes to an understanding of power.

Power and Society also introduces students to some of the central challenges facing American society: ideological conflict, crime and violence, racism and sexism, community problems, poverty and powerlessness, globalization, and international relations in a post–September 11 world. Each of these challenges is approached from an interdisciplinary viewpoint, with power as the integrating concept.

Power and Society facilitates the introduction of each of the social sciences to students. Hopefully, they find their interest piqued—by one discipline or an interdisciplinary area of inquiry—and that will help them focus their studies in their academic career. *Power and Society* provides a kind of "tasting menu" for the social sciences. Although we hope that students enjoy every chapter thoroughly, we also recognize, and hope that students recognize, the value of when one particular subject stimulates their intellect.

Addressing the theme of power is a useful tool in arousing students' interest because it allows for a real application of each of the social sciences. *Power* has been defined as the capacity to modify the conduct of individuals through the real or threatened use of rewards and punishments. Doubtless other central concepts or ideas in the social sciences might be employed to develop an integrated framework for an introduction to social science. But power certainly is a universal phenomenon that is reflected in virtually all forms of human interaction. Power is intimately related to many other key concepts and ideas in the social sciences—personality, behavior, aggression, role, class, mobility, wealth, income distribution, markets, culture, ideology, change, authority, oligarchy, and the elite. Power is also a universal instrument in approaching the various crises that afflict human beings and their societies—racism, sexism, poverty, violence, crime, urban decay, and international conflict.

Several special features are designed to arouse student interest in the social sciences as well as to help students understand the meaning of various concepts. The first such feature is the presentation of timely, relevant Case Studies in each chapter to illustrate important concepts. Topics include Scientific Research Design: An Experiment in Preventing PTSD; The Rise and Fall of Communism in Russia; Aboriginal Australians; Diagnosing Mental Illness; Achieving Economic Stability; Vietnam: A Political History; How Is Poverty Measured?; The Insanity Defense; and Iran.

In addition, illustrative Focus features throughout the text help maintain student interest. Topics include The Vocabulary of Social Science; Selected Direct Quotations from Ideologies; How to Tell if You're Liberal or Conservative; Social Science Asks: Is Marriage Becoming Obsolete in America?; Address Inequality or Expand the Economy?; Power and the Kingdom of Saudi Arabia; DNA as a Genealogical Tool; Inside the Brain; Evolutionary Psychology: The Mating Game; Posttraumatic Stress Disorder: Not Just a Soldier's Disease; Interest Rates and You; The Concentration of Corporate Power; Rating the Presidents; Explaining Presidential Approval Ratings; Media Power: The Presidential Debates; Dr. Martin Luther King Jr. and the Power of Protest; A Declaration of Women's Rights, 1848; Who Are the Poor?; A Cure for Poverty? The Gates Foundation; It's a Real Crime!; The Least-Developed Countries; Afghanistan; and Know Your Geography.

A third special feature is the International Perspective. Although this book introduces students to the social sciences with principal reference to the American experience, international and comparative perspectives are integrated into each chapter, and several chapters focus exclusively on these perspectives. International Perspective sections within those chapters include Polling the World; Women in the Workforce; Global Inequalities; Depression: A Worldwide Battle; A Look at Government Debt; The Multinationals' Global Economic Power; The Role of Government; The Basic Necessities: Water and Food; The Death Penalty; and Worldwide Urbanization.

A fourth special feature is Controversies in Social Science, designed to stimulate student interest in social science, inspire classroom discussion, and warn students that the social sciences deal with many controversial topics that remain largely unresolved. Topics include the following: Can the Social Sciences Be Scientific?; The World's Missing Girls; Direct versus Representative Democracy; The Occupy Movement; Charles Beard and the Economic Interests of the Founders; Affirmative Action and the Constitution; America's Shame: Our Poor Children; Incarceration versus Education; and When Should the United States Use Military Force?

Critical thinking skills and research methodologies receive greater attention throughout this new edition and are highlighted in a new feature that appears in every chapter, Research This! In Chapter 1, students are asked to analyze the concept of legitimacy as a source of power. Chapter 2 looks at how important religion is in various societies, while in Chapter 3 this feature examines how Americans describe their political ideology, while Chapter 4 asks students to compare the importance of religion in various nations. In Chapter 5, students analyze 2010 Census Bureau data, and in Chapter 6 students analyze and compare the Declaration of

Independence and the Declaration of Sentiments. In Chapter 7, we examine ideology and age, and Chapter 8 looks at bank bailouts. In Chapter 9, students examine the prevalence of serious mental illness in subsets of the population. Chapter 10 asks students to compare laws restricting abortion in the various states, while Social Security recipients are the Research This! topic in Chapter 11. In Chapter 12 this feature examines U.S. citizens' feelings of security where they live, how they have changed over the last decade, and whether this sense of security reflects the changes in national crime rates during this period. Chapter 13 asks students to analyze global population growth, and in Chapter 14, they are asked to think critically about the trend of Americans' confidence in the military.

Key vocabulary terms with definitions are placed in the margins throughout each chapter. The special feature On the Web at the end of each chapter continues to provide students with initial directions for further exploration on the Internet of the topics in each chapter. Updated Web addresses are provided with brief descriptions of the information available at various sites.

The thirteenth edition of *Power and Society* also strives to facilitate students' critical thinking and integrate self-assessment into the text. In the beginning of each chapter, new learning objectives frame that chapter's area of inquiry, helping students navigate each chapter by providing a critical thinking "roadmap." Each chapter ends with a Chapter Summary that has been reorganized to tie into the learning objectives as it recaps the most important concepts of each chapter. A Review Quiz at the end of each chapter enables students to test their own level of comprehension of key concepts within that chapter. These tools are meant to assist students in their studies by providing them with a clear path to the text's content in the beginning, along with an assessment tool to gauge their progress on that path at the end.

With its stimulating and provocative Focus, Case Study, and International Perspective sections, as well as the Controversies in Social Science and Research This! features—all of which provide timeliness, relevance, interest, and perspective to each chapter topic—*Power and Society* strives to be a "teachable" text. Rather than evade or dilute "hot topics"—for example, ideological conflict, genetics versus environmental influences on behavior, power and gender, sexual harassment, mental illness, the neglect of African American and Native American history, affirmative action, violence in American history, the death penalty, and drug legalization—it focuses on controversy as a means of developing student interest and appreciation for the social sciences. The thirteenth edition continues to resist the lamentable tendency in introductory texts to "dummy" material for undergraduate students and shows that social science research and scholarship are relevant to our current societal problems.

As always, coverage has been brought up to date to reflect current events and contemporary concerns. New content includes coverage of the Occupy Wall Street and Tea Party Movements (Chapter 3); coverage of the global economic recession and slow recovery (Chapters 8, 13); new 2010 Census data (Chapters 2, 5, 8, and 11); the 2012 presidential election (Chapter 7); and new developments in international affairs, including the U.S. withdrawal from Iraq (Chapter 14), the use of child soldiers (Chapter 13), and the Arab Spring movements of 2011 throughout the Middle East (Chapter 14).

Each chapter now introduces its discipline, its subfields, and concerns more systematically. Specifically, Chapter 3 includes an updated discussion of Modern Conservatism, and in Chapter 6, a new section that describes the process of historical analysis called, "How Historical Analysis Informs the Social Sciences" has been added. Chapter 12 now features streamlined coverage of violence. In addition, data has been meticulously updated in the narrative, tables, and figures throughout the book.

This edition continues the book's traditional focus on the condition of women and minorities in American society, with specific discussions of "Power and Gender," "Women in the Workforce," "Racism in American History," "The Civil Rights Movement," "Martin Luther King Jr. and the Power of Protest," and "Sexual Discrimination: Sexual Harassment and the Law." This edition also seeks to further integrate analysis of the role of women and racial and ethnic minorities into the text as a whole, not just in boxed features. New to the thirteenth edition is expanded coverage of the struggle for power and rights by people with disabilities and by gays and lesbians.

An instructor's manual filled with lecture ideas and test questions is available. Students may purchase the study guide that provides multiple-choice, true/false, completion, and essay questions to lead them through independent study of the text.

Though Tom Dye's name no longer appears on the cover, he created this book and I remain indebted to him for sharing his considerable intellect, his knowledge of numerous disciplines, and his understanding of the world of publishing with me. I would also like to thank the folks at Cengage for their continuing support, including Executive Editor, Carolyn Merrill; Senior Publisher, Suzanne Jeans; Jennifer Meyer Dare, Scott Greenan, Patrick Roach, and Eireann Aspell. Thanks also to Megan Lessard and Jyotsna Ojha at PreMedia Global. I wish to thank Jennifer Jacobson for her fine efforts in revising *Power and Society* into the thirteenth edition. Jennifer's kindness and sharp attention to detail made this revision a pleasure. Paul Meilak provided wonderful encouragement and support during this revision process. I also would like to thank Caroline, Alexandra, and John Harrison for their patience and good humor (and occasionally being quiet) while I was revising this edition. Able research assistance was provided by Taylor St. John. I would also like to thank Brenda Beach, Ph.D., who reviewed the text and provided valuable feedback, and authored the Test Bank, PowerPoint Slides, and Web Quizzes that accompany this edition. Many thanks to those who provided guidance on this and past editions:

Hugh M. Arnold, Clayton College and State University
Hal Bass, Ouachita Baptist University
Brenda Beach, Kaplan University
Janet Bennion, Lyndon State University
Brett Benson, Lewis-Clark State College
Liz Clark, Kaplan University
Charles Cotter, Florida State University
Kimberly Cowell-Meyers, Christopher Newport University
Michael S. Cummings, University of Colorado–Denver
Fred Dauser, Talladega College
William G. Davis, University of California at Davis
Sean Duffy, Quinnipiac University
Marcy Jean Everest, King's College

Geraldine Finn, University of Findlay
Paul George, Miami Dade Community College
Todd Hechtman, Eastern Washington University
Linda A. Jackson, Michigan State University
Nancy Johnson, Kaplan University
William E. Kelly, Auburn University
Howard Lucky, Prairie State College
Seth Mallios, San Diego State University
Sean Massey, Binghamton University
Charles Matzke, Michigan State University
Francis Moran, Jersey City College
Daniel W. O'Connell, Palm Beach Community College
Kristen Parris, Western Washington University
Joseph G. Rish, King's College
Christopher Robinson, University of Alabama at Birmingham
Gregg Santori, Coppin State College
William H. Taylor, Terra Community College
Frank J. Vattano, Colorado State University
Alex Velez, St. Mary's University
J. Russell Willis, Grambling State University
Otto Zinser, East Tennessee State University

Supplements for Instructors

Free Companion Website for Harrison *Power and Society: An Introduction to the Social Sciences*, 13e

- ISBN-13: 9781285058597
- This password-protected website for instructors features all of the free student assets plus an instructor's manual, book-specific PowerPoint® presentations, and a test bank. Access your resources by logging into your account at www.cengage.com/login.

Instructor's Manual and Test Bank online for Harrison *Power and Society: An Introduction to the Social Sciences*, 13e

- ISBN-13: 9781285058580
- This password-protected Instructor's Manual and Test Bank are accessible by logging into your account at www.cengage.com/login. The test bank, revised by Brenda Beach, Ph.D., is offered in Microsoft Word® and ExamView® formats and includes multiple-choice questions with answers and page references along with essay questions for each chapter. ExamView® features a user-friendly testing environment that allows you to not only publish traditional paper and computer based tests, but also Web-deliverable exams. The Instructor's Manual, revised by Dr. Charles Matzke, includes learning objectives, chapter outlines, summaries, discussion questions, class activities and projects suggestions, tips on integrating media into your class, and suggested readings and Web resources.

Power & Society

AN INTRODUCTION TO THE SOCIAL SCIENCES

Thirteenth Edition

Each of the disciplines in the social sciences concerns itself with the distribution of power in societies. During the Jasmine Spring rebellions throughout the Middle East in 2011, the power structures in many societies were changed through the force of mass rebellion. Here, in Tunis, Tunisia, protesters slept on the government square, paying tribute to the martyrs of the Jasmine Revolution and seeking to force the ouster of the Tunisian government.

PART 1

The Nature and Study of Power

The purpose of this book is to introduce you to the social sciences. Because power in society is a theme that pervades each of the social sciences, as well as the problems they study, we have chosen this theme as the focal point for our presentation. Part One is designed to familiarize you with the notion of power, with the nature of each of the social sciences, and with the scientific methods they employ. You will find that Chapter 1 reflects the structure of the entire text. Its first part examines the nature of power; its second part describes the individual social sciences and the particular ways in which they contribute to our understanding of power. Its third part focuses on the problems with which the social sciences are concerned. Chapter 2 is devoted to a discussion of the methods used in social science research—how social scientists gather data, how they endeavor to employ scientific and experimental methods of research, and the special problems they encounter in doing so. In Chapter 3, we explore how ideology shapes the context in which struggles for power occur, and we also examine some of the major ideological struggles in recent times.

CHAPTER 1

Power, Society, and Social Science

Learning Objectives

After reading this chapter, students will be able to:

- Explain how power is defined.
- List the defining characteristics of power.
- List the disciplines within the social sciences, and describe how each analyzes power.
- Explain what is meant by the interdisciplinary study of social problems.

The Nature of Power

Ordinary men and women are driven by forces in society that they neither understand nor control. These forces are embodied in governmental authorities, economic organizations and markets, social values and ideologies, accepted ways of life, and learned patterns of behavior. However diverse the nature of these forces, they have in common the ability to modify the conduct of individuals, to control their behavior, and to shape their lives. **Power** *is the capacity to affect the conduct of individuals through the real or threatened use of rewards and punishments.* Power is exercised over individuals and groups by offering them things they value or by threatening to deprive them of those things. These values are the base of power, and they can include physical safety, health, and well-being; wealth and material possessions; jobs and means to a livelihood; knowledge and skills; social recognition, status, and prestige; love, affection, and acceptance by others; and a satisfactory self-image and self-respect. To exercise power, then, control must be exercised over the things that are valued in society.

Power is a special form of influence. Broadly speaking, influence is the production of intended effects. People who can produce intended effects by any means are said to be influential. People who can produce intended effects by the real or threatened use of rewards and punishments are said to be powerful.

Power can rest on various resources. The exercise of power assumes many different forms—the giving or withholding of many different values. In many circumstances, the desire for power as well as wealth motivates people. Indeed, the English philosopher Bertrand Russell (1872–1970), regarded as one of the twentieth century's greatest thinkers, summarized his views about the

power
the capacity to affect the conduct of others through the real or threatened use of rewards and punishments

importance of power in society in a book significantly entitled *Power: A New Social Analysis*, in which he wrote:

> When a moderate degree of comfort is assured, both individuals and communities will pursue power rather than wealth: they may seek wealth as a means to power, or they may forgo an increase of wealth in order to secure an increase of power, but in the former case as in the latter, their fundamental motive is not economic.[1]

Yet power bases are usually interdependent—individuals who control certain valued resources and are likely to control other resources as well. Wealth, economic power, prestige, recognition, political influence, education, respect, and so on, all tend to "go together" in society.

Power is never equally distributed. "There is no power where power is equal." For power to be exercised, the "powerholder" must control some base values. By *control* we mean that the powerholder is in a position to offer these values as rewards to others or to threaten to deprive others of these values.

Power is a relationship among individuals, groups, and institutions in society. Power is not really a "thing" that someone possesses. Instead, power is a relationship in which some individuals or groups have control over resources valued by others. As Bertrand Russell writes:

> Like energy, power has many forms, such as wealth, armaments, civil authority, and influence on opinion. No one of these can be regarded as subordinate to any other, and there is no one form from which the others are derivative. The attempt to treat one form of power, say wealth, in isolation can only be partially successful. ... To revert to the analogy of physics, power, like energy, must be regarded as continually passing from any one of its forms into any other, and it should be the business of social science to seek the laws of such transformations.

Elites and Masses

The **elite** are the few who have power; the **masses** are the many who do not. The elite are the few who control what is valued in society and use that control to shape the lives of others. The masses are the many whose lives are shaped by institutions, events, and leaders over which they have little control. Political scientist Harold Lasswell wrote, "The division of society into elites and masses is universal," and even in a democracy, "a few exercise a relatively great weight of power, and the many exercise comparatively little."[2]

elite
the few who have power

masses
the many who do not have power

Power, Authority, and Legitimacy

Legitimacy is the belief that the exercise of power is "right" or "proper" and that people are morally obligated to submit to it. Legitimacy depends on people believing that the exercise of power is necessary and valuable to society. As long as people believe in the legitimacy of the institutions in which power is lodged and believe that power is being used rightfully and properly, force will seldom be required. People feel obliged to obey laws, follow rules, and abide by decisions that they believe to be legitimate. But if people begin to question the legitimacy of institutions (that is, governments, corporations, churches, the military, and so on) and if people come to believe that laws, rules, and decisions are no longer rightful or proper, then they will no longer feel morally obligated

legitimacy
belief that the exercise of power is right and proper

North Korean Dictator Kim Jong Un has power, but his authoritarian government lacks legitimacy. What are the sources of legitimate authority?

to abide by them. Institutional power will then rest on sheer force alone—as, for example, when unpopular, "illegitimate" governments rely on repression by police or military forces to exercise power over their populations.

Authority

authority
power that is exercised legitimately

Authority refers to power that is exercised legitimately. Not all power is legitimate: A thief who forces us to turn over money at gunpoint is exercising power, not authority. A tax collector from the Internal Revenue Service who forces us to turn over money under threat of a fine or jail sentence is exercising authority—power that is perceived as legitimate. Authority, then, is a special type of power that is believed to be rightful and proper. Political leaders in all societies surround themselves with elaborate symbols of office in order to help legitimize their authority. Symbols of authority surround us: your instructor's podium, a police officer's uniform, and a presidential entourage all connote authority. These symbols all seek to convey authority and legitimacy to the masses. Symbols of authority often rest on the perception by the masses that a particular symbol designates authority.

Sources of Legitimacy

What are the sources of legitimacy? Early in the twentieth century, a German sociologist named Max Weber (pronounced "Vayber") suggested three general sources of legitimacy:

1. *Tradition:* Legitimacy rests on established beliefs in the sanctity of authority and the moral need to obey leaders.
2. *Charisma:* Legitimacy rests on the personal heroic qualities of a particular leader.
3. *Legality:* Legitimacy is based on a commitment to rules that bind both leaders and the people.

Historically, most leaders have depended on tradition for their authority. The rule of tribal chieftains, pharaohs and kings, and feudal lords and ladies has been accepted as right because "it has always been that way." Some have relied on charismatic leadership—from Napoleon to Hitler to Gandhi to Mao Zedong. The authority of these leaders was based on personal appeal of an individual leader and the faith of their followers. Still other elites depend on legitimacy conferred by rules that are agreed on by both leaders and followers. Weber referred to this type of legitimacy as **rational-legal authority**. Leaders exercise their authority not because of tradition or personal charisma but because of the office or position they occupy—a position they assumed through legal means, such as through an election.

rational-legal authority
legitimacy conferred by rules that are agreed on by both leaders and followers

Institutional Power

Power is exercised in large institutions—governments, corporations, schools, the military, churches, newspapers, television networks, law firms, and so on. Power that stems from high positions in the social structures of society is stable and far-reaching. Sociologist C. Wright Mills once observed: "No one can be truly powerful unless he has access to the command of major institutions, for it is over these institutional means of power that the truly powerful are, in the first instance, powerful."[3] Not all power, it is true, is anchored in or exercised through institutions. But institutional positions in society provide a continuous and important base of power. As Mills explained,

> If we took the one hundred most powerful men in America, the one hundred wealthiest, and the one hundred most celebrated away from the institutional positions they now occupy, away from their resources of men and women and money, away from the media of mass communication that are now focused upon them—then they would be powerless and poor and uncelebrated. For power is not of a man. Wealth does not center in the person of the wealthy. . . . To have power requires access to major institutions, for the institutional positions men occupy determine in large part their chances to have and to hold these valued experiences.[4]

The Context of Power

Sometimes power is exercised to fulfill small, personal objectives. But on a societal level, often power is exercised in order to enact a specific agenda, and action takes place with greater goals in mind. One of the most common determinants of how power is exercised broadly is ideology—people are frequently motivated to exercise power because of their ideas and values about the nature of society. How these actions are remembered occurs through collecting recorded facts, organizing them into a narrative, and interpreting their meaning as history.

Power and Ideology

Ideas have power. Indeed, whole societies are shaped by systems of ideas that we call ideologies. An **ideology** is an integrated system of ideas about values in general, and the ideal role of government in particular. The study of ideologies—liberalism, conservatism, socialism, communism, fascism—is not a separate

ideology
integrated system of ideas about values in general, and the ideal role of government in particular

Mao Zedong led the Communist Revolution in China in 1949 and then was the leader of China until his death in 1976. His control over China's people and government is often attributed to his charismatic leadership ability. This 1938 photo shows Mao in Shensi Province speaking to fellow communist revolutionaries during a six thousand-mile "Long March" during that country's revolution. Are there any political leaders today who derive power from their charisma?

social science. Rather, the study of ideologies spans all the social sciences, and it is closely related to philosophy. Ideologies are integrated systems of ideas that rationalize a way of life, establish standards of "rightness" and "wrongness," and provide emotional impulses to action. Ideologies usually include economic, political, social, psychological, and cultural ideas, as well as interpretations of history.

Ideologies rationalize and justify power in society. By providing a justification for the exercise of power, the ideology itself becomes a base of power in society. Ideology "legitimizes" power, making the exercise of power acceptable to the masses and thereby adding to the power of the elite. However, ideologies also affect the behavior of the elite, because once an ideology is deeply rooted in society, powerholders themselves are bound by it.

In our study of power and ideology, we will first explore the ideology of *classical liberalism*—an ideology that attacked the established power of a hereditary aristocracy and asserted the dignity, worth, and freedom of the individual. Classical liberalism and capitalism justify the power of private enterprise and the market system. Whereas classical liberalism limits the powers of government, *modern liberalism* accepts governmental power as a positive force in freeing people from poverty, ignorance, discrimination, and sickness. It justifies the exercise of governmental power over private enterprise and the establishment of the welfare state. In contrast, *modern conservatism* doubts the ability of the governmental planners to solve society's problems; conservatism urges greater reliance on family, church, and individual initiative and effort (see Research This!).

We will then look at ideologies that have influenced other societies. *Fascism* is a power-oriented ideology that asserts the supremacy of a nation or race over the interests of individuals, groups, and other social institutions. *Marxism* attacks the

RESEARCH *THIS!*

The Gallup organization has been tracking the ideology of Americans for many years. The following figure presents the annual averages to responses to the question: How would you describe your political views—very conservative, conservative, moderate, liberal, or very liberal? The "verys" are condensed into the data shown.

How would you describe your political views—very conservative, conservative, moderate, liberal, or very liberal?

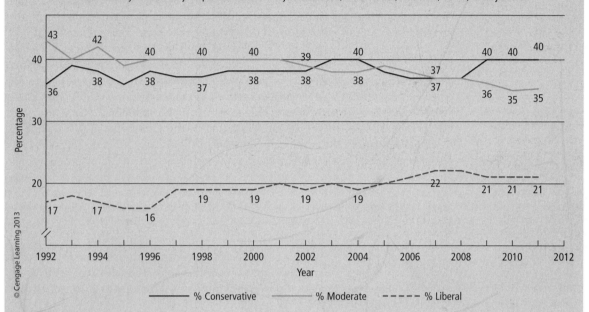

© Cengage Learning 2013

SOURCE: www.gallup.com/poll/152021/conservatives-remain-largest-ideological-group.aspx

YOUR ANALYSIS:

1. Based on the figure shown, what is the overall trend with regard to Americans' ideology between 1992 and 2008? Was ideology in the United States stable then?

2. Democrats, who are usually affiliated with a liberal ideology, were elected to the presidency in 1992, 1996, and 2008, while a Republican (typically conservative) was elected in 2000 and 2004. What happened to the ideologies of those parties after their respective presidents were elected?

3. What marked change occurred in Americans' ideology since 2008? Why do you think this might have occurred?

market system, free enterprise, and individualism; it justifies revolutionary power in overthrowing liberal capitalist systems and the establishment of a "dictatorship of the proletariat." *Communism* calls for the evolutionary democratic replacement of the private enterprise system with government ownership of industry.

We will describe the collapse of communism and the reasons for its failure in Eastern Europe and the former Soviet Union, as well as its evolution in China.

Power in History

History is the recording, narrating, and interpreting of human experience. The historian recreates the past by collecting recorded facts, organizing them into a narrative, and interpreting their meaning. History is concerned with change over time. It provides a perspective on the present by informing us of the way people lived in the past. History helps us understand how society developed into what it is today.

The foundations of power vary from age to age. As power bases shift, new groups and individuals acquire control. Thus, power relationships are continuously developing and changing. An understanding of power in society requires an understanding of the historical development of power relationships.

In our consideration of the historical development of power relationships, we will look at the changing sources of power in American history and the characteristics of the individuals and groups who have acquired power. We will describe the people of power in the early days of the Republic and their shaping of the Constitution and the government it established. We will discuss Charles Beard's controversial interpretation of the Constitution as a document designed to protect the economic interests of those early powerholders. We will also discuss how westward expansion and settlement created new powerholders and new bases of power. We will explore the power struggle between Northern commercial and industrial interests and Southern planters and slave owners for control of land in the West, and the Civil War, resulting from that struggle. In addition, we will explore the development of an industrial elite in America after the Civil War, the impact of the Great Depression on that elite, and the resulting growth of New Deal liberal reform. In our analysis of the Reconstruction Era and African American history, we will examine how history occasionally overlooks the experiences of powerless minorities and later reinterprets their contributions to society.

Power and the Social Sciences

Social science is the study of human behavior. Actually, there are several social sciences, each specializing in a particular aspect of human behavior and each using different concepts, methods, and data in its studies. Anthropology, sociology, economics, psychology, and political science have developed into separate "disciplines," but all share an interest in human behavior.

Power is *not* the central concern of the social sciences, yet all the social sciences deal with power in one form or another. Bertrand Russell notes:

> Those whose love of power is not strong are unlikely to have much influence on the course of events. The people who cause social changes are, as a rule, people who strongly desire to do so. Love of power, therefore, is a characteristic of the people who are causally important. We should, of course, be mistaken if we regarded it as the sole human motive, but this mistake would not lead us so much astray as might be expected in the search for causal laws in social science, since love of power is the chief motive producing the changes that social science has to study.[5]

Each of the social sciences contributes to an understanding of the forces that modify the conduct of individuals, control their behavior, and shape their lives. Thus, to fully understand power in society, we must approach this topic in an **interdisciplinary** fashion—using ideas, methods, data, and findings from all the social sciences.

interdisciplinary
the study of a topic using ideas, methods, and data from all of the social sciences

Anthropology

Anthropology is the study of people and their ways of life. It is the most holistic of the social sciences in that it studies all aspects of a **society**—a group of people who depend on one another for their well-being and who share a common culture. Many anthropologists focus their energies on describing humans, societies, and power structures at various points in time and in various places; others are concerned with using knowledge derived from anthropological studies to improve human existence. Within the discipline of Anthropology are four subfields. These include linguistics, archaeology, biological and physical anthropology, and socio-cultural anthropology.

anthropology
the study of people and their ways of life

society
a group of people who depend on one another and share a common culture

Linguistic anthropology is a method of analyzing societies in terms of their use of language, while **archaeology** is the study of both the physical and cultural characteristics of peoples and societies that existed in the distant past. It is similar to history but reaches further back in time, into **prehistory**, the time before written records. It endeavors to reconstruct the history of a society from the remains of its culture. Some of these remains are as impressive as the pyramids of Egypt and the Mayan temples of Mexico; some are as mundane as bits of broken pottery, stone tools, and garbage.

archaeology
the study of the physical and cultural characteristics of peoples and societies that existed prior to recorded history

prehistory
the time before written records

Biological anthropologists (sometimes called physical anthropologists) are concerned with the evolution of the human species. They examine how humans historically have interacted with their natural environment and with each other. Biological anthropologists also are concerned with contemporary issues concerning human growth, development, adaption, disease, and mortality.

Socio-cultural anthropologists study how people live within their environment. Cultural anthropologists describe and compare societies and cultures. They describe and explain a great many things: child rearing and education, family arrangements, language and communication, technology, ways of making a living, the distribution of work, religious beliefs and values, social life, leadership patterns and power structures, and culture, or the ways of life that are common to a society.

Power is part of the **culture** or the way of life of a people. Power is exercised in all societies because all societies have systems of rewards and sanctions designed to control the behavior of their members. Perhaps the most enduring structure of power in society is the family: Power is exercised within the family when patterns of dominance and submission are established between male and female and between parents and children. Societies also develop structures of power outside the family to maintain peace and order among their members, to organize individuals to accomplish large-scale tasks, to defend themselves against attack, and even to wage war and exploit other peoples.

culture
the ways of life that are common to a society

In our study of power and culture, we will examine how cultural patterns determine power relationships. We will also examine patterns of authority in traditional and modern families and the changing power role of women in society. We will focus special attention in Chapter 4 on whether marriage is becoming obsolete in America. We will also examine the origins and development of power relationships, illustrating these concepts with an example involving the kingdom of Saudi Arabia, a state that is also a chiefdom.

Political Science

political science
the study of government and politics

Political science is the study of government and politics. Governments possess *authority*, a particular form of power—that is, power that may include the legitimate use of physical force. Recall that by *legitimate*, we mean that people believe the exercise of power is "right" or "proper." In legitimate governments, the people generally consent to the government's use of this power. Of course, other individuals and organizations in society—for example, muggers, street gangs, terrorists, violent revolutionaries—use force. But only government can legitimately threaten people with the loss of freedom and well-being as a means of modifying their behavior. Moreover, governments exercise power over all individuals and institutions in society—corporations, families, schools, and so forth. Obviously the power of government in modern society is very great, extending to nearly every aspect of modern life "from womb to tomb."

Political scientists from Aristotle to the present have been concerned with the dangers of unlimited and unchecked governmental power. We will examine the American experience with limited, constitutional government and the meaning of democracy in modern society. We will observe how the U.S. Constitution divides power, first between states and the national government, and second among the legislative, executive, and judicial branches of government. We will review the continuing controversy over whether the people themselves should decide important issues by voting directly on them or whether elected representatives should do so. We will examine the growth of power in Washington, DC, and the struggle for power among the different branches of government. We will observe that the president of the United States enjoys more power than the writers of the Constitution envisioned. We will explore what factors appear to strengthen and weaken presidents and how scholars rate the performances of past presidents. Finally, in our look at "Media Power: The Presidential Debates," we will examine the growing power of television in American politics.

Economics

economics
the study of the production and distribution of scarce goods and services

Economics is the study of the production and distribution of scarce goods and services. There are never enough goods and services to satisfy everyone's demands, and because of this, choices must be made. Economists study how individuals, businesses, and nations make these choices about goods and services.

Economic power is the power to decide what will be produced, how much it will cost, how many people will be employed to produce it, what their wages will be, what the price of the good or service will be, what profits will be made, how these profits will be distributed, and how fast the economy will grow.

Capitalist societies rely heavily on the market mechanism to make these decisions. In our study of economic power, we will explore the strengths and weaknesses of this market system, as well as the ideas of economic philosophers Adam Smith and John Maynard Keynes. We will examine America's great wealth—how it is measured, how it is distributed, where it comes from, and where it goes. In addition, we will consider the role of government in the economy, where it gets its money, and how it spends it. We will also examine the concentration of corporate power in America and whether the corporate elite use that power to benefit the stockholders or themselves. Finally, we will describe the globalization of economic power and the emergence of giant multinational corporations.

Psychology

Psychology may be defined as the study of the behavior of people and animals. Behavior, we know, is the product of both "nature and nurture"—that is, a product of both our biological makeup and our environmental conditioning. We will examine the continuing controversy over *how much* of our behavior is a product of our genes versus our environment. There is great richness and diversity in psychological inquiry. **Biological psychology** examines the extent to which electrical and chemical events in the brain and nervous system determine behavior. **Behavioral psychologists** study the learning process—the way in which people and animals learn to respond to stimuli. Behavioral psychologists frequently study in experimental laboratory situations, with the hope that the knowledge gained can be useful in understanding more complex human behavior outside the laboratory. **Social psychologists**, on the other hand, study interpersonal behavior—the ways in which social interactions shape an individual's beliefs, perceptions, motivations, attitudes, and behavior. Social psychologists generally study the whole person in relation to the total environment. **Psychoanalytic (Freudian) psychologists** study the impact of subconscious feelings and emotions and of early childhood experiences on the behavior of adults. **Humanistic psychologists** are concerned with the human being's innate potential for growth and development. **Cognitive psychologists** emphasize how people learn about themselves and their environment. Many other psychologists combine theories and methods in different ways in their attempts to achieve a better understanding of behavior.

Personality consists of all the enduring, organized ways of behavior that characterize an individual. Psychologists differ over how personality characteristics are determined. Some psychologists study the impact of physical aspects of the brain—particularly chemicals and electrical impulses—on personality traits (biological psychology). Other branches of psychology explore whether characteristics are acquired through the process of reinforcement and conditioning (behavioral psychology), products of the individual's interaction with the significant people and groups in his or her life (social psychology), manifestations of the continuous process of positive growth toward "self-actualization" (humanistic psychology), the results of subconscious drives and long-repressed emotions stemming from early childhood experiences (Freudian psychology), or some combination of all these.

In our study of power and personality, we will examine various theories of personality determination in an effort to understand the forces shaping an individual's

psychology
the study of the behavior of people and animals

biological psychology
the study of electrical and chemical events in the brain and nervous system as determinants of behavior

behavioral psychology
the study of human and animal responses to stimuli

social psychology
the study of interpersonal behavior

psychoanalytic (Freudian) psychology
the study of the effects of subconscious feelings and early childhood experiences on behavior

humanistic psychology
the study of the growth and development of the human personality

cognitive psychology
an approach to psychology that emphasizes how people learn about themselves and their environment

personality
all the enduring, organized ways of behavior that characterize an individual

reaction to power. We will explore the recurring question of "nature versus nurture," biology versus environment, in determining the human condition. Using a Freudian perspective, we will study the "authoritarian personality"—the individual who is habitually dominant and aggressive toward others over whom he or she exercises power but is submissive and weak toward others who have more power; the individual who is extremely prejudiced, rigid, intolerant, cynical, and power oriented. We will explore the power implications of B. F. Skinner's ideas of behavioral conditioning for the control of human behavior. We will also describe the treatment of mental illness from these various psychological perspectives. In a case study, we will describe the startling results of an experiment designed to test the relationship between authority and obedience, and we'll also examine levels of stress worldwide.

Sociology

sociology
the study of relationships among individuals and groups

Sociology is the study of relationships among individuals and groups. Sociologists describe the structure of formal and informal groups, their functions and purposes, and how they change over time. They study social institutions (such as families, schools, and churches), social processes (for example, conflict, competition, assimilation, and change), and social problems (crime, race relations, poverty, and so forth). Sociologists also study social classes.

social stratification
the classification and ranking of members of a society

All societies have some system of classifying and ranking their members—a system of **stratification**. In modern industrial societies, social status is associated with the various roles that individuals play in the economic system. Individuals are ranked according to how they make their living and the power they exercise over others. Stratification into social classes is determined largely on the basis of occupation and control of economic resources.

Power derives from social status, prestige, and respect, as well as from control of economic resources. Thus, the stratification system involves the unequal distribution of power.

In our study of power and social class, we will explore stratification and the extent of inequality in America. We will discuss the differing lifestyles of upper, middle, working, and lower classes in America and the extent of class conflict. We will examine the ideas of sociologist C. Wright Mills about a "power elite" in America that occupies powerful positions in the governmental, corporate, and military bureaucracies of the nation. Taking our study of power relationships to an international level, we will look at global inequalities. We will examine the ideas of Karl Marx about the struggle for power among social classes. Finally, we will describe the differential in political power among social classes in America.

Social Sciences and Social Problems

Social problems—the major challenges confronting society—include racism, sexism, poverty, crime, violence, urban decay, increasing globalization, and international conflict. These problems do not confine themselves to one or another of the disciplines of social science. They spill over the boundaries of anthropology, economics, sociology, political science, psychology, and history—they are interdisciplinary in character. Each of these problems has its *historical* antecedents, its *social* and *psychological* roots, its *cultural* manifestations, its *economic* consequences, and its impact on *government* and public policy. The origins of these social problems, as well as the various solutions proposed, involve complex power relationships.

Inequality Based on Race, Ethnicity, Gender, Sexual Orientation, and Disability

In some power relationships, there is inequality because of discrimination against individuals because of their race, gender, sexual orientation, or disability. Historically, no social problem has challenged the United States more than racial inequality. It is the only issue over which Americans ever fought a civil war. We will describe the American experience with racism and the civil rights movement that brought about significant changes in American life. We want to understand the philosophy of that movement, particularly the "nonviolent direct action" philosophy of Nobel Peace Prize winner Dr. Martin Luther King Jr. However, we will also examine continuing inequalities between blacks and whites in income, employment, and other conditions of life in the United States. We will explore how the face of America continues to change, including the problems confronting Hispanic Americans, Muslim and Arab Americans, Native Americans, Asian Americans, and other groups.

In addition, we will look at sexism in American life, particularly in the economy. We will describe the successes and failures of the women's movement over the years and examine the issue of sexual harassment and the constitutional status of abortion as a privacy right. We will explore the controversies over "affirmative action" and "racial preferences" and their implications for how America is to achieve real equality. We also will examine the issue of women's participation in the workforce from an international perspective.

We will also examine other forms of discrimination, including discrimination based on sexual orientation, and discrimination based on disability. We will describe the struggle for equality undertaken by gay rights groups, and by groups who advocate for the disabled. We will also look at current efforts by these groups to secure equal treatment.

Poverty and Powerlessness

The American economy has produced the highest standard of living in the world, yet a significant number of Americans live in poverty. Poverty can be defined as **powerlessness**—a sociopsychological condition of hopelessness, indifference, distrust, and cynicism. We will discuss whether there is a "culture of poverty"—a way of life of the poor that is passed on to future generations—and, if so, what are the implications for government policy. We will describe governmental efforts to cope with poverty and discuss the controversial question regarding the effect of welfare reform policies on the poor. We will focus special attention on homelessness in America and on the problem of poverty among children in the United States.

powerlessness
a sociopsychological condition of hopelessness, indifference, distrust, and cynicism

Crime and Violence

Governmental power must be balanced against *individual freedom*. A democratic society must exercise police powers to protect its citizens, yet it must not unduly restrict individual liberty. We will explore the problem of crime in society and how crime is defined and measured. We will also describe the constitutional

Globalization has resulted in an increased awareness of the crises faced by many throughout the world. Today, social scientists examine issues including war, hunger, displacement, and lack of freedom, which have ripple effects throughout the world. Here, victims of the Darfur, Sudan genocide wait for the distribution of food at a refugee camp.

Daniel Pepper/Getty Images News/Getty Images

rights of defendants and the role of the courts in protecting these rights, including the implementation of the death penalty. We will describe the economics of crime and explore a controversial question of whether more prisons mean less crime. An even more controversial question that will be addressed is the relationship between drugs and crime and whether drug use should be legalized. We will summarize economic, psychological, and social explanations of crime and violence. We will describe briefly the history of violence in American society and the role that violence has played in American struggles for power.

Globalization

Globalization, the development of an increasingly integrated global economy, has sweeping and increasing influence on power distribution. This trend has broad implications in economic systems, in government, in culture, and beyond. Globalization is shaping both the issues that social scientists examine and the manner in which they examine them. In addition to our increased interconnectedness fostered by increasingly integrated economies and by technology, we will examine world population growth and worldwide urbanization. We will examine some of the most important crises facing people throughout the world, including war, poverty, hunger, warfare, disease, and lack of personal freedom.

International Conflict

sovereignty
a nation's authority over internal affairs, freedom from outside intervention, and recognition by other nations

The struggle for power is global, involving all the nations and peoples of the world, whatever their goals or ideals. Nearly two hundred nations in the world claim **sovereignty**: authority over their internal affairs, freedom from outside intervention, and political and legal recognition by other nations. But sovereignty is a legal fiction; it requires power to make sovereignty a reality. Over the years, nations have struggled for power through wars and diplomacy. The struggle has led to attempts to maintain a fragile balance of power among large and small nations, as well as attempts to achieve collective security through the United Nations and other alliances. We will provide a brief history of the long Cold War between two nuclear "superpowers"—the United States and the former Soviet Union. We will describe the especially dangerous issue of nuclear arms and efforts to bring them under control. The United States continues to face challenges related to global politics. We will take up the highly controversial question, "When should the United States use military force?"

Throughout the book, whether in discipline-specific discussions within the social sciences, or in the topical, interdisciplinary analysis, we see power as an important concept integral to all disciplines and issues in the social sciences. Chapters 2 and 3 continue to place the concept of power in perspective, and introduce the methodological and ideological framework that shapes the social sciences' analysis of this concept.

CHAPTER SUMMARY

- Ideology—that is, individuals' belief about the extent to which government should be involved in peoples' lives—and historical perspective provide the context in which power is exercised.

- Each of the social sciences—anthropology, political science, economics, psychology, and sociology—analyzes power within the framework of that discipline.

- Power is also a useful framework for examining various social problems in the United States, including inequality, poverty, crime and violence, and problems related to globalization and international conflict.

KEY TERMS

anthropology   the study of people and their ways of life

archaeology   the study of the physical and cultural characteristics of peoples and societies that existed prior to recorded history

authority   power that is exercised legitimately

behavioral psychology   the study of human and animal responses to stimuli

biological psychology   the study of electrical and chemical events in the brain and nervous system as determinants of behavior

cognitive psychology   an approach to psychology that emphasizes how people learn about themselves and their environment

culture   the ways of life that are common to a society

economics   the study of the production and distribution of scarce goods and services

elite and masses   the few who have power and the many who do not

history   the recording, narrating, and interpreting of human experience

humanistic psychology   the study of the growth and development of the human personality

ideology   integrated system of ideas about values in general, and the ideal role of government in particular

interdisciplinary   the study of a topic using ideas, methods, and data from all of the social sciences

legitimacy   belief that the exercise of power is right and proper

personality   all the enduring, organized ways of behavior that characterize an individual

political science   the study of government and politics

power   the capacity to affect the conduct of others through the real or threatened use of rewards and punishments

powerlessness   a sociopsychological condition of hopelessness, indifference, distrust, and cynicism

prehistory   the time before written records

psychoanalytic (Freudian) psychology   the study of the effects of subconscious feelings and early childhood experiences on behavior

psychology   the study of the behavior of people and animals

rational-legal authority   legitimacy conferred by rules that are agreed on by both leaders and followers

social psychology   the study of interpersonal behavior

social science   the study of human behavior

social stratification   the classification and ranking of members of a society

society   a group of people who depend on one another and share a common culture

sociology   the study of relationships among individuals and groups

sovereignty   a nation's authority over internal affairs, freedom from outside intervention, and recognition by other nations

ON THE WEB

EXPLORING POWER AND SOCIETY

The Internet is an invaluable tool for researching topics related to the study of power and society.

In this section at the end of each chapter, you will find suggestions for websites that can guide your research into topics discussed in that chapter. The website for this text, **www.cengagebrain.com**, offers many resources for each chapter. In addition, searching the Internet by using key terms on search engines will also yield an abundance of information. Of course, when using the Internet, one must be wary of the sources of information. Be skeptical of information that cannot be verified by several sources and consider the source of the information before relying on it in your research.

REVIEW QUIZ

MULTIPLE CHOICE

1. Legitimacy conferred by rules that are agreed on by both leaders and followers is called what?
   a. power
   b. legitimacy
   c. rational-legal authority
   d. ideology

2. _____ is an integrated system of ideas about values in general, and the ideal role of government in particular.
   a. Authority
   b. Ideology
   c. Power
   d. Legitimacy

3. The study of people and their ways of life is known as what?
   a. social science
   b. political science
   c. economics
   d. anthropology

4. What is known as the study of the physical and cultural characteristics of peoples and societies that existed prior to recorded history?
   a. prehistory
   b. archaeology
   c. cultural anthropology
   d. physical anthropology

5. The time before written records is called _____.
   a. prehistory
   b. archaeology
   c. cultural anthropology
   d. physical anthropology

6. What is the study of the behavior of people and animals?
   a. anthropology
   b. economics
   c. sociology
   d. psychology

7. What is the study of the production and distribution of scarce goods and services?
   a. anthropology
   b. economics
   c. political science
   d. psychology

8. Name the approach to psychology that emphasizes how people learn about themselves and their environment.
   a. social psychology
   b. psychoanalytic (Freudian) psychology
   c. humanistic psychology
   d. cognitive psychology

9. What is the study of the growth and development of the human personality called?
   a. social psychology
   b. psychoanalytic (Freudian) psychology
   c. humanistic psychology
   d. cognitive psychology

10. What is the study of government and politics called?
    a. anthropology
    b. economics
    c. political science
    d. psychology

FILL IN THE BLANK

11. _____ is the capacity to affect the conduct of others through the real or threatened use of rewards and punishments.

12. The few who have power and the many who do not are called _____.

13. The belief that the exercise of power is right and proper is called _____.

14. The study of a topic using ideas, methods, and data from all of the social sciences is said to be _____.

15. _____ is the classification and ranking of members of a society.

ANSWER KEY:
1. c; 2. b; 3. d; 4. b; 5. a; 6. d; 7. b; 8. d; 9. c; 10. c; 11. Power; 12. elites and masses; 13. legitimacy; 14. interdisciplinary; 15. Social stratification.

CHAPTER 2

Social Sciences and the Scientific Method

Learning Objectives

After reading this chapter, students will be able to:

- Explain the purpose of the scientific method.
- Describe some of the difficulties that social scientists from each discipline face in applying the scientific method to the study of social problems.
- Describe methods that social scientists use to conduct research.

Science and the Scientific Method

A **science** may be broadly defined as any organized *body of knowledge*, or it may be more narrowly defined as a discipline that employs the scientific method. If we use the broad definition, we can safely say that all the social sciences are indeed sciences. However, if we narrow our definition to only those disciplines that employ the scientific method, then some questions arise about whether the social sciences are really scientific. In other words, if science is defined as a *method of study*, rather than a *body of knowledge*, then not all studies in the social sciences are truly scientific.

science
broadly defined, any organized body of knowledge

The **scientific method** develops and tests theories about how observable facts or events are related in order to explain them. What does this definition really mean? How is this method of study actually applied in the social sciences? To answer these questions, let's examine each aspect of the scientific method separately.

scientific method
a method of explanation that develops and tests theories about how observable facts or events are related

Explaining Relationships

The goal of the scientific method is explanation. When using this method, we seek to answer *why*. Any scientific inquiry must begin by observing and classifying things. Just as biology begins with the careful observation, description, and classification of thousands upon thousands of different forms of life, the social sciences also must begin with the careful observation, description, and classification of various forms of human behavior. But the goal is explanation, not just description. Just as biology seeks to develop theories of evolution and genetics to explain the various forms of life upon the earth, the social sciences seek to develop theories to explain why human beings behave as they do.

The Vocabulary of Social Science

Social science researchers use many special terms in their work, some of which have already been defined. While reading social science research reports, it helps to understand the specific meanings given to the following terms:

- **THEORY:** A causal explanation of relationship between observable facts or events. A good theory fits the facts, explains why they occur, and allows us to predict future events.
- **HYPOTHESIS:** A tentative statement about a relationship between facts or events that should be derived from the theory and should be testable. Hypotheses typically are statements of relationships between variables.
- **VARIABLE:** A characteristic that varies among different individuals or groups.
- **INDEPENDENT VARIABLE:** Whatever is hypothesized to be the cause of something else.
- **DEPENDENT VARIABLE:** Whatever is hypothesized to be the effect of something else.
- **SIGNIFICANT:** Not likely to have occurred by chance.
- **CORRELATION:** Significant relationships found in the data.
- **CAUSATION:** A significant relationship wherein the presence of one variable (the independent variable) causes changes in another variable (dependent variable).
- **INFERENCE:** A causal statement based on data showing a significant relationship.
- **SPURIOUS:** Describing a relationship among facts or events that is not causal but is a product of the fact that both the independent and dependent variables are being caused by a third factor.

To answer the question of *why*, the scientific method searches for *relationships*. All scientific **hypotheses** assert some relationship between observable facts or events. The social sciences seek to find relationships that explain human behavior. The first question is whether two or more events or behaviors are related in any way—that is, do they occur together consistently? The second question is whether either event or behavior *causes* the other. Social scientists first try to learn whether human events have occurred together merely by chance or accident or whether they occur together so consistently that their relationship cannot be a mere coincidence. A relationship that is not likely to have occurred by chance is said to be **significant**. After observing a significant relationship, social scientists next ask whether there is a *causal relationship* between the phenomena (that is, whether the facts or events occurred together because one is the cause of the other) or whether both phenomena are being caused by some third factor. Focus: "The Vocabulary of Social Science" explains some of the terms used in scientific studies.

hypothesis
a tentative statement about a relationship between observable facts or events

significant
not likely to have occurred by chance

Deductive and Inductive Reasoning

The scientific method seeks to develop statements (hypotheses) about how events or behaviors might be related and then determines the validity of these statements by careful, systematic, and logical tests. This process begins using logic and observing the phenomenon around us.

Essentially, deductive reasoning is based on the observation of relationships using linear logic. So:

All X are Y (first premise)
All Y are Z (second premise)
Hence, all X are Z (deductive conclusion, or hypothesis)

deductive reasoning
to infer from a general theory to a particular case

inductive reasoning
to observe one phenomenon or series of phenomena and make general assertions based on that observation

In the example above, we relied on **deductive reasoning**—or inferring from a general theory to a particular case. Social scientists also use **inductive reasoning**—that is observing one phenomenon or series of phenomena and making general assertions based on that observation. So, deductive reasons from general to specific, while inductive reasons from specific to general.

To make the differences between these two forms of logical reasoning clear, let's use a tried and true example, called a *syllogism*:

- General observation: All men are mortals.
- Specific observation: Socrates is a man.
- Deductive-derived hypothesis: Therefore, Socrates must be mortal.

Using inductive logic, reasoning would be flipped:

- Specific observation: Socrates is mortal.
- General observation: Other men also are mortal.
- Inductive-derived tentative conclusion: All men are mortal.

Developing and Testing Hypotheses

Scientific tests are really exercises in deductive or inductive logic. For example, if we wanted to find out something about the relationship between people's race and political party preference in voting, we might collect and record data from a national sample of African American and white voters chosen at random.* If our data showed that *all* blacks voted Democratic and *all* whites Republican, it would be obvious that there was a perfect **correlation**, or a significant statistical relationship, between race and voting. In contrast, if both blacks and whites voted Republican and Democratic in the *same* proportions, then it would be obvious that there was no correlation.

correlation
a significant statistical relationship

But in the social sciences, we rarely have such obvious, clear-cut results. Generally our data will show a mixed pattern. For example, in the 2008 presidential election, with Barack Obama seeking to become the first African American president in U.S. history, 95 percent of all African American voters supported him, while 4 percent backed his opponent John McCain. Among white voters, 43 percent voted for Obama, while 57 percent supported McCain. And in the 2004 presidential election between Democrat John Kerry and Republican George W. Bush, polls indicated that 88 percent of African Americans voted Democratic and 11 percent voted Republican. In that same election, 58 percent of whites voted Republican and only 41 percent voted Democratic. If there had been *no* relationship between race and voting, then blacks and whites would have voted Democratic and Republican in roughly the *same* proportions.

---

* Throughout this book we use the term *African American* when referring to specific individuals or the racial group, but in text and tables that compare African Americans and whites, we use parallel terms, *black* and *white*.

TABLE 2-1 VOTING BY RACE IN PRESIDENTIAL ELECTIONS
Testing the Hypothesis: African Americans Tend to Vote Democratic

Election Year	Candidates	All (%)*	Whites (%)	Blacks (%)
2008	Republican McCain	47	57	4
	Democrat Obama	53	43	95
2004	Republican Bush	51	58	11
	Democrat Kerry	48	41	88
2000	Republican Bush	48	54	8
	Democrat Gore	48	42	90
1996	Republican Dole	41	46	12
	Democrat Clinton	49	43	84
	Independent Perot	8	9	4
1992	Republican Bush	38	41	11
	Democrat Clinton	43	39	82
	Independent Perot	19	20	7
1988	Republic Bush	54	60	11
	Democrat Dukakis	46	40	89
1984	Republican Reagan	59	66	9
	Democrat Mondale	41	34	90
1980	Republican Reagan	51	56	10
	Democrat Carter	41	36	86
	Independent Anderson	7	7	2
1976	Republican Ford	48	5	15
	Democrat Carter	50	46	85
1972	Republican Nixon	62	68	13
	Democrat McGovern	38	32	87

* Figures are percentages of the vote won by each candidate. Percentages in each election may not
  add up to 100 because of voting for minor-party candidates.
SOURCE: Data from the *Gallup Opinion Poll* surveys and CNN Exit Poll results (2008).

But as we have just noted, blacks voted Democratic in far heavier proportions in both elections (95 percent and 88 percent) than whites (43 and 41 percent). This difference is not likely to have occurred by chance—thus, we consider it "significant." The same pattern of heavy Democratic voting among African Americans can be observed in other elections (Table 2-1). So we can make the inference that race is related to voting.

Note, however, that correlation (two events occurring together in a statistically significant relationship) does not equal causation (that one event necessarily *caused* the other to occur). Rather, both events could be caused by a third, as yet unidentified, characteristic or event. We must employ additional logic to find out which fact or event caused the other, or whether both were caused by a third fact or event. We can eliminate as illogical the possibility that voting Democratic causes one to become an African American. That leaves us with two possibilities: Being African American may cause Democratic voting, or voting Democratic may be caused by some third condition shared by many African Americans. For example, the real causal relationship may be between

RESEARCH *THIS!*

Researchers in each of the social sciences rely on original data to help inform their theories of the world around us. In the United States, several important data sets are provided by the U.S. government. Every ten years (most recently in 2010), the federal government conducts a census, or survey, of the population. Data from this census, including details about the population, housing, poverty and income, and community information is available through the U.S. Census Bureau website: www.census.gov.

The following table shows the changes in the U.S. population over the 10-year period from 2000–2010.

YOUR ANALYSIS:

1. Examine the population for your geographic region, and based on your region's trend, use deductive reasoning to assert a hypothesis about how the population has changed in your state.

- General observation:
- Specific observation:
- Deductive-derived hypothesis:

2. Examine the data for your state, and solely on your state's trend, use inductive reasoning to assert a hypothesis about how the population has changed in your region.

- Specific observation:
- General observation:
- Inductive-derived tentative conclusion:

Are both forms of reasoning equally useful? In this case, did they produce accurate results?

Population Change for the United States, Regions, States, and Puerto Rico: 2000 to 2010

Area	Population		Change	
	2000	2010	Number	Percent
United States.........	281,421,906	308,745,538	27,323,632	9.7
REGION				
Northeast..................	53,594,378	55,317,240	1,722,862	3.2
Midwest.....................	64,392,776	66,927,001	2,534,225	3.9
South......................	100,236,820	114,555,744	14,318,924	14.3
West	63,197,932	71,945,553	8,747,621	13.8
STATE				
Alabama	4,447,100	4,779,736	332,636	7.5
Alaska	626,932	710,231	83,299	13.3
Arizona	5,130,632	6,392,017	1,261,385	24.6
Arkansas	2,673,400	2,915,918	242,518	9.1
California	33,871,648	37,253,956	3,382,308	10.0
Colorado	4,301,261	5,029,196	727,935	16.9
Connecticut	3,405,565	3,574,097	168,532	4.9
Delaware	783,600	897,934	114,334	14.6
District of Columbia	572,059	601,723	29,664	5.2
Florida	15,982,378	18,801,310	2,818,932	17.6
Georgia	8,186,453	9,687,653	1,501,200	18.3
Hawaii	1,211,537	1,360,301	148,764	12.3
Idaho	1,293,953	1,567,582	273,629	21.1
Illinois...................	12,419,293	12,830,632	411,339	3.3
Indiana....................	6,080,485	6,483,802	403,317	6.6
Iowa.......................	2,926,324	3,046,355	120,031	4.1
Kansas.....................	2,688,418	2,853,118	164,700	6.1
Kentucky	4,041,769	4,339,367	297,598	7.4
Louisiana..................	4,468,976	4,533,372	64,396	1.4
Maine......................	1,274,923	1,328,361	53,438	4.2
Maryland	5,296,486	5,773,552	477,066	9.0
Massachusetts..............	6,349,097	6,547,629	198,532	3.1
Michigan...................	9,938,444	9,883,640	−54,804	−0.6
Minnesota	4,919,479	5,303,925	384,446	7.8
Mississippi................	2,844,658	2,967,297	122,639	4.3
Missouri...................	5,595,211	5,988,927	393,716	7.0
Montana....................	902,195	989,415	87,220	9.7
Nebraska...................	1,711,263	1,826,341	115,078	6.7
Nevada.....................	1,998,257	2,700,551	702,294	35.1
New Hampshire..............	1,235,786	1,316,470	80,684	6.5
New Jersey	8,414,350	8,791,894	377,544	4.5
New Mexico.................	1,819,046	2,059,179	240,133	13.2
New York	18,976,457	19,378,102	401,645	2.1
North Carolina.............	8,049,313	9,535,483	1,486,170	18.5
North Dakota...............	642,200	672,591	30,391	4.7
Ohio.......................	11,353,140	11,536,504	183,364	1.6
Oklahoma	3,450,654	3,751,351	300,697	8.7
Oregon.....................	3,421,399	3,831,074	409,675	12.0
Pennsylvania...............	12,281,054	12,702,379	421,325	3.4
Rhode Island...............	1,048,319	1,052,567	4,248	0.4
South Carolina.............	4,012,012	4,625,364	613,352	15.3
South Dakota...............	754,844	814,180	59,336	7.9
Tennessee..................	5,689,283	6,346,105	656,822	11.5
Texas......................	20,851,820	25,145,561	4,293,741	20.6
Utah.......................	2,233,169	2,763,885	530,716	23.8
Vermont....................	608,827	625,741	16,914	2.8
Virginia...................	7,078,515	8,001,024	922,509	13.0
Washington	5,894,121	6,724,540	830,419	14.1
West Virginia..............	1,808,344	1,852,994	44,650	2.5
Wisconsin	5,363,675	5,686,986	323,311	6.0
Wyoming	493,782	563,626	69,844	14.1
Puerto Rico	3,808,610	3,725,789	−82,821	−2.2

Source: U.S. Census Bureau, 2010 Census and Census 2000.

lower household incomes and Democratic voting: People with lower household incomes tend to identify with the Democratic Party. And while of course not all African Americans have lower household incomes, in general, African Americans constitute a larger proportion of lower-income households than their proportion of the population as a whole.

We can test this new hypothesis by looking at the voting behavior of both black and white low-income groups. It turns out that low-income black voters vote more heavily Democratic than low-income white voters, so we can reject the lower household income explanation. We may therefore infer that race is *independently* related to voting behavior. But there may be other possible alternatives to our explanation of the relationship between race and voting behavior. For example, African American parents may socialize their children to be loyal Democrats. Social scientists must test as many alternative explanations as possible before asserting a causal relationship.

Every time that we can reject an alternative explanation for the relationship we have observed, we increase our confidence that the relationship (as between race and voting behavior) is a causal one. Of course, in the areas of interest to social scientists, someone can always think of new alternative explanations, so it is generally impossible to establish for certain that a causal relationship exists. Some social scientists react to the difficulties of proving "cause" by refusing to say that the relationships they find are anything more than correlations. The decision whether or not to call a relationship "causal" is difficult. Statistical techniques cannot guarantee that a relationship is causal; social scientists must be prepared to deal with probabilities rather than absolutes.

Dealing with Observable Phenomena

*The scientific method deals only with observable—***empirical***—facts and events.* In other words, the scientific method deals with what *is*, rather than what *should be*. It cannot test the validity of values, norms, or feelings, except insofar as it can test for their existence in a society, group, or individual. For example, the scientific method can be employed to determine whether voting behavior is related to race, but it cannot determine whether voting behavior *should be* related to race. The latter question is a *normative* one (dealing with "ought" and "should"), rather than an empirical one (dealing with "is"). The scientific method is *descriptive* and *explanatory*, but not **normative**. The social sciences can explain many aspects of human behavior but cannot tell human beings how they ought to behave. For guidance in values and norms—for prescriptions about how people should live—we must turn to ethics, religion, or philosophy.

empirical
referring to observable facts and events; what is

normative
referring to values or norms; what should be

Developing Theory

The scientific method strives to develop a systematic body of theory. Science is more than crude empiricism—the listing of facts without any statement of relationships among them. Of course, especially in the early stages of a science, research may consist largely of collecting data, but the ultimate goal of the scientific method is to develop **theory** verifiable statements about relationships among facts and events. It is the task of social scientists to find patterns and regularities in human

theory
verifiable statements about relationships among facts and events

behavior, just as it is the task of physicists and chemists to find patterns and regularities in the behavior of matter and energy. The social scientist's use of the scientific method, then, assumes that human behavior is not random, rather that it is regular and predictable. Social scientists' development of theory, however, must be more normative than in the natural sciences. For example, underlying much theory in the social sciences are assumptions about human nature—whether it is inherently good or inherently selfish. These assumptions oftentimes form the building blocks of theory.

Theories are developed at different *levels of generality*. Theories with low levels of generality explain only a small or narrow range of behaviors. For example, we might theorize that conservative Christian voters tend to vote Republican, and this theory has a fairly low-level generality about political behavior; that is, it is a narrow and quite specific theory about one group's voting behavior. Theories with higher levels of generality explain a greater or wider range of behavior. For example, the statement that religious differences cause political conflict has a higher level of generality. Strictly speaking, a theory is a set of interrelated concepts at a fairly high level of generality. Some social scientists concentrate on theory building rather than on empirical research; they try to develop sweeping social theories to explain all, or a large part, of human behavior. Still other social theorists provide insights, hunches, or vague notions that suggest possible explanations of human behavior, thus developing new hypotheses for empirical research.

Maintaining a Scientific Attitude

Perhaps more than anything else, *the scientific method is an attitude of doubt or skepticism*. It is an insistence on careful collection of data and systematic testing of ideas; a commitment to keep bias out of one's work, to collect and record all relevant facts, and to interpret them rationally regardless of one's feelings. Admittedly, it is difficult to maintain a truly **scientific attitude** when examining social behavior. (See Controversies in Social Science: "Can Social Science Be Scientific?") For the social scientist, it is the determination to test explanations of human behavior by careful observations of real-world experiences. It is a recognition that any explanation is tentative and may be modified or disproved by careful investigation. Even the scientific theories that constitute the core knowledge in any discipline are not regarded as absolutes by the true social scientist; rather, they are regarded as probabilities or generalizations developed from what is known so far.

scientific attitude
doubt or skepticism about theories until they have been scientifically tested

What Is a "Fact"?

In the social sciences, very few statements can be made that apply to *every* circumstance. We cannot say, for example, that "all evangelical/born-again Christians vote Republican." This is a **universal statement** covering every evangelical or born-again Christian, and universal statements are seldom true in the social sciences. Moreover, it would be difficult to examine the voting behavior of every evangelical or born-again Christian voter in the past and in the future to prove that the statement is true.

universal statement
a statement that applies to every circumstance

A more accurate statement might be "most white evangelical/born-again Christians vote Republican." This is a **probabilistic statement**; it does not exclude the possibility that some white evangelical/born-again Christians vote Democratic. An even more accurate statement would be that "74 percent of white evangelical/born-again Christians cast their ballots for Republican candidate John McCain in the 2008 presidential election." This means there was a 74 percent *probability* of a white evangelical/born-again Christian voter casting his or her ballot for Republican John McCain.

A probabilistic statement is a fact, just like a universal statement. Students in the physical sciences deal with many universal statements—for example, "Water boils at 100 degrees Celsius." Water always does this. But social science students must learn to think in probabilities rather than in absolute terms.

Social scientists must also beware of substituting individual cases for statements of probability. They must be careful about reasoning from one or two observed cases. A statement such as "I know an evangelical family who always votes Democratic" may be true, but it would be very dangerous to generalize about the voting habits of all evangelicals on the basis of this one case. We always build tentative generalizations from our own world of experiences. However, as social scientists, we must ensure that our own experiences are typical. We should keep in mind that the "facts" of the social sciences are seldom absolute—they rarely cover the complexity of any aspect of human behavior. So we must be prepared to study probabilities.

probabilistic statement
a statement that applies to some proportion of circumstances

The Classic Scientific Research Design

An **experiment** is a scientific test that is controlled by the researcher and designed to observe the effect of a program or treatment. The *classic scientific research design* involves the comparison of specific changes in two or more carefully selected groups, both of which are identical in every way, except that one has been given the program or treatment under study while the other has not.[1]

This design involves the following:

- Identification of the goals of the study and the selection of specific hypotheses to be tested.
- Selection of the groups to be compared—the **experimental group**, which will participate in the program or undergo the treatment being studied, and the **control group**, which is similar to the experimental group in every way, except that it will *not* participate in the program or undergo the treatment being studied.
- Measurement of the characteristics of both the experimental and control groups *before* participation in the experiment.
- Application of the program or treatment to the experimental group, but not to the control group. (Members of the control group may be given a *placebo*—some activity or program known to have no effect—to make them believe that they are participating in the experiment. Indeed, the scientific staff administering the experiment may not know which group is the real

experiment
a scientific test controlled by the researcher to observe effects of a specific program or treatment

experimental group
the group that will participate in the program or undergo the treatment under study

control group
a group, similar to the experimental group, that does not undergo treatment; used for comparison

CONTROVERSIES IN SOCIAL SCIENCE

Can Social Science Be Scientific?

The scientific method was devised in the physical and biological sciences. There are many difficulties in applying this method to the study of individuals, groups, economies, classes, governments, nations, or whole societies. Let's examine some of the obstacles to the development of truly scientific social sciences.

Personal Bias *Social science deals with subjective topics and must rely on interpretation of results.* Social scientists are part of what they investigate—they belong to a family, class, race, gender, political party, interest group, profession, and nation. If the topic is an emotional one, the social scientist may find it much harder to suppress personal bias than does the investigator in the physical sciences: It is easier to conduct an unbiased study of migratory birds than of migrant workers.

Researchers study what they think is important in society, and their personal values affect what they think is important. Moreover, researchers' values are also frequently reflected in their perceptions of the data, in their statement of the hypotheses, in their design of the test for the hypotheses, and in their interpretations of the findings. An extreme version of this criticism of the social sciences (sometimes referred to as *poststructuralism*) argues that no knowledge is free of the race, gender, and class bias of the researcher.

Public Attitudes *Another problem in the scientific study of human behavior centers on public attitudes toward social science.* Few people would consider arguing with atomic physicists or biochemists about their respective fields, but most people believe they know something about social problems. Many people think they know exactly what should be done about juvenile delinquency, welfare dependency, and race relations. Very often their information is limited, and their view of the problem is simplistic. When a social scientist suggests that a problem is very complex, that it has many causes, and that information on the problem is incomplete, people may believe that the social scientist is simply obscuring matters that seem obvious.

Social science sometimes develops explanations of human behavior that contradict established ideas. Of course, the physical and biological sciences have long faced this same problem: Galileo faced the opposition of the established church when he argued that the earth revolved around the sun, and Darwin's theory of evolution continues to be a public issue. But social science generates even more intense feelings when it deals with poverty, crime, sexual behavior, race relations, and other sensitive topics.

Researcher Attitudes *Researchers themselves, particularly historians and sociologists, must be wary of evaluating historical events with a present day lens.* Using present-days mores or standards, it would be easy to pass judgment on common practices historically, which, at the time, may have been commonplace. For example, founding father Thomas Jefferson has been harshly criticized as a slaveholder and as sexist. But during the era in which he lived slaveholding was commonplace, and there was little notion of equality between the sexes. Using present day standards to judge Jefferson constitutes presentism.

Logical Fallacies *In both history and psychology, social scientists must be careful to avoid logical fallacies unique to their discipline.* For example, looking retrospectively, a historian might easily conclude that the United States should have anticipated the attacks on the United States on September 11, 2001, but looking at a situation with perfect hindsight is different from having the information available to leaders beforehand. Similarly, a psychologist may conclude that most individuals are similar to themselves and may imbue their subjects with absent positive and negative traits (i.e., assuming that everyone is loyal and faithful, or that everyone is dishonest).

Limitations of Conducting Social Science Research *Another set of problems in social science centers on the limitations and design of social science research.* It is not really possible to conduct some forms of controlled experiments on human beings. For example, we cannot deliberately subject people to poverty and deprivation just to see if it makes them violent. Instead, social researchers must find situations of poverty and deprivation in order to make the necessary observations about causes of violence. In a laboratory, we can control all or most of the factors that go into the experimental situation. But in real-world observations, we cannot control many factors; this makes it difficult to pinpoint what it is that causes the behavior that we are studying.

Design Constraints of Social Science Research *In fields such as anthropology and sociology, where ethnographies are created by social scientists who engage in participant observation, the participants know they are being observed.* When an entity (including a government or corporation) facilitates the observation, the setting may not be representative of typical settings. For example, a foreign anthropologist studying toddler learning methods in China may be directed to conduct her observations in a model school for gifted children.

Moreover, even where some experimentation is permitted, human beings frequently modify their behavior simply because they know they are being observed in a social science experiment. This phenomenon, known as the *Hawthorne effect*, makes it difficult to determine whether the observed behavior is a product of the stimulus being introduced or merely a product of the experimental situation itself. The Hawthorne effect is so named because it was identified for the first time by a group of researchers led by Elton Mayo. The researchers were investigating the impact of various social and environmental conditions at the Western Electric Hawthorne plant. The researchers found that whatever they did (improve lighting, dim lighting) resulted in increases in productivity. It was later determined that the increases actually were due to the increased attention that the workers were getting from the researchers rather than the changes to the social and environmental conditions in the workplace.

experimental group and which group is the control group. When neither the staff nor the group members themselves know who is really receiving the treatment, the experiment is called a *double-blind experiment.*)

- Measurement of the condition of both the experimental and control groups *after* the program or treatment. If there are measurable differences between the experimental and control groups, the scientist can begin to infer that the program or treatment has a specific effect. If there are *no* measurable differences, then the scientist must accept the **null hypothesis**—the statement that the program or treatment has no effect.

null hypothesis
a statement that the program or treatment has no effect

- Comparison of the preprogram/pretreatment status versus the postprogram/ posttreatment status in both groups. This is a check to see if the difference between the experimental and control groups occurred during the experiment (see Case Study: "Scientific Research Design: An Experiment in Preventing PTSD"). If there is no control group and only the experimental group is studied, this method is often called a "before–after" study.
- A search for plausible explanations for differences after treatment between the control and experimental groups that might be due to factors other than the treatment itself.

The classic research design is not without its problems. Social scientists must be aware of the more difficult problems in applying this research design to social science research and must be prepared on occasion to change their procedures accordingly. These problems include the following:

- Members of the experimental group may respond differently to a program if they know it is an experiment. Members of a control group are often told they are participating in an experiment, even though nothing is really being done to the control group.
- If the experimental group is only one part of a larger city, state, or nation, the response to the experiment may be different from what it would have been had all parts of the city, state, or nation been receiving the program. For example, if only one part of a city receives streetlights, criminals may simply operate as usual (even with the lights), and total crime rates will be unaffected.
- If persons are allowed to *volunteer* for the experiment, then experimental and control groups may not be representative of the population as a whole.
- In some situations, political pressures may make it possible to provide one neighborhood or group with certain services while denying these same services to the rest of the city, state, or nation. If everyone *thinks* the program is beneficial before the experiment begins, no one will want to be in the control group.
- It may be considered morally wrong to provide some groups or persons with services, benefits, or treatment while denying the same to other groups or persons (control groups) who are identical in their needs or problems.
- Careful research is costly and time consuming. Public officials often need to make immediate decisions. They cannot spend time or money on research even if they understand the long-term benefits of careful investigation. Too often, politicians and other policy makers must operate on "short-run" rather than "long-run" considerations.

CASE STUDY

Scientific Research Design: An Experiment in Preventing PTSD

Let's consider an example of applying the classic scientific research design to a specific social problem—post-traumatic stress disorder (PTSD). Researchers are examining ways of preventing the onset of PTSD after a traumatic event. Several hypotheses have been developed: Some researchers assert that prolonged exposure therapy, which involves breath control training as victims of trauma imagine the trauma they have experienced, will help victims of trauma combat the onset of PTSD symptoms. Other researchers advocate cognitive training designed to teach those who have experienced trauma to reduce negative thoughts. Some researchers hypothesize that victims of trauma should undergo prolonged exposure therapy only if they still show signs of stress disorder problems after five months. Still others advocate for the prevention of PTSD through the use of antidepressant medications.

In order to determine the best course of action, researchers at Hadassah University Hospital in Jerusalem, Israel, selected 242 patients who had suffered from a recent traumatic event (an average of about 10 days prior), and then had experienced subsequent acute stress, to participate in a study. The participants were divided into four groups, and each group received one of five treatments.

Group	Treatment
1	Prolonged exposure therapy
2	Cognitive training
3	Prolonged exposure therapy (delayed five months)
4	Antidepressant medication Lexapro*
Control group	Placebo

After treatment and nine months of follow-up, researchers assessed the effectiveness of various treatments, essentially assessing the validity of the various hypotheses. The researchers found that between 21 percent and 23 percent of the participants in groups one, two, and three who received psychotherapy developed PTSD (including those who delayed treatment until five months after the event), while 42 percent of those in group four, the antidepressant group, and 47 percent of those who took the placebo developed symptoms.

In evaluating the treatment methods, researchers concluded that prolonged exposure, cognitive therapy, and delayed prolonged exposure effectively prevent chronic PTSD in recent survivors. They also stated that lack of improvement from treatment with the antidepressant medication requires further evaluation. These conclusions can now be further evaluated by other researchers, and practitioners can formulate new hypotheses concerning the best avenues for preventing PTSD, including therapies that combine treatments.

(continued)

SOURCE: Arieh Y. Shalev, Yael Ankri, Yossi Israeli-Shalev, Tamar Peleg, Rhonda Adessky, Sara Freedman. "Prevention of Posttraumatic Stress Disorder by Early Treatment: Results from the Jerusalem Trauma Outreach and Prevention Study," Archives of General Psychiatry. Published online October 3, 2011. (http://archpsyc.ama-assn.org/cgi/content/full/archgenpsychiatry.2011.127)

* The study received funding from Lundbeck Pharmaceuticals, the manufacturer of Lexapro, the U.S. National Institute of Health, and other sources.

Gathering Data: Survey Research

How do social scientists go about observing the behaviors of individuals, groups, and societies? There are a variety of methods for gathering data (Table 2-2); some fields rely more heavily on one particular method than on another. The *controlled experiment*, described earlier, is often used in psychology; the *survey* is frequently employed in political science and sociology; *field research*, or participant observation, is a major source of data in anthropology; and *secondary data analysis* is employed in all social sciences.[2]

Survey Research

Most surveys ask questions of a representative sample of the population rather than question the entire population. A selected number of people, the **sample**, is chosen in a way that ensures that this group is representative of the **universe**,

sample
in survey research, the people chosen to represent the opinions of a larger group

universe
the whole group about which information is desired

One common way the classic research design effects our everyday lives is its use in the federal drug approval process. Angel Raich (second from the left) 41, of Oakland, California, sued the U.S. Attorney General and Drug Enforcement Administration director to block them from interfering with her medical marijuana use and sought to end the federal monopoly on the supply of marijuana that can be used in FDA-approved research. Raich suffers from an inoperable brain tumor.

TABLE 2-2   GATHERING DATA IN THE SOCIAL SCIENCES

Research Method	Operationalization	Example
Classical scientific experiment	Uses the scientific method; includes both an experimental and a control group; measures the impact of the application of the program or treatment on both groups.	See Case Study: "Scientific Research Design: An Experiment in Preventing PTSD"
Survey research	Uses the scientific method; asks opinions of a randomly selected sample of the population.	Gallup polls.
Field research: participant observation	Researchers both observe and participate in the behavior being studied.	Political scientist works as a campaign consultant while researching the decision-making structure in campaigns.
Field research: unobtrusive observer	Researchers observe the behavior being studied but try not to intrude or partake in the behavior.	Sociologist researching children's sex roles at play observes children while going unnoticed.
Field research: ethnography	A systematic description of a society's customary behaviors, beliefs, and attitudes.	Anthropologist lives with, interviews, and observes people of another culture.
Secondary-source data	Data used by social scientists that have been collected by other organizations or governments or researchers	U.S. Census data (see *Research This!*).

© Cengage Learning

the whole group of people about which information is desired. To ensure that the sample is representative of the universe, most surveys rely on random selection. In a **random sample**, each person in the universe has an equal chance of being selected for interviewing. Random sampling improves the likelihood that the responses obtained from the sample would be the same as those obtained from the universe if everyone were questioned. Hypothetically, we must obtain a random sample of American voters by throwing every voter's name in a giant box and blindly picking out one thousand names to be interviewed. A more common method is to randomly select telephone area codes and then numbers from across the nation.

There is always the chance that the sample selected will *not* be representative of the universe (see International Perspective: "Polling the World"). But survey researchers can estimate this **sampling error** through the mathematics of probability. The sampling error is usually expressed as a range above and below the sample response, within which there is a 95 percent likelihood that the universe response would be found if the entire universe was questioned. For example, if 63 percent of the people questioned (the sample) say they approve of the way that the president is handling his job and the sampling error is calculated at ± 3 percent (said "plus or minus 3 percent"), then we can say that there is a 95 percent likelihood that the president's approval rating among the whole population (the universe) stands somewhere between 60 and 66 percent (63 − 3 and 63 + 3).

random sample
a subset of the population in which there is an equal chance of each person in the universe being selected in the sample for interviewing

sampling error
the range of responses in which a 95 percent chance exists that the sample reflects the universe

INTERNATIONAL PERSPECTIVE

Polling the World

Imagine surveying a Zambian about whether she experienced boredom yesterday. Or asking a Paraguayan if he would recommend the area he lives in to others as a place to live. Or perhaps inquiring of an Icelander if she had smiled or laughed in the last day.

Imagine collecting the data on over one hundred questions in a scientific manner that will allow for comparisons between nations, that are inclusive of various populations, that facilitate the creation of indices (such a Well Being Index, or a Law and Order Index) based on individuals' responses to questions. Imagine conducting such a survey in war-torn regions, in desert conditions, in respondents' native tongues, sometimes using telephones (in places where at least 80 percent of the population has a phone), or in face to face interviews. (See following table.)

As part of their World Poll, the Gallup organization continuously polls individuals in more than 150 nations and seeks to represent the opinions of 98 percent of the world's population. Gallup's sample in each country is approximately 1,000 residents, consisting of the entire civilian, non-institutionalized population, aged 15 and older. "Gallup asks everyone from Australia to Pakistan the same questions, every time, in the same way, with the same meaning, and asks them in his or her own language to produce statistically comparable results."[1] Accurate surveys enable social scientists, world leaders, and policymakers to understand citizens' concerns, attitudes, behaviors, and gauge their sense of well-being.

Gallup Worldwide Research Data Collected

Country	Data Collection Dates	Number of Interviews	Design Effect[a]	Margin of Error[b]	Mode of Interviewing	Languages	Over-sample[c]	Exclusions (Samples are Nationally Representative unless noted otherwise)
Afghanistan	Apr 13 – Apr 22, 2010	1,000	1.72	4.1	Face-to-Face	Dari, Pashto		Gender-matched sampling was used during the final stage of selection.
Albania	Jul 2 – Jul 19, 2010	1,000	1.7	4	Face-to-Face	Albanian		
Algeria (5.1)	Feb 1 – Mar 7, 2010	1,001	1.41	3.7	Face-to-Face	Arabic		The sparsely populated deep South and governorates that represent security risks within Algiers were excluded. The excluded areas represent approximately 25% of the population.
Algeria (5.2)	Sep 2 – Oct 22, 2010	1,000	1.29	3.5	Face-to-Face	Arabic		The sparsely populated deep South and governorates that represent security risks within Algiers were excluded. The excluded areas represent approximately 25% of the population.
Argentina	Jul 1 – Jul 30, 2010	1,000	1.45	3.7	Face-to-Face	Spanish		
Armenia	Jun 26 – Jul 28, 2010	1,000	1.25	3.5	Face-to-Face	Armenian		
Australia	Feb 17 – Mar 10, 2010	1,000	1.5	3.8	Landline and Cellular Telephone	English		
Azerbaijan	Jul 14 – Jul 28, 2010	1,000	1.3	3.5	Face-to-Face	Azeri, Russian		Nagorno-Karabakh and territories not included for safety of interviewers. These areas represent less than 10% of the total population.
Bahrain (5.1)	Mar 31 – Apr 30, 2010	1,031	1.5	3.7	Face-to-Face	Arabic		Includes Bahrainis and Arab expatriates; non-Arabs were excluded. It's estimated that approximately one-fourth of the adult population is excluded.

Source: www.gallup.com/se/128171/Country-Data-Set-Details-May-2010.aspx

FOR DISCUSSION:

1. Describe some of the obstacles researchers face in collecting data in the various countries described above.

2. What other issues might researchers face in collecting survey data internationally?

---

[1] http://www.gallup.com/poll/128189/Gallup-global-polling-work.aspx

Large samples are not really necessary to narrow the sampling error. Large samples are not much more accurate than small samples. A sample of a few thousand—even one thousand—is capable of reflecting the opinions of 1 million or 100 million voters fairly accurately. For example, a random sample of one thousand voters across the United States can produce a sampling error (plus or minus) of only 3 percent.

Problems in Survey Research

If a poll is constructed scientifically and thoughtfully, it can provide accurate information about the opinions about a population. When well-constructed polls are inaccurate, it is usually because public opinion is unformed, weakly held, or changing rapidly. If public opinion is really unformed on a topic, as may be the case in early presidential preference polls, people may choose a familiar name or a celebrity who is frequently mentioned in the news. As the campaign progresses and people learn about the candidates and form opinions on them, candidates who were once unknown and rated only a few percentage points in early polls can emerge as front-runners. Weakly held opinions are more likely to change than strongly held opinions. Political commentators sometimes say a particular candidate's support is "soft," meaning that his or her supporters are not very intense in their commitment; therefore, the polls could swing quickly away from the candidate. Finally, widely reported news events may change public opinion very rapidly. A survey can measure opinions only at the time it is taken. A few days later, public opinion may change, especially if major events are receiving heavy television coverage. Some political pollsters conduct continuous surveys until election night in order to catch last-minute opinion changes.

But today pollsters and public opinion researchers who rely on telephone polling face a large obstacle in the data collection process: Many people rely exclusively on cell phones and do not have landline telephones meaning that those "celly-onlys" tend to be severely underrepresented in most national polls. Most data suggest that these "celly-onlys" are disproportionately young and oftentimes have less income than those with landlines, or those with both landlines and cell phones. Pollsters are attempting to remedy this problem in several ways—some are conducting polls of celly-onlys. Others are attempting to rectify the underrepresentation of these individuals by including a larger number of landline-surveyed younger people and those with lower incomes polled in their samples.

Assessing Public Opinion

Public opinion in democracies is given a great deal of attention. Indeed, survey research on public opinion is a thriving industry. There are some "hot-button" issues about which virtually everyone has an opinion and many people feel very intensely. And survey results on these issues command the attention of politicians and the news media as well as social scientists. **Salient issues** are those that people think about most and about which they hold strong and stable opinions.

In assessing public opinion polls, the construction of a poll merits scrutiny. It is important to realize that the wording or phrasing of public opinion questions can often determine the outcome of a poll. Indeed, "loaded" or "leading" questions are often asked by unprofessional pollsters simply to produce results

public opinion
the aggregate of opinions of individuals on topics in survey research

salient issue
an issue about which most people have thoughts about and hold strong and stable opinions

One way that social scientists assess public opinion is through the use of public opinion polls, including election day exit polls. These surveys, which rely on random sampling, predict which candidate will win an election before polls close. One such poll was taken in Los Angeles, where respondents indicated which candidate they voted for. Exit polls also shed light in why individuals prefer one candidate over another.

push poll

a survey that asks leading questions in order to sway opinion for a particular candidate or position

favorable to their political candidate or to their side of an argument. Called **push polls**, these efforts really constitute more of a campaign tactic than a scientific public opinion survey. A push poll might sound something like this:

PUSH POLLER: *In Tuesday's upcoming election between Rose Fitzgerald and Fred Foley, would you say that you are more likely to vote for Rose Fitzgerald or Fred Foley for mayor?*
VOTER: *Fred Foley.*
PUSH POLLER: *If you were informed that Fred Foley had multiple arrests for disorderly conduct and lewd behavior, would you be more or less likely to vote for him?*

The purpose of a push poll, as you can see, is not to gauge public opinion about a candidate but to unscrupulously smear the name of a candidate, oftentimes with baseless charges. Note that the push poller is not claiming any of the statements are facts but is saying, "If they were. . . ." Nonetheless, the voter is left with the impression that the charges have merit.

In scientific public opinion polls, ideally, questions should be clear and precise, easily understood by the respondents, and as neutral and unbiased as possible. But because all questions have a potential bias, it is usually better to examine changes over time in responses to identically worded questions.

Even the most scientific surveys are not error free, however. We have already noted that weakly held opinions can change rapidly. Thus, by the time poll results are reported in the media, those results may no longer reflect public opinion. Also, many opinion surveys ask questions that people had not considered before being interviewed. Few people are willing to admit that they know nothing about the topic or that they really have "no opinion." They believe they should provide an answer even if they have little interest in the topic itself. The result is that polls often seem to "create" public opinion. Another problem is the **halo effect**—the tendency of respondents to give "good-citizen" responses, whether the responses are truthful or not. For example, people do not like to admit that they do not vote or that they do not care about politics. Surveys regularly report higher percentages of people *saying* they voted in an election than the *actual* number of ballots cast would indicate. Many people give socially respectable answers, even to an anonymous interviewer, rather than answers that suggest prejudice, hatred, or ignorance.

halo effect
the tendency of respondents to give "good-citizen" responses to pollsters

Field Research

Fieldwork is the cornerstone of modern anthropology. Many sociologists and political scientists also obtain their information through field work. These social scientists study by direct, personal observation of people, events, and societies. **Field research** is essentially going where the action is, watching closely, and taking notes.[3]

Fieldwork is usually less structured than either experimental or survey research. Oftentimes, field research enables a more in-depth examination of the causes of behaviors than quantitative research allows. However, in field research, the scientist cannot control many variables, as in experimental research. Nor can the scientist know whether the peoples or societies being studied are truly representative of all other peoples or societies, as in survey research. However, careful field reports can provide qualitative information that is often missing from experimental and survey research. Researchers can report on emotions, feelings,

field research
directly observing social behavior

Participant-observation research involves the integration of the researcher into the field. The researcher observes and actually participates in the behavior being studied. Here a French anthropologist studies Aru Island villagers in Indonesia. What are the advantages of this type of research?

and beliefs that underlie people's behavioral responses. Researchers can also report on attitudes, myths, symbols, and interpersonal relationships that could not be detected by other research methods. Most important, they can observe individuals, groups, and societies as they live in their subjects' environment.

participant observation
researchers both observe and participate in the behavior being studied

Field research often involves **participant observation**, where the researcher both observes and participates in the society being studied. Direct participation (moving to Appalachia and getting a job as a coal miner, for example) can provide insights that would otherwise escape a researcher. However, personal participation can also interfere with the detachment required for scientific inquiry. There is also the question of whether the scientist should identify himself or herself as a researcher, which could change the behavior of the people being studied, or conceal his or her identity, which could encourage people to act naturally but raises ethical questions. Some behavior simply cannot be observed if social scientists are identified as researchers.

Consider the dilemma of the sociologist who wanted to study homosexual behavior in public toilets. It was not really feasible for him to go on field trips to public toilets, identifying himself as a sociologist and asking people if they were homosexuals seeking contacts, and, if so, if he could observe their behavior. But he understood that, in some areas, public toilets had provided an important meeting ground for gay men who lacked access to other means of meeting gay men. So instead he began visiting public toilets where he suspected homosexual activity was taking place and volunteered to act as a "lookout" for those engaging in the action. He discovered that a lookout was an acceptable, even important, position, and he took advantage of it to study homosexual behavior. Later, after the publication of his study, he came under attack by homosexuals and others for deceiving his subjects.[4]

In other field research, a researcher will attempt to be as unobtrusive as possible in order not to influence or change the behavior of the subjects. For example, a sociologist researching the sex roles of children at play might push her own child on a swing while listening and observing another group of children playing "house" at a park.*

Anthropology relies heavily on field research. To describe cultures accurately, many anthropologists choose to live among the people they are studying, directly observing and participating in their lives. Many early anthropological studies were intuitive: They produced in-depth, first-hand observations of societies, but these observations were not very systematic. Some would focus on child rearing, religion, art, language, or a particular practice specific to the area being studied and foreign to researchers. Later, anthropological field work became more disciplined, and anthropologists began systematic comparisons of cultures.

ethnography
systematic description of a society's customary behaviors, beliefs, and attitudes

Ethnography is the systematic description of a society's customary behaviors, beliefs, and attitudes. Ethnographic studies are usually produced by anthropologists who have spent some time living with, interviewing, and observing the people. Anthropologists in the field can test hypotheses by directly asking and observing the people and learning about the context of their behavior and beliefs. For example, an anthropologist in the field may think that the society he or she is studying practices polygamy (one man marries more than one woman simultaneously) because it has

---

* Researchers typically must be granted consent by the human subjects of their research (or their parents or guardians).

more women than men. But as ethnographic studies are gradually acquired for a larger number of different cultures, anthropologists can begin to test hypotheses by cross-cultural comparisons. They may find reports of some societies that practice polygamy even though the number of men and women is equal. This finding would cast doubt on the hypothesis that polygamy is caused by gender-ratio imbalances.

A **case study** is an in-depth investigation of a particular event in order to understand it as fully as possible. A case study may involve an examination of a single government decision, a single business firm, a single town, or a single society. In anthropology, a case study often will examine a specific topic in a given culture—mating rituals among the Ibakharu tribe in Algeria, for example.

In the social sciences, case studies sometimes help future researchers analyze similar situations. In some ways, case studies can be thought of as using historical analysis to help inform the future. For example, an analysis of the passage of a piece of legislation might enable a researcher to create a hypothesis about that could help elucidate future decision-making patterns; a case study of the impact of change in a neighborhood—changes in crime rates or employment rates, ethnic population changes, or any other criteria—may help social scientists someday understand how other neighborhoods might face similar changes by generating hypotheses about the effect of change. But while a hypothesis may be tested in a case study, researchers know that a single case is not sufficient to make generalizations about other cases. A single case study is more useful for generating hypotheses to be explored later in comparative studies involving larger numbers of cases. However, some case studies involve limited comparisons, as when two, three, or four cases are studied simultaneously.

case study
an in-depth investigation of a particular event in order to understand it as fully as possible

CHAPTER SUMMARY

- The purpose of the scientific method is to explain relationships. The scientific method develops and tests theories about how observable facts or events are related in order to explain them. Through the scientific method, social scientists develop hypotheses and determine if correlations exist. As part of the scientific method, researchers strive to develop a systematic body of theory based on empirical facts or events. In engaging in social science research, it is important that the researcher maintain a scientific attitude—one of doubt or skepticism regarding theories until theories have been tested. Social scientists in each discipline face unique difficulties applying the scientific method to the study of social problems. Specifically, operationalizing the classic scientific research design method presents obstacles to anthropologists, sociologists, political scientists, psychologists, historians, and economics because of difficulties in design, including the availability of a random sample. Research design issues also include altered behavior by the control group, making inferences from one population to another, moral considerations in research—including withholding the value or treatment from a population—and the cost of careful research.

- Methods used by social scientists to conduct research include the classical scientific experiment, survey research, three types of field research including participant observation, unobtrusive observer, and ethnography, plus analysis of secondary source data.

KEY TERMS

case study   an in-depth investigation of a particular event in order to understand it as fully as possible

control group   a group, similar to the experimental group, that does not undergo treatment; used for comparison

correlation   a significant statistical relationship

deductive reasoning   to infer from a general theory to a particular case

empirical   referring to observable facts and events; what is

ethnography   systematic description of a society's customary behaviors, beliefs, and attitudes

experiment   a scientific test controlled by the researcher to observe effects of a specific program or treatment

experimental group   the group that will participate in the program or undergo the treatment under study

field research   directly observing social behavior

halo effect   the tendency of respondents to give "good-citizen" responses to pollsters

hypothesis   a tentative statement about a relationship between observable facts or events

inductive reasoning   to observe one phenomenon or series of phenomena and make general assertions based on that observation

normative   referring to values or norms; what should be

null hypothesis   a statement that the program or treatment has no effect

participant observation   researchers both observe and participate in the behavior being studied

probabilistic statement   a statement that applies to some proportion of circumstances

public opinion   the aggregate of opinions of individuals on topics in survey research

push poll   a survey that asks leading questions in order to sway opinion for a particular candidate or position

random sample   a subset of the population in which there is an equal chance of each person in the universe being selected in the sample for interviewing

salient issue   an issue about which most people have thoughts about and hold strong and stable opinions

sample   in survey research, the people chosen to represent the opinions of a larger group

sampling error   the range of responses in which a 95 percent chance exists that the sample reflects the universe

science   broadly defined, any organized body of knowledge

scientific attitude   doubt or skepticism about theories until they have been scientifically tested

scientific method   a method of explanation that develops and tests theories about how observable facts or events are related

significant   not likely to have occurred by chance

theory   verifiable statements about relationships among facts and events

universal statement   a statement that applies to every circumstance

universe   the whole group about which information is desired

ON THE WEB

EXPLORING THE SOCIAL SCIENCES

The website for this textbook offers resources for exploring the social sciences on the Internet, as well as study tools including a glossary, practice quizzes, discussion questions, and Internet exercises. Visit **www.cengagebrain.com**.

The U.S. government is the most reliable single source of information on American society. Virtually every U.S. government department and agency maintains a website with access to extensive information relevant to a particular sector of American society. Try searching the Internet using the various departments in the executive branch, including agriculture, commerce, defense, education, energy, environment, health and human services, housing and urban development, homeland security, interior, crime and justice, labor, state and international affairs, transportation, treasury, and veterans' affairs to find an abundance of information collected by the U.S. government.

• **U.S. Census Bureau** As depicted in the text, perhaps the most extensive U.S. government database is that maintained by the U.S. Census Bureau: **www.census.gov**. This site directs visitors to

information, from A to Z, on the United States. It even keeps a population clock, providing daily estimates of the U.S. and world populations.

Try this: Go to **2010.census.gov/2010census/data/** and click on your state. Examine the shifts in population that have occurred in the counties in your state. Use deductive and inductive reasoning to create hypotheses as to why these shifts have occurred.

• **Polling Organizations** Several of the nation's largest polling organizations, including Gallup (**www.gallup.com**), the Roper Center for Public Opinion Research (**www.ropercenter.uconn.edu**), and the National Organization for Research at the University of Chicago (**www.norc.org**) host websites that oftentimes provide intriguing, up-to-date poll data.

Try This: Go to **www.gallup.com/poll/101872/How-does-Gallup-polling-work.aspx** and explain Gallup's research design, including defining the universe, the sample, and their sampling error.

REVIEW QUIZ

MULTIPLE CHOICE

1. What is the method of explanation that develops and tests theories about how observable facts or events are related?
   a. social science
   b. the scientific method
   c. field work
   d. a case study

2. A tentative statement about a relationship between observable facts or events is called _____.
   a. a hypothesis
   b. significant
   c. a universal statement
   d. a scientific attitude

3. A significant statistical relationship is called a _____.
   a. correlation
   b. sample
   c. universal statement
   d. scientific attitude

4. Referring to observable facts and events is known as _____.
   a. a scientific attitude
   b. empirical
   c. a universal statement
   d. normative

5. What is the name for a statement that applies to some proportion of circumstances?
   a. a correlation
   b. a theory
   c. a universal statement
   d. a probabilistic statement

6. The group that will participate in the program or undergo the treatment under study is called the _____.
   a. halo group
   b. control group
   c. experimental group
   d. correlation group

7. In survey research, what is the name for the group of people chosen to represent the opinions of a larger group?
   a. the population
   b. the control group
   c. the experimental group
   d. the sample

8. The aggregate of opinions of individuals on topics in survey research is called _____.
   a. public opinion
   b. the universe
   c. a sample
   d. the halo effect

9. What is the systematic description of a society's customary behaviors, beliefs, and attitudes called?
   a. a case study
   b. field work
   c. ethnography
   d. participant observation

10. An in-depth investigation of a particular event in order to understand it as fully as possible is known as what?
    a. a case study
    b. field work
    c. ethnography
    d. participant observation

FILL IN THE BLANK

11. Broadly defined, any organized body of knowledge is called _____.

12. Doubt or skepticism about theories until they have been scientifically tested is known as a _____.

13. A scientific test controlled by the researcher to observe effects of a specific program or treatment is called _____.

14. Each person in the universe having an equal chance of being selected in the sample for interviewing occurs in a _____.

15. _____ reflects the range of responses in which a 95 percent chance exists that the sample reflects the universe.

CHAPTER 3

Power and Ideology

Learning Objectives

After reading this chapter, students will be able to:

- Explain the ways in which ideology can control people's behavior, and describe what functions ideologies serve in general.

- List the seven ideologies discussed in this chapter, and describe how they compare and contrast with each other.

- Explain where you think individual liberty fits in relation to the welfare of the society as a whole.

- Identify the ideology that best represents your ideal, or consider whether elements of different ideologies best represent your ideal.

The Power of Ideas

ideology
an integrated system of ideas or beliefs that rationalizes and justifies the exercise of power, influencing how power is exercised

Ideas have power. People are coerced by ideas—beliefs, symbols, doctrines—more than they realize. Indeed, whole societies are shaped by systems of ideas that we frequently refer to as ideologies. An **ideology** is an integrated system of ideas or beliefs that provides society and its members with rationalizations for a way of life, guides for evaluating "rightness" and "wrongness," and emotional impulses to action. Political ideology provides a framework for thinking about politics, about policy issues, and about how active a role government should have in society. In the United States, one key component of various ideologies is the extent to which adherents believe that the government should have a role in people's everyday lives, in particular the extent to which the government should promote economic equality in society.

Power and ideology are intimately related. Ideology rationalizes and justifies the exercise of power. By providing a justification of power, ideology itself becomes a source of control over people. Without the added *legitimacy* provided by ideology, powerholders would be confronted by an aroused populace who strongly resent what they regard as the naked power exercised over them. Nothing could be more dangerous to the stability of a power system. Yet the very ideology that legitimizes power also·governs the conduct of powerholders. Once an ideology is deeply rooted in a society, powerholders themselves are bound by it if they wish to retain power.[1]

Functions of Ideology

Ideologies control people's behavior in several ways: (1) Ideologies affect perception. Ideas influence what people "see" in the world around them. Ideologies frequently describe the character of human beings in society; they help us become aware of certain aspects of society but often impair our ability to see other aspects. Ideologies may distort and oversimplify in their effort to provide a unified and coherent account of society. (2) Ideologies rationalize and justify a way of life and hence provide legitimacy for the structure of society. An ideology may justify the status quo, or it may provide a rationale for change, or even for revolution. (3) Ideologies provide normative standards to determine "rightness" and "wrongness" in the affairs of society. Ideologies generally have a strong moral component. (4) Ideologies provide motivation for social and political action. They give their followers a motive to act to improve world conditions. Ideologies can even "convert" individuals to a particular social or political movement and arouse them to action.

The Risk of Oversimplification

It is difficult to summarize a modern ideology in a few brief paragraphs. The risk of oversimplification is great. And because ideologies themselves are oversimplifications, the problem is compounded. Moreover, ideologies are constantly changing. When old utopian hopes are disappointed, they are frequently revised or replaced by new ones. New ideologies compete with older ones in various stages of revision (see Focus: "Selected Direct Quotations from Ideologies"). To unravel the ideological forces operating in society at any given time is a highly complex affair. With these warnings in mind, however, let's consider some of the major ideologies that influence our contemporary world.

Classical Liberalism: The Least Government Is the Best Government

classical liberalism
asserting the dignity of the individual and limited government power

divine right of kings
Bossuet's idea that monarchies, as representatives of God's will, entitled them to rule absolutely, ignoring the will and well-being of their subjects

Classical liberalism asserted the worth and dignity of the individual. It emphasized the rational ability of human beings to determine their own destinies, and it rejected ideas, practices, and institutions that submerged individuals into a larger whole and deprived them of their essential dignity. In particular, classical liberalism rejected the notion prominent centuries ago when kings and emperors throughout Europe claimed that they reigned by divine sanction, or God's will. The French philosopher Jacques-Benigne Bossuet characterized this type of rule as the **divine right of kings**, stating that monarchies, as representatives of God's will, could rule absolutely, ignoring the will and well-being of their subjects.

Liberalism grew out of the eighteenth-century Enlightenment, the Age of Reason during which time scientists including Sir Isaac Newton drastically changed how people thought about the universe and their societies. In particular, Newton's ideas about **natural law**—the premise that the laws that govern human behavior come from the nature of humans themselves and can be universally applied—provided the foundation for more ideas that would see people exerting greater influence over governments. Some of liberalism's great philosophers such as John Locke and Adam Smith affirmed their faith in reason, virtue, and common sense. Liberalism originated as an attack on hereditary prerogatives and distinctions of a feudal society, the monarchy, the privileged aristocracy, the state-established church, and the restrictions on individual freedom associated with the feudal order. And it offered an alternative vision as to how individuals and governments should function.

natural law
the premise that the laws that govern human behavior come from the nature of humans themselves and can be universally applied

Classical Liberal Ideas

Classical liberalism helped motivate America's founders to declare their independence from England, to write the American Constitution, and to establish the Republic.[2] It rationalized their actions and provided ideological legitimacy for the new nation. John Locke, the English political philosopher whose writings most influenced the founders of the United States, argued that even in a "state of nature"—that is, a world in which there were no governments—an *individual* possesses **inalienable rights**, rights that are inherent in an individual because of their humanness, and rights that cannot legitimately be taken away by a government. Locke's idea of inalienable rights—the rights to life, liberty, and property—directly influenced American founding father Thomas Jefferson, who in writing the Declaration of Independence would include "life, liberty, and happiness" as "God-given and unalienable Rights." Locke's idea of natural law, or moral principle, guaranteed every person these rights. He believed that the very purpose of government was to protect individual liberty.

inalienable rights
rights not granted by government but belonging to individuals by virtue of their natural human condition

In order to accomplish this goal, Locke asserted that human beings form a **social contract** among themselves to establish a government to protect their rights; they agree to accept government authority in order to better protect life, liberty, and property. Implicit in the social contract and the liberal notion of liberty is the belief that government activity and restrictions over the individual should be kept to a minimum.

social contract
the idea that government arises from an implied contract among people as a means of protecting their rights

Thus, classical liberalism included a belief in **limited government**, the idea that government cannot violate the rights that it was established to protect. Because government is formed through the consent of the governed to protect individual liberty, it logically follows that government cannot violate the rights it was established to protect.

limited government
the idea that government cannot violate the rights that it was established to protect; government power over the individual is limited

Classical liberalism also affirmed the equality of all human beings. The Declaration of Independence expressed the conviction that "all men are created equal." The founders believed in equality for all *before the law*, notwithstanding the accused's circumstances. Over time, the notion of equality has also come to include *equality of opportunity* in all aspects of life—social, educational, and economic.

Today, the notion of equality often includes the idea that governments can be used to help achieve equal opportunities for all. That is, government programs sometimes serve as a mechanism to attempt to "level the playing field" so that barriers to advancement are eliminated. This role of government is based on the more modern notion of **equality of opportunity**, that each person should have an equal chance to develop individual capacities to his or her natural limits; there should be no artificial barriers to personal advancement.

equality of opportunity
each person should have an equal chance to develop individual capacities to his or her natural limits; there should be no artificial barriers to personal advancement

It is important to remember, however, that classical liberalism has always stressed equality of opportunity but not absolute equality. Thomas Jefferson recognized a "natural aristocracy" of talent, ambition, and industry, and classical liberals have always accepted inequalities that are a product of individual merit and hard work. Absolute equality, or "leveling," is not a part of classical liberalism.[3]

Classical Liberalism and the Economic Ideology of Capitalism

capitalism
an economic system that protects private property, private ownership of businesses, and the freedom to buy and sell goods and services, with a minimum of government intervention

Classical liberalism as a *political* ideology is closely related to **capitalism** as an *economic* ideology.[4] Capitalism asserts the individual's right to own private property and to buy, sell, rent, and trade in a free market. The economic version of liberty is the freedom to make contracts, to bargain for one's services, to move from job to job, to join labor unions, to start one's own business.

laissez-faire
French for "let it be," refers to a "hands off" approach or a limited role of the government in economic activity

Capitalism and classical liberal democracy are closely related as economic and political systems. Capitalism stresses individual rationality in economic matters; freedom of choice in working, producing, buying, and selling; and a **laissez-faire**, or "hands-off," approach to government intervention in economic affairs. Liberal democracy emphasizes individual rationality in voter choice; freedoms of speech, press, and political activity; and limitations on government power over individual liberty. In classical liberal politics, individuals are free to speak out, to form political parties, and to vote as they please—to pursue their political interests as they think best. In classical liberal economics, individuals are free to find work, to start businesses, and to spend their money as they please—to pursue their economic interests as they think best. The role of government is restricted to protecting private property, enforcing contracts, and performing only those functions and services that cannot be performed by the private market.

Modern Liberalism: Government Power to "Do Good"

modern liberalism
government power is seen as a positive force in protecting the individual

Modern liberalism rationalizes and justifies much of the growth of governmental power that occurred in the United States in the twentieth century. Modern liberalism emphasizes the importance of the social and economic security of a whole population as a prerequisite to individual self-realization and self-development. Classical liberalism looked with suspicion on government as a potential source of "interference" with personal freedom, but modern liberalism looks on the *power of government as a positive force* to be used to contribute to the elimination of social and economic conditions that adversely affect people's lives and impede their self-development. Modern liberals approve of the use of government power to ensure the general social welfare and to correct the perceived ills of society. They believe that they can change people's lives through the exercise of government power: end discrimination, abolish poverty, eliminate slums, ensure employment, uplift the poor, eliminate sicknesses, educate the masses, and instill humanitarian values in everyone. They emphasize the importance of civil liberties, including freedom of speech, assembly, and the press, as outlined in the Bill of Rights. The prevailing impulse is to *do good*, to perform public services, and to assist the least fortunate in society, particularly minorities and the poor.[5]

Reforming Capitalism

Modern liberalism is frequently critical of certain aspects of capitalism, but it proposes to *reform* capitalism rather than replace it with socialism. Modern liberalism continues to recognize the individual's right to own private property, but it imposes on the property owner many social and economic obligations (see Controversies in Social Science: Protesting Income Inequality). For example, it assumes that business will be privately owned but will be subject to considerable government regulation. Thus, the government intervenes to ensure fair labor standards, minimum wages, healthy working conditions, consumer protection, environmental protection, and so forth.

A Larger Role for Government

Modern liberals are also committed to support (and often expansion) of the *public (governmental) sector of society* in matters having to do with education, welfare, housing, the environment, transportation, urban renewal, medicine, employment, child care, and so on. Modern liberalism sees the government as playing an important role in the future: setting new goals, managing the economy, meeting popular wants, and redirecting national resources from private wants toward public needs.

Reduction of Inequalities

Modern liberalism defines equality somewhat differently from classical liberalism. Classical liberalism stresses the value of *equality of opportunity:* Individuals should be free to make the most of their talents and skills, but differences in wealth or power that are a product of differences in talent, initiative, risk taking, and skill are accepted as natural. In contrast, modern liberalism contends that individual dignity and equality of opportunity depend in some measure on *reduction of absolute inequality* in society. Modern liberals believe that true equality of opportunity cannot be achieved where significant numbers of people suffer from hunger, remediable illness, or extreme hardships in the conditions of life. In addition, they support political equality, advocating contemporary movements that promote the political rights of gay and lesbian couples and voting rights for the disenfranchised. Thus, modern liberalism supports government efforts to reduce various inequalities in society.

CONTROVERSIES IN SOCIAL SCIENCE

Protesting Income Inequality

O ccupy Wall Street is a movement formed by American citizens in response to the country's economic conditions following the 2008 financial crisis. Protesters first gathered on September 17, 2011, at Liberty Square in Manhattan's Financial District. Topping the list of occupiers' complaints were the high unemployment rate, the greed of American corporations, and the increasing divide between the country's rich and poor. After the first demonstrations began in New York, the Occupy movement spread to more than 100 cities throughout the country and has been linked to similar protests internationally in Asia, Europe, Africa, and Australia.

Though the Occupy movement has been characterized as disorganized and lacking a central agenda, one key theme that has emerged from the protests is opposition to increasing income inequality. The mantra of the movement is "We are the 99 percent," a reference to nearly all Americans who are not in the top 1 percent of earners. (The *Washington Post* calculated that the threshold for an individual to be a part of the top 1 percent was an income exceeding roughly $516,000 in 2011.) Since 1981, the margin between the rich and poor has continuously widened in the United States, with more money landing in the hands of the wealthy. In 2007, 43 percent of the country's financial wealth (total net worth not including home value) was held by the top 1 percent of the population; the bottom 80 held just

Modern Conservatism: Individualism and Traditional Values

conservatism
ideology emphasizing individual freedom from government controls and maximum personal liberty

In the United States today, *conservatism* is associated with classical liberalism (see Focus: "How to Tell if You're Liberal or Conservative"). Today, **conservatism** is an ideology that emphasizes individual freedom from government controls and maximum personal liberty. In this country, conservatives also stress the importance of reliance on individual initiative and effort for self-development rather than on government programs and projects; a free-enterprise economy with a minimum of government intervention; and rewards for initiative, skill, risk taking, and hard work, in contrast to government-imposed "leveling" of income. These views are consistent with the early classical liberalism of Locke, Jefferson, and the nation's founders. The result, of course, is a confusion of ideological labels: Conservatives today charge modern liberals with abandoning the principles of individualism, limited government, and free enterprise, and today's conservatives claim to be the true "liberals" in society.[6]

In 2009 a new manifestation of conservative ideology arrived on the American political scene. The Tea Party movement—an allusion to the 1773

7 percent. Since the housing market bubble burst, estimates figure that there has been a 36 percent drop in wealth for median American households, compared to an 11 percent drop for the top 1 percent.

While many people argue that income inequality fuels the fire of economic distress and instability, some believe it is necessary to inspire innovation and economic growth. Those who represent America's wealthiest argue that protesters are pointing their fingers in the wrong direction, saying that it is the government's job to regulate the financial industry and play watch-dog over big businesses. They also argue that many of those who have enjoyed financial success have worked hard and sometimes have created products—including products, such as iPhones and Facebook, used to organize the Occupy movement.

As protesters continue to occupy cities around the world, the controversy over who is to blame for a lagging economy and what changes could be made grow more complicated.

Should politicians and large corporations listen to those protesting the nature of our economic system? What should be done to start creating a healthier economy? In your view, does income inequality spawn economic growth? Explain how the Occupy movement fits into the American ideological perspective.

colonial protest in Boston on the British tax on tea, and an acronym for "taxed enough already"—is a conservative, libertarian movement. Some key agenda items for Tea Party members include reduction of the federal budget deficit and decreased taxation through reduced government spending, and decreasing the national debt. Tea Party activists often advocate for a free market economy. They also argue for limited powers for the federal government, a strengthening of states' rights, the protectionism of individual liberties, and a strict interpretation of the Constitution.

While the Tea Party movement began as a loosely-organized grassroots, populist movement, with little formal leadership, in the aftermath of the 2010 congressional elections, it emerged as a more formal organization. Today, Tea Party caucuses exist in both the U.S. House of Representatives and the U.S. Senate, and political personalities including former vice presidential candidate Sarah Palin and former presidential candidates Rep. Ron Paul (R-Texas) and Rep. Michelle Bachman (R-Minnesota) are often cited as the movement's ideological leaders. Most Americans who ascribe to the Tea Party philosophy identify themselves as Republicans but express dissatisfaction with the traditional Republican Party nationally.[7]

FOCUS

Selected Direct Quotations from Major Ideologies

Modern Liberalism "If the people cannot trust their government to do the job for which it exists—to protect them and to promote their common welfare—all else is lost."
—Barack Obama, 2008

Classical Liberalism "To understand political power aright, and derive it from its original, we must consider what estate all men are naturally in, and that is, a state of perfect freedom to order their actions, and dispose of their possessions and persons as they think fit, within the bounds of the law of Nature, without asking leave or depending upon the will of any other man."
—John Locke, *Treatise of Civil Government*, 1668

Modern Conservatism "Economic arrangements play a dual role in the promotion of a free society. On the one hand, freedom in economic arrangements is itself a component of freedom broadly understood, so economic freedom is an end in itself. In the second place, economic freedom is also an indispensable means toward the achievement of political freedom."
—Milton Friedman, *Free to Choose*, 1980

Fascism "The stronger must dominate and not blend with the weaker, thus sacrificing his own greatness. Only the born weakling can view this as cruel, but he after all is only a weak and limited man; for if this law did not prevail, any conceivable higher development of organic living beings would be unthinkable."
—Adolf Hitler, *Mein Kampf*, 1925

"Anti-individualistic, the Fascist conception of life stresses the importance of the State and accepts the individual only in so far as his interests coincide with those of the State, which stands for the conscience and the universal will of man as a historic entity."
—Benito Mussolini, *Fascism*, 1925

Communism "The history of all hitherto existing societies is the history of class struggles. Freeman and slave, patrician and plebeian, lord and serf, guild-master and journeyman, in a word, oppressor and oppressed, stood in constant opposition to one another, carried on an uninterrupted, now hidden, now open fight, a fight that each time ended, either in a revolutionary reconstitution of society at large, or in the common ruin of the contending classes."
—Karl Marx and Friedrich Engels, *Communist Manifesto*, 1888

Socialism "The aim of all socialist measures, even of those which appear outwardly as coercive measures, is the development and the securing of a free personality. Their more exact examination always shows that the coercion included will raise the sum total of liberty in society, and will give more freedom over a more extended area than it takes away. The legal day of a maximum number of hours' work, for example, is actually a fixing of a minimum of freedom, a prohibition to sell freedom longer than for a certain number of hours daily, and, in principle, therefore, stands on the same ground as the prohibition agreed to by all liberals against selling oneself into personal slavery."
—Edward Bernstein, Evolutionary Socialism, 1899

MLADEN ANTONOV/Staff/Getty Images

Conservatism is an ideology that emphasizes individual freedom from government controls and maximum personal liberty. Conservatives also stress self-reliance, a free-enterprise economy and rewards for initiative, skill, risk taking, and hard work. Rep. Ron Paul (R-Texas), who has twice sought the Republican nomination for president, often attracts staunchly conservative supporters.

Law and Tradition

Modern conservatism does indeed incorporate much of classical liberalism, but conservatism also has a distinct ideological tradition of its own. Conservatism, reflecting the political tradition of British philosopher Thomas Hobbes (1588–1670), is not as optimistic about human nature as is liberalism. Hobbes argued that in a state of nature, the strong prey upon the weak. In his 1651 book *Leviathan*, arguing the merits of an absolute monarch, Hobbes describes how a social contract can protect individuals from anarchy, a state of "continuall feare, and danger of violent death; And the life of man, solitary, poore, nasty, brutish, and short."[8]

Like Hobbes, traditionally, modern conservatives understood that human nature includes elements of irrationality, intolerance, extremism, ignorance, prejudice, hatred, and violence. Thus, they were more likely to place their faith in *law* and *tradition* than in the popular emotions of mass movements. Without the protection of law and tradition, people and societies are vulnerable to terror and violence. The absence of law does not mean freedom but rather exposure to the tyranny of terrorism and violence.

Preference for Evolutionary Change

Conservatism sets forth an *evolutionary* view of social progress. Revolutionary change is far more likely to set society back than to improve it. But over time, people can experiment in small ways with incremental changes; continued from generation to generation, this process of evolutionary change leads to a progressive improvement in the condition of humanity. No government possesses the wisdom to resolve all problems, but the cumulative experience of society does produce certain workable arrangements for the amelioration of social ills. Gradual progress is possible, but only if people do not destroy the painfully acquired wisdom of the past in favor of new, untried utopian solutions that jeopardize the well-being of society.

Tradition, Family, and Church as Guides

Conservatives hold that people are rational beings, but that they are also victims of passion. Without the guidance of law, tradition, and morality, people would soon come to grief by the unruliness of their passions, destroying both themselves and others in pursuit of selfish gain. Rationalism is far from a sufficient guide to action; law, tradition, and morality are also needed for the realization of human purposes. Strong institutions—family, church, and community—are needed to repress individuals' selfish and irrational impulses and to foster civilized ways of life.

Smaller Government

Conservatives believe that government should play a more limited role in people's everyday lives. They think that government should have a smaller role in regulating business and industry and that market forces, rather than the government, should largely determine economic policy. Conservatives believe that families, faith-based groups, and private charities should be more responsible for protecting the neediest and the government less so. When governments must act, conservatives prefer decentralized action by state governments rather than a nationwide federal policy.

Libertarianism

libertarianism
ideology that advocates that government should take a "hands-off" approach in most matters

To the right of conservatism, one finds the libertarian ideology. According to **libertarianism**, government should take a "hands-off" approach in most matters. This ideology can be found to the right of conservatism on a traditional ideological spectrum. Libertarians believe that the less government intervention, the better. They chafe at attempts by the government to foster economic equality or to promote a social agenda, whether that agenda is the equality espoused by liberals or the traditional values espoused by conservatives. Libertarians strongly support the rights of property owners and a *laissez-faire* capitalist economy. Figure 3-1 shows a spectrum of these ideologies that exist in the United States.

How Americans Describe Themselves

The terms *liberal* and *conservative* have been used with different meanings over the years, so it is difficult to know whether Americans are really liberal or conservative on the issues. One way of determining their stance is to ask questions such as. "How would you describe your own political philosophy—conservative, moderate, or liberal?" As can be seen from the results of recent surveys,

FOCUS

HOW TO TELL IF YOU'RE LIBERAL OR CONSERVATIVE

	You Are Liberal if You Agree That	You Are Conservative if You Agree That
Economic policy	Government should regulate business to protect the public interest	Free-market competition is better at protecting the public than government regulation
	The rich should pay higher taxes to support public services for all	Taxes should be kept as low as possible
	Government spending for social welfare is a good investment in people	Government welfare programs destroy incentives to work
Crime	Government should place primary emphasis on alleviating the social conditions (poverty, joblessness, etc.) that cause crime	Government should place primary emphasis on providing more police and prisons and stop courts from coddling criminals
Social policy	Government should protect the right of women to choose abortion and fund abortions for poor women	Government should restrict abortion and not use taxpayer money for abortions
	Government should pursue affirmative action programs on behalf of minorities and women in employment, education, etc.	Government should not grant preferences to anyone based on race or gender
	Government should keep religious prayers and ceremonies out of schools and public places	Government should allow prayers and religious observances in schools and public places
National security policy	Government should support "human rights" throughout the world	Government should pursue the "national interest" of the United States
	Military spending and further expansion of the war on terrorism should be cautious	Military spending must reflect a variety of new dangers in this post–September 11 period
You generally describe yourself as	"caring" "compassionate" "progressive"	"responsible" "moderate" "sensible"
And you describe your political opponents as	"extremists" "right-wing radicals" "reactionaries"	"knee jerks" "bleeding hearts" "left-wing radicals"

SOURCE: Adapted from Thomas R. Dye, *Politics in America*, 4th ed. (New York: Prentice Hall, 2001).

FIGURE 3-1   THE TRADITIONAL IDEOLOGICAL SPECTRUM

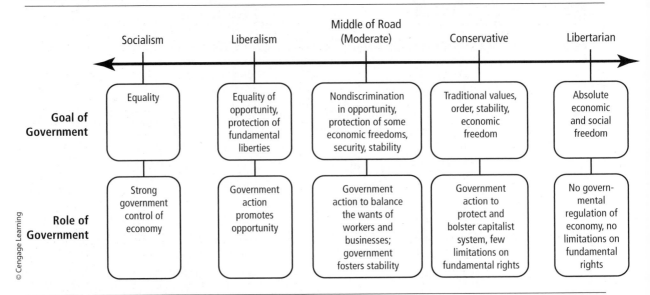

SOURCE: Brigid Callahan Harrison, Jean Wahl Harris, Susan J. Tolchin. *American Democracy Now.* (New York: McGraw-Hill, 2009) p. 28.

self-described conservatives outnumber liberals although it is important to note that many Americans prefer "moderate" and many others decline to label themselves at all (see Research This!).

What do Americans mean when they label themselves "liberal," "moderate," or "conservative"? There is no clear answer to this question. People who called themselves "conservatives" did not consistently oppose social welfare programs or government regulation of the economy. People who called themselves "liberals" did not consistently support social welfare programs or government regulation of the economy. And Americans, in comparison to Europeans, are much less ideological and less likely to hold strong or extreme ideological positions.

In trying to determine an individual's ideology, one useful question to ask is, "To what extent should government be involved in people's everyday lives?" When asked this question, many liberals would say that government should play a larger role—they believe that government should do more to ensure equality, provide services, regulate business and industry, and protect workers. Other the other hand, conservatives are likely to argue that government should be doing less—that the marketplace should be left to its own devices, and that private organizations should provide for the needy. Since 1992, the Gallup Poll asked people their views about the role of government, as shown in Figure 3-2. Figure 3-2 shows that while there is little change in people's views about whether the government is doing too much or should do more to solve the country's problems, there is some small difference during Democratic presidential administrations (between 1992 and 2000, and after 2008) and more people thinking that the government is doing too much.

RESEARCH *THIS!*

How would you describe your political views—very conservative, conservative, moderate, liberal, or very liberal?

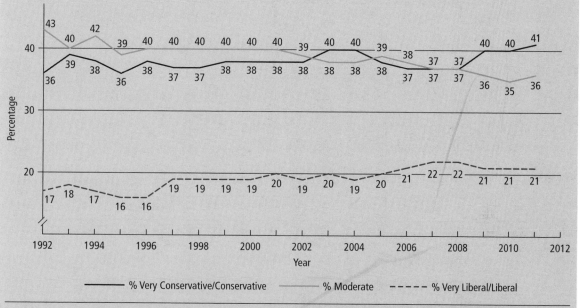

SOURCE: http://www.gallup.com/poll/148745/Political-Ideology-Stable-Conservatives-Leading.aspx

The Gallup Poll data above shows how Americans describe their own ideological positions since 1992. Over the course of nearly twenty years, the percentage of people who consider their political views to be conservative, moderate, or liberal has stayed remarkably consistent.

Since 2008, when President Obama took office, we have seen a slight uptick in the number of self-described conservatives, which grew from 37 percent in 2008 to 41 percent in 2011. Meanwhile, the number of liberals has stayed between 21 and 22 percent since 2006.

YOUR ANALYSIS:

1. What has been the trend with regard to the proportion of Americans who call themselves "moderates"?

2. Why do you think people relate more to a conservative or moderate ideology? Does the term "liberal" carry a certain connotation?

3. What may have led to conservatives outnumbering moderates in recent years? During what other period did conservatives hold the highest percentage in the poll, and what could have caused that?

4. Why do you think moderates ranked the highest in percentage for ten years?

FIGURE 3-2   SOME PEOPLE THINK THE GOVERNMENT IS TRYING TO DO TOO MANY THINGS THAT SHOULD BE LEFT TO INDIVIDUALS AND BUSINESSES. OTHERS THINK THAT GOVERNMENT SHOULD DO MORE TO SOLVE OUR COUNTRY'S PROBLEMS. WHICH COMES CLOSER TO YOUR OWN VIEW?

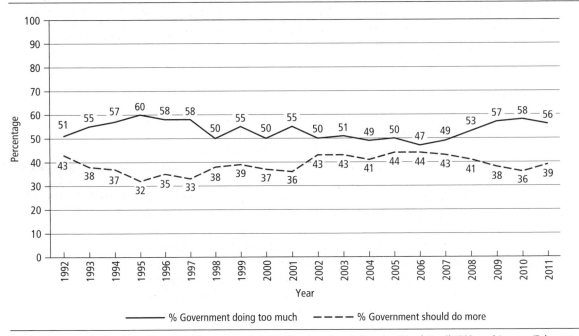

SOURCES: Surveys by CBS News/New York Times, as reprinted in The American Enterprise, March/April 1993; and January/February 2000, 51; by the Gallup Organization, October 2005; and by The Washington Post "Ideological Shift or Just Complicated?" http://voices.washingtonpost.com/behind-the-numbers/2008/11/ideological_shift_or_just_comp.html.

The Advent of Communism: "Workers of the World, Unite"

communism

an ideology critical of capitalism that asserts that the class structure created by the capitalist mode of production perpetuates various facets of society

Communism is a strain of the larger ideological movement of socialism. Both socialism and communism arose out of the Industrial Revolution and the "social evils" it generated. Even though the Industrial Revolution led to a rapid rise in standards of living in Western Europe, what impressed many early observers of this revolution was the economic inequalities it engendered. Throughout much of the nineteenth century, the real beneficiaries of the new industrialism seemed to be the successful manufacturers, bankers, merchants, and speculators; the lot of the slum-dwelling working classes showed little improvement. This was a bitter disappointment to the humanitarian hopes of many who had earlier embraced liberalism in the expectation that the rewards of economic progress would be shared by everyone. It appeared that liberalism and capitalism had simply substituted an aristocracy of wealth for an aristocracy of birth.

Karl Marx

Like many other socialists, Karl Marx (1818–1883) was an upper middle–class intellectual. When his radicalism barred academic advancement, he turned to journalism and moved from Berlin to Paris. There he met Friedrich Engels, a wealthy young intellectual who supported Marx financially and collaborated with him on many of his writings. The ***Communist Manifesto*** (1848) was a political pamphlet—short, concise, and full of striking phrases, such as "Workers of the world, unite. You have nothing to lose but your chains." It provided an ideology to what had previously been no more than scattered protest against injustices. The *Manifesto* set forth the key ideas of Marxism, which would be developed twenty years later in great detail in a lengthy work, *Das Kapital*.

Communist Manifesto
political pamphlet, written by Karl Marx, describing Marxism and calling for world revolution

Economic Determinism

Communists believe that the nature of the economy, or "mode of production," is basic to all the rest of society. The mode of production creates the class structure, the political system, religion, education, family life, law, and even art and literature, an idea called **economic determinism**. The economic structure of capitalism creates a class structure of a wealthy *bourgeoisie* (pronounced bore-zh-WA-zee) (a property-owning class of capitalists) who control the government and exercise power over the *proletariat* (the propertyless workers). Communists believe that the class structure created by this capitalist mode of production is perpetuated through various facets of society. For example, communists might assert that the education system in a capitalist nation socializes few students to be part of the elite ruling class—encouraging them to develop leadership skills and develop attributes of the ruling class—but instead that it socializes many to become part of the working class, by encouraging deference to authority and passivity.

economic determinism
the nature of the economy determines the social structure

Class Struggle

The first sentence of the *Communist Manifesto* exclaims, "The history of all hitherto existing society is the history of class struggles." The class that owns the mode of production is in the dominant position and *exploits* the other classes. Such exploitation creates antagonism, or **class struggle**, which gradually increases until it bursts into revolution. The capitalist exploits the worker to the point at which the worker is forced to revolt against the oppressors and overthrow the capitalist state.

class struggle
the basic conflict in any society is between economic classes; capitalists versus the proletariat

Inevitability of Revolution

Marx asserted that a proletarian revolution is inevitable. As capitalists try to maximize their profits, the rich become richer and the poor become poorer. As capitalists drive wages down to maximize profits, capitalism becomes plagued by a series of crises or depressions, each one worse than the one before. The result of these "internal contradictions" in capitalism is a great deal of human misery, which eventually explodes in revolution. Thus, in their drive for profit, capitalists really dig their own graves by bringing the revolution ever closer.

Dictatorship of Proletariat

Although Marx claimed that the coming of the revolution was inevitable, he nonetheless urged workers to organize for revolutionary action. The capitalists will never peacefully give up their ruling position. Only a violent revolution will place the proletariat in power. When the proletariat come to power, they, like ruling classes before them, will set up a state of their own—a dictatorship of the proletariat—to protect their class interests. This proletariat dictatorship will seize the property of the capitalists and place ownership of the mode of production in the hands of the proletariat. The bourgeoisie will be eliminated as a class.

The Classless Society

After the revolution, as a result of *common ownership* of everything, a *classless* society will emerge. Because the purpose of government is to assist the ruling class in exploiting and oppressing other classes, once a classless society is established the government will have no purpose and will gradually "wither away." In the early stages of the revolution, the rule of distribution will be "from each according to his ability, to each according to his work." But after the victory of communism and the establishment of a full classless society, the rule of distribution will be "from each according to his ability, to each according to his need" (see Case Study: "The Rise and Fall of Communism in Russia").

Socialism: Government Ownership, Central Planning

socialism
public ownership of the means of production, distribution, and service

There is a bewildering variety of definitions of **socialism**. Occasionally critics of government programs in the United States label as "socialist" any program or policy that restricts free enterprise in any way. But fundamentally, socialism means *public ownership of the means of production, distribution, and service.* Socialists agree on one point: Private property in land, buildings, factories, and stores must be transformed into social or collective property. The idea of *collective ownership* is the core of socialism.

Opposition to Capitalism

Socialism shares with communism a *condemnation of the capitalist system* as exploitive of the working classes. Communists and socialists agree on the evils of industrial capitalism: the exploitation of labor, the concentration of wealth, the insensitivity of the profit motive to human needs, the insecurities and sufferings brought on by the business cycle, the conflict of class interests, and the propensity of capitalist nations to involve themselves in war. In short, most socialists agree with the criticisms of the capitalist system set forth by Marx.

Commitment to Democracy

However, socialists are committed to the democratic process as a means of replacing capitalism with collective ownership of economic enterprise. They generally reject the desirability of violent revolution as a way to replace capitalism and instead advocate peaceful constitutional roads to socialism. Moreover, socialists have rejected the idea of a socialist "dictatorship"; they contend that the goal of socialism is a *free society* embodying the democratic principles of freedom of speech, press, assembly, association, and political activity. They frequently claim that socialism in the economic sector of society is essential to achieving democracy and equality in the political sector of society. In other words, they believe that true democracy cannot be achieved until wealth is evenly distributed and the means of production are commonly owned.

Government Ownership

Socialists believe that wealth must be redistributed so that all persons can share in the benefits created by society. Redistribution means a transfer of ownership of all substantial economic holdings to the government. But the transfer must be accomplished in a democratic fashion rather than by force or violence, and a socialist society must be governed as a true democracy.

Central Planning

Socialism relies on central planning by government bureaucrats to produce and distribute goods and services. Free markets are either outlawed or restricted to a few consumer items. Government bureaucrats decide how many shirts, televisions, autos, and so on should be produced. Factories are given quotas to meet, and their output is shipped to government stores. Workers' wages are also determined by government planners, as are decisions about new investments and developments. Government planners rely on their own judgment about what is needed, rather than relying on market demand. Planners set goals for each sector of the economy, usually in five-year plans.

Nationalization

Socialists envision a gradual change from private to public ownership of property. Thus, socialists may begin by "nationalizing" the railroads, the steel industry, the automobile industry, privately owned public utilities, or other specific segments of the economy. **Nationalization** involves government seizure of these industries from private owners.

nationalization
government seizure of industries from private owners

Fascism: The Supremacy of Race or Nation

Fascism is an ideology that asserts *the supremacy of the nation or race over the interests of individuals.* In the words of the former Italian fascist dictator, Benito Mussolini, "Everything for the state; nothing against the state; nothing outside of the state."

fascism
the supremacy of the nation over the individual

The Organic State

Fascism perceives the state as not merely a government bureaucracy but *the organic life* of a whole people. According to Mussolini, "The Italian nation is an organism having ends, life, and means of action superior to those of the separate individuals or groups of individuals which compose it." In *Mein Kampf*, written by Adolf Hitler before his assumption of power in Germany in the 1930s, Hitler added to the concept of an organic state, with his idea of the *Volk* (people), in which race and nation are united.[9]

Fascist Goal

The **goal of the fascist state** is not the welfare of the mass of people but the *development of a superior race of human beings.* The goal is the cultivation of bravery, courage, creativity, genius, intelligence, and strength. Fascism values the

goal of the fascist state
a superior race of human beings

superior individual who rises out of the mire of mass mediocrity and the superior nation that rises above the vast anthill of humankind. If life is a struggle for existence in which the fittest survive, then strength is the ultimate virtue and weakness is a fault.

Merger of Nationalism and Socialism

Though different from traditional socialism, which seeks to create a structure in which all persons can share in the benefits created by society, fascism offers itself as a *merger of nationalism and socialism*. Before World War II, fascism in Italy and Germany put itself forward as a socialist regime adopted to national purposes. The party of Adolf Hitler was the National Socialist, or "Nazi," party. Under fascism the nation is an organic whole; therefore, the economy ought to be *cooperative* rather than competitive. Every class and every interest ought to work together for the *good of the nation*. Against the rights of liberty or equality, national socialism established the duties of *service, devotion,* and *discipline.*

Totalitarian Power Structure

totalitarianism
incorporates all sections of society into the state

The power structure of a fascist regime is **totalitarian**, incorporating all sections of society into the state. Fascism strives for a totality of power in which all sectors of society—education, labor, art, science—are incorporated into the state and serve the purposes of the state.

Anti-Semitism

anti-Semitism
hatred of and prejudice against Jews

The origins of **anti-Semitism**—hatred and prejudice directed toward Jews—go back many centuries in Europe, through persecutions, exclusions, ghettoization,

In 1935, Adolf Hitler addressed 100,000 people in Nuremberg, Germany. Hitler's form of fascism emphasized the organic state in which race and nation are united.

Topham / The Image Works

and attacks (pogroms) against Jewish communities. But the racial theories developed under fascism brought anti-Semitism to a historically unprecedented scale of horror. In *Mein Kampf*, Hitler depicts the Jews as defilers of German racial purity—not human beings, but "maggots" "contaminating" the nation and state. The Nazis exploited anti-Semitism in their rise to power, encouraging discrimination, exclusion from schools and businesses, forced ghettoization, and violent attacks against Jews and Jewish-owned property. Later, Hitler implemented his "final solution" to the "Jewish problem"—the mass murder of an entire people, or **genocide**.

Genocide

Almost 6 million European Jews were systematically murdered (called the *Shoah*, or calamity, in Hebrew) during World War II, along with millions of other people, including gypsies, Catholics, homosexuals, and the disabled, who were defined as "inferior" by Nazi ideology. All told, an estimated 9 to 11 million people were killed in **the Holocaust**. The killing began with mass shootings by special *Einsatzgruppen* squads and later escalated into the systematic transportation of millions of Jews and others to a huge network of death camps including Auschwitz, Bergen-Belsen, Buchenwald, and Dachau. Huge gas chambers and furnaces for the burning of corpses enabled SS troops to kill many thousands in a single day; many others died from starvation, beatings, disease, and cruel medical experimentation. Evidence of this Holocaust is preserved in photos, artifacts, documents, and personal accounts at the Yad Vashem memorial in Jerusalem, Israel, as well as the records of the International Military Tribunal held in Nuremberg, Germany, after the war to try Nazi war criminals.

genocide
mass murder of an entire people

the Holocaust
the murder of millions of Jews, as well as millions belonging to other religious, ethnic, and cultural groups, in Nazi death camps during World War II

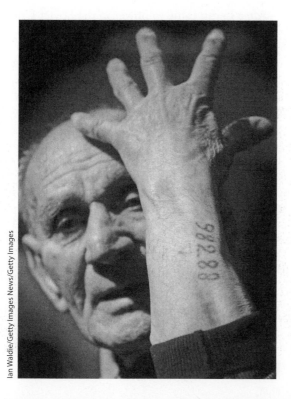

Ian Waldie/Getty Images News/Getty Images

Part of the evidence of the Holocaust is seen through survivors of that genocide. Auschwitz survivor Mr. Leon Greenman, prison number 98288, shows his prison number tattooed on his arm. Mr. Greenman, age 93 at the time of the photo, spent three years of his life in six different concentration camps during World War II, in which 6 million European Jews were systematically murdered.

CASE STUDY

The Rise and Fall of Communism in Russia

After the 1917 Russian Revolution that overthrew the tzar, Vladimir Lenin, a revolutionary leader who had reinterpreted Marxism as a revolutionary ideology, used that ideology to create a communist state in the Soviet Union. Lenin's thinking so greatly changed the ideas first posited by Karl Marx that Soviet-style modern communist ideology is frequently referred to as *Marxism-Leninism.*

The Totalitarian Party   According to Lenin, the key to a *successful* revolution was the creation of a new and revolutionary type of totalitarian political party composed of militant professional revolutionaries. This party would be organized and trained like an army to obey the commands of superior officers. While Western European socialist parties were gathering millions of supporters in relatively democratic organizations, Lenin constructed a small, exclusive, well-disciplined, elitist party. According to Lenin, the Communist Party is the true "vanguard of the proletariat"—the most advanced and class-conscious sector of the proletariat—which has an exclusive right to act as spokesperson for the proletariat as a whole and to exercise the dictatorial powers—"dictatorship of the proletariat"—over the rest of society.

Communism in One Country   After Lenin came to power in the Soviet Union in 1917, he found himself no longer in the position of revolutionary leader; he was the leader of a nation. Gradually abandoning their original hopes for an immediate world revolution, Lenin and his successor, Stalin, turned to the task of creating "communism in one country." With the Communist Party more centrally disciplined than ever, the Soviet leaders turned to the achievement of rapid industrialization through a series of five-year plans designed to convert a backward agrarian country into a modern industrial nation. The sweeping industrialization, brought about by the repression and terror of a totalitarian regime, came at great cost to the people.

The Police State   The Stalinist period saw brutality, oppression, imprisonment, purges, and murders—later officially admitted by the Soviet leaders. The Soviet regime held down the production of consumer goods in order to concentrate on the development of heavy industry. In part, the ideology of communism made it possible to call on the people for tremendous sacrifices for the good of the communist state.

The state never withered away in communist Russia. Indeed, to maintain the communist government, a massive structure of coercion—informants, secret police, official terrorism, and a giant prison system—was erected. (The brutality of the system is described by Nobel Prize-winning author and former Soviet political prisoner Aleksandr Solzhenitsyn in *The Gulag Archipelago.*)

Militarism   Following the "Great Patriotic War"—the Russian name for World War II, in which more than 20 million Soviet citizens were killed and Nazi Germany was defeated—Stalin and his successors directed the Soviet economy primarily toward military purposes. The Soviets maintained the world's largest and most heavily armed military forces, and they built a nuclear missile force that surpassed that of the United States in size and numbers. (Their rapid progress in heavy missiles allowed them to place the first satellite in orbit in 1957 and the first man in space in 1962.) But the huge military establishment was a heavy economic burden; consumer goods in the Soviet Union were generally shoddy and always in short supply. Long waiting lines at state-run stores became the symbol of the Soviet economy.

Perestroika* and *Glasnost   Mikhail Gorbachev ascended to power in the Soviet Union in 1985, committed to *perestroika* ("restructuring")—the reform and strengthening of communism in the nation. Gorbachev deviated from many of the earlier interpretations of Marxism-Leninism. He encouraged greater decentralization in industry and less reliance on centralized state direction. At the same time, he called for *glasnost* ("openness") in Soviet life and politics, removing many restrictions on speech, press, and religion and permitting elections with noncommunist candidates running for and winning elective office.

Gorbachev also reached agreements with the United States and Western European nations on the reduction of both nuclear and conventional weapons. Most important, he opposed the use of military force to keep communist governments in power in Eastern Europe. As a result of this decision, communist governments were ousted in Poland, Czechoslovakia, Hungary, Bulgaria, Romania, and East Germany in 1989. The Berlin Wall was torn down, and Germany was unified in 1990.

The Collapse of Communism   Gorbachev's economic and political reforms threatened powerful interests in the Soviet state—the Communist Party *apparatchiks* (bureaucrats) who were losing control over economic enterprises; the military leaders, who opposed the withdrawal of Soviet troops from Germany and Eastern Europe; the KGB police, whose terror tactics were increasingly restricted; and central government officials, who were afraid of losing power to the republics. When these hard-liners attempted the forcible removal of Gorbachev in August 1991, the democratic forces rallied to his support. Led by Boris Yeltsin, the first elected president of the Russian Republic, thousands of demonstrators took to the streets, Soviet military forces stood aside, and the coup crumbled. Gorbachev was temporarily restored as president, but Yeltsin emerged as the most influential leader in the nation. The failed coup hastened the demise of the Communist Party.

The Disintegration of the Soviet Union   Strong independence movements in the republics of the former Union of Soviet Socialist Republics (USSR) emerged as the authority of the centralized Communist Party in Moscow waned. Lithuania, Estonia, and Latvia—nations that had been forcibly incorporated into the Soviet Union in 1939—led

(continued)

the way to independence in 1991. Soon all of the fifteen republics of the USSR declared their independence, and the USSR officially ceased to exist after December 31, 1991. Its president, Mikhail Gorbachev, no longer had a government to preside over. The red flag with its hammer and sickle atop the Kremlin in Moscow was replaced with the flag of the Russian Republic.

Russia after Communism   The transition from a centralized state-run economy to free markets turned out to be more painful for Russians than expected. Living standards for most people declined, alcoholism and death rates increased, and even average life spans shortened. President Boris Yeltsin was confronted by both extreme nationalists, who believed democracy weakened the power of Russia in the world, and the continuing efforts of communists to regain their lost power. Ethnic conflict and political separatism, especially in the largely Muslim province of Chechnya, added to Russia's problems. (Only in 2000, after prolonged fighting, did Russian troops finally take control of most of the province.) Nevertheless, Yeltsin was able to overcome these political challenges and win reelection as president in 1996. But corruption, embezzlement, graft, and organized crime continued to undermine democratic reforms. Ill health eventually forced Yeltsin to turn over power to Vladimir Putin, who himself won election as president of Russia in 2000 and reelection in 2004. Constitutionally banned from seeking reelection in 2008, Putin was succeeded by his hand-picked successor and chief of staff Dmitry Medvedev. During his campaign for president, Medvedev announced that if elected, he would appoint Putin to the post of Prime Minister, in effect ensuring a way for the popular Putin to retain an influential role in Russian politics. Medvedev was easily elected and carried through on his promise.

The United States has a vital continuing interest in promoting democracy and economic reform in Russia. Russia remains the only nuclear power capable of destroying the United States.

Neofascism today can be observed in some extremist movements in Germany, France, Great Britain, and the United States. "Skinheads," often emblazoned with Nazi swastikas, preach and practice violence against non-whites, Jews, and foreigners. Extremist parties and politicians frequently echo fascist themes in their aggressive patriotism, racist rhetoric and actions, opposition to ethnic minorities, and calls for national and racial unity.

Why Communism Collapsed

The Allied victory over the Axis powers in World War II signaled the end of the Nazi state in Europe, but in the aftermath of the war, Communist Russia increased its hold in Eastern Europe, leading to the formation of the Communist Bloc in Eastern Europe. After a protracted arms race with the United States, however, communism collapsed in Russia and Eastern Europe in 1989.

Speculation about the causes of communism's collapse is risky. The fact that before 1989 very few Western social scientists had predicted these revolutionary events suggests that we do not fully understand their causes. Yet we can suggest some interesting hypotheses about the current crisis of communism.

Deteriorating Living Standards

Communist economies cannot provide an adequate standard of living for their people. The democratic revolutions in Eastern Europe and the Soviet Union were inspired principally by the realization that free-market capitalism was providing much higher standards of living in the Western world. The economies of the communist-bloc nations were falling further and further behind the economies of the capitalist nations of the West. Similar comparative observations of the successful economies of the free-market "Four Dragons"—South Korea, Taiwan, Singapore, and Hong Kong—inspired Chinese leaders to experiment with market forces.

Communist bureaucracies cannot determine production and allocate goods and services as effectively as free markets. In a communist system, central bureaucracies, not consumers, determine production. Production for elite goals (principally, a strong military) comes first; production for individual needs comes last. People serve the system instead of the other way around. Consumer goods are shoddily made and always in short supply. This results in long lines at stores, rampant black marketeering, and frequent bribery of bureaucrats and managers to obtain necessary consumer items.

Lack of Individual Incentives

Communism destroys the individual's incentive to work, produce, innovate, invent, save, and invest in the future. The absence of profit incentives leads to extravagant waste by enterprise managers. Employees have no incentives to work hard or to satisfy customers. Official prices are low, but shortages prevent workers from improving their standard of living. Bureaucrats try to order innovation, but innovation requires individual creativity and reward, not conformity to a central plan.

Popular Distrust and Cynicism

Over time, *communist systems lose the trust of the people.* Because the system promised a worker's paradise, the economic hardship imposed on the people inspires widespread cynicism. Because the system promised equality, the power and privilege enjoyed by the bureaucratic elite inspire resentment.

Absence of Political and Economic Freedoms

The concentration of both economic and political decision making in the hands of a central government bureaucracy is incompatible with democracy. Democracy requires limited government, individual freedom, and dispersal of power in society. *In communist nations, the government exercises virtually unlimited power over economic as well as political affairs, individual economic freedoms are curtailed, and great power is accumulated by the government bureaucracy.* In contrast, in capitalist nations, governmental intervention in the marketplace is limited, individuals are free to make their own economic decisions, and power is dispersed among many groups and institutions: governments, corporations, unions, press and television, churches, interest groups, and so forth.

Communism's Incompatibility with Democracy

Thus, democracy is closely tied to capitalism. Capitalism does not ensure democracy; some capitalist nations are authoritarian. But capitalism is a necessary condition for democracy. *All existing democracies have free-market economies, and no communist system is a democracy.* In other words, capitalism is a necessary although not a sufficient condition for democracy.

Above all, the communist system denies individual freedom, political pluralism, and democracy. Force, repression, and indoctrination can be effective over many years. But at some point, the universal human aspiration for personal freedom and dignity emerges to challenge the communist order.

CHAPTER SUMMARY

- Ideologies can be extremely powerful weapons that perform several functions, including affecting perception, rationalizing and justifying a way of life, providing normative standards to determine "rightness" and "wrongness" in the affairs of society, and in motivating social and political action.

- Classical liberalism emphasized the rational ability of human beings to determine their own destinies, and it rejected ideas, practices, and institutions that submerged individuals into a larger whole and deprived them of their essential dignity. It included a belief in limited government and a capitalist economic ideology.

- Modern liberalism rationalizes the growth of governmental power that occurred in the United States in the twentieth century. It emphasizes the importance of the social and economic security of a whole population as a prerequisite to individual self-realization and self-development, and urges the reform of capitalism.

- Conservatism is an ideology that emphasizes individual freedom from government controls and maximum personal liberty.

- Americans are more likely to describe themselves as conservative than liberal, though many Americans describe themselves as "moderate."

- Key tenets of communism include the idea that through economic determinism, the mode of production creates the class structure, the political system, religion, education, family life, law, and even art. Communists emphasize class struggle, and believe in the inevitability of class-based revolution, leading to a dictatorship of the proletariat and the eventual withering away of the state.

- Socialism argues for public ownership of the means of production, distribution, and service. Socialists oppose capitalism but are committed to the democratic process as a means of replacing capitalism with collective ownership of economic enterprise.

- Fascism's goal is the development of a superior race of human beings. Components of fascism include the creation of the totalitarian state, as well as anti-Semitism.

- Explanations as to why communism collapsed include its inability to provide a decent standard of living for its people, the lack of individual incentives, the loss of trust in the government by its people, the lack of political and economic freedom, and its incompatibility with democracy.

KEY TERMS

anti-Semitism hatred of and prejudice against Jews

capitalism an economic system that protects private property, private ownership of businesses, and the freedom to buy and sell goods and services, with a minimum of government intervention

class struggle the basic conflict in any society is between economic classes; capitalists versus the proletariat

classical liberalism asserting the dignity of the individual and limited government power

communism an ideology critical of capitalism that asserts that the class structure created by the capitalist mode of production perpetuates various facets of society

Communist Manifesto political pamphlet, written by Karl Marx, describing Marxism and calling for world revolution

conservatism ideology emphasizing individual freedom from government controls and maximum personal liberty

divine right of kings Bossuet's idea that monarchies, as representatives of God's will, entitled them to rule absolutely, ignoring the will and well-being of their subjects

economic determinism the nature of the economy determines the social structure

equality of opportunity each person should have an equal chance to develop individual capacities to his or her natural limits; there should be no artificial barriers to personal advancement

fascism the supremacy of the nation over the individual

genocide mass murder of an entire people

goal of the fascist state a superior race of human beings

the Holocaust the murder of millions of Jews, as well as millions belonging to other religious, ethnic, and cultural groups, in Nazi death camps during World War II

ideology an integrated system of ideas or beliefs that rationalizes and justifies the exercise of power, influencing how power is exercised

inalienable rights rights not granted by government but belonging to individuals by virtue of their natural human condition

laissez-faire French for "let it be," refers to a "hands off" approach, or a limited role of the government in economic activity

limited government the idea that government cannot violate the rights that it was established to protect; government power over the individual is limited

libertarianism ideology that advocates that government should take a "hands-off" approach in most matters

modern liberalism government power is seen as a positive force in protecting the individual

nationalization government seizure of industries from private owners

natural law the premise that the laws that govern human behavior come from the nature of humans themselves and can be universally applied

social contract the idea that government arises from an implied contract among people as a means of protecting their rights

socialism collective ownership of the means of production, distribution, and service

totalitarianism incorporates all sections of society into the state

ON THE WEB

EXPLORING IDEOLOGIES

The website for this textbook (www.cengagebrain.com) offers resources for exploring ideologies on the Internet. In addition, many ideological-based organizations maintain websites explaining their views and soliciting converts. You do not, however, have to agree with the views presented in order to learn something about ideological positions of these groups. Visit www.cengagebrain.com.

- **Americans for Democratic Action** and the **American Conservative Union** Among the more prominent liberal and conservative organizations with informative websites are the Americans for Democratic Action (ADA) and the American Conservative Union (ACU). The ADA site (**www.adaction.org**) describes the organization as "the voice of liberal activists" and provides liberal views on a wide variety of current social, economic, and political issues. The ACU describes itself as "your conservative voice in Washington"; its site (**www.conservative.org**) provides pro-family, anticrime, pro–free enterprise, anti–big government, and anti-tax views.

  Try this: Select an issue of interest to you, such as education funding, environmental policy, wage policy, abortion, the death penalty, or another issue. Then visit **www.adaction.org** and **www.conservative.org**. Compare the issue positions of liberals and conservatives. With which do you agree?

- **Think Tanks** Among the more interesting liberal think tank sites are those of the Brookings Institution (**www.brookings.edu**) and the Progressive Policy Institute (**www.ppionline.org**). And among the more interesting conservative think tank sites are those of the Heritage Foundation (**www.heritage.org**) and the American Enterprise Institute (**www.aei.org**). These two liberal and two conservative organizations present their respective viewpoints on current issues, offer subscriptions and publications, and solicit memberships and contributions.

  Try this: Go to one conservative and one liberal policy think tank, and examine their Web page to determine which issues are important to the think tanks right now. Why do you think these issues are important to them? Are they issues that concern the role of government in people's everyday lives?

REVIEW QUIZ

MULTIPLE CHOICE

1. Functions of ideology include _____.
   a. rationalizing a way of life
   b. providing standards of right and wrong
   c. motivating people to social and political action
   d. all of the above

2. Bossuet's idea that monarchs, as representatives of God's will, could rule absolutely, ignoring the will and well-being of their subjects is called _____.
   a. inalienable rights
   b. the divine right of kings
   c. natural law
   d. a social contract

3. The premise that the laws that govern human behavior come from the nature of humans themselves and can be universally applied is called _____.
   a. inalienable rights
   b. the divine right of kings
   c. natural law
   d. a social contract

4. Asserting the dignity of the individual and limited government power is a tenet of _____.
   a. socialism
   b. classical liberalism
   c. communism
   d. capitalism

5. An economic system that protects private property, private ownership of businesses, and the freedom to buy and sell goods and services, with a minimum of government intervention is called _____.
   a. socialism
   b. classical liberalism
   c. totalitarianism
   d. capitalism

6. Incorporating all sections of society into the state is called _____.
   a. socialism
   b. classical liberalism
   c. totalitarianism
   d. capitalism

7. Collective ownership of the means of production, distribution, and service is a characteristic of _____.
   a. socialism
   b. classical liberalism
   c. totalitarianism
   d. capitalism

8. The socialist idea that violent revolution will give all power to the workers and eliminate the bourgeoisie is called _____.
   a. the withering away of the state
   b. class struggle
   c. economic determinism
   d. the dictatorship of the proletariat

9. Government seizure of industries from private owners is _____.
   a. conservatism
   b. nationalization
   c. totalitarianism
   d. capitalism

10. Hatred and prejudice against Jews is called _____.
    a. the Holocaust
    b. anti-Semitism
    c. capitalism
    d. *Volk*

FILL IN THE BLANK

11. _____ is an integrated system of ideas or beliefs that rationalizes and justifies the exercise of power, influencing how power is exercised.

12. Rights not granted by government but belonging to individuals by virtue of their natural human condition are _____.

13. The idea that government arises from an implied contract among people as a means of protecting their rights is called a _____.

14. The supremacy of the nation over the individual is a component of _____.

15. _____ is race and nation united.

Each of the social sciences contributes to our understanding of power in society, including why states exercise power through warfare. In Afghanistan, U.S. Marines search for bomb-making materials in a small village in the Washir Valley, Helmand Province, taking five detainees who are suspected of operating mortars and/or building improvised explosive devices. Warfare involves anthropological, economic, political, sociological, and psychological components that are of interest to social science researchers.

PART 2

Power and the Social Sciences

In Part Two, we look at the ways that each of the social sciences contributes to our understanding of power in society. Not only will we gain some feel for different topics, theories, methods, and data of each of the social sciences, but we also will explore how each of the social sciences helps us better understand human behavior—a goal shared by each of the disciplines within the social sciences.

In Chapter 4, we focus on what *anthropology*, with its concern for culture, has to tell us about the growth of power relationships in our own society, as well as various societies worldwide. In Chapter 5, we examine the *sociology* of relationships between power and social class, particularly as evidenced by stratification in American society. In Chapter 6, we look at how the perspective of *history* can increase our understanding of how power in society changes over time. In Chapter 7, we examine government, politics, and power from the point of view of *political science*. Control of economic resources is an important base of power in any society, so in Chapter 8 we turn our attention to *economics*. Finally, in Chapter 9, we focus on *psychology* and its explanations as to how and why individuals react in characteristic and different ways to power and authority, using theories of personality from that discipline.

CHAPTER 4

Power and Culture: An Anthropologist's View

Learning Objectives

After reading this chapter, students will be able to:

- Understand how anthropologists view power.
- Explain the role values and beliefs play in ensuring cultural stability.
- Understand how power relationships begin and evolve.
- Describe how the American family has changed, and explain how these changes affected the power distribution within society.

The Origins of Power

Power is exercised in all societies. Every society has a system of sanctions, whether formal or informal, designed to control the behavior of its members. Informal sanctions may include expressions of disapproval, ridicule, or fear of supernatural punishments. Formal sanctions involve recognized ways of censuring behavior—for example, ostracism or exile from the group, loss of freedom, physical punishment, mutilation or death, or retribution visited upon the offender by a member of the family or group that has been wronged.

Power in society is exercised for four broad purposes:

- To maintain peace, order, and stability within the society
- To organize and direct community enterprises
- To conduct warfare, both defensive and aggressive, against other societies
- To rule and exploit subject peoples

Even in the least-developed societies, power relationships emerge for the purposes of maintaining order, organizing economic enterprise, conducting offensive and defensive warfare, and ruling over subject peoples.

At the base of power relationships in society is the family or kinship group. A **family** is traditionally defined as a residential kin group. Typically, a family consists of an adult female and an adult male, sometimes joined through marriage, as well as dependent children. Though this is typical, there are numerous variations including families with only one adult or families not related by blood. But within most families, power is exercised in some fashion. Typically this occurs when work is divided between male and female and parents and

functions of power in society
maintain internal peace, organize and direct community enterprises, conduct warfare, rule and exploit

family
traditionally defined as a residential kin group

72

children and when patterns of dominance and submission are established between male and female, parents and children.

In the simplest societies, power relationships are found partially or wholly within family and kinship groups. True political (power) organizations begin with the development of power relationships among and between family and kinship groups. As long as **kinship groups**, or people related to one another by blood, are relatively self-sufficient economically and require no aid in defending themselves against hostile outsiders, political organization has little reason to develop. But the habitual association of human beings in communities or local groups generally leads to the introduction of some form of a more formal political organization where power is exercised.

kinship group
people related to one another by blood

The basic power structures are voluntary alliances of families and clans who acknowledge the same leaders. They also habitually work together in economic enterprises. In order to maintain peaceful relations, they agree to certain standards of conduct. They also cooperate in the conduct of offensive and defensive warfare. Thus, power structures begin with the development of cooperation among families and kinship groups. This cooperation creates relationships that can be mutually advantageous both economically and in terms of safety.

Warfare frequently leads to another purpose for power structures: ruling and exploiting peoples who have been conquered in war. Frequently, traditional

In some societies, arranged marriages are the norm. Here, a bride and groom exchange vows in a traditional marriage ceremony in India.

Catherine Karnow/Encyclopedia/CORBIS

societies that have been successful in war learn that they can do more than simply kill or drive off enemy groups. Well-organized and militarily successful tribes learn to subjugate other peoples, retaining them as subjects, for purposes of political and economic exploitation. The power structure of the conquering group takes on another function—that of maintaining control over and exploiting conquered peoples.[1]

Anthropology's Examination of Power

Within the social sciences, anthropology examines humans, their societies, and the power structures described above through a broad perspective. Anthropology succeeds in integrating many disciplines of study, including some of the humanities, social sciences (including psychology, political science, and economics), as well as knowledge garnered through biology, geology, and other physical sciences. Many anthropologists focus their energies on describing humans, societies, and power structures at various points in time and in various places; others are concerned with using knowledge derived from anthropological studies to improve human existence. Within the discipline of anthropology are four subfields. These include archaeology, biological and physical anthropology, linguistic anthropology, and socio-cultural anthropology.

Archaeology

archaeology
the study of human cultures through their physical and material remains

Archaeology—the study of human cultures through their physical and material remains—relies on the examination of relics—the remnants of human experience—to analyze the behaviors of past cultures. For example, through the analysis of something as simple as pottery remains, anthropologists might learn a great deal about a society—the size of water jugs might indicate their access to potable water, utensils might shed light on the common foods that were consumed, decorations might demonstrate trade patterns with other societies, art depicted on the pottery might reflect common stories of the society.

Archaeologists examine a wide variety of artifacts—art, tools, costumes, animal remains, and dwellings—to learn how members of society interacted with one another, how their economies developed, their belief systems, and how they interacted with other societies and their natural environment.

Biological Anthropology

biological anthropology
the study of humans as biological organisms

Biological anthropology (sometimes called physical anthropology) is the study of humans as biological organisms.[2] Biological anthropologists are interested in the evolution of the human species. In their work, they examine the origin of humans, theories of evolution, how humans historically have interacted with the natural world and each other, and how humans have adapted to their environments. Biological anthropologists also are concerned with contemporary issues concerning human growth, development, adaption, disease, and mortality. Biological anthropologists typically use an interdisciplinary framework for their work: some might rely on the same types of archeological fossils studied by archeologists. Others might borrow methodologies and tools from the biological sciences, while still others will examine human behavior by looking at their closest genetic relatives in the animal world and study primates.

Linguistic Anthropology

Linguistic anthropology is a method of analyzing societies in terms of human communication, including its origins, history, and contemporary variation and change.[3] How individuals speak belies information about the structure and evolution of society. A simple example: If you have studied a romantic language, you will know that many romantic languages have a formal and informal noun meaning "you," and the level of formality used might be an indication about one's relationship with the person one is addressing. Studying communication patterns, the creation of dialects indicating the growth of subcultures, and the implicit meaning inherent in linguistic terms (about belief systems, ideologies, religion, and so on), linguistic anthropologists examine how language both reflects human experience with a society, and affects that experience.

linguistic anthropology
a method of analyzing societies in terms of human communication, including its origins, history, and contemporary variation and change

Socio-cultural Anthropology

Socio-cultural anthropology is the study of living peoples and their cultures, including how people live within a given environment. Focusing broadly on various aspects of society from family life to government structures, socio-cultural anthropologists are interested in how societies form and develop. They broadly examine **culture**, people's learned and shared behaviors and beliefs or the ways of life that are common to a society. Socio-cultural anthropology often relies on the research methodology of participant observation (as described in greater detail in Chapter 2), in that the researcher both observes and participates in the behavior being studied to gain an intimate look at how individuals within a society work within a certain context.

socio-cultural anthropology
the study of living peoples and their cultures

culture
people's learned and shared behaviors and beliefs

Because socio-cultural anthropology is particularly interested in similarities and differences between societies across time and space, and the similarities and differences between subsets of populations, we often see socio-cultural anthropological research in the form of comparative analyses. And so, a socio-cultural anthropologist might look at religion in developing versus modern cultures, or differences between men and women in a given tribal society; it provides a perfect framework for our examination of power relations within societies.

Culture: Ways of Life

The culture of any society represents generalizations about the behavior of many members of that society. Culture does not describe the personal habits of any one individual. Common ways of behaving in different societies vary enormously. For example, in some societies arranged marriages are the norm, but such practices are frowned upon in other societies. In some cultures, like those in New Guinea, people paint their entire bodies with intricate designs whereas in others, like the United States, only the faces of the female are painted.

The concept of culture is basic to what anthropology is all about. Anthropologist Clyde Kluckhohn once defined culture as all the "historically created designs for living, explicit and implicit, rational, irrational, and nonrational that may exist at any given time as potential guides for the behavior of man."[4] In contrast with psychologists, who are interested primarily in describing and explaining individual behavior, anthropologists tend to make **cultural generalizations**. These cultural generalizations focus on aggregate behaviors within a society or values and beliefs that are commonly shared.

cultural generalization
the description of commonly shared values, beliefs, and behaviors in a society

One method of viewing these cultural generalizations is the idea that different cultures are organized around characteristic purposes or themes, a notion popularized by cultural anthropologist Ruth Benedict (1887–1947) in her widely read book *Patterns of Culture*. According to Benedict, a professor of anthropology at Columbia University, each culture has its own patterns of thought, action, and expression dominated by a certain theme that is expressed in social relations, art, and religion.

For example, Benedict identified the characteristic themes of life among the Zuñi Pueblo Indians of the Southwestern United States as moderation, sobriety, and cooperation. There was little competition, contention, or violence among tribal members. In contrast, the Kwakiutls of the Northwestern United States engaged in fierce and violent competition for prestige and self-glorification. Kwakiutls were distrustful of one another, emotionally volatile, and paranoid. Yet Benedict was convinced that abnormality and normality were relative terms. What is "normal" in Kwakiutlan society would be regarded as "abnormal" in Zuñi society, and vice versa. She believed that there is hardly a form of abnormal behavior in any society that would not be regarded as normal in some other society. Hence, Benedict helped social scientists realize the great variability in the patterns of human existence. People can live in competitive as well as cooperative societies, in peaceful as well as aggressive societies, in trusting as well as suspicious societies.

Today, many anthropologists have reservations about Benedict's idea that the culture of a society reflects a single dominant theme. There is probably a multiplicity of themes in every society, and some societies may be poorly integrated. Moreover, even within a single culture, wide variations of individual behavior exist.

Subcultures

subculture
the variation in ways of life within a society

Generalizations about a whole society do not apply to every individual, or even to every group within a society. In virtually every society, there are distinct variations in ways of life among groups of people. These variations often are referred to as **subcultures**. They are frequently observed in such things as distinctive language, music, dress, and dance. Subcultures may center on race or ethnicity, or they may focus on age (the "youth culture") or class (see "Is There a Culture of Poverty?" in Chapter 11). Subcultures also may evolve out of opposition to the beliefs, values, or norms of the dominant culture of society—for example, a "drug culture," a "gang culture," or a "hip-hop culture."

Multiculturalism

Multiculturalism generally refers to acknowledging and promoting multiple cultures and subcultures. It seeks to protect and celebrate cultural diversity—for example, Spanish-language usage, African American history, and Native American heritage. Multiculturalism tends to resist cultural unification—for example, English-only education, an emphasis on the study of Western civilization, and the designation of "classic" books, music, and art.

    Multiculturalism invites students to formally explore the ways of life of their own subculture—Hispanic, African American, Native American, or Asian history, for example. Multiculturalism also enables students to learn about societies other than their own—for example, non-Western cultures of Asia or Africa or traditional cultures of the Mayas or Aztecs. But some criticisms of multiculturalism include that it may denigrate the unifying symbols, values, and beliefs of American society and that it may encourage ignorance of Western European culture, including the foundations of individual freedom and democracy. In doing so, multiculturalism may serve to weaken the dominant "American" culture.

multiculturalism
acknowledging, protecting, and promoting multiple cultures and subcultures

Culture Is Learned

Anthropologists believe that culture is learned, and it is transferred from one generation to another. Culture is passed down through the generations, and cultures vary from one society to another because people in different societies are brought up differently. The process by which culture is communicated is called the **socialization process**. Some agents that work to teach culture include family, schools, religious organizations, and the media. In these settings, individuals learn from other people how to speak, how to think, and how to act in certain ways.

socialization process
process by which culture is communicated to successive generations

The Components of Culture

Anthropologists often subdivide a culture into various components in order to simplify thinking about it. These components of culture—symbols, beliefs, values, norms, religion, sanctions, and artifacts—are closely related in any society.[5]

Symbols

Symbols are culturally created and play a key role in the development and maintenance of cultures. A heavy reliance on symbols—including words, pictures, and writing—distinguish human beings from other animals. A **symbol** is anything that has meaning bestowed on it by those who use it. Words are symbols and language is symbolic communication. Objects or artifacts can also be used as symbols: The symbol of a cross is a visual representation of Christianity; a burning cross is a symbol of hate. The color red may stand for danger, or it may be a symbol of revolution. The creation and use of such symbols enable human beings to transmit their learned ways of behaving to each new generation. Children

symbol
anything that communicates meaning, including language, art, and music

are not limited to knowledge acquired through their own experiences and observations; they can learn about the ways of behaving in society through symbolic communication, receiving in a relatively short time the result of centuries of experience and observation. Human beings can therefore learn more rapidly than other animals, and they can employ symbols to solve increasingly complex problems. Because of symbolic communication, human beings can transmit a body of learned ways of life accumulated by many people over many generations.

Beliefs

beliefs
generally shared ideas about what is true

Beliefs are generally shared ideas about what is true. Every culture includes a system of beliefs that are widely shared, even though there may be some disagreement with these beliefs. Culture includes beliefs about marriage and family, religion and the purpose of life, and economic and political organization (see Case Study: "Aboriginal Australians"). For example, in Saudi Arabia, cultural beliefs are strongly linked to Islam, that country's predominant religion. There, because Friday is the holy day, many businesses are closed on Thursday and Friday, rather than on Saturday and Sunday. The difference in this culture's "weekend" is reflective of how beliefs influence a society's culture.

In modern times, beliefs often are more fluid than they have been historically. For instance, in the United States long-held beliefs about many ideas—for example, the role of women in society, racial equality, and homosexuality—have evolved drastically in the past half century. This change in widespread beliefs came about partly because of the increased presence of a common media, but some changes also came about because of a change in values brought about by scientific research and the civil rights and women's rights movements.

Values

values
shared ideas about what is good and desirable

Values are shared ideas about what is good and desirable. Values tell us that some things are better than others. Values provide us with standards for judging ways of life. Values may be related to beliefs as beliefs can justify our values. One case in point: In the United States, the idea of nepotism—showing favoritism to one's relatives for employment, for example—is often frowned upon. But in Saudi Arabia, nepotism is viewed positively because it means that you are surrounding yourself with known and trusted individuals. This value reflects the belief in Saudi Arabia that family is extremely important, which emphasizes reliance on family as a support structure. There, families provide social and economic networks, and shape nearly all aspects of a Saudi's life. However, values can conflict with one another (that is, the value of individual freedom conflicts with the need to prevent crime), and not everyone in society shares the same values. Yet most anthropologists believe that every society has some widely shared values.

Norms

norms
shared rules and expectations about behavior

Norms are shared rules and expectations about behavior. Norms are related to values in that values justify norms. If, for example, we value freedom of speech, we allow people to speak their minds even if we do not agree with them.

CASE STUDY

Aboriginal Australians

Aboriginal Australians lay claim to being the oldest living culture in our world today. Their mark on Australia can be traced back at least 50,000 years when the first inhabitants migrated through Asia across to the ancient continent of Sahul, which once included Australia, New Guinea and Tasmania. Recent research suggests that today's Aborigines are direct descendants of the first modern humans to leave our ancestral home of North Africa.

The Aborigine belonged to separate bands of semi-nomadic hunter-gatherers, each with its own territory. Over time, they learned to acclimate themselves to Australia's often harsh environments, caring for the land that fed them and living in communion with their surroundings. Their tracking skills stemmed from an intimate knowledge of Australia's rivers, mountains, and vast desert land.

Travel Pictures/Alamy

(continued)

When early European settlers first arrived in 1788, there were somewhere between 300,000 to one million indigenous Australians and an estimated 600 different clan groups.

Today, the Aborigine's connection to the land is the cornerstone of their cultural heritage. They are a deeply spiritual people and the Dreaming, or the Dreamtime, is a complex web of stories that represents their spiritual beliefs as well as their law. In the Dreaming, Ancestor Spirits walked over the land creating animals, plants, bodies of water, and landforms. The Spirits stayed on Earth once they had finished creating, and so the Dreaming never ends. Throughout Australia there are sacred places that represent where Ancestor Spirits have come to rest. Uluru, or Ayers Rock, located in the center of Australia, is the most famous of these. Music, dance, and art are also integral parts of Aboriginal cultural history. They often represent stories of the Dreaming and are created to express the Aborigines' fight for survival overtime and the kinship they have with all living things.

folkways
a trivial norm that guides actions

mores
important norms that carry moral authority

The norm of tolerance derives from the value that we place on individual freedom. Fairly trivial norms, like lining up at ticket windows instead of pushing to the front, or "staying to the right" in a crowded corridor, are called **folkways**. Folkways may determine our style of clothing, our diet, or our manners. **Mores** (pronounced "morays") are more important norms. These are rules of conduct that carry moral authority; violating these rules directly challenges society's values. For example, a young Indian couple might challenge an important norm, like arranged marriage, by opting to marry for romantic love. Like values and beliefs, some norms within a given culture conflict with one another and there is substantial variation within individuals' belief in society's norms.

Religion

religion
a set of beliefs and practices pertaining to supernatural powers and the origins and meaning of life

Religion is evident in all known cultures. Although there are differences between societies in the nature of their religious beliefs, all cultures include some beliefs about supernatural powers (powers that are not human and not subject to the laws of nature) and about the origins and meaning of life and the universe. Anthropologists, in their professional roles, do not speculate about the truth or falsehood of religious beliefs. Rather, anthropologists are concerned with why religion is found in all societies and how and why religion varies from one society to another.

Various theories have arisen about why religious beliefs are universal. Some theories contend that religious beliefs arise out of human anxieties about death and the unknown or out of human curiosity about the meaning, origins, and purpose of life. Religions help us answer universal questions, such as "Why am

FIGURE 4-1   IS RELIGION AN IMPORTANT PART OF YOUR DAILY LIFE

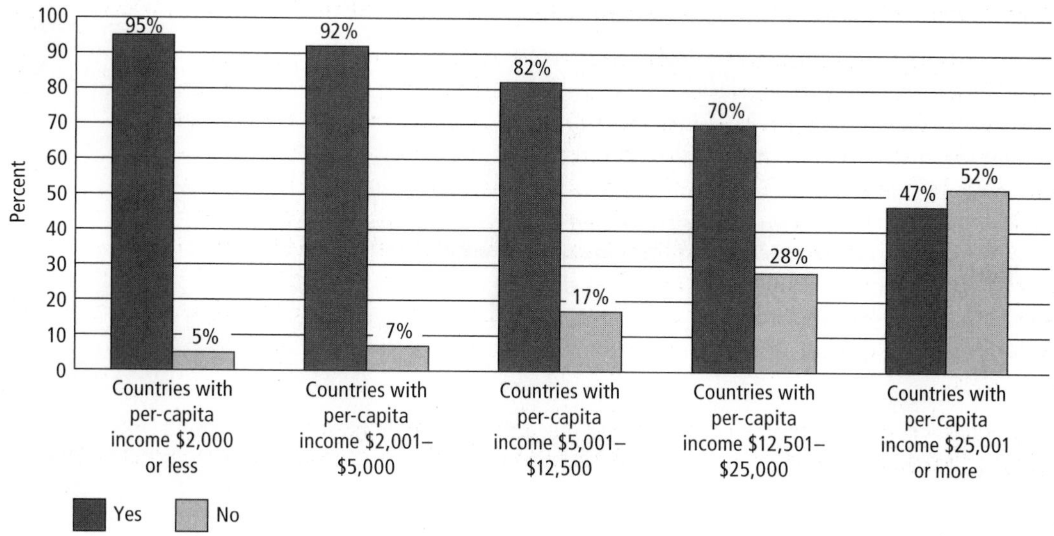

SOURCE: http://www.gallup.com/poll/142727/Religiosity-Highest-World-Poorest-Nations.aspx

I here?", "What is the meaning and purpose of life?", and "What happens when we die?" Other theories stress the social functions of religion—that it provides goals, purposes, rituals, and norms of behavior for people. Some also assert that for many in the world, particularly the most vulnerable, religion provides hope in what may otherwise be a rather dire existence. For example, Figure 4-1 shows that religion is more important in poorer countries: 95 percent of respondents living in countries with a per capita income of under $2,000 say religion is an important part of their daily life. As income increases, levels of religiosity decrease, with only 47 percent of those in countries with per capita income over $25,000 saying that religion is an important part of their life (see Research This!).

More than 80 percent of the world's population identify themselves with an organized set of religious beliefs. About 33 percent of the world's population is Christian. Islamic (Muslims), Hindu, and Buddhist religions combined account for about 40 percent of the world's population, while Judaism accounts for about 0.2 percent of the world's population.

Sanctions

Sanctions are the rewards and punishments for conforming to or violating cultural norms. Rewards—for example, praise, affection, status, wealth, and reputation—reinforce cultural norms. Punishments—for example, criticism, ridicule, ostracism, penalties, fines, jail, and executions—discourage violations of cultural norms. But conformity to cultural norms does not depend exclusively on sanctions. Most of us conform to our society's norms of behavior even when

sanction
a reward or punishment for conforming to or violating cultural norms

RESEARCH *THIS!*

The table below shows the proportion of people in a given country who indicate that religion is an important part of their everyday lives.

Is religion an important part of your daily life?

Country	Percent Responding "Yes"
Bangladesh	99+
Niger	99+
Yemen	99
Indonesia	99
Malawi	99
Sri Lanka	99
Somaliland region	98
Djibouti	98
Mauritania	98
Burundi	98
Estonia	16
Sweden	17
Denmark	19
Japan	24
Hong Kong	24
United Kingdom	27
Vietnam	30
France	30
Russia	34
Belarus	34

SOURCE: www.gallup.com/poll/142727/religiosity-highest-world-poorest-nations.aspx

YOUR ANALYSIS:

1. Describe the trend in general with regard to the importance of religion to people in various countries when considering income. What might explain this trend?

2. Data not shown on the table is that about two-thirds of Americans—65 percent—say religion is important in their daily lives. How does this information buck the trend indicated by your analysis above? What might explain this?

3. Do you believe that as countries develop, religion becomes less important? Why?

no sanctions are pending and even when we are alone. For example, do you close the bathroom door when you are home alone, with no chance of anyone else entering the house? For society, conformity to society's norms absent of sanctions means a more orderly existence. For example, most people stop for a red light even at a deserted traffic intersection, making it less likely that an accident will occur. We do so because we have been taught to do so, because we do not envision any alternatives, because we share the values on which the norms are based, or because we view ourselves as part of society.

Artifacts

An **artifact** is a physical product of a culture. An artifact can be anything from a piece of pottery or a religious object from an ancient society to a musical composition, a high-rise condominium, or a beer can from a modern society. But usually we think of an artifact as a physical trace of an earlier culture about which we have little written record. As discussed earlier in this chapter, archeologists try to understand what these early cultures were like from the study of the artifacts they left behind.

artifact
a physical product of a culture

The Nature of Culture

Culture assists people in adapting to the conditions in which they live. Even ways of life that at first glance appear quaint or curious may play an important role in helping individuals or societies cope with problems. Cultural anthropologists rely on four key approaches when examining culture: *functionalism*, *the materialist perspective*, *idealism*, and *cultural relativism*.

Functionalism

Many anthropologists approach the study of culture by asking what functions a particular institution or practice performs for a society. How does the institution or practice serve individual or societal needs? Does it work? How does it work? Why does it work? This approach is known as **functionalism**.[6]

Functionalism assumes that there are certain minimum biological needs, as well as social and psychological needs, that must be satisfied if individuals and society are to survive. For example, biological needs might include food, shelter, bodily comfort, sexual needs, reproduction, health maintenance, physical movement, and defense.

Social and psychological needs are less well defined, but they probably include affection, communication, education in the ways of the culture, material satisfaction, leadership, social control, security, and a sense of unity and belonging. Given that humans have few inborn instincts on how to meet these biological, social, and psychological needs, culture provides the mechanisms—including social groups and institutions, rules of conduct, and tools—that structure meeting one's needs within a society. Despite great variety in the way that these needs are met in different cultures, we can still ask how a culture goes about fulfilling them and how well it does so. Functionalists tend to examine

functionalism
a perspective in anthropology that emphasizes that cultural institutions and practices serve individual or societal needs

every custom, material object, idea, belief, and institution in terms of the task or function that it performs.

To understand a culture functionally, we have to find out how a particular institution or practice relates to biological, social, or psychological needs and how it relates to other cultural institutions and practices. For example, in modern societies, families still can perform numerous biological, social, or psychological functions. Or a society might fulfill its biological need for food by hunting and fulfill its psychological needs by worshiping animals. Although functionalism is not the predominant perspective used by most anthropologists today, it shaped some of the methods and perspectives that are prevalent in contemporary times.

Materialism

Another approach to the study of culture emphasizes the importance of the ways in which humans relate to their social and natural environments. These anthropologists believe that acquiring the materials essential for survival shape the relations that people have with one another and with their environment. Securing their material well-being means that people will attempt to maximize the natural resources at their disposal. Thus, humans form groups to organize the acquisition of material goods, whether through bands of hunters, farming communities, or modern stockbrokers. Anthropologists using the **materialist perspective** focus on how people make their living in their specific environmental setting.

materialist perspective
a perspective in anthropology that focuses on how people make their living in a specific environmental setting

technology
both the tools and the knowledge humans use to overcome their environment and meet their material needs

Some materialist anthropologists emphasize the role of **technology**, defined as both the tools and the knowledge humans use to overcome their environment and meet their material needs. Technology and the environment impact culture. Thus, technology and the effort to use the environment to fulfill one's material needs influence a wide variety of practices and social institutions, including marriage practices, family structure, religious practices, economic structures, and political systems. For example, marriage practices within many societies have been regarded in materialist terms, with male suitors evaluated in terms of assets, wealth, and earning potential and females evaluated on the size of the dowry they bring into the marriage. In modern societies today, technology (or the legal and political structure) has codified this materialist view of marriage, allowing for the creation of prenuptial agreements (or "pre-nups") that specify the distribution of assets should a marriage end.

Modern materialists also assert that the relationship among technology, the environment, and culture is circular. That is, technology and the environment shape the culture, and the culture adopts practices that may then change technology and the environment, which then reshapes the culture, and so on. The relationship among the three variables is constantly evolving. An example of this can be seen in fishing cultures. When people fished for subsistence, fish were plentiful and the means of catching were relatively simple (net, rod, or spear). As the product of fish becomes more of a commodity, technology changes: bigger fishing vessels, industrial nets, and so on. This also changes the society: Some fishers own boats and can become wealthier; others do not and have a more difficult time making a living. And, of course, the environment changes: Fish become scarcer. But the impact does not stop there: Technology responds by the growth of industrial fisheries rather than private fishers. And the environment continues to respond: Fewer fish still. Culture also responds: Rules on minimum catch size and eventually the replacement of fishing as an occupation with other tasks.

When a population grows and in response to that growth exploits the environment and uses it more intensely, this is a process known as **intensification**. With intensification, populations use their environment and detrimentally impact it. They then are forced to use energy to meet their material need in other ways and develop creative means of doing so. In short, they use both their environment and their knowledge or labor more "intensely." This forces cultural change because (1) societies must respond to the changes in technology and use and (2) social relations have necessarily changed between individuals during this process.

intensification
when population growth causes increased use and exploitation of the environment

Idealism

While the materialist approach is important for modern anthropologists, another important perspective in anthropology is idealism. **Idealism** focuses on the importance of ideas in determining culture. Proponents of idealism believe that the inherent uniqueness of humans and their desire for meaning beyond material well-being is defining and essential to what shapes culture. Indeed, idealists assert that the components of needs and the resources to meet them all are socially constructed (by a culture of ideas). Think of the idea of hunger. In an affluent society, you might ask someone, "Are you hungry for a slice of pizza?" The individual might accept or reject the offer of pizza, depending on absolute hunger or on craving (perhaps she felt like eating a turkey sandwich instead). In other cultures, hunger is hunger and food (whatever is available) satisfies that hunger.

idealism
a perspective in anthropology that focuses on the importance of ideas in determining culture

Idealists assert that people's perceptions of their environment are important in shaping their relation to it. For example, one society might place a house of worship on the most fertile land or sacrifice valuable resources to a deity. Idealists also assert that how people view resources is culturally determined. Many cultures reject a wide variety of food for religious or cultural reasons: Americans typically reject horsemeat, reptiles, dog and cat meat, insects, and many plants. Both Muslims and Jews reject pork, and Hindus reject beef. To idealists, the social construction of resources that meet material needs indicates the importance of ideas, whether they are religious, cultural, or political, in shaping all other aspects of life. To idealists, the struggle for meaning, the importance of relations between individuals, and the creation of culture and of symbols and intellectual needs drive humans in the creation of culture. Idealists view materialism as a limited (and Western-biased) viewpoint of human motivation.

Using any of these perspectives, anthropology helps us appreciate other cultures. It requires impartial observation and testing of explanations of customs, practices, and institutions. Anthropologists cannot judge other cultures by the same standards that we use to judge our own. **Ethnocentrism**, or

ethnocentrism
judging other cultures solely in terms of one's own culture

judging other cultures solely in terms of one's own culture, is an obstacle to good anthropological work.

Cultural Relativity

cultural relativity
suspending judgment of other societies' customs, practices, and institutions

Cultural relativity—suspending judgment of other societies' customs, practices, and institutions—enables anthropologists to examine aspects of culture and determine their function within that society. For example, many criticize the policy of the government of the People's Republic of China that mandates that each couple may have only one child. When examined through an ethnocentric American prism, we would think that such a policy violates one of the fundamental freedoms of individuals. But if we suspend judgment and look at the policy using a cultural relativist perspective, we might determine that given that society's focus on the needs of the community (rather than individual liberties), the enormous population growth previously seen without population-control policy and the fear on the part of the state that it might not be able to support uncontrolled population growth (with food, jobs, transportation, and housing), then we can see the function that the policy performs within that culture.

However, cultural relativism can lead to moral dilemmas for scholars and students. Although it is important to assess the elements of a culture in terms of how well they work for their own people in their own environment,[7] an uncritical or romantic view of other cultures is demoralizing. For example, in China the one-child policy has resulted in rampant abandonment of baby girls. (Sons bear the responsibility of caring for one's elders in China, thus having a son ensures that the parents will be cared for in their old age.) There also are reports of abortions being performed for the purpose of sex selection in China. In other cultures, a preference for sons has resulted in the practice of female infanticide. Anthropologists might explain the preference for sons in terms of economic production based on hard manual labor in the fields. But understanding the functional relationship between female infanticide and economic conditions must not be viewed as a moral justification of the practice (see Controversies in Social Science: "The World's Missing Girls").

Some elements of a culture not only differ from those of another culture but also are better. The fact that all peoples—Asians, Europeans, Africans, Native Americans, and others—have often abandoned features of their own culture in order to replace them with elements from other cultures implies that the replacements served peoples' purposes more effectively.[8] For example, Arabic numerals are not simply different from Roman numerals; they are more efficient. It is inconceivable today that we would express large numbers in Roman numerals; for example, the year of American independence—MDCCLXXVI—requires more than twice as many Roman numerals as Arabic numerals and requires adding numbers. This is why the European nations, whose own culture derived from Rome, replaced Roman numerals with numerals derived from Arab culture (which had learned them from the Hindus of India). So it is important for scholars and students to avoid the assumption of cultural relativity—that all cultures serve their people equally well.[9]

Authority in the Family

The family is the principal agent of socialization into society. It is the most intimate and important of all social groups. Of course, the family can assume different shapes in different cultures, and it can perform a variety of functions and meet a variety of needs. But in all societies, the family relationship centers on procreative and child-rearing functions. A cross-cultural comparison reveals that in all societies, most families possess these common characteristics:[10]

- Sexual mating
- Childbearing and child rearing
- A system of names and a method of determining kinship
- A common habitation (at some point)
- Socialization and education of the young
- A system of roles and expectations based on family membership

These common characteristics indicate why the family is so important in human societies. It replenishes the population and rears each new generation.

Within the family, the individual personality is formed. The family transmits and carries forward the culture of the society. It establishes the primary system of roles with differential rights, duties, and behaviors. And it is within the family that the child first encounters authority.

Marriage

To an anthropologist, marriage does not necessarily connote a wedding ceremony and legal certificate. Rather, **marriage** means a socially approved sexual and economic union between a man and a woman, intended to be more or less permanent and implying social roles between the spouses and their children. Marriage is found in all cultures, and anthropologists have offered a variety of explanations for its universality (see Focus: "Social Science Asks: Is Marriage Becoming Obsolete in America?"). One theory explaining marriage focuses on the prolonged infant dependency of humans. In many cultures, infants are breast-fed for up to two years. This results in a division of roles between the female nurturer and the male protector that requires some lasting agreement between the partners. Another theory focuses on sexual competition among males. Marriage minimizes males' rivalry for female sexuality and thus reduces destructive conflict. Still another theory focuses on the economic division of labor between the sexes. Males and females in every culture perform somewhat different economic activities; marriage is a means of sharing the products of their divided labor.

Marriage is found in all cultures, but the institution varies from culture to culture. In some cultures, common practice holds that a girl should be married by the time she is 18 years old. Although UNICEF, the United Nations Children's Fund, has lobbied against this practice as a violation of human rights, the practice nonetheless continues and is particularly widespread in areas of Africa (Figure 4-2). Oftentimes, parents of girls encourage the marriage of very young daughters—hoping that the marriage, typically to an older and oftentimes better educated man—will benefit both the child and the family

marriage
a socially approved sexual and economic union between a man and a woman, intended to be lasting, and implying social roles between the spouses and their children

CONTROVERSIES IN SOCIAL SCIENCE

The World's Missing Girls

I n China, there are an estimated 32 million more males than females, an imbalance that appears to be increasing.* In Pakistan, a woman's in-laws compel her to abort a 4-month-old fetus—her third abortion—because the fetus that she is carrying is female. Newspapers report the new "middle-class trend" in India: relatively inexpensive ultrasound technology used for sex selection. In Zambia, a promising HIV treatment program, antiretroviral therapy (ART), is introduced, but only one-third of the patients are female, despite the higher prevalence of the virus in women there. The following table shows the projected population-to-sex ratio for selected countries for 2011, based on census figures within those nations. The figure for each nation is the number of males per one hundred females. In most industrialized democracies, the number of boy and girl babies born in a given year is roughly equal, with a slight skew toward a few more boy babies. But because women's life expectancy is longer, the cumulative ratio of females to males is skewed toward there being more females. For instance, on average, females in the United States live about six years longer than men; thus there are more women than men in total.

The table also shows the extent of the problem of missing girls in the selected countries. In parts of some nations—like China, India, and Pakistan—the sex ratio is imbalanced because female fetuses are being aborted. Infant girls also are more likely to be victims of infanticide. The preference for sons is common in many societies. In many agricultural societies, sons are desirable because they will provide labor. In China and parts of India, sons are responsible for their parents' well-being during old age. Without a government-supported old-age benefit program and with daughters traditionally responsible for the care of their in-laws, many believe that they *need* a son to survive later in life.

In some societies, the sex imbalance is exacerbated by government policies. For example, for many years China's one-child policy—intended to control that country's population growth—was blamed for the sex-ratio imbalance and the abandonment of girls. That policy was called into question when in 2008 a powerful earthquake hit Sichuan Province, killing 70,000 people, including thousands of only children who were buried in the rubble of their schools when the quake hit. In the aftermath of the earthquake, China revised that policy, granting exception to families affected by the earthquake. Families who had lost a child, or whose child was severely injured or disabled in the earthquake, were granted approval to bear another child.

---

*http://newsweek.washingtonpost.com/postglobal/pomfretschina/2009/04/abortions_in_china_girls.html

India also offers incentives for smaller families, leaving many to charge that such policies encourage sex-selective abortions because prospective parents limiting the number of children they will have more frequently chose to have male children.

In other societies, the problem of missing girls is due to an inherent lack of value on female life. In some parts of Africa, female children are less likely to be given the basic necessities—including food, potable water, and medicine—in favor of their brothers.

The impact of sex imbalance looks similar despite its numerous causes. In China, "bachelor villages"—inhabited exclusively by bachelor men who cannot find wives—are cropping up. Tens of thousands of women and girls have been kidnapped in China in recent years. The victims are sometimes forced to marry their captors or are sold to another man to become his wife. Experts also say that the sex-ratio imbalance could have dire political consequences, pointing to rebellions that have historically fomented when the sex ratio became imbalanced as groups of young men without the prospect of a family or a future turned against the political system that spawned their situation.

POPULATION SEX RATIO FOR SELECTED COUNTRIES, 2010 (PROJECTED) (MALES PER ONE HUNDRED FEMALES)

United States	97.5
Niger	101.2
Pakistan	103.4
India	106.8
Saudi Arabia	124
China	108

SOURCE: Population Division of the Department of Economic and Social Affairs of the United Nations Secretariat, *World Population Prospects: The 2008 Revision and World Urbanization Prospects: The 2008 Revision* (http://esa.un.org/unpp/).

FIGURE 4-2   PROPORTION OF WOMEN AGED 20–24 YEARS WHO WERE MARRIED BY THE AGE OF 18 YEARS, SELECTED COUNTRIES

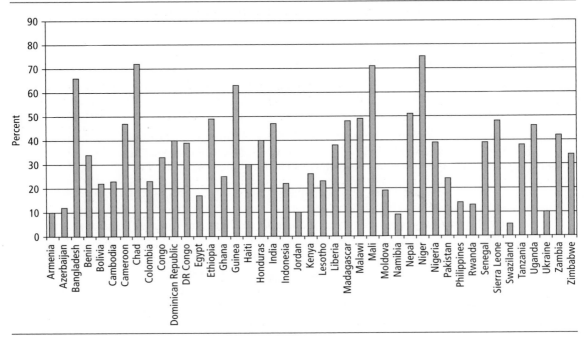

SOURCE: http://www.measuredhs.com/

financially and socially. At the very least, the marriage of a daughter while still a child alleviates some of the financial burden on the family by placing the financial burden for the upkeep of the girl on the husband. Research indicates that early marriage is detrimental to girls. Girls who married before the age of 18 years are less educated, have more children, and are more likely to experience domestic violence then those who married after age 18.[11]

Romantic Love

Most Americans believe that romantic love should be the basis of a marriage, but this ideal does not characterize marriages in many other societies. On the contrary, in many societies, like India and among some Inuit of Greenland, romantic love is believed to be a poor basis for marriage and is strongly discouraged. (Nonetheless, in most of the world's societies, romantic love is depicted in love songs and stories.) Marriages based on romance are far less common in less developed societies where economic and kinship factors are important considerations in marriage.[12]

Monogamy

monogamy
a marriage union of one husband and one wife

Family arrangements vary and the marriage relationship may take on such institutional forms as monogamy, polygyny, and polyandry. **Monogamy** is the union of one husband and one wife; *polygyny* is the union of one husband and two or more wives; *polyandry* is the union of one wife and two or more husbands.

Throughout the world, monogamy is the most widespread marriage form, probably because the gender ratio (number of males per one hundred females) has been near one hundred in all societies, meaning there is about an equal number of men and women.

The Family in Agricultural Societies

In most agricultural societies, the family is **patriarchal** and patrilineal: The male is the dominant authority, and kinship is determined through the male line. The family is an economic institution as well as a sexual and child-rearing one; it owns land, produces many artifacts, and cares for its old as well as its young. Male family heads exercise power in the wider community; patriarchs may govern the village or tribe. Male authority frequently means the subjugation of both women and children. This family arrangement is buttressed by traditional moral values and religious teachings that emphasize discipline, self-sacrifice, and the sanctity of the family unit.

    Women face a lifetime of childbearing, child rearing, and household work. Families of ten or fifteen children are not uncommon. The property rights of a woman are vested in her husband. Women are taught to serve and obey their husbands and are not considered as mentally competent as men. The husband owns and manages the family's economic enterprise. Tasks are divided: Men raise crops, tend animals, and perform heavy work; women make clothes, prepare food, tend the sick, and perform endless household services.

patriarchal family
the male is the dominant authority, and kinship is determined through the male line

The Family in Industrialized Societies

Industrialization alters the economic functions of the family and brings about changes in the traditional patterns of authority. In industrialized societies, the household is no longer an important unit of production, even though it retains an economic role as a consumer unit. Work is to be found outside the home, and industrial technology provides gainful employment for women as well as for men. Typically, this means an increase in opportunities for women outside the family unit and the possibility of economic independence. The number of women in the labor force is increasing today in the United States; about 71 percent of adult women are employed outside the home.

    The patriarchal structure that typifies the family in an agricultural economy is altered by the new opportunities for women in advanced industrial nations (see International Perspective: "Women in the Workforce"). Not only do women acquire employment alternatives, but their opportunities for education also expand. Independence allows them to modify many of the more oppressive features of patriarchy. Women in an advanced industrialized society have fewer children, and divorce becomes a realistic alternative to an unhappy marriage.

    In advanced industrial societies, governments perform some of the traditional functions of the family, further increasing opportunities for women. For example, the government steps into the field of formal education—not just in the instruction of traditional skills like reading, writing, and arithmetic, but in support of home economics, driver training, health care, and perhaps even sex

Social Science Asks: Is Marriage Becoming Obsolete in America?

During the past 50 years, there has been a steep decline in the percentage of American adults who are marrying. Part of the explanation is that Americans are marrying later: According to a recent Pew study, the median age for first marriages for both women (26.5) and men (28.7) has never been higher. In 1960, 72 percent of Americans 18 and older were married. Contrast that to 51 percent of Americans today.

American culture has changed over the past few decades, and these changes have spawned some of the decline in marriage. The sexual revolution and women's movements of the 1960s

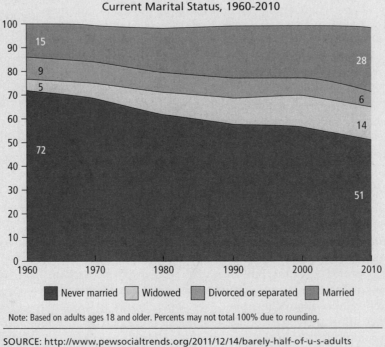

Current Marital Status, 1960-2010

Note: Based on adults ages 18 and older. Percents may not total 100% due to rounding.

SOURCE: http://www.pewsocialtrends.org/2011/12/14/barely-half-of-u-s-adults-are-married-a-record-low/?src=prc-headline

education, all areas that were once the province of the family. Government welfare programs provide assistance to dependent children when a family breadwinner is absent, unemployed, or cannot provide for the children. The government undertakes to care for the aged, the sick, and others incapable of supporting themselves, thus relieving families of still another traditional function.

Despite these characteristics of industrial society, however, *the family remains the fundamental social unit.* The family is not disappearing; marriage and family life are as popular as ever. But the father-dominated authority structure, with its traditional duties and rigid gender roles, is changing. The family is becoming an institution in which both husband and wife seek individual happiness rather and 1970s meant that premarital sex became more acceptable and women's entry into the paid workforce in mass numbers meant that economically independent women had less incentive to marry early. As society continues to change, many college-educated young adults decide to focus on their careers before settling down. There are also a number of alternative living situations that weren't as prevalent 20, 30, or 50 years ago. Many couples may have children but choose not to get married. There is also a higher number of single-person households and single parenting. Divorce rates are also a factor, though those have leveled off in recent years.

But more startling is that between 2009 and 2010, new marriages decreased five percent in the United States. That is a drastic change for a one-year period. One explanation for the drastic decline in nuptials that year? The stagnant economy may mean that many young people do not have the financial means for a wedding and for independent living, demonstrating the interrelated nature of various aspects of culture influence society's behavior and institutions.

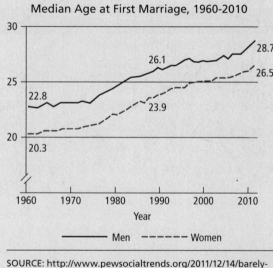

Median Age at First Marriage, 1960-2010

SOURCE: http://www.pewsocialtrends.org/2011/12/14/barely-half-of-u-s-adults-are-married-a-record-low/?src=prc-headline

than the perpetuation of the species and economic efficiency. Many women still choose to seek fulfillment in marriage and child rearing rather than in outside employment; others decide to do this temporarily. The important point is that now this is a choice and not a cultural requirement.

The American Family

The American family endures. Its nature may change, but the family unit none-theless continues to be the fundamental unit of society.

Today, there are more than 79 million families in America, and 270 million of the nation's nearly 312 million people live in these family units.[13] About

INTERNATIONAL PERSPECTIVE

Women in the Workforce

Over time, more and more women have joined the workforce throughout the world. Even in the last twenty years, international statistics indicate that the world's female workforce has increased rapidly.

In the United States, the percentage of women working outside the home rose from 31 percent in 1950 (not shown in the accompanying table) to nearly 60 percent in 1980 and over 70 percent today. Virtually all other industrialized nations have experienced similar increases in the percentage of women in the workforce. Nonetheless, fewer than half of women in some nations (for example, Italy, Mexico, and Turkey) are included in the workforce. In contrast, women in Scandinavian nations (Finland, Iceland, Norway, and Sweden) have long had higher workforce participation rates than American women.

Female Labor Force Participation Rates, by Country [in percent]

Country	1980	1990	2000	2009	Country	1980	1990	2000	2009
Australia	52	62	66	71	Korea, South	46	51	55	58
Austria	49	55	62	70	Luxembourg	40	50	70	96
Belgium	47	52	57	61	Mexico	34	23	43	47
Canada	57	68	70	74	Netherlands	36	53	66	74
Czech Republic	(X)	69	64	62	New Zealand	45	65	68	74
Denmark	71	78	76	77	Norway	62	71	76	78
Finland	70	74	72	74	Poland	(NA)	(NA)	61	57
France	54	60	65	66	Portugal	55	62	67	73
Germany[1]	53	57	64	71	Slovakia	(X)	(X)	63	61
Greece	33	44	50	55	Spain	32	42	52	65
Hungary	(NA)	(NA)	52	55	Sweden	74	81	75	78
Iceland	(NA)	(NA)	83	80	Switzerland	54	66	77	83
Ireland	36	44	57	64	Turkey	(NA)	37	30	29
Italy	40	46	47	52	United Kingdom	58	66	68	70
Japan	55	60	64	69	United States	60	69	71	70

SYMBOL:
NA Not available.
X Not applicable.

FOOTNOTES:
[1]Prior to 1991, data are for former West Germany.

SOURCE: Organization for Economic Cooperation and Development (OECD), 2011, "Labour Market Statistics: Labour Force Statistics by Sex and Age: Indicators," OECD Employment and Labour Market Statistics database (copyright).

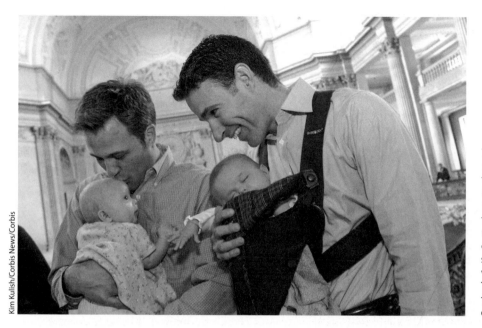

The rapidly changing nature of families in the United States can be seen in this photo. Here, a gay couple cares for their children. In the middle of the twentieth century, divorce and single-parent families were relatively rare. Today, the American family is a flexibly defined unit.

32 percent of the population lives in nonfamily households, including people with nonfamily roommates and people who live alone.

However, the nature of the family unit has indeed been changing. Husband–wife families comprise 70 percent of all families with children, whereas 30 percent of all families consist of a single adult and children. Female-headed families with no spouse present have risen from 10 percent of all families with children in 1970 to 26 percent of all families in 2010 (Figure 4-3). The birth rate also demonstrates how American families are changing: In the 1950s, the fertility rate for the average woman of childbearing age was 3.7 births. In the 1970s, that dropped to 2.4, and continued to fall, reaching a low of only 1.8 in 2000, which is below the projected zero-population growth rate (2.1 children per female of childbearing age). By 2011, the birth rate had climbed to 2.06, reflecting another change in the structure of the American family, with record numbers of births to unmarried women of all ages.[14]

It is not really clear what factors are contributing to these changes in the American family. Certainly, new opportunities for women in the occupational world have increased the number of women in the workforce and altered the traditional patterns of family life. Economic concerns may be an even more important factor: Families must increasingly depend on the incomes of both husband and wife to maintain a middle-class lifestyle.

Divorce

Almost all societies allow for the separation of husband and wife. Many developing societies have much higher divorce rates than the United States and other advanced industrialized societies. In 2011 in the United States, there were

FIGURE 4-3   THE CHANGING AMERICAN FAMILY

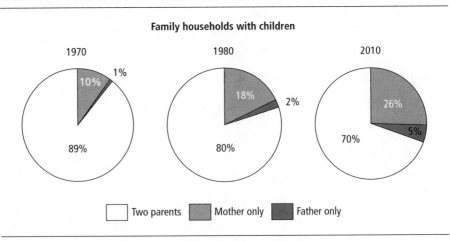

SOURCE: http://www.census.gov/compendia/statab/2012/tables/12s0067.pdf

3.4 divorces for every 7.5 marriages (per 1000 total population).[15] At this rate, we would expect half of all marriages to end in divorce. The U.S. divorce rate has decreased somewhat in recent years; it was higher at 5.2 divorces per 1000 population in 1970. The median duration of marriages that end in divorce is seven years, but not all marriages are created equal: First marriages are less likely to end in divorce, while the odds of divorce increase with subsequent marriages. Researchers believe that part of the explanation for the declining divorce rate in the United States is because Americans are more likely to live together without marrying today than in earlier decades, and those who do marry are likely to marry at an older age—on average five years older—than in the 1960s. Both of these factors also help explain why the United States' divorce rate is lower than that found in many developing nations, where people are likely to marry younger and not live together without marrying.

Women are more heavily burdened by divorce than men. Most mothers retain custody of children. Although both spouses confront reduced family income from the separation, the burden falls more heavily on the mother who must both support herself and rear the children. Divorced fathers are generally required by courts to provide child support payments; however, these payments rarely amount to full household support, and significant numbers of absent fathers fail to make full payments. Most divorced persons eventually find new spouses, but these remarriages are even more likely to end in divorce than first marriages.

Power and Gender

sex-based differences
biologically rooted
differences between
men and women

Although some societies have reduced sexual inequalities, no society has entirely eliminated male dominance.[16] Role differentiation in work differs among cultures. Sometimes, role differentiation occurs because of **sex-based differences**, or biologically rooted differences, between men and women. For example, the practice of women working close to home sometimes stems from women's biological need to be close to their young children in order to nurse them. Other differences are **gender-based differences** derived from society's cultural expectations based on accepted norms. For example, the historical tendency of men becoming physicians while women became nurses was based on gendered expectations. Moreover, historically, comparisons of numbers of different cultures studied by anthropologists reveal that men rather than women traditionally have dominated in political leadership and warfare. Though women are an increasing presence in world politics, even today, women on the average make up only about 17 percent of the representatives in national legislative bodies (congresses and parliaments) around the world,[17] and in no country have women achieved representation comparable to their proportion of the population.

Why have men dominated in politics and war in most cultures? There are many theories on this topic. Many theories link men's and women's participation in politics to their participation in war. For example, a theory of physical strength suggests that men prevail in warfare, particularly in primitive warfare, which relies mainly on physical strength of the combatants. Because men did the fighting, they also had to make the decisions about whether or not to engage in war; thus, men were dominant in politics. Decisions about whether to fight or not were vital to the survival of the culture; therefore, decisions about war were the most important political decisions in a society. Dominance in those decisions assisted men in other aspects of societal decision making and led to their general political dominance.

A related hunting theory suggests that in most societies, men do the hunting, wandering far from home and using great strength and endurance. The skills of hunting are closely related to the skills of war; people can be hunted and killed in the same fashion as animals. Because men dominated in hunting, they also dominated in war.

A childcare theory argues that women's biological function of bearing and nursing children prevents women from going far from home. Infants cannot be taken into potential danger. (As we stated earlier in this chapter, in most cultures women breastfeed their children for up to two years.) This circumstance explains why women in most cultures perform functions that allow them to remain at home—for example, cooking, harvesting, and planting—and why men in most cultures undertake tasks that require them to leave home—hunting, herding, and fishing. Warfare of course requires long stays away from home. In addition, the different nature of these functions—that men's work tends to take place in public and in groups and women's work tends to center around children and the home—leads to the evolution of what has been called the **public–private split**. The public–private split is the idea that men dominate in the public sphere and women focus on the private or domestic sphere. Thus, men are more likely to dominate in politics because they have more experience in the public sphere.

Still another theory, an aggression theory, proposes that men on the average possess more aggressive personalities than women. Some anthropologists

gender-based differences
the cultural characteristics linked to male and female that define people as masculine and feminine

public–private split
the theory that men dominate in the public sphere and women focus on the private or domestic sphere

contend that male aggression is biologically determined and occurs in all societies. They point to evidence that even at very young ages, boys try to hurt others and establish dominance more frequently than girls; these behaviors seem to occur without being taught and even when efforts are made to teach boys just the opposite.[18]

All these theories are arguable, of course. Some theories may be thinly disguised attempts to justify an inferior status for women—for keeping women at home and allowing them less power than men. Moreover, these theories do not go very far in explaining why the status of women varies so much from one society to another.

Although these theories help explain male dominance, we still need to explain the following: Why do women participate in politics in some societies more than in others? Generally, women exercise more political power in societies where they make substantial contributions to economic life. Thus, women have less power in societies that depend on hunting or herding and appear to have less power in societies that frequently engage in warfare. They also exercise more power in societies where societal views determine that women's participation in politics is acceptable and in societies where women have the opportunity to take part in educational and economic activities that lead to participation in politics. Some evidence suggests that the type of electoral system influences women's participation in politics. Finally, some evidence shows that women have more power in societies that rear children with greater affection and nurturance because women's work is held in higher esteem.[19]

Saudi women shop for wedding dresses in Riyadh, Saudi Arabia. Although Saudi women must wear the abaaya in public places, they can dress more liberally at private family gatherings.

John Moore / The Image Works

Power and Political Systems

The **political system** is the way that power is organized and distributed in a society, whether it is organizing a hunt and designating its leader or raising and commanding an army of millions. Some form of political system exists in all societies.[20]

Anthropologists have identified various types of political systems. These systems can be arranged according to the extent to which power is organized and centralized, from family and kinship groups to bands, tribes, chiefdoms, states, and nations.

political system
the organization and distribution of power in society

Family and Kinship Groups

In some societies, no separate power organization exists outside the family or kinship group. In these societies, there is no continuous or well-defined system of leaders over or above those who head the individual families. These societies do not have any clear-cut division of labor or economic organization outside the family, and there is no structured method for resolving differences and maintaining peace among members of the group. Further, these societies do not usually engage in organized offensive or defensive warfare. They tend to be small and widely dispersed, have economies that yield only a bare subsistence, and lack any form of organized fighting force. Power relationships are present, but they are closely tied to family and kinship. An example of this type of society is the Inuit, a people who inhabit the coastal areas of Arctic North America, Siberia, and Greenland. Family and kinship groups are the most important structure: The division of labor is based at the family level (and is determined by sex). Ostracism is the most prevalent method of social control.

Bands

Bands are small groups of related families of usually fewer than 75 people who occupy a common territory and come together periodically to hunt, trade, and make marriage arrangements. Bands are often found among nomadic societies where groups of families move about the land in search of food, water, game, and subsistence.

band
a small group of related families who occupy the same territory and interact with one another

Anthropologists believe that bands were the oldest form of political organization outside of the family and that all humans were once food foragers who moved about the land in small bands numbering at most a hundred people.

Authority in the band is usually exercised by a few senior heads of families; their authority most often derives from achievements in hunting or fighting. The senior headmen must decide when and where to move and choose a site for a new settlement. People follow the headmen's leadership primarily because they consider it in their own best interest to do so. Sanctions may range from contempt and ridicule to ostracism or exile from the band.

Tribes

tribe
a group of separate bands or villages sharing a common language and culture who come together for greater security

Anthropologists describe **tribes** as groups of bands or villages that share a common language and culture and unite for greater security against enemies or starvation. (*Tribe* also has a distinct legal definition in the United States, referring to recognized political organizations of Native Americans. See "Native Americans: An Historical Overview" in Chapter 10.) Typically, tribes are engaged in hunting, herding, or farming, and they live in areas of greater population density than bands. Tribal authorities must settle differences between bands, villages, and kinship groups. They must organize defenses as well as plan and carry out raids on other tribes. They must pool resources when needed and decide upon the distribution of common resources—the product of an organized hunt, for example. Authority may rest in the hands of one or more leaders respected for age, integrity, wisdom, or skills in hunting and warfare.

Chiefdoms

chiefdom
a centralized society in which power is concentrated in a single chief who heads a ranked hierarchy of people

Anthropologists also identify **chiefdoms**—highly centralized, regional societies in which power is concentrated in a single chief who is at the head of a ranked hierarchy of people. An example of a chiefdom is Akan, a chiefdom that dominated politics in areas now part of Ghana and the Ivory Coast. The position of chief is usually hereditary. People's status in the chiefdom is decided by their kinship to the chief; those closest to him are ranked socially superior and receive deferential treatment from those in lower ranks. The chief's responsibilities extend to the distribution of land and resources, the recruitment and command of warriors, and control over the goods and labor of the community. The chief may amass considerable personal wealth and other evidence of his high status.

States

state
a permanent centralized organization with a defined territory and recognized authority to make and enforce rules

The most comprehensive and complex system of power relationships is the **state**. A state is a permanent, centralized organization with a well-defined territory and the recognized authority to make and enforce rules of conduct. The power of the state is legitimate; that is, the state has the rightful use of power within a society. In state societies, populations are large and highly concentrated; the economy produces a surplus; and there are recognized rules of conduct for the members of the society, with positive and negative sanctions. These societies have an organized military establishment for offensive and defensive wars. In war, conquered people are not usually destroyed but instead are held as tributaries or incorporated as inferior classes into the state. In the vast majority of these societies, power is centered in a small, hereditary elite (see Focus: "Power and the Kingdom of Saudi Arabia" on p. 102).

Power in the state is employed to maintain order among peoples and to carry on large-scale community enterprises, just as in the band or tribe. But power in the state is also closely linked to defense, aggression, and the exploitation of conquered peoples. Frequently, states emerge in response to attacks by others.

Where there is a fairly high density of population, frequent and continuing contact among bands, and some commonality of language and culture, there is the potential for "national" unity in the form of a state. But a state may not emerge if there is no compelling motivation for large-scale cooperation. Motivation is very often provided initially by the need for defense against outside invasion.

Nations

A nation differs from a state in important ways. A **nation** is a society that sees itself as "one people" with a common culture, history, institutions, ideology, language, territory, and (often) religion. By this definition, there are probably five thousand or more nations in the world today. (The United Nations has only 192 member states; see Chapter 14.) Only rarely do nation and state coincide, as in Japan, which has a relatively homogenous population within its territory. Because of migration, trade, and war, many states are much more heterogeneous. Some states do not have a nation of their own but exist within the borders of other nations. An example of a stateless nation is that of the Kurds, who occupy land in a variety of states, including Iraq and Turkey. Many states are multinational, that is, they include within their territorial boundaries more than one nation. When a state and nation do coincide, it is usually referred to as a nation-state.

The United States declares itself to be "one nation, indivisible, under God," yet it encompasses multiple nationalities, languages, and cultures. The claim to nationhood by the United States rests primarily on a common allegiance to the institutions of democracy. Similarly, the nations of Russia and China are composed of a variety of peoples who identify with national institutions. Other nation-states base their claim to nationhood on common ethnicity and ancestry as well as language and territory.

nation
a society that sees itself as one people with a common culture, history, ideology, language, set of institutions, and territory

Power and Society: Some Anthropological Observations

Let's summarize the contributions that anthropological studies can make to our understanding of the growth of power relationships in societies. First, it is clear that the *physical environment* plays an important role in the development of power systems. Where the physical environment is harsh and the human population must out of necessity be spread thinly, power relationships are restricted to the family and kinship groupings. Larger political groupings are essentially impossible. The elite emerge only after there is some concentration of population where food resources permit groupings of people larger than one or two families.

Second, power relationships are linked to the economic patterns of a culture. In subsistence economies, power relationships are limited to the band or tribal level. Only in surplus-producing economies do we find states or statelike power systems. Developed power systems are associated with patterns of settled life, a certain degree of technological advance, and economic surplus.

FOCUS

Power and the Kingdom of Saudi Arabia

The Kingdom of Saudi Arabia is a state: It has a defined territory and recognized authority to make and enforce laws. But the Kingdom of Saudi Arabia is also an excellent example of a chiefdom. In 1902 Abd al-Aziz Ibn Saud captured the city of Riyadh (now the capital) and began a quest to unite the Arabian Peninsula, which occurred on September 23, 1932. It is within the Kingdom of Saudi Arabia that one finds two of Islam's holiest cities: Mecca and Medina.

Saudi Arabia is currently ruled by King Fahd bin Abd al-Aziz Al Saud, who serves as both *chief of state and the head of government.* That is, the king acts as both the ceremonial head of state, like the queen of England, and government leader, like the prime minister. In Saudi Arabia, there are no elections. Rather, there is a *hereditary monarchy* that is bound by tenets of Islam, and the descendants of Abd al-Aziz Ibn Saud have succeeded him to the throne. Next in the line of succession is Crown Prince Abdallah bin Abd al-Aziz Al Saud. But the Saudi monarchy does not operate like many monarchies based on primogeniture. *Primogeniture* means that the oldest son will inherit title and/or possessions. Rather, the older and most widely respected princes decide which prince will become king. Thus, power comes as the result of having favor with one's peers.

In the 1930s, the discovery of oil meant the transformation of the kingdom and the Saudi Royal family. Since the 1950s, the United States and the rest of the world have become increasingly dependent on Saudi Arabia as a primary source of cheap oil. Now, Saudi Arabia has the largest proved reserves of petroleum in the world (26 percent) and is the world's largest exporter of petroleum. There is no doubt that the kingdom's petroleum reserves have enhanced it with power not seen by other countries that do not have such important natural resources.

Saudi Arabia is governed by *Shari'a*, or Islamic law. In 1992 and 1993, a series of reforms was implemented, creating some secular rules. These rules, however, only supplement the religious law in effect. By Western standards, law in Saudi Arabia is quite strict, and the Islamic state exercises a strong degree of power over its populace. Women are prohibited from driving cars or getting driver's licenses. Drug traffickers are subjected to the death penalty, and in 1995

Third, patterns of warfare are linked to the development of power relationships. Warfare is rare or lacking among people who have no real power system outside the family. Where power relationships emerge at the band or tribal level, warfare appears to be continuous, in the form of periodic raiding for small economic gains or the achievement of personal glory and status; victory assumes the form of killing or driving off enemy groups. Only at the state level is warfare well organized and pursued for the purpose of conquest and economic exploitation. This does not mean necessarily that statelike power systems cause war but that some common factor underlies both the rise of state power systems and organized warfare. Warfare and conquest are not essential to the maintenance of the state; in fact, in the modern world, warfare between major states may slowly give way to other forms of competition, if only because of the increasing threat of total destruction.

alone, more than 150 criminals were publicly beheaded with a sword. Thieves are punished with amputation of the offending hand.

Assisting the king in governing is the *Majlis-al-Shura*, or Shura Council, which the king can use to consult on various issues. The council is designed to increase the level of consideration given to various decisions and highlights the value placed on experience and wisdom. The ninety members of the council are appointed by the king, and most of them are members of the royal family. They serve a four-year term and can be reappointed.

Members of the Saudi Royal family enjoy the fruits of the nation's wealth and are entitled to a variety of privileges. Many receive stipends from the king, some live rent-free in numerous compounds, and all are entitled to free air travel on Saudi Arabian Airlines. Even nonroyal Saudis enjoy a high standard of living; all are entitled to interest-free loans to purchase homes or start-up businesses. Health care is free for all, as is a college education. Some utilities, like water, are free. Others, like telephone service, are subsidized and cost average citizens far less than in other places.

One problem faced by the Saudis, however, is their expanding numbers. Some estimates put the numbers of the royal family at 30,000, meaning that the resources of the royal family are being taxed and will continue to be as the number of royals grows. In addition, the population of Saudi Arabia itself is growing, with a birth rate nearly double that of the United States. This means that the oil reserves held by the nation will need to support a burgeoning population in the future.

Another problem is the esteem with which the royal family is held in some circles in Saudi Arabia. Though an Islamic state, Saudi royals are renowned for their lifestyles and vices that often contradict Islamic law. In an effort to quell that criticism, the Saudi royals have made concessions to Islamic fundamentalists. The Saudi education system, for example, is administered by *Wahhabi* fundamentalists. Indeed, two-thirds of all doctorate degrees awarded in Saudi Arabia are awarded in Islamic studies. And some contend that in an effort to deflect criticism and instability from internal politics, the Saudi royals have supported fundamentalist efforts at *jihad*, or Islamic holy war, in other parts of the world.

Fourth, anthropological research makes it clear that power relationships exist in simple forms in primitive societies and that no society is void of a power structure. Power structures become more complex and hierarchical and more impersonal and based on physical force as societies move from the subsistence level with simple technology to a surplus-producing level with advanced technology and large cooperative enterprises. The simpler power systems are frequently headed by chiefs and councils selected for their age, wisdom, or demonstrated capacity as hunters or warriors. These leaders tend to rule more by example and persuasion than by formal decree or force. As more complex state systems emerge, leaders are endowed with the exclusive right to coerce. Characteristically, political and economic power in the state is concentrated in a small hereditary elite. Modern representative government, in the form of European and American democracies, is relatively rare in the history of human societies.

CHAPTER SUMMARY

- Anthropologists, in their study of human culture, have documented that the exercise of power and the division of labor within the family constitute the most basic power relationship, the one from which true political power structures develop.

- Within the social sciences, anthropology examines humans, their societies, and power structures through a broad perspective. Within the discipline of anthropology are four subfields. These include archaeology, biological and physical anthropology, linguistic anthropology, and socio-cultural anthropology.

- In their examination of cultures, anthropologists tend to make cultural generalizations that focus on aggregate behaviors within a society or values and beliefs that are commonly shared.

- Anthropologists often subdivide a culture into various components, including symbols, beliefs, values, norms, religion, sanctions, and artifacts in order to simplify cultural analysis.

- Culture assists people in adapting to the conditions in which they live. Cultural anthropologists rely on four key approaches when examining culture: functionalism, the materialist perspective, idealism, and cultural relativism.

- The family is the principal agent of socialization into society. In all societies, the family relationship centers on procreative and child-rearing functions, and shares other common characteristics. The family transmits and carries forward the culture of the society. It establishes the primary system of roles with differential rights, duties, and behaviors. And it is within the family that the child first encounters authority.

- Sex role differentiation in work differs among cultures. Sometimes, role differentiation occurs because of sex-based differences, or biologically rooted differences, between men and women. Other differences are gender-based differences derived from society's cultural expectations based on accepted norms.

- Anthropologists have identified various types of political systems based on the way that power is organized and distributed in a society. These systems can be arranged according to the extent to which power is organized and centralized, from family and kinship groups to bands, tribes, chiefdoms, states, and nations.

- Anthropological studies indicate that the physical environment plays an important role in the development of power systems, that power relationships are linked to the economic patterns of a culture, that patterns of warfare are linked to the development of power relationships, and that power relationships exist in simple forms in primitive societies and that no society is void of a power structure.

KEY TERMS

archaeology   the study of human cultures through their physical and material remains

artifact   a physical product of a culture

band   a small group of related families who occupy the same territory and interact with one another

beliefs generally shared ideas about what is true

biological anthropology the study of humans as biological organisms

chiefdom a centralized society in which power is concentrated in a single chief who heads a ranked hierarchy of people

cultural generalization the description of commonly shared values, beliefs, and behaviors in a society

cultural relativity suspending judgment of other societies' customs, practices, and institutions

culture people's learned and shared behaviors and beliefs

ethnocentrism judging other cultures solely in terms of one's own culture

family traditionally defined as a residential kin group

folkways a trivial norm that guides actions

functionalism a perspective in anthropology that emphasizes that cultural institutions and practices serve individual or societal needs

functions of power in society maintain internal peace, organize and direct community enterprises, conduct warfare, rule and exploit

gender-based differences the cultural characteristics linked to male and female that define people as masculine and feminine

idealism a perspective in anthropology that focuses on the importance of ideas in determining culture

intensification when population growth causes increased use and exploitation of the environment

kinship group people related to one another by blood

linguistic anthropology a method of analyzing societies in terms of human communication, including its origins, history, and contemporary variation and change

materialist perspective a perspective in anthropology that focuses on how people make their living in a specific environmental setting

mores important norms that carry moral authority

multiculturalism acknowledging, protecting, and promoting multiple cultures and subcultures

norms shared rules and expectations about behavior

marriage a socially approved sexual and economic union between a man and a woman, intended to be lasting, and implying social roles between the spouses and their children

monogamy a marriage union of one husband and one wife

nation a society that sees itself as one people with a common culture, history, ideology, language, set of institutions, and territory

patriarchal family the male is the dominant authority, and kinship is determined through the male line

political system the organization and distribution of power in society

public–private split the theory that men dominate in the public sphere and women focus on the private or domestic sphere

religion a set of beliefs and practices pertaining to supernatural powers and the origins and meaning of life

sanction a reward or punishment for conforming to or violating cultural norms

sex-based differences biologically rooted differences between men and women

socialization process process by which culture is communicated to successive generations

subculture the variation in ways of life within a society

socio-cultural anthropology the study of living peoples and their cultures

state a permanent centralized organization with a defined territory and recognized authority to make and enforce rules

symbol anything that communicates meaning, including language, art, and music

technology both the tools and the knowledge humans use to overcome their environment and meet their material needs

tribe a group of separate bands or villages sharing a common language and culture who come together for greater security

values shared ideas about what is good and desirable

ON THE WEB

EXPLORING ANTHROPOLOGY

• The website for this textbook offers resources for exploring anthropology on the Internet. See **www.cengagebrain.com**. Other resources such as federal government and international organization websites, including the United Nations Statistics Division (**http://unstats .un.org/unsd/default.htm**) site, provide a wealth of comparative statistical information, including demographic and social statistics, that can offer data sets that facilitate anthropological research.

The following are good websites to start with:

• **The American Anthropological Association** (**www.aaanet.org**) This is the website of the professional association for anthropologists. It contains links to many anthropological sites

and provides additional information about the study of anthropology.

Try this: Go to **www.aaanet.org/** and under Resources click on the RACE: Are We So Different? tab. Take an interactive virtual tour of this travelling exhibit that examines anthropological research on the meaning of race.

• **Society for Applied Anthropology** (**www. sfaa.net**) This site is a tool for facilitating applied anthropological research. It includes student forums, links to other anthropological websites, and anthropological publications.

Try this: Go to http://community.sfaa.net/, click on the community page and view the various community groups on the Society for Applied Anthropology's page. Pick one group and examine in-depth the areas of study on which they focus.

REVIEW QUIZ

MULTIPLE CHOICE

1. What are people related to one another by blood called?
   a. family
   b. a band
   c. a kinship group
   d. a more

2. What is the description of commonly shared values, beliefs, and behaviors in a society called?
   a. multiculturalism
   b. culture
   c. cultural generalization
   d. subculture

3. What is the variation in ways of life within a society called?
   a. multiculturalism
   b. culture
   c. cultural generalization
   d. subculture

4. Anything that communicates meaning, including language, art, and music is a _____.
   a. symbol
   b. value
   c. belief
   d. religion

5. Generally shared ideas about what is true is called a _____.
   a. symbol
   b. value
   c. belief
   d. religion

6. Shared ideas about what is good and desirable are known as _____.
   a. symbols
   b. values
   c. beliefs
   d. religions

7. What is the perspective in anthropology that emphasizes that cultural institutions and practices serve individual or societal needs?
   a. functionalism
   b. materialist perspective
   c. idealism
   d. ethnocentrism

8. What is suspending judgment of other societies' customs, practices, and institutions called?
   a. ethnocentrism
   b. idealism
   c. intensification
   d. cultural relativity

9. What is a small group of related families who occupy the same territory and interact within the group called?
   a. a tribe
   b. a band
   c. a chiefdom
   d. a state

10. What is a society called that sees itself as one people with a common culture, history, and institutions?
    a. a tribe
    b. a band
    c. a nation
    d. a state

FILL IN THE BLANK

11. _____ is all the ways of life common to a society.

12. A set of beliefs and practices pertaining to supernatural powers and the origins and meaning of life is called _____.

13. A trivial norm that guides actions is known as a _____.

14. _____ is both the tools and the knowledge humans use to overcome their environment and meet their material needs.

15. When population growth causes increased use and exploitation of the environment, it is called _____.

CHAPTER 5

Power and Sociology: The Importance of Social Class

Learning Objectives

After reading this chapter, students will be able to:

- Explain how social class is defined.
- Explain the theories that inform sociology's examination of social class.
- Describe how social class influences the exercise of power in the United States.

Power Relations and Social Stratification

All known societies have some method of classifying their members using some system of rankings. Although many societies claim to grant "equality" to their members, in no society have people in fact been considered equal. The **stratification** of society involves the classification of individuals and the ranking of classifications on a superiority–inferiority scale. This system of classification and ranking is itself a source of prestige, wealth, income, authority, and power. In some societies, there is greater mobility of individuals between different strata; in other societies, individuals remain in the strata to which they were born.

stratification
classifying individuals and ranking the classifications on a superiority–inferiority scale

Individuals can be classified based on a wide variety of characteristics—physical strength, fighting prowess, family lineage, ethnicity or race, age, gender, religion, birth order, and so on. But the most important bases of stratification in a modern industrial society are the various roles that individuals play in the economic system.

Individuals are ranked according to how they make their living and how much control they exercise over the livelihood of others. Ranking by occupation and control of economic resources occurs in not only the United States but also most other modern nations.[1]

The evaluation of individuals along a superiority–inferiority scale means a differential distribution of prestige. Thus, the top strata will receive the *deference* of individuals who are ranked below them. Deference may take many forms: acquiescence in the material advantages or privileges of the elite (the use of titles and symbols of rank, distinctive clothing, housing, and automobiles), accordance of influence and respect, acceptance of leadership in decision making, and so on.

The stratification system also involves different lifestyles: foods eaten, magazines and books read, places of residence, favorite sports, schools attended, pronunciation and accent, recreational activities, and so forth. The stratification system is also associated with the *uneven distribution of wealth and income*: In every society, higher-ranking persons enjoy better housing, clothing, food, automobiles, and other material goods and services than persons ranked lower on the scale.

Finally, the stratification system involves the *unequal distribution of power*—the ability to control the acts of others. Sociologists agree that power and stratification are closely related, but they disagree on the specific value of this relationship. Some theorize that power is a *product* of economic well-being, prestige, or status. Others believe that power *determines* the distribution of wealth, prestige, and status.[2] Some sociologists see the merits of both arguments and contend that while power does determine the distribution of wealth, prestige, and status, it also is self-perpetuating in that these attributes also create power.

The stratification system creates social classes. The term **social class** refers to all individuals who occupy a broadly similar category and ranking in the stratification system. Members of the same social class may or may not interact or even realize that they have much in common. Because all societies have stratification systems, all societies have social classes.

social class
a category and ranking in the stratification system

Stratification in American Society

Social classes are of interest to sociologists, with their concern for the relationships among individuals and groups. Sociologists have devised several methods of identifying and measuring social stratification. These include (1) the subjective method, in which individuals are asked how they see themselves in the class system; (2) the reputational method, in which individuals are asked to rank positions in the class system; and (3) the objective method, in which social scientists observe characteristics that discriminate among patterns of life that they associate with social class.

Subjective Self-Classification

The American ideology encompasses the notion that status should be based on personal qualities and achievements. Individuals in a free society should have the opportunity to achieve the social rankings that they can earn by ability, effort, and moral worth. These individuals are supposed to rise or fall according to their merits. In view of this ideology, it is not surprising that traditionally, overwhelming majorities of Americans think of themselves as middle class. Through **subjective identification** in which individuals self-classify their own social class, nearly nine out of ten will describe themselves as middle class when they are forced to choose between this term and either upper or lower class. Even when the choices are broadened, more people identify themselves as middle class than any other class (Table 5-1). It is apparent that characterizing oneself as upper class is regarded as "snobbish" (only 2 percent identified themselves as

subjective identification
individuals identify their own social class

TABLE 5-1 SOCIAL CLASS SELF-IDENTIFICATION

"If you were asked to use one of five names for your social class, in which would you say you belong?"

	2008	2010
Upper class (Total)	21	20
Upper	2	2
Upper middle	19	18
Middle class	53	50
Lower class (Total)	25	29
Lower middle	19	21
Lower	6	8

SOURCE: pewsocialtrends.org/files/2010/11/759-recession.pdf

upper class) and that a stigma is attached to viewing oneself as lower class. Even people who admit to being poor consider it an insult to be called lower class.[3]

The Great Recession and Self-Classification

From Table 5-1, we also can see the impact that the recent economic recession has had on Americans' subjective self-evaluation of social class. Notably, we see that between 2008 and 2010, there was a marked downward adjustment of Americans' self-classification of social class. In fact, only 50 percent of Americans saw themselves as middle class (though this figure increases to 89 percent if allowing the qualifiers of "upper middle" and "lower middle"). Between 2008 and 2010, both the proportion of individuals identifying themselves as upper middle class and middle class shrunk, with one percent fewer Americans identifying themselves as upper middle class. On the other hand, the proportion identifying themselves as lower middle class increased between 2008 and 2010.

One explanation for these changes is the detrimental effect the economic recession had on factors that contribute to individuals' perception of social class. One of the factors is income: As earned income decreases (because of lower wages, fewer hours worked, or unemployment) so too do people's perceptions of their class status. In addition, higher levels of unemployment also may contribute to a decrease in rank in self-classification measures because people no longer participate in the occupation on which their workplace identity was based.

Reputational Prestige

reputational prestige the general level of respect associated with a specific job title

Occupations differ in their **reputational prestige,** or the general level of respect associated with a specific job title. The prestige rankings of occupations are often used as a measure of the stratification system of modern societies. It is not polite to ask people how much money they make or how much money they have accumulated, but it is socially acceptable to ask what they do for a living. Often people ask others this question in order to identify social ranking.

Occupational prestige scores obtained from national surveys are fairly consistent (Table 5-2). Note that prestige is not exactly the equivalent of income although occupations near the top generally pay more than those at the bottom. Prestigious occupations, in addition to paying well, also tend to involve substantial authority; in contrast, close supervision and taking orders lower the prestige of occupations. Responses in Table 5-2 reflect this trend, with firefighters, police officers, and military officers enjoying comparatively high levels of prestige.

TABLE 5-2 OCCUPATIONAL PRESTIGE RANKINGS

"I am going to read off a number of different occupations. For each, would you tell me if you feel it is an occupation of very great prestige, considerable prestige, some prestige, or hardly any prestige at all?"

	Percentages			
Occupation	Very Great Prestige	Considerable Prestige	Some Prestige	Hardly Any at All
Firefighter	62	21	13	5
Scientist	57	22	14	7
Doctor	56	28	13	3
Nurse	54	24	18	4
Military officer	51	24	17	7
Teacher	51	22	17	10
Police officer	44	24	24	7
Priest/Minister/Clergy	41	21	28	10
Engineer	39	27	28	5
Farmer	36	22	28	14
Architect	29	30	31	10
Member of Congress	28	21	27	22
Lawyer	26	22	33	19
Business executive	23	15	46	16
Athlete	21	18	42	19
Journalist	17	20	40	22
Union Leader	17	17	34	30
Entertainer	17	17	40	25
Banker	16	21	43	18
Actor	15	19	33	33
Stockbroker	13	11	43	31
Accountant	11	23	46	19
Real estate agent/broker	5	14	50	30

SOURCE: www.harrisinteractive.com/vault/Harris-Interactive-Poll-Research-Pres
Occupations-2009-08.pdf

Interestingly, many of the occupations that Americans tend to focus great deals of attention on—athletes, actors, and entertainers—rank comparatively low when gauging prestige, at least in the abstract. Instead, many highly ranked occupations require extensive education; indeed, some sociologists believe that education is the most important single factor influencing occupational prestige rankings.[4] Occupations like doctor, nurse, and scientist all require extensive training and tend to rank as prestigious occupations. Finally, it is interesting to note that most prestigious jobs are white-collar occupations that involve mental activity rather than blue-collar occupations that require physical labor. These rankings have remained stable for several decades.

Objective Classifications

objective criteria
determining social class
by ranking income,
occupation, or education

The principal **objective criteria** of social class are income, occupation, and education. If sociologists are correct in assuming that occupation and control of economic resources are the source of stratification in society, then these indexes are the best available measures of class. Certainly, income, jobs, and education are unequally distributed in American society as they are in all other societies.

College graduates comprise nearly 30 percent of the adults in the United States (Figure 5-1). Over 85 percent are high school graduates, and about 15 percent dropped out of formal education without a high school diploma. This is a dramatic increase in formal education over previous generations.

Income is closely related to education. Generally, individuals who have acquired higher education tend to enjoy higher annual incomes. While there are

FIGURE 5-1   EDUCATIONAL ATTAINMENT

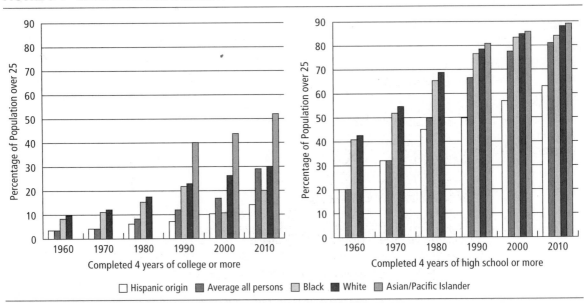

SOURCE: www.census.gov/compendia/statab/cats/education/educational_attainment.html

some disparities in income related to race (for example, Asians and whites in general tend to earn more than blacks and Hispanics), by far *the biggest factor determining income is education.* Higher levels of educational achievement are linked to higher earnings across racial groups.

Race and Ethnicity

Ethnic and racial stratification is visible in virtually all measures of social class: income, education, and occupation. For example, in Figure 5-2 showing adult educational attainment levels since 1960, while all groups have gained in education, African American and especially Hispanic high school and college completion percentages remain below those of whites. (On the other hand, the educational attainment of Asian Americans and Pacific Islanders surpasses other races, particularly in the percentage of completion of four years of college or more.) The educational gap between blacks and whites has narrowed somewhat over the years, but not the gap between Hispanics and whites. Of course, given the previously noted importance of education's impact on income and occupational prestige, we can see that unequal levels of educational attainment create continued inequality in American society. (We examine "Power, Race, and Gender" in greater detail in Chapter 10.)

Sociology and the Study of Social Classes

Sociologists disagree on why societies distribute wealth, power, and prestige unequally. On the one side are the functional theorists, who argue that stratification is necessary and perhaps inevitable for maintaining society. On the other side are the conflict theorists, who argue that stratification results from the selfish interests of groups trying to preserve their advantages over others.[5] Still yet

FIGURE 5-2 EDUCATION, EARNINGS, AND RACE

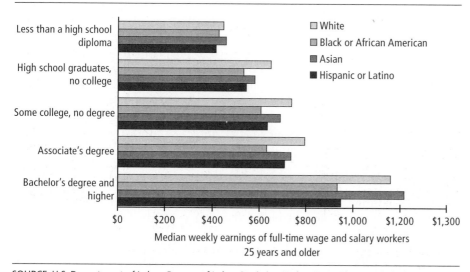

Median weekly earnings of full-time wage and salary workers 25 years and older

SOURCE: U.S. Department of Labor, Bureau of Labor Statistics. "Labor Force Characteristics by Race and Ethnicity, 2010" www.bls.gov/cps/cpsrace2010.pdf.

another perspective, the symbolic interactionists, argue that social stratification is the result of interactions between individuals. And postmodernists cite the inability of the three previous perspectives to adequately address social stratification in a postindustrial society.

Functional Theory

functional theory
inequality is necessary to get people to work harder in more demanding jobs that require longer training and greater skills

Functional theory assumes that society is stable and orderly and that a stable society requires inequality within it. Functionalism might be summarized as follows:

- Certain positions are more important to a society's survival than other positions and require special skills. For example, in most societies, occupations such as governor, physician, teacher, and priest are considered vital.
- Only a few persons in society have the ability (intelligence, energy, and personality) to perform well in these positions.
- These positions require persons who have ability to undergo extensive training and education before they occupy these positions.
- To motivate able people to endure the training and to sacrifice their time and energy for education, society must provide them with additional rewards.
- The result is social inequality with some classes of people receiving more rewards than others. Inequality is inevitable and essential to ensure "that the most important positions are conscientiously filled by the most qualified persons."[6]

In other words, an expectation of inequality is essential in getting people to work harder in more difficult jobs that require longer training and greater skill.[7]

division of labor
individuals perform distinct, assigned functions

manifest function
the acknowledged and expected function of societal relations or an institution

latent function
the unrecognized or unanticipated function of societal relations or an institution

dysfunction
the undesirable by-product of relations or institutions

Sociologists who advocated functionalist theory include Talcott Parsons and Robert Merton. Parsons stressed the need for a **division of labor** (when individuals perform distinct, assigned functions) within families and within society. If individuals and institutions perform their tasks, society can remain stable. Merton described various aspects of function within society, including **manifest functions** (the acknowledged and expected functions of societal relations or an institution), **latent functions** (unrecognized or unanticipated functions of societal relations or an institution), and **dysfunctions** (the undesirable by-products of relations or institutions). For example, the media is a social institution whose manifest function is to inform and entertain. Its latent function may be to socialize young Americans and immigrants to a common culture. But its dysfunctional impact may be that it discourages social and civic interaction by providing a "too convenient" form of entertainment.

Conflict Theory

conflict theory
inequality is imposed on society by those who want to retain their wealth and power

In contrast, **conflict theory** focuses on the struggle among competing groups in society over scarce resources. Conflict theorists assert the following:

- People who possess property, income, power, or prestige—the upper classes—simply wish to protect their position in society. Thus, the stratification system is perpetuated.

- There are many "functionally important" positions in society that are not highly rewarded. It might be argued that a garbage collector, an electrician, an auto mechanic, or a plumber is just as important to the survival of society as is a physician or a lawyer.
- Many people in the lower classes have the ability to perform in high-status occupations, but because of unequal educational opportunities, they never get the chance to do so.
- Wealth is not the only way of motivating people. Conceivably, societies might reward people merely by recognizing their services. Cooperation could then replace competition as a motivating force.
- Stratification negatively affects the thinking of members of the lower class. Stratification may even be "dysfunctional" to society if it fosters feelings of suspicion, hostility, and disloyalty to society among those in the lower classes.

In short, the stratification system is imposed on society by those at the top. It allows them to use their power and prestige to keep what they have.

Sociologists who used the conflict perspective in their research include Max Weber (pronounced VAY-ber) and C. Wright Mills. Weber argued that power is the ability of an individual in a social relationship to carry out his or her will despite resistance from others in the social relationship. Mills saw society as competition between groups in society, and he argued that in the United States a ruling class exists. That is, the power structure is composed of a small **power elite** that includes top business executives, media moguls, and military and government leaders who dominate decision making in this country. (Elite theory is discussed in greater detail in Chapter 3, "Power and Ideology.") Later in this chapter, we examine the ideas of Karl Marx, who argued that the struggle between classes was the driving force in history and politics.

power elite
Mills's term for a ruling class that dominates decision making

Feminist theory, which regards society through a gendered prism and emphasizes the male-dominated, or patriarchical, nature of society, is considered a form of conflict theory. Feminist theory emphasizes the struggle for equality of women with men and the transformative nature a change in relations between the sexes could have on society.

feminist theory
a form of conflict theory, a theory of social stratification that uses a gendered prism and emphasizes the struggle for equality of women with men

Symbolic Interaction Theory

Symbolic interaction theory differs from both the functionalist and conflict theories in that it focuses on a micro level of analysis; that is, whereas functionalism and conflict theory analyze large groups and institutions within societies, symbolic interaction theory focuses on individuals and small groups in society. Specifically, symbolic interaction theory examines the role that symbols play in creating meaning for communication between individuals (interaction). There are a few key tenets of symbolic interaction theory:

- Symbols include not only written language but also facial expressions, gestures, signs, and common meanings.
- Symbols help people assign meanings to social situations. For example, a couple flirting might engage in behaviors like increased eye contact,

According to Symbolic Interaction Theory, symbols, including non-verbal communication, help people assign meanings to social situations. The touching hands, bodies turned toward each other, eye contact, and smiles all indicate that these individuals are flirting.

Thomas Michael Corcoran / PhotoEdit

subjective reality
one individual's idea of what occurred in a social interaction; that individual's interpretation of events

smiling, tilting of the head, and close physical contact. Flirting can occur with spoken language.

- The assessment of social interaction is through a **subjective reality**, that is, one individual's idea of what occurred in a social interaction is just that—an individual's interpretation of events.
- Our assessment of social interaction prescribes our behavior.

Our identities and concept of self are shaped by social interactions and our perceptions of these interactions.

Symbolic interactionists view social class as the result of individuals' actions. That is, social structures, classes, and institutions come from the interaction between individuals and the use of symbols in their everyday communications. Symbolic interactionists concede that these interactions can be structured and defined by larger political and economic structures, but they argue that interaction between individuals and the meaning ascribed to that interaction is constantly changing. For example, even in a brief encounter, one individual can discern a great deal about another. We often evaluate individuals and subjectively compare them to ourselves by using such symbols as:

- Possessions: What kind of car does the person drive? What kind of clothing does she wear? Is it neatly pressed or rumpled? Are her nails manicured? What kind of shoes and sunglasses does she wear; what handbag does she carry?
- Language: Does she sound educated? Have a large vocabulary? Have an accent associated with rich or poor areas?
- Facial expression and demeanor: Is she commanding or reticent, proud or meek?

Oftentimes our interaction is impacted by our subjective perception of who we are interacting with. We might respond to someone in a higher social class with deference and might respond to someone in a lower social class with a lack of respect.

Theorists using the symbolic interaction theory include George Herbert Mead and Herbert Bloomer. Both Mead and Bloomer, who coined the term *symbolic interaction*, were part of the Chicago School. The **Chicago School** refers to the Sociology Department at the University of Chicago—the first sociology department in the United States. This faculty was instrumental in nurturing the new discipline and also formed the professional sociological organization now called the American Sociological Society.

Chicago School
the first sociology department in the United States at the University of Chicago

Postmodernism

Postmodernism asserts that the functionalist theory, conflict theory, and symbolic interaction theory have proven inadequate in analyzing societies in a postindustrial world. Postmodernism rejects these theories as unsuccessful and asserts that discipline—specific borders within the social sciences (for example, psychology, political science, and economics)—undermine the ability of the social sciences to effectively analyze postmodern societies. Postmodern societies typically have certain characteristic traits including

- An information explosion facilitated by the print and electronic media.
- An economy with high levels of information and service-related jobs.
- An emphasis on consumerism.
- Increased globalization in artistic, cultural, and economic aspects of life.

Postmodernism is an emerging theory in sociology and the rest of the social sciences. While rejecting older theories, it also calls into question key assumptions on which those theories are based. Critics of postmodernism contend that, although the theory succeeds in forcing a reevaluation of old assumptions, it ignores some object realities within society, including inequality in power relationships within and between societies.

Inequality in America

Income is a key component of stratification, and income is unequally distributed in all societies. As long as societies reward skills, talent, knowledge, hard work, innovation, initiative, and risk taking, there will be inequalities of income. But the question remains: How much inequality is required to provide adequate rewards and incentives for education, training, work, enterprise, and risk?

Income Distributions

Let's try to systematically examine income inequality in America. Table 5-3 divides all American families into five groups—from the lowest one-fifth in income to the highest one-fifth—and shows the percentage of total family income received by each group over the years. (If perfect income equality existed, each

TABLE 5-3 INCOME INEQUALITY

Percentage Distribution of Family Income, by Quintiles, and Top 5 Percent

Quintiles	1929	1970	1980	1990	2000	2010
Lowest	3.5	5.4	5.2	3.8	3.6	3.3
Second	9.0	12.2	11.6	9.6	8.9	8.5
Third	13.8	17.6	17.5	15.9	14.8	14.6
Fourth	19.3	23.9	24.1	24	23	23.4
Highest	54.4	40.9	41.5	46.6	49.8	50.2
Top 5 percent	30.0	15.6	15.6	18.5	22.1	22.4

SOURCES: U.S. Bureau of the Census, *Statistical Abstract of the United States 2002* (Washington, DC: Government Printing Office, 2003), Table 659, and U.S. Bureau of the Census, *Statistical Abstract of the United States 2009*, Table 675. Share of Aggregate Income Received by Each Fifth and Top 5 Percent of Households: 1990 to 2006 www.census.gov/compendia/statab/tables/09s0675.pdf, and www.census.gov/prod/2011pubs/p60-239.pdf.

fifth would receive 20 percent of all family income, and it would not even be possible to rank fifths from highest to lowest.) The poorest one-fifth received 3.5 percent of all family personal income in 1929; by 1970 this group had increased its share of all family personal income to 5.4 percent. (Most of the increase occurred during World War II.) The highest one-fifth received 54.4 percent of all family personal income in 1929; by 1970 this percentage had declined to 40.9. The income share received by the top 5 percent of families declined from 30 percent in 1929 to 15.6 percent in 1970.

Rising Income Inequality

Note, however, an increase in inequality in the United States since 1970. The income share of the lowest group of families has declined from 5.4 percent in 1970 to 3.3 percent in 2010, while the income share of the highest group has risen from nearly 41 percent in 1970 to over 50 percent in 2010. That is to say that the highest 20 percent of income-earning families in the United States earn more than half of the income received. Included in that top-earner category is the highest 5 percent, who earn more than 20 percent of the income earned in the United States. The income share of that top 5 percent of American families has risen from over 15 percent in 1970 to over 22 percent in 2010.

While rising income inequality in the United States garnered widespread attention from the media in the wake of the Occupy movement protests in 2011, social scientists, policy makers, and advocates for the poor have voiced concern over this reversal of the historical trend toward greater income equality for the past several decades (see Focus: "Address Inequality or Expand the Economy?").

This recent increase in inequality appears to be a product of several social and economic trends: (1) the relative decline of the manufacturing sector of the economy, with its middle-income, blue-collar jobs, and the ascendancy of the information and service sectors, with a combination of high-paying and low-paying jobs; (2) an increase in the number of two-wage families, making single-wage households relatively less affluent; (3) demographic trends that include

FOCUS

Address Inequality or Expand the Economy?

In the 2012 presidential election, one top issue was equality. That year, many Democrats, including President Obama, advocated increasing taxes on wealthy Americans in an effort to reduce income inequality. The issue became a popular one in the context of a sour economy and then a snail's pace recovery, which was compounded by widespread reports of CEOs of banks and financial services corporations earning millions of dollars in bonuses after their companies had received federal bailout monies. The Occupy movements, with their mantra of "we are the 99 percent" (meaning not the top one percent of income earners), also focused considerable attention on the issue of income inequality. Yet many Americans think growing the economy is more important than reducing income inequality.

When asked to gauge their priorities, most Americans (82 percent) say that the government should grow and expand the economy. Many Americans (70 percent) also believe in increasing equality of opportunity, but reducing income inequality and disparities in wealth is a less popular issue, with 46 percent of Americans saying it is an extremely or very important priority.

How important is it that the federal government in Washington enacts policies that attempt to do each of the following—extremely important, very important, somewhat important, or not important. How about policies designed to . . .				
	Extremely important	**Very important**	**Somewhat important**	**Not important**
	%	%	%	%
Grow and expand the economy	32	50	12	6
Increase the equality of opportunity for people to get ahead if they want to	29	41	18	12
Reduce the income and wealth gap between the rich and the poor	17	29	26	28

SOURCE: www.gallup.com/poll/151568/Americans-Prioritize-Growing-Economy-Reducing-Wealth-Gap.aspx larger proportions of aged and larger proportions of female-headed families; (4) global competition, which lowers wages in unskilled and semiskilled jobs while rewarding people in high-technology, high-productivity occupations; (5) the concentration of wealth by a handful of ultra-high income earners, sometimes called the superrich, whose work as corporate CEOs, heads of technological start-up companies, and hedge fund managers garner them top salaries.

Inequality of Wealth

Inequalities of wealth in the United States are even greater than inequalities of income. Wealth is the total value of a family's assets—bank accounts, stocks, bonds, mutual funds, business equity, houses, cars, and major appliances—minus outstanding debts such as credit card balances, mortgages, and other loans. The top 1 percent of families in the United States own almost 40 percent of all family wealth. Inequality of wealth appeared to be diminishing until the mid-1970s, but in recent years it has surged sharply. Not surprisingly, age is the key determinant of family wealth; persons 55 to 64 years old are by far the wealthiest, with persons 65 to 74 years old close behind; young families generally have less than one-fourth of the assets of older retirees. Many of those in the bottom fifth have a negative family net worth. This means that their family debt in bank loans, mortgages, credit cards, and automobile loans, and other debts exceeds the value of their assets.

Equality of Opportunity

equality of opportunity
equal chances for success based on ability, work, initiative, and luck

Most Americans are concerned more with **equality of opportunity** than with equality of results. Equality of opportunity refers to the ability to make of oneself what one can, to develop talents and abilities, and to be rewarded for work, initiative, and achievement. Equality of opportunity means that everyone comes to the same starting line in life with the same chance of success and that whatever differences develop over time do so as a result of abilities, talents, initiative, hard work, and perhaps good luck. Americans do not generally resent the fact that physicians, engineers, airline pilots, or others who have spent time and energy acquiring particular skills make more money than those whose jobs require fewer skills and less training. Nor do most Americans resent the fact that people who risk their own time and money to build a business, bring new or better products to market, and create jobs for others make more money than their employees. Nor do many Americans begrudge multimillion-dollar incomes to sports figures, rock singers, or movie stars, whose talents entertain the public. Indeed, few Americans object when someone wins a million-dollar lottery, as long as everyone had an equal chance at winning.

Equality of Results

equality of results
equal incomes regardless of ability, work, or initiative

Equality of results refers to the equal sharing of income and material rewards regardless of one's condition in life. Equality of results means that everyone starts and finishes the race together, regardless of ability, talent, initiative, or work. Most Americans support a "floor" on income and material well-being—a

FIGURE 5-3 VIEWS OF DISTRIBUTION OF WEALTH IN THE U.S.

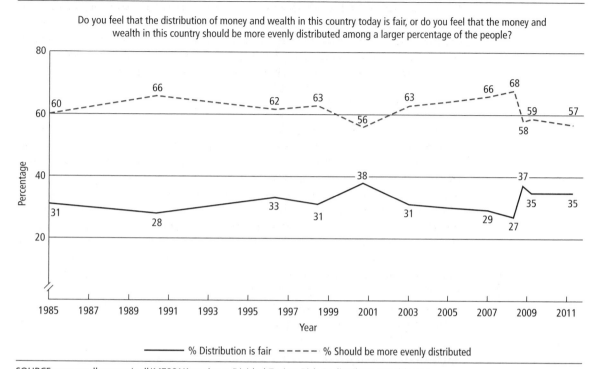

Do you feel that the distribution of money and wealth in this country today is fair, or do you feel that the money and wealth in this country should be more evenly distributed among a larger percentage of the people?

SOURCE: www.gallup.com/poll/147881/Americans-Divided-Taxing-Rich-Redistribute-Wealth.aspx

level below which no one, regardless of his or her condition, should be permitted to fall. But very few Americans want to place a "ceiling" on income or wealth, though Figure 5-3 indicates that Americans' opinions on the distribution of wealth is a divisive issue, with 58 percent of all poll respondents saying that wealth should be more evenly distributed. Nonetheless, unwillingness to limit top income extends to nearly all groups in America, the poor as well as the rich. Generally, Americans want people who cannot provide for themselves to be well cared for, especially children, the elderly, the ill, and the disabled. However, most Americans believe that a "fair" economic system rewards people for ability and hard work.

Social Mobility: The Ups and Downs

Although all societies are stratified, societies differ greatly in **social mobility**— that is, in the opportunity people have to move from one class to another. The social mobility of individuals may be upward, when they achieve a status higher than that of their parents, or downward, when their status is lower. In the United States, there is a great deal of social mobility, both upward and downward.

The United States describes itself as the land of opportunity. The really important political question may be how much real opportunity exists for

social mobility
the movement of people upward or downward in social class

individual Americans to improve their conditions in life relative to others. The impression given earlier by Table 5-3 is one of a static distribution system, with families permanently placed in upper or lower fifths of income earners.

But there is considerable evidence of both upward and downward movement by people among income groups. Children do not always end up in the same income category as their parents, and many young people believe that their prospects of becoming rich are good (see Research *This!*).

Traditional Upward Mobility

Throughout most of the twentieth century, Americans experienced more upward mobility than downward mobility. As the economy grew and changed, most Americans were able to improve their conditions in life or, at least, see their children do better than themselves. Early in the century, higher-paid factory jobs replaced farm work. With the growth of the American organized labor movement in the 1940s, many factory jobs paid a living wage—a wage that could enable workers to afford a satisfactory standard of living. Later, the ranks of professional, managerial, sales, and other white-collar workers grew. By 1970 white-collar workers outnumbered blue-collar workers—machine operators, mechanics, trade and craft workers, and laborers. Many sons and daughters of working-class parents were able to go to college and prepare themselves for careers in white-collar occupations.

The Shrinking Middle Class

deindustrialization
a decline in the manufacturing sector of the economy

In recent years, however, this general movement of upward social mobility has been replaced by a pattern of both upward and downward mobility. Today's young people can no longer assume that they will be better off than their parents, as the recent economic downturn disproportionately affected younger Americans who in 2012 had the highest unemployment rate of any age group. Over the long haul, the middle class in the United States has shrunk because of **deindustrialization**—a decline in its manufacturing sector accompanied by increases in its financial, technical, information, and service sectors. Deindustrialization had resulted in the loss of millions of well-paying, mostly unionized, blue-collar jobs in manufacturing, including the once-dominant American steel and auto industries. In the 1950s and 1960s, these jobs allowed non-college-educated workers to own their own homes in the suburbs and send their children to college. But the new information age economy replaced many of these jobs with two very different categories of jobs. The first category consists of such highly skilled, highly paid technical jobs as computer engineer, systems analyst, information specialist, financial and investment adviser, accountant, and science technician. The second category consists of such unskilled and semiskilled, low-paying service jobs as data processor, healthcare aide, food server, and packager. This division of the occupational structure into high-paying and low-paying jobs adds to both inequality in society and to a pattern of upward and downward mobility.

RESEARCH *THIS!*

Looking ahead, how likely is it that you will ever be rich? Would you say it is—very likely, somewhat likely, not very likely, or not at all likely?

Asked of those who do not consider themselves rich

	Very likely	Somewhat likely	Not very likely	Not at all likely
	%	%	%	%
2012	7	21	40	32
2003^	10	21	37	31
1996	10	24	37	27
1990	9	23	32	35

^Question was asked of all respondents; data for respondents who said they were "already rich" was excluded.

Looking ahead, how likely is it that you will ever be rich? Would you say it is—very likely, somewhat likely, not very likely, or not at all likely?

Asked of those who do not consider themselves rich

	Likely (very/somewhat)	Not very likely (not very/not at all)
	%	%
18 to 29	47	52
30 to 49	35	64
50 to 64	17	83
65+	8	91
2012		

SOURCE: www.gallup.com/poll/154619/Americans-Having-Rich-Class-Years-Ago.aspx

YOUR ANALYSIS:

1. Based on the data shown, do most people believe that they will become rich?

2. Are older people more or less likely to believe that they will become rich? Why might this be the case?

3. When were people the most pessimistic about their chances of becoming rich?

globalization
increasing exchanges
of goods and services
by firms in different
countries

Deindustrialization has been accompanied by economic **globalization**—increasing exchanges of goods and services by firms in different countries. Today, about one-quarter of the world's total economic output is sold in a country other than the one in which it was produced. Global competition heavily impacts the American economy and social structure. The opening of world markets benefits America's most productive workers—its highly skilled, well-educated, high-tech workers who are capable of competing and winning in the global marketplace. But at the same time, America's unskilled and semiskilled workers are placed at a serious disadvantage in competition with workers in less-developed countries. It is difficult to maintain the wage levels of American manufacturing jobs in the face of competition from huge numbers of extremely low-paid workers in economies such as Mexico, China, and India. Thus, the benefits of globalization flow unequally: Upper middle-class Americans benefit, while lower middle-class Americans suffer.

Mobility and Education

Education is the most common path to social mobility. As indicated earlier, education is closely related to earnings (see Figure 5-1). It is not surprising, then, that leaders in business and government in the United States argue that the "solution" to worsening inequality in downward social mobility is for American workers to improve their productivity through better education and increased training. And it is not surprising that many middle-class American families emphasize education as a means of upward mobility. But increasingly, the cost of education has proven an impediment to many middle-class Americans. The cost is compounded by the fact that in the current economic climate high-paying, entry level jobs tend to be concentrated in certain fields (including information technology and the sciences).

Class as a Determinant of Lifestyle

Life in each social class is different. Differences in ways of life mean differences in culture or (because the lifestyle in each class is really a variant of one common culture in American society) a division of the culture into subcultures. Many sociologists have described class subcultures. Class differences exist in almost every aspect of life: health, vocabulary, table manners, recreation and entertainment, religion, family and child-rearing practices, political beliefs and attitudes, club memberships, dress, birth rates, attitudes toward education, reading habits, and so on. It is impossible to provide a complete description of all the class differences that have been reported by sociologists. Moreover, class lifestyles overlap, and in America there are no rigid boundaries between classes. Class subcultures should be thought of as being on a continuous scale with styles of life that blend; thus there are many in-between positions. Finally, it should be remembered that any generalizations about broad classes in the United States do not necessarily describe the lifestyle of any particular individuals; the following paragraphs are merely a general summary of the subcultures.

The Upper Class

The typical upper-class individual is future oriented and cosmopolitan. Persons of this class expect a long life, look forward to their future and the future of their children and grandchildren, and are concerned about what lies ahead for the community, the nation, and humanity. They are self-confident, believing that within limits they can shape their own destiny and that of the community. They are willing to invest in the future—that is, to sacrifice some present satisfaction in the expectation of enjoying greater satisfaction in time to come. They are self-respecting; they place great value on independence and creativity and on developing their potential to the fullest. The goals of life include individuality, self-expression, and personal happiness. Wealth permits a wide variety of entertainment and recreation: theater, concerts, art, yachting, tennis, skiing, exotic travel abroad, and so on. Upper-class individuals generally take a tolerant attitude toward unconventional behavior in sex, the arts, fashions, lifestyles, and so forth. They feel they have a responsibility to "serve" the community and to "do good." They are active in public service and contribute time, money, and effort to worthy causes. This "public-regardingness" inclines them toward liberal politics; the upper classes provide the leadership for the liberal wings of both the Republican and Democratic parties.

The upper class relies on publications like the *New York Times*, the *Wall Street Journal*, and the *New Yorker* magazine for news and information. They also are more likely to listen to National Public Radio (NPR) shows like *All Things Considered* and *Marketplace* and watch public television (PBS).

Although the presence of an American upper class is obvious, political scientists and sociologists question whether the upper class actually constitutes a ruling class. One of the most popular and controversial analyses of this subject is *The Power Elite*, by sociologist C. Wright Mills. Since its appearance in 1956, most writers have been unable to discuss national power without reference to this important study.

According to Mills, power in the United States is concentrated at the top of the nation's corporate, government, and military organizations, which closely interlock to form a single structure of power: a **power elite**. Power rests in these three domains: "the corporation chieftains, the political directorate, and the warlords." Occasionally there is tension among them, but they share a broad consensus about the general direction of public policy. Other institutions (the family, church, schools, and so forth) are subordinate to the three major institutions of power.

power elite
Mills's term for a ruling class that dominates decision making

Mills asserts that the power elite hold power because of their position at the top of the institutional structures of society. These people are powerful not because of any individual qualities—wealth, prestige, skill, or cunning—but because of the institutional positions that they occupy. As society has concentrated more and more power in a few giant institutions, the people in command of these institutions have acquired enormous power over all of us.

As Mills explains it,

> The history of modern society may readily be understood as the story of the enlargement and the centralization of the means of power—in economic, in political, and in military institutions.[8]

pluralist
a theorist who argues
that groups are the
dominant influence in
public policy making

Other scholars argue that an American upper class exists but little evidence points to a power elite. These theorists, called **pluralists,** emphasize the role that groups play in influencing public policy. They point to policies that do not benefit the upper class as evidence of a lack of the existence of a power elite. Political scientist Nelson Polsby argued that competition, even within the upper class, results in a lack of unity that means there can be no cohesive, unified power elite.[9]

The Middle Class

Middle-class individuals are also future oriented; they plan ahead for themselves and their children. They are not likely to be as cosmopolitan as the upper-class person, however, because they are more concerned with their immediate families than with "humanity" in the abstract. They are confident about their ability to influence their own futures and those of their children, but they do not really expect to have an effect on community, state, or national events. Investing time, energy, and effort in self-improvement and getting ahead are principal themes of life. Middle-class people strongly want their children to go to college and acquire the kind of formal training that will help them get ahead. Recreation and entertainment often includes golf, swimming, movies, sports events, and travel often within the United States. Middle-class individuals tend to be middle-of-the-road or conservative in politics. Though they join voluntary organizations, many of which are formally committed to community service, they give less of their money and effort to public causes than do those in the upper class.

This said, it would be untrue to paint a picture of a unified American middle class. Although many of the above characteristics are true for most members of the middle class, we actually can refer to multiple middle classes in America. The upper middle class—composed largely of professionals employed in stable occupations like medicine, architecture, advanced education, the law, and engineering—often have annual incomes well over $100,000 and often more than double the income of others who consider themselves "middle class." This group enjoys a good deal of economic stability, and their leisure activities may include some "upper-class" activities.

At the other end of the middle class spectrum are those who struggling to maintain a middle-class existence in the face of economic uncertainty. Often, these are single-income families (either because one person is staying at home or because the income earner is not part of a couple). Sometimes, the presence of two income earners means the difference between a working-class and a middle-class lifestyle. Politically, the middle class is probably the most important social class because it is the largest class in American society, therefore a large (though not unified) voting bloc.

The Working Class

Working-class people are obliged to concern themselves more with the present than the future. They expect their children to make their own way in life. They are self-respecting and self-confident, but these feelings extend over a narrower range of matters than they do in middle-class individuals. The horizon of the working class is limited by job, family, immediate friends, and neighborhood.

Working-class individuals work to maintain themselves and their families; they do not look at their jobs as a means of getting ahead or as a means of self-expression. Their deepest attachment is to family; most visiting is done with relatives rather than friends. Working-class persons usually do not belong to many organizations other than union and church. In their views toward others in the community, they are "private regarding"; they believe that they work hard for a living and feel others should do the same. They tend to look down on people who accept welfare unless those people are forced to do so by circumstances over which they have no control. When they vote, they generally vote Democratic, but they are often apathetic about politics and are less likely to vote than members of the other classes. The working-class position in politics is motivated not by political ideology but by ethnic and party loyalties, by the appeal of personalities, or by occasional favors. For recreation the working-class individual turns to television, bowling, stock-car racing, circuses, fairs, and carnivals.

The Lower Class

Lower-class individuals must live from day to day. They have little confidence in their ability to influence what happens to them. Things happen to them; they do not make them happen. When they work, it is often from payday to payday, and they frequently drift from one unskilled job to another. Their self-confidence is low, they feel little attachment to community, and they tend to resent authority (for example, that of police officers, social workers, teachers, landlords, and employers). (For a look at the lower class in other countries, see International Perspective: "Global Inequalities.")

The lower-class family is frequently headed by a woman. For the male offspring of a lower-class matriarchal family, the future is often depressing, with defeat and frustration repeating throughout his life. He may drop out of school in the eighth or ninth grade because of lack of success. Without parental supervision, and having little to do, he may get into trouble with the police. The police record will further hurt his chances of getting a job. With limited job skills, few role models, little self-discipline, and low aspiration levels, the lower-class male is not likely to find a steady job that will pay enough to support a family. Yet he yearns for the material standard of living of higher classes—a car, an iPhone, a television set, and other conveniences. Frequently, to compensate for defeat and frustration, the lower-class male will resort to risk taking, conquest, and fighting to assert his masculinity. Entertainment may be limited to drinking and gambling. Many aspects of lower-class culture are unattractive to women. Sociologist Herbert Gans wrote, "The woman tries to develop a stable routine in the midst of poverty and deprivation; the action-seeking man upsets it."[10]

Social Classes: Conflict and Conciliation

An awareness of class membership is not the same as class consciousness. **Class consciousness** is the belief that all members of one's social class have similar economic and political interests that are adverse to the interests of other classes and ought to be promoted through common action. The conflict that emerges between

class consciousness
believing that all members of one's class have similar political and economic interests, adverse to those of other classes

INTERNATIONAL PERSPECTIVE

Global Inequalities

Three of every four persons in the world today live in less-developed countries (LDCs).* Traditionally, these countries encompass most of the globe: South and Central America; Africa; parts of the Middle East; and Asia, with the exception of Japan and the rapidly developing "Four Dragons"—Hong Kong, South Korea, Taiwan, and Singapore.

While this broad category of LDCs is commonly used by social scientists and others, it is important to remember that it encompasses societies with different languages, diverse people, and distinct cultures. Nonetheless, there are common characteristics of LDCs that can be observed by visitors as well as by social scientists. Americans can better appreciate their own society by knowing how the majority of the world's population lives.

Poverty

Poverty in LDCs is widespread and severe. The vast majority of the world's population lives well below the standard of living of America's poorest families. In fact, of the world's 6 billion people, 1.2 billion live on less than $1 per day. Of those, about 60 percent live in South Asia or sub-Saharan Africa. Hunger and ill health are common. It is estimated that one out of every five persons in the world today does not eat enough to enable him or her to work; one child in four dies before reaching 5 years old. Life expectancy is short (see the accompanying table).

Inequality

The limited resources of most LDCs are unequally distributed, with small elites controlling large proportions of land and wealth. In some societies, a caste system determines one's social position at birth with no opportunity for upward social mobility. The subordination of women in these societies is very pronounced; women are commonly denied education, land ownership, and a voice in public affairs.

Traditionalism

The cultures of LDCs generally place great value on traditional ways of life passed down, virtually unchanged, from generation to generation. Traditionalism also means the acceptance of one's life and one's fate, however poor. It also means resisting innovation and change.

---

*A note on terminology: Less-developed countries were once referred to as the "Third World." This term was used during the Cold War (see Chapter 14) to distinguish between industrialized Western democracies ("First World"); the stagnating communist economies of Eastern Europe ("Second World"); and poorer, non-industrialized societies in Asia, Africa, and Latin America ("Third World").

High Fertility

Birth rates are generally very high in LDCs. Family reliance on human labor, high infant mortality rates, the low status of women, and the absence of birth control information or technology all contribute to high birthrates. Because of its enormous population and fears that the government would be unable to feed and support unfettered population growth, China has attempted to force families to have only one child; sterilization and abortion are common, as are abortions of female fetuses and the abandonment of female babies.

Primitive Technology

Most energy in these societies is directly supplied by human and animal muscle power. A lifetime of hard manual labor, just to meet minimum needs, confronts most of the people of the world. Animal labor is more common than farm machinery.

LIFE IN THE LESS-DEVELOPED WORLD

	GDP per capita ($U.S.) 2008	Birth Rate** 2010 (proj.)	Life expectancy (years) 2010 (projected)	Infant Mortality Rate[†] 2010 (projected)
United States	47,000	14	78	6
Mexico	14,200	19	76	18
Colombia	8,900	19	73	18
Venezuela	13,500	20	74	21
Egypt	5,400	21	72	26
Nigeria	2,300	36	47	93
Vietnam	2,800	16	72	22
Sri Lanka	4,300	16	75	18
China	6,000	14	74	19
India	2,800	21	71	28
Pakistan	2,600	27	65	63
Bangladesh	1,500	28	64	54
Angola	8,800	24	39	178
Afghanistan	800	19	45	149

** Live births per one thousand population per year.

[†]Number of deaths of children under 1 year of age per one thousand live births per year.

SOURCE: U.S. Bureau of the Census, *Statistical Abstract of the United States 2009,* Table 1295. Births, Deaths, and Life Expectancy, by Country or Area: 2008 and 2010, www.census.gov /compendia/statab/tables/09s1295.pdf, and the CIA World FactBook, www.cia.gov/library /publications/the-world-factbook/geos/XX.html.

social classes because of class consciousness is a central feature of communist ideology. In the opening of his famous Communist Manifesto, Karl Marx wrote:

> The history of all hitherto existing society is the history of class struggles. Freeman and slave, patrician and plebeian, lord and serf, guild-master and journeyman, in a word, oppressor and oppressed....[11]

According to Marx, social classes develop on the basis of the different positions that individuals fulfill in the prevailing "mode of production"—that is, the economy. In an agricultural economy, the principal classes are landowner and tenant, serf, or slave; and in an industrial economy, the capitalist or "bourgeois" (pronounced BOO-jwah) (owner of the factory) and the non-property-owning worker, or "proletarian." The bourgeoisie have an interest in maximizing profit and seek to keep for themselves the surplus of profit that has been created by the worker. Workers are exploited in that they produce more than they receive in wages; this "surplus value" is stolen from the workers by the capitalists.

Marx viewed class consciousness as an important prerequisite to successful proletarian revolution. Class consciousness would increase as the proletariat grew in numbers, as workers communicated among themselves and achieved solidarity in unions and political organizations, and as conflict between workers and owners

Poor children's opportunities for recreation are limited and may involve greater risk than the activities of middle- or upper-class children. What kinds of activities were commonplace during your childhood? What do these activities indicate about your own social class growing up?

JOEL NITO/AFP/Getty Images

Jim West / Alamy

Over the past several years, social class has become and increasingly important dividing line in American society. The Occupy movement sought to highlight increasing income inequality in the United States, as well as tax policies they viewed as unfair to average working Americans. As the economy improves, do you think social class will become more important or less important to most Americans?

intensified. The bourgeoisie would not relinquish their control over the means of production without a fight, and therefore violent revolution was necessary and inevitable. Marx said little about the details of revolution; this aspect of communist ideology was developed later by Lenin (see Chapter 6). But after the successful proletarian revolution, Marx envisioned a society without social classes.

Historically Americans have been aware of class membership, but members of the same class have not always shared political interests, felt that collective class action is necessary, or have seen themselves as locked in a struggle against opposing classes. In short, few Americans believe in the militant Marxist ideology of class struggle.

Yet over the past several years, there is evidence that social class is becoming an increasingly important dividing line in American society. Figure 5-4 shows that part of the reason for this increasing sentiment of conflict comes from individuals' declining assessment of their own social class—as people are forced down the social class ladder, they feel resentment and in conflict with those on

FIGURE 5-4   PUBLIC PERCEPTIONS OF CONFLICT BETWEEN
RICH AND POOR

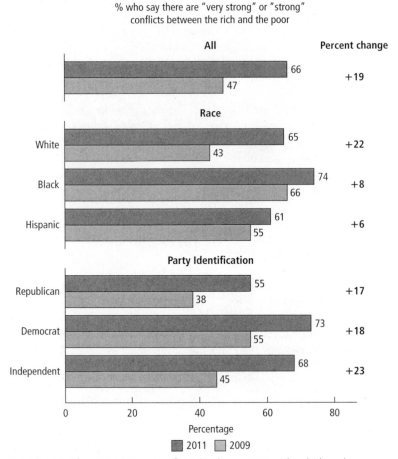

% who say there are "very strong" or "strong"
conflicts between the rich and the poor

Question wording: "In America, how much conflict is there between poor people and rich people: very strong conflicts, strong conflicts, not very strong conflicts, there are not conflicts?

Notes: For results from the 2011 survey, n=2,048; for the 2009 survey, n=1,701. Whites and blacks included only non-Hispanics. Hispanics are of any race.

SOURCE: www.pewsocialtrends.org/2012/01/11/rising-share-of-americans-see-conflict-between-rich-and-poor/

the top. In 2011, this consciousness was heightened by the Occupy movement, a protest organization that started out as a long-term rally against corporate greed on Wall Street and grew into an international movement protesting income inequality—or against the top one-percent of income earners. The Occupy movement also generated a great deal of media coverage, which in turn increased peoples' awareness of class issues.

Figure 5-4 shows that increasing proportions of Americans believe there are "very strong" or "strong" conflicts between the rich and the poor. In 2011,

66 percent believed this to be true, an increase of 19 percent in only two years. In addition, there is increasingly sentiment that class conflict is intense: twice as many Americans (30 percent) said there are "very strong conflicts" between the rich and poor people in 2011 versus 2009.

Despite the fact that increasing proportion of Americans believe intense class conflict exists in the United States, historically we know that class conflict often has been tamped down by several factors that typically serve to stabilize the existing class system in America and reduce class conflict:

- A relatively high standard of living of Americans of all social classes
- A great deal of upward mobility in the American system, which diverts lower-class attention away from collective class action and focuses it toward individual efforts at "getting ahead"
- The existence of a large middle-income, middle-prestige class
- Widespread belief in the legitimacy of the class structure and the resulting acceptance of it
- Many cross-cutting allegiances of individuals to churches, races, unions, professional associations, voluntary organizations, and so forth, which interfere with class solidarity

In stabilizing the class system, these factors also stabilize the existing distribution of power in America.

The American system has produced a high level of material comfort for the great majority of the population. Historically, the real possibilities of acquiring greater income and prestige have reinforced efforts to strive within the system rather than to challenge it. Even individuals who realize that their own social mobility is limited can transfer their hope and ambition to their children. A large middle class, diverse in occupation and ambiguous in political orientation, helps blur potential lines of class identification and conflict. This class stands as a symbol and an embodiment of the reality of opportunity. Finally, cross pressuring cleavages caused by religious affiliations, ethnic backgrounds, and racial categories, as well as by other types of diversity (for example, region, skill level, and occupational group), have all worked against the development of unified class movements.

Social Class and Political Power

Government leadership is recruited mainly from the upper and upper middle social classes. For example, although millionaires comprise less than 1 percent of all Americans, about one-third of the members of Congress are millionaires. Most government officials, particularly at the national level (cabinet officers, presidential advisers, congressional representatives, Supreme Court judges, and so on) are well educated, prestigiously employed, successful, and affluent—part of the upper or upper middle classes. With few exceptions, they are the children of professionals, business owners and managers, or successful farmers and landowners. Only a small minority are the children of hourly wage earners.

The occupational characteristics of representatives also show that they are generally of higher social standing than their constituents; professional and business occupations dominate the halls of Congress. One reason is that congressional candidates are more likely to win election if their occupations are socially "respectable" and provide opportunities for extensive public contacts. The lawyer, insurance agent, and real estate agent establish in their businesses the wide circle of friends necessary for political success. Another, subtler reason is that candidates and elected legislators must come from occupational groups with flexible work responsibilities. Lawyers, landowners, and business owners can adjust their work to the campaign and legislative schedules, whereas office and factory workers cannot. We know that political power is largely exercised by individuals from upper social classes, but what does this really mean for the great majority of Americans? We might infer that people drawn from upper social classes share values and interests different from those of the majority of people. On the other hand, several factors may modify the impact of upper social classes in politics.

First, there may be considerable conflict among members of upper social classes about the basic directions of public policy; that is, despite similarity in social backgrounds, individuals may not share a consensus about public affairs. Competition rather than consensus may characterize their relationships.

Second, the elite may be very "public regarding" in their exercise of power; they may take the welfare of the masses into account as an aspect of their own sense of well-being. Indeed, there is a great deal of evidence that America's upper classes are liberal and reformist and that "do-goodism" is a widespread impulse. Many public leaders from very wealthy families of the highest social status (for instance, Franklin D. Roosevelt, Adlai Stevenson, and John F. Kennedy) have championed the interests of the poor and the downtrodden. Thus, upper-class values may foster public service rather than political exploitation.

Third, upper-class leaders, whatever their values, can be held accountable for their exercise of power by the majority in elections. Our system of parties and elections forces public officials to compete for mass support to acquire public office and the political power that goes with it. This competition requires them to modify their public statements and actions to fit popular preferences. Hence, in a democracy, the fact that the upper social classes tend to hold public office does not necessarily mean that the masses are oppressed, exploited, or powerless.

CHAPTER SUMMARY

- All known societies have some method of stratifying members on a superiority–inferiority scale. The most important bases of stratification in a modern industrial society are the various roles that individuals play in the economic system.

- Sociologists have devised several methods of identifying and measuring social stratification, including the subjective method, the reputational method, and the objective method.

- Functional theorists argue that stratification is necessary and perhaps inevitable for maintaining society. Conflict theorists assert that stratification results from the selfish interests of groups trying to preserve their advantages over others. Symbolic interactionists stress that social stratification is the result of interactions between individuals. Postmodernists cite the inability of the three previous perspectives to adequately address social stratification in a postindustrial society.

- Income is a key component of stratification, and income is unequally distributed in all societies. In the United States, income and wealth are both increasingly unequally distributed. Many Americans, however, believe that equality of opportunity is an important component of equality.

- Societies differ greatly in social mobility. In the United States, there is a great deal of social mobility, both upward and downward, but the shrinking size of the middle class has meant that mobility for some in recent years has been downward.

- Class differences exist in almost every aspect of life: health, vocabulary, table manners, recreation and entertainment, religion, family and child-rearing practices, political beliefs and attitudes, club memberships, dress, birth rates, attitudes toward education, reading habits, and so on.

- Historically Americans have been aware of class membership, but over the past several years, there is evidence that social class is becoming an increasingly important dividing line in American society.

- Government leadership is skewed to include more individuals from the upper and upper middle social classes than the working and lower classes.

KEY TERMS

Chicago School   the first sociology department in the United States at the University of Chicago

class consciousness   believing that all members of one's class have similar political and economic interests, adverse to those of other classes

conflict theory   inequality is imposed on society by those who want to retain their wealth and power

deindustrialization   a decline in the manufacturing sector of the economy

division of labor   individuals perform distinct, assigned functions

dysfunction   the undesirable by-product of relations or institutions

equality of opportunity   equal chances for success based on ability, work, initiative, and luck

equality of results   equal incomes regardless of ability, work, or initiative

feminist theory   a form of conflict theory, a theory of social stratification that uses a gendered prism and emphasizes the struggle for equality of women with men

functional theory   inequality is necessary to get people to work harder in more demanding jobs that require longer training and greater skills

globalization   increasing exchanges of goods and services by firms in different countries

latent function   the unrecognized or unanticipated function of societal relations or an institution

manifest function   the acknowledged and expected function of societal relations or an institution

objective criteria   determining social class by ranking income, occupation, or education

pluralist   a theorist who argues that groups are the dominant influence in public policy making

power elite   Mills's term for a ruling class that dominates decision making

reputational prestige   the general level of respect associated with a specific job title

social class   a category and ranking in the stratification system

social mobility   the movement of people upward or downward in social class

stratification   classifying individuals and ranking the classifications on a superiority–inferiority scale

subjective identification   individuals identify their own social class

subjective reality   one individual's idea of what occurred in a social interaction; that individual's interpretation of events

ON THE WEB

EXPLORING SOCIOLOGY

- The website for this textbook offers resources for exploring power and social class on the Internet. Sociology covers a very broad range of subject matter—social life, social change, and the social causes and consequences of human behavior. This chapter has focused on power and social class, but the subject matter of social class ranges from the intimate family to the hostile mob, from organized crime to religious cults, and from the sociology of work to the sociology of sports. Visit **www.cengagebrain.com**.

  Here are some other useful sources:

- **American Sociological Association/Society for Applied Sociology** For a better understanding of the full range of sociology, begin visiting the websites maintained by the American Sociological Association (ASA, www.asanet.org) and the Society for Applied Sociology (SAS, **www.appliedsoc.org**). The ASA site is oriented toward academic sociology, primarily teachers of sociology in colleges and universities, but it also provides student career information including resources for those with an undergraduate degree in sociology. The SAS site is oriented toward practicing sociologists in government, health care, law enforcement, and human resources.

  Try This: Go to **www.asanet.org/journals /journals.cfm** and click one of the links for ASA journals. Browse through the contents of the featured essays or articles. What area of sociology does the journal examine? What kind of information is included? What type of professionals would find this journal most useful?

• **U.S. Census Bureau** Current information on income, education, and occupation of Americans, as well as information on poverty and inequality, can be found in U.S. Census Bureau data (**www.census.gov**). An "A to Z" index includes direct links to data on "income," "poverty," "inequality," and so on.

Try This: Go to **http://quickfacts.census .gov/qfd/** and click on your state. Read through the facts to get a clearer picture of economic conditions, household dynamics, state poverty levels, etc. Do the "quick facts" match your impression of current conditions in your area?

REVIEW QUIZ

MULTIPLE CHOICE

1. Classifying people and ranking the classifications on a superiority–inferiority scale is called _____.
   a. social stratification
   b. operationalization
   c. socialization
   d. social objectification

2. Methods of identifying and measuring stratification *do not* include _____.
   a. societal assessment
   b. reputational prestige
   c. objective criteria
   d. subjective identification

3. The idea that inequality is necessary to get people to work harder in more demanding jobs that require longer training and greater skills is a key component of _____.
   a. Marxism
   b. conflict theory
   c. functional theory
   d. symbolic interaction theory

4. What are the unrecognized or unanticipated functions of societal relations or an institution?
   a. manifest functions
   b. dysfunction
   c. deviated functions
   d. latent functions

5. What are the acknowledged and expected functions of societal relations or an institution?
   a. manifest functions
   b. dysfunction
   c. deviated functions
   d. symbolic interaction theory

6. The idea that inequality is imposed on society by those who want to retain their wealth and power is a key component of what?
   a. democratic theory
   b. conflict theory
   c. functional theory
   d. symbolic interaction theory

7. What is Mills's term for a ruling class that dominates decision making?
   a. the bourgeoisie
   b. the power elite
   c. the ruling class
   d. the dominant cadre

8. Having equal chances for success based on ability, work, initiative, and luck is a characteristic of _____.
   a. equality of result
   b. marginal equality
   c. equality of opportunity
   d. equality of intent

9. The examination of the role that symbols play in creating meaning for communication between individuals is a key component of

   _____.
   a. Marxism
   b. conflict theory
   c. functional theory
   d. symbolic interaction theory

10. Factors in American life that reduce class conflict *do not* include which of the following?
    a. a low standard of living
    b. upward mobility
    c. a large middle class
    d. widespread belief in the system

FILL IN THE BLANK

11. Talcott Parsons and Robert Merton were proponents of _____

12. When individuals identify their own social class, it is called _____

13. When individuals perform distinct, assigned functions, there is said to be a _____

14. _____ is a form of conflict theory, a theory of social stratification that uses a gendered prism and emphasizes the struggle for equality of women with men.

15. The _____ is the name given to the faculty of the first sociology department in the United States who were instrumental in nurturing the new discipline and also formed the professional sociological organization now called the American Sociological Society.

CHAPTER 6

Power and History

Learning Objectives

After reading this chapter, students will be able to:

- Describe how historical analysis informs the social sciences.
- Explain how historical analysis is done.
- List the ways in which elites dominated in early American life.
- Explain how Western expansion changed power relationships in the United States.
- Describe how modern liberalism changed government's functions.

History and Social Science

Can history inform the social sciences? The purpose of this chapter is not to teach American history but to examine the work of historians to see what contribution they can make to our understanding of power and the social sciences.

history
the recording, narrating, and interpreting of all past human actions and events

recording
the documentation of events

narrating
the description of events based on documentation

interpretation
the analysis of the underlying causes and outcomes of past events

History refers to all past human actions and events. The study of history includes **recording**, that is, the documentation of events; **narrating**, the description of events based on documentation; and **interpretation**, the analysis of the underlying causes and outcomes of these events. History includes the discovery of facts about past events, as well as the interpretation of the events. Many historians contend that their primary responsibility is the reporting of facts about the past: the accurate presentation of what actually happened, unbiased by interpretive theories or philosophies.

But however carefully historians try to avoid bias, they cannot report all the facts of human history. Facts do not select and arrange themselves. The historians must select and organize facts that are worthy of interest, and this process involves personal judgment of what is important about the past. The historian's judgment about the past is affected by present conditions. So the past is continually reinterpreted by each generation of historians. History is "an unending dialogue" between the present and the past; it is "what one age finds worthy of note in another."

In selecting and organizing their facts, historians must consider the causes of wars and revolutions, the reasons for the rise and fall of civilizations, and the consequences of great events and ideas. They cannot marshal their facts without some notion of *interrelations* among human events. Because they must consider what forces have operated to shape the past, they become involved in economics, sociology, psychology, anthropology, and political science. Historian Henry Steele Commager has observed that "no self-respecting modern historian is content merely with recording what happened; he [*sic*] wants to explain why it happened."[1] Thus, history and social science are intimately related.

How Historical Analysis Informs the Social Sciences

Oftentimes, we view history as a linear progression of facts. From elementary school on, history books present a definitive view, frequently one that portrays an element of inevitability about historic events. But from our own experiences, we know that major events are rarely linear or predictable. Rather, they are complex and the result of many interactions, and often individuals will attribute important events to differing causes depending on their perspectives. While a rudimentary view of history sometimes conveys a sense that the outcomes of events are predetermined, historical analysis frequently conveys the importance of individuals and groups in determining outcomes.

In recording events, historians recognize that perspective is an important component of historical analysis and interpretation. Because perspective matters, historians often rely on numerous **original source documents**, including official documents, but also diaries and journals, legal documents, publications specific to a particular period or event, and sometimes even oral accounts in recording historical events.

Recognizing that perspective influences narrative and interpretation, many historians view historical analysis as a dialogue between perspectives. Consider, for example, the modern Occupy movement, in which protesters gathered in many U.S. cities to rail against corporate greed, government bail-outs for corporations, and income inequality. Years from now, historians may provide the narrative of this movement by examining photographs of the protests, news accounts, statements made by elected officials, public opinion polls, arrest reports of protestors, police accounts, and the accounts by protestors themselves. Those interpreting the movement would recognize that elites would have a different view of the movement than the working class. Similarly, nearly every event in U.S. history is subject to the perspective of the historic analyst.

Historical Interpretation and the American Experience

In most societies, there is a great temptation to interpret national history in a romanticized fashion. Many national histories are self-congratulating, patriotic exercises. Many historical biographies rely on the **great man paradigm**, which narrates history as the actions of larger-than-life individuals who are

original source documents
publications, including official documents, but also diaries and journals, legal documents, and sometimes even oral accounts in recording historical events that historians often rely on to record historic events

great man paradigm
a method of viewing history which focuses on the actions larger-than-life individuals who are free of the faults of common people, and who shape the course of events themselves rather than merely respond to the world in which they live

free of the faults of common people, and who shape the course of events themselves rather than merely respond to the world in which they live. National leaders of the past—Washington, Jefferson, Jackson, Lincoln, Franklin D. Roosevelt—are portrayed as noble people, superior in character and wisdom to today's politicians. Even with the myth of the cherry tree discarded, generations of historians have looked with awe on the gallery of national heroes.

Some national histories do not rely on great man explanations but instead narrate history as the origin and growth of democratic institutions. **Institutionalist perspectives** focus on the structures that spawned democracy from its ancient Greek beginnings, through English constitutional development, to the colonies and the American constitutional system. Frequently, these national histories reinforce reverence for existing political and governmental institutions.

But historians have also been critical of American institutions. At the beginning of the twentieth century, reform politicians and muckraking journalists brought a new skepticism to American life, and historians who emphasized what would come to be known as **elite theory** stressed the disproportionate role that elites had in shaping American society. The Progressive Era was critical of the malfunctioning of many government institutions that had become sacred over time and even of the preeminent position of the nation's founders. In 1913 Charles A. Beard created an uproar by suggesting that economic motives played a part in leading the founders to write the Constitution (see Controversies in Social Science: "Charles Beard and the Economic Interests of the Founders").

Nevertheless, for the most part the quest for the American past has been carried on in a spirit of sentiment and nostalgia rather than of critical analysis. Historical novels, fictionalized biographies, pictorial collections, and books on American regions all appeal to our fondness for looking back to what we believe was a better era.

institutionalist perspective
a method of viewing history which focuses on the structures that spawned democracy from its ancient Greek beginnings, through English constitutional development, to the colonies and the American constitutional system

elite theory
a method of viewing history that stresses the disproportionate role that elites had in shaping American society

Examining Power Relations in U.S. History

Our own bias about the importance of power in society leads us to focus attention in this chapter on *changing sources of power over time* in American history and on the characteristics of the people and groups who have acquired power (see Research This!). We contend that the Constitution and the national government it established reflected the beliefs, values, and interests of the people of power—the elite—of the new republic and that a changing elite has continued to exert influence in the government since the nation's founding. If we are to have a true understanding of the Constitution, the basis of the structure of that government, we must investigate the political interests of the founders and the historical circumstances surrounding the Philadelphia convention in 1787. That is, in the narrative that follows, we combine the great man paradigm with institutionalist and elitist approaches to U.S. history in an effort to increase comprehension of key events so that interpretation of these events can occur.

RESEARCH *THIS!*

DECLARATION OF INDEPENDENCE

We hold these truths to be self-evident, that all men are created equal, that they are endowed by their Creator with certain unalienable Rights, that among these are Life, Liberty and the pursuit of Happiness . . .

. . . The history of the present King of Great Britain is a history of repeated injuries and usurpations, all having in direct object the establishment of an absolute Tyranny over these States. To prove this, let Facts be submitted to a candid world.

He has refused his Assent to Laws, the most wholesome and necessary for the public good.

He has forbidden his Governors to pass Laws of immediate and pressing importance, unless suspended in their operation till his Assent should be obtained; and when so suspended, he has utterly neglected to attend to them. . .

DECLARATION OF SENTIMENTS

. . . We hold these truths to be self-evident: that all men and women are created equal; that they are endowed by their Creator with certain inalienable rights; that among these are life, liberty, and the pursuit of happiness; that to secure these rights governments are instituted, deriving their just powers from the consent of the governed . . .

. . . The history of mankind is a history of repeated injuries and usurpations on the part of man toward woman, having in direct object the establishment of an absolute tyranny over her. To prove this, let facts be submitted to a candid world.

He has never permitted her to exercise her inalienable right to the elective franchise.

He has compelled her to submit to laws, in the formation of which she had no voice . . .

Having deprived her of this first right as a citizen, the elective franchise, thereby leaving her without representation in the halls of legislation, he has oppressed her on all sides.

The Declaration of Independence shows a list of grievances that the American colonists had against the British King George III. These grievances were the cause of the American Revolution, through which the colonies eventually won independence from Great Britain. The Declaration of Sentiments shows a list of grievances that women and men at the Seneca Fall Convention had against the U.S. government. Seneca Falls is widely viewed as the beginning of the modern struggle for women's suffrage, or the right to vote.

YOUR ANALYSIS:

1. Based on the excerpt of the original source document, what generally was the nature of the grievances against King George III in 1776?

2. Based on the excerpt of original source document, what generally was the nature of the grievances against the U.S. government in 1876?

3. How are these claims similar? Do you believe that this similarity was intentional? Why? What is the effect of these similar lists of grievances?

Sources of Change in Power Relationships

Power structures change over time. As an expanding American economy created new sources of wealth, power in the United States shifted to those groups and individuals who acquired the new economic resources. First, Western expansion and settlement; then industrialization, immigration, and urbanization; and now technological and information innovation created new sources of wealth, new bases of power, and new powerholders.

But power in the United States has changed hands, without any serious break in the ideas and values underlying the American political and economic institutions. The nation has never experienced a true revolution in which national leadership is forcefully replaced by groups or individuals who do not share the values of the system itself. Instead, *changes have been slow and incremental.* New national leaders have generally accepted the national consensus about private enterprise, limited government, and individualism. Historian Richard Hofstadter argues effectively that many accounts of the American past overemphasize the political differences in every era:

> The fierceness of the political struggles has often been misleading; for the range of vision embraced by the primary contestants in the major parties has always been bounded by the horizons of property and enterprise. However much at odds on specific issues, the major political traditions have shared a belief in the rights of property, the philosophy of economic individualism, the value of competition; they have accepted the economic virtues of capitalist culture as necessary qualities of man. Even when some property right has been challenged—as it was by followers of Jefferson and Jackson—in the name of the rights of man or the rights of the community, the challenge, when translated into practical policy, has actually been urged on behalf of some other kind of property.[2]

The Rise of Western Elites

According to historian Frederick Jackson Turner, "The rise of the New West was the most significant fact in American history."[3] Certainly, the American West had a profound impact on the political system of the new nation. People went west because of the vast wealth of fertile lands that awaited them there; nowhere else in the world could one acquire wealth so quickly. Because landed families of the Eastern Seaboard seldom had reason to migrate westward, the Western settlers were mainly middle- or lower-class immigrants. With hard work and good fortune, a penniless migrant could become a rich plantation owner or cattle rancher in a single generation. Thus, the West meant rapid upward social mobility.

Jacksonian Democracy

A new elite arose in the West and had to be assimilated into America's governing circles. This assimilation had a profound effect on the character of America's elite. No one exemplifies the new entrants better than Andrew Jackson. Jackson's victory in the presidential election of 1828 was not a victory of the common man over the propertied classes but a victory of the new Western elite over established leadership in the East, and his political career has been held up as the epitome of a great man triumph. It forced the established elite to recognize the growing importance of the West and to open their ranks to the new rich who were settling west of the Alleghenies.

CONTROVERSIES IN SOCIAL SCIENCE

Charles Beard and the Economic Interests of the Founders

Charles Beard, historian and political scientist, provided the most controversial historical interpretation of the origin of American national government in his landmark book, *An Economic Interpretation of the Constitution*.* Beard argued that to understand the Constitution we must understand the economic interests of the national elite, which included the writers of the document:

> Did the men who formulated the fundamental law of the land possess the kinds of property which were immediately and directly increased in value or made more secure by the results of their labors in Philadelphia? Did they have money at interest [loans outstanding]? Did they own public securities [government bonds]? Did they hold Western lands for appreciation? Were they interested in shipping and manufactures?†

Beard was *not* charging that the founders wrote the Constitution exclusively for their own benefit. But he argued that they personally benefited immediately from its adoption and that they did not act only "under the guidance of abstract principles of political science." Beard closely studied old unpublished financial records of the U.S. Treasury Department and the personal letters and financial accounts of the fifty-five delegates to the Philadelphia convention. The accompanying table summarizes his findings of the financial interests of the nation's founders.

Beard then turned to an examination of the *Constitution* itself, in the original form in which it emerged from the Convention, to observe the *relationship between economic interests and political power.* The first, and perhaps the most important, enumerated power is the power to "lay and collect taxes, duties, imposts, and excises." The *taxing power* was of great benefit to the holders of government bonds, particularly when it was combined with the provision in Article VI that "all debts contracted and engagements entered into, before the adoption of this Constitution, shall be as valid against the United States under this Constitution, as under the Confederation." This meant that the national government would be obliged to pay off all those investors who held bonds of the United States and that the taxing power would give the national government the ability to do so on its own (see Beard's "Classification of the Founders of the American Nation," columns "Public Security Interests, Major and Minor").

Following the power to tax and spend, to borrow money, and to regulate commerce in Article I, there is a series of *specific powers designed to enable Congress to protect money and property.* Congress is given the power to make bankruptcy laws, to coin money and regulate its value, to fix standards of weights and measures, to punish counterfeiting, to establish post offices and post roads, to pass copyright and patent laws to protect authors and inventors, and to punish piracies and felonies committed on the high seas. Each of these powers is a specific asset to bankers, investors, merchants, authors, inventors, and shippers (see Beard's "Classification of the Founders of the American Nation," columns "Real Estate and Land Speculation," "Lending and Banking Investments," and "Mercantile, Manufacturing, and Shipping Interests").

The Constitution provided an explicit advantage to slaveholders in Article I V, Section 2 (later altered by the Thirteenth Amendment, which abolished slavery; see Beard's "Classification of the Founders of the American Nation," column "Plantations and Slaveholdings"):

---

* Charles Beard, *An Economic Interpretation of the Constitution* (New York: Macmillan, 1913).
† Ibid., p. 73.

No person held to Service or Labour in one State, under the Laws thereof, escaping into another, shall, in Consequence of any Law or Regulation therein, be discharged from such Service or Labour, but shall be delivered up on Claim of the Party to whom such Service or Labour may be due.

Many historians disagree with Beard's emphasis on the economic motives of the founders. For example:

The Constitution was adopted in a society which was fundamentally democratic, not undemocratic; and it was adopted by people who were primarily middle-class property owners, especially farmers who owned realty, not just by the owners of personalty. . . . The Constitution was not just an economic document, although economic factors were undoubtedly important. Since most of the people were middle-class and had private property, practically everybody was interested in the protection of property.**

Moreover, in the struggle over ratification of the new Constitution, influential anti-Federalists deplored its undemocratic features, and their criticism about the omission of a Bill of Rights led directly to the inclusion of the first ten amendments.

BEARD'S CLASSIFICATION OF THE FOUNDERS OF THE AMERICAN NATION BY ECONOMIC INTERESTS

Public Security Interests (Owners of U.S. Bonds)		Real Estate and Land Speculation	Lending and Banking Investments	Mercantile Manufacturing and Shipping Interests	Plantations and Slaveholdings
Major	Minor				
Baldwin	Bassett	Blount	Bassett	Broom	Butler
Blair	Blount	Dayton	Broom	Clymer	Davie
Clymer	Brearley	Few	Butler	Ellsworth	Jenifer
Dayton	Broom	FitzSimons	Carroll	FitzSimons	A. Martin
Ellsworth	Butler	Franklin	Clymer	Gerry	L. Martin
FitzSimons	Carroll	Gerry	Davie	King	Mason
Gerry	Few	Gilman	Dickinson	Langdon	Mercer
Gilman	Hamilton	Gorham	Ellsworth	McHenry	C. C. Pinckney
Gorham	L. Martin	Hamilton	Few	Mifflin	C. Pinckney
Jenifer	Mason	Mason	FitzSimons	G. Morris	Randolph
Johnson	Mercer	R. Morris	Franklin	R. Morris	Read
King	Mifflin	Washington	Gilman		Rutledge
Langdon	Read	Williamson	Ingersoll		Spaight
Lansing	Spaight	Wilson	Johnson		Washington
Livingston	Wilson		King		Wythe
McClurg	Wythe		Langdon		
R. Morris			McHenry		
C. C. Pinckney			Manson		
C. Pinckney			C. C. Pinckney		
Randolph			C. Pinckney		
Sherman			Randolph		
Strong			Read		
Washington			Washington		
Williamson			Williamson		

**Robert E. Brown, *Charles Beard and the Constitution* (Princeton, NJ: Princeton University Press, 1956); 200.

Jacksonian democracy
a philosophic ideal of
the frontier society that
emphasized the self-made
individual, and wealth
and power won by
competitive skill

Because Jackson was a favorite of the people, it was easy for him to believe in the wisdom of the masses. But **Jacksonian democracy** was by no means a philosophy of leveling egalitarianism, meaning the absolute equality of humankind and the desirability of political, economic, and social equality. The ideal of the frontier society was the self-made individual, and wealth and power won by *competitive skill* were much admired. Wealth and power obtained through special privilege offended the frontier people. They believed in a *natural aristocracy* rather than an aristocracy by birth, education, or special privilege. It was *not* absolute equality that Jacksonians demanded but a *more open elite system*—a greater opportunity for the rising middle class to acquire wealth and influence through competition.

Seeking Mass Support

In their struggle to open America's elite system, the Jacksonians appealed to mass sentiment. Jackson's humble beginnings, his image as a self-made man, his military adventures, his frontier experience, and his rough, brawling style endeared him to the masses. As beneficiaries of popular support, the new Western elite developed a strong faith in the wisdom and justice of popular decisions. The new Western states that entered the Union granted universal white male suffrage, and gradually the older states fell into step. (Though some states granted voting rights to women who owned property early on, the ratification of the U.S. Constitution actually meant the elimination of that right.) The rising elite, themselves often less than a generation away from the masses, saw in a widened electorate a chance for personal advancement that they could never have achieved under the old regime.

Jacksonians sought to exploit these opportunities by changing American political institutions. The Jacksonians became noisy and effective advocates of the principle that all free men should have the right to *vote* and that no restrictions should be placed on *office holding*. They also launched a successful attack on the congressional caucus system of nominating presidential candidates, substituting instead nomination by national party conventions. In 1832 when the Democrats held their first national convention, Andrew Jackson was renominated by acclamation.

Other institutional changes included the method of selecting presidential electors. The Constitution left to the various state legislatures the right to decide how presidential electors should be chosen, and in most cases the legislatures themselves chose the electors. But after 1832, all states elected their presidential electors by popular vote. In most states, the people voted for electors who were listed under the name of their party and their candidate and pledged to cast their electoral vote for the listed candidate.

The Civil War and Elite Division

Social scientists can gain insight into societal conflict and the *breakdown of elite consensus* through the study of history, particularly the history of the U.S. Civil War. The United States' elite were in substantial agreement about the character and direction of the new nation during its first sixty years. In the 1850s, however, the issues of slavery and, more broadly, the issues of the power of states versus the power of the federal government—the most divisive issues in the history of American politics—became urgent questions that drove a wedge between the elite groups and ultimately led to the nation's bloodiest war. The political system was unequal to the task of negotiating a peaceful settlement to the problem of slavery because America's elite were deeply divided over the question.

Southern Elite

It was the white **Southern elite** and not the white masses who had an interest in the slave and cotton culture. On the eve of the Civil War, probably not more than one in four southern families held slaves, and many of those families held only one or two slaves each. The number of great planters (men who owned fifty or more slaves and large holdings of land) was probably not more than seven thousand. Yet the views of these planters dominated Southern politics.

Southern elite
plantation owners dependent on slave labor

Northern Elite

The **Northern elite** consisted of merchants and manufacturers who depended on wage labor. The Northern elite had no direct interest in the abolition of slavery in the South. Some Northern manufacturers were making good profits from Southern trade, and with higher tariffs they stood a chance to make even better profits. Abolitionist activities imperiled trade relations between North and South and were often looked on with irritation in Northern social circles.

Northern elite
manufacturers dependent on wage labor

Elite Conflict over Western Land

However, both the Northern and the Southern elite realized that control of the West was the key to future dominance of the nation. The Northern elite wanted a West composed of small farmers who produced food and raw materials for the industrial and commercial East and provided a market for Eastern goods. But Southern planters feared the voting power of a West composed of small farmers and wanted Western lands for the expansion of the cotton and slave culture. Cotton ate up the land, and because it required continuous cultivation and monotonous rounds of simple tasks, cotton growing was suited to slave labor. Thus, to protect the cotton economy, it was essential to expand westward and to protect slavery in the West. The conflict over Western land eventually precipitated the Civil War.

Attempts at Compromise

Yet despite such differences, the underlying consensus of the American elite was so great that compromise after compromise was devised to maintain unity. Both the Northern and the Southern elite displayed a continued devotion to the principles of constitutional government and the protection of private property. In the *Missouri Compromise of 1820*, the land in the Louisiana Purchase exclusive of Missouri was divided at 36° 30' north latitude, with slavery legal in areas south of that line and illegal north of it. The Missouri Compromise also compromised on slavery in two other states: Maine and Missouri were admitted to the Union as free and slave states, respectively.

After the war with Mexico, the elaborate *Compromise of 1850* caused one of the greatest debates in American legislative history, with "great men," including Senators Henry Clay, Daniel Webster, John C. Calhoun, Salmon P. Chase, Stephen A. Douglas, Jefferson Davis, Alexander H. Stephens, Robert Toombs, William H. Seward, and Thaddeus Stevens all participating. Cleavage within the elite was apparent, but it was not yet so divisive as to split the nation. A compromise was achieved, providing for the admission of California as a free state; for the creation of two new territories, New Mexico and Utah, out of the Mexican Cession of 1848; for a drastic fugitive slave law to satisfy Southern planters; and for the prohibition of the slave trade in the District of Columbia. Even the *Kansas–Nebraska Act of 1854* was intended to be a compromise; each new territory was supposed to decide for itself whether it should be slave or free, the expectation being that Nebraska would vote free and Kansas slave. Gradually, however, the spirit of compromise gave way to divergence and conflict.

Elite Consensus Breaks Down

Beginning in 1856, proslavery and antislavery forces fought it out in "bleeding Kansas." Senator Charles Sumner of Massachusetts delivered a condemnation of slavery in the Senate and was beaten almost to death on the Senate floor by Congressman Preston Brooks of South Carolina. Intemperate language in the Senate became commonplace, with frequent threats of secession, violence, and civil war. In 1857 a Southern-dominated U.S. Supreme Court decided, in *Dred Scott v. Sanford*, that the Missouri Compromise was unconstitutional because Congress had no authority to forbid slavery in any territory. Slave property, said Chief Justice Roger B. Taney, was as much protected by the Constitution as was any other kind of property. In 1859, John Brown and his followers raided the U.S. arsenal at Harper's Ferry as a first step to freeing the slaves of Virginia by force. Brown was captured by Virginia militia under the command of Colonel Robert E. Lee, tried for treason, found guilty, and executed. Southerners believed that Northerners had tried to incite the horror of slave insurrection, whereas Northerners believed that Brown died a martyr.

Lincoln's Views and Slavery

Abraham Lincoln never attacked slavery in the South; his exclusive concern was to halt the spread of slavery in the Western territories. He wrote in 1845, "I hold it a paramount duty of us in the free States, due to the Union of the States, and perhaps to liberty itself (paradox though it may seem), to let the slavery of the other states alone."[4] Throughout his political career, Lincoln consistently held this position. On the other hand, with regard to the Western territories, he said, "The whole nation is interested that the best use shall be made of these territories. We want them for homes and free white people. This they cannot be, to any considerable extent, if slavery shall be planted within them."[5] In short, Lincoln wanted the Western territories to be tied economically and culturally to the Northern system.

Preserving the Union

Historian Richard Hofstadter believed that Lincoln's political posture was essentially conservative: He wished to preserve the long-established order and consensus that had protected American principles and property rights so successfully in the past. He was not an abolitionist and he did not seek the destruction of the Southern elite or the rearrangement of the South's social fabric.

His goal was to bring the South back into the Union, to restore orderly government, and to establish the principle that states cannot resist national authority with force. At the beginning of the Civil War, Lincoln knew that a great part of conservative Northern opinion was willing to fight for the Union but might refuse to support a war to free slaves. Lincoln's great political skill was his ability to gather all the issues of the Civil War into one single over-riding theme: *the preservation of the Union.* However, he was bitterly attacked throughout the war by radical Republicans who thought he had "no antislavery instincts."

As the war continued and casualties mounted, opinion in the North became increasingly bitter toward Southern slave owners. Many Republicans joined the abolitionists in calling for emancipation of the slaves simply to punish the "rebels." They knew that the power of the South was based on the labor of slaves. Lincoln also knew that if he proclaimed to the world that the

The costs of preserving the Union. This photo, taken after the Battle Antietam, shows the "Bloody Lane" where two Union regiments trapped Confederates in a barrage of rifle fire. The photo was taken by the famous Civil War photographer Matthew Brady, whose images were the first that Americans had ever seen of the horrors of war.

Library of Congress

war was being fought to free the slaves, there would be less danger of foreign intervention.

The Emancipation Proclamation

On September 22, 1862, Lincoln issued his preliminary Emancipation Proclamation. Claiming his right as commander-in-chief of the army and navy, he promised that "on the first day of January . . . , 1863, all persons held as slaves within any State or designated part of a State the people whereof shall then be in rebellion against the United States shall be then, thenceforward, and forever free." Thus, one of the great steps forward in human freedom in this nation, the Emancipation Proclamation, did not come about as a result of demands by the people and certainly not as a result of demands by the slaves themselves. Hofstadter contended that *the Emancipation Proclamation was a political action taken by the president for the sake of helping to preserve the Union.* It was not a revolutionary action but a conservative one.

Power in the Post–Civil War Era

In the post–Civil War era, the nation faced the problem of reunification and reconstruction. The nation had been devastated, both physically and psychologically, and it would take massive efforts to fix the remnants of the War Between the States. Largely, these efforts were entrusted to the Congress, who had the budgetary authority to fund the massive reconstruction efforts. Traditionally, historians viewed this Reconstruction Congress as vindictive against the South, and the Reconstruction Era is considered destructive, oppressive, and corrupt. Military rule was imposed on the South. "Carpetbaggers" and "scalawags" confiscated the property of helpless Southerners and retarded the economic progress of the South for decades. Maladministration and corruption in the federal government were portrayed as being greater than ever before in American history.

Despite this rampant corruption, the Reconstruction Congress did make several well-intentioned efforts to improve the quality of life and ensure equality for African Americans. Historian C. Vann Woodward's work records the progress of African Americans during Reconstruction and explains the reimposition of segregation in terms of class conflict among whites. (Alex Haley's popular book *Roots*, together with the dramatic television series based on it, is another example of historical interpretation. Whereas many older histories of the pre–Civil War South romanticized plantation life, *Roots* described the cruelties and brutality of slavery.)

Reconstruction and the Empowerment of African Americans

When the Republicans gained control of Congress in 1867, African Americans momentarily seemed destined to attain their full rights as U.S. citizens. Under military rule, Southern states adopted new constitutions that awarded them the vote and other civil liberties. African American men were elected to state legislatures and to the U.S. Congress. In 1865, nearly 10 percent of all federal troops were black.[6]

The accomplishments of the Reconstruction Congress were considerable. Even before the Republicans gained control, the Thirteenth Amendment, which abolished slavery, had become part of the Constitution. But it was the Fourteenth and Fifteenth Amendments and the important Civil Rights Act of 1875 that attempted to secure a place for the blacks in the United States equal to that of the whites.

The Civil Rights Act of 1875 declared that all persons were entitled to the full and equal enjoyment of all public accommodations, inns, public conveniences, theaters, and other places of public amusement. In this act, the Reconstruction Congress committed the nation to a policy of nondiscrimination in all aspects of public life.

But by 1877, support for Reconstruction policies began to crumble. In what has been described as the "Compromise of 1877," the national government agreed to end military occupation of the South, thereby giving up its efforts to rearrange Southern society and lending tacit approval to white supremacy in that region. In return, the Southern states pledged their support for the Union, accepted national supremacy, and enabled the Republican candidate, Rutherford B. Hayes, to assume the presidency following the much-disputed election of 1876, in which his opponent, Samuel Tilden, had received a majority of the popular vote.

The Development of the White Supremacy Movement

The withdrawal of federal troops from the South in 1877 did not bring about an instant change in the status of African Americans. In the South, African Americans voted in large numbers well into the 1880s and 1890s. Certainly, we do not mean to suggest that discrimination was nonexistent during that period. Perhaps the most debilitating of all segregation—that in the public schools—appeared immediately after the Civil War under the sanction of Reconstruction authorities. Yet segregation took shape only gradually.

The first objective of the *white supremacy movement* was to disenfranchise African American voters. There were several standard devices developed for achieving this feat. In the South, those who wanted to vote might be subject to a **literacy test**, often one in which the test administered to blacks was exponentially more difficult than the one for white voters, and anyone whose grandfather had voted prior to 1865 was exempted from the test. Called the **grandfather clause**, this tactic facilitated the participation of whites and prevented the participation of blacks whose grandfathers would have been ineligible to vote prior to 1865. Some areas also used a **poll tax**, in which voters not exempted by the grandfather clause would have to pay a large fee to vote. Because the Democratic Party largely controlled the South, the use of the **white primary**, which allowed only white voters to vote in the party's primary election, meant that there would be no real element of choice for voters voting only in the general election. White supremacists also relied on various forms of intimidation to prevent blacks from voting.

literacy test
a discriminatory test used to prevent African Americans from voting

grandfather clause
exempted anyone whose grandfather had voted before 1865 from literacy tests for voting and from poll taxes

poll tax
voters not exempted by the grandfather clause would have to pay a large fee to vote

white primary
allowed only white voters to vote in the party's primary election

This 1956 photo taken in Dallas, Texas, shows the extent of Jim Crow laws, which required the segregation of the races.

Following the disenfranchisement of African Americans, the white supremacy movement established segregation and discrimination as public policy by the adoption of a large number of "Jim Crow" laws, designed to prevent the mingling of whites and blacks. (Jim Crow was a stereotypical African American in a nineteenth-century song-and-dance show.) Between 1900 and 1910, laws were adopted by Southern state legislatures requiring segregation of the races in streetcars, hospitals, prisons, orphanages, and homes for the aged and indigent. In 1913 the federal government itself adopted policies that segregated the races in federal office buildings, cafeterias, and restroom facilities.

Social policy followed (indeed, exceeded) public policy. Signs reading "White Only" or "Colored" appeared everywhere, with or without the support of law.

Early U.S. Supreme Court Approval of Segregation

The Fourteenth Amendment had been passed by the Reconstruction Congress and ratified in 1868. Its guarantee of "equal protection of the laws" was clearly designed to protect newly freed African Americans from discrimination in state laws. But in 1896, in the infamous case of *Plessy v. Ferguson*, the U.S. Supreme Court held that the separation of the races did *not* violate the equal protection clause so long as people of each race received equal treatment. Schools and other public facilities that were "separate but equal" were held to be constitutional. In the words of the Court,

> The object of the amendment was undoubtedly to enforce the absolute equality of the two races before the law, but in the nature of things it could not have been intended to abolish distinctions based upon color, or to enforce social, as distinguished from political, equality, or a commingling of the two races upon terms unsatisfactory to either. Laws permitting, and even requiring, their separation in places where they are liable to be brought into contact do not necessarily imply the inferiority of either race to the other, and have been generally, if not universally, recognized as within the competency of the state legislatures in the exercise of their police power.[7]

The effect of this decision was to give constitutional approval to segregation. The decision would not be reversed until 1954 in *Brown v. Board of Education of Kansas* (see Chapter 10).

Response by African Americans to Segregation

Many early histories of Reconstruction paid little attention to the response of African Americans to the imposition of segregation. But there were at least three distinct types of response: (1) accommodation to a subordinate position in society, (2) the formation of an African Americans protest movement, and (3) migration out of the South to avoid some of the consequences of assertions of white supremacy.

The foremost African American advocate of accommodation to segregation was the well-known educator Booker T. Washington, one of many African-Americans included in "great man" analyses of U.S. history. Washington enjoyed wide popularity among both black and white Americans. He was an adviser to two presidents (Theodore Roosevelt and William Howard Taft) and was highly respected by white philanthropists and government officials. In his famous Cotton States' Exposition speech in Atlanta in 1895, Washington assured whites that blacks were prepared to accept a separate position in society: "In all things that are purely social we can be as separate as the fingers, yet one as the hand in all things essential to mutual progress."[8]

Washington's hopes for African Americans lay in a program of self-help through education. He himself had attended Hampton Institute in Virginia where the curriculum centered on practical trades for African Americans. Washington obtained some white philanthropic support in establishing his own Tuskegee Institute in Tuskegee, Alabama, in 1881. His first students helped build the school. Training at Tuskegee emphasized immediately useful vocations such as farming, preaching, and blacksmithing. Washington urged his students to stay in the South, to acquire land, and to build homes, thereby helping eliminate ignorance and poverty among their fellow African Americans. One of Tuskegee's outstanding faculty members was George Washington Carver, who researched and developed uses for Southern crops. Other privately and publicly endowed black colleges were founded that later developed into major universities, including Fisk and Howard (both started by the Freedmen's Bureau) and Atlanta, Hampton, and Southern.

While Washington was urging African Americans to make the best of segregation, a small band of blacks was organizing themselves behind a declaration of black resistance and protest that would later rewrite American public policy. The leader of this group—another "great man"—was W. E. B. Du Bois, a brilliant historian and sociologist at Atlanta University. In 1905 Du Bois and a few other African American intellectuals met in Niagara Falls, Canada, to draw up a platform intended to "assail the ears" and sear the consciences of white Americans. In rejecting moderation and compromise, the Niagara statement proclaimed: "We refuse to allow the impression to remain that the Negro American assents to inferiority, is submissive under oppression and apologetic before insults." The platform listed the major injustices perpetrated against African Americans since Reconstruction: the loss of voting rights, the imposition of Jim Crow laws and segregated public schools, the denial of equal job opportunities, the existence of inhumane conditions in Southern prisons, the exclusion of African Americans from West Point and Annapolis, and the failure on the part of the federal government to enforce the Fourteenth and Fifteenth Amendments. Out of the Niagara meeting came the idea for a nationwide organization dedicated to fighting for African Americans, and on February 12, 1909, the one-hundredth anniversary of Abraham Lincoln's birth, the National Association for the Advancement of Colored People (NAACP) was founded.

Du Bois himself was on the original board of directors of the NAACP, but a majority of the board consisted of white liberals. In the years to follow, most of the financial support and policy guidance for the association was provided by whites rather than blacks. However, Du Bois was the NAACP's first director of research and the editor of its magazine, *Crisis.* The NAACP began a long and eventually successful campaign to establish rights for African Americans through legal action. Over the years, hundreds of court cases were brought at the local, state, and federal court levels on behalf of African Americans denied their constitutional rights.

World War I provided an opportunity for restive blacks in the South to escape the worst abuses of white supremacy by migrating en masse to Northern cities. In the years 1916 to 1918, an estimated half-million African Americans moved to the North to fill the labor shortage in industrial cities caused by the war effort. Most migrating African Americans arrived in big Northern cities only to find more poverty and segregation. But at least they could vote and attend better schools, and they did not encounter laws requiring segregation in public places.

The progressive "ghettoization" of African Americans—their migration from the rural South to the urban North and their increasing concentration in central-city ghettos—had profound political as well as social implications. The ghetto provided an environment conducive to political action. Even as early as 1928, the black residents of Chicago succeeded in getting a black man elected to the House of Representatives. The election of Oscar de Priest, who served in Congress from 1929 until 1935, and was the first African American congressman from the North, signaled a new turn in American urban politics by demonstrating the potential power of the African American vote in Northern cities both to white politicians and to African American voters and candidates. And the black ghettos would soon provide an important element in a new political coalition that was about to take form—namely, the Democratic Party of Franklin Delano Roosevelt.

Power and the Industrial Revolution

The importance of the Civil War for the power structure of the United States lay in the commanding position that the new industrial capitalists won during the course of that struggle. Even before 1860, Northern industry had been altering the course of American life; the economic transformation of the United States from an agricultural to an industrial nation reached the crescendo of a revolution in the second half of the nineteenth century. Canals and steam railroads had been opening up new markets for the growing industrial cities of the East. The rise of corporations and of stock markets for the accumulation of capital upset old-fashioned ideas about property. The introduction of machinery in factories revolutionized the conditions of labor and made the masses dependent on industrial capitalists for their livelihood. Civil War profits compounded the capital of the industrialists and placed them in a position to dominate the economic life of the nation. Moreover, when the Southern planters were removed from the national scene, the government in Washington became the exclusive domain of the new industrial leaders.

Social Darwinism

The new industrial elite found a new philosophy to justify its political and economic dominance. Drawing an analogy from Darwinian biology, Herbert Spencer undertook to demonstrate that, just as an elite was selected in nature through evolution, so also society would near perfection as it allowed a natural *social* elite to be selected by *free competition*. Spencer hailed the accumulation of new industrial wealth as a sign of "the survival of the fittest." The **social Darwinists** found in the law of survival of the fittest an admirable defense for the emergence of a ruthless ruling elite, an elite that defined its own self-interest more narrowly, perhaps, than any other in American history. It was a conservative philosophy that permitted the conditions of the masses to decline to the lowest depths in American history.

social Darwinism competition selects the best; a philosophy justifying great accumulations of wealth

Industrialists Acquire Political Power

After the Civil War, industrialists became more prominent in Congress than they had ever been. They had little trouble in voting high tariffs and hard money, both of which heightened profits. Very little effective regulatory legislation was permitted to reach the floor of Congress. After 1881 the Senate came under the spell of Nelson Aldrich, son-in-law of John D. Rockefeller, who controlled Standard Oil. Aldrich served thirty years in the Senate. He believed that geographical representation in that body was old-fashioned and openly advocated a Senate manned officially by representatives from the great business "constituencies"—steel, coal, copper, railroads, banks, textiles, and so on.

The Rise of the Modern Corporation

The *corporate form of business* facilitated the amassing of capital by limiting the liability of capitalists to their actual investments and thereby keeping their personal fortunes safe in the event of misfortunes to their companies. The corporate form also encouraged capitalists to take risks in expanding industrial capital through the stock market. "Wall Street," the address of the nation's busiest securities market, the New York Stock Exchange, became a synonym for industrial capitalism. The markets for corporation stocks provided a vast and ready money source for new enterprises or for the enlargement and consolidation of old firms.

The New Deal and the Emergence of the "Liberal Establishment"

The *economic collapse of the Great Depression* undermined the faith of both rich and poor in the idea of social Darwinism. Following the stock market crash of October 1929 and despite assurances by President Herbert Hoover that prosperity lay "just around the corner," the American economy virtually stopped. Prices dropped sharply, factories closed, real estate values declined, new construction practically ceased, banks went under, wages were cut drastically, unemployment figures mounted, and welfare rolls swelled.

The election of Franklin D. Roosevelt (another "great man") to the presidency in 1932 ushered in a new era in American political philosophy. The Great Depression did *not* bring about a revolution, it did *not* result in the emergence of a new elite, but it did have an important impact on the *thinking* of America's governing circles. The economic disaster that had befallen the nation caused the elite to consider the need for economic reform. The Great Depression also reinforced the notion that the elite must acquire a greater public responsibility. The victories of fascism in Germany and communism in the Soviet Union and the growing restlessness of the masses in the United States made it plain that *reform and regard for the public welfare* were essential to the continued maintenance of the American political system and the dominant place of the elite in it.

The New Deal

New Deal philosophy based on the idea that governments has the responsibility to provide an economic safety net for citizens, particularly in tough economic times

Roosevelt, himself a member of the wealthy power elite, sought to elaborate a **New Deal philosophy,** based on the idea that governments has the responsibility to provide an economic safety net for citizens, particularly in tough economic times.

This philosophy that would permit government to devote much more attention to the public welfare than did the philosophy of Hoover's somewhat discredited "rugged individualism." The New Deal was not a revolutionary system but rather a necessary *reform* of the existing capitalist system. In the New Deal, the American elite accepted the principle that the entire community, through the agency of the national government, has a *responsibility for mass welfare*. Roosevelt's second inaugural address called attention to "one-third of a nation, ill housed, ill clad, ill nourished." Roosevelt succeeded in preserving the existing system of private capitalism and avoiding the threats posed to the established order by fascism, socialism, communism, and other radical movements.

Historian Richard Hofstadter commented on Roosevelt's liberal, public-regarding philosophy:

> At the beginning of his career he took to the patrician reform thought of the progressive era and accepted a social outlook that can best be summed up in the phrase "noblesse oblige." He had a penchant for public service, personal philanthropy, and harmless manifestos against dishonesty in government; he displayed a broad easy-going tolerance, a genuine liking for all sorts of people; he loved to exercise his charm in political and social situations.[9]

Roosevelt's personal philosophy was soon to become the prevailing ethos of the new liberal establishment.

Bettmann/CORBIS

President Franklin D. Roosevelt signs the Social Security Bill of 1935.

CASE STUDY

The Vietnam War: A Political History

Histories of the Vietnam War, like all histories, reflect the historian's judgment about what facts are most important to be recorded, the perspective of the narrative, and how the narrative should be interpreted. Debate over histories of the war reflects many of the same controversies that occurred during the war itself.

The account of the Vietnam War presented here reflects the notion that history can inform the social sciences, and in this case it is the writer's view that a historical narrative of the war informs a political analysis. This is reflective of the idea that the loss in Vietnam was a political, not a military, defeat, and that responsibility for the tragic results lies with the nation's political leadership—their failure to set forth clear objectives in Vietnam, to develop a strategy to achieve those objectives, and to rally mass support behind the effort.

Initially, the United States sought to resist communist aggression from North Vietnam and ensure a strong and independent democratic South Vietnamese government. President John F. Kennedy sent a force of more than twelve thousand advisers and counterinsurgency forces to assist in every aspect of training and support for the Army of the Republic of Vietnam (ARVN). Kennedy also personally inspired the development and deployment of Special Forces ("Green Berets") to deal directly with a guerrilla enemy and help "win the hearts and minds" of the Vietnamese people.

By 1964 units of the North Vietnamese Army (NVA) had begun to supplement the communist guerrilla forces (Vietcong) in the south. President Lyndon B. Johnson, informed that the South Vietnamese government was on the "verge of collapse," authorized major increases in U.S. supporting forces and began planning for a U.S. combat role. In February 1965, Johnson ordered U.S. combat troops into South Vietnam and authorized a gradual increase in air strikes against North Vietnam.

The fateful decision to commit U.S. ground combat forces to Vietnam was made without any significant effort to mobilize American public opinion, the government, or the economy for war. And the failure of the nation's leadership to set forth a clear military objective in Vietnam made "victory" impossible. Nonetheless, by late 1967, more than 500,000 U.S. troops were committed to Vietnam. Washington committed these military forces to a war of attrition, a war in which U.S. firepower was expected to inflict sufficient casualties on the enemy to force them to negotiate a settlement. But the enemy relied on guerilla warfare tactics: attacking, then quickly melting into the civilian population, hiding in tunnels, or retreating back to "sanctuaries" in Cambodia and Laos.

The failure to achieve any decisive military victories eroded support for the war among both elites and masses. The *Pentagon Papers*,* composed of official memos and documents of the war, reveal increasing disenchantment with military results throughout 1967 by Secretary of Defense Robert McNamara and others who had originally initiated U.S. military actions. But Johnson sought to rally support for the war by claiming that the United States was "winning." The U.S. commander in Vietnam, General William Westmoreland, was brought home to tell Congress that there was light at the end of the tunnel.

But these pronouncements only helped set the stage for the enemy's great political victory—the Tet offensive. The offensive was a massive, coordinated attack against all major cities of South Vietnam, during which Vietcong forces blasted their way into the U.S. embassy compound in Saigon and held the courtyard for six hours.

The Vietcong failed to hold any of the positions that they captured, the people did not rise up to welcome them as "liberators," and their losses were high. By any *military* measure, the Tet offensive was a "defeat" for the enemy and a "victory" for U.S. forces. Yet the Tet offensive was Hanoi's greatest political victory because it called into question the administration's assertions that the United States was winning the war. The media launched a long and bitter campaign against the war effort and elite support for the war plummeted.

Deserted by the very elite who had initiated American involvement in the war, hounded by hostile media, and confronting a bitter and divisive presidential election, Johnson made a dramatic announcement on national television on March 31, 1968. He halted the bombing of North Vietnam, asked Hanoi for peace talks, and concluded: "I shall not seek, and I will not accept, the nomination of my party for another term as your president."

American objectives in Vietnam shifted again with the arrival in Washington of the new president, Richard M. Nixon, and his national security adviser, Henry A. Kissinger. Nixon and Kissinger knew the war must be ended, but they sought to end it "honorably." They sought a peace settlement that would give South Vietnam a reasonable chance to survive. But even in the absence of a settlement, they began the withdrawal of U.S. troops under the guise of "Vietnamization" of the war effort.

Unable to persuade Hanoi to make even the slightest concession at Paris, Nixon sought to demonstrate American strength and resolve. In the spring of 1970, Nixon authorized an attack on an NVA sanctuary inside the territory of Cambodia—an area known as the Parrot's Beak—not far from Saigon. The Cambodian operation was brief and probably achieved very little militarily, but it mobilized the antiwar movement in the United States. Demonstrations centered on American campuses, and four students were killed in an angry confrontation with National Guardsmen at Kent State University.

When North Vietnam launched a new, massive, conventional invasion of the south in March 1972, Nixon authorized the heaviest bombing campaign of the war as well as a naval blockade of North Vietnam and the mining of its Haiphong Harbor. The NVA suffered heavy casualties, and the attack was thrown back. Meanwhile, National Security Adviser Henry Kissinger and Hanoi's Le Duc Tho had begun meeting secretly in Paris, away from the formal negotiations, to work out "the shape of a deal." U.S. prisoners of war were a major bargaining chip for Hanoi. In the presidential election of 1972, the war became a partisan issue. Democratic candidate George McGovern had earlier stated that he would

(continued)

"crawl on his hands and knees to Hanoi" for peace, while Nixon continued his "peace with honor" theme. Nixon's landslide re-election strengthened his position in negotiations.

The United States unleashed a devastating air attack directly on Hanoi for the first time in December 1972. When negotiations resumed in Paris in January, the North Vietnamese quickly agreed to peace on the terms that Kissinger and Le Duc Tho had worked out earlier. Both Nixon and Kissinger contended that the Christmas bombing secured the final peace.**

The Paris Peace Agreement of 1973 called for a cease-fire in place, with NVA troops remaining in their areas of control in the south. The South Vietnamese government and its troops also remained in place. All U.S. forces were withdrawn from South Vietnam and U.S. prisoners returned.

The South Vietnamese government lasted two years after the Paris Agreement. Congress refused to provide significant military aid to the South Vietnamese. The Watergate affair forced Nixon's resignation in August 1974. In early 1975, Hanoi decided that the Americans would not "jump back in," and therefore "the opportune moment" was at hand. President Gerald Ford never gave serious consideration to the use of U.S. military forces to repel the new invasion, and his requests to Congress for emergency military aid to the South Vietnamese fell on deaf ears.

U.S. Ambassador Graham Martin, embarrassed by his government's abandonment of Vietnam, delayed implementation of escape plans until the last moment. The United States abandoned hundreds of thousands of loyal South Vietnamese who had fought alongside the Americans for years.[†] The spectacle of U.S. Marines using rifle butts to keep desperate Vietnamese from boarding helicopters on the roof of the U.S. embassy "provided a tragic epitaph for twenty-five years of American involvement in Vietnam."[‡]

America's humiliation in Vietnam had lasting national and international consequences. The United States suffered 47,378 battle deaths and missing-in-action cases among the 2.8 million who fought in Vietnam. More than 1 million Vietnamese, military and civilian, in both the north and south, were killed during the war years. But the "peace" was bloodier than the war. In Cambodia more than 2 million people were murdered by victorious communist forces in genocidal "killing fields." More than 1.5 million South Vietnamese were forcibly relocated to harsh rural areas and "re-education camps." Nearly 500,000 "boat people" tried to flee their country; eventually, the United States took in nearly 250,000 Vietnamese refugees. Unlike past wars, there were no victory parades, and no one could answer the question of the mother whose son or daughter was killed in Vietnam: "What did he (she) die for?"

Thirty-five years after the last American soldier left Vietnam, American presidents using troops abroad are scrutinized by both the media and the public, who remain wary of becoming entangled in "another Vietnam."

* *The New York Times, The Pentagon Papers* (New York: Bantam Books, 1971).

** Henry Kissinger, *The White House Years* (Boston: Little, Brown, 1979), 1461; Richard Nixon, *RN: The Memoirs of Richard Nixon*, vol. 2 (New York: Warner Books, 1978), 251.

† Frank Snepp, *Decent Interval* (New York: Random House, 1977).

‡ George C. Herring, *America's Longest War* (New York: Random House, 1979), 262.

SOURCE: Taken from Thomas R. Dye and Harmon Zeigler, *The Irony of Democracy,* 7th. ed. (Pacific Grove, CA: Brooks/Cole, 1987): 78–88.

The New Deal brought a lasting commitment of the national government to social welfare. Prior to its passage, the poor, the unemployed, the disabled, infirmed, or elderly relied exclusively on the benevolence of friends, family, and charities. But the Social Security Act of 1935 established a basic framework of national social policy that remains in place today (see Chapter 11). It established a compulsory insurance program for workers to provide cash assistance on retirement, disability, or death. It provided assistance to the states for cash welfare payments to the poor and to the unemployed. Modern American liberalism remains indebted to the legacy of Franklin D. Roosevelt.

The Origins of Modern Liberalism

Thus, *modern liberalism* in the United States is a product of elite response to economic depression at home and the rising threats of fascism and communism abroad. Its historical origin can be traced to elite efforts to *preserve* the existing political and economic system through reform. Included in these reforms have been programs that have expanded the functions and powers of the national government and drastically altered how Americans perceive what the government's role should be. This historical perspective on the liberal tradition gives us a better understanding of the origins of change and reform within society and the power exerted by elites in implementing policies that serve to create long-term stability in the United States.

Modern Liberalism in Modern History

Building on the New Deal, President Lyndon B. Johnson's "Great Society" initiatives in 1965 reflected the continued influence modern liberalism had on the national policy agenda in the United States. It also reflected a transformation of what functions Americans expected their government to perform. As a result of modern liberalism, many Americans believe that the government should provide a safety net for the neediest citizens. Thus during President Lyndon Johnson's administration (1963–1969), the role of government expanded, creating the federal Medicare program for the aged and the Medicaid program for the poor. While facing criticism concerning escalation of the Vietnam War, the Johnson administration also heralded in a federal food-stamp program, and began Head Start federally funded preschool programs (see Case Study: "The Vietnam War: A Political History").

Since Franklin Roosevelt's administration, modern liberalism and its implication for the size and role of government have been at the heart of most political struggles in the United States. During the early days of the Obama administration, we again saw questions being raised as to the appropriate level of government intervention when important components of the economic system—including the banking, financial services, and auto industries—were failing. And similar to elite policymakers during the Great Depression, President Obama, his administration, and Congress sought to preserve the existing political and economic system through reform and government intervention and assistance.

CHAPTER SUMMARY

- The study of history is the recording, narrating, and interpretation of historic events. Historians must select and organize facts that are worthy of interest, and this process involves personal judgment of what is important about the past. History is "an unending dialogue" between the present and the past; it is "what one age finds worthy of note in another."

- Historical analysis is not merely the interpretation of opinion. Historians must first understand events before they are to interpret their meaning. A solid comprehension of historical facts and the ability to critically evaluate and assess original source documents to determine credibility and accuracy are crucial components of historical analysis.

- Paradigms for studying history include the great man paradigm, which narrates history as the actions of larger-than-life individuals;

institutionalist perspectives, which focus on the structures that spawned democracy; and elite theory, which emphasizes the disproportionate role that elites had in shaping American society.

- During the rise of the New West, we could see greater influence of self-made Western elites through the advent of Jacksonian democracy and populism. The Civil War represented a struggle for power in many arenas: Northern versus Southern elites; slaveholders versus abolitionists; and union forces versus conferral forces.

- The post–civil war era generally can be described as a period of increased segregation, while the Industrial Revolution brought increased power to modern corporations.

- Modern liberalism, including efforts by elites to protect the status quo, characterized the New Deal era.

KEY TERMS

elite theory   a method of viewing history that stresses the disproportionate role that elites had in shaping American society

grandfather clause   exempted anyone whose grandfather had voted before 1865 from literacy tests for voting and from poll taxes

great man paradigm   a method of viewing history which focuses on the actions larger-than-life individuals who are free of the faults of common people, and who shape the course of events themselves rather than merely respond to the world in which they live

history   the recording, narrating, and interpreting of all past human actions and events

institutionalist perspective   a method of viewing history which focuses on the structures that spawned democracy from its ancient Greek beginnings,

through English constitutional development, to the colonies and the American constitutional system

interpretation   the analysis of the underlying causes and outcomes of past events

Jacksonian democracy   a philosophic ideal of the frontier society that emphasized the self-made individual, and wealth and power won by competitive skill

literacy test   a discriminatory test used to prevent African Americans from voting

narrating   the description of events based on documentation

New Deal philosophy   based on the idea that governments has the responsibility to provide an economic safety net for citizens, particularly in tough economic times

Northern elite manufacturers dependent on wage labor

original source documents publications, including official documents, but also diaries and journals, legal documents, and sometimes even oral accounts in recording historical events that historians often rely on to record historic events

poll tax voters not exempted by the grandfather clause would have to pay a large fee to vote

recording the documentation of events

social Darwinism competition selects the best; a philosophy justifying great accumulations of wealth

Southern elite plantation owners dependent on slave labor

white primary allowed only white voters to vote in the party's primary election

ON THE WEB

EXPLORING HISTORY

The website for this textbook offers resources for exploring power and history on the Internet. An almost endless variety of websites are also available to assist students in the study of history. Indeed, in using standard search engines, it is best to designate the category of history that you wish to review, for example, "U.S. History: Civil War." Visit **www.cengage.com**.

- **Smithsonian Institution** The Smithsonian Institution in Washington, DC, is one of the nation's most valuable resources. Visit the museum's extensive archives (**www .siris.si.edu/**), with specific categories listed for such things as social and cultural history, ethnic and religious history, historical photographs, and the history of sports, entertainment, business, technology, and medicine.

- **Try this:** Go to the Smithsonian Archives at **www.siris.si.edu/** where you can access 7.4 million records, including images, voice recordings, and so on pertaining to events in American history. Search a key term of interest to you or the date you were born to discover the various records housed in the Smithsonian Archives.
- **African American History** African American history can be accessed at the site maintained by the Library of Congress, "The African American Odyssey," **http://lcweb2.loc.gov/ ammem/aaohtml/exhibit/**.
- **Try this:** Go to **lcweb2.loc.gov/ammem/ aaohtml/exhibit/** and explore the narrative concerning African American history. Evaluate how the accompanying original source documents bolster the narrative. Look for examples of the great man paradigm, an institutionalist approach, and elite theory in the interpretation.

REVIEW QUIZ

MULTIPLE CHOICE

1. Approaches to American history *do not* include _____.
   a. the external review approach
   b. the "great man" approach
   c. the democratic institutions approach
   d. critical approaches

2. Charles Beard argued that the founders _____.
   a. were socialists
   b. lacked a cohesive ideology
   c. pursued their economic interests
   d. sacrificed their own economic interests for the good of the masses

3. In general, change in the power structure of the United States has been _____.
   a. incremental
   b. rapid
   c. revolutionary
   d. anarchic

4. American beliefs shared over time *do not* include _____.
   a. individualism
   b. importance of private property
   c. enterprise
   d. cooperation

5. Influences of the West on American history *do not* include _____.
   a. a more open elite system
   b. new wealth and opportunity
   c. greater educational opportunity
   d. upward social mobility

6. The Missouri Compromise of 1820 and the Kansas-Nebraska Act of 1854 were two of many attempts _____.
   a. to sell land to foreign investors to generate revenue for the U.S. Treasury
   b. to distribute public lands
   c. at compromise to maintain unity in the U.S.
   d. to end segregation in the U.S.

7. Booker T. Washington was best known as an advocate of _____.
   a. migration out of the South by African Americans
   b. the formation of an African American power movement
   c. cooperation between suffragists and abolitionists
   d. accommodation to segregation

8. W. E. B. Du Bois was best known as an advocate of _____.
   a. migration out of the South by African Americans
   b. the formation of an African American power movement
   c. cooperation between suffragists and abolitionists
   d. accommodation to segregation

9. Roosevelt's New Deal philosophy was to _____.
   a. reform capitalism, not replace it
   b. grant civil rights to African Americans
   c. protect economic elites at the expense of the masses
   d. eliminate capitalism

10. Modern liberalism can be seen in _____.
    a. President Johnson's Great Society programs
    b. President Obama's economic reforms
    c. President Reagan's New Federalism
    d. a and b

FILL IN THE BLANK

11. The recording, narrating, and interpreting of all past human actions and events is called _____.

12. The _____ were plantation owners dependent on slave labor.

13. The _____ were manufacturers dependent on wage labor.

14. A philosophy justifying great accumulation of wealth that argues that competition selected the best is called _____.

15. The _____ brought a lasting commitment of the national government to social welfare.

CHAPTER 7

Power and Politics

Learning Objectives

After reading this chapter, students will be able to:

- Describe the discipline of political science and explain what it is concerned with.
- Define democracy.
- Describe the kind of democracy that exists in the United States.
- List the branches of the U.S. government.
- Explain the source of each branch's power and how that power is exercised.

Politics, Political Science, and Government Power

politics
the study of power

A distinguished American political scientist, Harold Lasswell, defined **politics** as "who gets what, when, and how." "The study of politics," he said, "is the study of influence and the influential. The influential are those who get the most of what there is to get. . . . Those who get the most are the *elite;* the rest are *mass.*"[1] He went on to define *political science* as the study of "the shaping and sharing of power." Admittedly, Lasswell's definition of political science is very broad. Indeed, if we accept Lasswell's definition of political science as the *study of power,* then political science includes cultural, economic, social, and personal power relationships—topics that we have already discussed in chapters on anthropology, economics, sociology, and psychology.

political science
the study of government and how individuals influence government action

Although some political scientists have accepted Lasswell's challenge to study power in all its forms in society, most limit the definition of **political science** to the study of government and how individuals influence government action. This chapter focuses primarily on the study of government and how individuals influence government action in the United States.

government power
the legitimate use of force; coverage of the whole society

What distinguishes **government power** from the power of other institutions, groups, and individuals? The power of government, unlike that of other institutions in society, is distinguished by (1) *the legitimate use of physical force* and (2) *coverage of the whole society* rather than only segments of it. By *legitimate,* we mean the right or power of the government to exercise authority. By *physical force,* we mean that the government can legitimately compel action, sometimes through law enforcement agencies and sometimes through the threat of punishment, including incarceration. Because government decisions extend to the

Democracy means individual participation in the decisions that affect one's life, often through voting. Here Egyptian soldiers stand guard as voters leave a polling station in Cairo in 2011, the first Egyptian elections held after the popular uprising that ousted long-time dictator Hosni Mubarak from power.

ALFRED / SIPA/News.com

whole of society and because only government can legitimately use physical force, government has the primary responsibility for maintaining order and for resolving differences that arise *between* segments of society. Thus, government must regulate conflict by establishing and enforcing general rules by which conflict is to be carried on in society, by arranging compromises and balancing interests, and by imposing settlements that the parties in the dispute must accept. In other words, government lays down the "rules of the game" in conflict and competition between individuals, organizations, and institutions within society.

The Meaning of Democracy

democracy
individual participation in the decisions that affect one's life

Ideally, **democracy** means *individual participation* in the decisions that affect one's life. In traditional democratic theory, popular participation has been valued as an opportunity for individual self-development. Responsibility for governing one's own conduct develops character, self-reliance, intelligence, and moral judgment—in short, dignity. Even if a benevolent king could govern in the public interest, the true democrat would reject him.[2]

Procedurally, popular participation was to be achieved through *majority rule* and *respect for the rights of those with a minority view*. Self-development means *self-government*, and self-government can be accomplished only by encouraging each individual to contribute to the creation of public policy and by resolving conflicts over public policy through majority rule. Minorities who had had the opportunity to influence policy but whose views had not succeeded in winning majority support would accept the decisions of majorities. In return, majorities would permit minorities to attempt openly to win majority support for their views. Freedom of speech and press, freedom to dissent, and freedom to form opposition parties and organizations are essential to ensure meaningful individual participation.

John Locke and the Idea of Limited Government

Oftentimes, majority rule and respect for the rights of minorities occurs by limiting the power of the government through a social contract. **Constitutionalism** is the belief that government power should be *limited*. A fundamental ideal of constitutionalism—"a government of laws and not of men"—suggests that those who exercise government authority are restricted in their use of it by a higher law. A constitution governs government.

constitutionalism
the belief that government power should be limited

A famous exponent of the idea of constitutional government was the English political philosopher John Locke (1632–1704). Perhaps more than anyone else, Locke inspired the political thought of our nation's founders in that critical period of American history in which the new nation won its independence and established its constitution. Locke's ideas are written into both the Declaration of Independence and the Constitution of the United States.

According to Locke, all people possess **natural rights**. These rights are not granted by government but derive from human nature itself. Governments cannot deprive people of their "unalienable rights to life, liberty, and property." People are rational beings, capable of self-government and able to participate in political decision making. Locke believed that human beings formed a contract among themselves to establish a government in order to better protect their natural rights, maintain peace, and protect themselves from foreign invasion.

natural rights
rights are not granted by government but derive from human nature itself

Because government was instituted as a contract to secure the rights of citizens, government itself could not violate individual rights. If government did so, it would dissolve the contract establishing it. Revolution, then, was justified if government was not serving the purpose for which it had been set up. However, according to Locke, revolution was justified only after a long period of abuses by government, not over any minor mismanagement.

A **social contract** is the idea (not an actual written contract) that people consent to be governed and voluntarily give up some of their liberties so that the remainder of their liberties can be protected. For example, in the United States, people enjoy the right of freedom of speech, but this right is limited: One cannot exercise freedom of speech if it means joking to airport security personnel about bringing a bomb onboard an aircraft. But this rule protects people from the inconvenience of more delayed flights if security had to identify and search the bags of every prankster.

social contract
the idea that people consent to be governed and in doing so agree to give up some of their liberties so that the remainder of their liberties can be protected

The social contract that established government made for safe and peaceful living and for the secure enjoyment of one's life, liberty, and property. Thus, the ultimate legitimacy of government derived from a contract among the people themselves and not from gods or kings. It was based on the consent of the governed. To safeguard their individual rights, the people agree to be governed.

Thomas Jefferson eloquently expressed Lockean ideals in the Declaration of Independence:

> We hold these truths to be self-evident, that all men are created equal, that they are endowed by their Creator with certain unalienable Rights, that among these are Life, Liberty, and the pursuit of Happiness. That to secure these rights, Governments are instituted among Men, deriving their just powers from the consent of the governed.

Democratic Ideals of Liberty and Equality

The underlying value of democracy is *individual dignity*. In the Declaration of Independence, Thomas Jefferson wrote that human beings, by virtue of their existence, are entitled to life, liberty, and the pursuit of happiness. Government control over the individual should be kept to a minimum; this means the removal of as many external restrictions, controls, and regulations on the individual as possible without infringing on the freedom of other citizens.[3]

Another vital aspect of classic democracy is a belief in the *equality* of all people. The Declaration of Independence expresses the conviction that "all men are created equal." The founders believed in equality *before the law*, notwithstanding the circumstances of the accused. Although the founders' view of *who* was equal was limited—women and racial minorities were not afforded the same political rights as white males—the notion of equality informed early American political life. Eventually, the idea of equality has come to mean that a person is not to be judged by social position, sex, economic class, creed, or race. Many early democrats also believed in *political equality*, that is, equal opportunity to influence public policy.[4] Political equality is expressed in the concept of "one person, one vote."

Over time, the notion of equality has also come to include *equality of opportunity* in all aspects of American life—social, educational, and economic, as well as political—and to encompass employment, housing, recreation, and public accommodations. All people are to have equal opportunity to develop their individual capacities to their natural limits.

In summary, democratic thinking involves the following ideas:

- Popular participation in the decisions that shape the lives of individuals in a society, including consent of the governed
- Limited government formed by a social contract, which establishes the right of revolution if the government consistently tramples the rights of individuals
- Government by majority rule, with recognition of the rights of minorities to try to become majorities; these rights include the freedoms of speech, press, assembly, and petition, and the freedom to dissent, to form opposition parties, and to run for public office
- A commitment to individual dignity and the preservation of the liberal values of liberty and property
- A commitment to equal opportunity for all to develop their individual capacities

Power and the American Constitution

A **constitution** establishes government authority. It sets up government bodies (such as the House of Representatives, the Senate, the presidency, and the Supreme Court in the United States). It grants them powers, determines how their members are to be chosen, and prescribes the rules by which they make decisions. Constitutional decision making is deciding how to decide, that is, it is deciding on the rules for policy making. It is not policy making itself. Policies will be decided later, according to the rules set forth in the Constitution.[5]

A constitution cannot be changed by the ordinary acts of government bodies; change can come only through a process of general popular consent. The U.S. Constitution, then, is superior to ordinary laws of Congress, orders of the president, decisions of the courts, acts of the state legislatures, and regulations of the bureaucracies. Indeed, the Constitution is "the supreme law of the land."

constitution
the establishment of government authority; the creation of government bodies, granting their powers, determining how their members are selected, and prescribing the rules by which government decisions are to be made; considered basic or fundamental, a constitution cannot be changed by ordinary acts of government bodies

Constitutionalism: Limiting Government Power

As we noted, constitutions govern government. To place individual freedoms beyond the reach of government and beyond the reach of majorities, a constitution must truly limit and control the exercise of authority by government. It does so by setting forth individual liberties that the government—even with majority support—cannot violate. In the United States, many of these individual liberties can be found in the first ten amendments to the Constitution.

The Bill of Rights

The U.S. Constitution contains many specific written restrictions on government power. The original text of the Constitution that emerged from the Philadelphia Convention in 1787 did *not* contain a **Bill of Rights**—a listing of individual freedoms and restrictions on government power. The nation's founders originally argued that a specific listing of individual freedoms was unnecessary because the national government possessed only enumerated powers; the power to restrict free speech or press or religion was not an enumerated power, so the national government could not do these things. But **Anti-Federalists** (who did not favor ratifying the Constitution and argued for states' rights) in the state ratifying conventions were suspicious of the power of the new national government.[6] They were not satisfied with the mere inference that the national government could not interfere with personal liberty; they wanted specific written guarantees of fundamental freedoms. The **Federalist** supporters of the new Constitution agreed to add a Bill of Rights as the first ten amendments to the Constitution in order to win ratification in the state conventions. This is why our fundamental freedoms—speech, press, religion, assembly, petition, and due process of law—appear in the Constitution as *amendments* (Table 7-1).

Bill of Rights
the first ten amendments to the U.S. Constitution listing individual freedoms and restrictions on government power

Anti-Federalists
those who argued against ratification of the U.S. Constitution; they were wary of a strong national government and favored states' rights

Federalists
advocates for ratification of the U.S. Constitution

TABLE 7-1   THE BILL OF RIGHTS

The Bill of Rights limits the power of government by proscribing what it cannot do, and it also specifies some individual rights citizens enjoy. In recommending the rights to be included in the Bill of Rights, James Madison chose from among more than two hundred suggestions.* That the rights he selected still have applicability today is a testament to his forethought and understanding of human nature and the nature of governments.

Amendment I
Congress shall make no law respecting an establishment of religion, or prohibiting the free exercise thereof; or abridging the freedom of speech, or of the press; or the right of the people peaceably to assemble, and to petition the government for a redress of grievances.

Amendment II
A well regulated militia, being necessary to the security of a free state, the right of the people to keep and bear arms, shall not be infringed.

Amendment III
No soldier shall, in time of peace be quartered in any house, without the consent of the owner, nor in time of war, but in a manner to be prescribed by law.

Amendment IV
The right of the people to be secure in their persons, houses, papers, and effects, against unreasonable searches and seizures, shall not be violated, and no warrants shall issue, but upon probable cause, supported by oath or affirmation, and particularly describing the place to be searched, and the persons or things to be seized.

Amendment V
No person shall be held to answer for a capital, or otherwise infamous crime, unless on a presentment or indictment of a grand jury, except in cases arising in the land or naval forces, or in the militia, when in actual service in time of war or public danger; nor shall any person be subject for the same offense to be twice put in jeopardy of life or limb; nor shall be compelled in any criminal case to be a witness against himself, nor be deprived of life, liberty, or property, without due process of law; nor shall private property be taken for public use, without just compensation.

Amendment VI
In all criminal prosecutions, the accused shall enjoy the right to a speedy and public trial, by an impartial jury of the state and district wherein the crime shall have been committed, which district shall have been previously ascertained by law, and to be informed of the nature and cause of the accusation; to be confronted with the witnesses against him; to have compulsory process for obtaining witnesses in his favor, and to have the assistance of counsel for his defense.

Amendment VII
In suits at common law, where the value in controversy shall exceed twenty dollars, the right of trial by jury shall be preserved, and no fact tried by a jury, shall be otherwise reexamined in any court of the United States, than according to the rules of the common law.

Amendment VIII
Excessive bail shall not be required, nor excessive fines imposed, nor cruel and unusual punishments inflicted.

Amendment IX
The enumeration in the Constitution, of certain rights, shall not be construed to deny or disparage others retained by the people.

Amendment X
The powers not delegated to the United States by the Constitution, nor prohibited by it to the states, are reserved to the states respectively, or to the people.

* Leonard W. Levy, Origins of the Bill of Rights (New Haven, CT: Yale University Press, 1999).

The Constitution Structures Government

The Constitution that emerged from the Philadelphia convention on September 17, 1787, founded a new government with a unique structure. That structure was designed to implement the founders' belief that government rested on the consent of the people, that government power must be limited, and that the purpose of government was the protection of individual liberty and property. But the founders were political realists; they did not have any romantic notions about the wisdom and virtue of "the people." James Madison wrote: "A dependence on the people is, no doubt, the primary control on the government; but experience has taught mankind the necessity of auxiliary precautions."[7] The key structural arrangements in the U.S. Constitution—national supremacy, federalism, republicanism, separation of powers, checks and balances, and judicial review—all reflect the founders' desire to create a strong national government while ensuring that it would not become a threat to liberty or property.

National Supremacy

National supremacy simply means that when state and federal law conflict in an area in which both have jurisdiction, federal (national) laws are superior. The heart of the Constitution is the National Supremacy Clause of Article VI:

> This Constitution, and the Laws of the United States which shall be made in Pursuance thereof; and all Treaties made, or which shall be made, under the Authority of the United States, shall be the supreme Law of the Land; and the Judges in every State shall be bound thereby, any Thing in the Constitution or Laws of any State to the Contrary notwithstanding.

This sentence ensures that the Constitution itself is the supreme law of the land. Laws made by Congress must not conflict with the Constitution. The Constitution and the laws of Congress supersede state laws.

national supremacy
when state and federal law conflict in an area in which both have jurisdiction, federal (national) laws are superior

Federalism

The Constitution divides power between the nation and the states, creating a federalist system. **Federalism** recognizes that both the national government and the state governments have independent legal authority over their own citizens: Both can pass their own laws, levy their own taxes, and maintain their own courts.[8] The states have an important role in the selection of national officeholders—in the apportionment of congressional seats and in the allocation of electoral votes for president. Most important, perhaps, both the Congress and three-quarters of the states must consent to changes in the Constitution itself.

federalism
the division of power between states and nations

Republicanism

To the founders, a **republican government** (**republicanism**, not to be confused with the name of the Republican political party) meant the delegation of powers by the people to a small number of representatives "whose wisdom may best discern the true interest of their country, and whose patriotism and love of justice, will be least likely to sacrifice it to temporary or partial considerations." The founders believed that government rests ultimately on "the consent of the

republican government (republicanism)
government by elected representatives of the people

direct democracy
people themselves vote directly on issues, rather than their representatives

governed." But their notion of republicanism envisioned decision making by *representatives* of the people, not the people themselves. The U.S. Constitution does not provide for **direct democracy**—voting by the people on national questions—that is, unlike many state constitutions today, it does not provide for national *referenda* (see Controversies in Social Science: "Direct Democracy versus Representative Democracy"). Moreover, in the original Constitution of 1787, only the House of Representatives are elected directly by voters in the states. Members of the Senate were elected by state legislatures; not until the ratification of the Seventeenth Amendment in 1913 would voters directly elect their U.S. senators. The president is elected by "electors" (chosen in a way prescribed by state legislatures) and the U.S. Supreme Court and other federal judges are appointed by the president with the consent of the Senate.

These republican arrangements may appear undemocratic from our perspective today, but in 1787 this Constitution was more democratic than any other governing system in the world. Most other nations of that time were governed by monarchs, emperors, chieftains, and hereditary aristocracies. Later democratic impulses in America greatly altered the original Constitution and reshaped it into an even more democratic document. Specifically, the Constitution has reflected the increasing democratization of American society through the expansion of suffrage—the right to vote. Constitutionally, we see suffrage expanding to African Americans, women, and those 18 to 20 years old, mirroring the changes in society's notions about who is qualified to elect the nation's leaders.

The Separation of Powers

separation of powers
the principle of dividing government powers among the executive, legislative, and judicial branches

The **separation of powers** in the national government—separate legislative, executive, and judicial branches—was intended by the nation's founders as an additional safeguard for liberty. Number 51 of *The Federalist Papers*, written to convince colonists of the merits of ratifying the Constitution, expresses the logic behind creating separate branches of government and giving them checks over each other:

> Ambition must be made to counteract ambition. . . . It may be a reflection on human nature, that such devices should be necessary to control the abuses of government. But what is government itself, but the greatest of all reflections on human nature? If men were angels, no government would be necessary. If angels were to govern men, neither external nor internal controls on government would be necessary. In framing a government which is to be administered by men over men, the great difficulty lies in this: you must first enable the government to control the governed; and in the next place oblige it to control itself.[9]

In practical terms, this has meant that the power to create, administer, and judge the laws has rested with the legislative, executive, and judicial branches, respectively.

Checks and Balances

checks and balances
the principle whereby each branch of the government exercises a check on the actions of the others, preventing too great a concentration of power in any one person or group of persons

Each of the major decision-making bodies of American government possesses important **checks and balances** (Figure 7-1) over the decisions of the others. No bill can become law without the approval of both the House and the Senate.

ZUMA Press, Inc. / Alamy

The president shares legislative power by setting the congressional agenda through his State of the Union address, shown here in 2012. Sitting behind President Obama are Vice President Joe Biden and House Speaker John Boehner (far right).

The president shares in legislative power through the veto and the responsibility of the office to "give to the Congress information of the State of the Union, and recommend to their consideration such measures as he shall judge necessary and expedient." The president also can convene sessions of Congress. But the president's powers to make appointments and treaties are shared by the Senate. Congress also can override executive vetoes.

The president must execute the laws, but to do so he or she must rely on the executive departments, and they must be created by Congress. Moreover, the executive branch cannot spend money that has not been appropriated by Congress.

Federal judges, including members of the U.S. Supreme Court, must be appointed by the president, with the consent of the Senate. Congress must create lower and intermediate courts, establish the number of judges, fix the jurisdiction of lower federal courts, and make "exceptions" to the appellate jurisdiction of the Supreme Court.

Perhaps the keystone of the system of checks and balances is the idea of **judicial review**, an original contribution by the nation's founders to the science of government. Judicial review is the power of the courts to strike down laws that they believe conflict with the Constitution. Article VI grants federal courts the power of judicial review of *state* decisions, specifying that the Constitution and the laws and treaties of the national government are the supreme law of the land, superseding anything in any state laws or constitutions. However, nowhere does the Constitution specify that the U.S. Supreme Court has power of judicial review of executive action or of federal laws enacted by Congress. This principle was instead established in the case of *Marbury v. Madison* in 1803, when Chief Justice John Marshall argued convincingly that the founders had intended

judicial review
the power of the courts to strike down laws they believe conflict with the Constitution

CONTROVERSIES IN SOCIAL SCIENCE

Direct Democracy versus Representative Democracy

Democracy means popular participation in government. (The Greek roots of the word mean "rule by the many.") But "popular participation" can have different meanings. To our nation's founders, who were quite ambivalent about the wisdom of democracy, it meant that the voice of the people would be *represented* in government. *Representational democracy* means the selection of government officials by vote of the people in periodic elections open to competition in which candidates and voters can freely express themselves.

Direct democracy means that the people themselves can initiate and decide policy questions by popular vote. The founders were profoundly skeptical of this form of democracy. *The U.S. Constitution has no provision for direct voting by the people on national policy questions.* It was not until over one hundred years after the U.S. Constitution was written that widespread support developed in the American states for direct voter participation in policy making. Direct democracy developed in states and communities, and it is to be found today *only* in state and local government.

Initiative and Referendum   The *initiative* is a form of direct democracy whereby a specific number or percent of voters, through the use of petition, may have a proposed state constitutional amendment or state law placed on the ballot for adoption or rejection by the electorate of a state. This process bypasses the legislature and allows citizens to both propose and adopt laws and constitutional amendments.

The *referendum* is a device by which the electorate must approve citizen initiatives or decisions of the legislature before these become law or become part of the state constitution. Most states require a favorable referendum vote for a state constitutional amendment. Referenda on state laws may be submitted by the legislature (when legislators want to shift decision-making responsibility to the people), or referenda may be demanded by popular petition (when the people wish to change laws passed by the legislature).

Arguments for Direct Democracy   Proponents of direct democracy make several strong arguments on behalf of the initiative and referendum devices.

- Direct democracy enhances government responsiveness and accountability. The threat of a successful initiative and referendum drive—indeed, sometimes the mere circulation of a petition—encourages officials to take the popular actions.

- Direct democracy allows citizen groups to bring their concern directly to the public. For example, taxpayer groups have been able through the initiative and referendum devices to place their concerns on the public agenda.
- Direct democracy stimulates debate about policy issues. In elections with important referendum issues on the ballot, campaigns tend to be more issue oriented.
- Direct democracy stimulates voters' interest and improves election-day turnout. Controversial issues on the ballot—the death penalty, abortion, gun control, taxes, gay rights, a ban on racial preferences, and so on—bring out additional voters.

Arguments for Representative Democracy   Opponents of direct democracy, from our nation's founders to the present, argue that representative democracy offers far better protection for individual liberty and the rights of minorities than direct democracy. The founders constructed a system of checks and balances not so much to protect against the oppression of a ruler but to protect against the tyranny of the majority. Opponents of direct democracy echo many of the founders' arguments:

- Direct democracy encourages majorities to sacrifice the rights of individuals and minorities. This argument supposes that voters are generally less tolerant than elected officials.
- Voters are not sufficiently informed to cast intelligent ballots on many issues. Many voters cast their vote in a referendum without ever having considered the issue before going into the polling booth.
- A referendum does not allow consideration of alternative policies or modifications or amendments to the proposition set forth on the ballot. In contrast, legislators devote a great deal of attention to writing, rewriting, and amending bills and seeking out compromises among interests.
- Direct democracy enables special interests to mount expensive initiative and referendum campaigns. Although proponents of direct democracy argue that these devices allow citizens to bypass legislatures dominated by special-interest groups, in fact, only a fairly well-financed group can mount a statewide campaign on behalf of a referendum issue.

SOURCE: See Thomas E. Cronin, *Direct Democracy* (Cambridge, MA: Harvard University Press, 1989).

FIGURE 7-1   CHECKS AND BALANCES IN THE U.S. GOVERNMENT

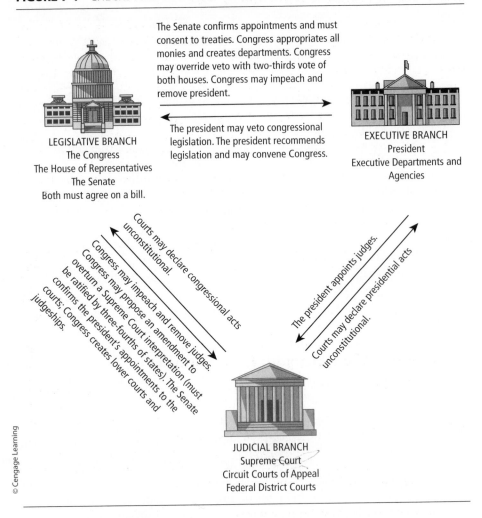

the Supreme Court to have the power of invalidating not only state laws and constitutions but also any laws of Congress or executive actions that came into conflict with the Constitution of the United States. Thus, the Court stands as the final defender of the constitutional principles against the encroachments of popularly elected legislatures and executives.

Federalism and the Growth of Power in the Federal Government

Since the founding of the United States, the power of the national government has increased significantly.[10] Major developments in the history of American federalism have contributed to this increase in national power.

Expansion of Implied National Power

Chief Justice John Marshall added immeasurably to national power in *McCulloch v. Maryland* (1819) when he broadly interpreted the "necessary and proper" clause of Article I, Section 8, of the Constitution, which states that the Congress has the power "to make all laws necessary and proper for carrying into Execution the foregoing powers, and all other Powers vested in this Constitution in the Government of the United States . . . ." Marshall asserted powers for the federal government that were not explicitly expressed in the Constitution. In approving the establishment of a national bank (a power not specifically delegated to the national government in the Constitution), Marshall wrote:

> Let the end be legitimate, let it be within the scope of the Constitution, and all means which are appropriate, which are plainly adopted to that end, which are not prohibited but consistent with the letter and the spirit of the Constitution, are constitutional.[11]

Since then, the "necessary and proper" clause has been called the "implied powers" clause or even the "elastic" clause, suggesting that the national government can do anything not specifically prohibited by the Constitution. Given this tradition, the courts are unlikely to hold an act of Congress unconstitutional simply because no formal constitutional grant of power gives Congress the power to act.

The Civil War as a Victory for Federalism

Although we often view the Civil War as a war about slavery, the war also was the nation's greatest crisis in federalism. A key question decided by the war was whether a state has the right to oppose federal action by force of arms. The same issue was at stake when, to enforce desegregation, the federal government sent troops to Little Rock, Arkansas, in 1957; to Oxford, Mississippi, in 1962; and to Tuscaloosa, Alabama, in 1963. In these confrontations, it was clear that the federal government held the military advantage.

Growth of Interstate Commerce

The growth of national power under the interstate commerce clause is also an important development in American federalism. The Industrial Revolution created a national economy governable only by a national government. Yet, until the 1930s, the U.S. Supreme Court placed many obstacles in the way of government regulation of the economy. Finally, in *National Labor Relations Board v. Jones & Laughlin Steel Corporation* (1937), the Supreme Court recognized the principle that Congress could regulate production and distribution of goods and services for a national market under the interstate commerce clause. As a result, the national government gained control over wages, prices, production, marketing, labor relations, and all other important aspects of the national economy. Today, we can see government regulation of interstate commerce in our everyday lives, whether in the minimum wages paid by employers or the federal regulations on workplace conditions.

Federal Civil Rights Enforcement

Over the years, the U.S. Supreme Court has built a national system of civil rights based on the Fourteenth Amendment, ratified after the Civil War: "No State shall . . . deprive any person of life, liberty, or property, without due process of law; nor deny to any person within its jurisdiction the equal protection of the laws." In early cases, the Supreme Court held that the general guarantee of *liberty* in the first phrase (the due process clause) prevents state and local governments from interfering with free speech, press, religion, and other personal liberties. Later, particularly after *Brown v. Board of Education of Topeka* in 1954, the Court also used the equal protection clause to prohibit state and local government officials from denying equality of opportunity.

Federal Grants-in-Aid

grants-in-aid
payments of funds from the national government to state or local governments, usually with conditions attached to their uses

The federal government also exerts power through the use of money. The income tax (established in 1913) gave the federal government the authority to raise large sums of money, which it spent for the "general welfare," as well as for defense. Gradually, the federal government expanded its power in states and communities by use of **grants-in-aid**. During the Great Depression of the 1930s, the national government used its taxing and spending powers in a number of areas formerly reserved to states and communities. Congress began grants-in-aid programs to states and communities for public assistance, unemployment compensation, employment services, child welfare, public housing, urban renewal, highway construction, and vocational education and rehabilitation.

Today, federal grants-in-aid might pay for more police officers in your town, the creation of a bike path in your county, textbooks in your public schools, or highway improvement programs in your state. Table 7-2 shows the number of governments that exist in the United States. Nearly every government receives federal monies to provide services, though oftentimes these monies are channeled through the states to counties, municipalities, and school and special districts.

TABLE 7-2   THE NUMBER OF GOVERNMENTS IN THE UNITED STATES TODAY

Federal (national) government	1
State governments	50
County governments	3,043
Municipal and township governments	36,011
School districts	13,051
Special Services districts*	37,381

* Includes governments that administer natural resources, fire protection services, or housing and community development.

SOURCE: www.census.gov//govs/cog/GovOrgTab03ss.html.

Federalism Today

Today, federal grants-in-aid are the principal source of federal power over states and communities. Nearly one-quarter of all state and local government revenues are from federal grants. These grants almost always come with detailed conditions regarding how the money can be used. *Categorical grants* specify particular projects or particular individuals eligible to receive funds; *block grants* provide some discretion to state or local officials in using the money for a particular government function, such as law enforcement. Federal grant money is distributed in hundreds of separate programs, but welfare (including Temporary Assistance for Needy Families, or TANF) and health (including Medicaid) account for nearly two-thirds of federal aid money.

Federal mandates, which are requirements issued by the national government that state and local governments must comply with, also centralize power in Washington. The federal government often passes laws requiring state and local governments to perform functions or undertake tasks that Congress deems in the public interest. Many of these federal mandates are "unfunded," that is, Congress does not provide any money to carry out these mandated functions or tasks even though they impose costs on states and communities. For example, environmental protection laws passed by Congress require local governments to provide specified levels of sewage treatment, and the Americans with Disabilities Act requires state and local governments to build ramps and alter curbs in public streets and buildings.

federal mandate
a requirement issued by the national government with which state and local governments must comply

Devolution?

Over the years, various efforts have been made to return power to states and communities. President Ronald Reagan was partially successful in his "New Federalism" efforts; many categorical grant programs were consolidated into block grants with greater discretion given to state and local governments.

In recent decades, Congress has considered the **devolution** of some government responsibilities from the national government to the states and their local governments. So far, welfare cash assistance is the only major federal program to "devolve" back to the states. Since Franklin D. Roosevelt's New Deal, with its federal guarantee of cash Aid to Families with Dependent Children (AFDC), low-income mothers and children had enjoyed a legal "entitlement" to welfare payments. Welfare reform in 1996, however, increased the power of state government by devolving responsibility for determining eligibility to the state. This is a major change in federal social welfare policy (see Chapter 11) and may become a model for future shedding of federal entitlement programs.

devolution
the transfer of federal programs to state and local governments

During the George W. Bush administration, some evidence indicates a trend away from devolution and toward increased federal involvement, particularly in education policy. The federal No Child Left Behind Act has created a vast array of federal mandates that local school districts must comply with to continue to receive federal funding. Some of these requirements, including mandatory yearly assessment testing of students, have been met with criticism by teachers and administrators. Nonetheless, the act represents a radical departure from the devolutionary trend of previous administrations.

Power and the Branches of the Federal Government

The changes in federalist relations and the increase in size of the national government have necessarily resulted in changes in the powers of the branches of the federal government—the Congress, the presidency, and the judiciary. When the founders drafted the Constitution, the powers of the Congress were quite strong, while their fear of a tyrannical king-type leader made them limit the powers of the presidency. The powers of the judiciary were barely defined. Over the years, the powers of all three branches of government have grown considerably, both because of circumstance and because of the authority exerted by individuals who have served in these branches.

Presidential Power

Americans look to their president for "greatness." Great presidents are those associated with great events—George Washington with the founding of the nation, Abraham Lincoln with the preservation of the Union, Franklin D. Roosevelt with the nation's emergence from economic depression and victory in World War II (see Focus: "Rating the Presidents"). People tend to believe that the president is responsible for "peace and prosperity" as well as "change." They expect their president to present a "vision" of America's future and to symbolize the nation.

Providing National Leadership

The president personifies American government for most people.[12] People expect the president to act decisively and effectively to deal with national problems. They expect the president to be compassionate—to show concern for problems confronting individual citizens. The president, while playing these roles, is the focus of public attention and is the nation's leading celebrity. Presidents receive more media coverage than any other person in the nation, for everything from their policy statements to their favorite foods.

The nation looks to the president for leadership. The president has the capacity to mobilize public opinion, to communicate directly with the American people, to offer direction and reassurance, and to advance policy initiatives in both foreign and domestic affairs.

One source of presidential power is being viewed favorably by the American people. Presidential popularity is an important asset in giving presidents power and providing national leadership. Popular presidents cannot *always* transfer their popularity into power in the way of policy successes, but popular presidents usually have more success than unpopular presidents. Presidential popularity is regularly tracked in national opinion polls. Over the years, national surveys have asked the American public the following: "Do you approve or disapprove of the way the current president is handling his job?" (see Focus: "Explaining Presidential Approval Ratings"). Generally, presidents have been more successful in providing leadership in both foreign and domestic affairs when they have enjoyed high approval ratings.

Managing Crises

In time of crisis, the American people look to their president to take action, to provide reassurance, and to protect the nation and its people. For example, when the economic crisis hit in 2008, expectations were high for President Barack Obama, who had just been elected president. It is the president, not the Congress or the courts, who is expected to speak on behalf of the people in time of national triumph and tragedy. The president also gives expression to the nation's sadness in tragedy and strives to help the nation go forward. For example, in the aftermath of September 11, 2001, then–President George W. Bush addressed the nation and also attended memorial services where he performed in a ceremonial capacity as the nation's "chief mourner." The president also gives expression to the nation's pride in victory. The nation's heroes are welcomed and its championship sports teams are feted in the White House Rose Garden.

Providing Policy Leadership

The president is expected to set policy priorities for the nation. Most policy initiatives originate in the White House and various departments and agencies of the executive branch and then are forwarded to Congress with the president's approval. Presidential programs are submitted to Congress in the form of messages, including the president's annual State of the Union Address to Congress and the Budget of the United States Government, which the president presents each year to Congress.

As a political leader, the president is expected to mobilize political support for policy proposals. It is not enough for the president to send policy proposals to Congress. The president must rally public opinion, lobby members of Congress, win legislative battles, and perhaps even fend off judicial challenges to policy proposals. Take, for example, President Obama's reform of the nation's health care system. In addition to fighting a scathing battle to get the measure passed in Congress, President Obama had to court the public on this matter and fend off legal challenges that questioned the constitutionality of the new law. To avoid being perceived as weak or ineffective, presidents must get their key legislative proposals through Congress. Presidents use the threat of a veto to prevent Congress from passing bills that they oppose; when forced to veto a bill, they fight to prevent an override of the veto. The president thus is responsible for "getting things done" in the policy arena.

Managing the Economy

The American people hold the president responsible for maintaining a healthy economy, or for fixing a damaged one. Presidents are blamed for economic downturns, whether or not government policies had anything to do with market conditions. The president is expected to "Do something!" in the face of high unemployment, declining personal income, high mortgage rates, rising inflation, or even a stock market crash. Herbert Hoover in 1932, Gerald Ford in 1976, Jimmy Carter in 1980, and George H. W. Bush in 1992—all incumbent presidents defeated for reelection during recessions—learned the hard way that the

FOCUS

Rating the Presidents

From time to time, historians and political scientists have been asked to rate U.S. presidents. The ratings given the presidents have been remarkably consistent. Abraham Lincoln, George Washington, Franklin Roosevelt, Woodrow Wilson, and Thomas Jefferson are universally recognized as the greatest American presidents. Ulysses S. Grant and Warren G. Harding both dominate on the bottom, or "failure" side, of most rating lists. It is more difficult for historians to rate recent presidents; the views of historians are influenced by current political controversies. Often the passage of time allows scholars to make more objective evaluations. Richard Nixon may be evaluated higher by future historians than he is today. How would you rate Bill Clinton? Barack Obama?

Schlesinger (1948)	Schlesinger (1962)	Dodder (1970)	Murray (1982)	Ridings & McIver (1996)
Great	**Great**	**Accomplishments of Administration**	**Presidential Rank**	**Overall Ranking**
1. Lincoln	1. Lincoln	1. Lincoln	1. Lincoln	1. Lincoln
2. Washington	2. Washington	2. F. Roosevelt	2. F. Roosevelt	2. F. Roosevelt
3. F. Roosevelt	3. F. Roosevelt	3. Washington	3. Washington	3. Washington
4. Wilson	4. Wilson	4. Jefferson	4. Jefferson	4. Jefferson
5. Jefferson	5. Jefferson	5. T. Roosevelt	5. T. Roosevelt	5. T. Roosevelt
6. Jackson	**Near Great**	6. Truman	6. Wilson	6. Wilson
Near Great	6. Jackson	7. Wilson	7. Jackson	7. Truman
7. T. Roosevelt	7. T. Roosevelt	8. Jackson	8. Truman	8. Jackson
8. Cleveland	8. Polk, Truman (tie)	9. L. Johnson	9. J. Adams	9. Eisenhower
9. J. Adams	9. J. Adams	10. Polk	10. L. Johnson	10. Madison
10. Polk	10. Cleveland	11. J. Adams	11. Eisenhower	11. Polk
Average	**Average**	12. Kennedy	12. Polk	12. L. Johnson
11. J. Q. Adams	11. Madison	13. Monroe	13. Kennedy	13. Monroe
12. Monroe	12. J. Q. Adams	14. Cleveland	14. Madison	14. J. Adams
13. Hayes	13. Hayes	15. Madison	15. Monroe	15. Kennedy
			16. J. Q. Adams	16. Cleveland

Schlesinger (1948)	Schlesinger (1962)	Dodder (1970)	Murray (1982)	Ridings & McIver (1996)
14. Madison	14. McKinley	16. Taft	17. Cleveland	17. McKinley
15. Van Buren	15. Taft	17. McKinley	18. McKinley	18. J. Q. Adams
16. Taft	16. Van Buren	18. J. Q. Adams	19. Taft	19. Carter
17. Arthur	17. Monroe	19. Hoover	20. Van Buren	20. Taft
18. McKinley	18. Hoover	20. Eisenhower	21. Hoover	21. Van Buren
19. A. Johnson	19. Arthur, Eisenhower (tie)	21. A. Johnson	22. Hayes	22. G. H. W. Bush
20. Hoover		22. Van Buren	23. Arthur	23. Clinton
21. B. Harrison	20. B. Harrison	23. Arthur	24. Ford	24. Hoover
	21. A. Johnson	24. Hayes	25. Carter	25. Hayes
Below Average	22. B. Harrison	25. Tyler	26. B. Harrison	26. Reagan
22. Tyler	23. A. Johnson	26. B. Harrison	27. Taylor	27. Ford
23. Coolidge		27. Taylor	28. Tyler	28. Arthur
24. Fillmore	**Below Average**	28. Buchanan	29. Fillmore	29. Taylor
25. Taylor	24. Taylor	29. Fillmore	30. Coolidge	30. Garfield
26. Buchanan	25. Tyler	30. Coolidge	31. Pierce	31. B. Harrison
27. Pierce	26. Fillmore	31. Pierce	32. A. Johnson	32. Nixon
Failure	27. Coolidge	32. Grant	33. Buchanan	33. Coolidge
28. Grant	28. Pierce	33. Harding	34. Nixon	34. Tyler
29. Harding	29. Buchanan		35. Grant	35. W. Harrison
			36. Harding	36. Fillmore
	Failure			37. Pierce
	30. Grant			38. Grant
	31. Harding			39. A. Johnson
				40. Buchanan
				41. Harding

Note: These ratings result from surveys of scholars ranging in numbers from 55 to 950.

SOURCES: Arthur Murphy, "Evaluating the Presidents of the United States," *Presidential Studies Quarterly* 14 (1984): 117–126; William J. Ridings Jr., and Stuart B. McIver, *Rating the Presidents* (Secaucus, NJ: Citadel Press, 1997).

FOCUS

Explaining Presidential Approval Ratings

President-watching is a favorite pastime among political scientists. Regular surveys of the American people ask the question "Do you approve or disapprove of the way the current president is handling his job?" By asking this same question over time about presidents, political scientists can monitor the ups and downs of presidential popularity. Then they can attempt to explain presidential popularity by examining events that correspond to changes in presidential approval ratings.

One hypothesis that helps explain presidential approval ratings centers on the election cycle. The hypothesis is that presidential popularity is usually highest immediately after election or reelection, but it steadily erodes over time. Note that this hypothesis tends to be supported by the survey data in the accompanying figure. This simple graph shows, over time, the percentage of survey respondents who say they approve of the way the president is handling his job. Presidents usually begin their administrations with high approval ratings—Barack Obama started out his presidential term in 2009 with a 69 percent approval rating. Presidents and their advisors generally know about this "honeymoon"-period hypothesis and try to use it to their advantage by pushing hard for their policies in Congress early in the term.

P<small>RESIDENTIAL</small> A<small>PPROVAL</small> R<small>ATINGS</small>

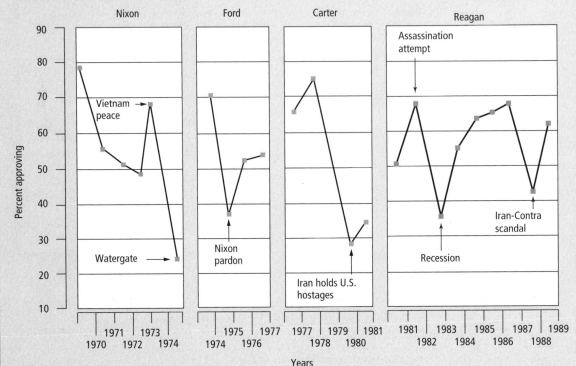

Another hypothesis centers on the effects of international crises. Initially, people "rally 'round the flag" when the nation is confronted with an international threat and the president orders military action. President George H. W. Bush registered an all-time high in presidential approval ratings during the Persian Gulf War in 1991. But prolonged, indecisive warfare erodes popular support for a president. The public approved of President Johnson's handling of his job when he first sent U.S. ground combat troops into Vietnam in 1965, but support for the president waned over time as military operations mounted.

Major scandals may hurt presidential popularity and effectiveness. The Watergate scandal produced a low of 22 percent approval for Nixon just prior to his resignation. Reagan's generally high approval ratings were blemished by the Iran–Contra scandal in 1987. Yet Clinton's ratings continued their upward trend despite a White House sex scandal and a vote for impeachment by a Republican-controlled House of Representatives.

Finally, it is widely hypothesized that economic recessions erode presidential popularity. Every president in office during a recession has suffered loss of popular approval, including Reagan during the 1982 recession. But no president suffered a more precipitous decline in approval ratings than George H. W. Bush, whose popularity plummeted from its Gulf War high of 89 percent to a low of 37 percent in only a year, largely as a result of recession. Barack Obama did rival Bush though, with a high honeymoon approval rating of 69 percent in 2009, followed by a low of 38 in August 2011, an evaluation many believed was a reflection of the poor economy.

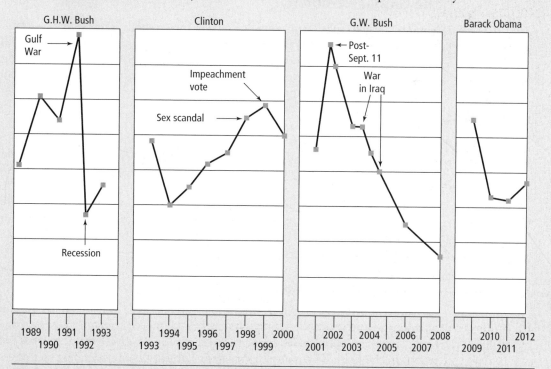

general public holds the president responsible for hard economic times. Presidents must have an economic strategy to stimulate the economy—tax incentives to spur investments, spending proposals to create jobs, and plans to lower interest rates. In today's economy, they must also develop programs to improve America's international competitiveness. Presidents also manage the economy through their appointment of the Federal Reserve Board, as is discussed in Chapter 8.

Presidents themselves are partly responsible for these public expectations. Incumbent presidents have been quick to take credit for economic growth, low inflation, low interest rates, and low unemployment. And presidential candidates in recessionary times invariably promise "to get the economy moving again."

Managing the Government

As the chief executive of a mammoth federal bureaucracy with 2.8 million civilian employees, the president is responsible for implementing policy—that is, for achieving policy goals. Policy making does not end when a law is passed. Policy implementation involves issuing orders, creating organizations, recruiting and assigning personnel, disbursing funds, overseeing work, and evaluating results. It is true that the president cannot perform all these tasks personally. But the ultimate responsibility for implementation—in the words of the Constitution, "to take Care that the Laws be faithfully executed"—rests with the president. Or as the sign on Harry Truman's desk put it: "The Buck Stops Here."

The Global President

Nations strive to speak with a single voice in international affairs; for the United States, the global voice is that of the president. As commander-in-chief of the armed forces of the United States, the president is a powerful voice in foreign affairs.[14] Efforts by Congress to speak on behalf of the nation in foreign affairs and to limit the war-making power of the president have been generally unsuccessful. It is the president who orders American troops into combat. It is the president's finger that rests on the nuclear trigger.

As the "leader of the free world" the president of the United States has the unique ability to make an imprint not only on the United States' foreign policy, but also on the entire international political environment. For example, during the George W. Bush administration, U.S. foreign policy was shaped by the notion that a "clash of civilizations" characterized relations between the United States and many Muslim nations, while the Obama presidency stressed a more conciliatory relationship with these countries (see Chapter 14 for further discussion of U.S. foreign policy under these presidents).

Commander-in-Chief

Global power derives primarily from the president's role as commander-in-chief of the armed forces of the United States. Presidential command over the armed forces is not merely symbolic; presidents may issue direct military orders to troops in the field. For example, President Barack Obama's decision to increase troops in Afghanistan in a military surge strategy was a manifestation of his role of commander-in-chief. This role is one of the defining aspects of the presidency: As president, George Washington personally led troops to end the Whiskey Rebellion in 1794; Abraham Lincoln issued direct orders to his generals in the Civil War; Lyndon Johnson personally chose bombing targets in Vietnam; and George H. W. Bush personally ordered the Gulf War cease-fire after one hundred hours of ground fighting. As commander-in-chief, President George W. Bush issued a military order concerning the detention, treatment, and trial of noncitizen "combatants" believed to be involved in terrorism. All presidents, whether they are experienced in world affairs or not, soon learn after taking office that their influence throughout the world heavily depends on the command of capable military forces.

Modest Constitutional Powers

Popular expectations of presidential leadership far exceed the formal constitutional powers granted to the president. Compared with the Congress, the president has only modest constitutionally expressed powers (Table 7-3). Nevertheless, presidents over the years have consistently exceeded their specific grants of power in Article II, from Thomas Jefferson's decision to double the land area

TABLE 7-3   CONSTITUTIONAL POWERS OF THE PRESIDENT

Chief Administrator
Implement policy: "take Care that the Laws be faithfully executed" (Article II, Section 3)
Supervise executive branch of government
Appoint and remove executive officials (Article II, Section 2)
Prepare executive budget for submission to Congress (by law of Congress)
Chief Legislator
Initiate policy: "give to the Congress Information of the State of the Union, and recommend to their Consideration such Measures as he shall judge necessary and expedient" (Article II, Section 3)
Veto legislation passed by Congress, subject to override by a two-thirds vote in both houses
Convene special session of Congress "on extraordinary Occasions" (Article II, Section 3)
Chief Diplomat
Make treaties "with the Advice and Consent of the Senate" (Article II, Section 2)
Exercise the power of diplomatic recognition: "receive Ambassadors" (Article II, Section 3)
Make executive agreements (by custom and international law)
Commander-in-Chief
Command U.S. armed forces: "The president shall be Commander in Chief of the Army and Navy" (Article II, Section 2)
Appoint military officers
Chief of State
"The executive Power shall be vested in a President" (Article II, Section 1)
Grant reprieves and pardons (Article II, Section 2)
Represent the nation as chief of state
Appoint federal court and Supreme Court judges (Article II, Section 2)

of the United States with the Louisiana Purchase to William Jefferson Clinton's decision to send U.S. troops to keep the peace in Bosnia and Kosovo.

Limits on Presidential Power

Despite the great powers of the office, no president can monopolize policy making. The president functions within an established political system and can exercise power only within its framework.[15] The president cannot act outside existing political consensus, outside the "rules of the game." To ensure that the president does not overstep constitutionally-prescribed boundaries, both the Congress and the courts provide checks on the president, as described earlier in this chapter. So presidents may face a Congress that overrides a presidential veto, or fails to confirm judicial appointments; or a Court that declares a presidential action unconstitutional.

Electing the President

The 2008 presidential election proved to be historical, with Barack Obama succeeding in his quest to become the first African American elected president of the United States. Obama came to be the Democratic nominee for the presidency via another historic contest: He and Sen. Hillary Rodham Clinton vied for their party's nomination, each seeking to make history (she attempted to be the first woman major party nominee and U.S. president). Obama won the Democratic nomination with a well-organized and well-financed campaign that targeted young and first-time primary voters, and made savvy use of new technologies, including social networking sites like Facebook and MySpace.

These technologies would prove even more important in the 2012 contest between Obama and Republican Governor Mitt Romney. That year, we saw both campaigns rely on technology as tool of campaigning. The Republicans and Democrats each used the Internet and cellular technology to communicate with voters, mobilize supporters, organize their campaigns, and to raise money.

While the 2012 election was groundbreaking in terms of the campaigns' use of technology, back in the year 2000 another dramatic election took place. That year, Americans were given a dramatic reminder that the president of the United States is *not* elected by nationwide popular vote but rather by a majority of votes in the Electoral College. In most states, electors are chosen in winner-take-all system, whereby the candidate who receives the most popular votes wins all of that states' electoral votes. This system typically serves to exaggerate the popular margin of victory. But in 2000, Democrat Al Gore won 500,000 more votes nationwide (out of over 100 million cast) than his opponent Republican George W. Bush. But Bush won a majority of the states' electoral votes—271 to 267—the narrowest margin in modern American history. And Florida's crucial 25 electoral votes were decided by the U.S. Supreme Court more than a month after election day.

The Electoral College

The U.S. Constitution provides that the president will be chosen by the majority of the number of "electors" chosen by the states. Article II says "Each state shall appoint, in such Manner as the Legislature thereof may direct, a Number of Electors, equal to the whole Number of Senators and Representatives to which the State may be entitled in the Congress . . ." This means that each state gets a number of electors to the Electoral College equal to the size of their congressional delegation. Each state's congressional delegation is composed of two U.S. senators and a number of members of the House of Representatives based on the state's population. Although the number of each state's electors is equal to the size of their congressional delegation, the members of Congress themselves are not the actual electors. The number of members of the House of Representatives is determined every ten years after the U.S. census is taken. Thus, the number of electoral votes of each state is subject to change after each ten-year census. The Twenty-Third Amendment granted three electoral votes to the District of Columbia even though it has no voting members in Congress. Winning the presidency requires winning enough states to garner at least 270 of the 538 total electoral votes.

The U.S. Constitution specifically gives state legislatures the power to determine how electors in their states are to be chosen. By 1840 the spirit of Jacksonian democracy (see Chapter 6) had inspired state legislatures to allow the voters of their states to choose slates of presidential electors pledged to vote for one or another party's presidential and vice-presidential candidates. The slate that wins a plurality of the popular vote in a state (more than any other slate, but not necessarily a majority) casts all of the state's votes in the Electoral College.

It is possible for a presidential candidate to win more popular votes nationwide and yet lose the election by failing to win a majority of the electoral votes. That is, a candidate could win by large margins of the popular vote in some states, yet lose by small margins in states with a majority of electoral votes, and thus lose the presidency despite having more popular votes nationwide.

Presidential candidates are well aware of the necessity to garner a majority of the electoral votes of the states. So in their campaigns they generally concentrate their efforts on the "swing" states—those that are judged to be close and that could swing either way—and give less attention to states that they feel are solidly in their column or hopelessly lost. Presidential candidates also focus on the larger states. Indeed, it is possible to win the presidency by winning the electoral vote in just eleven states. (As shown in Figure 7-2, the electoral votes of California, Texas, Florida, New York, Pennsylvania, Illinois, Ohio, Georgia, Michigan, North Carolina, and New Jersey total 270 electoral votes, just enough to win the presidency.)

The Historical Record

The Constitution specifies that if no candidate wins a majority of the electoral votes, the House of Representatives chooses the president, with each state delegation casting one vote. But the Constitution does not specify what happens if competing slates of electors are submitted by one or more states. This problem is left up to the full Congress to resolve.

Only two presidential elections have ever been decided formally by the House of Representatives. In 1800 Thomas Jefferson and Aaron Burr tied in the Electoral College because the Twelfth Amendment had not yet

FIGURE 7-2   THE ELECTORAL COLLEGE, 2012

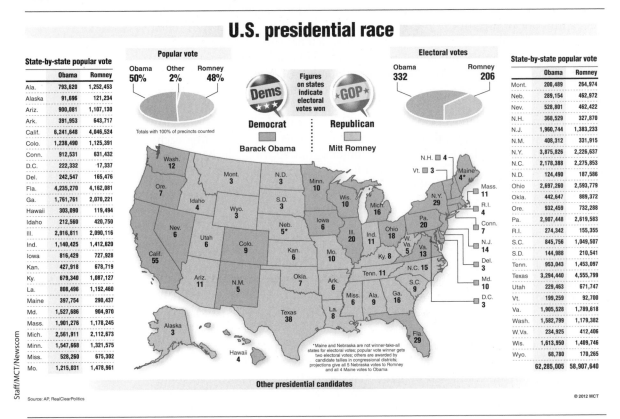

been adopted to separate presidential from vice-presidential voting; all the Democratic–Republican electors voted for both Jefferson and Burr, creating a tie. In 1824 Andrew Jackson won the popular vote and more electoral votes than anyone else but failed to get a majority. The House chose John Quincy Adams over Jackson, causing a popular uproar and ensuring Jackson's election in 1828. In addition, in 1876 the Congress was called on to decide which electoral results from the Southern states to validate; a Republican Congress chose to validate enough Republican electoral votes to allow Republican Rutherford B. Hayes to win, even though Democrat Samuel Tilden had won more popular votes. Hayes promised the Democratic southern states that in return for their acknowledgment of his presidential claim, he would end the military occupation of the South.

In 1888 the Electoral College vote failed to reflect the popular vote. Benjamin Harrison received 233 electoral votes to incumbent president Grover Cleveland's 168, even though Cleveland won about 90,000 more popular votes than Harrison (with fewer states in the union, there were fewer members of the House of Representatives and electors in the Electoral College). Cleveland was elected for a second time in 1892, the only president to serve two nonconsecutive terms.

The 2000 Presidential Election

In 2000, the battleground states were Pennsylvania, Ohio, Michigan, Illinois, Wisconsin, and especially Florida. Bush's younger brother, Jeb Bush, had been elected governor of Florida in 1998, and Republicans controlled both houses of the legislature. Early in the campaign, Bush had been so certain of winning Florida that he made very few appearances there. Only late in the campaign, when Gore was showing a lead in the Florida polls, did Bush mount a serious effort in that state.

Early in the evening on election night, the television networks "called" all of the battleground states for Gore, in effect declaring him the winner. But by 9 P.M. on the East Coast, Florida was yanked back into the undecided column; the Electoral College vote looked like it was splitting down the middle. Then around 1 A.M., Florida was "called" for Bush, and the networks pronounced him the next president of the United States. Gore telephoned Bush to concede, but after learning that the gap in Florida was closing fast, Gore called again and withdrew his concession. For the second time, the television networks pulled Florida back into the "Too Close to Call" column.

The Count Continues

The morning after election day, it was clear that Gore had won the nationwide popular vote. But the Electoral College outcome depended on Florida's 25 electoral votes. Bush's lead in Florida, after several machine recounts and the count of absentee ballots, was 930 votes out of 6 million cast in that state.

Armies of lawyers descended on Florida. The Gore campaign demanded *hand* recounts of the votes in the state's three most populous and Democratic counties—Miami-Dade, Broward (Fort Lauderdale), and Palm Beach. Bush's lawyers argued that the hand counts in these counties were late, unreliable, subjective, and open to partisan bias. Gore's lawyers argued that the Palm Beach "butterfly" ballot was confusing (the Gore–Lieberman punch hole was positioned third instead of second under Bush/Cheney; Pat Buchanan's punch hole was positioned second). They also argued that partially detached and indented "chads" (small perforated squares in the punch cards that should fall out when the voter punches the ballot) should be inspected to ascertain the "intent" of the voter.

A President Chosen by the Supreme Court

Gore formally protested the Florida vote, expecting that his protest would eventually be decided by the Florida Supreme Court, with its seven Democratic-appointed justices. And, indeed, by a four-to-three vote the Florida high court agreed. It ordered a hand recount of all "undervotes" in the state—ballots that failed to register a presidential selection on machines—to determine the "intent" of the voter.

However, Bush appealed to the U.S. Supreme Court, arguing that the Florida Supreme Court had overreached its authority under the U.S. Constitution when it substituted its own deadline for the deadline enacted by the state's legislature. (Article II, Section 1, declares that "Each State shall appoint [presidential electors] in such Manner as the *Legislature* thereof may direct. . . .") Bush's lawyers also argued that without specific standards to determine the "intent" of the voter, different vote counters would use different standards (counting or not counting chads that were "dimpled," "pregnant," "indented," and so on). Without uniform rules, such a recount would violate the equal protection clause of the Fourteenth Amendment.

In *Bush v. Gore*, the U.S. Supreme Court agreed (by a seven-to-two vote) that the Florida court had created "constitutional problems" involving the equal protection clause, and the Court ordered (by a five-to-four vote) that the hand count be ended altogether. The effect of the decision was to reinstate the Florida secretary of state's certification of Bush as the winner of Florida's 25 electoral votes and consequently the winner of the Electoral College vote for president by the narrowest of margins—271 to 267.

For the first time in the nation's history, a presidential election was decided by the U.S. Supreme Court. Perhaps only the Supreme Court possesses sufficient legitimacy in the mind of the American public to bring about a resolution to the closest presidential electoral vote in history.

The Power of the Courts

The founders of the United States viewed the federal courts as the final bulwark against threats to individual liberty. Since *Marbury v. Madison* first asserted the U.S. Supreme Court's power of judicial review over congressional acts, the federal courts have struck down more than eighty congressional laws and uncounted state laws that they believed conflicted with the Constitution.

Judicial review and the right to interpret the meaning and decide the application of the Constitution and laws of the United States are great sources of power for judges.[16]

Key Court Decisions

Some of the nation's most important policy decisions have been made by courts rather than by executive or legislative bodies. The federal courts took the lead in eliminating racial segregation in public life, ensuring the separation of church and state, defining relationships between citizens and law enforcers, and guaranteeing voters equal voice in government. Today, the federal courts grapple with the most controversial issues facing the nation: abortion, affirmative action, the death penalty, religion in schools, the rights of criminal defendants, and so on. Courts are an integral component of America's government system, for sooner or later most important policy questions are brought before them.[17]

Democracy and the U.S. Supreme Court

The undemocratic nature of judicial review has long been recognized in American politics. Nine Supreme Court justices—who are not elected to office, whose terms are for life, and who can be removed only for "high crimes and misdemeanors"—possess the power to void the acts of popularly elected presidents, Congresses, governors, and state legislators. Why should the views of an appointed court about the meaning of the Constitution prevail over the views of *elected* officials? Presidents and members of Congress are sworn to uphold the Constitution, and it can reasonably be assumed they do not pass laws that they believe to be *un*constitutional. Why should the Supreme Court have judicial review of the decisions of these bodies?

The answer appears to be that the founders distrusted both popular majorities and elected officials who might be influenced by popular majorities. They believed that government should be limited so it could not attack principle and property, whether to do so was the will of the majority or not. So the courts were deliberately insulated against popular majorities; to ensure their independence, judges were not to be elected but appointed for life terms. Only in this way, the writers of the Constitution believed, would they be sufficiently protected from the masses to permit them to judge courageously and responsibly. Insulation is, in itself, another source of judicial power.

Judicial Restraint

The power of the courts, especially the U.S. Supreme Court, is limited only by the justices' own judicial philosophy. The doctrine of **judicial restraint** argues that because justices are not popularly elected, the Supreme Court should defer to the decisions of Congress and the president unless their actions are in clear conflict with the plain meaning of the Constitution. Former Justice Felix Frankfurter once wrote, "The only check upon our own exercise of power is our own sense of self-restraint. For the removal of unwise laws from the statute books, appeal lies not with the Courts but to the ballot and to the processes of democratic government."[18] One should not confuse the wisdom of a law with its constitutionality; the courts should decide only the constitutionality of laws, not the wisdom or fairness.

A related limitation on judicial power is the principle of *stare decisis*, which means the issue has already been decided in earlier cases. Reliance on precedent is a fundamental notion in law; it gives stability to the law. If every decision ignored past precedents and created new law, no one would know what the law is from day to day.

judicial restraint judges should defer to the decision of elected representatives unless it is in clear conflict with the plain meaning of the Constitution

stare decisis reliance on precedent to give stability to the law

Judicial Activism

However, much of the history of the Supreme Court has been one of **judicial activism**, not restraint. The dominant philosophy of the Supreme Court under Chief Justice Earl Warren (1953–1969) was that judges should interpret the meaning of the Constitution to fit the needs of contemporary society. By viewing the Constitution as a broad and flexible document, the nation can avoid new constitutional amendments and still accomplish changes in society. Precedents can be overturned as society grows and changes.

Judicial activism was reflected in the Supreme Court's famous *Brown v. Board of Education of Topeka* decision in 1954 that declared that racially segregated schools violated the equal protection clause of the Fourteenth Amendment. This decision contradicted the legal precedent that had been set in 1857 when the Court ruled in the *Dred Scott* decision that "separate but equal" facilities *did not* violate the equal protection clause.

judicial activism judges may interpret the meaning of the Constitution to fit the needs of contemporary society

The Supreme Court's power to interpret the Constitution means that the legacy of a president's appointments to the Court may be felt for decades. Today's Supreme Court includes Sonia Sotomayor, Stephen Breyer, Samuel Alito, Elena Kagan; (seated) Clarence Thomas, Antonin Scalia, Chief Justice John Roberts, Anthony Kennedy, and Ruth Bader Ginsburg.

The Supreme Court also overturned precedent in requiring that the states apportion their legislatures so as to guarantee equal voter representation in *Baker v. Carr* in 1962. It struck down long-established practices of prayer and Bible reading in public schools in *Engle v. Vitale*, also in 1962. The Court under Earl Warren also greatly expanded the rights of criminal defendants.

The Supreme Court under President Richard Nixon's appointee, Chief Justice Warren Burger (1969–1986), was only slightly less activist. The Court's 1973 decision in *Roe v. Wade*, invoking privacy rights in declaring that abortion was a constitutional right of women, was perhaps the most sweeping reinterpretation of individual liberty in the Court's history.

Presidents Ronald Reagan and George H. W. Bush sought to strengthen the doctrine of judicial restraint in their appointments to the Supreme Court (Table 7-4). Chief Justice William Rehnquist (first appointed to the Court by President Nixon in 1971, elevated to chief justice by President Reagan in 1986, and served as chief justice until his death in 2005) was less activist than his predecessors. However, none of the major decisions of the Warren or Burger Courts was reversed during Rehnquist's tenure. Chief Justice John Roberts, who was appointed to the court as chief justice in 2005 by President George W. Bush, has followed in Rehnquist's footsteps, providing staunchly conservative but generally less activist leadership than earlier chief justices.

In 2009, with the retirement of Associate Justice David Souter, as shown in Table 7-4, Barack Obama became the first Democrat to appoint a member of the Supreme Court in 15 years. He appointed the third woman and first Latina to serve on the Court, Sonia Sotomayor. In 2010, he also would appoint Elena Kagan to the Court, succeeding Justice John Paul Stevens. Obama's predecessor, George W. Bush, was able to appoint both Chief Justice Roberts and Associate

TABLE 7-4   MEMBERS OF THE U.S. SUPREME COURT

Justice	Law School Graduated from	President Who Appointed
Elena Kagan	Harvard	Obama (2010)
Sonia Sotomayor	Yale	Obama (2009)
Samuel Alito	Yale	G. W. Bush (2005)
John G. Roberts, Jr.	Harvard	G. W. Bush (2005)
Ruth Bader Ginsburg	Columbia	Clinton (1993)
Stephen G. Breyer	Harvard	Clinton (1994)
Clarence Thomas	Yale	G. H. W. Bush (1991)
Antonin Scalia	Harvard	Reagan (1986)
Anthony Kennedy	Harvard	Reagan (1988)

Justice Samuel Alito, because of the death of Rehnquist and the retirement of Sandra Day O'Connor, who was the first woman to serve on the Supreme Court. President Clinton's appointments of Ruth Bader Ginsburg (the second woman to serve on the Court) and Stephen Breyer strengthened the moderate to liberal voice of the Supreme Court, while Bush appointees Roberts and Alito swung the court back to right. Obama's appointments of Sotomayor and Kagan add a more liberal voice.

The Powers of Congress

What are the powers of Congress in the American political system? The Congress is a **bicameral**, or two-chambered body. The upper house, called the U.S. Senate, consists of 100 members, with each state electing two senators. The lower house, called the U.S. House of Representatives, consists of 435 members, each of whom represents a congressional district. The number of House seats allocated to each state depends on that state's population.

> **bicameral**
> a two-chambered body

Policy proposals are usually initiated outside Congress; it is the role of Congress to respond to proposals from the president, executive agencies, and interest groups. Congress does not merely ratify or "rubber-stamp" decisions; it plays an independent role in the policy-making process. But this role is essentially a deliberative one in which Congress accepts, modifies, or rejects the policies initiated by others. Congress functions as an arbiter rather than an initiator of public policy.

Many of the decisions that Congress makes, or powers it exercises, emanate from the powers granted to it explicitly in the U.S. Constitution (see Table 7-5). We can see that the Constitution grants Congress many powers outright. But Congress also has powers not explicitly listed in the Constitution. These powers, called **implied powers**, come from the Supreme Court's interpretation of the "necessary and proper clause" of the Constitution in *Marbury v. Madison*.

> **implied powers**
> congressional powers coming from the Supreme Court's interpretation of the "necessary and proper clause"

TABLE 7-5 CONSTITUTIONAL POWERS GRANTED TO CONGRESS

Judicial Powers
- Establish federal courts
- Punish counterfeiters
- Punish illegal acts on the high seas

Economic Powers
- Impose taxes
- Establish import tariffs
- Borrow money
- Regulate interstate commerce
- Coin and print money, determine the value of currency

National Security Powers
- Declare war
- Raise and regulate national armed forces
- Call up and regulate state national guard
- Suppress insurrections
- Repel invasions

Regulatory Powers
- Establish standards of weights and measures
- Regulate copyrights and patents

Administrative Powers
- Establish procedures for naturalizing citizens
- Establish post offices
- Govern the District of Columbia

And while the powers of the federal government in general expanded because of the *Marbury* decision, Congress's power increased greatly because of this interpretation. The necessary and proper clause has meant that the Congress has a great deal of power, and can act in passing laws concerning matters that the founders could not even imagine.

Domestic Affairs

Congress is more influential in domestic affairs than it is in foreign and military affairs. The Constitution grants presidents greater authority in foreign affairs, whereas Congress traditionally has exercised more authority in the domestic policy realm. Citing their own expertise and views, or the views of their constituents, members of Congress are more likely to reject presidential proposals regarding business, labor, agriculture, education, welfare, urban affairs, civil rights, taxation, and appropriations. The president and executive departments must go to Congress for needed legislation and appropriations. Congressional committees can exercise power in domestic affairs by giving or withholding the appropriations and the legislation that these executive agencies want.

Foreign and Military Affairs

In the Constitution, the president and Congress share power over foreign and military affairs. The president is "Commander in Chief of the Armed Forces," but Congress "declares war." The president "sends and receives ambassadors" and "makes treaties," but the Senate must confirm appointments and "advise and consent" to treaties. Nevertheless, strong presidents have generally led the nation in both war and peace (see the Case Study in Chapter 6, "The Vietnam War: A Political History").

Until the Vietnam War, no congressional opposition to undeclared war was evident. But military failure and public opposition to the war in Vietnam led Congress to try to curtail the war power of the president. Congress passed the controversial **War Powers Act** in 1973 over a weakened President Nixon's veto. The act specifies that if the president sends U.S. troops into combat, this must be reported to Congress within forty-eight hours. American forces can remain in a combat situation for only sixty days unless Congress by specific legislation authorizes their continued engagement. The act also states that Congress can withdraw troops at any time by passing a resolution in both houses, and the president cannot veto a resolution.

War Powers Act
Congress's effort to limit presidential war-making power

Congressional Elections

The founders' views of the House and Senate are also reflected in the structure of congressional elections. Members of the House of Representatives, the branch of government designed to be closest to the people, are elected every two years in even-numbered years (2012, 2014, and so on). Originally, the Constitution required that members of the U.S. Senate were chosen by state legislators, but this structure was changed with ratification of the Seventeenth Amendment to the Constitution in 1913, which mandated popular elections of senators. Thus, members of the U.S. Senate serve six-year terms, with one-third of the Senate elected every two years. One of the best predictors of a candidate's chances of success in a congressional election is **incumbency**, or whether the person running for office already holds that office: On average, about 95 percent of incumbent members of the House of Representatives running for re-election win, and about 88 percent of their Senate counterparts do.

incumbency
when the person running for office already holds that office

Reapportionment

There are circumstances, however, when the impact of incumbency can be mitigated. Typically, this occurs in election years after reapportionment and redistricting. **Reapportionment** (sometimes called apportionment) is the process of allocating seats in the House of Representatives to each state based upon changes in their population since the last census. Every ten years, in the year ending in zero (2010, 2020, and so on), the federal government conducts a census counting the number of people throughout the country. If the state's population changes significantly, it may gain or lose seats in the House of Representatives.

reapportionment
the process of allocating seats in the House of Representatives to each state based upon changes in their population since the last census

Redistricting

redistricting
the redrawing of
congressional district
boundaries within
each state

Redistricting, the redrawing of congressional district boundaries within each state, is based on the reapportionment from the census. Because the composition of a congressional district can change after reapportionment and redistricting, this process can mitigate the impact of incumbency. Frequently, the greatest changes in the composition of the House of Representatives occur in election years ending in 2 (2012, 2022, and so on), the first elections that incorporate the changes from reapportionment and redistricting. When states lose seats, the result is that an incumbent member of Congress is likely to lose a seat. When states gain seats, there is an open seat in which a new member of Congress can be elected.

Power and Political Behavior in the United States

Although power certainly rests in the three branches of government, the exercise of power is not limited to elected or appointed officials. Indeed, every day, ordinary Americans have the opportunity to exercise political power in a wide variety of ways. Popular participation in the political system is the very definition of democracy. Individuals in a democracy may

- Run for public office.
- Participate in marches and demonstrations.
- Make financial contributions to political candidates and causes.
- Attend political meetings, speeches, and rallies.
- Write letters to public officials and newspapers.
- Join, form, or belong to organizations that support or oppose particular candidates and take stands on public issues.
- Wear political buttons and place bumper stickers on their cars.
- Attempt to influence friends while discussing candidates and issues.
- Vote in elections.
- Follow an issue or campaign in the mass media.

This list of activities constitutes a ranking of the forms of political participation, in inverse order of their frequency. Figure 7-3 shows graphically the percentage of people who engage in the various activities. Each form of political participation is an attempt by individuals to exert some power over government—to have their voice heard. The effectiveness of these efforts varies according to the context in which the behavior occurs. The activities at the beginning of the list require greater expenditure of time and energy and greater personal commitment; consequently, far fewer people engage in those activities, as we can see in Figure 7-3. Fully one-third of the population is politically apathetic: They do not vote, and they are largely unaware of and indifferent to the political life of the nation.

Voter Turnout

Voter turnout is greatest in presidential elections, but even in those contests turnout is only about 50 to 55 percent of eligible people. "Off-year" congressional elections—congressional elections held in years in which there is no

FIGURE 7-3 PERCENT OF PEOPLE WHO PARTICIPATE IN VARIOUS POLITICAL ACTIVITIES

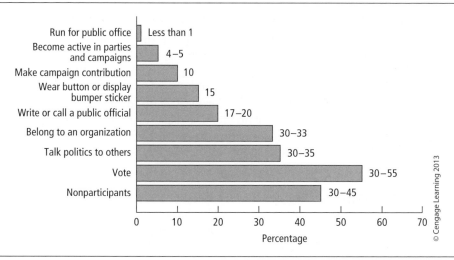

Source: Brigid Callahan Harrison, Jean Wahl Harris and Susan Tolchin. American Democracy Now. (McGraw-Hill Publishers, 2008).

presidential election—attract only 35 to 40 percent of eligible people to the polls. Yet in these off-year contests, the nation chooses all of its U.S. representatives, one-third of its U.S. senators, and about one-half of its governors. Local government elections—for mayor, council members, school board, and so forth—frequently attract only one-quarter to one-third of eligible voters.

Nonvoting

Who votes and who doesn't?[19] Some groups of people are more likely to vote than others. Education appears to be the most important determinant of voter turnout. It may be that schooling promotes an interest in politics, instills the ethic of citizen participation, or gives people a better awareness of public affairs and an understanding of the role of elections in a democracy. Education is associated with a sense of confidence and **political efficacy**—the feeling that one can indeed have a personal impact on public affairs.

Age is another factor affecting voter participation. While nonvoting is greatest among those who are 18 to 21 years old, voter participation by young people has increased over the past several presidential elections. In fact, in the 2008 presidential election, the turnout rate among those aged 18–29 rivaled the record-setting turnout rate of 1974, the presidential election that followed the United States granting 18- to 21-year-olds the right to vote. Why are young people less likely to vote? Many political scientists note that young people are less likely to own property or be settled in a community, and therefore may feel less connection to local and even national politics. Others assert that young people have more distractions; more demands on their time in schooling, work, or new family responsibilities. In contrast, older Americans are politically influential in part because elected officials know they turn out at the polls, and both public policy and political campaigns respond to their preferences.

High-income people are more likely to vote than are low-income people. Most of this difference is a product of the fact that high-income people are

political efficacy
the feeling that one can indeed have a personal impact on public affairs

more likely well educated and older. Poor people, however, may also feel alienated from the political system. The poor may lack a sense of political efficacy—they may feel they have little control over their own lives, let alone over public affairs. Or the poor may simply be so absorbed in the problems of life that they have little time or energy to spend on registering and voting.

Historically, race was a major determinant of nonvoting. Black voter turnout, especially in the South, was markedly lower than white voter turnout. But today, blacks and whites at the *same* educational and income levels register and vote with the same frequency. The greatest racial disparity in voter turnout is between Hispanics and non-Hispanic voters. Low voter participation by Hispanics may be a product of language differences, late cultural assimilation, or noncitizenship status.

The Voter Decides

Perhaps no other area of political science has been investigated so thoroughly—by political candidates, campaign strategists, and political scientists—as the reasons behind the voters' choices at the polls.[20] Voters cast ballots for and against candidates for a variety of reasons, including their party affiliation, their membership in social and economic groups, their positive and negative evaluations of the images of the candidates, their view of the goodness or badness of the times (especially the economy), and sometimes even the positions of the candidates on important issues.

Although party ties have weakened somewhat over time, party affiliation remains an important influence over voter choice. People who identify themselves as Democrats or Republicans usually vote for their party's candidate. Membership in various social, economic, and demographic groups also affects voting; for example, African American voters and women voters regularly are more likely to support to Democratic candidates than whites or men.

Candidates spend a great deal of time and money during a campaign trying to project a favorable image of themselves (or a negative image of their opponent) through television and the press (see Focus: "Media Power: The Presidential Debates"). Challengers attack the record of incumbents seeking re-election, holding them responsible for anything bad that happened during their term, especially any weaknesses that developed in the economy. Incumbents are more likely to be re-elected when the nation enjoys "peace and prosperity." Relatively few voters cast their ballot exclusively on a particular policy position of a candidate although some "hot-button" issues—health care reform or economy, for example—influence the choice of some voters.

Political Parties in the United States

Democracy is ultimately based on majority rule, and one function of political parties is to *put majorities together*. Political parties organize voters for effective political expression at the polls. Voters, in turn, use party labels to help them identify the general political viewpoints of the candidates.[21] Political parties are the most important voter cue because they provide voters with a tool that screens candidates to ensure that the candidate's view loosely reflects the party ideology and voters perceive the parties as having different strengths

FOCUS

Media Power: The Presidential Debates

Presidential debates attract more viewers than any other campaign activity. Debates allow people to directly compare the responses of each candidate. Even if issues are not really discussed in depth, people see how presidential candidates react as human beings under pressure.

The Kennedy–Nixon Debates   *Televised presidential debates began in 1960 when John F. Kennedy and Richard M. Nixon confronted each other on a bare stage before an America watching on black-and-white television sets.* Nixon was the vice president in the popular presidential administration of Dwight Eisenhower; he was also an accomplished college debate team member. He prepared for the debates as if they were college debates, memorizing facts and arguments. But he failed to realize that image triumphs over substance on television. Nixon was shifty eyed and clearly in need of a shave or more makeup to hide his pronounced "five o'clock shadow." By contrast, Kennedy was handsome, cool, and confident. Television viewers preferred the glamorous young Kennedy. The polls shifted in Kennedy's direction after the debate, and he won in a very close general election. Nixon blamed his makeup man.

The Carter–Ford Debates   *President Lyndon Johnson avoided debating in 1964, and Nixon, having learned his lesson, declined to debate in 1968 and 1972.* Thus, televised presidential debates did not resume until 1976, when incumbent President Gerald Ford, perceiving that he was behind in the polls, agreed to debate challenger Jimmy Carter. Ford made a series of verbal slips—saying, for example, that the nations of Eastern Europe were free from Soviet domination. Carter was widely perceived as having "won" the debates, and he went on to victory in the general election.

The Reagan–Carter and Reagan–Mondale Debates   *It was Ronald Reagan who demonstrated the true power of television.* Reagan had lived his life in front of a camera. Carter talked rapidly and seriously about programs, figures, and budgets. But Reagan was master of the stage; he was relaxed, confident, joking. He appeared to treat the president of the United States as an overly aggressive, impulsive younger man, regrettably given to exaggeration ("There you go again"). When the debate was over, it was clear to most viewers that Carter had been bested by a true professional in media skills.

However, in the first of two televised debates with Walter Mondale in 1984, Reagan's skills of a lifetime seemed to desert him. He stumbled over statistics and groped for words. His poor performance raised the only issue that might conceivably defeat him—his age. The president had looked and sounded *old*.

In preparation for the second debate, Reagan decided, without telling his aides, to lay the perfect trap for his questioners. When asked about his age and capacity to lead the nation, he responded with a serious deadpan expression to a hushed audience and waiting America: "I want you to know that I will not make age an issue in this campaign. I am not going to exploit for political purposes [pause] my opponent's youth and inexperience." The studio audience broke into uncontrolled laughter. Even Mondale had to laugh. With a classic one-liner, the president buried the age issue and won not only the debate but also the election.

The Bush–Dukakis Debates   *In 1988 Michael Dukakis ensured his defeat with a cold, detached performance in the presidential debates, beginning with the very first question.* When CNN anchor Bernard Shaw asked, "Governor, if Kitty Dukakis were raped and murdered, would you favor an irrevocable death penalty for the killer?" The question demanded an emotional reply. Instead, Dukakis responded with an impersonal recitation of his stock positions on crime, drugs, and law enforcement. George H. W. Bush seized the opportunity to establish an intimate, warm, and personal relationship with the viewers: "I do believe some crimes are so heinous, so brutal, so outrageous . . . I do believe in the death penalty." Voters responded to Bush, electing him.

The Clinton–Bush–Perot Debates   *The three-way presidential debates of 1992 drew the largest television audiences in the history of presidential debates.* In the first debate, Ross Perot's Texas twang and down-home folksy style stole the show. But it was Bill Clinton's smooth performance in the second debate, with its talk-show format, that seemed to wrap up the election. Ahead in the polls, Clinton appeared at ease walking about the stage and responding to audience questions with sympathy and sincerity. By contrast, George H. W. Bush appeared stiff and formal and somewhat ill at ease with the "unpresidential" format.

The Clinton–Dole Debates   *A desperate Bob Dole, running twenty points behind, faced a newly "presidential" Bill Clinton in their two 1996 debates.* (Perot's poor standing in the polls led to his exclusion.) Dole tried to counter his image as a grumpy old man in the first encounter; his humor actually won more laughs from the audience than the president's more stately comments. Dole injected more barbs in the second debate, complaining of "ethical problems in the White House" and repeating the mantra "I keep my word," suggesting that Clinton did not. But Clinton remained cool and comfortable, ignoring the challenger and focusing on the nation's economic health. Viewers, most of whom were already in Clinton's court, judged him the winner of both debates.

The Bush–Gore Debates   *Separate formats were agreed upon for three debates—the traditional podium, a conference table, and a town-hall setting.* Vice President Al Gore was assertive, almost to the point of rudeness, but both candidates focused on policy differences rather than personal attacks. Viewers gave Gore the edge in these debates, but they found George W. Bush more likable. Bush appeared to benefit more in the post-debate polls. An estimated 47 million people watched the first debate, and viewership fell to 36 million for the second and third debates. Most observers rated the single vice-presidential debate between Dick Cheney and Joe Lieberman as friendlier and more informative than the Bush–Gore encounters.

The Bush–Kerry Debates   *A thirty-two-page document agreed to by both the Kerry and Bush campaigns defined the terms of the three presidential debates in 2004.* The first debate, sponsored by the

Miccosukee Tribe of Indians of Florida, was held at the University of Miami, Florida. This debate, which had a standard debate format, focused on issues concerning foreign policy and homeland security. The second debate, held at Washington University in St. Louis, Missouri, was a town-hall style debate; the third debate, held at Arizona State University in Tempe, Arizona, had the same format as the first but focused on domestic policy issues.

Before these debates, the reputations of the candidates—President George W. Bush as not particularly well spoken and Senator John Kerry as a well-spoken intellectual—shaped the expectations of their debate performances. Indeed, many in the Bush camp appeared to be *lowering* expectations of the president. Public opinion polls after the debates indicated that most Americans who watched the debates believed that Kerry had won each debate, but that Bush held his own against Kerry, putting in a respectable performance.

The Obama–McCain Debates   *The 2008 presidential debates were billed as the opportunity for the voters to see the differences between the youthful Democratic Senator Barack Obama and the experienced Republican Senator John McCain.* In the end, however, neither candidate committed gaffes significant enough to discredit his candidacy. Three debates were scheduled, two hosted by moderators who posed questions to the candidates, and one a town hall format debate.

Assessing the first debate, CBS News polls revealed that most people thought Obama had won (40 percent) or that it was a draw (38 percent). In the second debate, many questioned whether Obama would succeed in getting his message across in the town hall format. He did, according to a CNN poll, which showed that 50 percent of viewers thought he had won. Controversial during this debate was McCain's use of the term "that one" to refer to Obama. During the third presidential debate, McCain used "Joe the Plumber" as the example of someone who would wind up paying more taxes under Obama's proposal. Despite the attacks, most viewers said they believed Obama had won.

The Obama-Romney Debates   *The candidates split the debates.* In the first presidential debate, an assertive Mitt Romney challenged President Obama's record on the economy, and Obama's response was largely viewed as dispassionate. In the second debate, Obama was more commanding and was viewed by most as having won. The third debate, which centered on foreign policy, was largely viewed as a draw.

(see Research This!) . And so, to the extent that a voter holds a cohesive ideology, parties provide that voter with a convenient, time-saving mechanism to evaluate every candidate standing for office.

Because American parties are necessarily rather loose coalitions of interests, they do not command the total loyalty of every officeholder elected under a party's banner. The fact that candidates run under a Republican or Democratic label does not clearly indicate where they will stand on every public issue, but party labels offer a general idea of where candidates fall on the ideological continuum. Even so, these coalitions do have considerable cohesion and historical continuity. The *party label discloses the coalition of interests and the policy views with which candidates have* generally associated themselves. At the least, the party label tells more about a candidate's politics than would a strange name, with no party affiliation, on the ballot.

Especially in two-party systems, such as we have in the United States, parties also *structure the choice of candidates* for public office and thus relieve voters of the task of choosing among dozens of contending candidates on election day. The preliminary selecting and narrowing of candidates, by conventions and primary elections, are indispensable in a large society.

Political parties *educate voters* about the candidates and the issues that are important in a given election. After educating voters, parties also *mobilize the masses*, through get-out-the-vote efforts.

Political parties help *define the major problems and issues* confronting society. In attempting to win a majority of the voters, parties inform the public about the issues facing the nation. The comparisons that parties make during political campaigns have an important educational value: Voters come to "know" the opposing candidates for public office, and the problems of national interest are spotlighted.

Finally, the party out of office performs an important function for democratic government by *providing a loyal opposition*. That is, members of the party that is out of government can be counted on to provide criticism of actions and policies made by the party in government, thus providing a valuable "check" on those in government. Moreover, the very existence of a recognized party outside the government helps make criticism of government legitimate and effective.

Differences between Democrats and Republicans

It is sometimes argued that there are few significant differences between the two main American parties. It is not uncommon in European nations to find authoritarian parties competing with democratic parties, capitalist parties with socialist parties, Catholic parties with secular parties, and so on. However, within the context of American political experience, the Democratic and Republican Parties can be clearly differentiated. There are at least three ways in which to discern the differences: (1) by examining differences in the *coalitions of voters* supporting each party, (2) by examining differences in the *policy views of the leaders* in each party, and (3) by examining differences in the *voting records of the representatives and senators* of each party.

In ascertaining party differences according to support from different groups of voters, we must note first that major groups are seldom *wholly* within one party or the other. For example, in presidential elections, all major social groups divide their votes between the parties. Yet differences between the parties are

RESEARCH *THIS!*

Periodically the Gallup Organization asks poll respondents their views on the capabilities of the Democratic and Republican parties. The data shown in this table indicates that there are some similarities and some differences in the perceived strengths of the parties.

	Applies %	Does not apply %
Can bring about the changes this country needs		
Democrats	50	47
Republicans	48	48
Has mostly honest and ethical members in Congress		
Democrats	45	50
Republicans	42	52
Looks out for the country's long-term future as well as current problems		
Democrats	52	44
Republicans	53	43
Has a clear plan for solving the country's problems		
Democrats	33	62
Republicans	32	63
Is able to manage the federal government effectively		
Democrats	39	56
Republicans	42	52

SOURCE: www.gallup.com/poll/24655/Party-Images.aspx#3

YOUR ANALYSIS:

1. Based on the data shown, where do Democrats' strengths lie? Republicans?

2. In which categories do voters evaluate the parties most similarly?

3. Are there differences between the parties? How do you think that impacts the parties' electability?

revealed *in the proportions of votes given by each major group to each party* (see "Sex," "Race," and "Religion" in Table 7-6). Thus, the Democratic Party receives a disproportionate amount of support from Catholics, Jews, African Americans, women, lower-income groups, blue-collar workers, union members, and big-city residents. The Republican Party receives disproportionate support from Protestants, whites, men, higher-income groups, professionals and managers, white-collar workers, nonunion members, and rural and small-town residents.

Differences in Views of Party Leaders

The second way of discerning Democratic and Republican Party differences involves an examination of the political opinions of the leaders of each party. Political scientists have studied party differences by presenting a series of policy

TABLE 7-6   VOTING BY GROUPS IN RECENT PRESIDENTIAL ELECTIONS

	2012 Election		2008 Election		2004 Election	
	Democrat Obama	Republican Romney	Democrat Obama	Republican McCain	Democrat Kerry	Republican G.W. Bush
National	50	48	53%	46%	48%	51%
Sex						
Male	48	52	49	48	44	55
Female	55	45	56	43	51	48
Race						
White	41	59	43	55	41	58
African American	93	7	95	4	88	11
Latino	71	29	67	31	53	44
Asian	73	27	62	35	56	44
Age						
Under 30 years	60	39	66	32	54	45
30-49	52	47	53	45	47	52
50 and older	47	53	49	50	46	53
Religion						
Protestant	42	57	45	54	40	59
Catholic	50	48	54	45	47	52
Jewish	69	30	78	21	74	25
Political Party						
Republican	6	93	9	90	6	93
Democrat	92	7	89	10	89	11
Independent	45	50	52	44	49	48

* Not available.

SOURCE: Based on data from the *Gallup Poll* surveys and voter exit polls, 2000, and CNN polls, 2004, 2008, 2012.

questions to the delegates to the Democratic and Republican National Conventions. They have found substantial differences of opinion between Democratic and Republican leaders on important public issues. In general, Democratic party leaders are more "progressive" and attempt to elevate the poor and underprivileged by using redistributive policies, and Republican leaders emphasize personal responsibility and a more laissez faire government.[22] During the administration of President George W. Bush, the Republican Party's ideology did undergo a significant change with the dominance of neoconservative Republicans (see Chapter 3 for further discussion of the role of ideology).

Party Differences in Congressional Voting

The third indication of party differences in the United States is the roll-call voting behavior of the representatives and senators of each party on controversial

	2000 Election			1996 Election		
	Democrat Gore	Republican G.W. Bush	Green Nader	Democrat Clinton	Republican Dole	Independent Perot
National	48%	48%	3%	49%	41%	8%
Sex						
Male	42	53	3	43	44	10
Female	54	43	2	54	38	7
Race						
White	42	54	3	43	46	9
Nonwhite	90	8	1	84	12	4
	62	35	2			
	NA*	NA	NA			
Age						
Under 30 years	48	46	5	53	34	10
30-49 years	48	49	2	48	41	9
50 years and older	51	47	2	48	41	9
Religion						
Protestant	42	56	2	41	50	8
Catholic	50	47	2	53	32	9
	79	19				
Political Party						
Republican	8	91	2	13	80	6
Democrat	86	11	1	84	10	5
Independent	45	47	6	43	35	17

issues. About half of all roll-call votes in Congress are party votes, votes in which a majority of Democrats oppose a majority of Republicans. Party votes occur most frequently on well-publicized, high-conflict issues. Party voting also occurs on presidential recommendations, with the president's party in Congress supporting the president's position and the opposition party opposing it. Bipartisan votes, those roll calls in which party majorities are found on the same side, usually occur on less-publicized, low-conflict issues. On many issues, voting follows party lines during roll calls on preliminary amendments but swings to a bipartisan vote on the final legislation. This occurs when the parties disagree on certain aspects of a bill but compromise on its final passage.

Power and American Government

Although it is clear that the government exercises a great deal of power over its citizens, it is important to remember that legitimate governments derive their power from those citizens, in the form of consent of the governed. In addition, democracies offer up a multitude of ways for citizens to impact the government and policies. Some forms of participation cost little in terms of time or energy; other forms of participation, like running for public office, involve serious commitment and lifestyle change. As with other forms of power described in this text, political power is distributed unevenly in the United States. Those who are economically powerful are more likely to be politically powerful, but political power does offer opportunities for average citizens to exercise power.

CHAPTER SUMMARY

- The power of government, unlike that of other institutions in society, is distinguished by the legitimate use of physical force and coverage of the whole society rather than only segments of it.

- Ideally, democracy means individual participation in the decisions that affect one's life. Procedurally, popular participation was to be achieved through majority rule and respect for the rights of those with a minority view. Oftentimes, majority rule and respect for the rights of minorities occurs by limiting the power of the government through a social contract, a form of constitutionalism.

- The U.S. Constitution sets up government bodies, including the House of Representatives, the Senate, the presidency, and the Supreme Court in the United States. It grants them powers, determines how their members are to be chosen, and prescribes the rules by which they make decisions.

- The separation of powers in the national government—separate legislative, executive, and judicial branches—was intended by the nation's founders as an additional safeguard for liberty

- Since the founding of the United States, the power of the national government has increased significantly. Major developments in the history of American federalism, including *Marbury v. Madison*, the Civil War, the growth in interstate commerce, the use of federal law to enforce civil rights laws, and federal grants-in-aid, have contributed to this increase in national power.

- Today, federal grants-in-aid are the principal source of federal power over states and communities. Nearly one-quarter of all state and local government revenues are from federal grants.

- The roles that a president must perform include managing crisis, providing policy leadership, managing the economy and the government, and acting as global leader and commander-in-chief.

- The founders of the United States viewed the federal courts as the final bulwark against threats to individual liberty. Since *Marbury v. Madison* first asserted the U.S. Supreme Court's power of judicial review over congressional acts, the federal courts have struck down more than eighty congressional laws and uncounted state laws that they believed conflicted with the Constitution.

- The Congress is a bicameral, or two-chambered body. The upper house, called the U.S. Senate, consists of 100 members, with each state electing two senators. The lower house, called the U.S. House of Representatives, consists of 435 members, each of whom represents a congressional district. The number of House seats allocated to each state depends on that state's population.

- Although power certainly rests in the three branches of government, the exercise of power is not limited to elected or appointed officials. Indeed, every day, ordinary Americans have the opportunity to exercise political power in a wide variety of ways, including running for public office and voting in elections, but there are many other ways for individuals to participate in political life.

- Political parties organize voters for effective political expression at the polls. Voters, in turn, use party labels to help them identify the general political viewpoints of the candidates.

KEY TERMS

Anti-Federalists those who argued against ratification of the U.S. Constitution; they were wary of a strong national government and favored states' rights

bicameral a two-chambered body

Bill of Rights the first ten amendments to the U.S. Constitution listing individual freedoms and restrictions on government power

constitution the establishment of government authority; the creation of government bodies, granting their powers, determining how their members are selected, and prescribing the rules by which government decisions are to be made; considered basic or fundamental, a constitution cannot be changed by ordinary acts of government bodies

constitutionalism the belief that government power should be limited

checks and balances the principle whereby each branch of the government exercises a check on the actions of the others, preventing too great a concentration of power in any one person or group of persons

democracy individual participation in the decisions that affect one's life

direct democracy people themselves vote directly on issues, rather than their representatives

devolution the transfer of federal programs to state and local governments

federalism the division of power between states and nations

Federalists advocates for ratification of the U.S. Constitution

grants-in-aid payments of funds from the national government to state or local governments, usually with conditions attached to their uses

federal mandate a requirement issued by the national government with which state and local governments must comply

government power the legitimate use of force; coverage of the whole society

implied powers congressional powers coming from the Supreme Court's interpretation of the "necessary and proper clause"

incumbency when the person running for office already holds that office

judicial activism judges may interpret the meaning of the Constitution to fit the needs of contemporary society

judicial restraint judges should defer to the decision of elected representatives unless it is in clear conflict with the plain meaning of the Constitution

judicial review the power of the courts to strike down laws they believe conflict with the Constitution

national supremacy when state and federal law conflict in an area in which both have jurisdiction, federal (national) laws are superior

natural rights rights are not granted by government but derive from human nature itself

politics the study of power

political efficacy the feeling that one can indeed have a personal impact on public affairs

political science the study of government and how individuals influence government action

reapportionment the process of allocating seats in the House of Representatives to each state based upon changes in their population since the last census

redistricting the redrawing of congressional district boundaries within each state

republican government (republicanism) government by elected representatives of the people

separation of powers the principle of dividing government powers among the executive, legislative, and judicial branches

social contract the idea that people consent to be governed and in doing so agree to give up some of their liberties so that the remainder of their liberties can be protected

stare decisis reliance on precedent to give stability to the law

War Powers Act Congress's effort to limit presidential war-making power

ON THE WEB

EXPLORING GOVERNMENT AND POLITICS

The website for this textbook (**www.cengagbrain .com**) offers online resources for exploring power and government on the Internet. The Internet overflows with information about government, politics, and public affairs. The real problem with finding specific information is in sorting through the overabundance of political news and commentary. Internet users should be cognizant of the *sources* of political information and be prepared to adjust for political bias.

- **Library of Congress** The Library of Congress (**http://thomas.loc.gov**) contains a wealth of information about politics, government organizations, and the history of the government. It also provides links to many practical sites.

  Try this: Go to **http://thomas.loc.gov/cgi -bin/bssQuery/?Opt=t&Db=112** and pick a current bill from the list. Click through the links to see the text of the legislation. Explain what the bill seeks to do if passed. Who is sponsoring the bill?

- **White House** A frequent starting place for browsing through government and politics is with the White House itself (**www.whitehouse.gov**). The news, speeches, reports, and other items carried on this site reflect the political views of the president. But the site also links with all other executive departments and agencies.

  Try this: From the **main** White House site, hover over the "Issues" tab. Pick an issue and read what work the executive branch is doing to improve it. Then, using outside resources, find information on the same subject—for example,

from news sources or political opposition—that discuss the president's work on the issue you chose.

- **Project Vote Smart** Project Vote Smart (**www.votesmart.org**) is a nonprofit voter education service that provides a wide range of information about voting and candidates, including local elections. You may also register to vote via the website.

  Try this: Go to the Project Vote Smart site and, again, hover over the "Issues" button. Click on a similar issue that you did for the White House, and browse through bills and public statements on the issue. Are the views and findings the same or different **from** what you discovered on the White House site?

REVIEW QUIZ

MULTIPLE CHOICE

1. Which of the following is *not* a feature of democracy?
   a. popular participation in government
   b. individual dignity
   c. minority rule
   d. equality of opportunity

2. What is the belief that government power should be limited?
   a. constitutionalism
   b. natural rights
   c. eminent domain
   d. implied powers

3. Those who argued against ratification of the U.S. Constitution, were wary of a strong national government, and favored states' rights were called _____.
   a. Federalists
   b. Anti-Federalists
   c. Democrats
   d. Constitutionalists

4. What are the first ten amendments to the U.S. Constitution listing individual freedoms and restrictions on government power?
   a. *The Federalist Papers*
   b. natural rights
   c. the Bill of Rights
   d. the Social Contract

5. What is the requirement issued by the national government with which state and local governments must comply?
   a. the supremacy doctrine
   b. federal grant-in-aid
   c. a block grant
   d. federal mandate

6. Congressional powers coming from the Supreme Court's interpretation of the "necessary and proper clause" are called what?
   a. implied powers
   b. statutory powers
   c. inherent powers
   d. enumerated powers

7. What is the principle of dividing government powers among the executive, legislative, and judicial branches?
   a. separation of powers
   b. judicial review
   c. checks and balances
   d. direct democracy

8. What is the idea that judges should defer to the decision of elected representatives unless it is in clear conflict with the plain meaning of the Constitution?
   a. judicial restraint
   b. judicial activism
   c. judicial review
   d. *stare decisis*

9. Reliance on precedent to give stability to the law is called _____.
   a. judicial restraint
   b. judicial activism
   c. judicial review
   d. *stare decisis*

10. Which of the following is *not* discussed as one of the main reasons why voters cast ballots for and against candidates?
    a. citizenship of the candidate
    b. candidate image
    c. candidate membership in social and economic groups
    d. candidate party affiliation

FILL IN THE BLANK

11. The idea that people consent to be governed and in doing so agree to give up some of their liberties so that the remainder of their liberties can be protected is called a _____.

12. Advocates for ratification of the U.S. Constitution were called _____.

13. _____ is the idea that when state and federal law conflict in an area in which both have jurisdiction, federal (national) laws are superior.

14. The division of power between states and nations is called _____.

15. _____ is the feeling that one can indeed have a personal impact on public affairs.

ANSWER KEY:

1. c; 2. a; 3. b; 4. c; 5. d; 6. a; 7. a; 8. a; 9. d; 10. a; 11. social contract; 12. Federalists; 13. National supremacy; 14. federalism; 15. Political efficacy.

Power and the Economy

Learning Objectives

After reading this chapter, students will be able to:

- Understand the key theories of how governments can exercise power in the economic system.
- Describe the tools that governments use to influence the economy.
- Explain the major trends regarding the American and global and economic systems today.

Power and Economic Organization

A great deal of power in the United States is centered in large economic organizations—corporations, banks, utilities, investment firms, and government agencies charged with the responsibility of overseeing the economy. Not all power is anchored in or exercised through these institutions; power is also embodied in class, cultural, political, and ideological institutions and processes, as discussed elsewhere in this volume. *But control of economic resources provides a continuous and important base of power in any society.*

economics
the study of the production and distribution of scarce resources

Economics is the study of the production and distribution of scarce goods and services. Economics decides the following questions:

- *What should be produced?* What goods and services should be produced and in what quantities? Should we produce more automobiles or more trains and subways, more food and fertilizer or more clean air and water, more police protection or higher Social Security benefits? Should we produce more for immediate consumption, or should we save and invest more now in order to be able to enjoy even more later? Every economic system must answer questions like these.
- *How will goods and services be produced?* The decision to produce particular goods and services does not accomplish the task. Resources must be organized and allocated, and people must be motivated to work. Various combinations of resources—land, labor, capital (factories, machinery, and supplies), and technology—might be used to produce a particular item. All these resources must be organized for production, either by providing economic incentives (wages and profits) or by threats of force.

• *For whom will goods and services be produced?* Who will consume these products and services? Economists refer to this question as the question of *distribution*. Should people be paid according to their skills, knowledge, or contribution to the production of goods and services? Or should everyone be paid equally regardless of their skills, knowledge, or contribution to production? Should people be allowed to bid for goods and services, with the most going to the highest bidders? Or should goods and services be distributed by government, with the most going to those who are best able to influence government decisions?

market system
a method of making economic decisions that allows individuals and firms to decide who gets what and how using a voluntary exchange

In general, there are two ways of making these economic decisions: (1) individually through the market system, or (2) collectively through governments. The **market system** allows individuals and firms to make their own decisions about who gets what and how. Markets implement decisions through voluntary exchange. Markets work through decentralized decisions of many separate individuals and businesses. A simple example within the market system is the Internet-based marketplace eBay. On eBay, individuals voluntarily decide to sell goods, and other individuals may decide to purchase those goods.

collective decision making a method of making economic decisions in which governments implement decisions through coercion (fines, penalties, and imprisonment) and threats of coercion

Governments also decide who gets what and how by **collective decision making**. Governments implement decisions through coercion (fines, penalties, and imprisonment) and threats of coercion. In democracies, collective decisions are influenced by individual voters, interest groups, and parties; in nondemocratic governments, the decisions are influenced primarily by ideology and the interests of government leaders themselves. An example of government collective decision making includes the creation and enforcement of minimum-wage laws.

In most economies, including that of the United States, economic decisions are made by *both* the market system and the government.[1]

The Market System, Hard Boiled and Impersonal

economic system
institutions and processes by which society produces and distributes scarce resources

The **economic system** consists of the institutions and processes by which a society produces and distributes scarce resources. There is not enough of everything for all of us to have all we want. If nature provided everything that everyone wanted without work, an economic system would be unnecessary.

But resources are scarce, and some scheme must be created to decide who gets what. Scarcity, together with the problem of choice it raises, is the fundamental question of economics.

private enterprise economy
private individuals in search of wages and profits, acting on their own, without government direction

The American economic system is a market, or free-enterprise, system. It is largely unplanned; no government bureau tells all 135 million workers in the United States where to work, what to do, or how to do it. On the whole, the **private enterprise economy** organizes itself with a minimum of centralized planning or direction. The American system relies chiefly on private individuals, in search of wages and profits, to get the job done. No government agency directs that shirts be produced: If people want shirts, then profit can be made in producing them, and businesspeople who recognize the potential profit will begin turning them out. No government agency directs how many shirts will be produced: As shirt output increases, a point is reached at which there are so many shirts that the price that people are willing to pay falls below the cost of producing them. Then, businesspeople begin curtailing their production of shirts. This same production-in-search-of-profits goes on as well for thousands of other products simultaneously.

Markets

A private enterprise economy decides what is to be produced, how it is to be produced, and how it is to be distributed, all in a fashion that is for the most part impersonal. Everyone, by following self-interest, decides who gets what. The absence of planning and control does not mean chaos. Rather, it means a complex system of production and distribution that no single mind, and probably no government planning agency, could organize or control in all its infinite detail.

A **market** is any place or arrangement that enables people to exchange money for goods, services, or labor. The rate at which money is exchanged for goods and services is called the **price**. Under the private enterprise system, the *market determines what is to be produced, how much it will cost, and who will be able to buy it.* Consumers decide what should be produced by expressing their preferences in terms of the amount of money they spend on various goods and services, thus creating **consumer demand**. When consumers are willing to pay for something, they will bid up the price of that item. The price is an indication of how much of the item consumers want produced.[2]

market
arrangement that enables people to exchange money for goods, services, and labor

price
the rate at which money is exchanged for goods and services

consumer demand
preferences for goods and services, expressed by willingness to pay

Imaginechina/Corbis

Demand for Apple products, including its iPhones and iPads, has sometimes resulted in product shortages. Here, Chinese workers labor on a production line at the plant of Foxconn in Shenzhen, China, where human rights activists charged that nearly a quarter-million workers there have been subject to long hours, obligatory overtime, and harsh conditions.

Profits

profits
motivate producers to
satisfy consumer demand
and to produce goods
and services in the most
efficient way possible

Business firms are out to make **profits**, the monetary gains that motivate producers to satisfy consumer demand and to produce goods and services in the most efficient way possible. Profits occur when selling prices are higher than the costs of production. Profits drive the free enterprise system because businesspeople move into industries in which consumers bid up prices. Then, when consumer demand bids up prices, businesspeople can afford to pay higher wages; and workers tend to move toward those industries with higher pay and better working conditions. Thus, consumer demand shifts both business and labor into industries in which prices are high. Business firms play a key role in a private enterprise system because they channel production toward industries having the strongest consumer demand and organize productive activity in the most efficient (lowest-cost) way possible. Profits are the mainspring of the market system. In seeking profits, business firms perform a vital economic function.

Prices

Who gets the goods that are produced? The price system allocates goods to those who have both the *willingness* and the *ability to pay*. The willingness to pay determines the desirability of producing a certain item. No government agency determines whether we "need" goods and services; the market reveals whether individuals are willing to pay for them. Consumers, however, must also have the ability to pay: They must earn incomes by working to produce goods and services that consumers want.

The *labor market* largely determines where people will work and how much they will be paid. The income received for their labor depends primarily on their worth to the businesses that employ them. They are worth more when they contribute more to production and profit. Where production and profits are low, wages will be low, and individuals frequently will be unemployed. The market is hard boiled and impersonal. If a business produces too much of a particular item—more than consumers are willing to buy at a particular price—the price will have to be lowered or production (supply) will have to be cut back. Competition among businesses also checks prices; a business that sets a price higher than that set by competitors will lose sales.

Thus, *consumer demand, product supply, and competition determine prices.* In the absence of interfering factors, prices depend on a relationship of supply and demand at any given time. If demand increases, prices tend to rise; if demand decreases, prices tend to fall. If supply increases, prices tend to fall; if supply decreases, prices tend to rise.

The Ideal Market

The market reconciles the interests of buyers and sellers, labor and business, in the process of getting people to agree on prices. The market in a free enterprise system undertakes this reconciliation automatically, without assistance from outside individuals or forces. The **ideal conditions for a market operation** are these:

- *Competition:* The existence of a perfect competition, in which the market has so many buyers and sellers that no single trader has any control over the price of the good or service being exchanged, and the price is made by the market through the impersonal forces of supply and demand. (If one or a few sellers have control over supply, the market is said to be *monopolistic*; if one or a few buyers have control over demand, the market is said to be *monopolistic.*)
- *Exclusion:* The ability of a buyer of the good to exclude others from the satisfactions that good provides so that no one can enjoy the benefits of someone else's purchase. (When people benefit from the purchases of others, *spillover effects* result, as, for example, in the case of national defense products, which cannot be sold on the open market.)
- *Mobility:* The complete mobility of resources and labor so they can move in response to changes in prices. In a completely mobile economy, each individual and business is prepared to alter the pattern of spending and working in response to changes in prices of goods and labor.

ideal conditions for a market operation
competition among many buyers and sellers; ability of buyer to exclude others from benefits of purchase; mobility of resources and labor

In other words, an ideal market has a great deal of competition, and prices are determined solely by supply and demand. All must pay for the goods and benefits that they receive, and resources and labor shift easily in response to changes in prices and wages.

Supply, Demand, and the Market Price

In order to understand the market, we must consider the decisions of both suppliers and consumers simultaneously. In other words, we must consider supply and demand and how both are reconciled by price.

An Example of Market Pricing

Let's illustrate what happens in a true market economy where price is governed by supply and demand.

Along with many other commodities, millions of bushels of wheat are bought and sold every day at the Chicago Board of Trade. Let's suppose that the first buyer of the day offers $6 per bushel for wheat with buyers for 20 million bushels of wheat at this low price (demand). However, few owners are willing to sell at this price, so only 10 million bushels of wheat are offered at $6 per bushel (supply). The result is an imbalance in supply and demand, a 10-million-bushel shortfall in supply at the low $6 price. Those still wishing to buy must therefore raise their price to attract more wheat to the market. Let's suppose that the price then shoots up to $8 per bushel. At this price, there are fewer buyers (let's say only an 8-million-bushel demand) and many more sellers (let's say an 18-million-bushel supply). The result is an excess supply of 10 million bushels at the high price; this excess will eventually push prices back down.

FIGURE 8-1   AN EXAMPLE OF SUPPLY, DEMAND, AND PRICE

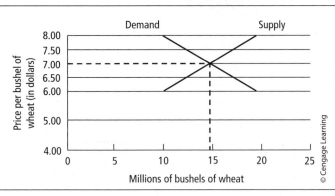

Thus, the price tends to stabilize at a point low enough to attract sufficient demand for wheat but high enough to attract an equivalent supply of wheat. In our example, this price is $7 per bushel, where 14 million bushels are demanded and 14 million bushels are offered.

Figure 8-1 shows our example of supply and demand in graphic form. The supply curve is low at a low price, but it increases as the price increases. Demand is high at a low price, but it declines as the price increases. The two lines for supply and demand intersect at a price where the amount demanded just matches the amount supplied. This will tend to be the market price. In our example, it is $7 per bushel. Any other price will produce either an excess supply (at a higher price) or an excess demand (at a lower price).

Product, Labor, and Capital Markets

labor market
decisions of employers and employees to offer and accept jobs at specified wages (prices)

Consumer products are only one type of market.[3] The **labor market** consists of the decisions of employers and employees to offer and accept jobs at specified wages. Wages represent the price of labor in the labor market. As with the product market, the price of labor (wages) depends on the available supply of labor and the demand for it. This explains the differences in wages for jobs that require little skill versus those that require great skill or training. Because a large supply of unskilled labor is capable of performing certain jobs—for example, retail work, many service jobs, or some manufacturing work—these jobs will pay lower wages than other jobs that require more skill or training, like a neurosurgeon, a concert pianist, or an astronaut.

capital market
decisions of lenders and borrowers to make and accept loans at specified interest rates (prices)

The **capital market** refers to money made available by banks and other lenders as loans, primarily to business firms but to consumers as well. The interest rate charged by lenders is really the price of money. It is the price that businesses and consumers are willing to pay lenders in order to borrow money (see Focus: "Interest Rates and You").

All three of these types of markets—product, labor, and capital markets—function simultaneously in the economy. Prices, wages, and interest rates regulate the supply and demand for products, labor, and capital, respectively. We can envision the economy as the interaction of supply and demand in all three of these types of markets (Figure 8-2). One of the largest actors in this interaction

Interest Rates and You

In the capital market, interest rates are the price of borrowing money; that is, interest rates reflect the price that businesses and consumers are willing to pay lenders in order to borrow money. Usually, interest is calculated as percentage of the amount of money borrowed.

Suppose you are interested in purchasing a car and need to budget what your monthly payments will be. Your monthly car payment will be a function of your interest rate, the amount you are borrowing, the length of the loan, and method used to calculate the interest. The interest rate available to you depends on several factors. One important factor is the Federal Funds Rate, which is the interest rate that your bank is paying other banks to borrow money, so that it can lend you the money. Another important factor is your credit score, based on your credit history. If you have little or no credit, or a poor credit history, you will pay a higher interest rate than someone with good credit.

Many loans have a fixed rate of interest; that is, the interest rate is "locked in" and stays the same for the life of the loan, so your monthly payments can be accurately calculated for the entire life of the loan. Other loans have variable interest rates, meaning that the interest rate could fluctuate (both up and down) over time. When you assume a variable rate loan, your monthly payments will change depending on the interest rate.

The following tables provide the monthly payments and the total amount for a $15,000 loan that would be paid over the life of the loan, given various interest rates. The first table shows the payments for a thirty-six-month loan, and the second table shows payments for a forty-eight-month loan. Clearly, the interest rate paid affects both the monthly payment and the total amount paid. The shorter-term loan results in higher monthly payments but less total money paid over the life of the loan.

Interest Rate (%)	Term	Monthly Payment ($)	Total Paid ($)
3	36 months	436	15,696
3.5	36 months	440	15,840
4	36 months	443	15,948
4.5	36 months	446	16,056
5	36 months	450	16,200

Interest Rate (%)	Term	Monthly Payment ($)	Total Paid ($)
3	48 months	332	15,936
3.5	48 months	335	16,080
4	48 months	339	16,272
4.5	48 months	342	16,416
5	48 months	345	16,560

In securing a loan, you would need to decide the amount of the monthly payment that you could afford, and the prevailing interest rates and your credit history would determine the interest rate that you could get on your loan. Someone with better credit history who managed a shorter-term loan could save nearly $1000 (or 15 percent) over the life of the loan.

FIGURE 8-2   PRODUCT, LABOR, AND CAPITAL MARKETS

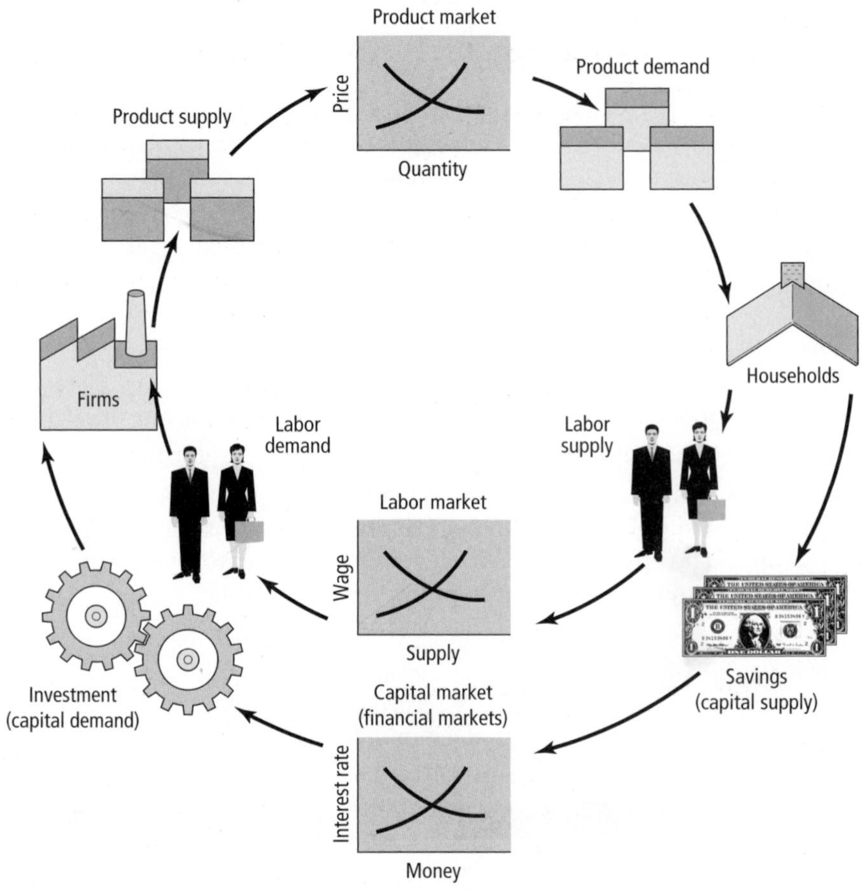

is the government, which sets interest rates, and makes many policies that affect prices and wages. The policies and extent of government involvement in these markets is decided by economic policymakers.

Government in a Free-Market Economy

The free-enterprise system that was previously described is subject to major modifications by the activities of government. In fact, government is now so involved in the economy that we might call the American economic system a *mixed* economy rather than a *private enterprise* economy. Government intervenes in the free market for many reasons:

- To protect private property and enforce contracts
- To provide a stable money supply
- To ensure competition among businesses by breaking up monopolies and prohibiting unfair competitive practices

- To set minimum standards for wages and working conditions
- To regulate industries (like banking, communications, broadcasting, and transportation) with a strong public interest
- To protect the consumer from phony goods and services and false or misleading advertising
- To provide a wide range of public services (for example, defense, education, highways, and police protection) that cannot be reasonably provided on a private-profit basis
- To provide support and care (for example, welfare, Social Security, unemployment compensation, and health care) to individuals who cannot supply these things for themselves through the market system to ensure that the economic system functions properly and avoids depression, inflation, or high levels of unemployment

The extent to which and the methods by which governments intervene in the economy vary. Oftentimes, the reason for this variation centers on the beliefs of key policymakers about the best ways for governments to support a prosperous economy.

Economic Theories That Inform Economic Policy

In making these economic decisions, policymakers tend to rely on several different theories about how power should be exercised by governments concerning the economy. In the United States, the initial consensus was that the federal government should play a very limited role in the economy. But as the national economy grew, economic actors, including workers and corporations, sought greater government involvement in the economy, including protections for both workers and for corporations. Economic conditions—especially the Great Depression—created an environment in which citizens sought even greater governmental involvement in economic matters. Throughout these developments, economists developed new theories about the proper role for governments in creating and maintaining a healthy economy: Keynesian economics, supply-side economics, and monetarism.

Laissez-Faire Economics: Government's "Hands-Off" Economic Policy

Until the late 1800s, a majority of the American people believed that the government should take a relatively **laissez-faire**, or "hands-off," stance with regard to the marketplace. That is, they thought that the government should neither encourage nor discourage business practices that affected economic health. In his *Wealth of Nations* (1776), economist Adam Smith described the principles underlying the theory of laissez-faire. Smith's classical capitalist argument emphasized that the most effective means of supporting a strong and stable economy in the long term is to allow unregulated competition in the marketplace. According to Smith, people's pursuit of their self-interest in an unregulated marketplace would yield a healthy economy. While supporting a hands-off approach in general, the national government became involved in economic activity not long after the Constitution went into effect in 1789.

laissez-faire
"hands-off" stance of a government in regard to the marketplace

Today, the economic model set forth by Adam Smith is frequently referred to as classical economics, or laissez-faire economics (from the French phrase meaning "allow to do as one pleases"). Smith wrote *The Wealth of Nations* as an attack on the mercantilism of nations in his day—that is, the attempt of governments to intervene in the economy with special tariffs, regulations, subsidies, and exclusive charters to businesses, all designed to maximize the accretion of gold and silver in government treasuries.

> It is the highest impertinence and presumption, therefore, in kings and ministers, to pretend to watch over the economy of private people, and to restrain their expense, either by sumptuary laws, or by prohibiting the importation of foreign luxuries. They are themselves always, and without any exception, the greatest spendthrifts in the society. Let them look well after their own expence, and they may safely trust private people with theirs. If their own extravagance does not ruin the state, that of their subjects never will.[4]

Smith argued against mercantilism and for free competition in the marketplace. He believed that a worldwide market, unfettered by government restrictions or subsidies, would result in lower prices and high standards of living for all. A free market would allow the businesses and nations most capable of producing particular goods cheaply and efficiently to do so. The outcome of the specialization and efficiency created by free competition would be a high standard of living for everyone. Thus, pursuit of private profit was actually in the public interest.

Smith objected to government interference in the natural operations of the marketplace. According to Smith, government should do only two things: (1) create an environment for an orderly marketplace—that is, maintain law and order, protect private property, enforce contracts, and provide a monetary system; and (2) supply those services that the marketplace cannot provide, such as defense, public works, and care of widows, orphans, and other helpless people.

Today many "classical" economists echo Adam Smith's ideas. Although it is now widely recognized that government must play an important role in stabilizing the economy (avoiding both inflation and depression), protecting consumers, regulating business and labor practices, and assisting individuals who cannot care for themselves, classical economists nonetheless argue that economic planning by government is incompatible with personal freedom. They contend that bureaucratic intervention in the economy not only is inefficient and wasteful but also gradually erodes individual freedom and initiative. Thus, the appeal of laissez-faire economics is based not only on the efficiency of the marketplace in channeling labor and resources into their most productive uses but also on the personal freedom this system guarantees.

Nonetheless, in the nineteenth century, as a manufacturing economy replaced the farming-dominated economy, the general laissez-faire stance of the national government disappeared. Technological advances fueled industrialization and the movement of workers from farms to manufacturing jobs in the cities. As immigrants flocked to the United States, the supply of cheap labor ballooned. Giant corporations formed, and individuals with money to invest accumulated great wealth. Monopolies and trusts also developed, limiting competition in a variety of industries. **Income inequality**, the gap in the proportion

income inequality
the gap in the proportion of national income held by the richest compared to that held by the poorest

of national income held by the few at the top of the income ladder compared to the many on the lower rungs of the ladder, grew. At the same time, the quality of life for the majority of working-class citizens deteriorated as additional family members, including children, needed to work to pay for life's basic necessities. Because of this decline in the quality of life, many Americans began to look to the federal government for solutions.

In the late nineteenth century, the federal government began to respond to workers' demands for better wages and working conditions and to business owners' calls for uniform rules and regulations for business practices to replace the existing hodgepodge of state-imposed regulations, abandoning the idea of a "hands off" federal economic policy. Moreover, by the early twentieth century, the national government took steps to protect public health by passing laws regulating the processing of foods and drugs, and the cleanliness and safety of manufacturing plants, indirectly affecting the economy by increasing the cost of doing business. Americans accepted and even called for a mixed economy featuring regulated capitalism.

Today, consensus continues on the need for some level of government involvement in the marketplace in order to ensure a healthy and sustainable economy, environment, and standard of living. But debate continues as well over how much government involvement is appropriate and what specific policies the government should enact, particularly in the wake of the recent economic recession, and the slow economic recovery that followed. Nonetheless, the U.S. government is committed to preserving economic prosperity and using fiscal and monetary policies to try to offset the effects of inflation and recession (see Case Study: "Achieving Economic Stability").

Keynesian Economics

The Great Depression of the 1930s significantly altered American thinking about laissez-faire economics. It is difficult to realize today what a tremendous economic disaster befell the nation in those days. Following the stock market crash of October 1929, the American economy virtually collapsed. Businesses failed, factories shut down, new construction practically ceased, banks closed, and millions of dollars in savings were wiped out. One out of four American workers was unemployed, and one out of six was receiving welfare relief. Many lost faith in the free-enterprise system and urged the abandonment of the market economy. The "solutions" of fascism in Italy and Germany and communism in the Soviet Union were looked to as alternatives to a "doomed" capitalist system.

In 1936 John Maynard Keynes, a British economist, wrote a landmark book called *The General Theory of Employment, Interest and Money*. Keynes attacked the basic notion of classical economics—that the free-enterprise system was a self-adapting mechanism that tended to produce full employment and maximum use of resources.

He believed that not all savings went into investment. When there was little prospect of profit, savings were likely to be hoarded and not used. This removal of money from the economy brought depression. Moreover, he argued, low interest rates would not necessarily stir businesses to reinvest; the expectation of profit,

CASE STUDY

Achieving Economic Stability

Socialist critics of free-market economies have long argued that the "internal contradictions of capitalism" would eventually bring about the downfall of free markets. They contended that economic cycles of inflation and depression would undermine public support for free markets and pave the way for socialism. And indeed, before 1950, economic cycles in the United States produced extreme ups and downs, with double-digit swings in real gross domestic product (GDP). In recent decades, however, economic fluctuations have been more moderate.

We still experience economic cycles, but many economists believe that countercyclical government fiscal and **monetary policy**, the government's influence over the supply of money and credit and interst rates, including the policies implemented in the Obama administration's economic stimulus package, has succeeded in achieving greater stability (see the accompanying graph).

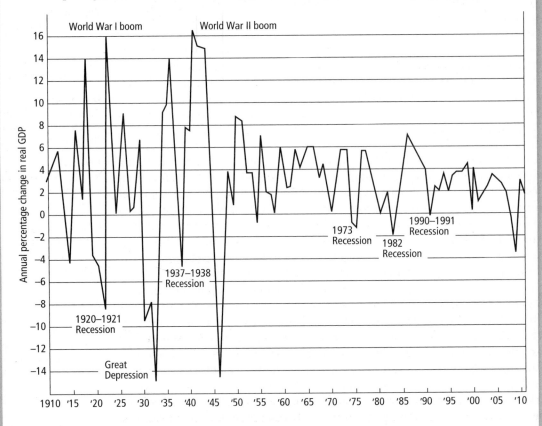

SOURCE: www.bea.gov/national/xls/gdpchg.xls

not the availability of money, motivated investment. Keynes believed that as confidence in the future diminishes, investment will decline, regardless of interest rates.

Keynesian economics recommends that during a **recession**—an economic downturn during which unemployment is high and the production of goods and services is low—the national government should increase its spending (to create jobs) and decrease taxes (so that people have more money to spend) to stimulate the economy. Based on this theory, during a **depression**, which is a long-term and severe recession, deficit spending is justified. During times of rapid economic growth—an **economic boom**, which is the opposite of a recession/depression—Keynesian theory recommends cutting government spending and possibly increasing taxes. In the long term, deficit spending during recessions and collecting a surplus when the economy is booming should lead to a balanced budget. Hence, Keynesian economic theory advocates using **fiscal policy**, the combination of tax policy and spending policy, to ensure a healthy economy.

In Keynes's view, only government could reverse a downward economic cycle. Private businesses cannot be expected to invest when consumer demand is low and no prospect of profit exists. And consumers cannot be expected to increase their purchases when their incomes are falling. So the responsibility rests on the government to take countercyclical action to increase income and consumption. In recessions, government can *increase its own expenditures or lower taxes or do both* to raise total demand and private income. Of course, increasing expenditures or lowering taxes or both means an increase in government debt, but only in this fashion can government pump money into the economy.

Keynes also argued that governments should pursue countercyclical fiscal policies to offset inflation as well as depression. **Inflation** refers to a rising price level for consumer goods and services, which results in decreased purchasing power of money. Inflation occurs when total demand exceeds or nears the productive capacity of the economy. An excess of demand over supply forces prices up. Keynes believed that when inflation threatens, government should gear its fiscal policy toward *reducing its own expenditures or increasing taxes or both*.

Before the Great Depression of the 1930s, government officials and economists believed that a **balanced budget**, a budget in which the government's expenditures (costs of doing business) are equal to or less than its revenues (money raised), was important for a healthy economy. Yet officials and economists recognized that during wartime the government might need to engage in **deficit spending**, spending more than is raised through taxes, to pay for the military effort.

Historically the national government had been willing to put aside the goal of a balanced budget only in order to finance war. That changed when President Franklin D. Roosevelt (1933–1945) and Congress supported deficit spending to address the severe economic depression that engulfed the nation in the 1930s, when unemployment rates soared as high as 25 percent. In response to the Depression's heavy toll on Americans, the Roosevelt administration implemented numerous economic regulations and also proposed and put into practice a number of innovative work and public assistance programs. These policies drove up government spending at a time of shrinking government revenues. A key objective of the government's increased spending was to trigger economic growth by lowering unemployment rates, thereby increasing demand for goods

monetary policy
the government's influence over the supply of money and credit and interest rates

Keynesian economics
theory that recommends that during a recession the national government should increase its spending and decrease taxes, and during a boom, it should cut spending and increase taxes

recession
an economic downturn during which unemployment is high and the production of goods and services is low

depression
a long-term and severe recession

economic boom
rapid economic growth

fiscal policy
the effect of government spending and taxation on the economy

inflation
the decreased value of money as evidenced by increased prices

balanced budget
a budget in which the government's expenditures are equal to or less than its revenues

deficit spending
government expenditures costing more than is raised in taxes, leading to borrowing and debt

(because more employed people means more people with money to spend), thus boosting the national economy. Deficit spending, Roosevelt said, would provide the solution to the American people's economic woes by increasing demand for goods and services. Keynes and Roosevelt were not revolutionaries. On the contrary, they wished to preserve the private enterprise system by developing effective government measures to overcome disastrous economic cycles.

Automatic Stabilizers

automatic stabilizer
a government program that acts to counter economic cycles

Part of Keynesian philosophy includes the idea of **automatic stabilizers**, which are government programs that act automatically to counter the effects of economic cycles. For example, because income taxes increase in proportion to one's earnings, the income tax automatically restricts spending habits in times of prosperity by taking larger bites of income. In times of adversity and low earnings, taxes drop automatically. Welfare programs also act automatically to counter economic cycles: In recessions more people apply for welfare and unemployment payments, and those payments help offset declines in income.

The Employment Act of 1946

Employment Act of 1946
pledges the federal government to promote maximum employment, production, and purchasing power

Council of Economic Advisers
advises the president on national economic policies

stagflation
an economic condition in which the high unemployment of a recession occurs with large increases in prices of consumer goods (high inflation) typical of economic boom

supply-side economics
using government policies to affect the supply side of the economy; that is, to increase the supply of goods and services through incentives to work, save, and produce

Roosevelt's use of fiscal policy to reinvigorate the national economy was followed by passage of the landmark **Employment Act of 1946**, which established the national government's responsibility for ensuring the low unemployment rate characteristic of a healthy economy. The act specifically pledges the federal government "to promote maximum employment, production, and purchasing power." The act created the **Council of Economic Advisers** (CEA) to "develop and recommend to the president national economic policies." The CEA is composed of three economists, appointed by the president, and a staff of analysts who collect data on the economy and advise the president on what to do to offset cycles of inflation or recession. The act also requires the president to submit to Congress an annual economic report assessing the state of the economy and recommending economic legislation.

Keynesian economics emphasizes the *demand side* of the economy—increasing government spending and expanding the money supply in periods of recession and doing the opposite in periods of inflation. In other words, Keynesian economics calls for government manipulation of aggregate (total) demand for goods and services. While Keynesian economics has informed the economic policies of Democratic and Republican administrations since Roosevelt's administration, it did not provide a clear direction for economic policy during the economic downturn beginning in the late 1970s. Labeled **stagflation**, the economy during the late 1970s and most of the 1980s experienced the high unemployment of a recession and large increases in the prices of consumer goods (high inflation) typical of an economic boom. Republican President Ronald Reagan (1981–1989) implemented a different economic theory in his efforts to deal with stagflation.

Supply-Side Economics

President Reagan introduced the nation to a competing economic theory, **supply-side economics**, or using government policies to affect the supply side of the economy; that is, to increase the supply of goods and services through incentives to work, save, and produce. Advocates of supply-side economics believe in tax cuts and decreases in government regulation to stimulate the economy in times of recession. Supply-siders argue that the high government tax rates and costly regulations reduce incentives for Americans to work, save, invest, and produce (as any extra effort will just mean they pay more in taxes). Supply-side economists believe that government should act to increase incentives to produce. Increased production will keep prices down (reduce inflation) and open up new employment opportunities (avoid recession). In addition, high taxes drain the economy because they diminish people's ability to save and corporations' ability to invest to increase productivity. Therefore, the theory goes, if the government cuts taxes, workers will be more productive and people will have more money to save and invest, thus stimulating economic growth. Supply-siders also argue that because government regulation increases the cost of producing goods, **deregulation**—reducing or eliminating restrictions on business—will contribute to increased production at the same cost, thus increasing the supply of goods.

deregulation
reduction or elimination of regulatory restrictions on firms and industries

Reducing Tax Rates

Central to supply-side economics is the idea of reducing marginal rates of taxation. (The marginal rate of taxation is the rate at which *additional* income is taxed.) Before 1981 the marginal rates of the federal personal income tax ranged from 14 to 70 percent. Supply-side economists argued that these high marginal rates of taxation (especially the 50 to 70 percent brackets) reduced economic output and productivity. People prefer leisure time over extra work if, for example, 50 percent of the additional money they make from the extra work is "snatched away" by income taxes. Individuals avoid risking their money in new business investments if, for example, 70 percent of the income from the investment will be taken away by income taxes. High marginal tax rates also encourage people to seek out tax shelters, unproductive investments that are favored by special provisions in the tax laws that reduce personal income taxes. In addition, a large underground economy flourishes when tax rates are high; in the underground economy, people hide their real incomes and/or trade goods and services rather than conduct transactions out in the open where they will be subject to taxation.

Monetarism

Economist Milton Friedman, a one-time supporter of Keynesian economics, is today best known for yet another economic theory, **monetarism**, which advocates that the government's proper role in promoting a healthy economy is using its power to regulate the money supply to ensure that the rate of inflation remains low. Government influences the supply of money by making it easy or difficult to borrow money from banks. The **Federal Reserve Board** (the Fed) was created in 1913 to regulate the nation's supply of money through its power to control the amount of money that commercial banks can lend. The Fed is headed by a seven-person board of governors, appointed by the president, for overlapping terms of fourteen years.

monetarism
theory that says the government's proper economic role is to control the rate of inflation by controlling the amount of money in circulation

Federal Reserve Board
controls the supply of money and credit and interest rates (sets monetary policy)

In periods of recession, the Fed can loosen controls on lending and encourage banks to lend more money to businesspeople at lower interest rates. During inflation the Fed can pursue tight money policies, policies that make it more difficult for banks to lend money, and thus reduce inflationary pressures.

Monetarists believe that *too much* money in circulation leads to a high inflation rate, which slows economic growth as people spend less because of higher prices. In addition, as the rate of inflation increases, investors begin to worry about the health of the economy, and investments may decline as a result, ultimately limiting economic growth. On the flip side, the monetarists say, *too little* money in circulation means there is not enough for new investments and that consequently new jobs are not created; this situation, too, retards economic growth. Today, monetarists target an inflation rate of 1–3 percent per year to ensure an adequate money supply for a healthy economy. They believe that the national government must use its monetary policy to maintain this level of inflation.

Although economists, government officials, and citizens broadly agree that the government should act to ensure a healthy economy, perpetual debate occurs over how involved the government should be in the economy and what specific policy actions it should take. Where people stand in this debate depends on which economic theory they advocate. Each theory supports the use of different government policies to promote a healthy economy.

The Contemporary American Economy

In examining the American economy in recent times, we can see that these economic theories have had important influence on decisions made by government policymakers. In particular, supply-side economics and Keynesianism have made significant impact on economic decision-making in recent presidential administrations.

Reagan Tax Cuts

When the Reagan administration arrived in Washington in 1981, its first priority was to reduce high marginal rates of income taxation in the hope of stimulating economic growth. In two tax cut acts (1981 and 1986) pushed through Congress by President Ronald Reagan, the top marginal tax rate came down from 70 to 28 percent (Figure 8-3). These tax rate reductions succeeded in stimulating the economy. Runaway inflation was halted, unemployment was reduced from double-digit levels, and the number and proportion of Americans with jobs reached all-time highs. However, the incentive effects of the tax cuts did not produce enough new tax revenues to make up for lower rates. Tax revenues lagged far behind federal expenditures. Neither President Reagan, nor President George H. W. Bush, nor Congress was willing to cut expenditures enough to reduce the gap between lower taxes and continued high spending levels. This resulted in the largest deficits in the nation's history, and these deficits are now part of the nation's debt, which exceeds $16 trillion.

FIGURE 8-3 TOP MARGINAL INCOME TAX RATES

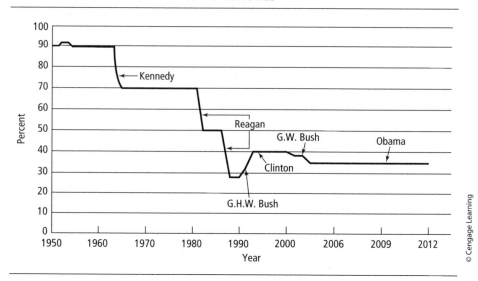

© Cengage Learning

Bush and Clinton Tax Increases

Neither President George H. W. Bush nor President Bill Clinton was fully convinced by the arguments of supply-side economics. At the Republican National Convention in 1988, George H. W. Bush made a firm pledge to the American people that he would veto any tax increase passed by the Democratic-controlled Congress, speaking the famous words: "Read my lips. No new taxes." But the pressure of continuing high deficits and the unwillingness to cut spending caused former President Bush to reverse course and agree to an increase in the top marginal income tax rate to 31 percent, thereby abandoning the supply-side economic policies of his predecessor, Ronald Reagan. By breaking his solemn pledge on taxes, Bush contributed heavily to his own defeat in the 1992 presidential election.

Bill Clinton won the presidency largely on his pledge to revive the economy. (At his campaign headquarters, aides posted a large sign, "It's the economy, stupid," to help maintain the focus of the campaign.) Clinton repeatedly referred to the supply-side economics of the Reagan years as "failed, trickle-down" economics. Soon after taking office, he presented Congress with a new economic plan calling for a large tax increase; cuts in defense spending; increases in spending for health, education, communications, and transportation; and a schedule for gradually lowering annual federal deficits. Clinton succeeded in getting the Democratic-controlled Congress to raise top marginal income tax rates for high-income earners to 36 and 39.6 percent.

Prosperity and Decline

The United States experienced its longest continuous period of GDP growth beginning in 1991. The economic prosperity of the 1990s created more jobs and lowered the **unemployment rate**—the percentage of the workforce not working

unemployment rate
percentage of the labor force not working but looking for work or waiting for a job to open

but looking for jobs or waiting to return to a job. At the same time, inflation—rises in the general level of prices—was kept in check. This prosperity confounded supply-side economic theory, inasmuch as it came after *increases* in marginal tax rates. During the Clinton administration, economic growth combined with increases in tax rates succeeded in turning annual federal deficits into annual surpluses.

The Bush Economy

The prosperity prevalent during the Clinton administration came to an end in early 2001 when unemployment rates started to increase. The problem worsened after the terrorist attacks on September 11 of that year. And so during President George W. Bush's first term, his administration had to grapple with increased unemployment, falling stock prices and skittish investors, and higher prices in some sectors of the economy. Working with a Republican-dominated Congress for most of his presidency, Bush pursued many supply-side policies by cutting taxes and deregulating. Bush's strategy to address the nation's economic woes was to change the tax code, relying on policies reminiscent of the supply-side economics of the 1980s. These changes focused on reducing taxes for those making the most money in hopes of spurring the economy into recovery. The Federal Reserve Board also sought to inject money into the hurting post–September 11, 2001, economy by slashing interest rates.

Bush succeeded in winning tax cuts for corporations, the wealthiest Americans, and the lowest-earning Americans during his first term in office. One result of these tax changes was that taxpayers who made more than $1 million in 2004 saw their tax bill fall by an average of $123,592.[5] Bush reduced the tax rate (the top earners, those earning over $311,950 would pay $90,514.50 [29 percent] plus 35 percent on all earnings over $311,950) and increased the per-child tax credit from $600 to $1000. Using supply-side theory, Bush also reduced the top capital gains tax rate (tax rate paid when profit is realized on the sale of property or other assets) and the dividend income tax rate (the rate paid on dividends paid to stockholders), seeking to free up more money for investment. Bush implemented these policies, which primarily affected the wealthiest Americans, in the hope that increased investment by the top economic tiers would spur economic growth, benefiting those on the lower rungs of the economic ladder. Though many economists would not credit the Bush tax policies, by the middle of Bush's second term, unemployment rates had fallen, and the stock market was at a record high.

But the economy would again start to falter, starting with a burst in the housing bubble, characterized by a readjustment in unsustainable increases in the prices of real estate. Coupled with the real estate bubble bursting was the realization that many banks and lending institutions—in an effort to profit during the hey-day of the real estate boom—had made risky loans to many home purchasers with poor credit history, or who had assumed mortgages too high for their income levels. With the burst of the real estate market, the unemployment rate began to creep up (with employment in new housing construction being hit first, then spawning declines in connected industries) and mortgage defaults increased. Many of these risky mortgages—called sub-prime because the borrowers typically would not qualify for a traditional prime mortgage—had been purchased by financial institutions, and as their losses accumulated, investors sold off stocks, leaving some banks insolvent, forcing the collapse of once-giant financial services corporations, including Bear Stearns and Lehman Brothers. The stock sell-off resulted in a spiraling decline in the stock market, decreasing the value of private investment and retirement portfolios. This in turn marked a decline in consumer confidence, and an accompanying reluctance by consumers to spend. The decrease in consumer spending in turn caused less demand for goods and services, exacerbating the already grim unemployment numbers.

In response to this spreading crisis, President Bush asked Congress to intervene, and Congress passed the Emergency Economic Stabilization Act of 2008 (see Research This!). This act, widely referred to as the bank bailout, sought to restore confidence in the banking industry, and sought to provide relief to banks and lending institutions by providing up to $700 billion for the federal government to purchase mortgage-backed securities through the Troubled Assets Relief

RESEARCH *THIS!*

The accompanying table shows the banks that were the top recipients of bank bailout money. Those figures in italics note that the money has been repaid to the government.

Bank	City	State	Amount
Wells Fargo & Co.	San Francisco	Calif.	$25,000,000,000
Citigroup Inc.	New York	N.Y.	$25,000,000,000
JPMorgan Chase & Co.	*New York*	*N.Y.*	*$25,000,000,000*
Bank of America Corp.	*Charlotte*	*N.C.*	*$15,000,000,000*
Morgan Stanley	*New York*	*N.Y.*	*$10,000,000,000*
Goldman Sachs Group Inc.	*New York*	*N.Y.*	*$10,000,000,000*
Bank of America Corp.	*Charlotte*	*N.C.*	*$10,000,000,000*
The PNC Financial Services Group Inc.	Pittsburgh	Pa.	$ 7,579,200,000
U.S. Bancorp	*Minneapolis*	*Minn.*	*$ 6,599,000,000*
Capital One Financial Corp.	*McLean*	*Va.*	*$ 3,555,199,000*
SunTrust Banks Inc.	Atlanta	Ga.	$ 3,500,000,000
Regions Financial Corp.	Birmingham	Ala.	$ 3,500,000,000
Fifth Third Bancorp	Cincinnati	Ohio	$ 3,408,000,000
Hartford Financial Services Group, Inc.	Hartford	Conn.	$ 3,400,000,000
American Express Company	*New York*	*N.Y.*	*$ 3,388,890,000*
BB&T Corp.	*Winston-Salem*	*N.C.*	*$ 3,133,640,000*
Bank of New York Mellon Corp.	*New York*	*N.Y.*	*$ 3,000,000,000*

SOURCE: http://money.cnn.com/news/specials/storysupplement/bankbailout/

YOUR ANALYSIS:

1. Have most of the top recipients paid back their loans?

2. In your view, is it the responsibility of the government to shore up the banking industry? What would be the danger of not shoring up these banks?

3. Should the government impose increased restrictions on how recipient banks do business? Should these restrictions apply only before they have repaid borrowed monies, or continue after payback?

(TARP) Program. The bank bailout would be subjected to great criticism when it was revealed that executives employed by several of the bailed out banks earned enormous, multi-million dollars salaries, leading some critics to question whether government money should have been used to shore up these companies.

Obama's Economic Policies

economic stimulus bill
fiscal policy designed to pump money into the ailing economy

It was in this complex and sweeping economic firestorm that Barack Obama assumed the presidency. Modeling his economic recovery proposal on the New Deal programs of Franklin D. Roosevelt, the original Keynesian president, Obama requested that Congress pass an **economic stimulus bill**, a fiscal policy designed to pump money into the ailing economy, called the American Recovery and Reinvestment Act of 2009. Obama's $787 billion economic stimulus act sought to curtail the recession by cutting individual and small business taxes, and by creating one to two million jobs by spending $185 billion in 2009 on health care, education, energy, infrastructure, and research and technology. Through the stimulus package, President Obama and the Congress sought to spur growth in the U.S. economy. The stimulus act was meant to shorten the recession, which is defined as negative GDP growth, and also to create hope, stemming the panic that gripped investors in 2008. In response to the mistrust that many people feel toward the finance industry, it further limited bonuses for senior executives for companies that receive TARP funds. Heading into his bid for re-election in 2012, President Obama also sought to change the nation's tax policy, advocating for a higher marginal tax rate for millionaires. In his corner was the iconic billionaire financier Warren Buffett, whose advocacy for Obama's proposal (Buffett decried the idea that he was subjected to a lower tax rate than his own secretary) lead it to be dubbed "The Buffett Rule."

Measuring America's Wealth

Underlying the power of nations is the strength of their economy—their total productive capacity. The United States can produce $11 trillion worth of goods and services in a single year for its 313 million people. Even in times of economic crisis, the United States plays a dominant role in the global economy. To understand America's vast wealth, we must learn how to measure it. We need to know where the wealth comes from and where it goes. This measuring is done through the **national income accounting** system, whereby the federal government collects data that describe the nation's income and outputs. The U.S. government, like the governments of other advanced industrialized nations, collects extensive data on economic activity.

national income accounting
data collected by government that describe the nation's income and output

Let's begin with the **gross domestic product** (GDP), the nation's total production of goods and services for a single year valued in terms of market prices.* It is the sum of all the goods and services that people have been willing to pay for, from wheat production to bake sales, from machine tools to maid service, from aircraft manufacturing to bus service, from automobiles to chewing gum, from wages and salaries to interest on bank deposits.

gross domestic product
the total value of production of goods and services for a year

* Occasionally, economists use a slightly different measure of national output: the gross national product (GNP). The GNP measures output attributable to U.S. residents, in other words the total output attributable to production located in the United States. The GNP is often used in cross-national comparisons.

Computing the GDP

To compute the GDP, economists sum up all the expenditures on goods and services, plus government purchases. Care is taken to count *only the final product* sold to consumers so that raw materials will not be counted twice—that is, in the original sale to a manufacturer and in the final price of the product. Business investment includes *only new investment goods* (buildings, machinery, and so on) and does not include financial transfers such as the purchase of stocks and bonds. Government purchases for goods and services include the money spent on *goods* (weapons, roads, buildings, parks, and so on), as well as the *wages* paid for the *services* of government employees. Transfer payments such as welfare payments, unemployment insurance, and Social Security payments are *not* part of the GDP because they are not payments for currently produced goods or services. The GDP ignores *all* transactions of money and goods in which *no new* goods or services are produced. Thus, the GDP becomes a measure of the nation's production of goods and services. It can be thought of as the total national economic pie for a given year.

Current Dollars versus Constant Dollars

Because prices have increased over time through inflation, to get a meaningful measure of actual growth in output, we must view the gross domestic product in **chained dollars**. Doubling the GDP merely by doubling prices signifies no real gain in production, so to separate *real increases* in the GDP from mere *dollar increases*, we must adjust for changes in the value of the dollar over the years. Economists account for changes in the value of a dollar by establishing the value of a dollar in a particular time base (for example, 2005) and then using *chained dollars* to measure the value of goods over time. Figure 8-4 shows that the GDP has grown both in current dollars *and* in chained dollars. Thus, America's economic growth is not just a product of inflation.

chained dollars
dollars valued from a particular year in order to account for changes in the value of dollars—that is, inflation

Per Capita GDP

The GDP is sometimes measured in per capita terms—the GDP divided by the population. **Per capita GDP** is a better measure of the well-being of the average person in a country. Cross-national comparisons are generally made in gross national product (GNP)—a slightly different measure that includes goods and services produced by citizens outside of their own country.

per capita GDP
GDP divided by the population; a measure of economic well-being

Limitations of the GDP Measure

The GDP does *not* measure nonmarket activities—for example, household work or child rearing (unless these tasks are performed by paid employees). It does not measure well-being as it is reflected in leisure time. Indeed, an increase in leisure may be associated with a decrease in GDP because less time is devoted to producing goods and services. Yet we might consider ourselves better off for having more time for leisure activities. Moreover, the GDP does not directly measure social ills—for example, crime or pollution. And it does not measure the *distribution* of income or output among individuals in a society. It is not a measure of inequality; it does not tell us what proportions of people are wealthy or poor.

FIGURE 8-4   GDP GROWTH IN THE UNITED STATES

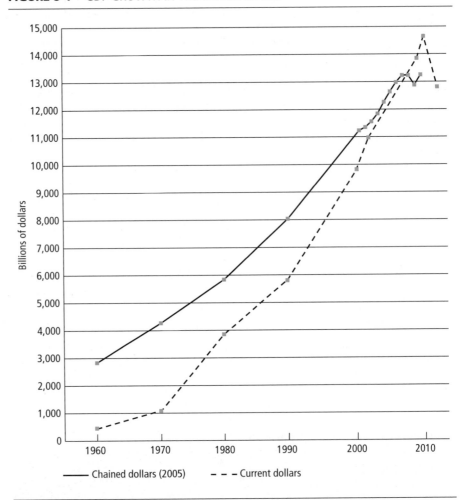

──── Chained dollars (2005)   – – – Current dollars

SOURCE: http://www.census.gov/foreign-trade/index.html.

The GDP values all goods and services equally in dollar items. It does not distinguish, for example, between cigarette sales, Bible sales, football-game ticket sales, grocery-store sales, or handgun sales. Arguably, some goods and services benefit society more than others, yet the GDP is neutral in its valuation of all goods and services.

underground economy
economic activities that
are unreported and not
counted in the GDP

Finally, some economic activities escape measurement. The **underground economy** involves activities that are unreported to government and therefore not counted in the GDP. For example, illegal drug transactions are not counted as part of the GDP even though they may constitute a significant portion of economic activity in the nation. Likewise, income that is not reported for tax purposes—that is, tax-evasion income—generally goes unreported into GDP. For example, cash received in private transactions, including tips, is often unreported or underreported. Studies estimate that the size of the U.S. underground economy is anywhere from 5 to 30 percent of the GDP.

Government Money: Where It Comes from and Where It Goes

The U.S. government currently receives about $2 *trillion* each year in revenues, an amount equal to about 22 percent of the GDP.[6] It currently spends a bit more than it receives (Figure 8-5).

Revenues

Where does all this money come from? Federal revenues come primarily from the federal personal income tax (42 percent) and the Social Security payroll tax (40 percent). These taxes are paid to the federal government directly by the American people. The corporate income tax has declined as a source of federal revenue (9 percent) over the years. Federal excise taxes on various products, including alcohol, tobacco, and gasoline, provide an additional source of revenue (3 percent); and the government also collects miscellaneous revenues, including customs duties on imported goods, fines, penalties, and forfeitures.

Expenditures

Most U.S. government spending goes into entitlement programs. These programs provide all classes of people with legally enforceable rights to government benefits. Entitlements now account for over 50 percent of all federal spending,

AP Photo/Jim Prisching, File

In 2009, states received billions of dollars to create jobs in order to stimulate the economy. Billions of dollars were spent in road repaving and infrastructure improvements, which many analysts said was an efficient use of such money. In creating the stimulus package, the Obama administration relied on a Keynesian approach to solving the recession.

FIGURE 8-5   U.S. GOVERNMENT REVENUES AND EXPENDITURES

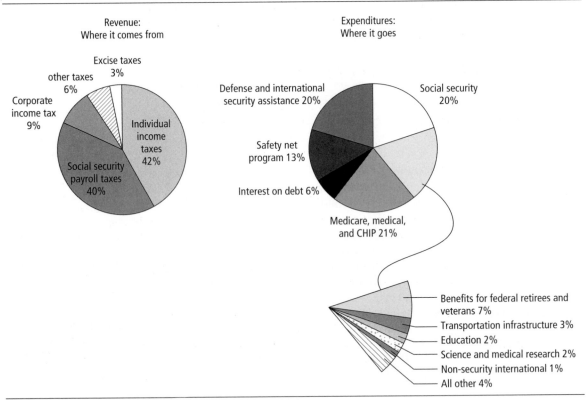

SOURCE: www.usgovernmentrevenue.com.

including Social Security (20 percent), Medicare, Medicaid, the Children's Health Insurance Program (CHIP) (21 percent), and various public assistance programs (13 percent), including food stamps, supplemental security income, and tax credits. These entitlement programs were enacted by past Congresses and represent continuing commitments of federal spending. Of course, future Congresses could reduce or cancel these previously promised benefits, but doing so would be regarded by many voters as a breach of trust. Social Security and Medicare benefits are especially sacrosanct. In addition to these entitlement programs, the federal government is committed to other mandatory spending, including interest payments on the national debt. With the aging U.S. population, each year more people become entitled to Social Security and Medicare—the two largest entitlement programs—and federal government spending rises accordingly. Between 1990 and 2011, the federal outlay for Social Security nearly tripled, growing from about $250 billion to about $731 billion.

In the years immediately following the end of the Cold War, spending for national defense had declined dramatically from an average of about $300 billion annually to about $275 billion annually (see Chapter 14). During the

George W. Bush administration, however, defense spending increased significantly in order to finance post–September 11 military operations in Afghanistan and Iraq, a trend that continued under President Obama. In 2011, defense spending totaled more than $718 billion.

Government Debt, Deficits, and Surpluses

For many years the federal government spent more than it received in revenues (Figure 8-6). This trend temporarily ended with the Clinton administration's policies that increased tax revenues, and in 1998 Congress passed the first balanced budget (a budget in which expenditures were less than revenues) since 1969. This trend continued until 2001. In 2002, the government again began running a **federal deficit**, the name for the negative imbalance that occurs when the government spends more than it collects. Since that time, the federal government has continued to engage in deficit spending, with the budgets from 2002 reflecting some of the largest federal budget deficits in history. This and the cumulative annual federal deficits drove up the accumulated debt of the U.S. government to over $16 *trillion*. Both deficit spending and the accumulating national debt were the centerpiece of a disagreement between President Obama and many conservative Republican members of Congress, who sought lower federal spending—particularly on education and some safety net programs in order to decrease the deficit and slow the accumulating debt. The **national debt**, the sum total of all annual federal deficits, now totals about $42,000 for every man, woman, and child in the nation, or about $212,000 for every one of America's 66 million families (see International Perspective: "A Look at Government Debt").

federal deficit
the annual negative imbalance between revenues and expenditures of the U.S. government, or when the government spends more than it collects in any given year; the sum of the deficits plus interest equals the national debt

national debt
the total of all annual federal deficits, money owed to others due to borrowing

FIGURE 8-6   ANNUAL FEDERAL DEFICITS AND SURPLUSES

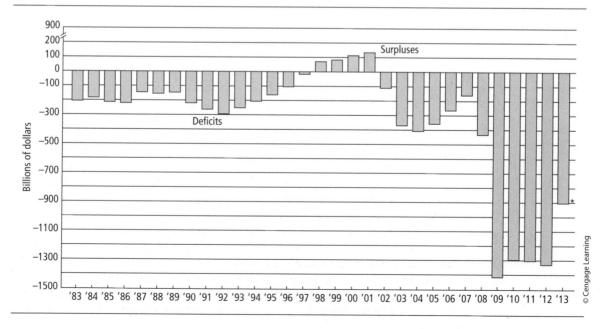

© Cengage Learning

INTERNATIONAL PERSPECTIVE

A Look at Government Debt

Much is made of the accumulating debt of the U.S. government. Politicians speak of "mortgaging our children's future." And in recent years, the debt has increased significantly, with burgeoning deficits resulting from increased payout for Social Security and increased military expenditures. The accompanying table places the U.S. public debt in perspective and shows that although the federal debt is not as high as some industrialized nations (say, Japan's at 208 percent), it also is markedly higher than others. As the table shows, some nations' debt is several times their GDP, whereas others' debts are a relatively insignificant proportion. Examining debt as proportion of the GDP is a good idea because it conveys debt as a proportion of the relative size of the economy. For example, suppose one individual had credit card and personal loan debt of $70,000 and had an annual income of $35,000. His debt is equal to 200 percent of his income. But suppose that same $70,000 debt was owed by an individual with an annual income of $140,000. Then the debt would constitute only 50 percent of her annual income. The proportion of debt to income, or in the case of nations, debt to GDP, places the debt in the framework of the overall economy.

Rank	Country	Public Debt (% of GDP)	Rank	Country	Public Debt (% of GDP)
1	Zimbabwe	231	19	Belize	84
2	Japan	208	20	Canada	84
3	Saint Kitts and Nevis	200	21	Hungary	83
4	Greece	165	22	Germany	82
5	Lebanon	137	23	United Kingdom	80
6	Iceland	130	24	Bhutan	79
7	Antigua and Barbuda	130	25	Sri Lanka	79
8	Jamaica	127	26	Dominica	78
9	Italy	120	27	Saint Lucia	77
10	Singapore	118	28	Bahrain	75
11	Ireland	107	29	Israel	74
12	Barbados	104	30	Austria	72
13	Portugal	103	31	Nicaragua	71
14	Sudan	101	32	United States	69
15	Belgium	100	33	Spain	68
16	Saint Vincent and the Grenadines	90	34	Malta	68
			35	Cyprus	67
17	Egypt	86			
18	France	86			

SOURCE: *CIA World FactBook*, 2012.

The U.S. government debt is owed mostly to American banks and financial institutions and private citizens who buy Treasury bonds. About 47 percent of this debt is owed to foreign banks, firms, and individuals. As old debt comes due, the Treasury Department sells new bonds to pay off the old; that is, it continues to "roll over," or "float," the debt. While many object to the large federal debt (particularly conservative Republicans in Congress), the debt today is a smaller percentage of the GDP than at some periods in U.S. history. Indeed, to pay the costs of fighting World War II, the U.S. government ran up a debt of 110 percent of GDP; the current debt is the highest in history in dollar terms but only about 70 percent of the GDP. This suggests that the debt is manageable because of the size and strength of the U.S. economy.

The ability to float such a debt depends on public confidence in the U.S. government—confidence that it will continue to pay interest on its debt, that it will pay off the principal of bond issues when they come due, and that the value of the bonds will not decline over time because of inflation.

Debt Burdens

Interest payments on the national debt come from current taxes and divert money from *all* other government programs. Even if the federal government manages to continue to balance its current annual budgets, these payments will remain obligations of the children and grandchildren of the current generation of policy makers and taxpayers.

The federal debt requires the U.S. Treasury Department to borrow large amounts of money. This money is diverted from the private sector where it would otherwise be available as loans for new and expanding businesses, for modernizing industrial plants and equipment, and for financing the purchase of homes, cars, appliances, and other credit items for consumers. In other words, the federal government's borrowing "crowds out" capital markets. The less capital available in the private sector, the slower the growth rate of the economy will be.

The Politics of Deficits

For many years, despite pious rhetoric in Washington about the need to "balance the budget," neither presidents nor Congresses, Democrats nor Republicans were willing to reduce expenditures or raise taxes enough to produce a balanced budget. Congressional leaders consistently sidetracked proposed amendments to the U.S. Constitution that would require a balanced budget. It was more expedient politically to shift the burden of current government spending to future generations by incurring deficits than it was to cut favorite programs or raise taxes. Politicians were (and still are) especially reluctant to challenge the politically powerful older citizens who receive the largest proportions of federal spending through the Social Security and Medicare programs.

The nation's booming economy in the 1990s added more revenues to the federal treasury and gradually reduced annual deficits. In 1998 when President Clinton presented the first balanced federal budget in thirty years to the Congress, he projected surpluses for future years. With the economic downturn that subsequently arose in 2001, combined with increased government spending for the wars in Iraq and Afghanistan, plus defense and homeland security and decreased tax revenue because of the tax cuts, the Bush administration's budgets again engaged in deficit spending. This trend continued during the Obama administration, but with the emergence of a vocal group of conservative Republicans in the House of Representatives (some of whom had won election in 2010 based on their opposition to the growing debt), Obama faced opposition in Congress for continuing the established pattern of deficit spending.

In planning the 2013 budget, President Obama proposed a spending measure that would include infrastructure improvements designed to create jobs, and job-training programs. He advocated raising $1.5 trillion from the wealthiest Americans over 10 years to offset the costs of these programs. He also sought to close some corporate tax breaks, many targeted at oil and gas companies. And advocating the Buffett Rule, he also proposed higher taxes on dividend income.

House Republicans opposed most of President Obama's proposal and created their own plan that cut domestic spending, reformed Medicare and Medicaid, and transformed the federal tax code. As part of their proposal, the House approved cutting $310 billion from projected deficit spending over the next decade by cutting programs for the poor and using the savings to offset military spending cuts scheduled for 2013. Deficit spending and the debt remained a central issue throughout the 2012 presidential and congressional campaigns.

The Concentration of Economic Power

Economic power in America is highly concentrated. Large economic and financial institutions decide what will be produced in the United States and increasingly what will be produced outside of it. They decide how many people will be employed and what their wages will be. They determine how goods and services will be distributed and what new products will be developed.

They decide how much money will be available for capital investment and where these investments will be made. Decisions made in the boardroom of these institutions affect our lives as much as those typically made by governments (see Focus: "The Concentration of Corporate Power").

Power in the Corporation

The modern corporation is governed by its board of directors. The directors include the chairman of the board, the president or CEO (chief executive officer), selected senior vice presidents, and some "outside" members who are not managers of the corporation. The "inside" directors, who are also full-time presidents or vice presidents of the corporation, tend to dominate board proceedings because they know more about the day-to-day operations of the corporation than do the outside directors.

Outside directors may sit on the corporate board as representatives for families who still own large blocks of stock or as representatives for banks that have

Reuters/Mike Segar

Over the past several years, revelations that financial services companies had been improperly run and had engaged in shoddy business practices while corporate CEOs profited handsomely riled the American public. Among these scandals was the MF Global scandal, which was alleged to have mishandled $1.6 billion. Artist Geoffrey Raymond (right), famous for his paintings of troubled Wall Street figures, stands by his work "Corzine Agonistes," protesting the company's treatment of its investors.

lent money to the corporation. Occasionally, outside directors are prominent citizens, members of minority groups, or representatives of civic associations. Outside directors are usually chosen by the CEO and the inside directors. All directors are officially elected by the corporation's stockholders. However, the CEO and inside directors draw up the "management slate," which usually wins because top management casts many proxy votes, which they solicit in advance from stockholders.

Corporate power does *not* rest in the hands of masses of corporate employees or even in the hands of millions of middle- and upper-middle-class Americans who own corporate stock. When confronted with mismanagement, these stockholders simply sell their stock, rather than try to challenge the power of the directors.

Managerial Power

Following the Industrial Revolution in America in the late nineteenth century and well into the twentieth century, the nation's largest corporations were controlled by the tycoons who created them—Andrew Carnegie (Carnegie Steel, later United States Steel, and today USX), Andrew Mellon (Alcoa and Mellon banks), Henry Ford (Ford Motor), J. P. Morgan (J.P. Morgan), and John D. Rockefeller (Standard Oil Company, later broken into Exxon, Mobil, Chevron, Atlantic Richfield, and other large oil companies). But by the 1930s, control of most large corporations had passed from owners to professional managers. The theory of **managerialism** became the conventional wisdom about corporate governance.[7]

managerialism
control of the corporation by professional managers rather than stockholders

FOCUS

The Concentration of Corporate Power

Control over the nation's economic resources is becoming increasingly concentrated in the hands of very few people, largely because of the consolidation of economic enterprise into a small number of giant corporations. The following statistics can only suggest the scale and concentration of modern corporate enterprise in the United States: The United States has more than two hundred thousand industrial corporations, but the one hundred largest corporations hold over two-thirds of the nation's industrial assets. Indeed, just ten industrial corporations hold one-third of the nation's industrial assets (see the accompanying table). Banking is also highly concentrated. The United States has nearly fifteen thousand banks, but the ten largest banks hold over one-third of all banking assets. The rate of corporate and banking mergers in recent years suggests that this concentration of economic resources is increasing.

The Largest U.S. Industrial Corporations*	The Largest U.S. Commercial Banks (ranked by revenues and profits)
1. ExxonMobil	1. Bank of America
2. Wal-Mart Stores	2. JPMorgan Chase
3. Chevron	3. Citigroup
4. Conoco Phillips	4. Wells Fargo
5. General Motors	5. Goldman Sachs Group
6. General Electric	6. Morgan Stanley
7. Berkshire Hathaway	7. American Express Corp
8. Fannie Mae	8. U.S. Bancorp
9. Ford Motor	9. Capital One Financial
10. Hewlett-Packard	10. Ally Financial

* Ranked by a composite index comprised of sales, profits, assets, and market value.

SOURCE: http://www.sigtarp.gov/Quarterly%20Reports/April_25_2012_Report_to_Congress.pdf

principal–agent problem
ensuring that managers (agents) operate firms in the best interest of the owners (principals) rather than themselves

It was recognized early on that corporate managers might run their firms to best serve their own interests rather than those of the owners—for example, paying themselves multimillion-dollar annual salaries and providing themselves with lavish corporate-paid lifestyles. But for decades, individual and institutional stockholders largely ignored this potential **principal–agent problem**. Stockholders' power was fragmented and dispersed; stockholders could not do much, other than sell their stock, even if they knew that managers were taking personal advantage of their position. But perhaps a more important reason that managers were largely unchallenged was that the American economy prospered from the 1940s through the 1970s. Governance of the U.S. corporation seemed to be working well, rewarding both managers and owners.

Corporate Counterrevolution

Traditionally, the top managers of large corporations were considered invincible; nothing short of bankruptcy could dislodge them. Corporate managers ran the American economy, perpetuating themselves in office; they ruled without much interference from outside directors, stockholders, employees, or consumers. But beginning in the 1980s, new challenges to the imperial position of top management arose, most notably from (1) a new activism by outside directors and large stockholders, checking the power of corporate chief executives and occasionally forcing their retirement; and (2) a rise in **hostile takeovers** led by corporate raiders, who acquire corporate stock and voting power in order to force the ouster and replacement of existing management.

A hostile takeover involves the purchase of enough stock in a publicly held corporation to force the ouster and replacement of existing corporate management. Usually, a hostile takeover begins with a **corporate raider** buying the stock of a corporation on the open market, often with money borrowed for this purpose. After establishing a stock ownership position in the corporation, the raider may then offer a takeover bid to existing management. Management may reject the bid outright or try to buy back the stock purchased by the raider at a higher price—that is, to offer the raider "greenmail." If the raider and management cannot reach an agreement, the hostile takeover proceeds. The raider arranges to borrow additional money—perhaps several billion dollars—to make a purchase offer to the target corporation's stockholders, usually at a price higher than the current stock exchange price. If the raider wins control of the corporation, the old managers are replaced.

Following a successful takeover, the corporation is heavily laden with new debt. The raider may have borrowed billions to buy out shareholders. The investment firms that provided the loans to finance the corporation's purchase may issue junk bonds with high interest rates to attract investors to these risky ventures. The corporation must pay off these bonds with its own revenues. Additionally, many millions of dollars may be in bond-sale commissions and attorneys' fees to pay out. The raider may be forced to sell off parts of the corporation or some of its valuable assets in order to help pay off part of the debt. Thus, the target corporation itself must eventually bear the burden of the takeover battle.

Are corporate takeovers good or bad for America? The raiders claim that their activities force improvements in efficiency and productivity. Even the potential threat of a takeover forces corporate managers to streamline their operations, eliminate waste, increase revenues, raise profits, and distribute profits to their shareholders rather than spend them on the management comforts.

Opponents of the corporate takeover movement argue that fear of the raider forces management to focus on short-range profits at the expense of long-range research and development. Management may resort to "poison pills" to deliberately weaken its own corporation to make it unattractive to raiders: It

hostile takeover
the purchase of stock in a corporation by an outsider and the subsequent ousting of the prior management

corporate raider
an investor who arranges to purchase stock in a hostile takeover

may increase its debt, buy other poorly performing corporations, devalue stock-holders' voting powers, or provide itself with "golden parachutes" (rich sever-ance benefits) in the event of ouster. While the original stockholders are paid handsomely by the raider, the corporation must labor intensively to pay off the debt incurred.

The corporation may be broken apart and its separate pieces sold, which may disrupt and demoralize employees. If the corporation cannot meet the high-interest payments, bankruptcy threatens. And the diversion of American capital from productive investments to takeovers threatens to weaken national productivity.

The Principle–Agent Problem Revisited

In recent years, a wave of corporate scandals in the United States left many employees and investors again facing the principle–agent problem. Over the past several years, revelations that financial services companies, insurance com-panies, and American automotive companies had been mismanaged, improperly run—had engaged in shoddy business practices while corporate CEOs profited handsomely—riled the American public.

Among the worst of these scandals was that of the American International Group (AIG) insurance company. Caught in a liquidity crisis and faced with a downgraded credit rating, the federal government bailed out the insurance giant in September 2008, enabling AIG to borrow $182 billion in exchange for equity in the company. But when media reports revealed that the company had paid more than $150 million in bonuses to employees who stayed with the com-pany, backlash ensued. High-level employees received hate mail, death threats, and faced protestors outside their homes. When Congress passed the economic stimulus package in 2009, one component of the act was limiting allowable bonuses to employees of corporations bailed out by the federal government. Yet scandals, including the 2011 revelation that executives at MF Global had misap-propriated $1.6 billion in customer's investments, continued to rock the banking and financial services sectors.

The Globalization of Economic Power

Today, almost one-quarter of the world's total economic output is sold in a country other than the country in which it was produced. The United States currently exports about 13 percent of the value of its GDP and imports about16 percent. Exports and imports were only about 3 percent of GDP as late as 1970.[8]

Historically, America's corporate and financial institutions supported **tariffs**, which are taxes on goods imported into a country in order to protect their domestic marketplace. Tariffs on foreign imports forced prices up and gave U.S. firms sheltered markets. This not only improved the profit mar-gins of U.S. corporations but also allowed them to operate less efficiently: Management became top-heavy; its products, especially automobiles, were

tariff
a tax on goods imported into a country

frequently poor in quality; and the workforce was larger, and wages for workers were higher than they otherwise would be if U.S. firms had to face foreign competition.

Expanding World Trade

America's corporate and financial powers gradually came to see the economic advantages of expanding world trade (Figure 8-7). U.S. firms that dominated the domestic market in the 1950s and 1960s—steel, automobiles, aircraft, computers, drugs, electronics, agriculture, and so on—began to look abroad to expand their own sales. American corporations became multinational corporations (see International Perspective: "The Multinationals' Global Economic Power"). They began by expanding their sales and distribution staffs worldwide and then later began to shift manufacturing itself to low-wage, low-cost countries. Globalization of economic power required reductions in tariffs and trade barriers around the world. America's corporate and financial elites began to lobby Congress for reductions in U.S. tariffs. The result was a dramatic decline in average U.S. tariff rates. In effect, the United States became an open market.

FIGURE 8-7   THE GROWTH OF WORLD TRADE IN THE U.S. ECONOMY

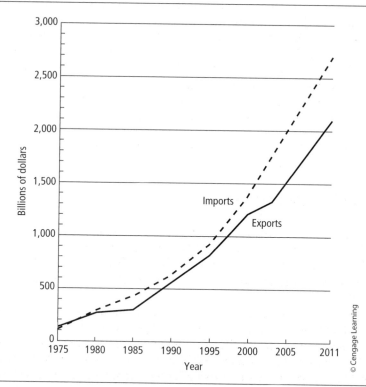

INTERNATIONAL PERSPECTIVE

The Multinationals' Global Economic Power

The concentration of economic power in relatively few large institutions is not an exclusively American phenomenon. On the contrary, the trend toward corporate concentration of resources is worldwide. It is not only large American corporations that have expanded their markets throughout the world, invested in overseas plants and banks, and merged with foreign corporations; large Chinese, European, and Japanese firms also compete very effectively for world business. Just as American companies have greatly expanded investments abroad, so too have foreign companies sharply increased their business in the United States. The result is the emergence of truly multinational corporations, which not only trade worldwide but also build and operate plants in many nations.

The world's largest corporations are listed in the accompanying table. Wal-Mart and ExxonMobil are among the world's largest nonbanking corporations, but only ten of the world's twenty-five largest corporations are headquartered in the United States; three of the top twenty-five are Chinese, two are French, two Japanese, two are German. The remaining are Korean, Dutch, Spanish, Italian or Swiss.

Among the companies that dominate the world economy, we can notice a trend in the types of goods and services they provide: Nine of the top twenty-five are oil and gas corporations, another five are consumer durables (primarily automotive). Thus, fourteen of the top twenty-five corporations worldwide are concentrated in those two industries. In brief, the central feature of the American and world economy is the concentration of resources in relatively few large corporations.

Comparative Advantage

comparative advantage
the argument that
countries benefit most
when they concentrate
on producing the goods
that they are most
efficient at producing

The classic argument for free trade is based on the principle of **comparative advantage**. If nations devote more of their resources to the production of those goods that they produce most efficiently, then all trading nations benefit.[9] Comparative advantage focuses on what each nation does *relatively* better than the other. Trade shifts resources (investment capital, jobs, technology, raw materials, and so on) in each nation toward what each does best. (Imagine a lawyer who is also a faster typist than her secretary. Even though the lawyer is better than her secretary at both law *and* typing, it makes more sense for her to concentrate on law and leave the typing to her secretary. Their combined output of "lawyering" and typing will be greater than if each did some of the other's work.) Similarly, if one nation has large petroleum reserves while

THE WORLD'S LARGEST CORPORATIONS

Rank	Company	Country	Industry
1	Wal-Mart Stores	United States	Retail
2	Royal Dutch Shell	Netherlands	Oil and Gas
3	Exxon Mobil	United States	Oil and Gas
4	BP	United Kingdom	Oil and Gas
5	Sinopec Group	China	Oil and Gas
6	China National Petroleum	China	Oil and Gas
7	State Grid	China	Energy
8	Toyota Motor	Japan	Consumer Durables
9	Japan Post Holdings	Japan	Delivery Service
10	Chevron	United States	Oil and Gas
11	Total	France	Oil and Gas
12	ConocoPhillips	United States	Oil and Gas
13	Volkswagen	Germany	Consumer Durables
14	AXA	France	Insurance
15	Fannie Mae	United States	Financial Services
16	General Electric	United States	Conglomerate
17	ING Group	Netherlands	Financial Services
18	Glencore International	Switzerland	Commodities
19	Berkshire Hathaway	United States	Diversified Financials
20	General Motors	United States	Consumer Durables
21	Bank of America Corp.	United States	Financial Services
22	Samsung Electronics	South Korea	Electronics
23	ENI	Italy	Oil and Gas
24	Daimler	Germany	Consumer Durables
25	Ford Motor	United States	Consumer Durables

SOURCE: http://www.forbes.com/sites/scottdecarlo/2012/04/18/the-worlds-biggest-companies/

another has abundant vineyards, each nation benefits by producing what it can most efficiently—oil and wine, respectively—and trading with each other for the other product.

The Benefits of Trade

The efficiencies achieved by trading are said to directly benefit consumers by making available cheaper imported goods. Export industries also benefit when world markets are opened to their products. American exporters benefit directly from sales abroad, and they also benefit indirectly when foreign firms are allowed to sell in the American market. This is because sales of foreign goods in America provide foreigners with U.S. dollars that they can use to purchase the goods of America's exporting industries.

It is also argued that the pressure of competition from foreign-made goods in the American marketplace forces our domestic industries to become more efficient—cutting their costs and improving the quality of their own goods. Trade also quickens the flow of ideas and technology, allowing nations to learn from each other. Finally, trade expands the menu of goods and services available to trading countries. American consumers gain access to everything from exotic foods and foreign-language movies to Porsches, BMWs, and Jaguars.

Trade Organizations and Agreements

World Trade Organization
an international organization that adjudicates trade disputes among countries and monitors and enforces trade agreements

International economic agreements and organizations have been arranged to facilitate the new global economy. The **World Trade Organization** (WTO) was created in 1993 with 117 member nations. The WTO has the power to adjudicate trade disputes among countries and monitor and enforce trade agreements.

General Agreement on Tariffs and Trade
a multinational agreement covering trade relations among nations

The most important worldwide trade agreement is the multinational **General Agreement on Tariffs and Trade** (GATT). Created after World War II, GATT has undergone various revisions. The latest version—the Uruguay Round—was completed in 1993. Among other things, it eliminated quotas on textile products; established more uniform standards for proof of dumping; set rules for the protection of intellectual-property rights (patents and copyrights on books, movies, videos, and so on); reduced tariffs on wood, paper, and some other raw materials; and scheduled a gradual reduction of government subsidies for agricultural products.

North American Free Trade Agreement
an agreement in which the United States, Mexico, and Canada agree to eliminate all barriers among themselves

In 1993 the United States, Canada, and Mexico signed the **North American Free Trade Agreement** (NAFTA). Objections by labor unions in the United States (and independent presidential candidate Ross Perot) were drowned out in a torrent of support by the American corporate community, Democrats and Republicans in Congress, President Bill Clinton, and former President George H. W. Bush. NAFTA envisioned the removal of tariffs on virtually all products by all three nations over a period of ten to fifteen years. It also allows banking, insurance, and other financial services to cross these borders. Most studies of the impact of NAFTA indicate that the agreement has helped both the U.S. and the Mexican economies, perhaps the Mexican economy in particular. And despite the fears of labor unions before its enactment, NAFTA has had little impact on the U.S. labor market.

The Case for Protectionism

protectionism
maintaining high tariffs to protect domestic producers from foreign competition

Although most economists favor worldwide free trade, arguments can also be made for **protectionism**—maintaining high tariffs to protect domestic producers from foreign competition. The principal argument for protectionism is that unlimited foreign competition costs Americans their jobs. When Americans buy Japanese or Korean steel, steelworkers in Pittsburgh lose their jobs. When Americans buy shoes from Taiwan or Hong Kong, millworkers in South Carolina become unemployed.

Some foreign producers, especially those in the less-developed world, gain comparative advantage by paying their workers extremely low wages. American producers cannot compete effectively with companies that pay wages that may be less than a quarter of those paid in the United States. Moreover, foreign producers are not subject to the same environmental protection laws as producers in the United States. These laws raise the cost of production in the United States and thereby give comparative advantage to foreign producers who do not incur such costs.

CHAPTER SUMMARY

- Economics is the study of the production and distribution of scarce goods and services. Economics decides what should be produced, how will goods and services be produced, and for whom will goods and services be produced. In general, there are two ways of making these economic decisions: (1) individually through the market system, or (2) collectively through governments.

- The economic system consists of the institutions and processes by which a society produces and distributes scarce resources. In an ideal market there is a great deal of competition, and prices are determined solely by supply and demand. All must pay for the goods and benefits that they receive, and resources and labor shift easily in response to changes in prices and wages.

- Three types of markets—product, labor, and capital markets—function simultaneously in the economy. Prices, wages, and interest rates regulate the supply and demand for products, labor, and capital, respectively, and the interaction of supply and demand in all three of these types of markets. One of the largest actors in this interaction is the government, which sets interest rates and makes many policies that affect prices and wages.

- The free-enterprise system that was previously described is subject to major modifications by the activities of government. Government is now so involved in the economy that we might call the American economic system a *mixed* economy rather than a *private enterprise* economy.

- Economic theories about the proper role for governments in creating and maintaining a healthy economy include Keynesian economics, supply-side economics, and monetarism.

- In recent presidential administrations, including those of Reagan, George H.W. Bush, Clinton, George W. Bush, and Obama, supply-side economics and Keynesianism have made significant impact on economic decision-making.

- Measuring the strength of their economy is done through the national income accounting system, whereby the federal government collects data that describe the nation's income and outputs. One key indicator is the gross domestic product (GDP), the nation's total production of goods and services for a single year valued in terms of market prices.

- The federal government spends more than it receives in revenues, creating a federal deficit, the name for the negative imbalance that occurs when the government spends more than it collects. The cumulative annual federal deficits drove up the accumulated debt of the U.S. government to more than $16 *trillion*.

- Economic power in America is highly concentrated. Large economic and financial institutions decide what will be produced in the United States and increasingly what will be produced outside of it. This concentration of economic power has fostered resistance by many outside the concentrated power structure.

KEY TERMS

automatic stabilizer   a government program that acts to counter economic cycles

balanced budget   a budget in which the government's expenditures are equal to or less than its revenues

capital market   decisions of lenders and borrowers to make and accept loans at specified interest rates (prices)

chained dollars   dollars valued from a particular year in order to account for changes in the value of dollars—that is, inflation

collective decision making   a method of making economic decisions in which governments implement decisions through coercion (fines, penalties, and imprisonment) and threats of coercion

comparative advantage   the argument that countries benefit most when they concentrate on producing the goods that they are most efficient at producing

consumer demand   preferences for goods and services, expressed by willingness to pay

corporate raider   an investor who arranges to purchase stock in a hostile takeover

Council of Economic Advisers   advises the president on national economic policies

deficit spending   government expenditures costing more than is raised in taxes, leading to borrowing and debt

depression   a long-term and severe recession

deregulation   reduction or elimination of regulatory restrictions on firms and industries

economic boom   rapid economic growth

economic stimulus bill   fiscal policy designed to pump money into the ailing economy

economic system   institutions and processes by which society produces and distributes scarce resources

Economics   the study of the production and distribution of scarce resources

Employment Act of 1946   pledges the federal government to promote maximum employment, production, and purchasing power

federal deficit   the annual negative imbalance between revenues and expenditures of the U.S. government, or when the government spends more than it collects in any given year; the sum of the deficits plus interest equals the national debt

Federal Reserve Board   controls the supply of money and credit and interest rates (sets monetary policy)

fiscal policy   the effect of government spending and taxation on the economy

General Agreement on Tariffs and Trade   a multinational agreement covering trade relations among nations

gross domestic product   the total value of production of goods and services for a year

hostile takeover   the purchase of stock in a corporation by an outsider and the subsequent ousting of the prior management

ideal conditions for a market operation   competition among many buyers and sellers; ability of buyer to exclude others from benefits of purchase; mobility of resources and labor

income inequality   the gap in the proportion of national income held by the richest compared to that held by the poorest

inflation   the decreased value of money as evidenced by increased prices

Keynesian economics   theory that recommends that during a recession the national government should increase its spending and decrease taxes, and during a boom, it should cut spending and increase taxes

labor market   decisions of employers and employees to offer and accept jobs at specified wages (prices)

laissez-faire   "hands-off" stance of a government in regard to the marketplace

managerialism   control of the corporation by professional managers rather than stockholders

market   arrangement that enables people to exchange money for goods, services, and labor

market system   a method of making economic decisions that allows individuals and firms to decide who gets what and how using a voluntary exchange

monetarism   theory that says the government's proper economic role is to control the rate of inflation by controlling the amount of money in circulation

monetary policy   the government's influence over the supply of money and credit and interest rates

national debt   the total of all annual federal deficits, money owed to others due to borrowing

national income accounting   data collected by government that describe the nation's income and output

North American Free Trade Agreement   an agreement in which the United States, Mexico, and Canada agree to eliminate all barriers among themselves

per capita GDP   GDP divided by the population; a measure of economic well-being

price   the rate at which money is exchanged for goods and services

principal–agent problem   ensuring that managers (agents) operate firms in the best interest of the owners (principals) rather than themselves

private enterprise economy   private individuals in search of wages and profits, acting on their own, without government direction

profits   motivate producers to satisfy consumer demand and to produce goods and services in the most efficient way possible

protectionism   maintaining high tariffs to protect domestic producers from foreign competition

recession   an economic downturn during which unemployment is high and the production of goods and services is low

stagflation   an economic condition in which the high unemployment of a recession occurs with large increases in prices of consumer goods (high inflation) typical of economic boom

supply-side economics   using government policies to affect the supply side of the economy; that is, to increase the supply of goods and services through incentives to work, save, and produce

tariff   a tax on goods imported into a country

underground economy   economic activities that are unreported and not counted in the GDP

unemployment rate   percentage of the labor force not working but looking for work or waiting for a job to open

World Trade Organization   an international organization that adjudicates trade disputes among countries and monitors and enforces trade agreements

ON THE WEB

EXPLORING ECONOMICS

The website for this textbook (**www.cengagebrain .com**) offers resources for exploring power and the economic order on the Internet. News and information about business and economics also abounds on the Web. Individual corporations, business and trade associations, securities firms, labor unions, and a variety of government agencies all post valuable economic information on the Web.

- **Bureau of Economic Analysis** Probably the best place to start browsing for economic information is the site maintained by the Bureau of Economic Analysis of the U.S. Department of Commerce (**www.bea.gov**). It provides up-to-date information on the GDP, prices, income, exports and imports, government revenues and expenditures, and more, in current and constant dollars, annually and for the last four quarters, and by industry and by region of the United States.

  Try This: Go to **www.bea.gov/regional/ index.htm** and look for the "GDP by state" data. Look up your state and find out which quintile you fall in. Compare your state GDP to your regional GDP. How does it rank?

- **Bureau of Labor Statistics** Information on careers in economics is available at the website maintained by the Bureau of Labor Statistics of the U.S. Department of Labor entitled "Occupational Outlook Handbook" (**www.bls.gov/ oco**). It describes the work of economists (as well as that of other occupations from A to Z), their training and employment opportunities, earnings, and job outlook. Employment opportunities for economics majors are usually much better than those for majors in other social sciences. Average earnings for economists are also higher. Applied economics is useful in business and in a wide variety of other organizations, including labor unions and governments.

  Try This: Go to **www.bls.gov/oco/ooh_index .htm** and look at the list of occupations. Pick two or three and explain the position, the training involved, the general salary, and the outlook of the position economically.

REVIEW QUIZ

MULTIPLE CHOICE

1. What is the rate at which money is exchanged for goods and services?
   a. market
   b. profit
   c. price
   d. inflation

2. Ideal conditions for a market operation *do not* include which of the following?
   a. competition among many buyers and sellers
   b. the ability of the buyer to exclude others from benefits of purchase
   c. deregulation
   d. mobility of resources and labor

3. The preferences for goods and services, expressed by willingness to pay, is called _____.
   a. consumer demand
   b. price
   c. profit
   d. inflation

4. The decisions of employers and employees to offer and accept jobs at specified wages comprise _____.
   a. the capital market
   b. the labor market
   c. fiscal policy
   d. monetary policy

5. What is the theory that recommends that during a recession the national government should increase its spending and decrease taxes, and during a boom, it should cut spending and increase taxes?
   a. monetarism
   b. laissez-faire economics
   c. Keynesianism
   d. supply-side economics

6. Using government policies to increase the supply of goods and services through incentives to work, save, and produce is called _____.
   a. monetarism
   b. laissez-faire economics
   c. Keynesianism
   d. supply-side economics

7. What is the theory that says the government's proper economic role is to control the rate of inflation by controlling the amount of money in circulation?
   a. monetarism
   b. laissez-faire economics
   c. Keynesianism
   d. supply-side economics

8. What is the total value of nation's production of goods and services for a year?
   a. the per capita gross domestic product
   b. the gross domestic product
   c. national income accounting
   d. the deficit

9. The annual negative imbalance between revenues and expenditures of the U.S. government, or when the government spends more than it collects in any given year, is called _____.
   a. deficit
   b. the national debt
   c. national income accounting
   d. the trade deficit

10. Ensuring that managers operate firms in the best interest of the owners rather than themselves is called _____.
    a. managerialism
    b. comparative advantage
    c. takeover theory
    d. the principal–agent problem

FILL IN THE BLANK

11. The arrangement that enables people to exchange money for goods, services, and labor is called a _____.

12. Economic activities that are unreported and not counted in the GDP are part of the _____.

13. The _____ controls the supply of money and credit and interest rates (sets monetary policy).

14. The purchase of stock in a corporation by an outsider and the subsequent ousting of the prior management is called a _____.

15. The international organization that adjudicates trade disputes among countries and monitors and enforces trade agreements is called the _____.

ANSWER KEY:
1. c; 2. c; 3. a; 4. b; 5. c; 6. d; 7. a; 8. b; 9. a; 10. d; 11. market; 12. underground economy; 13. Federal Reserve Board; 14. hostile takeover; 15. World Trade Organization.

CHAPTER 9

Power and Psychology

Learning Objectives

After reading this chapter, students will be able to:

- Explain the nature-versus-nurture controversy over the determination of personality.
- List the different approaches to explaining and understanding personality.
- Describe how power is related to the study of personality.

Psychology and the Study of Personality

Personality is all the characteristic ways of behaving that an individual exhibits; it is the characteristic, enduring and organized patterns of thought, emotion, and behavior an individual habitually exhibits when subjected to particular stimuli. By *characteristic*, we mean that individuals tend to respond in a similar fashion to many different situations. For example, their attitudes toward authority in general may lead them to respond in a similar fashion to supervisors, directors, or other authority figures in different situations. By *enduring*, we mean that these characteristic ways of behaving tend to operate over a long time, perhaps through youth, young adulthood, and maturity. Attitudes toward authority in the home may carry over to school, university, job, church, government, and so forth. By *organized*, we mean relationships exist between various elements of an individual's personality.

A change in one element (for example, a growing need for social approval) would bring about a change in another element (perhaps an increased willingness to conform to group norms).

Thus, personality is not just a bundle of traits but an integrated pattern of behaviors. Psychology is the discipline in the social sciences that analyzes personality. It does so both by examining the personality of individuals and how individuals affect and are affected by other people and by their social and physical environments. In this chapter, we will examine a large-scale debate in both society and the discipline of psychology: the extent to which biological nature versus social environmental factors influence personality. We then will examine how personality is studied within the varied subfields of psychology, and how each of them considers the notion of power within their examination of personality.

personality
the characteristic ways of behaving; the characteristic, enduring, and organized patterns of thought, emotion, and behavior

Personality and Individual Responses to Power

Personality is linked to our examination of power because individual responses to authority are a product of personality. In addition, the nature of authority, whether elected leaders, the police, teachers, clergy members, or whatever other form it takes, is a product of the personality of the authority figure.

Individuals react toward and exercise power and authority in characteristic ways. In many different situations, their responses to power and authority are fairly predictable. Some individuals regularly seek power and authority, whereas others avoid seeking them. Some individuals are submissive to authority, whereas others are habitually rebellious. Some individuals try to conform to the expectations of other people, and others are guided by internalized standards. Some individuals feel powerless, helpless, and isolated; they believe that they have little control over their own lives. Other individuals are self-assured and aggressive; they speak out at meetings, organize groups, and take over leadership positions. Some individuals are habitually suspicious of others and are unwilling to compromise; they prefer simple, final, and forceful solutions to complex problems. Some individuals are assertive, strong willed, and self-confident; others are timid, submissive, and self-conscious. There are as many different ways of responding to power as there are types of personalities.

Nature versus Nurture

Children often have the same personality characteristics as their parents. Is the similarity a result of what they learned in the home? Or do children inherit personality characteristics from their parents? Actually, this is not an "either/or" question: Psychologists generally acknowledge that personality is affected by both heredity and environment. The only question is, what is the relative influence of these factors on personality?

The questions of the relative influence of heredity versus environment on personality, as well as how the interaction between nature and nurture influence behavior, are part of a larger controversy about the influence of genetics on behavior. Some psychologists attribute greater influence to heredity in determining many personality characteristics by chemical and hormonal balances, the functioning of the senses (sight, hearing, smell, taste, and touch), and physique. Other psychologists attribute greater influence to environment. The influence of the environment may begin even before birth, depending, for example, on whether the mother has a good diet; avoids smoking, alcohol, and drugs; is active or inactive; and is in good emotional health. Research shows that infants respond to their earliest environment and acquire characteristic ways of responding—that is, personality—very early in life.

It is very difficult to determine whether a specific personality characteristic shared by a parent and child has been genetically inherited or transmitted through social interaction in the home.[1] However, some studies of twins have suggested that heredity plays an important role in personality. **Identical twins** (who have the same genetic composition) score more alike on standard personality tests than **fraternal twins** (whose genetic composition is different).[2]

identical twins
twins who develop from a single fertilized egg and who are genetically identical

fraternal twins
twins who develop from separate eggs and are no closer genetically than brothers and sisters

Research on the behavior of identical twins suggests the importance of genetic influences. Identical twins Gerald Levey and Mark Newman, for example, were separated at birth and raised in different homes. When reunited at age 31, they discovered that they had both become firefighters.

Thomas Wanstall/The Image Works

Identical twins reared in separate families tend to share more personality and behavior characteristics than fraternal twins raised in the same household. For example, researchers at the University of Minnesota conducted a study of identical twins separated at birth. One set of twins, Oskar Stohr and Jack Yufe, were born in Trinidad and were separated shortly after birth. Oskar moved to Germany with his mother and was raised by his maternal grandmother as a Catholic and a Nazi. Jack remained in Trinidad with his father and was raised Jewish. Yet when they were reunited, researchers found startling similarities between the twins. Both Jack and Oskar came to the interviews sporting mustaches, blue double-breasted suits, and similar wire-rimmed glass frames. They also shared many general personality traits, according to researchers. But some of the similarities between the two men were startling because of their oddness and their specificity. For example, both men would surprise people by sneezing on elevators, and both men flushed the toilet before using it.[3] According to various studies, separated identical twins shared the same smoking and eating habits and scored similarly on tests of intelligence, extroversion, and neuroticism.[4]

Our Genetic Code

gene
an inherited unit of life, composed of DNA, found in every cell

DNA
deoxyribonucleic acid—a code of instructions to cells determining their structure, appearance, and function

Every cell of the human body contains **genes** that instruct its growth and development. Genes are composed of **DNA**—or deoxyribonucleic acid, the complex code of instructions that determine the cell's structure and appearance. Among humans, our genetic code is nearly—99.9 percent—identical. It is difficult to estimate how much of our personality can be attributed to our genes versus our environment. A common estimate is that **hereditability**—differences among groups of people that are attributable to genetics—accounts for about 50 percent of the variation in personalities among people. This does not mean that 50 percent of any individual's personality is inherited but that 50 percent of differences among people are inherited (see Focus: "DNA as a Genealogical Tool").

Genes and Sexuality

How much of the differences in the behaviors of men and women can be attributable to genetic differences between males and females? The genetic differences between males and females essentially are the product of the level of the hormone **androgen**, which determines whether an embryo will develop male or female genitalia. Increased levels of **testosterone** in the embryo's sex glands produce male genitalia; lower levels result in the development of female genitalia. It is difficult for researchers to assess what influence hormones have on behavior compared with the influence of the environment because typically these factors work in concert to produce a unified sexual identity. That is, hormones determine whether a baby will be a boy or a girl. Then, the social environment treats that child in a manner consistent with society's gender expectation.

The social environment consists of parents, other relatives, friends, and so on. In examining differences between males and females in areas like proclivity toward violence, occupational preferences, cognitive abilities, aggression, personality, and sexuality, some theorists assert that nature and nurture comprise "inseparable threads" that create gender.[5]

Recent developments in genetics research have revealed the complex nature of gender. For example, studies of mice show that genes drive the brains of male and female embryos in different directions as early as midway through a full-term mouse pregnancy, leading researchers to question if men's and women's brains are hardwired differently early on in their development.[6] Other researchers have shown that the livers of male and female mice host different subsets of recently identified genes, which figure prominently in both reproductive function and in the ability to metabolize certain drugs.[7]

Researchers also have analyzed the impact of hormones on sexuality and sexual arousal. Data on the impact of chemical and surgical castration (the removal of the testes or rendering them useless via chemicals) are mixed. Such procedures result in a loss of interest in sexual activity in some men but not others.[8] Typically, however, higher levels of testosterone are linked to increased sexual desire among both men and women, but higher levels appear to have little bearing on sexual performance.[9]

When considering the impact of biology versus environment on the behaviors of men and women and their sexuality, it is clear that both have some impact. Indeed, with regard to sex-role behaviors, many researchers believe that environment plays a more dominant role than hormones. Some species' sexual activity is the singular result of hormones; however, in general, humans clearly are influenced less by hormonal changes and more by environmental and emotional factors. Indeed, an oft-repeated axiom is that a human's most important sexual organ is the brain through which environment and emotions are processed.

hereditability
differences among groups of people that are attributable to genetics

androgen
the hormone produced in an embryo's sex glands that determines whether the embryo will develop as a male or a female

testosterone
the male sex hormone (found in varying levels in both men and women)

DNA as a Genealogical Tool

We know that DNA helps determine a lot about a person—their appearance, their intellect, and even part of their personality. Now researchers say that DNA also can tell us about our genealogy—our family history.

Currently, two forms of DNA testing are available. The first, Y-DNA, which can only be used on males, examines the Y chromosome that is passed on in virtually identical form from father to male offspring. This test can provide information about the direct male line of descent—the son's father, the father's father, and so on.

The second test examines the mitochondrial DNA that is passed on from a mother to all of her offspring. This test traces the female line of descent—a son or daughter's mother, her mother, her mother, and so on. Both tests can usually determine the ethnicity of the line of descent being tested.

Typically, a genetic test is done in the privacy of one's home. An interested individual pays a genetic testing company, which then sends a kit in the mail that contains toothbrushlike brushes. After rubbing the brush on the inside of the cheek for ninety seconds, the brush is placed in a test tube. The test is then replicated eight hours later and mailed to the testing company, which notifies the subject of the results.

DNA testing has proven popular among some African Americans, who, because of the legacy of slavery, lack information about their ancestry. Celebrities, including Oprah Winfrey and Whoopi Goldberg, have had their DNA tested, sometimes with surprising results.

In 2006 a PBS documentary, *African American Lives*, featured Henry Louis "Skip" Gates, Jr., who chairs the African and African American Studies program at Harvard University. Gates had researched his family history, and, combined with oral history, had what he believed was the story of his family tree: that he was descended from a freed slave and her former owner. Gates sought out white descendants of the former slave owner to compare their Y-DNA results. But Gates was shocked at the outcome—the results did not match. When Gates had his mitochondrial DNA tested, it revealed that he also had a white maternal ancestor. In all, Gates estimated that he is probably about 50 percent white.

Another experiment in tracking genetic ancestry is "The Genographic Project," which is being undertaken by National Geographic. DNA evidence indicates that all humans are descended from a common ancestor who lived in Africa sixty thousand years ago. Indeed, all human genomes are 99.9 percent identical. But as our ancestors began migrating to the Middle East, India, Asia, and Northern Europe, a series of genetic mutations occurred in the DNA accounting for that 0.1 percent difference. Each mutation is associated with a place and time in history, so these mutations indicate the location to which our ancestors migrated.

To track DNA, National Geographic seeks to collect DNA from one hundred thousand indigenous and traditionally isolated people throughout the world. In addition, members of the general public can also submit their DNA (for a fee) to help researchers add to their data so that individuals can learn about their ancestral roots.

Genes and Intelligence

Perhaps no other aspect of the biology versus environment argument generates as much controversy as that of intelligence. There are serious political implications in the nature of intelligence: If mental abilities are primarily inherited, then efforts to equalize education are not likely to be successful. If, on the other hand, mental abilities are primarily nurtured by the environment, then efforts to erase disadvantaged educational environments are worthwhile.

Research on twins again suggests that genetics contributes heavily to intelligence: Identical twins raised together are closer in intelligence scores than fraternal twins raised together. Indeed, identical twins raised apart are closer in intelligence scores than fraternal twins raised together. And by inserting an "intelligence" gene into fertilized mouse eggs, researchers have produced smarter mice.[10]

However, early experiences of newborns and even unborn fetuses can have profound effects on mental abilities. Malnutrition, sensory deprivation (absence of cuddling, talking to, and stimulating babies), and social isolation have profound effects on brain development. An example from nature brings home this point: Consider the development of two genetically identical seedlings. One is planted in rich soil and is tended to, the other planted in poor soil and neglected. Despite the seeds' identical genetics, one seed will thrive, and the other languish.

Nurture and Human Development

The mother (usually the primary caregiver) is the single most important influence in anyone's early environment. We cannot deprive human babies of contact with their mothers for the sake of experimentation, but psychologists have placed newborn monkeys in isolation and observed their development. The results showed abnormal and irreversible behavior: extreme fear, anxiety, avoidance of all social contact with other monkeys, and emotional and intellectual retardation.

Newborn Instincts

Some psychologists argue that early mother–child relationships are instinctual. Newborns possess five instinctual responses: sucking, crying, smiling, clinging, and following. Together, these responses foster attachment of the child to the mother and the mother to the child. Some psychologists contend that these inherited responses were acquired over millions of years by natural selection. Also, evidence shows that clinging and following are inherited responses. Infant monkeys reared in isolation from their mothers were supplied with two surrogate mother figures. One was made of wire mesh, while the other was made of soft "cuddly" cloth. The baby monkeys chose to be near the soft surrogate even though the wire mesh surrogate had a bottle attached to it for feeding.

Nurture and Brain Activity

But newer technology, notably PET (positron-emission tomography) scanning of brain activity in infants, has provided convincing evidence of the significance of very early learning. Simple activities—like cuddling and rocking, and singing and talking to babies—stimulate electrical activity in a baby's brain and actually

FIGURE 9-1 PET SCANS OF (A) NURTURED AND (B) NEGLECTED BRAINS

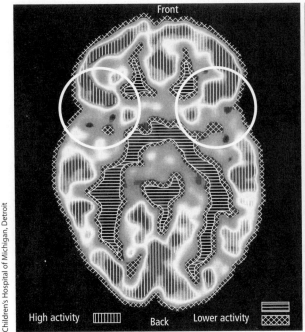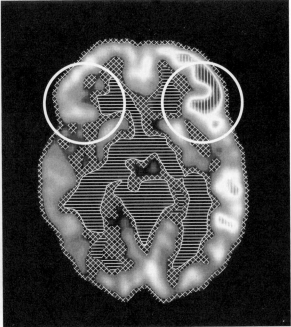

Children's Hospital of Michigan, Detroit

(a) PET scan of the healthy brain of a normal child shows regions of high and low activity.

(b) This PET scan of the brain of a Romanian orphan institutionalized shortly after birth shows the effects of extreme deprivation; areas of high activity are few. Circles show temporal lobes.

build connections between neurons. In the first few months of life, the number of these connectors (synapses) increases over twenty fold from 100 billion to more than 1 trillion. While neuronal connections continue to form throughout the life span, an infant's earliest experiences exert a dramatic impact on the brain's growth, physically determining the number and strength of neuronal connections (see Focus: "Inside the Brain"). These connections govern everything from language and music to mathematics and emotions. The brain of a baby not only grows bigger, but its actual wiring is also set in place. Infants who are deprived of human interaction fail to develop as many active areas of the brain and as many neuronal connections as infants who experience more stimulation.

Early traumas elevate stress hormones in an infant's brain. These hormones actually reduce electrical activity. Neglected and abused children have smaller brains than normal children and fewer neuronal connections (see Figure 9-1). These conditions are associated with later language, cognitive, learning, and emotional problems.

Approaches to Psychology and Personality

Psychologists differ over the precise conditions contributing to the development of personality. Within psychology are varying approaches that explain how individuals gain power over their behaviors, thoughts, and feelings as well as over other

Inside the Brain

A newborn's brain is already wired for rudimentary behaviors—breathing, heartbeat, reflexes, crying, sucking, and so on. But in higher regions of the brain, neuronal connections are still being created (see the accompanying figure). These connections are stimulated and reinforced by an infant's exposure to language, images, sounds, and even facial expressions.

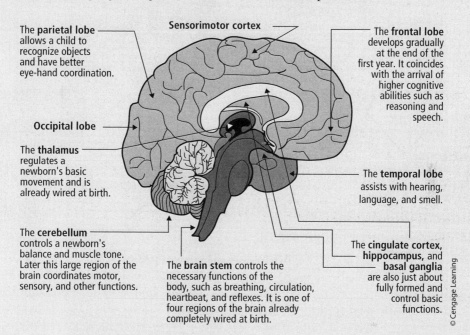

The **parietal lobe** allows a child to recognize objects and have better eye-hand coordination.

Sensorimotor cortex

The **frontal lobe** develops gradually at the end of the first year. It coincides with the arrival of higher cognitive abilities such as reasoning and speech.

Occipital lobe

The **thalamus** regulates a newborn's basic movement and is already wired at birth.

The **temporal lobe** assists with hearing, language, and smell.

The **cerebellum** controls a newborn's balance and muscle tone. Later this large region of the brain coordinates motor, sensory, and other functions.

The **brain stem** controls the necessary functions of the body, such as breathing, circulation, heartbeat, and reflexes. It is one of four regions of the brain already completely wired at birth.

The **cingulate cortex, hippocampus,** and **basal ganglia** are also just about fully formed and control basic functions.

© Cengage Learning

As we examine some of the theories and perspectives of personality in this chapter, we should remember that heredity and environment, *nature* and *nurture*, play important roles in shaping human beings. We examine some theories of personality that emphasize instincts and heredity, others that emphasize early childhood experiences, and still others that emphasize continuing growth and development over a lifetime. There is no single "right" theory of personality, and all can provide insight as to how individuals perceive, relate to, and use power.

individuals. These approaches are not necessarily exclusive; many psychologists employ more than one approach in their efforts to understand behavior (Figure 9-2).

The Cognitive Approach

Today, most research on personality employs the cognitive approach. The **cognitive approach** is a methodology that emphasizes how people learn about themselves and their environment. Cognitive theorists assert that differences in personality are the result of differences in how individuals mentally represent information derived from their environment, including the behavior of others. One cognitive theorist, Albert Bandura, developed **social-learning theory,**

cognitive approach
a methodology that emphasizes how people learn about themselves and their environment

social-learning theory
behavior is shaped by internal cognitive processes and observing the behavior of others

FIGURE 9-2   APPROACHES TO PSYCHOLOGY

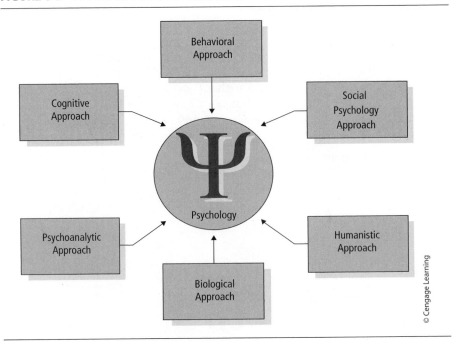

© Cengage Learning

cognitive neuroscience
explores how mental
activities are executed in
an individual's brain

biological psychology
the study of electrical and
chemical events in the
brain and nervous system

neuron
a cell in the human brain
that transmits impulses
to other cells, muscles,
and glands

dendrite
a branch of neurons
where the cell receives
impulses from other
neurons

axon
a long, tubelike structure
that protrudes from the
cell body of a neuron

neurotransmitter
a chemical in the brain
that crosses synapses in
order to stimulate the
next neuron

synapse
a connector between
neurons

which states that behavior is shaped by internal cognitive processes and observing the behavior of others as well as the environment that behavior occurs in.
Bandura cites intuitive evidence for this approach—one does not teach an ado-
lescent to drive by giving that person the car keys. In a famous experiment,
Bandura demonstrated that children are more likely to engage in aggressive
behavior toward an inflatable Bobo doll when they had witnessed adult role models beating the inflatable doll with a mallet.[11] Another example of the cognitive
approach is **cognitive neuroscience**, which explores how mental activities are
executed in an individual's brain. Cognitive neuroscientists might study a person's
brain while he or she is performing a mental activity such as problem solving.

Biological Psychology

Biological psychology attempts to explain behaviors as the results of electrical and chemical events taking place within the brain and nervous system.
Cells in the human brain, called **neurons**, transmit impulses to other cells as
well as muscles and glands. Neurons receive impulses on branches of the cell
called **dendrites** (from the Greek *dendron* for "tree"). Electrical and chemical
processes travel down the **axon**, a long, tubelike structure. **Neurotransmitters**,
which are chemical messengers, carry messages across **synapses** from one neuron to the next. Given these processes, biological psychologists sometimes use
electrical stimulation and chemical therapies to change mental processes and
behaviors (Figure 9-3).

FIGURE 9-3 SYNAPSES AT THE CELL BODY OF A NEURON

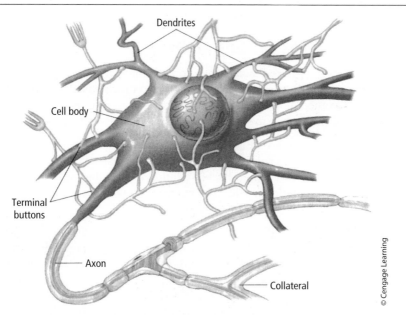

Many different axons, each of which branches repeatedly, synapse on the dendrites and cell body of a single neuron. Each branch of an axon ends in a swelling, called a synaptic *terminal*, which contains neurotransmitters. When released, neurotransmitters transmit the nerve impulse across the synapse to the dendrites or cell body of the receiving cell.

Biological psychologists also are interested in the impact of genetics on personality and the heredibility of traits. Personality traits as varied as shyness, curiosity, risk taking, and aggressiveness have been identified in genetic research. There also appear to be genetic predispositions to alcoholism, schizophrenia, depression, and other mental disorders.

A related field of **evolutionary psychology** describes relationships between biological needs, genetic coding, and psychological traits of humans. It assumes that psychological traits have evolved over millions of years through the process of natural selection—that is, the development of genetic traits that improve survival and are passed on to future generations (see Focus: "Evolutionary Psychology: The Mating Game"). Some evolutionary psychologists examine the biological origins of differences between the sexes in relation to propensity for violence, aggression, parenting styles, and sexual inclinations.

But genes provide only a probability for a specific personality trait. Synapses must be formed, and neurotransmitters must stimulate neurons before genes can do their job. The effect of early childhood experiences can be profound. Genetics may increase the probability of personality traits and even predict the likelihood of various mental illnesses. But experiences largely determine whether the wiring for these genes will be developed or not. It is very difficult to estimate what proportion of an adult's personality is determined by genes versus that which is developed by interaction with his or her environment.

evolutionary psychology
the study of relationships between biological needs, genetic coding, and psychological traits of humans

Evolutionary Psychology: The Mating Game

Understanding sexual behavior has long posed a challenge to psychologists as well as the rest of us. Why do some men ogle women's breasts and evaluate women so much based on their physical attractiveness? Why do some women judge men more on their power, resources, and earnings potential? Why are men more likely to engage in short-term and extramarital affairs than women?

Evolutionary psychologists are proposing answers to these and similar questions about sexual behavior by reference to the mating concerns of our prehistoric ancestors. They argue that human sexual behavior, and human behavior generally, has been shaped by biological challenges confronting men and women and the evolutionary development of mental devices for coping with these challenges.

Evolutionary psychologists contend that men and women are as different psychologically as they are physically. In every culture, men consistently value youth and physical attractiveness in a mate more than women do. Women are consistently more concerned with a man's power, status, and resources. These preferences evolved from the different biological challenges facing men and women. Women invest far more time and energy in child rearing than men; human infants require years of nurturing. Over millions of years, women evolved a psychology that preferred men who appeared to have the power and resources to offer protection and assistance in the tasks of child rearing. In contrast, men's reproductive success depends on the fertility of their mates. So men have developed a mind-set that searches for signs of fertility—youth, large breasts, and good looks. (Cultures where food is less plentiful may prefer heavier women, while more affluent cultures may prefer slimness. But in all cultures, the hips should be roughly one-third larger than the waist, a ratio that suggests high fertility and good health.) Women also appreciate men's physical attractiveness because it promises good genes for their offspring. Thus, men as well as women in most cultures, modern as well as ancient, "beautify" themselves.

However, women must balance good looks against men's willingness and ability to provide continuing subsistence for the nest. Women must be concerned with men's commitment to a relationship long enough to nurture children.

While men have a stake in maintaining a long-term relationship with women to help ensure the survival of offspring, another strategy available to men is to impregnate as many women as possible to increase the likelihood that their genes will be continued. Thus, men, even those with long-term mates, are psychologically more predisposed toward short-term anonymous affairs than women. Women in long-term relationships may also engage in affairs, but it is likely to be part of a search for a new, more attractive, more resourceful, or more committed mate.

Male-oriented erotica, as in pornographic videos, feature lust-driven females willing to engage in sex acts with multiple partners with no emotional attachment. Female-oriented erotica, as in romance novels, feature handsome, powerful males with fiercely passionate commitments to the heroines.

Evolutionary psychology does not offer any solution to differences between the sexes, but it suggests that a better understanding of the contrasting psychologies of men and women will shed light on those differences.

Psychoanalytic (Freudian) Psychology

Psychoanalytic (Freudian) psychology views behavior as a product of the interaction between biologically based instincts (for example, hunger, sex, survival, and aggression) and our efforts to satisfy these instincts in socially acceptable ways. Early childhood experiences that forbid immediate gratification of instinctual drives tend to force them into the unconscious where they remain to affect dreams, speech, and mannerisms and to create anxieties, some of which may develop into emotional problems or mental illness.

Psychoanalysis is a type of insight-oriented therapy that encourages patients to think about themselves—their problems, dreams, and memories—so that they can gain insight into the causes of their own difficulties. Psychoanalysis encourages patients to talk about early childhood experiences, thus revealing unconscious thoughts and processes (most concerning early-childhood conflicts and sex). The revelations may result in greater insight as to the impact of these experiences on personality development. Although traditionally the practice of psychoanalysis has been the domain of the Freudian-trained psychiatrist, many clinical psychologists employ certain aspects of psychoanalytic psychology in their approach to therapy.

The Authoritarian Personality

The Freudian approach to power relationships focuses on early-childhood determinations of habitual responses to power and authority. Power motives—for example, a need to dominate others or, the opposite, comfort in accepting direction—are organized into the personality early in life.

An early influential study of power, authority, and personality, one that was conducted mainly within the framework of Freudian theory, was the landmark study *The Authoritarian Personality*.[12] This study was undertaken after World War II by a group of psychologists who sought to identify potentially antidemocratic individuals—those whose personality structures render them particularly susceptible to authoritarian appeals. The central attitudes of authoritarianism are *dominance* and *submission*—dominance over subordinates in any power hierarchy and submissiveness toward superiors. Authoritarians are highly ambivalent in their attitudes toward authority. They are outwardly servile toward those they perceive as their superiors, but in fact they also harbor strong negative feelings toward these same people. Their repressed rage toward their superiors is redirected into hostility toward the weak and inferior.

Authoritarians are *oriented toward power*. They tend to think in power terms, to be acutely sensitive in any situation to questions of who dominates whom. They are very uncomfortable when they do not know what the chain of command is. They need to know whom they should obey and who should obey them.

Authoritarians are *rigid*. They are "intolerant of ambiguity." They like order and are uncomfortable in the presence of disorder. When matters are complex, they impose their own rigid categories on them. Their thinking is therefore largely in stereotypes.

psychoanalytic (Freudian) psychology a theory in psychology that explains behavior as a product of the interaction of biological instincts and social learning, especially early childhood experiences; named for its founder, Sigmund Freud

psychoanalysis insight-oriented therapy, often focused on early-childhood experiences

Authoritarians show *exaggerated concern with strength*. Feelings of personal weakness are covered with a facade of toughness. They are unusually preoccupied with masculine virtues, and they stereotype women as feminine and soft.

Authoritarians are *cynical*. They distrust the motives of others and are generally pessimistic about human nature. They are disposed to believe that the world is a jungle and that various conspiracies exist to threaten them and their ways of life.

Authoritarians are *ethnocentric*. They view members of social groups other than their own as outsiders who are different, strange, unwholesome, and threatening. They hold an exalted opinion of their own groups. They reject outsiders and project many of their own aggressive impulses onto them. They place stereotyped labels on outsiders.

Social Psychology

social psychology
the study of the individual's relationships with other individuals and groups

Social psychology is concerned with the individual's relationships with other individuals and groups as they impact individual behavior. Social psychologists study social cognition, social influence, and social relations, or how we think about, influence, and relate to one another. Social psychologists examine power relations between individuals. They study the whole person and the impact of the social world on the person—the world of social interaction and group life, which constantly shapes and modifies the individual's goals, perceptions, attitudes, and behavior. The social-psychological approach to personality emphasizes the individual's **socialization**—the development of individual identity through interpersonal experiences and the internalizing of the expectations of significant others.

socialization
in psychology, the development of individual identity through interpersonal experiences and the internalizing of the expectations of significant others

Humanistic Psychology

humanistic psychology
the study of human experience and human fulfillment

Humanistic psychology focuses on human experience and human fulfillment; it emphasizes the individual's innate potential to grow and develop. According to the humanists, human beings are unique among animals because they alone have both psychological and biological needs. The individual is internally motivated to fulfill those needs, to grow and develop, and to expand the capacity for creativity. Humanistic psychology views personality development as a continuous process of positive growth in which the individual, having fulfilled a lower need, pursues the fulfillment of a higher one.

Behavioral Psychology

behavioral psychology
the study of how people and animals learn to respond to different stimuli

Behavioral psychology, another major approach to psychology, is concerned with the scientific study of the behavioral responses of human beings to various stimuli. Behavioral psychology focuses on observed behavior; its research setting is frequently the academic laboratory, and rats and pigeons (and college sophomores!) often are subjects of experimentation. It emphasizes careful observation, quantitative data, and statistical methods. Behavioral psychology relies heavily on learning theory (stimulus–response theory), which views all behavior as a product of learning or conditioning. Behavioral patterns are learned through a process whereby a stimulus evokes a response that is either rewarded or punished, and as a consequence, habits are formed. The behavioral approach to personality views personality as a pattern of learned, reinforced responses and minimizes internal psychological events in determining and explaining behavior.

Behaviorism and Learning Theory

Behavioral psychology views psychology as the study of human behavior. Traditionally, **behaviorism** is rooted in classical stimulus–response (SR) theory. It is not an overstatement to say that rats have had more to do with shaping this theory than human beings; SR theory grew out of experimental laboratory studies with animals. Academic psychology is based largely on SR theory; many college courses in psychology are oriented toward this approach.

Behavioral psychology asserts that the goal of psychologists should be to study behavior by employing the same scientific tests as the natural sciences. For the behaviorists, one is what one does; personality is behavior, a pattern of learned, reinforced responses. Behaviorists emphasize the role that an individual's environment or situation plays in determining that individual's behavior. Behavioral psychologists discount Freudian notions about the mind or the personality, which cannot be directly observed. Behaviorists differentiate between **operant conditioning**, or how individuals learn when they discover the connection between their behavior and resultant outcomes, and **observational learning**, or the type of learning that occurs when an individual observes the behavior of others and the resultant outcomes of their behavior. Behaviorists also acknowledge the emotional component of actions through classical conditioning. **Classical conditioning** is the type of learning that occurs when, consistently, situations are emotionally associated with specific responses. For example, if an individual engages in immoral behavior and is caught, the individual might feel embarrassment, guilt, and remorse. If that individual continues the immoral conduct, he or she might feel embarrassment, guilt, and remorse even in the absence of being caught.

The Learning Process

The learning process is a bit more complex than it first appears. To establish a **conditioned stimulus–response linkage**, a drive, a cue, a response, and reinforcement must be present. Learning depends on the establishment of this stimulus–response (SR) linkage. In simple terms, in order to learn, one must want something as a result of one's action (**drive**). Hunger, thirst, or curiosity may also provide the drive to learn. For example, if a child takes a cookie, hunger or the desire for a cookie is the drive. The sight of the cookie is the **cue** (or stimulus) that stimulates the response of reaching for a cookie. The stimulus may be visual (for example, objects, colors, lights, designs, and printed words), auditory (for example, bells, whistles, and spoken words), or related to any of the other senses. If the child eats the cookie and experiences satisfaction, the child learns that cookies satisfy hunger and taste good.

behaviorism
an approach to psychology that asserts that only observable behavior can be studied

operant conditioning
how individuals learn when they discover the connection between their behavior and resultant outcomes

observational learning
the type of learning that occurs when an individual observes the behavior of others

classical conditioning
the type of learning that occurs when, consistently, situations are emotionally associated with specific responses

conditioned stimulus–response (SR) linkage
drive, cue, response, and reinforcement

drive
a want for something

cue
the stimulus associated with the response

Of course, for a response to be linked to a cue, a response must first occur. A critical stage in the learning process is the production of the appropriate response. A young child might put many non-food objects in his mouth until learning that food satisfies hunger. The particular response that satisfies the drive is likely to recur the next time the same situation is encountered. Learning takes place not so much through "trial and error" as through "trial and success." Sometimes success might be accidental, but from the accidental behavior, learning can occur.

Conditioned Responses

The founder of modern SR theory was the Russian physiologist Ivan Petrovich Pavlov (1849–1936), who had already won a Nobel Prize for his studies of digestive glands before he undertook his landmark experiments with salivating dogs. Pavlov's early experiments established the notion of *conditioning*. Saliva flows when meat is placed in a dog's mouth. If a bell is consistently sounded just a moment before the meat is placed in its mouth, the dog will soon begin to salivate merely upon hearing a bell even if the meat is not given. Dogs do not normally salivate at the sound of a bell, so such a response is a **conditioned response**. The bell and the meat have become associated in the dog's mind by their occurring together.

conditioned response
a behavior that is elicited by a previously neutral stimulus

Reinforcement

The key to the learning process is the reinforcement of the appropriate behavior. **Reinforcement** occurs each time the behavior is accompanied by reduction in the drive. The cue itself will eventually elicit the same response as the original drive. For example, the sight of a cookie might create desire for it rather than hunger. In this way, a previously neutral stimulus (the cookie) becomes a *conditioned stimulus*, the child having learned to respond to it in a particular way. The *strength* of the SR linkage depends on (1) the strength of the original drive, (2) the closeness of the drive reduction to the response, and (3) the number of consistently reinforced trials.

reinforcement
repeating conditioned stimulus and response

Behavioral Therapy

In recent years, behavioral psychologists have come out of the laboratory to engage in some types of treatment for mental disorders. Behaviorists define disorders in terms of the undesirable behaviors that are exhibited. Behavioral psychologists seldom talk about anxiety or repression; they talk in terms of *functional* (desirable) and *dysfunctional* (undesirable) behaviors. They believe that neurotic behavior has been learned—generally by inconsistent use of rewards and punishment. (Hungry rats that are shocked when they pull a lever that previously produced food develop symptoms similar to nervous breakdowns.)

Undesirable behaviors can be extinguished by withholding rewards or by administering punishment. Neurotic behavior can be unlearned by the same combination of principles by which it was taught. **Behavioral psychotherapy** establishes a set of conditions in which neurotic habits are unlearned

behavioral psychotherapy
treatment based on learning or unlearning behavior

and non-neurotic habits are learned. The behavioral therapist is regarded as a kind of teacher and the patient as a learner. Thus, the behavioral therapist may reward patients in mental hospitals for good behavior with tokens to be used to buy small luxuries. A therapist of this school believes that smokers can learn avoidance reaction by having thick, obnoxious cigarette smoke blown in their faces or that bed wetters can unlearn their habit by sleeping on a wire blanket that produces a mild shock when it becomes wet. Even repression (viewed by the behaviorists as "learned nonthinking") can be overcome by forcing individuals to confront situations, events, or experiences that they have repressed.

Social Psychology: The Self in Relation to Others

Social psychology is concerned primarily with interpersonal interactions—how the individual interacts with others. The social psychologist studies the individual as a whole person interacting with the environment rather than studying particular responses, behaviors, or reflexes. Social psychologists also consider the social influence on an individual's thoughts, feelings, and other internal states. Although some social psychologists are critical of the "reductionism" of behavioral psychology—the tendency to reduce individual behavior to a series of SR linkages—others incorporate principles of behavioralism to gain a better understanding of social thought and action. Social psychology is strongly influenced by early **Gestalt psychologists**, who argued that the whole person is an entity that cannot be understood by breaking it into sensory elements. (The German word *Gestalt* means "whole," "pattern," or "configuration.")

Gestalt psychology
the study of the whole individual

Self-Awareness

Social psychologists view *interpersonal interaction* as the critical determinant of personality development. Indeed, an individual develops an awareness of self only by interaction with the environment. A newborn cannot distinguish his or her own body from the outer world. The infant acquires an identity—a sense of **self**—only by moving out into the world and relating to other people. As the infant observes and responds to his or her mother, the mother becomes a meaningful object, bringing pleasure, frustration, pain, and so on. The infant becomes aware of self only in relation to others. An infant who is totally ignored withdraws to a corner of the crib, does not talk or develop in any way, and withers away physiologically and psychologically. The emergence of self-identity requires interpersonal interaction; without others, there is no self.

self
the individual's awareness of himself or herself derived from interpersonal interaction

Socialization

The process by which an individual internalizes the values, attitudes, and judgments of others is called *socialization*. By interacting with others, people come to understand what is expected of them and internalize these expectations as part of their personalities. George Herbert Mead conceived the notion of roles to explain how the individual internalizes the expectations of others and acquires the values of society. The essential process in the development of self is the individual's taking on the roles of others in the social context.

Through interaction with its parents, the child learns that certain sounds, such as "Mama" and "Daddy," gain favorable attention. The child begins to

Young children often engage in role playing, a process that increases self-realization. Role playing also enables children to internalize the expectations of others that accompany different roles.

role playing
developing a sense of self by trying on a variety of roles

repeat these sounds because of the response they evoke in others and in this way begins to learn language. Children also learn that the things they do are meaningful to those around them, and thus they develop a sense of self. Infants who are ignored fail to develop either language or self-identity. Later, the small child at play tries on a variety of **roles**—for example, "mother," "father," "firefighter," and "soldier"—and increases self-realization in the process. Even such basic social roles as male and female may be viewed as products of socialization rather than biology. Through the process of gender typing, masculine and feminine traits develop through the child's internalization of the expectations of others and through role playing. Schools, games, and group activities provide more and more role-playing opportunities. Of course, not all the "others" in one's life are equally influential in shaping self-identity; each person has some significant others whose judgments carry more weight than the judgments of others. As socialization continues, knowledge of roles and attitudes of others becomes more generalized, and we gradually unify and consolidate the many roles that we have played into a generalized self-conception. At this point, the mature personality emerges.

Personality as Interpersonal Response Traits

interpersonal response traits
the sum of all of an individual's socializing experience, or personality

Over time, an individual acquires a distinctive pattern of **interpersonal response traits**, relatively consistent and stable dispositions to respond in a distinctive way toward others. These interpersonal response traits constitute the *personality*. They represent the sum of one's socialization, one's role experiences, and one's history of successes and failures with various interpersonal responses. Table 9-1 presents twelve interpersonal response traits.

TABLE 9-1   SOME INTERPERSONAL RESPONSE TRAITS*

Role dispositions

Ascendance (social timidity): defends one's rights; does not mind being conspicuous; is not self-reticent; is self-assured; forcefully puts self forward

Dominance (submissiveness): assertive; self-confident; power oriented; tough; strong willed; order-giving or directive leader

Social initiative (social passivity): organizes groups; does not stay in background; makes suggestions at meetings; takes over leadership

Independence (dependence): prefers to do own planning, to work things out in own way; does not seek support or advice; emotionally self-sufficient

Sociometric dispositions

Acceptance of others (rejection of others): nonjudgmental in attitude toward others; permissive; believing and trustful; overlooks weaknesses and sees best in others

Sociability (unsociability): participates in social affairs; likes to be with people; outgoing

Friendliness (unfriendliness): genial, warm; open and approachable; approaches other people easily; forms many social relationships

Sympathy (lack of sympathy): concerned with the feelings and wants of others; displays kindly, generous behavior; defends underdog

Expressive dispositions

Competitiveness (noncompetitiveness): sees every relationship as a contest in which other people are rivals to be defeated; self-aggrandizing; noncooperative

Aggressiveness (nonaggressiveness): attacks others directly or indirectly; shows defiant resentment of authority; quarrelsome; negativistic

Self-consciousness (social poise): embarrassed when entering a room after others are seated; suffers excessively from stage fright; hesitates to volunteer in group discussions; bothered at work when people watch; feels uncomfortable if different from others

Exhibitionism (self-effacement): is given to excess and ostentation in behavior and dress; seeks recognition and applause; shows off and behaves in odd ways to attract attention

---

* Opposite trait appears in parentheses.

Many social psychologists believe that interpersonal-interaction theory provides a basis for the treatment of *personality disorders*. They define an *integrated personality* as one in which the individual plays fairly well-defined and stable roles that are not incompatible or conflicting and that are consistent with the values of the groups and culture in which the individual lives. *Personality disorganization* occurs when people find themselves in highly conflicting roles. Most people can handle mildly conflicting roles, such as being mother and office worker simultaneously, but serious role conflicts, such as an inability to assume fully either a male or a female identification, may create deeper problems. Another source of personality disorganization may be an abrupt change in roles caused, for example, by the loss of a job by a breadwinner, the loss of a wife or husband, and even war and natural disaster. Failure to be adequately socialized in the first place is another recognized source of personality disorder; an example is the adult who exhibits childlike behavior or adolescents who cannot "find themselves"—that is, find mature responsible roles for themselves in society. Desocialization occurs when an individual, encountering consistent defeat and frustration in interpersonal situations, withdraws from contact with others. Thus, social psychologists tend to view mental disorders in terms of people's relationships to their social environment—whether they are well adjusted and capable of functioning in a socially acceptable fashion.

Humanistic Psychology: The Innate Human Potential

humanistic psychology focuses on individual development and self-fulfillment

Humanistic psychology, like social psychology, focuses on the whole person rather than on particular defensive structures or behavioral responses. However, whereas social psychology focuses on the process of socialization as the key factor in determining personality, humanistic psychology emphasizes the individual's innate potential for development, the human need for self-fulfillment.

Humanistic psychology represents a reaction against behaviorism and psychoanalytic theory, the two forces that dominated psychology for many years. Humanistic psychology rejects behaviorism's insistence on using the strictly scientific, objective, value-free methods of the natural sciences. It views behaviorism, with its narrow focus on behavior itself and its disregard of the subjective human experience, as unable to explain the totality of the person. Humanistic psychology also rejects the Freudian emphasis on the biological needs, or drives, of the body and on the defensive structure of the personality. For the humanists, the basic "self" is not a negative force that must be repressed or controlled; the self is good and has the innate and unique capacity to grow and to develop and expand its creativity.

The Need to Self-Actualize

According to the humanists, our needs include the need for safety and security, for friendships and intimacies, and for self-esteem and self-expression. The highest psychological need is the need for *self-actualization*. Human beings are internally motivated to fulfill these needs, to realize their potential; they have an innate propensity toward self-actualization. Personality development is the continuous process of positive growth in search of fulfilling ever-higher needs, the ultimate goal being self-actualization.

Self-actualization requires first of all that individuals be aware of their own feelings; without such self-awareness they can never know themselves, let alone realize their innate potential. In addition, self-actualization is affected by social, or environmental, factors. Like the social psychologists, humanistic psychologists believe that an individual's concept of self is in large measure socially determined, that others in one's world have an important impact on the way one feels about oneself. If one is fully and unconditionally accepted as a person, then one develops positive feelings about oneself; on the other hand, if acceptance is contingent upon certain types of behavior, then one may experience anxiety and the need to function defensively, to close oneself off from feelings and a subjective experience of the world. This type of functioning interferes with the process of self-actualization.

Hierarchy of Needs

From the point of view of humanistic psychology, the ultimate power of the individual might be regarded as the ability to achieve self-actualization. Abraham Maslow, one of the foremost spokespersons of the humanistic movement, devised a hierarchy of needs that distinguishes between the "higher" and "lower" needs inherent in each individual. The highest need is self-actualization. However, before one can fulfill the higher needs, one must first satisfy the lower needs. Individual behavior at any time is determined by the individual's strongest need at that time. The higher needs reflect later stages of personality development. At the base of Maslow's hierarchy are **physiological needs** (for example, food, clothing, and shelter). Above physiological needs are the needs for **safety and security**. These needs may not always be apparent to the individual; they may be subconscious and not easily identified. A need for safety or security may become highly motivating, depending on early childhood experiences. For example, the insecure child may later prefer occupations that offer insurance, retirement, protection from layoffs, and a predictable life. Once physiological and safety needs are fairly well satisfied, **social needs** become dominant. The individual, according to Maslow, now seeks group acceptance, friendships, and intimacies.

Assuming that an individual's social needs are reasonably well satisfied, a fourth need comes into prominence: *esteem*. Failure to understand this need may lead parents to complain, "We've given our child everything—a good home, stable family, all the things she ever asked for, even our own time and assistance—yet she is still dissatisfied." However, it may be that it is precisely because such children have had the three basic needs sufficiently satisfied that a fourth need emerges—recognition of worth as an individual. Like the need for security or social needs, the need for personal esteem appears in a variety of forms; a search for *recognition* is one manifestation of the need for personal esteem. Although salary carries some prestige value, often an impressive-sounding title (for example, "vice president for operations," "director of planning," or "deputy secretary") is even more important. Many individuals will sacrifice salary to achieve these symbols of esteem.

When the first four needs are more or less satisfied, we can expect to witness the emergence of Maslow's fifth and final need: *self-actualization*. According to Maslow, "Self-actualizing people are, without one single exception, involved in a cause outside of their own skin, in something outside of themselves."[13] Despite problems in defining self-actualization, it does seem true that at some point in life, frequently in the late 30s or early 40s, many individuals experience what is commonly called a "midlife crisis." At this point in their lives, some people feel that something is missing even though they have provided well for themselves and their families, faced no serious threats to their security, have won recognition in their field of work, and are well accepted by their family, friends, and neighbors. They ask, "Is that all there is?" According to Maslow, these individuals have reached a point at which they must turn to their fifth and final need, self-actualization.

Because Maslow's theory argues that in order to reach the stage of self-actualization, one must have met most of the more basic needs, there are enormous implications as to who can become self-actualized. Poor people struggling to meet basic physiological and safety needs and the working class who may not be able to meet esteem needs because of low-prestige occupations may be unable to become self-actualized.

physiological needs
the most basic cluster of needs, including water, food, oxygen, sleep, elimination, and sex

safety and security needs
include order and predictability

social needs
include affiliation with others and the feeling of being loved

The Study of Psychology and Power

In examining the various approaches in the field of psychology, we can see numerous and competing explanations as to how personality develops and the causes of human behavior. Each perspective, however, sheds light on power relations between individuals. Personality is defined by genetics and the environment. Our relations with others, how we learn, and how we have evolved—all impact what we think, feel, and do. Each perspective contributes to our understanding of power relations between individuals. In looking at the theme of power in psychology, mental illness also warrants examination as a determinant of structure of power relations.

Powerlessness and Mental Health

There is a common adage that "power tends to corrupt, and absolute power corrupts absolutely." It reflects our negative view of power and our association of power with abuse. But the distinguished psychologist Rollo May, whose contributions to the humanistic movement are highly significant, contends that power is a fundamental aspect of the life process. Indeed, he believes that *powerlessness* corrupts the human personality by robbing the individual of a sense of meaning and significance.

For those who suffer from mental illness, May's argument that power occurs in an individual's life in five functional forms may explain the powerlessness that often accompanies mental illness.[14] May's first form is the *power to be.* The word *power* comes from the Latin root meaning "to be able." The newborn must have the power to make others respond to his needs: He cries and waves his arms violently as signs of his discomfort. An infant who cannot elicit a response from others fails to develop as a separate personality. *Power as self-affirmation* is the recognition of one's own worth and significance in life. Some power is essential for self-esteem and self-belief. Power as self-assertion makes it clear who we are and what we believe. It gives us the potential to react to attack and protect ourselves from becoming victims. Power also occurs in everyone's life as *aggression*—striking out against a person or thing seen as an adversary.

The constructive aspects of aggression include cutting through barriers to initiate relationships; confronting another person, not with the intent to hurt but to penetrate that individual's consciousness; and actualizing one's own self in a hostile environment. The destructive side of aggression includes thrusting out to inflict injury and taking power simply to increase one's own range of control. Finally, power occurs as *violence.* May believes that violence is an attempt to exercise power. Violence may result from a failure at self-affirmation or self-assertion, or it may accompany aggression. Nonetheless, it can be regarded as functional to the individual if no other way is available for that person to gain significance in life. It is May's belief that modern mass society impairs the individual's self-esteem and self-worth. The feeling of personal powerlessness is widespread:

> To admit our own individual feelings of powerlessness—that we cannot influence many people; that we count for little; that the values to which our parents devoted their lives are to us insubstantial and worthless; that we feel ourselves to be "faceless others," insignificant to other people and therefore not worth much to ourselves—that is, indeed, difficult to admit.[15]

May believes that much irrational violence—for example, riots, assassinations, and senseless murders—is a product of feelings of powerlessness.

Treating Mental Illness

It is not always easy to distinguish mental health from mental illness. Generally, people are said to have a mental disorder when they feel distressed by their condition *and* it impairs their ability to pursue their normal functions in life. Brief stresses and strains of daily living usually do not require treatment, but severe, lasting, and incapacitating mental suffering clearly does so. Most symptoms of mental illness, however, are less than completely incapacitating (see Research This! for an examination of the prevalence of various mental illnesses in demographic groups). How much sadness indicates depression? How much suspicion

RESEARCH *THIS!*

While mental disorders are common in the United States, not every demographic group is equally likely to have mental illness. Following are data from the National Survey on Drug Use and Health (NSDUH), which defines a serious mental illness (SMI) as a diagnosable mental, behavioral, or emotional disorder (excluding developmental and substance use disorders) that occurs over sufficient duration to meet diagnostic criteria.

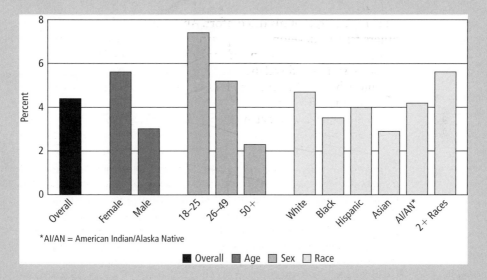

*AI/AN = American Indian/Alaska Native

■ Overall ■ Age ▨ Sex ☐ Race

YOUR ANALYSIS:

1. Based on the data shown, which sex is most likely to suffer from mental illness?

2. Why might mental illness rates decrease according to age?

3. What would be the most common demographic characteristics of someone suffering from mental illness?

INTERNATIONAL PERSPECTIVE

Depression: A Worldwide Battle

In America today, it seems a greater importance is placed on mental wellbeing than in the past, and less of a stigma exists around issues like depression. Perhaps because depression is better understood with more channels for people to seek help, it would appear that a larger percentage of Americans suffer from the illness.

But a look at the global landscape shows that Americans may be happier from day to day than people in many other countries. A recent Gallup poll asked people across the world, "Did you experience the following feelings during a lot of the day yesterday…? How about depression?" Compared to the highest rate of 41 percent, a moderate 12 percent of Americans polled answered "yes."

HIGHEST DEPRESSION RATES

Country	Percent Depressed
Ethiopia	41
Yemen	37
Palestinian Territory	32
Iraq	31
Hungary	30
Afghanistan	29
Pakistan	28

LOWEST DEPRESSION RATES:

Country	Percent Depressed
Central African Republic	1
Mauritania	2
Indonesia	2
Lao People's Democratic Republic	2
Denmark	3
Poland	3
Cote D'Ivoire	3
Austria	4
Switzerland	4

SOURCE: Gallup worldview. www.worldview.gallup com/default.aspx.

indicates paranoia? How much self-confidence indicates mania? Most of us bear some mental stress without seeking professional help (see International Perspective: "Depression: A Worldwide Battle"). But some people do not recognize their need for treatment even in the midst of acute mental illness.

Clinical Psychology

clinical psychology
focuses on treatment of
psychological disorders

Clinical psychology focuses on the treatment of psychological disorders. It is closely related to psychiatry in that both clinical psychologists and psychiatrists deal with the diagnosis and treatment of psychological disorders. (The psychiatrist, however, is also a medical doctor.) Clinicians deal with real people with real psychological problems. They enter the patient's world and concern themselves with the subjective human experience, including wishes, fears, anxieties, and ambitions. Clinical psychology stresses therapy, ranging from chemical therapy and shock treatment to various behavior therapies and insight therapies.

Professional Care

Professional assistance can be rendered by a **psychiatrist**—a medical doctor (MD) who specializes in the diagnosis and treatment of mental disorders; or a **clinical psychologist**—a therapist with graduate training, usually a PhD in psychological testing and treatment; or a **psychological counselor**—often a person with graduate training in psychology, marriage and family life, alcohol and drug-abuse treatment, social work, or related fields.

Diagnosing mental illness requires psychiatrists and psychologists to recognize a pattern of symptoms that correspond to an illness. This is often done by asking questions or giving written tests concerning a person's mental state. The American Psychiatric Association publishes *The Diagnostic and Statistical Manual* (DSM), which defines various mental disorders, describing typical observable behavior and responses to examiners' questions. Although the DSM can be very helpful in the diagnosis and treatment of mental disorders, seldom do patients' symptoms and responses fit perfectly with a recognized disorder. Indeed, sometimes fully qualified professionals render very different diagnoses of the same patients. (See Case Study: "Diagnosing Mental Illness.")

psychiatrist
an MD who specializes in the treatment of mental disorders

clinical psychologist
a therapist with a PhD in psychological treatment and testing

psychological counselor
a therapist with graduate training in psychology or related fields

CASE STUDY

Diagnosing Mental Illness

The American Psychiatric Association has tried to increase public awareness of the symptoms of mental illness as well as to remove the social stigma that surrounded mental illness in the past. Mental illness is not a character weakness but a treatable illness. Increasingly, psychiatrists are having great success in treating a wide range of psychiatric illnesses.

Addiction Disorders

Addiction disorders are one of the most common forms of mental illness. Addiction occurs when an individual cannot control his or her behavior. A wide variety of substances and behaviors can be addictive, including drugs (for example, alcohol or nicotine), opiates (for example, morphine or heroin), and stimulants (for example, amphetamines or cocaine). Behaviors such as using the Internet or video games, gambling, shopping, and having sexual relations also can be addictive. Because of the wide variety of addictions, estimates of the number of individuals addicted to substances and behaviors vary widely. Symptoms of addiction include the following:

- An overwhelming, destructive pattern of compulsion for the substance or behavior
- Greater tolerance required for satisfaction (particularly with substance addiction)
- Withdrawal symptoms when the behavior is stopped
- Secretive behaviors to mask the addiction
- Denial of the problem

Schizophrenia

Schizophrenia is one of the most debilitating mental illnesses. Often characterized by distorted thinking, hallucinations, delusions, and a dulling of normal emotions, schizophrenia is considered a brain disease. An estimated 2.4 million Americans suffer from this mental illness.

The following symptoms are sometimes associated with schizophrenia:

- Hearing nonexistent sounds
- Seeing nonexistent images
- Thoughts that dart uncontrollably from subject to subject
- Unfounded fears that one is being plotted against or watched
- Loss of self-esteem
- Withdrawal from friends and family
- Inappropriate emotions/reactions to situations
- Deteriorating work and school performance
- Neglect of social relationships and personal appearance

Depression

The most common and treatable mental illness, major and minor depression affects 8 million to 14 million Americans each year. Characterized by feelings of sadness, helplessness, hopelessness, and irritability, depression affects one in four women and one in ten men at some point during their lifetime.

If four or more of the following symptoms persist for more than two weeks, an individual should seek professional help:

- Change in appetite (significant weight loss or gain)
- Change in sleeping patterns
- Loss of interest in pleasurable activities
- Loss of energy; fatigue
- Feelings of worthlessness
- Feelings of inappropriate guilt
- Inability to concentrate; indecisiveness
- Recurring thoughts of death or suicide
- Melancholia (overwhelming feelings of sadness and grief)
- Disturbed thinking (out of touch with reality)
- Physical symptoms (headaches or stomachaches)

Manic Depression

Manic depression (bipolar illness) is a more severe form of depression. An estimated 2 million to 3 million people will suffer from this disorder at some time in their lives. People with manic depression experience mood swings from euphoria to depression.

All symptoms of depression can also be symptoms of manic depression. These are some of the typical symptoms of the manic (euphoric) phase of the disorder:

- An "on top of the world" mood that appears overly euphoric
- Expressions of unwarranted optimism

(continued)

- Lack of judgment
- Grandiose delusions of connections with God, celebrities, or political leaders
- Hyperactivity and excessive participation in numerous activities
- Racing, uncontrollable thoughts
- Decreased need for sleep
- Attention easily diverted to inconsequential or unimportant details
- Sudden irritability, rage, or paranoia

Postpartum Depression

Postpartum depression is a severe form of depression that occurs in some women after the birth of a child. Nearly all women who give birth experience the "baby blues"—a period of a week or two of depression—but postpartum depression lasts longer, and the symptoms may be more severe. In many cases, postpartum depression is caused by hormonal changes or imbalances.

Symptoms include the following:

- Irritability
- Sadness
- Crying
- Appetite changes
- Changes in sleep pattern
- Lack of energy
- Loss of interest in activities

In its more severe forms, those who suffer from postpartum depression may entertain thoughts of harming themselves or their babies. Those suffering from postpartum depression should seek help from a physician.

Anxiety Disorders

Anxiety disorders are very common, affecting an estimated 10 to 15 percent of the population. Of the several types of anxiety disorders, each has somewhat different symptoms:

- *Social phobia:* an intense fear of being scrutinized or evaluated by others
- *Simple phobia:* an intense fear of a particular object or situation
- *Posttraumatic stress disorder:* undesired recollections or re-experiences of a prior intense experience, often accompanied by chronic anxiety, angry outbursts, sleep disturbances, and emotional distress
- *Panic disorder:* repeated bouts of intense anxiety not necessarily related to any particular situation, often causing shortness of breath, dizziness, sweating, fainting, vomiting, racing and pounding heart
- *Obsessive–compulsive disorder:* obsessions are recurrent and persistent ideas, thoughts, or images that cannot be ignored or suppressed or stopped; compulsions are repetitive and persistent behaviors usually performed in a ritualistic manner that are not connected in any reasonable fashion with subjective circumstances
- *Generalized anxiety disorder:* generalized anxiety experienced for six months or longer that is not associated with life circumstances or a particular stimulus; symptoms include shakiness, restlessness, fatigue, shortness of breath, heart palpitations, sweating, dizziness, hot flashes, difficulty concentrating, and irritability

Treatment may come in the form of psychotherapy, drug therapy, or some combination of the two. (See Focus: "Posttraumatic Stress Disorder: Not Just a Soldier's Disease.") **Psychotherapy**, or "talk" therapy, involves communication between patient and therapist designed to help the patient better understand and deal effectively with troubling feelings and behavior. Psychotherapy includes a wide variety of techniques—some that depend on developing the patient's understanding of deeply ingrained motives and conflicts and others that help patients cope with their problems without necessarily exploring their underlying causes.

psychotherapy
"talk" therapy, involving communication between patient and therapist; includes a wide variety of techniques

Psychoanalysis

Traditional psychoanalysis is a therapy based on the Freudian notion that mental illness is most often a product of unconscious conflicts. If patients can acquire an insight into their own motives and needs, presumably they can develop more effective ways of handling their problems. When patients can freely express previously repressed emotions or relive intense emotional experiences, they are believed to be better equipped to face their current problems effectively. Sometimes insights are found in spontaneous talk or "free association," in the interpretation of dreams, or in hypnosis. But psychoanalysis is very time consuming and expensive. It may require weekly sessions over several years and thousands of dollars spent over that time.

Behavioral Therapies

Behavioral therapy assumes that disturbed behavior has been learned and that it can be unlearned or modified by a variety of conditioning techniques. Behavioral therapists are more concerned with changing specific behavioral patterns than with understanding or analyzing a patient's underlying personality. For example, in relaxation training, people learn to relax various muscles and eventually learn to relax their entire body. After learning to relax, they may be asked to confront a previously anxiety-producing stimulus. *Desensitization* occurs when people are able to maintain their relaxed condition while gradually encountering fears and phobias. *Assertiveness training* is another form of behavioral therapy in which people are taught to "speak up" or "say no" when others try to take advantage of them. *Positive reinforcement* is sometimes employed in mental hospitals when patients are rewarded for socially acceptable behavior. *Negative reinforcement*, or adverse conditioning, also can be effective in modifying alcohol and substance abuse.

Humanistic Therapies

Humanistic therapies tend to emphasize client-centered solutions to individual problems. The humanistic therapist does not try to interpret patients' behavior (as would a psychoanalyst) or modify it (as would a behavioral therapist), but rather, allows patients to develop their own self-actualizing solution to their problems. The therapist does not render judgments or opinions but instead tries to create an open and accepting atmosphere for the patient's self-expression. The goal is to enable patients to clarify their feelings. Group therapy is a

FOCUS

Posttraumatic Stress Disorder: Not Just a Soldier's Disease

Posttraumatic stress disorder (PTSD) is the psychological consequence of having experienced an extraordinarily stressful event—typically the fear or threat of one's death, the witnessing of the death of another, or the threat or occurrence of physical or psychological harm. PTSD was once thought of as a "combat" disease afflicting those on the front lines—for example, soldiers seeing wartime battle or police officers on the frontlines of crime fighting. But today, psychologists are just as likely to be diagnosing PTSD in the civilian population.

Among the first episodes prompting widespread PTSD diagnoses among civilian populations was the aftermath of the April 1995 bombing of the Alfred P. Murrah Federal Building in Oklahoma City. In that domestic terrorist attack, at least 168 people, including 19 children attending a child-care facility in the building, were killed, and another 800 people were injured. The enormous rescue efforts that occurred in days following the attack—an estimated 12,000 people volunteered to help the efforts—meant that many people, both those trained as first responders to a disaster and untrained civilian volunteers, were exposed to a horrifying situation that frequently led to PTSD.

Many of those who survived the terrorist attacks of September 11, 2001, on the World Trade Center in New York and the Pentagon in Washington, DC, also were diagnosed as suffering from PTSD. Symptoms of PTSD include insomnia, irritability, nightmares, flashbacks, memory loss, dissociation (separating thoughts of the trauma from the rest of the psyche), detachment (distancing oneself emotionally from people or situations), avoidance of triggers (reminders of the trauma), extreme stress response to triggers, and extreme startle response (to loud noises, or sounds or smells associated with the event).

In 2005 Hurricane Katrina fell on New Orleans and devastated the city as well as other communities in Louisiana and Mississippi. Psychologists have seen many diagnoses of PTSD stemming from this natural disaster as well.

But combat, war, terrorist attacks, and natural disasters are not the only traumas that can result in PTSD. The American Psychological Association lists childhood abuse and/or sexual assault, adult rape, and assaults as events that could prompt a PTSD reaction.

What can be done to treat PTSD? In some cases, the symptoms disappear on their own. But if someone suffers from symptoms of PTSD for more than two weeks, he or she should consult a doctor. Two primary methods of treatment include exposure therapy whereby a victim of PTSD is taught to process the memories of the events in a manageable way so that the event can become part of the past rather than a continually recurring event. Sometimes antidepressant medications also have proven effective in treating PTSD.

means of encouraging people to express their feelings in the presence of others with similar problems. Group therapy saves time and money because one therapist can work with six to twelve patients at once. People may derive some comfort and support from observing others with similar or perhaps even worse problems. And people may learn vicariously—by watching how others deal with their problems.

Drug Therapies

Drug therapy has had a revolutionary impact on mental health care. Beginning in the late 1950s, psychiatric drugs dramatically improved the effectiveness of treatment for a vast array of disorders. Prior to the advent of drug therapies, mental hospitals were very dismal places; physicians were able to offer little more than custodial care. Hallucinating patients talked to "voices"; catatonic patients sat in stupors; and manic patients paced the floors. The most agitated patients were sedated or placed in restraints. There were few "cures." But drug therapies changed these scenes. Currently, hospital stays are relatively brief; patients are medically and psychologically evaluated; drug therapies are initiated and are closely supervised. Patients who pose no danger to themselves or others are treated as outpatients.

The impact of the drug revolution is apparent in the depopulation of mental hospitals. During the first half of the twentieth century, the number of mental hospital patients rose steadily. But the introduction of drug therapies reversed this trend, and mental hospitals were emptied of all but temporary patients and a few very severe cases.

Indeed, the drug revolution was exploited as a means of reducing public spending for mental health care. Many patients are being released into the community with instructions for drug therapies and outpatient care. But they often have been unable to follow their instructions, and community care frequently has been lacking. It is estimated that one-quarter to one-third of the nation's street-wandering "homeless" population suffers from serious mental illness.

Schizophrenia, mania, and depression are the categories of mental illness that are frequently and successfully treated with drugs.[16] Four classes of drugs are commonly used in psychiatry today: antianxiety drugs, antipsychotics, antidepressants, and mood stabilizers. These drugs can provide immediate and effective relief for those who suffer the discomfort of mental disorders. Patients are medically monitored for potential unwanted side effects, but the newer drugs have proven very effective with only minimal side effects.

The Sociology of Psychological Disorders

Psychological disorders appear to vary by ethnicity and gender. Men are much more likely than women to suffer alcohol abuse and dependence. Women are more likely to report mood disorders. Men are more likely to develop antisocial personalities. Psychological disorders of various sorts are somewhat more prevalent among minorities in America. Minorities are also more likely to experience poverty. (See Focus: "Who Are the Poor?" in Chapter 11.) Poverty may therefore be the real factor affecting ethnic differences in disorders. The stress of poverty may precipitate psychological disorders, especially depression among women and alcoholism among men.[17]

CHAPTER SUMMARY

- Personality is all the characteristic ways of behaving that an individual exhibits; it is the characteristic, enduring, and organized patterns of thought, emotion, and behavior an individual habitually exhibits when subjected to particular stimuli. Psychology examines the relative influence of heredity versus environment on personality, as well as how the interaction between nature and nurture influence behavior.
- Every cell of the human body contains genes that instruct its growth and development. A common estimate is that hereditability—differences among groups of people that are attributable to genetics—accounts for about 50 percent of the variation in personalities among people.
- Nurturing also influences growth and development. An infant's earliest experiences exert a dramatic impact on the brain's growth, physically determining the number and strength of neuronal connections.
- Within psychology are varying approaches that explain how individuals gain power over their behaviors, thoughts, and feelings as well as over other individuals. These approaches include the cognitive approach, biological psychology, psychoanalytic psychology, social psychology, humanistic psychology, and behavioralistic psychology.
- Behavioral psychology asserts that the goal of psychologists should be to study behavior by employing the same scientific tests as the natural sciences, including the role that an individual's environment or situation plays in determining that individual's behavior. Social psychology is concerned primarily with interpersonal interactions—how the individual interacts with others—while humanistic psychology emphasizes the individual's innate potential for development, the human need for self-fulfillment.
- For those who suffer from mental illness, Rolland May's argument that power occurs in an individual's life in five functional forms may explain the powerlessness that often accompanies mental illness.
- Diagnosing mental illness requires psychiatrists and psychologists to recognize a pattern of symptoms that correspond to an illness. This is often done by asking questions or giving written tests concerning a person's mental state. Mental illness may be treated through clinical psychology, psychiatry, psychoanalysis, behavioral training, humanistic therapies, or drug therapies.

KEY TERMS

androgen   the hormone produced in an embryo's sex glands that determines whether the embryo will develop as a male or a female

axon   a long, tubelike structure that protrudes from the cell body of a neuron

behavioral psychology   the study of how people and animals learn to respond to different stimuli

behavioral psychotherapy   treatment based on learning or unlearning behavior

behaviorism   an approach to psychology that asserts that only observable behavior can be studied

biological psychology   the study of electrical and chemical events in the brain and nervous system

classical conditioning   the type of learning that occurs when, consistently, situations are emotionally associated with specific responses

clinical psychologist   a therapist with a PhD in psychological treatment and testing

clinical psychology   focuses on treatment of psychological disorders

cognitive approach   a methodology that emphasizes how people learn about themselves and their environment

cognitive neuroscience   explores how mental activities are executed in an individual's brain

conditioned response   a behavior that is elicited by a previously neutral stimulus

conditioned stimulus–response (SR) linkage   drive, cue, response, and reinforcement

cue   the stimulus associated with the response

dendrite   a branch of neurons where the cell receives impulses from other neurons

DNA   deoxyribonucleic acid—a code of instructions to cells determining their structure, appearance, and function

drive   a want for something

evolutionary psychology   the study of relationships between biological needs, genetic coding, and psychological traits of humans

fraternal twins   twins who develop from separate eggs and are no closer genetically than brothers and sisters

gene   an inherited unit of life, composed of DNA, found in every cell

Gestalt psychology   the study of the whole individual

hereditability   differences among groups of people that are attributable to genetics

humanistic psychology   focuses on individual development and self-fulfillment

identical twins   twins who develop from a single fertilized egg and who are genetically identical

interpersonal response traits   the sum of all of an individual's socializing experience, or personality

neuron   a cell in the human brain that transmits impulses to other cells, muscles, and glands

neurotransmitter   a chemical in the brain that crosses synapses in order to stimulate the next neuron

observational learning   the type of learning that occurs when an individual observes the behavior of others

operant conditioning   how individuals learn when they discover the connection between their behavior and resultant outcomes

personality   the characteristic ways of behaving; the characteristic, enduring, and organized patterns of thought, emotion, and behavior

physiological needs   the most basic cluster of needs, including water, food, oxygen, sleep, elimination, and sex

psychiatrist   an MD who specializes in the treatment of mental disorders

psychological counselor   a therapist with graduate training in psychology or related fields

psychoanalysis   insight-oriented therapy, often focused on early-childhood experiences

psychoanalytic (Freudian) psychology   a theory in psychology that explains behavior as a product of the interaction of biological instincts and social learning, especially early childhood experiences; named for its founder, Sigmund Freud

psychotherapy   "talk" therapy, involving communication between patient and therapist; includes a wide variety of techniques

reinforcement repeating conditioned stimulus and response

role playing developing a sense of self by trying on a variety of roles

safety and security needs include order and predictability

self the individual's awareness of himself or herself derived from interpersonal interaction

social-learning theory behavior is shaped by internal cognitive processes and observing the behavior of others

social needs include affiliation with others and the feeling of being loved

social psychology the study of the individual's relationships with other individuals and groups

socialization in psychology, the development of individual identity through interpersonal experiences and the internalizing of the expectations of significant others

synapse a connector between neurons

testosterone the male sex hormone (found in varying levels in both men and women)

ON THE WEB

EXPLORING PSYCHOLOGY

The website for this textbook (**www.cengagebrain.com**) offers resources for exploring power and personality. Psychology encompasses a wide variety of subjects. The official site of the American Psychological Association lists fifty-two "branches" of psychology, including developmental, personality, clinical, educational, behavioral, experimental, and humanistic psychology; psychoanalysis; psychopharmacology; and sport. Most of these have their own websites.

- **American Psychological Association** The best place to begin your exploration of psychology is the official site (**www.apa.org**) of the American Psychological Association (APA). It provides information for students, parents, teenagers, the media, and others about a wide variety of topics related to psychology, including common psychological disorders. For students, this site provides career-planning information, employment data, programs and degrees in graduate education, financial assistance, and more relating to psychology. Student membership in the APA is inexpensive and

includes subscriptions to *Monitor on Psychology* and *American Psychologist*. A search engine at the site provides an index of topics from "addiction" to "women."

Try This: Go to **www.apa.org/topics/index.aspx** and click one of the psychology topics. Read the overview and "What You Can Do" sections. How is psychology applied to that particular subject? In the "News" section, examine the latest psychology news pertaining to your topic.

- **Psychology.com** Several commercial sites invite browsers to view topics in psychology. Psychology.com (**www.psychology.com**) contains current articles, psychological tests, the directory of therapists, and even an "Ask a therapist" interactive link.

Try This: Go to **www.psychology.com/assessments/** and click on the "Simple Career Interest" survey. Follow the instructions for the short assessment and click through to see your results. Click on your three letter codes to view careers compatible to your personality.

REVIEW QUIZ

MULTIPLE CHOICE

1. What is the methodology that emphasizes how people learn about themselves and their environment?
   a. social learning theory
   b. the cognitive approach
   c. psychoanalytic psychology
   d. evolutionary psychology

2. What is the methodology that emphasizes that behavior is shaped by internal cognitive processes and observing the behavior of others?
   a. social learning theory
   b. the cognitive approach
   c. psychoanalytic psychology
   d. evolutionary psychology

3. What is the hormone produced in an embryo's sex glands that determines whether the embryo will develop as a male or a female?
   a. DNA
   b. testosterone
   c. androgen
   d. dendrite

4. Which of the following does NOT describe a characteristic of the authoritarian personality?
   a. dominance and submission
   b. orientation toward power
   c. flexibility
   d. exaggerated concern with strength

5. What is the theory in psychology that explains behavior as a product of the interaction of biological instincts and social learning, especially early childhood experiences?
   a. social learning theory
   b. the cognitive approach
   c. psychoanalytic psychology
   d. evolutionary psychology

6. How individuals learn when they discover the connection between their behavior and resultant outcomes is called what?
   a. operant conditioning
   b. observant conditioning
   c. conditioned stimulus–response (SR) linkage
   d. classical conditioning

7. Which of the following is not one of the causes of personality disorder?
   a. abrupt changes in roles
   b. inadequate socialization
   c. consistent defeat, frustration, and withdrawal
   d. nurturing and positive reinforcement

8. What is the most basic cluster of needs, including water, food, oxygen, sleep, elimination, and sex called?
   a. physiological needs
   b. safety and security needs
   c. social needs
   d. civic needs

9. What does the strength of the stimulus–response (SR) linkage depend on?
   a. strength of drive
   b. immediate drive reduction
   c. the number of trials
   d. all of the above

10. What is the name of the medical doctor who specializes in the treatment of mental disorders?
    a. clinical psychologist
    b. psychiatrist
    c. psychological counselor
    d. social worker

FILL IN THE BLANK

11. _____ is described as the characteristic, enduring, and organized patterns of thought, emotion, and behavior.

12. A _____ is an inherited unit of life.

13. _____ explores how mental activities are executed in an individual's brain.

14. An approach to psychology that asserts that only observable behavior can be studied is called _____.

15. _____ is "talk" therapy, involving communication between patient and therapist.

In Part Three, we focus on how power can be used to confront the crises that afflict human societies, including income inequality which was the focus of the Occupy Movement. Here, members of Occupy Wall Street protest in Zuccotti Park, New York, NY.

PART 3

The Uses of Power

In Part Three, we explore the major social problems confronting society. These problems are interdisciplinary in nature, not confined to any of the social science disciplines in particular. The problem of crime and violence, for example, is of as much interest and concern to the psychologist as it is to the sociologist. Because it is a question of human behavior and its consequences, it is also of concern to the political scientist, the historian, the economist, and the anthropologist. Each of these social scientists would approach the study of crime and violence from a somewhat different perspective. Our unifying perspective continues to be power in society, but our main focus here is on how power can be used to confront the crises that afflict human societies, for the betterment or to the detriment of humanity.

CHAPTER 10

Power, Race, and Gender

Learning Objectives

After reading this chapter, students will be able to:

- Describe how discrimination based on race, ethnicity, gender, disability, or sexual orientation diminishes individuals' power.

- Understand the role government has had in discriminating and in rectifying discrimination.

- Explain the similarities in different groups' struggles for equal treatment.

Racism in American History

Race has been a central issue in American society throughout the nation's history. African slaves were introduced to the earliest colonial settlements in 1619. In 1863 the Emancipation Proclamation, issued by President Abraham Lincoln in the midst of the Civil War, applied to slaves living in the Confederate states, and slavery was constitutionally abolished in the United States by the Thirteenth Amendment in 1865. But within a generation, racial segregation replaced slavery as a means of subjugation. In the decision *Plessy v. Ferguson*, segregation won constitutional approval by the U.S. Supreme Court in 1896; not until the historic *Brown v. Board of Education* case in 1954 did the Supreme Court formally reverse itself and declare segregation unconstitutional. Slavery and segregation left social, economic, and political scars that remain visible in American society today.[1]

Following the Civil War, Congress passed and the states ratified the Fourteenth Amendment to the U.S. Constitution, declaring that

> no State shall make or enforce any law which shall abridge the privileges or immunities of citizens of the United States; nor shall any State deprive any person of life, liberty, or property, without due process of law; nor deny to any person within its jurisdiction the equal protection of the laws.

The language and historical context leave little doubt that the purpose of the Fourteenth Amendment was to secure for blacks a place in American society equal to that of whites. Yet for a full century, these promises went unfulfilled.

Segregation became the social instrument by which blacks were denied social, economic, educational, and political equality. Segregation was enforced

FIGURE 10-1   SEGREGATION LAWS IN THE UNITED STATES IN 1954

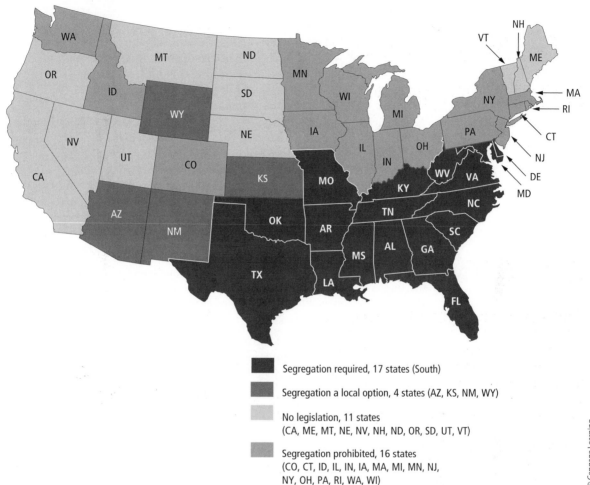

Segregation required, 17 states (South)

Segregation a local option, 4 states (AZ, KS, NM, WY)

No legislation, 11 states
(CA, ME, MT, NE, NV, NH, ND, OR, SD, UT, VT)

Segregation prohibited, 16 states
(CO, CT, ID, IL, IN, IA, MA, MI, MN, NJ,
NY, OH, PA, RI, WA, WI)

© Cengage Learning

by a variety of private sanctions, from lynching mobs to segregated help-wanted ads to private school and country club admission committees. But government was a principal instrument of segregation in both the Southern and border states of the nation. (Figure 10-1 shows school segregation laws in the United States in 1954.) In the Northern states, government was seldom used to enforce segregation, but it was also seldom used to prevent it. The results sometimes were similar.

The constitutional argument made on behalf of segregation—that the phrase "equal protection of the laws" did not prohibit the enforced separation of races so long as the races were treated equally—became known as the **separate-but-equal doctrine**. In 1896 the U.S. Supreme Court, in *Plessy v. Ferguson*, made this doctrine the official interpretation of the equal protection clause, thus giving segregation constitutional approval. But in fact, separate

separate-but-equal doctrine

interpreting the equal protection clause of the Fourteenth Amendment to allow segregation of the races if facilities were equal (1896–1954) facilities were never equal, and the ruling had the effect of legalizing a system in which facilities for African Americans—including everything from water fountains and restrooms to schools, colleges, and even graveyards—were consistently inferior to those provided to whites.

The initial goal of the civil rights movement was the elimination of direct legal segregation (also called *de jure* **segregation**). Discrimination and segregation practiced by governments had to be prohibited, particularly in voting and public education. Led by Thurgood Marshall, the chief counsel for the National Association for the Advancement of Colored People (NAACP) who later became the first African American Supreme Court justice, the newly emerging civil rights movement of the 1950s pressed for a court decision stating that *de jure* segregation violated the guarantee of equal protection of the laws granted by the Fourteenth Amendment. The civil rights movement sought a complete reversal of the separate-but-equal interpretation of *Plessy v. Ferguson*; it wanted a decision that laws separating the races were unconstitutional.

On May 17, 1954, the Court rendered its historic ***Brown v. Board of Education of Topeka, Kansas*** decision:

> Segregation of white and colored children in public schools has a detrimental
> effect upon the colored children. The impact is greater when it has the sanction
> of law, for the policy of separating the races is usually interpreted as denoting
> the inferiority of the Negro group.[2]

The Supreme Court's decision in *Brown* was very important symbolically. Although it would be many years before any significant number of black children would attend previously all-white schools, the decision by the nation's highest court stimulated black hopes and expectations. Indeed, many credit the *Brown* decision with starting the modern civil rights movement. The African American psychologist Kenneth Clark wrote, "This [civil rights] movement would probably not have existed at all were it not for the 1954 Supreme Court school desegregation decision which provided a tremendous boost to the morale of blacks by its clear affirmation that color is irrelevant to the rights of American citizens."[3]

The Civil Rights Movement

As long as the civil rights movement was combating government discrimination, it could employ the U.S. Constitution as a weapon in its arsenal and rely on judicial action to accomplish its objective. But when the civil rights movement turned its attention to combating private discrimination, it had to carry its fight into the legislative branch of government. Only Congress could restrict discrimination practiced by private owners of restaurants, hotels, and motels; private employers; and other individuals who were not government officials.

In the early 1960s, the civil rights movement stepped up its protests and demonstrations and attracted worldwide attention with organized

Margin notes:

***de jure* (pronounced day-juray) segregation** segregation permitted or required by law

Brown v. Board of Education of Topeka, Kansas (1954) landmark Supreme Court decision declaring that segregation itself violates the equal protection clause of the Fourteenth Amendment

Carl Iwasaki / Time Life Pictures / Getty Images

Linda Brown (front, center), the plaintiff in *Brown v. Board of Education*, in her segregated classroom at the Monroe School. The landmark 1954 Supreme Court decision made school segregation illegal.

sit-ins, freedom rides, picketing campaigns, boycotts, and mass marches. (See Focus: "Martin Luther King Jr. and the Power of Protest.") Figure 10-2 shows the most important events of the civil rights movement.

Civil Rights Legislation

After the massive "March on Washington" in August 1963, led by Martin Luther King Jr., President Kennedy asked Congress for the most comprehensive civil rights legislation it had ever considered. After Kennedy's assassination in 1963, both houses of Congress finally passed the **Civil Rights Act of 1964** with more than a two-thirds vote and with the overwhelming support of members of both the Republican and Democratic parties. It can be ranked with the Emancipation Proclamation, the Fourteenth Amendment, and *Brown v. Board of Education* as one of the most important steps toward full equality for African Americans.

Civil Rights Act of 1964 prohibits discrimination in public accommodations, in programs receiving federal funds, and in employment; established the EEOC to enforce its provisions

FIGURE 10-2   MAJOR EVENTS OF THE CIVIL RIGHTS MOVEMENT

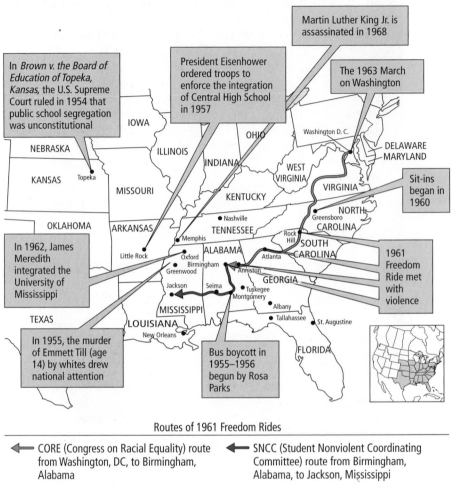

Routes of 1961 Freedom Rides

⟵ CORE (Congress on Racial Equality) route from Washington, DC, to Birmingham, Alabama

⟵ SNCC (Student Nonviolent Coordinating Committee) route from Birmingham, Alabama, to Jackson, Mississippi

SOURCE: Jacqueline Jones et al., *Created Equal: A Social and Political History of the United States,* 2nd ed. (New York: Pearson Longman, 2006), 855.

The act includes the following key provisions:

- It is unlawful to discriminate against or segregate persons on the grounds of race, color, religion, or national origin in any place of public accommodation, including hotels, motels, restaurants, movies, theaters, sports arenas, entertainment houses, and other places offering to serve the public.
- Each federal department and agency will take appropriate action to end discrimination in all programs or activities receiving federal financial assistance in any form. These actions may include the termination of assistance.
- It is unlawful for any firm or labor union to discriminate against any individual in any fashion because of his or her race, color, religion, sex, or national origins; an Equal Employment Opportunity Commission will be established to enforce this provision by investigation, conference, conciliation, or civil action in federal court.

On April 4, 1968, Martin Luther King Jr. was shot and killed in Memphis, Tennessee. The murder of the nation's leading advocate of nonviolence was a tragedy affecting all Americans. Before his death, King had campaigned in Chicago and other northern cities for an end to de facto segregation of blacks in ghettos and for the passage of legislation prohibiting discrimination in the sale or rental of houses and apartments. "Fair housing" legislation had consistently failed in Congress; there was no mention of discrimination in housing even in the comprehensive Civil Rights Act of 1964; and the prospects of a national fair housing law at the beginning of 1968 were not promising. With the assassination of King, however, the mood of the nation and of Congress changed dramatically. Congress passed a fair housing law as a tribute to the slain civil rights leader.

The **Civil Rights Act of 1968** prohibited the following forms of discrimination:

Civil Rights Act of 1968 prohibits discrimination in the sale or rental of a dwelling or in advertising the sale or rental

- Refusal to sell or rent a dwelling to any person because of race, color, religion, or national origin
- Discrimination against a person in the terms, conditions, or privileges of the sale or rental of a dwelling
- Indication of a preference or discrimination on the basis of race, color, religion, or national origin in advertising the sale or rental of a dwelling

Continuing Inequalities

With the election of President Barack Obama, the first African American president, some argue that racial equality has been achieved. But the statistics, including those presented in Table 10-1, indicate that stark differences remain in the average quality of life for whites and blacks in the United States. Despite progress toward equality in law, social and economic inequalities between blacks and whites persist. Median income of black families is only about 63 percent of that of white families (Table 10-1). The black poverty percentage is more than twice the white poverty percentage. Blacks have made notable progress in education, but the proportion of college graduates is still two-thirds the white population. Female-headed households have increased among both whites and blacks, but the proportion of households headed by a single black woman is increasing faster than those headed by single white women—today nearly half of all black households are headed by a female without a spouse present. Life expectancy among black men and women lags behind that of whites although the gap is closing over time. The infant mortality rate for blacks remains more than twice as high as for whites.

So while President Obama's election does mark an important watershed for Americans and it demonstrates that the civil rights movement succeeded in creating many new opportunities for African Americans, the statistics demonstrate that substantial inequalities between the races remain in the United States. Equality of *opportunity* is not the same as equality of *results*. The statistics lead us to ask what public policies should be pursued to achieve greater equality between the races. Is it sufficient that government eliminate discrimination, guarantee equality of opportunity, and apply "color-blind" standards to both blacks and whites? Or should government undertake **affirmative action**—preferential or compensatory treatment of minorities—to narrow the gap between whites and

affirmative action compensatory or preferential treatment of minorities

FOCUS

Martin Luther King Jr. and the Power of Protest

The civil rights movement developed new techniques for minorities to gain power and influence in American society. Mass protest is a technique by which groups seek to obtain a bargaining position for themselves that can induce desired concessions from established powerholders. It is a means of acquiring a bargaining leverage for those who would otherwise be powerless.

The nation's leading exponent of nonviolent protest was Dr. Martin Luther King Jr. Inspired by the ideas of Mohandas Gandhi, who advocated nonviolence, King developed a philosophy of nonviolent, direct-action protest on behalf of African Americans, which won him international acclaim and the Nobel Peace Prize in 1964.

King first came to national prominence in 1955 when he was only 25 years old; he led a year-long bus boycott in Montgomery, Alabama, to protest discrimination in seating on public buses. In 1957 he formed the Southern Christian Leadership Conference (SCLC) to provide encouragement and leadership to the growing nonviolent protest movement in the South.

In 1963 a group of Alabama clergymen petitioned King to call off mass demonstrations in Birmingham, Alabama. King, who had been arrested in the demonstrations, replied in his famous "Letter from Birmingham Jail":

> *One may well ask, "How can you advocate breaking some laws and obeying others?" The answer is found in the fact that there are unjust laws. I would be the first to advocate obeying just laws.*
>
> *One has not only a legal but a moral responsibility to obey just laws. Conversely, one has a moral responsibility to disobey unjust laws....*
>
> *One who breaks an unjust law must do it openly, lovingly ... and with a willingness to accept the penalty. I submit that an individual who breaks a law that conscience tells him is unjust, and willingly accepts the penalty by staying in jail to arouse the conscience of the community over its injustice, is in reality expressing the very highest respect for law.**

* A public letter by Martin Luther King Jr., Birmingham, Alabama, April 16, 1963.

blacks in employment, education, and income?[4] (See Controversies in Social Science: "Affirmative Action and the Constitution.") Although the government can attempt to eliminate discrimination on the basis of race in many areas, can the government even attempt to deal with the broader issue of racism in society and the cyclical effect that racism has on generations of African Americans?

Hispanic Power

Hispanic
referring to Spanish-speaking ancestry and culture

The term **Hispanic** refers to Mexican Americans, Puerto Ricans, Cubans, and others of Spanish-speaking ancestry and culture. Hispanics will soon become the nation's largest minority group (Table 10-2). The largest subgroup is Mexican Americans. Some are descendants of citizens who lived in the Mexican territory

Nonviolent direct action is mass action directed against laws regarded as unjust. Mass demonstrations, sit-ins, and other nonviolent direct-action tactics often involve disobedience to state and local laws. The political purpose of nonviolent direct action and civil disobedience is to call attention or "to bear witness" to the existence of injustices. Only laws regarded as unjust are broken, and they are broken openly, without hatred or violence. Punishment is actively sought rather than avoided because punishment will further emphasize the injustices of the law. The object of nonviolent civil disobedience is to stir the conscience of an apathetic majority and to win support for measures that will eliminate the injustices. By accepting punishment for the violation of an unjust law, persons practicing civil disobedience demonstrate their sincerity. They hope to shame the majority and to make it ask itself how far it will go to protect the status quo.

Perhaps the most dramatic application of nonviolent direct action occurred in Birmingham, Alabama, in the spring of 1963. Under King's direction, thousands of African Americans, including schoolchildren, staged protest marches. In response, police and firefighters, under the direction of Police Chief "Bull" Connor, attacked the demonstrators with fire hoses, cattle prods, and police dogs, all in clear view of national television cameras. Pictures of police brutality were flashed throughout the nation and the world, doubtless touching the consciences of many white Americans. The demonstrators conducted themselves in a nonviolent fashion. Thousands were dragged off to jail, including King. (It was at this time that King wrote his "Letter from Birmingham Jail," explaining and defending nonviolent direct action.)

The most massive application of nonviolent direct action was the great "March on Washington" in August 1963, during which more than 200,000 black and white marchers converged on the nation's capital. The march ended in a formal program at the Lincoln Memorial in which King delivered his most eloquent appeal, entitled "I Have a Dream":

> *I still have a dream. It is a dream deeply rooted in the American dream. I have a dream that one day this nation will rise up and live out the true meaning of its creed: "We hold these truths to be self-evident, that all men are created equal."*

annexed to the United States in 1848, but most have come to the United States in accelerating numbers in recent years. The largest Mexican American populations are found in Texas, Arizona, New Mexico, and California. Puerto Ricans constitute the second-largest Hispanic subgroup. Many still retain ties to the commonwealth and move back and forth from the island to New York. Cubans make up the third-largest subgroup; most have fled from Fidel Castro's Communist regime in Cuba and live mainly in the Miami metropolitan area.

Each of these Hispanic groups has encountered a different experience in American life. Indeed, some evidence shows that these groups identify themselves separately rather than as Hispanics.[5] Many Cuban Americans, especially early refugees from Castro's revolution in 1959, were skilled professionals and

TABLE 10-1 CONTINUING RACIAL INEQUALITIES

		White	Black
Median family income (current dollars)	1970	$10,236	$6,279
	2009	$51,861	$32,584
Poverty	1970	10%	35%
(percentage of population below poverty line)	2011	10%	27%
College education*	1970	11%	4%
	2010	30%	20%
Female-headed household†	1970	9%	33%
	2010	19%	49%
Life expectancy	1970	72	64
	2015 (proj.)	79	75
Infant mortality‡	1970	18	33
	2005	6	13

* Percentage of the population 25 years old and over.
† With children, no spouse present (percentage of all families of identified or specified race).
‡ Deaths per one thousand live births.

SOURCES: U.S. Bureau of the Census, *Statistical Abstract of the United States 2012* (Washington, DC: Government Printing Office, 2012), and *Statistical Abstract of the United States 2012,* www.census.gov/compendia/statab/2012/tables/12s0691.pdf. Persons Below Poverty Level by Selected Characteristics: 2012, www.census.gov/compendia/statab/cats/income_expenditures_poverty_wealth/poverty.html. Educational Attainment by Race and Hispanic Origin: 1960 to 2010, www.census.gov/compendia/statab/2012/tables/12s0229.pdf. Families by Type, Race, and Hispanic Origin: 2012, www.census.gov/compendia/statab/2012/tables/12s0066.xls. Expectation of Life at Birth, 1970 to 2005, and Projections, 2010 to 2020, www.census.gov/compendia/statab/2012/tables/12s0104.pdf. Infant, Neonatal, and Maternal Mortality Rates by Race: 1980 to 2007, www.census.gov/compendia/statab/2012/tables/12s0115.pdf.

businesspeople who rapidly set about rebuilding Miami's dormant economy. In politics Cuban Americans tend to vote Republican; they have succeeded in electing Cuban Americans to state and local offices in Florida and to the U.S. Congress.

The Mexican American population in the southwestern United States is growing very rapidly. For many years, agricultural businesses encouraged immigration of Mexican farm laborers willing to endure harsh conditions for low pay. Because until 1971 Hispanics were not legally considered a racial minority group, antidiscrimination laws, such as the 1964 Civil Rights Act, did not apply to them. In the landmark case *Corpus Christi Independent School District v. Cisneros* (1971), the Supreme Court upheld a lower court's ruling that Hispanics are a racial minority group; therefore, they are covered by laws protecting the rights of minority groups.

Despite this ruling, Hispanics may also still be subject to discrimination in employment. In the Immigration Reform Act of 1987, Congress offered amnesty to all undocumented workers who had entered the United States prior to 1982. But the act also required employers, under threat of penalties, to hire only people who could provide documentation of their legal status in the country. In order to comply with this law, some employers refuse to hire—and thus

CONTROVERSIES IN SOCIAL SCIENCE

Affirmative Action and the Constitution

The civil rights movement opened new opportunities for minorities and women in America. But equality of *opportunity* is not the same as equality of *results*. The early emphasis of government policy was nondiscrimination. Over time, however, the goal of public policy shifted from the traditional aim of equality of opportunity through nondiscrimination to equality of results through "goals and timetables" established by affirmative action. Although carefully avoiding the term *quota*, the notion of affirmative action tests the success of equal opportunity by observing whether minorities and women achieve admissions, jobs, and promotions in proportion to their numbers in the population.

However, a constitutional question arises as to whether affirmative action programs discriminate against whites and males and therefore violate the equal protection clause of the Fourteenth Amendment. The U.S. Supreme Court has wrestled with this question in several important cases.

The Bakke Case* After several years of premedical courses and volunteer work in a hospital, Allan Bakke, a 32-year-old white male who was also a Vietnam veteran, applied to the University of California at Davis Medical School. He was rejected two years in a row. He later learned that his college grades and medical aptitude test scores ranked well above those of many who had been accepted. All who had been accepted with lower scores were African American or Mexican American. Bakke filed a lawsuit arguing that the university had discriminated against him because of race—a violation of the Fourteenth Amendment's guarantee of equal protection of the laws. The university, which accepted one hundred applicants to medical school per year, admitted that it set aside sixteen places for "disadvantaged students," a category that never included any whites.

Candidates for those sixteen positions were placed in a separate admissions pool and competed only against one another. White applicants with grade-point averages below 2.5 (out of a possible 4.0) were always rejected, but many minority students were accepted with averages as low as 2.1 and 2.2. Bakke's average was 3.5.

The university argued that using race as a favorable criterion was in the best interest of the state and the nation. By increasing the number of minority students, the university hoped eventually to improve medical care among the poor and black. Minority doctors would also provide role models for young African Americans and Mexican Americans, giving them something to aspire to in their career development. The university contended that its separation of black and white candidates was "benign" discrimination (meant to help) rather than "invidious" (meant to hurt).

However, the U.S. Supreme Court held that the affirmative action program at the University of California at Davis Medical School violated Bakke's rights to equal protection of the laws under the Fourteenth Amendment. The Court ordered the university to admit Bakke to medical school.

---

* *Regents of the University of California v. Bakke*, 438 U.S. 265 (1978).

(*continued*)

CONTROVERSIES IN SOCIAL SCIENCE

The Court was careful to specify the discriminatory aspects of the university's affirmative-action program:

> *The Davis special admission program involves the use of an explicit racial classification…. No matter how strong their qualifications… they [whites] are never afforded the chance to compete with applicants from the preferred groups for the special admission seats.*

The Court went on to describe how an affirmative-action program could be constitutional:

> *Race or ethnic background may be deemed a "plus" in a particular applicant's file… [as long as] it does not insulate the individual from comparison with all other candidates for the available seats.*

The Supreme Court generally approved of the goal of achieving racial and ethnic diversity in the student body. Thus, the Bakke case set some limits on affirmative action programs, but it still permitted schools to consider race as a "plus" factor in competition for admission.

Since *Bakke*, the Court has considered many challenges to affirmative action plans on a case-by-case basis. No clear or consistent policy has emerged. In some cases, racial quota systems have been upheld as constitutional, and in other cases, they have been struck down as violations of the U.S. Constitution or the Civil Rights Act. Many of these cases have been decided by close 5–4 votes of the justices.

Strict Scrutiny   In 1995 the *U.S.* Supreme Court held that racial classifications in law must be subject to "strict scrutiny." This means that race-based actions by government—any disparate treatment of the races by federal, state, or local public agencies—must be found necessary to remedy past proven discrimination or to further clearly identified, compelling, and legitimate government objectives. Moreover, it must be "narrowly tailored" so as not to adversely affect the rights of individuals. In striking down a federal construction contract "set-aside" program for small businesses owned by racial minorities, the Court expressed skepticism about government racial classifications: "There is simply no way of determining what classifications are 'benign' and 'remedial' and what classifications are in fact motivated by illegitimate notions of racial inferiority or simple racial politics."*

Later, the Court affirmed an appellate court decision that "diversity" in the student body of a university is not a sufficiently compelling interest to justify the use of race or ethnicity in admissions decisions.†

The California Civil Rights Initiative   Opposition to racial and gender preferences inspired a citizen's initiative to be placed on the ballot in California in 1996. The California Civil Rights Initiative added the following key phrase to that state's constitution:

---

* *Aderand Construction v. Pena, 132 L. Ed.* 158 (1995).

† *Hopwood v. Texas* 78 F. 3d 932 (1996).

Neither the state of California nor any of its political subdivisions or agents shall use race, sex, color, ethnicity or national origin as a criterion for either discriminating against, or granting preferential treatment to, any individual or group in the operation of the State's system of public employment, public education or public contracting.

Supporters argued that this initiative extends protection to all of the state's citizens and eliminates racial preferences. The initiative was approved by 54 percent of California's voters. Opponents argued that it set back the civil rights movement and that it will end the progress of minorities in education and employment.

A federal court of appeals upheld the decision of California's voters to ban racial and gender preferences: "Impediments to preferential treatment do not deny equal protection.... That the Constitution permits rare race-based or gender-based preferences hardly implies that the state cannot ban them altogether."[*] In 1998 voters in Washington state followed California's lead and adopted a similar ban on affirmative action there.

But the constitutionality of various affirmative-action programs continues to be a topic for the U.S. Supreme Court. In 2003 the constitutionality of the affirmative-action programs at the University of Michigan was scrutinized. The Court struck down a practice used by the school, in which undergraduate applicants were awarded "points" based on their minority status.[†] But the Court did approve the University of Michigan Law School's practice of taking an applicant's race into consideration as a component of the applicant's entire application.[‡] The impact of many of these policy changes can be seen relatively quickly. In California the percentage of African American students enrolled at the more prestigious universities in the University of California system did decline in the aftermath of Proposition 209. For example, the percentage of African American undergraduate and graduate students at Berkeley declined from 6.6 percent in 1995 to 4.2 percent in 2003 to 2.9 percent in 2011, and enrollment of African Americans at UCLA dropped from 7.3 percent in 1995 to 3.1 in 2003.[§] In 2012, it stood at 4.04 percent.[^] And on the whole, statistical indicators show that the percentage of African American students enrolled in the entire University of California system has declined by about 1 percent.[‖]

---

[*] *Coalition for Economic Equity et al. v. Pete Wilson et al.,* Ninth Circuit Court of Appeals, April 1997.

[†] *Gratz v. Bollinger* 539 U.S. 244 (2003).

[‡] *Grutter v. Bollinger* 539 U.S. 306 (2003).

[§] University of California, Berkeley, Office of the President, Application, Admission, and Enrollment of California Resident Freshman, 1995–2003 (www.ucop.edu/news/factsheets/fl owfrc9503.pdf).

[^] www.admissions.ucla.edu/campusprofile.htm

[‖] University of California, Statistical Summary of Students and Staff, Fall 2000 (www.ucop.edu/ucophome/uwnews/stat/fall2000/statsumm2000.pdf).

discriminate against—any applicants for whom English is a second language and any who look Hispanic under the assumption that all such people could be undocumented immigrants. This means that employers are violating the equal employment rights of Latino citizens in many cases, for they are mistakenly assuming they are undocumented immigrants. The result has been a booming business in counterfeit green cards (employment) and Social Security cards.

Economic conditions in Mexico and elsewhere in Central America continue to fuel immigration, legal and illegal, to the United States. With lower educational levels, however, average incomes of Mexican American families are lower, and the poverty rate is higher than the general population. Although Mexican Americans have served as governors of Arizona and New Mexico and won election to the U.S. Congress, their political power, while steadily increasing, does not yet match their population percentages. Mexican American voter turnout is lower than other ethnic groups, perhaps because many are resident aliens or illegal immigrants not eligible to vote or perhaps because cultural factors discourage political participation, though the 2012 election suggests this is changing.[6]

Puerto Ricans are American citizens. Puerto Rico is a commonwealth of the United States with a government that resembles that of a state with a constitution and elected governor and legislature. However, Puerto Rico has no voting members of the U.S. Congress and no electoral votes for president. Median family income in Puerto Rico is higher than anywhere else in the Caribbean but only half that of the poorest state in the United States. As citizens, Puerto Ricans can move anywhere in the United States.

Asian Americans' Pursuit of Equality

Asian American citizens come from, or have ancestors from, a number of different countries with diverse cultures, religions, histories, and languages. Today, the largest percentage of Asian Americans have Chinese origins, followed by those of Filipino, Asian Indian, Vietnamese, Korean, and Japanese ancestry. Large numbers of immigrants from Japan came to the United States around the turn of the twentieth century, but it was not until the 1940s that the flow of immigrants from other Asian countries began to increase, beginning with the Philippines. In the 1960s the number of immigrants from Korea and India began to increase significantly, and in the 1970s—as the Vietnam War ended—immigrants from Vietnam began to arrive in large numbers. Today, 4 percent of the U.S. population is of Asian descent, and immigrants from China, the Philippines, India, Vietnam, and Korea rank among the top motherlands of immigrants to the United States (see Figure 10-3).

Like other U.S. citizens with non-white European ancestry, Asian Americans have had to fight for equal protection under the law and particularly for equal access to educational and employment opportunities as well as citizenship. One successful result of these efforts was the 1952 Immigration and Nationality Act, which allowed Asian immigrants to become citizens for the first time. Before passage of this law, only U.S.-born children of Asian immigrants could be citizens.

One of the most egregious examples of discrimination of Asian Americans occurred during World War II when Americans of Japanese ancestry were forced

FIGURE 10-3 THE MOST PREVALENT COUNTRIES OF BIRTH OF LEGAL IMMIGRANTS

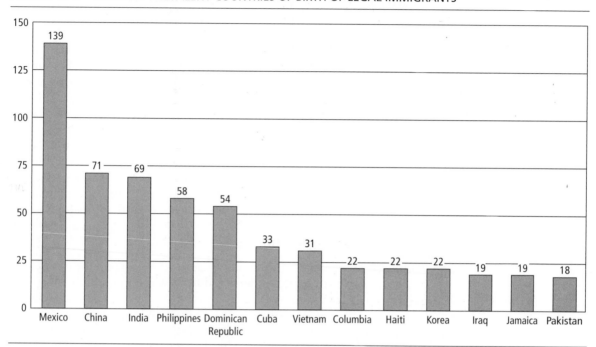

SOURCE: U.S. Census Bureau, Statistical Abstract of the United States: 2012, www.census.gov/compendia/statab/2012/tables/12s0042.pdf

to move to government-established internment camps. Under President Franklin Roosevelt's Executive Order 9066, over 120,000 Japanese Americans, two-thirds of whom were native-born U.S. citizens, were relocated from the West Coast of the United States after Japan's attack on Pearl Harbor. Many Japanese Americans who were forced to abandon their properties while by forcibly detained in the camps lost their homes and businesses, despite the fact that no Japanese American was ever convicted of treasonous acts against the United States.

Japanese American organizations fought for reparations for the citizens who were interned and for the repeal of a section of the 1950 Internal Security Act that allowed the government to imprison citizens deemed enemy collaborators during a crisis. Congress repealed the section of the 1950 law targeted by the Japanese American Citizens League, and in 1987 President Ronald Reagan (1981–1989) signed a bill providing $1.2 billion in reparations.

With the exception of Korean Americans and Vietnamese Americans, Asian Americans have the highest median income compared to the population as a whole. Asian Americans are also twice as likely as the population as a whole to earn a bachelor's degree or higher. Moreover, Asian Americans are better represented in professional and managerial positions than any other racial or ethnic group, including white Americans. Yet like women, Asian American citizens appear to hit a glass ceiling, for they are not as well represented in the very top positions as their high levels of educational achievement would seem to predict.

Immigration to America

The United States accepts more immigrants than all other nations of the world combined. The vast majority of immigrants in recent years have come from less-developed nations of Asia and Latin America (Figure 10-4). Most immigrants come to the United States for economic opportunity. Most personify the traits that we typically think of as American: opportunism, ambition, perseverance, initiative, and a willingness to work hard. As immigrants have always done, they frequently take dirty, low-paying, thankless jobs that other Americans shun. When they open their own businesses, they often do so in blighted, crime-ridden neighborhoods long since abandoned by other entrepreneurs. Since the terrorist attacks on September 11, 2001, those seeking to immigrate to the United States have undergone much stricter scrutiny than in years past; for many, immigrating has become a much more difficult process.

Economic and Cultural Change?

The politics of immigration center on both cultural and economic issues. The nation's business and corporate leaders tend to view immigration in economic terms, principally as an increase in the supply of low-wage workers in the United States. Many middle-class Americans view immigration in cultural terms, principally its impact on the ethnic composition of their communities. But in tougher economic times, some working and middle class Americans may view immigrant populations as an economic and cultural threat: to some Americans, immigrants may represent competitors in the labor market. That perception of economic competition may result in an "us versus them" mentally when it comes to larger cultural and political issues, including acceptance of diversity of multiculturalism in one's community, support of English as a Second Language programs, and national and state immigration policy.

FIGURE 10-4   SOURCES OF LEGAL IMMIGRATION TO THE UNITED STATES

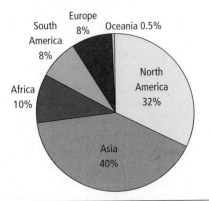

SOURCE: U.S. Census Bureau, The Statistical Abstract of the United States. No. HS-10. Native and Foreign-Born Population by Place of Birth. www.census.gov/statab/hist/HS-10.pdf.

Immigration Policy

Immigration policy is a responsibility of the national government. In 1882 Congress passed the first legislation restricting entry into the United States of persons alleged to be "undesirable" as well as virtually all Asians. Asians—particularly Chinese immigrants who came to the western United States to work in the California gold mines and the transcontinental railroad—as well as Irish fleeing the potato famine endured the brunt of early anti-immigrant sentiment. Following the end of World War I, Congress passed a comprehensive Immigration Act of 1921 that established maximum numbers of new immigrants each year and set a quota for each foreign country at 3 percent (later reduced to 2 percent) of the number of that nation's foreign born living in the United States in 1890. These restrictions reflected newer anti-immigration feelings that were generally directed at the large wave of southern and eastern European, Catholic, and Jewish immigrants (Poland, Russia, Hungary, Italy, and Greece) who had entered the United States prior to World War I. It was not until the Immigration and Nationality Act of 1965 that national origin quotas were abolished, replaced by preference categories for relatives and family members and professional and highly skilled persons. Today, the varied background of immigrants to the United States can be seen in their countries of origin (see Figure 10-4).

Immigration "reform" was the announced goal of Congress in the Immigration Reform and Control Act of 1986, also known as the Simpson–Mazzoli Act. It sought to control immigration by placing principal responsibility on employers; it set fines for knowingly hiring an illegal alien, with prison terms for repeat offenders. However, it allowed employers to accept many different forms of easily forged documentation and subjected them to penalties for discriminating against legal foreign-born residents. To win political support, the act granted amnesty to illegal aliens who had lived in the United States since 1982. But the act failed to reduce the flow of immigrants.

The climate regarding immigration heated up considerably in 2006. In December 2005, Representative James Sensenbrenner (R-Wisconsin) introduced a bill in the House of Representatives that sought to "amend the Immigration and Nationality Act to strengthen enforcement of the immigration laws, to enhance border security, and for other purposes."[7] Sensenbrenner's bill came about as the result of a crisis playing out in communities throughout the nation. The need for cheap labor—in cities as restaurant workers, landscapers, and laborers and in the countryside as farm workers who plant and harvest the majority of the nation's produce—has created a sub-economy in which immigration law is largely ignored by the businesses that need the labor. The supply of cheap labor has benefited consumers who are paying less for goods and services than they would be paying without cheap immigrant labor. Businesses and consumers largely have benefited from a vast supply of cheap labor, but communities have been forced to pay the price, with low-wage immigrant workers increasing the demand for social services and taxing the resources of schools.

House Resolution 4437 passed in the House but died in the Senate. If it had become law, it would have classified all undocumented workers and U.S. citizens who harbor and employ them as "aggravated felons." But H.R. 4437 galvanized a wide array of activist groups who sought to prevent the proposal from becoming law. In cities across the United States, immigrants and their supporters organized protests, rallies, and demonstrations against the proposed measure. In several cities, "A Day without Latinos" was organized, urging Latino immigrant workers to strike so as to demonstrate the impact on the city's economy. After the nationwide controversy surrounding the bill, the measure was blocked when the House and Senate failed to reconcile their different versions of immigration reform legislation. As a free society, the United States is not prepared to undertake massive roundups and summary deportations of millions of illegal residents. The Fifth and Fourteenth Amendments to the U.S. Constitution require that every *person* (not just *citizen*) be afforded due process of law.

U.S. Customs and Border Protection (CBP) may turn back persons at the border or even hold them in detention camps. The Coast Guard may intercept boats at sea and return persons to their country of origin.[8] Aliens have no constitutional right to come to the United States. However, *once in the United States, whether legally or illegally, every person is entitled to due process of law and equal protection of the laws.* People are entitled to a fair hearing prior to any government attempt to deport them. Aliens are entitled to apply for asylum and present evidence at a hearing of their "well-founded fear of persecution" if returned to their country.

Legal Immigration

Today, roughly 1 million people per year are admitted *legally* to the United States as "lawful permanent residents" (persons who have relatives who are U.S. citizens, are lawful permanent residents, or who have needed job skills) or as "refugees" or "asylees" (persons with "a well-founded fear of persecution" in their country of origin). In addition, over 20 million people are awarded visas each year to enter the United States for study, pleasure, or business. Federal law recognizes the following categories of noncitizens admitted into the United States:

- *Legal immigrants* (also "lawful permanent residents" or "permanent resident aliens"). Some of these immigrants are admitted to the United States on the basis of job skills, but most come as family members of persons legally residing in the United States. Legal immigrants may work in the United States and apply for citizenship after five years of continuous residence.
- *Refugees and asylees.* These are persons admitted to the United States because of "a well-founded fear of persecution because of race, religion, nationality, political opinion, or membership in a social group." (Refugees are persons not yet in the United States; asylees are persons who have already arrived and apply for refugee protection.) They may work in the United States.
- *Parolees* (or persons enjoying "temporary protected status"). These are persons admitted to the United States for humanitarian or medical reasons or whose countries are faced with natural or human-made disasters.
- *Legalized aliens* (also called "amnesty aliens"). These formerly illegal aliens were given legal status (amnesty) under the Immigration Reform and

Control Act of 1986. To qualify, they must show some evidence of having resided in the United States since 1982. They may work in the United States.

- *Nonimmigrants* (also "nonresident legal aliens"). Over 20 million people are awarded visas to enter the United States for pleasure and business. Time limits are placed on these visas usually by stamping a passport. Additionally, students, temporary workers and trainees, transient aliens, and foreign officials are eligible for temporary visas.

Illegal Immigration

The United States is a free and prosperous society with over five thousand miles of borders (two thousand with Mexico) and hundreds of international airports and seaports. In theory a sovereign nation should be able to maintain secure borders, but in practice the United States has been unwilling and unable to do so. Estimates of illegal immigration vary wildly, from the official U.S. Citizenship and Immigration Services (USCIS) estimate of four hundred thousand per year (about 45 percent of the legal immigration), to unofficial estimates ranging up to 3 million per year. The USCIS estimates that about 4 million illegal immigrants currently reside in the United States; unofficial estimates range up to 38 million or more. Many illegal immigrants slip across U.S. borders or enter ports with false documentation, and many more overstay tourist or student visas (and are not counted by the USCIS as illegal immigrants).[9]

Native Americans: An Historical Overview

Christopher Columbus, having erred in his estimate of the circumference of the globe, believed he had arrived in the Indian Ocean when he first came to the Caribbean. He mistook the Arawaks for people of the East Indies, calling them "Indios," and this Spanish word passed into English as *Indians*—a word that came to refer to all Native American peoples. But at the time of the first European contacts, these peoples had no common ethnic identity; hundreds of separate cultures and languages were thriving in the Americas. Although estimates vary, most historians believe that 7 to 12 million people lived in the land that is now the United States and Canada; 25 million more lived in Mexico; and as many as 60 to 70 million in all lived in the Western Hemisphere, a number comparable to Europe's population at the time.

In the centuries that followed, the native population of the Americas was devastated by warfare, by famine, and, most of all, by epidemic diseases brought from Europe. Overall, the native population fell by 90 percent, the greatest human disaster in world history. Smallpox was the Europeans' most effective weapon, followed by measles, bubonic plague, influenza, typhus, diphtheria, and scarlet fever. Superior military technology, together with skill in exploiting hostilities between tribes, gradually overcame native resistance. By 1910 only 210,000 Native Americans were in the United States.[10] Their population has slowly grown to the current 3 million.

The Trail of Broken Treaties

In the Northwest Ordinance of 1787, Congress, in organizing the Western territories of the new nation, declared that "the utmost good faith shall always be observed toward the Indians. Their lands and property shall never be taken from them without their consent." And later in the **Intercourse Act of 1790**, Congress declared that public treaties between the U.S. government and the independent Indian "nations" would be the only legal means of obtaining Indian land.

Intercourse Act of 1790 law that declared that public treaties between the U.S. government and the independent Indian "nations" would be the only legal means of obtaining Indian land

As president, George Washington forged a treaty with the Creeks: In exchange for land concessions, the United States pledged to protect the boundaries of the "Creek Nation" and allow the Creeks themselves to punish all violators of their laws within these boundaries. This semblance of legality was reflected in hundreds of treaties to follow. (And, indeed, in recent years some Indian tribes have successfully sued in federal court for reparations and return of lands obtained in violation of the Intercourse Act of 1790 and subsequent treaties.)

Yet Indian lands were constantly invaded by whites. Indian resistance would typically lead to wars that would ultimately result in great loss of life among warriors and their families and the further loss of tribal land. The cycle of invasion, resistance, military defeat, and further land concessions continued for a hundred years.

"Indian Territories"

Following the purchase of the vast Louisiana Territory in 1801, President Thomas Jefferson sought to "civilize" the Indians by promoting farming in "reservations" offered to eastern tribes west of the Mississippi River. But soon Indians who had been forced to move from Ohio to Missouri were forced to move again to survive the relentless white expansion. In 1815 President James Monroe designated as "Indian Territory" most of the Great Plains west of the Missouri River. Indians increasingly faced three unattractive choices: assimilation, removal, and extinction.

In 1814 the Creeks, encouraged by the British during the War of 1812 to attack American settlements, faced an army of Tennessee volunteer militia led by Andrew Jackson. At the Battle of Horseshoe Bend, Jackson's cannon fire decimated the Creek warriors. In the uneven Treaty of Fort Jackson, the Creeks, Choctaws, and Cherokees were forced to concede millions of acres of land.

By 1830 the "Five Civilized Tribes" of the southeastern United States (Choctaws, Cherokees, Creeks, Chickasaws, and Seminoles) had ceded most but not all of their lands. When gold was discovered on Cherokee land in northern Georgia in 1829, whites invaded their territory. Congress, at the bequest of the old Indian fighter Andrew Jackson, passed a Removal Act, ordering the forcible relocation of the tribes to "Indian Territory" (now Oklahoma). The Cherokees tried to use the white man's law to defend their land, taking their case, *Cherokee Nation v. Georgia* (1831), to the U.S. Supreme Court. When Chief Justice John Marshall held that the tribe was a "domestic dependent nation" that could not be forced to give up its land, President Jackson replied scornfully, "John Marshall has made his decision. Now let him enforce it." A seven thousand–man army pursued Seminoles into the huge Florida Everglades swamp and forced sixteen thousand Seminoles, Cherokees, and other Indians on the infamous "**Trail of Tears**" march to Oklahoma in 1838.

Encroachment upon the "Indian Territory" of the Great Plains was not long in coming. First, the territory was crossed by the Santa Fe and Oregon trails and a series of military forts built to protect travelers. In 1854 under pressure from railroad interests, the U.S. government abolished much of the original Indian Territory to create the Kansas and Nebraska territories that were immediately opened to white settlers. The tribes in the land—including Potawatomis, Kickapoos, Delawares, Shawnees, Miamis, Omahas, and Missouris—were forced to sign treaties accepting vastly reduced land reservations. But large buffalo-hunting tribes remained in the northern Dakotas and western Great Plains: the Sioux, Cheyennes, Arapahos, Comanches, and Kiowas. (Other smaller tribes inhabited the Rockies to California and the Pacific Northwest; and sedentary tribes—Pueblos, Hopis, and Pimas—and migrating tribes—Apaches and Navajos—occupied the Southwest.) The Plains Indians took pride in their warrior status, often fighting among themselves.

Trail of Tears
The forced march of 16,000 Indians from the Florida Everglades to Oklahoma in 1838

Indian Wars

The "Indian Wars" were fought between the Plains Indian tribes and the U.S. Army between 1864 and 1890. Following the Civil War, the federal government began to assign boundaries to each tribe and created a Bureau of Indian Affairs (BIA) to "assist and protect" Indian peoples on their "reservations." But the reservations were repeatedly reduced in size until subsistence by hunting became impossible. Malnutrition and demoralization of the native peoples were aided

Reuters/CORBIS

Chief Crazy Horse was one of the leaders who defeated Civil War General George Custer's forces in 1876, but Crazy Horse would surrender the following year. By 1910, the population of Native Americans had dwindled to 210,000, down from an estimated 7 million to 12 million. Shown here is the study for the Crazy Horse Memorial in front of the real memorial, which is under construction in South Dakota.

by the mass slaughter of the buffalo; vast herds, numbering perhaps as many as 70 million, were exterminated over the years. The most storied engagement of the long war occurred at the Little Big Horn River in South Dakota on June 25, 1876, where Civil War hero General George Armstrong Custer led elements of the U.S. Seventh Cavalry to destruction at the hands of Sioux and Cheyenne warriors led by Chief Crazy Horse, Chief Sitting Bull, and Chief Gall. But Custer's Last Stand inspired renewed army campaigns against the Plains tribes; the following year, Crazy Horse was forced to surrender. In 1881 destitute Sioux under Sitting Bull returned from exile in Canada to surrender themselves to reservation life. Among the last tribes to hold out were the Apaches, whose famous warrior Geronimo finally surrendered in 1886. Sporadic fighting continued to 1890 when a small malnourished band of Lakota Sioux was wiped out at Wounded Knee Creek.

The Attempted Destruction of Tribal Life

Dawes Act of 1887
attempted forced assimilation

The **Dawes Act of 1887,** also called the General Allotment Act, was a policy that forced Native Americans to assimilate into the dominant culture and governed federal Indian policy for decades. The thrust of the policy was to break up tribal lands, allotting acreage for individual homesteads in order to assimilate Indians into the white agricultural society. Farming was to replace hunting, and tribal life and traditional customs were to be shed for English language and schooling. But this effort to destroy Indian culture never really succeeded. Although Indian peoples lost over half of their 1877 reservation land, they neither lost their communal ties nor accumulated much private property. The Dawes Act remained federal policy until 1934 when Congress finally reversed itself and reaffirmed tribal ownership of land.

Life on the reservations was often desperate. Indians suffered the worst poverty of any group in the nation, with high rates of infant mortality, alcoholism, and other diseases. The BIA, notoriously corrupt and mismanaged, encouraged dependency and regularly interfered with Indian religious affairs and tribal customs.

The New Deal

Indian Reorganization Act of 1934
recognized tribes as legal governments

The New Deal under President Franklin D. Roosevelt came to Native Americans in the form of the **Indian Reorganization Act of 1934**. This act sought to restore tribal structures by recognizing tribes as instruments of the federal government. Tribal land ownership was restored, and elected tribal councils were recognized as legal governments. Efforts to force assimilation were largely abandoned. The BIA became more sensitive to Indian culture and began employing Indians in larger numbers.

Yet the BIA remained "paternalistic," frequently interfering in tribal "sovereignty." Moreover, in the 1950s Congress initiated a policy of "termination" of sovereignty rights for specific tribes who consented to relinquish their lands in exchange for cash payments. Only a few tribes chose this course, but the results were often calamitous: After the one-time cash payments were spent, Indian peoples became dependent on state social welfare services and often slipped further into poverty and alcoholism.

The American Indian Movement

The civil rights movement of the 1960s inspired a new activism among Native American groups. The American Indian Movement (AIM), sometimes called the "Red Power Movement," was founded in 1968 and attracted national headlines by occupying Alcatraz Island in San Francisco Bay. Violence flared in 1972 when AIM activists took over the site of the Wounded Knee battle and fought with FBI agents. Several tribes succeeded in federal courts and the Congress to win back lands and/or compensation for lands taken in treaty violations. Indian culture was revitalized, and Vine Deloria's *Custer Died for Your Sins* and Dee Brown's *Bury My Heart at Wounded Knee* became national bestsellers. A national policy victory came in 1975 when Congress passed the Self-Determination and Education Assistance Act that allowed for the control of federal programs, including federal education and health-care programs, on reservations by tribe members. By 2010, about 3 million people—less than 1 percent of the nation's population—identified themselves as American Indians. More than 1 million of these people lived on tribal reservation and trust land, the largest of which is the Navajo and Hopi enclave in the southwestern United States (Figure 10-5). Yet these peoples remain the poorest and least healthy in America, with high incidences of infant mortality, suicide, and alcoholism. Approximately half of all Indians live below the poverty line.

FIGURE 10-5 NATIVE AMERICAN SETTLEMENTS

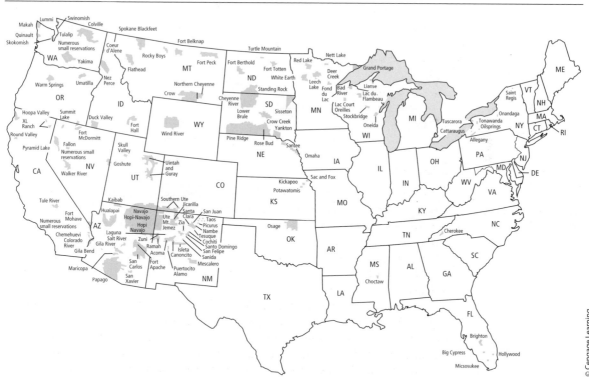

© Cengage Learning

Power and Gender

Gender roles involve power relationships. The traditional American family was patriarchal, and many cultural practices continue to reflect male dominance (see Chapter 4). Men still hold most of the major positions in industry, finance, academia, the military, politics, and government. Authority in many families still rests with the man. Today more than half of all married women work; more than half of women with children under 6 years of age work. Nonetheless, stereotyped gender roles continue to assign domestic service and child care to women, whether they work or not, and human achievement, interest, and ambition to men. Despite increases in the number and proportion of working women, on average, women continue to earn less money than men. Figure 10-6 shows that over time, the earnings gap between men and women is closing. But on average, women still make less than 80 cents for every dollar a man makes. This gap *usually is not caused by overt wage discrimination*—wherein men and women who perform the exact same jobs, with the exact

FIGURE 10-6   THE EARNINGS GAP: MEDIAN WEEKLY EARNINGS OF MEN AND WOMEN

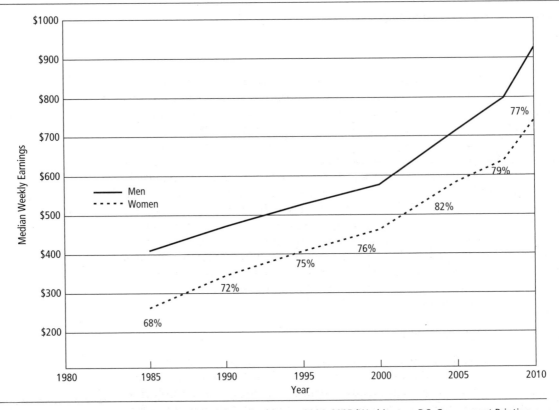

SOURCE: U.S. Census Bureau, Statistical Abstract of the United States, 2004–2005 (Washington, DC: Government Printing Offi ce, 2004), 411 and http://www.bls.gov/bls/blswage.htm.

TABLE 10-2 WOMEN'S WORK

	1960	1983	2010
"White Collar"			
Accountants and auditors			60
Environmental scientists and geoscientists			26
Lawyers	4	16	31
Physicians and surgeons	10	16	32
"Pink Collar"			
Registered nurses	97	96	88
Waiters and waitresses	91	88	71
Secretaries and administrative assistants	98	99	96
Hairdressers, hairstylists, and cosmetologists			92
"Blue Collar"			
Laborers	17	19	21
Electricians			2
Truck Drivers	1	2	5
Carpenters	1	1	1
Auto Mechanics	1	1	1

SOURCE: U.S. Department of Labor, *Employment in Perspective: Working Women* (Washington, DC: U.S. Government Printing Office, 1983); National Research Council, National Academy of Sciences, *Women's Work, Men's Work* (Washington, DC: National Academy Press, 1985); **http://www.census.gov/compendia/statab/2012/tables/12s0616.pdf**

same experience, and the exact same seniority receive different levels of pay. Historically, overt wage discrimination was a primary cause of the earning gap, but today most of the difference between men's and women's average pay can be explained by the fact that *the nation's occupational fields are still divided between traditionally male and female jobs* and that jobs typically dominated by women pay less on average than those dominated by men. In the top income-producing sectors, including science and technology, women's participation in those fields lags behind men's. Yet women continue to dominate the traditional "pink-collar" jobs (Table 10-2). Women have made important inroads in traditionally male white-collar occupations—physicians, lawyers, and engineers, for example—although men still remain in the majority in these professions. However, women have only begun to break into the blue-collar occupations traditionally dominated by men. Blue-collar jobs usually pay more than pink-collar jobs. This circumstance accounts for much of the earnings gap between men and women (Figure 10-6).

Sex Inequality: Culture or Biology?

How much of male dominance can be attributed to *biology* and how much to *culture*? When we speak of **sex**, we are referring to one's biology and whether one is born with male or female reproductive organs. With regard to our biological differences, many scholars assert that biological differences do not necessitate any distinctions between male and female in domestic service or child-care

sex
whether one is born with male or female reproductive organs

gender
culturally imposed
sex-role stereotypes

responsibilities, authority in the family, economic roles in society, or political or legal rights. Rather, they argue that the creation of sex-role stereotypes, or **gender**, *are culturally imposed on children from earliest childhood.*

The very first item in personality formation is the assignment of gender roles (you are a boy, you are a girl) and the encouragement of "masculine" and "feminine" traits. Traditionally, aggression, curiosity, intelligence, initiative, and force are encouraged in the boy; oftentimes passivity, refinement, shyness, and virtue are encouraged in the girl. Traditionally, girls were encouraged to think in terms of domestic and child-care roles, whereas boys were urged to think of careers in industry and the professions. Deeply ingrained symbols, attitudes, and practices are culturally designated as masculine or feminine. ("What a big boy!" "Isn't she pretty!") Traditionally, subjects in school were either masculine or feminine: Science, technology, and business were male; teaching, nursing, and secretarial studies were female. Boys have been portrayed in roles in which they master their environment; girls, in roles in which they admire the accomplishments of men. It is this *cultural* conditioning that led women to accept a family and child-centered life and an inferior economic and political role in society—not their *physiology.*

Many writers have deplored the *sociopsychological barriers* to a woman's full human development.[11] In a double standard of sexual guilt women are subject to greater shame for any sexual liaison, whatever the circumstances. Yet, while denied sexual freedom herself, the woman is usually obliged to seek advancement through the approval of men. She may try to overcome her powerlessness by using her own sexuality, perhaps at the cost of her dignity and self-respect. Historically, the prevailing male attitude was to value women for their sexual traits rather than for their qualities as human beings. Even today, women frequently are portrayed as "sex objects" in advertising, magazines, literature, and movies and on television. They are supposed to entertain, please, gratify, and flatter men with their sexuality; it is seldom the other way around. There is even evidence of self-rejection among women: Female children are more likely to wish they had been born boys than male children are to wish they had been born girls.[12] The power aspects of gender roles are also ingrained in male psychology. Young men are deemed feminine (inferior) if they are not sufficiently aggressive, physical, or violent (think of the commonality of the insult to a boy: "you throw (or run) like a girl").

In contrast to these arguments about *culturally* imposed gender roles, other observers have contended that *physiological differences* between men and women account for different gender roles.[13] The woman's role in the reproduction and care of the young is biologically determined. To the extent that she seeks to protect her young, she also seeks family arrangements that will provide maximum security and support for them. In the past, men have acquired dominant positions in industry, finance, government, and so forth, largely because women were exclusively preoccupied with family and child-care tasks. On average, men are physically stronger than women, and their role as economic providers is rooted in this biological difference. Whether any biologically determined mental or emotional differences exist between men and women is a disputed point, but the possibility of such differences exists. Thus, differential gender roles may be partly physical in origin.

The Long History of Women's Protests

The movement for women's rights in America is nearly as old as the nation itself. In 1776 Abigail Adams wrote to her husband John Adams at the Second Continental Congress while it was debating whether to declare American independence:

> If particular care and attention is not paid to the ladies, we are determined to foment a rebellion and will not hold ourselves bound by any laws in which we have no voice or representation.[14]

Despite Mrs. Adams's warnings the founders in fact paid little attention to the concerns of women. In fact, with the ratification of the U.S. Constitution in 1789, many women who had participated in the political life of the communities by voting were *disenfranchised* with the national constitution supplanting state laws that had allowed women the right to vote. And the political movement forecast by Abigail Adams did not really emerge until a generation later. The origins of the women's rights movement lie in the pre–Civil War antislavery crusade in which women played the major role (see Focus: "A Declaration of Women's Rights, 1848"). The first generation of feminists, including Lucretia Mott, Elizabeth Cady Stanton, Lucy Stone, and Susan B. Anthony, learned to organize, hold public meetings, and conduct petition campaigns as abolitionists.

After the Civil War, the feminist movement concentrated on winning civil rights and the franchise for women. The women suffragists employed mass demonstrations, parades, picketing, and occasional disruptions and civil disobedience—tactics similar to those of the civil rights movement of the 1960s. The more moderate wing of the American suffrage movement became the League of Women Voters; in addition to the women's vote, they sought protection of women in industry, child-welfare laws, honest election practices, and the elimination of laws discriminating against the rights of women.

It would take well more than half a century for the movement to succeed in accomplishing its most important goal: women's right to vote. The culmination of the early feminist movement was political equality, the passage in 1920 of the Nineteenth Amendment to the Constitution:

> The right of citizens of the United States to vote shall not be denied or abridged by the United States or by any State on account of sex.

The movement was also successful in changing many state laws that abridged the property rights of the married woman and otherwise treated her as the "chattel" (property) of her husband. But active feminist politics declined after the goal of women's voting rights had been achieved.

Renewed interest and progress in women's rights came with the civil rights movement of the 1960s.[15] The Civil Rights Act of 1964 prevents discrimination on the basis of gender, as well as of race, in employment, salary, promotion, and other conditions of work. The Equal Employment Opportunity Commission (EEOC), the federal agency charged with eliminating discrimination in employment, has established guidelines barring stereotyped classifications of "men's jobs" and "women's jobs." State laws and employer practices that differentiate between men and women in terms of hours, pay, retirement age, and so on have been struck down. Under active lobbying from feminist organizations, federal agencies, including the U.S. Office of Education and the Office of Federal Contract Compliance, have established affirmative-action guidelines for government agencies, universities, and private businesses doing work for the government. These guidelines set goals and timetables for employers to alter their workforce to achieve higher percentages of women at all levels.

For many years, feminist activity focused on the **Equal Rights Amendment (ERA)** to the Constitution, which would have struck down *all* existing legal inequalities in state and federal laws between men and women. The proposed amendment stated simply:

> Equality of rights under the law shall not be denied or abridged by the United States or by any State on account of sex.

The ERA passed the Congress easily in 1972 and was sent to the states, but it fell three states short of the three-fourths (thirty-eight) needed for ratification.

Why Are So Few Women in Power?

No discussion of gender and politics or of power in the United States would be complete without an assessment of women's role in the policy process. When we look at women's participation in government, in elected office in particular, the figures demonstrate the progress that women have made and the work that still needs to be done to achieve equitable representation in government. To date, just 18 percent of the members of Congress are women, including 20 of the 100 U.S. senators and 78 of the 435 members of the House of Representatives. In the states, 74 women (or about 23 percent) serve in statewide elective executive posts—including governors, lieutenant governors, attorneys general, state auditors, treasurers, and so on—while about 24 percent of state legislative seats are held by women.[16]

For several decades now, scholars have explored the question: Why are so few women elected to government posts in the United States? Researchers have looked at explanations including voter bias, the impact of money on women's election rates, and levels of political ambition of women considered to be part of the **eligibility pool**—people with the characteristics that voters deem suitable for elective office. In looking at these explanations, a few surprising conclusions can be made. First, the sex of a candidate has very little impact on the difference between the number of votes that candidates receives. That is, in most cases voter bias against women candidates is negligible.[17] In addition, researchers also have concluded that when controlling for the incumbency status of the candidate, women candidates are not at a disadvantage when it comes to campaign fund-raising.[18]

Two factors, however, are significant in determining the number of women elected to government office in the United States. Perhaps the most important factor is **incumbency advantage**—the benefit derived from already having been voted into a particular office once. At all levels of government—from local school boards, to state legislatures, to Congress, to the presidency—incumbent candidates hold an advantage over their challengers. Incumbents have greater

Equal Rights Amendment (ERA)
a proposed amendment to the U.S. Constitution guaranteeing equality of rights of the sexes

eligibility pool
people with the characteristics that voters deem suitable for elective office

incumbency advantage
the benefit derived from already having been voted into a particular office once

A Declaration of Women's Rights, 1848

When a delegation of American women was excluded from the World Anti-Slavery Convention in London in 1840, they realized that the cause of emancipation affected them as well as slaves. On July 19, 1848, they met in Seneca Falls, across the New York border in Canada, to draw up "The Seneca Falls Declaration of Sentiments and Resolutions." The Resolution parallels the Declaration of Independence and reads in part:

> *We hold these truths to be self-evident: that all men and women are created equal; that they are endowed by their Creator with certain inalienable rights; that among these are life, liberty, and the pursuit of happiness....*

> *The history of mankind is a history of repeated injuries and usurpations, on the part of man toward woman, having in direct object the establishment of an absolute tyranny over her. To prove this, let facts be submitted to a candid world.*

> *He has never permitted her to exercise her inalienable right to the elective franchise. He has compelled her to submit to laws, in the formation of which she had no voice....*

> *Having deprived her of this first right of a citizen, the elective franchise, thereby leaving her without representation in the halls of legislation, he has oppressed her on all sides.*

> *He has made her, if married, in the eye of the law, civilly dead.*

> *He has taken from her all rights in property, even to the wages she earns....*

> *He has monopolized nearly all the profitable employments, and from those she is permitted to follow, she receives but a scanty remuneration.*

> *He closes against her all the avenues to wealth and distinction which he considers most honorable to himself. As a teacher of theology, medicine, or law, she is not known.*

> *He has denied her the facilities for obtaining a thorough education, all colleges being closed against her.*

> *He allows her in Church, as well as State, but a subordinate position, claiming Apostolic authority for her exclusion from the ministry, and, with some exceptions, from any public participation in the affairs of the Church.*

> *He has created a false public sentiment by giving to a world a different code of morals for men and women, by which moral delinquencies which exclude women from society, are not only tolerated, but deemed of little account in man...*

> *He has endeavored, in every way that he could, to destroy her confidence in her own powers, to lessen her self respect and to make her willing to lead a dependent and abject life.*

> *Now, in view of this entire disfranchisement of one-half the people of this country, their social and religious degradation—in view of the unjust laws above mentioned, and because women do feel themselves aggrieved, oppressed, and fraudulently deprived of their most sacred rights, we insist that they have immediate admission to all the rights and privileges which belong to them as citizens of the United States.**

---

* Seneca Falls Declaration (1848), http://usinfo.state.gov/usa/infousa/facts/democrac/17.htm

name recognition, an easier time raising money for their campaigns, a greater ability to attract media attention, and a track record to stand on. In a typical congressional election year, 95 percent of all House members who choose to run for re-election win; about 90 percent of U.S. senators do. With men holding 85 percent of the seats in the House and Senate, women's ability to get elected to Congress is seriously challenged.

Researchers also conclude that another factor affecting women's ability to get elected has to do with women themselves. Several studies indicate that women express less political ambition than similarly situated male counterparts.[19] Some researchers conclude that professional responsibilities coupled with the responsibilities of home life, including child rearing, render qualified women less ambitious than men.

The causes of the relative lack of women in elected office may be multifaceted, and impact has many implications as well. From a purely representational perspective, researchers argue that diverse representatives are more likely to create policies that are more responsive to the needs of diverse constituencies. Research into how male and female legislators differ in creating policy also indicate that the presence of female legislators might mean the prioritization of different issues and different legislative processes, including more cooperative solutions and management styles.[20] Fewer women elected also mean fewer role models to shape the aspirations of young girls considering potential career choices. Beyond role modeling, diversity in leadership also colors the expectations of both boys and girls as they mature. Finally, the relative lack of women in elected office also has serious implications for women's increasing participation in higher levels of government. In many cases, political office holding tends to work like stepping stones—a local government official gains experience and gets elected to state office, a state office holder gets elected to Congress, and so on. The lack of women throughout these rungs makes it less likely that women will comprise a proportionate percentage of seats in higher offices.

Sexual Discrimination: Sexual Harassment and the Law

The women's movement has succeeded in placing the issues of sexual discrimination and sexual harassment on the national agenda. Title VII of the Civil Rights Act of 1964 protects employees from sexual discrimination "with respect to compensation, terms, conditions, or privileges of employment." In other words, the government and employers are prohibited from discriminating on the basis of sex in hiring, promoting, and paying their employees. Before the Civil Rights Act, help-wanted ads were segregated by sex, and women only would apply for work in the "Help Wanted—Women" section. In general, these jobs offered considerably less opportunity, prestige, and pay than those available to men. Today, if individuals believe that they are being discriminated against because of their sex when applying for a job, they can file a complaint with the Equal Employment Opportunity Commission, which was established by Title VII of the Civil Rights Act of 1964.

The U.S. Supreme Court held in 1986 that sexual harassment of employees could be "sufficiently severe" to alter the "conditions" of employment and therefore violate Title VII. Sexual harassment may take various forms. There seems to be little doubt that it includes (1) conditioning employment or promotion or privileges of employment on the granting of sexual favors by an employee and (2) "tangible" acts of touching, fondling, or forced sexual relations. But sexual harassment has also been defined to include (3) the creation of a "hostile working environment." This phrase may include offensive utterances, sexual innuendoes, dirty jokes, the display of pornographic material, and unwanted proposals for dates.

Several problems arise with this definition. First, it would appear to include speech and hence raise First Amendment questions regarding how far speech may be curtailed by law in the workplace. Second, the definition depends more on the subjective feelings of the individual employee about what is "offensive" and "unwanted" rather than on an objective standard of behavior that is easily understood by all.

In 1991 sexual harassment became a topic of national interest during the confirmation hearings of Judge Clarence Thomas, who had been nominated as Associate Justice by President George H. W. Bush. On October 11, 1991, Professor Anita Hill testified before the Senate Judiciary Committee—then comprised exclusively of men—which would vote on Thomas's nomination before sending the nomination to the full Senate. Hill testified about Thomas's behavior while he was her supervisor in the Department of Education at the Equal Employment Opportunity Commission, asking her for a date, and his explicit descriptions of pornography and his own sexual prowess. Despite Hill's testimony, Thomas won approval by the committee and was confirmed by the Senate. He now sits as an Associate Justice on the Supreme Court. Hill is a law professor at Brandeis University. Although Thomas was confirmed, Hill's testimony helped shape a national debate about the prevalence of sexual harassment and

© Brooks Kraft/Corbis

In January, 2009 President Obama signed the Lilly Ledbetter (left) Bill into law. Ledbetter's claim of discrimination was denied by the U.S. Supreme Court because she did not filed a claim 180 days after the initial act of wage discrimination statute of limitations on gender-based wage discrimination claims, making each paycheck an act of discrimination.

hostile work environments. Charges made to the Equal Employment Opportunity Commission (the arm of the federal government charged with enforcing sexual harassment law) sky-rocketed. The hearings also sparked outrage among many women candidates and voters in the 1992 election, dubbed "The Year of the Women," because of the higher than average number of women candidates, many of whom went on to win election that year.

The Supreme Court itself would tackle the issue in 1993. Specifically, the Court wrestled with the definition of a "hostile work environment" in *Harris v. Forklift* in 1993. It held that a plaintiff need not show that the utterances caused psychological injury but only that a "reasonable person" would perceive the work environment to be hostile or abusive. Presumably a single incident would not constitute harassment; rather, courts should consider "the frequency of the discriminatory conduct," "its severity," and whether it "unreasonably interferes with an employee's work performance."

Reproductive Rights

Reproductive rights are an issue of paramount importance to many women because control over one's body represents the most basic form of freedom, and the struggle for control over that power continues. In modern times, the debates surrounding reproductive freedoms have centered on the issues of birth control and abortion. Specifically, in 2012, birth control emerged as an issue when President Obama advocated for the coverage of birth control under employer-sponsored health insurance plans, even when the employer opposed the usage of birth control on religious grounds (primarily religious institutions). The debate became a firestorm of controversy when conservative radio talk show host Rush Limbaugh inserted himself into the controversy by repeatedly denigrating a young Georgetown University Law School student who had testified before a congressional panel about the need for birth control coverage through the university's health care insurance. The issue—and the role of government in regulating insurance mandates for birth control—remained a hot topic in the 2012 presidential campaign.

That year, the United States also saw debate re-emerge on the abortion issue with the major party candidates standing at opposite sides on the issue. Abortion is not an issue that can be easily compromised. The arguments touch on fundamental moral and religious principles. Proponents of abortion rights, who generally refer to themselves as "pro-choice"—including President Obama—argue that a woman should be permitted to control her own body and should not be forced by law to have unwanted children. They cite the heavy toll in lives lost because of criminal abortions and the psychological and emotional pain of an unwanted pregnancy and the potential poor quality of life of unwanted children born to mothers who were ill-equipped to care for them.

Opponents of abortion, who often refer to themselves as "pro-life" base their belief on the sanctity of life, including the life of the unborn child, which they insist deserves the protection of law—"the right to life." They believe that the killing of an unborn child for any reason other than the preservation of the life or health of the mother is murder.

One of the most controversial decisions in the Supreme Court's history was its ruling in **Roe v. Wade** (1973), which recognized abortion as a *constitutional*

Roe v. Wade
U.S. Supreme Court decision that recognized abortion as a constitutional right (1973)

right of women. In this historic decision, the Court determined that a fetus is not a "person" within the meaning of the Constitution, and therefore a fetus's right to life is not guaranteed by law. Moreover, the Court held that the "liberty" guaranteed by the Fifth and Fourteenth Amendments encompassed the privacy right of a woman to decide whether or not to terminate her pregnancy.

The Supreme Court's decision did not end the controversy over abortion. Congress banned the use of federal funds under Medicaid (medical care for the poor) for abortions except to protect the life of a woman (and later in cases of rape and incest as well). The Supreme Court upheld the constitutionality of federal and state *laws denying tax funds for abortions*. Although women retained the right to an abortion, the Court held that government has no constitutional obligation to pay for abortions.[21] The decision about whether to pay for abortion from tax revenues was left to Congress and the states.

About 1.2 million abortions are performed each year in the United States. This is about 42 percent of the number of live births. Figure 10-7 shows that

FIGURE 10-7 SELECTED CHARACTERISTICS OF WOMEN WHO HAVE ABORTION

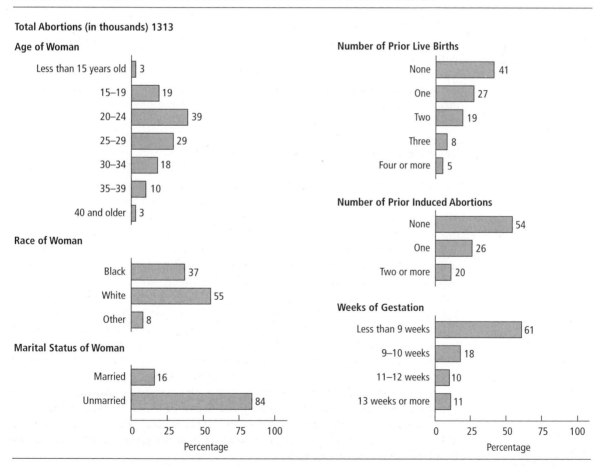

Total Abortions (in thousands) 1313

Age of Woman

Less than 15 years old	3
15–19	19
20–24	39
25–29	29
30–34	18
35–39	10
40 and older	3

Race of Woman

Black	37
White	55
Other	8

Marital Status of Woman

Married	16
Unmarried	84

Number of Prior Live Births

None	41
One	27
Two	19
Three	8
Four or more	5

Number of Prior Induced Abortions

None	54
One	26
Two or more	20

Weeks of Gestation

Less than 9 weeks	61
9–10 weeks	18
11–12 weeks	10
13 weeks or more	11

Percentage

SOURCE: www.census.gov/compendia/statab/2012/tables/12s0102.pdf.

nearly 90 percent of these abortions are performed in the first three months, and 11 percent are performed after the third month. Unmarried white women 20–24 years of age are most likely to have an abortion.

The Supreme Court has upheld *some* restrictions on abortion—those that do not impose an undue burden on the exercise of a woman's privacy right to choose abortion. In *Planned Parenthood v. Casey* (1992), the Court reaffirmed *Roe v. Wade* but upheld Pennsylvania requirements for physician counseling prior to an abortion, a twenty-four-hour waiting period, and parental notification when minors seek an abortion. Justice Sandra Day O'Connor wrote the Court's opinion, establishing a new standard for constitutionally evaluating state restrictions on abortion: They must not impose an undue burden on women seeking abortion. In the ensuing years, states have passed various laws restricting access to abortion in a variety of ways (see Research This!). Despite outcries from both pro-choice and pro-life forces, the *Casey* decision appears to place the Court's position on abortion almost exactly where public opinion polls suggest most Americans are: generally supporting a woman's right to choose an abortion but also supporting reasonable restrictions on the exercise of that right.

Violence at abortion clinics inspired Congress to pass federal legislation in 1994 restricting demonstrations at these sites. Federal laws now supplement state and local laws prohibiting interference in access to abortion clinics. Anti-abortion activists have sustained serious criticism in recent years when some groups began publishing "hit lists" of doctors who perform abortions. Several of these physicians, their bodyguards, and other clinic staffers have been killed by anti-abortion activists.

Disabled Americans

The women's and civil rights movements of the 1960s and 1970s made society more aware of the lack of equal protection of the laws for diverse groups of citizens, including people with disabilities. The first law to mandate equal protection for people with physical and mental disabilities was the 1973 Rehabilitation Act, which prohibited discrimination against people with disabilities in federally funded programs. In 1990, people with disabilities achieved a significant enhancement of this earlier victory in their fight to obtain protection of their civil rights. The **Americans with Disabilities Act (ADA)**, enacted in that year, extends the ban on discrimination against people with disabilities in education, employment, health care, housing, and transportation to all programs and organizations, not just those receiving federal funds. The ADA defines a disability as any "physical or mental impairment that substantially limits one or more of the major life activities of the individual." The ADA does not enumerate every disability that it covers, resulting in much confusion over which conditions it covers and which it excludes.

Disability advocates disagree with recent Court decisions that specify a definition of "disability" that they believe is too narrow. The Court has determined that if an individual can take an action to mitigate an impairment (such as wearing

Americans with Disabilities Act (ADA) bans discrimination against people with disabilities in education, employment, health care, housing, and transportation with regard to all programs and organizations

RESEARCH *THIS!*

The accompanying graph shows the various restrictions on abortions in each state.

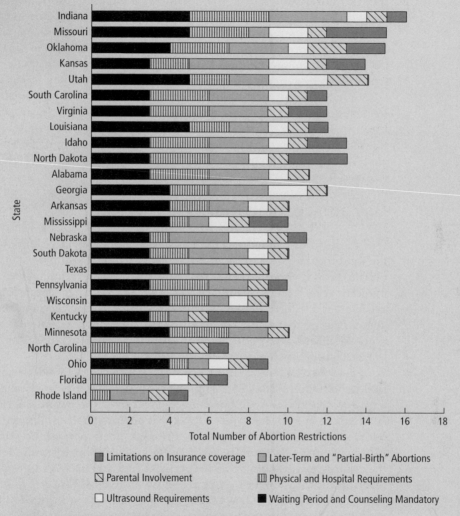

Number of abortion restrictions, by state and category of restriction.

SOURCE: http://www.guttmacher.org/statecenter/spibs/spib_OAL.pdf

YOUR ANALYSIS:

1. Which restrictions does your state have?

2. Which are the most prevalent restrictions?

3. Which states have the fewest restrictions? Why do you think those states have fewer restrictions?

eyeglasses for severe near-sightedness or taking medication for high blood pressure), then the impairment is not a disability requiring reasonable accommodation.

Despite disagreement about the breadth of the law's coverage, there is no question that the ADA has enhanced the civil rights of citizens with disabilities. Before the ADA was enacted, people with disabilities who were fired from their jobs or denied access to schools, office buildings, or other public places had no recourse. Cities were under no obligation to provide even the most reasonable accommodations to people with disabilities who sought employment or the use of public transportation systems. And employers were under no obligation to make even the most minor modifications to their workplaces for employees with disabilities. For example, if a qualified job applicant was wheelchair bound, an employer did not have to consider installing ramps or raising desks to accommodate the wheelchair but could simply refuse to hire the individual. The ADA changed this situation by requiring employers and governmental organizations to make it possible for people with disabilities to participate meaningfully in their communities through reasonable accommodations.

Gay and Lesbian Rights

One of the most contentious debates in contemporary U.S. politics centers on the fight for the rights of gays and lesbians. Although homosexuality has traditionally been a taboo subject—ignored in many places, criminalized in others—in recent years, homosexuality has lost much of its "taboo" status, particularly in urban areas. Historically, gays and lesbians were labeled "deviant," but research demonstrating that sexual orientation is biologically determined has mitigated much criticism, and public opinion—historically hard line against gay and lesbian rights—has tempered significantly.

Several LGBT civil rights organizations were founded after the Stonewall Rebellion. In June 1969, groups of gay men and lesbians clashed violently with police in New York City in a protest over the routine harassment by law enforcement of members of the lesbian and gay community. This influential conflict, which started at the Stonewall bar, marked the first time that members of this community acted collectively and in large numbers to assert their rights. Shortly after this event, in 1970, Lambda Legal, a national organization fighting for full recognition of the civil rights of LGBT citizens, was founded. Within a few years, gays and lesbians began to hold gay pride marches throughout the country, and many new groups such as the Human Rights Campaign and the National Gay and Lesbian Task Force began advocating for LGBT rights.

Among the most vocal struggles has been the fight for the right to marry or enter into a civil union, in which a gay or lesbian couple could enjoy the legal and financial benefits as heterosexual married couples. In 2012, President Obama announced that he supported the right of gay couples to marry, though the likelihood of federal legislation codifying this position appears slim. More likely, however, is the continued evolution of the right for gays to marry in various states. This issue represents a key battleground for gay rights advocates, and their opponents who have waged many successful efforts at legally defining marriage as a heterosexual union within a state.

The Supreme Court of Hawaii ruled in 1993 that it was a violation of the Hawaii state constitution to deny same-sex couples the right to marry. Opponents of same-sex marriage succeeded in their subsequent efforts to get a state constitutional amendment banning same-sex marriage on the ballot, and in 1996 the majority of Hawaiian voters approved it. The conflict over same-sex marriage that began in Hawaii quickly spread to other states. Since 1998, about 30 states have banned same-sex marriage through constitutional amendment or legislation. What this means for gay and lesbian couples is that they are not able to obtain the same rights and benefits that are available to opposite-sex couples through marriage, including tax benefits, the right to receive joint mortgages, the right to make medical decisions for a partner who is unable to make such decisions, spousal Social Security benefits, and rights of heritance when a deceased partner has no will.

In contrast, by 2012 the states of Maine, Maryland, Vermont, Massachusetts, Connecticut, Iowa, New Hampshire, New York, Washington, and the District of Columbia allow same-sex marriages. Oregon, Nevada, California, Colorado, Illinois, Wisconsin, Delaware, New Jersey, Rhode Island, and Maine allow for civil unions or domestic partnerships. Civil unions provide same-sex couples with many of the protections that married couples enjoy. However, the 1996 national Defense of Marriage Act states that the federal government does not recognize same-sex marriages, or civil unions, legalized by any state and that states do not need to recognize same-sex marriages that were legalized in other states.

The struggle for the rights of gays and lesbians in many ways mirrors the struggles of groups that have gone before them, struggles that continue today on many fronts—in the states, Congress, the courts, and the court of public opinion.

CHAPTER SUMMARY

- The legacy of slavery meant that significant forms of discrimination were embedded into both the U.S. legal system and the American psyche.

- Buoyed by the U.S. Supreme Court ruling *Brown v. Board of Education*, the modern Civil Rights Movement relied on protests and other means to persuade the federal government to correct legal forms of discrimination.

- Despite legislation, inequalities remain for many African Americans, and also Hispanic and Asian Americans.

- Among those facing discrimination are legal and illegal immigrants, who often are viewed as economic competition by American citizens. National immigration policy in recent years is reflective of both an economic perspective as well as the distrust skepticism that sometimes greets new immigrant cultures in the United States.

- Since the earliest years of America's settlement, Native Americans have faced a multitude of discriminatory practices that have decimated Native American populations.

- Gender remains a modern source of disparity, especially in terms of economic power and political power. Reproductive rights also remain a source of contention in the modern political arena.

- Disabled Americans also face discrimination, but the Americans with Disabilities Act has enhanced the rights of these citizens.

- At the forefront of the struggle for power are gays and lesbians. Chief among their agenda items today is the right to marry, bringing with it the accompanying economic and legal rights afforded spouses in the United States.

KEY TERMS

affirmative action   compensatory or preferential treatment of minorities

Americans with Disabilities Act (ADA)   bans discrimination against people with disabilities in education, employment, health care, housing, and transportation with regard to all programs and organizations

Brown v. Board of Education of Topeka, Kansas   landmark Supreme Court decision declaring that segregation itself violates the equal protection clause of the Fourteenth Amendment (1954)

Civil Rights Act of 1964   prohibits discrimination in public accommodations, in programs receiving federal funds, and in employment, and established the EEOC to enforce its provisions

Civil Rights Act of 1968   prohibits discrimination in the sale or rental of a dwelling or in advertising the sale or rental

Dawes Act of 1887   attempted forced assimilation

de jure (pronounced day-juray) segregation   segregation permitted or required by law

eligibility pool   people with the characteristics that voters deem suitable for elective office

Equal Rights Amendment (ERA)   a proposed amendment to the U.S. Constitution guaranteeing equality of rights of the sexes

gender   culturally imposed sex-role stereotypes

Hispanic   referring to Spanish-speaking ancestry and culture

incumbency advantage   the benefit derived from already having been voted into a particular office once

Indian Reorganization Act of 1934   recognized tribes as legal governments

Intercourse Act of 1790   law that declared that public treaties between the U.S. government and the independent Indian "nations" would be the only legal means of obtaining Indian land

Roe v. Wade   U.S. Supreme Court decision that recognized abortion as a constitutional right (1973)

separate-but-equal doctrine   interpreting the equal protection clause of the Fourteenth Amendment to allow segregation of the races if facilities were equal (1896–1954)

sex   whether one is born with male or female reproductive organs

Trail of Tears   The forced march of 16,000 Indians from the Florida Everglades to Oklahoma in 1838

ON THE WEB

EXPLORING POWER, RACE, AND GENDER

The website for this textbook (**www.cengagebrain.com**) offers resources for exploring power, race, and gender on the Internet. As well, a great deal of information and a wide variety of points of view on race, ethnicity, gender issues, and civil rights are available on the following websites. Internet homes for organizations like the NAACP, National Organization for Women (NOW), and the Human Rights Campaign also provide a wealth of knowledge in their respective areas.

- **U.S. Commission on Civil Rights** The U.S. Commission on Civil Rights is the federal government's official clearinghouse for information regarding discrimination or the denial of equal protection of the laws. Its website (**www.usccr.gov**) includes a wide variety of public reports and studies on civil rights matters; all are available to the public free of charge.

Try This: Go to **www.usccr.gov/pubs/index.php** and pick a publication of current importance. Browse through the report and share what new information you learn about the progression of civil rights in today's society.

- **U.S. Equal Employment Opportunity Commission** The U.S. Equal Employment Opportunity Commission also maintains a website (**www.eeoc.gov**) with facts about employment discrimination as well as instruction on how to file a charge under Title VII of the Civil Rights Act of 1964, the Americans with Disabilities Act, and the Equal Pay Act.

Try This: Go to **www.eeoc.gov/eeoc/initiatives/index.cfm** and read about the EEOC's recent initiatives for equal opportunity employment. In what ways are these initiatives fighting discrimination in the workplace?

REVIEW QUIZ

MULTIPLE CHOICE

1. The Supreme Court interpreted the equal protection clause of the Fourteenth Amendment to allow segregation of the races if facilities were equal in the _____.
   a. separate-but-equal doctrine
   b. Jim Crow doctrine
   c. equal protection doctrine
   d. Lincoln doctrine

2. Segregation permitted or required by law is called _____.
   a. de facto segregation
   b. redlining
   c. *de jure* segregation
   d. Fourteenth Amendment segregation

3. What was the landmark 1954 Supreme Court decision that declared that segregation itself violates the equal protection clause of the Fourteenth Amendment?
   a. *Roe v. Wade*
   b. *Plessy v. Ferguson*
   c. *Brown v. Board of Education of Topeka, Kansas*
   d. *Cherokee Nation v. Georgia*

4. The Civil Rights Act of 1964 *does not* prohibit discrimination in _____.
   a. public accommodations.
   b. the sale or rental of a dwelling.
   c. programs receiving federal funds.
   d. employment.

5. The Civil Rights Act of 1968 prohibits discrimination in _____.
   a. public accommodations
   b. the sale or rental of a dwelling
   c. programs receiving federal funds
   d. employment

6. The Intercourse Act of 1790 _____.
   a. recognized Indian nations
   b. prohibited separate-but-equal public accommodations
   c. banned interracial marriage
   d. banned gay marriage

7. In general, women earn about _____ cents for every dollar earned by men.
   a. 50
   b. 70
   c. 80
   d. 99

8. Secretaries, nurses, waitresses, and office clerks are examples of _____ jobs.
   a. white-collar
   b. blue-collar
   c. green-collar
   d. pink-collar

9. People with the characteristics that voters deem suitable for elective office are said to be part of the _____.
   a. power elite
   b. ruling class
   c. eligibility pool
   d. incumbency advantage

10. The 1973 Supreme Court decision that recognized women's constitutional right to an abortion was called _____.
    a. *Roe v. Wade*
    b. *Plessy v. Ferguson*
    c. *Planned Parenthood v. Casey*
    d. *Griswold v. Connecticut*

FILL IN THE BLANK

11. Compensatory or preferential treatment of minorities is called _____.

12. The forced march of 16,000 Indians from the Florida Everglades to Oklahoma in 1838 is known as the _____.

13. Whether one is born with male or female reproductive organs determines _____.

14. _____ is culturally imposed sex-role stereotypes.

15. The _____ bans discrimination against people with disabilities in education, employment, health care, housing, and transportation with regard to all programs and organizations.

Answer Key

1. a; 2. c; 3. c; 4. b; 5. b; 6. a; 7. c; 8. d; 9. c; 10. a; 11. affirmative action; 12. Trail of Tears; 13. sex; 14. Gender; 15. Americans with Disabilities Act.

CHAPTER 11

Poverty and Powerlessness

Learning Objectives

After reading this chapter, students will be able to:

- Explain the relationship between poverty and powerlessness.
- Describe who the poor are, and understand how poverty is defined.
- Describe the programs the government relies on to end poverty, and evaluate these programs' effectiveness.

Poverty as Powerlessness

powerlessness
the inability to control the events that shape one's life

Powerlessness is the inability to control the events that shape one's life. The poor lack economic resources and are hence largely dependent on others for the things they need. Their lack of power derives from their dependency. But powerlessness is also an attitude, a feeling that no matter what one does it will have little effect on one's life. An attitude of powerlessness reinforces the condition of powerlessness. Persistent poverty generates a lack of motivation and feelings of meaninglessness, hopelessness, distrust, and cynicism. Constant defeat causes many of the poor to retreat into a self-protective attitude characterized by indifference and a pervasive sense of futility.

alienation
a feeling of separation from society

The poor often experience **alienation**—feeling separated from society—because of their lack of success in realizing important life goals. Persons who are blocked consistently in their efforts to achieve life goals are most likely to express powerlessness and alienation. These attitudes in turn become barriers to effective self-help, independence, and self-respect.[1]

Poverty in the United States

How much poverty really exists in America? According to the U.S. Bureau of the Census, in 2011 there were more than 43 million poor people (those below the official poverty level) in the United States, or over 14 percent of the population (Figure 11-1). This marks the highest poverty rate in a decade, reflecting the damage inflicted on American families by the economic downturn. The increase in the official poverty rate was not the only indicator of the negative impact that the recent recession had on families in the United States.

FIGURE 11-1 POVERTY IN THE UNITED STATES

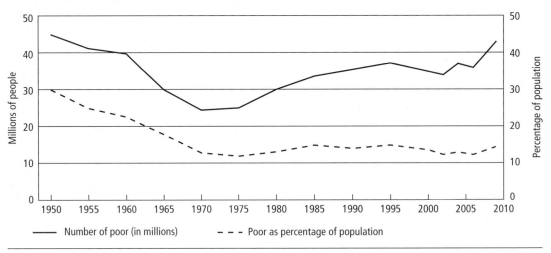

SOURCE: www.census.gov/prod/3/98pubs/p60-203.pdf

According to Census Bureau, households of all races saw declines in their median adjusted income, meaning that, on average, many Americans earned less money in 2011 than they had in previous years, on average less than what they earned in 2000.

The official poverty level is derived by calculating the minimum cash income required to maintain families of different sizes. The dollar amounts change each year to take into account the effect of inflation. (See Case Study: "How Is Poverty Measured?")

official definition of poverty

government estimates each year of the minimum cash income required for families of various sizes to subsist

This **official definition of poverty** emphasizes *subsistence levels*; it seeks to describe poverty objectively as the lack of enough income to acquire the minimum necessities of life. Liberals frequently view the subsistence definition of poverty as insensitive to a variety of needs including entertainment, recreation, and the relief of monotony. Items that were "luxuries" a generation ago are now considered "necessities." Liberals also note that the official definition *includes* cash income from welfare and Social Security. Without this government assistance, the number of poor would be higher.

Conservatives also challenge the official definition of poverty: It does not include the value of family assets. People (usually older people) who own their own houses and automobiles may have incomes below the poverty line yet not suffer any real hardship. (More than 43 percent of the official "poor" own their own homes, and more than 65 percent own automobiles.) Many persons who are ranked as poor do not think of themselves as "poor people"— students, for example. More important, the official definition of poverty *excludes* "in-kind" (noncash) benefits provided by government, benefits that include, for example, free medical care under Medicaid and Medicare, food stamps, public housing, and school lunches. If these benefits were "costed out" (that is, calculated as cash income), fewer persons might be classified as poor.

CASE STUDY

How Is Poverty Measured?

The U.S. government, specifically the U.S. Census Bureau, defines poverty by using a series of income thresholds that vary by family size. The accompanying table shows the income threshold for 2008. If a family's total income is less than the family's threshold, then that family and every individual in it is considered in poverty. One problem with the official poverty thresholds is that they do not vary geographically within the contiguous states (Alaska and Hawaii have separate thresholds taking into account higher costs of living). The impact of this is that, in places with a high cost of living, more people are probably "in poverty" but do not meet the official definition. The income thresholds are updated for inflation using the Consumer Price Index. The official poverty definition uses money income before taxes and does not include capital gains or non-cash benefits (such as public housing, Medicaid, and food stamps).

THE 2012 POVERTY GUIDELINES FOR THE 48 CONTIGUOUS STATES
AND THE DISTRICT OF COLUMBIA

Persons in Family / Household	Poverty Guideline
1	$11,170
2	15,130
3	19,090
4	23,050
5	27,010
6	30,970
7	34,930
8	38,890

For families/households with more than 8 persons, add $3,960 for each additional person.

Income Used to Compute Poverty Status

Money income is based on the following:

- Includes earnings, unemployment compensation, workers' compensation, Social Security, Supplemental Security Income, public assistance, veterans' payments, survivor benefits, pension or retirement income, interest, dividends, rents, royalties, income from estates, trusts, educational assistance, alimony, child support, assistance from outside the household, and other miscellaneous sources.
- Noncash benefits (such as food stamps and housing subsidies) do not count.
- Before taxes.

(continued)

- Excludes capital gains or losses.
- If a person lives with a family, add up the income of all family members (nonrelatives, such as housemates, do not count).

What Are the Poverty Thresholds?

Poverty thresholds are the dollar amounts used to determine poverty status:

- Each person or family is assigned one out of forty-eight possible poverty thresholds.
- The same thresholds are used throughout the contiguous United States, with separate thresholds for Alaska and Hawaii.
- Thresholds are updated annually for inflation using the Consumer Price Index for All Urban Consumers (CPI-U).

How Is Poverty Computed?

If total family income is less than the threshold appropriate for that family, then the following apply:

- The family is in poverty.
- All family members have the same poverty status.
- For individuals who do not live with family members, their own income is compared with the appropriate threshold.
- If total family income equals or is greater than the threshold, the family (or unrelated individual) is not in poverty.

Example

Family A has five members: two children, their mother, their father, and a great-aunt. Their threshold was $27,000 in 2012 (see poverty thresholds for 2012). Suppose the members' incomes in 2012 were as follows:

Mother	$10,000
Father	9,000
Great-aunt	10,000
First child	0
Second child	0
Total family income:	$29,000

Compare total family income with their family's threshold: income/threshold = $29,000/$27,000 = 1.07. Because their income was greater than their threshold, family A is not "in poverty" according to the official definition.

The income divided by the threshold is called the ratio of income to poverty. Family A's ratio of income to poverty is 1.07.

The difference in dollars between family income and the family's poverty threshold is called the income deficit (for families in poverty) or income surplus (for families above poverty). Family A's income surplus is $2,000 (or $29,000 – $27,000).

SOURCE: "How the Census Bureau Measures Poverty," http://aspe.hhs.gov/poverty/12poverty.shtml#thresholds

Is There a Culture of Poverty?

It is sometimes argued that the poor have a characteristic lifestyle, or **culture of poverty**, that assists them in adjusting to their world (see Focus: "Who Are the Poor?"). Like other aspects of culture, it is passed on to future generations, setting in motion a self-perpetuating cycle of poverty. The theory of the poverty cycle is as follows: Deprivation in one generation leads, through cultural impoverishment, indifference, apathy, or misunderstanding of their children's educational needs, to deprivation in the next generation. Lacking the self-respect that comes from earning an adequate living, some young men cannot sustain responsibilities of marriage, and father children out of wedlock with multiple women. Lacking role models of success, some poor young women succumb to a life characterized by instability, poverty, and hopelessness. Within the culture of poverty, some parents then hand down to their children the same burden of family instability and female-headed households that they themselves carried. Children born into a culture of alienation, apathy, and lack of motivation learn these attitudes themselves. Thus, the poor are prevented from exploiting any opportunities that are available to them.

culture-of-poverty thesis the idea that a lifestyle of poverty, alienation, and apathy is passed on from one generation to another

Poverty as Subculture

It is probably more accurate to talk about a *subculture* of poverty. The prefix *sub* is used because most of the poor subscribe to the "middle-class American way of life," at least as a cultural ideal and even as a personal fantasy. Most poor people do not reject American culture but strive to adapt its values to the realities of economic deprivation and social disorganization in their own lives.

Another view of the culture of poverty emphasizes the **present-orientedness** of many poor people.[2] Advocates of this explanation of the culture of poverty argue that poverty is the byproduct of the present-orientedness that occurs among poor people. Within the culture of poverty, despair runs so deep that individuals cannot envision a successful future and plan for it. Thus, they are less likely to sacrifice present-day wants for long-term needs—to forgo purchasing items today to save for a larger purchase, like a home or college education, in the future.

the culture of poverty as present-orientedness the inability to plan or sacrifice for the future

FOCUS

Who Are the Poor?

Poverty occurs in many kinds of families and in all races and ethnic groups. However, some groups experience poverty in proportions that are greater than the national average. The following statistics indicate the percentage of Americans in various groups who were living below the poverty level in 2010:

Total population	**15**
Male	13
Female	16
People in families	13
Female-headed families	32
White (non-Hispanic)	13
Black	27
Hispanic	26
Asian	12
Under 18 years	22
18–64 years	14
Over 65 years	9

SOURCES: Current Population Survey (CPS), www.census.gov/hhes/www/poverty/data/incpovhlth/2010/figure6.pdf.

Poverty is most common among female-headed families. In 2010 the incidence of poverty among these families was 13 percent, compared with only 6 percent for married-couple families. These women and their children constitute over two-thirds of all of the persons living in poverty in the United States. These figures describe the "feminization of poverty" in America. Clearly, poverty is closely related to family structure. Today, the disintegration of the traditional husband-wife family is the single most influential factor contributing to poverty.

Blacks experience poverty in much greater proportions than whites. Over the years, the poverty rate among blacks in the United States has been well over twice as high as the poverty rate among whites. Poverty among Hispanics is also significantly greater than among whites, and parallels the

It is true that some people experience poverty because of involuntary unemployment, prolonged illness, death of the breadwinner, or some other misfortune. But even when severe, this kind of poverty is not self-perpetuating. It ends once the external cause no longer exists. Other people will be poor no matter what their "external" circumstances are. They live in a culture rate among blacks. Asians are among the least likely of any minority group to experience poverty, with a poverty rate of 12 percent.

The accompanying figure also indicates that those over age 65 experience *less* poverty than younger people. Specifically, the figure shows the impact of the War on Poverty social welfare programs of the 1960s. But importantly, the figure shows that the poverty rate for senior citizens aged 65 and older (9 percent) is *less than* the national average of 15 percent (see the preceding table) and nearly half the average of those under age 18.

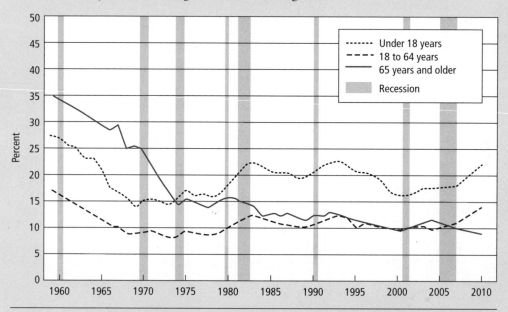

SOURCE: Current Population Survey Annual Social and Economic Supplement (CPS-ASEC) *Historical Poverty Tables* (Table 3), www.census.gov/apsd/techdoc/cps/cpsmar12.pdf

Moreover, the aged are much wealthier than younger age groups. They are more likely than younger people to own homes with paid-off mortgages. Medicare pays a large portion of their medical expenses. With fewer expenses, the aged, even with relatively smaller cash incomes, experience poverty differently from a younger mother with children. Continuing increases in Social Security benefits over the years are largely responsible for this singular "victory" in the war against poverty.

Finally, we should note that children are more likely to experience poverty than people of any other age. More than one in five American children, or 22 percent, live in poverty. (See Controversies in the Social Sciences: "America's Shame: Our Poor Children.")

of poverty that continues for generations because they psychologically cannot provide for the future. Particularly within a consumer-oriented society, where poor people are surrounded by the symbols of wealth on television and in the media, the temptation to feel a part of society is strong. Thus, proponents of the culture of poverty observe that increased income is not likely to

CONTROVERSIES IN THE SOCIAL SCIENCE

America's Shame: Our Poor Children

I n the United States, politicians are quite likely to advocate for and protect programs that serve the elderly, including Social Security and Medicare. One reason might be that the elderly are a vocal and effectively organized constituency. But political leaders are less likely to embrace policies that affect a less-organized constituency: children.

In the United States, the most likely people to be poor are children. Nationwide, nearly 22 percent, or one of every five children, live in poverty; 24 percent of children under age 5 live in poverty. Of the nearly 16 million American children who live in poverty, over 9 million live in families with incomes of less than half the poverty level.

The accompanying map shows that children living in southern states also comprise a disproportionate percentage of the poor: Alabama, Arkansas, Kentucky, Louisiana, Mississippi, South Carolina, Tennessee, and West Virginia all have child poverty rates of more than 25 percent, as do the New Mexico and Texas in the Southwest, and the District of Columbia.

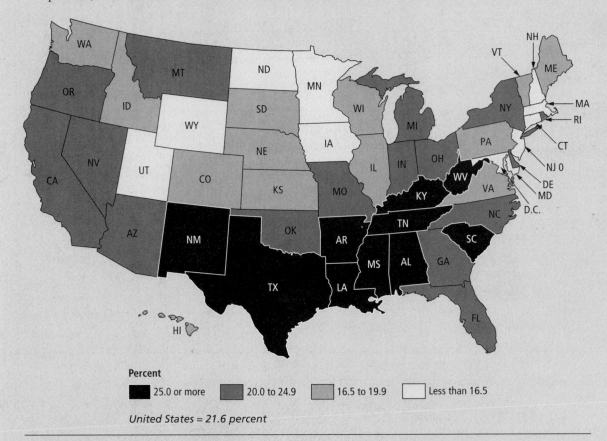

Percent

■ 25.0 or more   ■ 20.0 to 24.9   ■ 16.5 to 19.9   □ Less than 16.5

United States = 21.6 percent

SOURCE: www.census.gov/hhes/www/cpstables/032011/pov/new46_100125_10.htm

The following figure shows that black and Latino children are more likely to live in poverty. The figure shows that 38 percent of black children and 32 percent of Latino children live in families whose incomes fall below the federal poverty threshold. These statistics do not reflect the reality that black and Latino children are more likely to be poor, but because more whites are in the population as a whole, greater numbers of white children are living in poor families. Of all children whose family income falls below the federal poverty threshold, 53 percent are white.

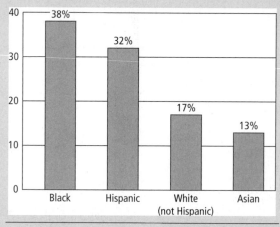

SOURCE: http://aspe.hhs.gov/hsp/12/povertyandincomeest/ib.shtml

The impact of poverty on children is enormous and can be life altering. Children who live in poverty often lack the most basic necessities for a healthy and productive life. They are more likely to lack adequate nutrition and are more likely to experience hunger. Malnutrition and malnourishment place children at increased risk for a host of physical and cognitive maladies. They also place children at risk for delayed physical and cognitive development. Poor children also have less access to quality health care and preventive medicine programs.

Children in poverty are more likely to face stressful living environments. These environments are characterized by unstable and unsafe housing, frequent moves, and overcrowded and unsanitary conditions. Poor children's neighborhoods also are more likely to be violent, and poor children are more likely to have access to illegal drugs, come in contact with urban gangs, and be pressured to commit crimes.

The schools that poor children attend are not as good as those attended by wealthier children. They are more likely to be in disrepair, overcrowded, and have fewer resources including books, teachers, computers, sports programs, extracurricular programs, and after-school programs.

Facing these obstacles renders poor children less likely to succeed in adulthood. Because of health issues, violence, poorly equipped schools, and fewer resources, poor children are less likely to succeed in school, impacting their ability to secure and maintain a good job in adulthood. They will then earn less money over their lifetimes, thus perpetuating the cycle of poverty.

A Cure for Poverty? The Gates Foundation

One enormous effort to address the conditions of poverty throughout the world has been under-taken by the richest man in the world. On June 15, 2006, Microsoft founder Bill Gates, with a current net worth of $61 billion, announced his plans to step down from his day-to-day responsi-bilities at Microsoft effective July 31, 2008, to enable him to devote more time to working at the Bill & Melinda Gates Foundation. In its 18 years of operation, the foundation has donated $26 billion in grants, including a $1.5 billion grant to the Global Alliance (GAVI) to help fund a pro-gram to provide childhood vaccinations in underdeveloped countries over a ten-year span.

The foundation employs about 1,000 people and boasts an endowment of $33.5 billion, thanks in part to a 2006 donation to the foundation by the world's second richest man, Warren Buf-fett. Buffett pledged 10 million shares of Berkshire Hathaway Class B stocks with a market value of nearly $31 billion at the time of his contribution. Before Buffett's donation, the foundation donated roughly $1.5 billion each year to four major areas: education, global health initiatives, libraries, and community and educational organizations in the United States' Pacific Northwest. Its mission:

> Guided by the belief that every life has equal value, the Bill & Melinda Gates Foundation works to reduce inequities and improve lives around the world. In developing countries, it focuses on improving health, reducing extreme poverty, and increasing access to technology in public libraries. In the United States, the foundation seeks to ensure that all people have access to a great education and to technology in public libraries. In its local region, it focuses on improving the lives of low-income families.*

Gates and his wife, Melinda, have spent considerable energy and money on efforts to eradicate disease, particularly those found in developing areas, and prevent the spread of and find a cure for HIV/AIDS. In an annual letter, Bill Gates wrote:

> A surprising but critical fact we learned was that reducing the number of deaths actually reduces population growth.... Contrary to the Malthusian view that population will grow to the limit of however many kids can be fed, in fact parents choose to have enough kids to give them a high chance that several will survive to support them as they grow old. As the number of kids who survive to adulthood goes up, parents can achieve this goal without having as many children.

remedy poverty when the poor are present oriented. Extra income is likely to be spent rather than saved, invested, or managed in ways that would improve one's financial security in the future. This culture of poverty may involve no more than a small portion of all families who live below the poverty line, but it generally continues regardless of what is done in the way of remedial action.[3] Perhaps the greatest danger in the idea of a culture of poverty is that poverty in this light can be seen as an unbreakable, puncture-proof cycle, which may lead to a relaxation of efforts to ameliorate the conditions of poverty. In other

This means that improved health is critical to getting a country into the positive cycle of increasing education, stability, and wealth. When health improves, people have smaller families and the government has more resources per person, so improving nutrition and education becomes much easier. These investments also improve health, and a virtuous cycle begins that takes a country out of poverty. This was a huge revelation for Melinda and me. It is why we expanded our focus from reproductive health to all of the major infectious diseases. Today the foundation's Global Health Program, which accounts for about 50 percent of our total spending, focuses on 20 diseases. The top five are: diarrheal diseases (including rotavirus), pneumonia, and malaria—which mostly kill kids—and AIDS and TB, which mostly kill adults.[†]

In 2009 alone, some of the foundation's initiatives included the following grants:

- GAVI Alliance, expanding childhood immunization: $1.5 billion
- United Negro College Fund, Gates Millennium Scholars Program: $1.37 billion
- PATH Malaria Vaccine Initiative (MVI): $456 million
- Rotary International, supporting polio eradication: $355 million
- Intensive Partnerships for Effective Teaching, supporting plans to transform how teachers are recruited, developed, rewarded, and retained: $290 million
- Hillsborough County Public Schools: $100 million
- Memphis City Schools: $90 million
- The College-Ready Promise, Los Angeles: $60 million
- Pittsburgh Public Schools: $40 million
- Alliance for a Green Revolution in Africa (AGRA), improving seeds and soil for African farmers: $264.5 million
- Save the Children, saving newborn lives: $112 million

The Gates Foundation's budget now exceeds the gross domestic product of many of the nations in which it works. In 2010, it allocated more than $2.8 billion in grants, surpassing some of the world's most important international philanthropic organizations, including the International Red Cross.

---

*The Gates Foundation. "Foundation Fact Sheet." www.gatesfoundation.org/MediaCenter/FactSheet.
†www.gatesfoundation.org/annual-letter/Pages/2009-agricultural-development-africa-asia.aspx.
SOURCE: The Gates Foundation (www.gatesfoundation.org), and http://www.gatesfoundation.org/about/Pages /foundation-fact-sheet.aspx.

words, it is feared that the "culture of poverty" idea may become an excuse for inaction.

In contrast with the cultural explanation of poverty we explored above—that parental transmission of values is responsible for the perpetuation of poverty—the **situational explanation thesis** argues that poverty can be explained by the social conditions of the poor, particularly the differences in financial resources that determine individual behavior. (See Focus: "A Cure for Poverty? The Gates Foundation" for one description of addressing the conditions of poverty.)

situational explanation thesis

poverty as a result of current social and economic conditions, or parental transmission of values and beliefs.

INTERNATIONAL PERSPECTIVE

The Basic Necessities: Water and Food

In the comparatively affluent United States where purchasing a 16 oz. bottle of water for upwards of $1 is a relatively common experience, and where ample food is not an issue for many, it may be difficult for some to fathom the scarcity of necessities like food and water. But for many residents living in parts of Africa, such scarcity is a relatively common phenomenon. The following table shows that about one-third of those polled in a Gallup survey of more than 17 nations have gone without enough clean drinking water. Among those most likely to have faced water scarcity are residents of Burkina Faso and Chad, where less than half of the population had enough clean water. Access to potable water is one of the key issues outlined in the U.N. Millennium Goals agenda for 2015, and from the accompanying table, we can see that one of the challenges facing the United Nations is the fact that rural dwellers nearly always face more water scarcity that urban dwellers, with rural dwellers in Zimbabwe being the only residents polled who had greater access

Thinking about yesterday, did you have enough clean drinking water?
Among all adults aged 15 and older who say "yes"

	Total %	Urban %	Rural %
MEDIAN	67	77	63
Botswana	89	99	87
Ghana	85	87	84
Senegal	83	91	81
Zimbabwe	79	64	84
Uganda	76	86	75
Mali	74	81	73
South Africa	72	93	63
Kenya	70	87	67
Niger	67	91	65
Cameroon	64	65	63
Nigeria	63	77	59
Liberia	63	66	62
Central African Republic	57	68	54
Tanzania	53	67	50
Sierra Leone	52	62	48
Burkina Faso	47	77	44
Chad	46	68	38

Source: www.gallup.com/poll/153191/Clean-Drinking-Water-Linked-Food-Security-Africa.aspx

(continued)

to potable water than urban dwellers in that nation. Water scarcity presents a serious public health threat, as the consumption of not-potable water increases the likelihood of illnesses, especially rotavirus, one of the leading killers of children under age five in developing areas.

The situation is similarly dire when it comes to adequate food. According to Gallup, one billion adults worldwide do not have enough money at times to buy the food they or their families needed, or 26 percent of those surveyed in 113 countries. Percentages were significantly higher in sub-Saharan African, where 40 percent reported struggling to have enough food. Of the 22 countries in which a majority of the population reported difficulty affording food, 15 countries were in sub-Saharan Africa. While of course the problem of food scarcity is connected to death rates and quality of life issues, it also is connected to issues of crime, violence, and political instability, as those desperate for food resort to any means to attain it.

Countries in Which Half or More Residents Struggle to Afford Food

Have there been times in the past 12 months when you did not have enough money to buy food that you or your family needed?

	Yes (2008)	Yes (2009)
Cameroon	66%	73%
Zimbabwe	79%	73%
Comoros	–	72%
Niger	68%	71%
Zambia	67%	69%
Philippines	58%	68%
Burundi	74%	67%
Kenya	67%	64%
Congo (Kinshasa)	–	61%
Azerbaijan	60%	60%
Tanzania	62%	60%
Malawi	–	60%
Nigeria	55%	59%
Ecuador	46%	58%
Georgia	51%	56%
Chad	54%	56%
South Africa	56%	55%
Dominican Republic	59%	55%
Cambodia	53%	55%
Ivory Coast	–	53%
Uganda	62%	52%
Honduras	48%	51%

- Survey not conducted in 2008.

Source: www.gallup.com/poll/143255/Estimated-Billion-Adults-Struggled-Afford-Food-2009.aspx

RESEARCH *THIS!*

SOCIAL SECURITY BENEFITS

Type of Beneficiary	Beneficiaries		Total Monthly Benefits (millions of d ollars)	Average Monthly Benefit (dollars)
	Number (thousands)	Percent		
All beneficiaries	56,158	100.0	63,243	1,126.16
Old-Age Insurance				
Retired workers	36,121	64.3	44,545	1,233.21
Spouses	2,287	4.1	1,395	609.76
Children	619	1.1	375	605.49
Survivors Insurance				
Widow(er)s and parents [a]	4,223	7.5	4,898	1,159.93
Widowed mothers and fathers [b]	152	0.3	134	875.85
Children	1,949	3.5	1,532	786.13
Disability Insurance				
Disabled workers	8,707	15.5	9,675	1,111.17
Spouses	165	0.3	49	298.11
Children	1,933	3.4	640	330.97

SOURCE: Social Security Administration, Master Beneficiary Record, 100 percent data.

NOTES: Data are for the end of the specified month. Only beneficiaries in current-payment status are included.

Some Social Security beneficiaries are entitled to more than one type of benefit. In most cases, they are dually entitled to a worker benefit and a higher spouse or widow(er) benefit. If both benefits are financed from the same trust fund, the beneficiary is usually counted only once in the statistics, as a retired-worker or a disabled-worker beneficiary, and the benefit amount recorded is the larger amount associated with the auxiliary benefit. If the benefits are paid from different trust funds the beneficiary is counted twice, and the respective benefit amounts are recorded for each type of benefit.

a. Includes nondisabled widow(er)s aged 60 or older, disabled widow(er)s aged 50 or older, and dependent parents of deceased workers aged 62 or older.

b. A widow(er) or surviving divorced parent caring for the entitled child of a deceased worker who is under age 16 or is disabled.

YOUR ANALYSIS:

1. Which group is the greatest proportion of Social Security recipients?

2. Which group receives, on average, the greatest monthly benefit?

3. Which group costs the government the most in benefits overall?

Poverty as Economic Deprivation

Opponents of the idea of a culture of poverty argue that this notion diverts attention from the conditions of poverty that foster family instability and present-orientedness. The question is really whether the conditions of poverty create a culture of poverty or vice versa. Reformers are likely to focus on the economic deprivation as the fundamental cause of the social pathologies that afflict the poor. They note that the idea of a culture of poverty can be applied only to groups who have lived in poverty for several generations. It is not relevant to those who have become poor during their lifetime because of sickness, accident, or old age. (See International Perspective: "The Basic Necessities: Water and Food.")

Government and Social Welfare

Public welfare has been a recognized responsibility of government in English-speaking countries for many centuries. As far back as the Poor Relief Act of 1601, the English Parliament provided workhouses for the "able-bodied poor" (the unemployed) and poorhouses for widows and orphans, the aged, and the handicapped. Today nearly one-third of the U.S. population receives some form of direct government benefit (Table 11-1). Among the most prevalent is Social Security, with approximately 10,000 baby boomers applying for benefits each day. Other Americans are recipients of Medicare or Medicaid, disability insurance, unemployment compensation, government employee retirement, veterans' benefits, food stamps, school lunches, job training, public housing, and cash public assistance payments. Thus, the "welfare state" now encompasses a very large part of our society.[4]

Social Insurance

In the Social Security Act of 1935, the federal government undertook to establish a basic framework for social welfare policies at the federal, state, and local levels in America. The **social insurance** concept was designed to *prevent* poverty resulting from individual misfortune—unemployment, old age, death of the family breadwinner, or physical disability. Social insurance was based on the same notion as private insurance: the sharing of risks, the setting aside of money for a rainy day, and legal entitlement to benefits on reaching retirement or on occurrence of specific misfortunes. Social insurance was *not* to be charity or public assistance. Instead, it relied on people's (compulsory) financial contribution through payroll deductions to their own protection.

social insurance
compulsory savings for all with legal entitlement to benefits

The key feature of the Social Security Act is the Old-Age, Survivors, Disability Insurance program; this is a compulsory social insurance program financed by regular deductions from earnings, which gives individuals the legal right to benefit in the event that their income is reduced by old age, death of the head of the household, or permanent disability. It is not public charity but a way of compelling people to provide insurance against loss of income. Another feature of the Social Security Act was that it induced states to enact unemployment compensation programs. Unemployment compensation is also an *insurance* program, only in this case the costs are borne solely by the employer. In 1965 Congress amended Social Security to add comprehensive health insurance for persons over 65—Medicare. Medicare provided for prepaid hospital insurance for the aged under Social Security and for low-cost voluntary medical insurance for the same group under federal administration. Medicare, too, is based on the insurance principle: Individuals pay for their medical insurance during their working years and enjoy its benefits after age 65. Thus, the program resembles private medical hospital insurance, except that it is compulsory.

Public Assistance

The distinction between the *social insurance* program and a *public assistance* (welfare) program is an important one that has on occasion become a major political issue. If the beneficiaries of a government program are required to have made contributions to it before claiming any of its benefits and if they are entitled to the benefits regardless of their personal wealth, the program is said to be financed on the *social insurance* principle. If the program is financed out of general tax revenues and if the recipients are required to show that they are poor before claiming its benefits, the program is said to be financed on the *public assistance* principle.

TANF
Temporary Assistance for
Needy Families (replaced
AFDC)

The purpose of public assistance is clearly to *alleviative;* the idea is simply to provide a minimal level of subsistence to certain categories of needy persons. The federal government, under its Supplemental Security Income (SSI) program, directly aids three categories of recipients: the aged, the blind, and the disabled. The federal government, under its Temporary Assistance for Needy Families (**TANF**; formerly Aid to Families with Dependent Children) program, gives money to the states to assist them in providing welfare payments to families with children under 18 years of age. Welfare aid to persons who do not fall into any of these categories but who, for one reason or another, are poor is referred to as *general assistance* and is paid for entirely from state funds.

In-Kind Welfare Benefits

**major public assistance
in-kind programs**
food stamps, school
lunches, Medicaid, public
housing

The federal government also provides many **in-kind** (noncash) **public assistance programs**. The Food Stamp Program was begun in 1965; originally, the poor were allowed to purchase food stamps at large discounts and use the stamps to buy food at stores; after 1977 the stamps were distributed free of charge. Free school lunches (and in some cities, breakfasts as well) are made available to children of the poor by federal payments to school districts, greatly alleviating the problem of hunger among the poor. In 1965 Congress also authorized federal funds to enable states to guarantee medical services to all public assistance recipients. This program is known as Medicaid. Unlike Medicare, Medicaid is a public assistance program designed for needy persons; no prior contributions are required, but recipients of Medicaid must be eligible for welfare assistance. In other words, they must be poor. Federal and state governments also provide funds for the Children's Health Insurance Program (CHIP), which provides health coverage to nearly 8 million children in families with incomes too high to qualify for Medicaid but who can't afford private coverage. Created in 1997, CHIP gives federal matching funds to states to provide this coverage. Finally, the federal government assists in providing job training and low-cost public housing for the poor and educational programs for needy students.

Welfare Reform

In 1996 Congress passed and President Clinton signed a welfare reform act that ended the 61-year-old guarantee of federal cash assistance to needy families with children. (The Social Security Act of 1935 had established Aid to Families with Dependent Children, AFDC, as a federal **entitlement**, a guarantee of benefits to anyone who meets eligibility requirements set by law.)

The Welfare Reform Act replaced AFDC with a **block grant**: funds provided by the federal government to states and municipalities for a specific use. The welfare block grant, called Temporary Assistance for Needy Families, or TANF, gave money to the states and increased the states' power in administrating welfare monies.

States were given wide discretion to determine eligibility for cash assistance. But the focus of welfare reform was on "welfare to work"—moving welfare recipients off public aid and into jobs. Among major provisions of welfare reform were work requirements, restrictions on aid, Medicaid, and state flexibility.

entitlement
programs that include a guarantee of benefits to anyone who meets eligibility requirements set by law

block grant
funds provided by the federal government to states and municipalities for a specific use, such as education, transportation, or welfare

Work Requirements

Adults receiving welfare benefits are now required to begin working within two years of receiving aid. States can exempt from this work requirement a parent of a child 12 months of age or younger.

Restrictions on Aid

TANF grant funds cannot be used for adults who have *received welfare for more than five years*, although state and local funds can be used. States can exempt up to 20 percent of their caseload from this time limit. States can also opt to impose a shorter time limit on benefits. None of the funds can be used for adults who do not work *after receiving welfare for two years*. In addition, states will have the option to

- Deny welfare assistance to children born to welfare recipients.
- Deny welfare to unwed parents under age 18 unless they live with an adult and attend school.

Medicaid

States will be required to continue to offer medical coverage for one year to welfare recipients who lose their welfare benefits because of increased earnings.

State Flexibility

States are permitted to align their food stamp program with other revamped welfare programs. They can establish a single set of eligibility and work requirements for food stamps, welfare checks, and other welfare programs.

Homelessness in America

The most visible social welfare problem in America is the nation's homeless "street people," suffering exposure, alcoholism, drug abuse, crime, violence, and chronic mental illness while wandering the streets of the nation's larger cities.

homeless
persons living on street and in public places; persons accepting housing in public shelters

The term **homeless** is used to describe many different situations.[5] Street people sleep in subways, bus stations, parks, or the streets. Some of them are temporarily traveling in search of work; some have left home for a few days or are young runaways; others have roamed the streets for months or years. The sheltered homeless obtain housing in shelters operated by local governments or private charities. As the number of shelters has grown in recent years, the number of sheltered homeless has also grown. But most of the sheltered homeless come from other housing, not the streets. These are people who have been recently evicted from rental units or have previously lived with family or friends. These sheltered homeless often include families with children; the street homeless are virtually all single persons.

Street People

The ranks of the street homeless expand and contract with the seasons.[6] These homeless are difficult subjects for systematic interviewing; many do not wish to admit to alcoholism, drug dependency, or mental illness. Serious studies indicate that close to half of the street homeless are chronic alcohol and drug abusers, and an additional one-fourth to one-third are mentally ill.[7] Alcohol and drug abusers, especially "crack" cocaine users, are a large portion of the homeless, who, in recent years, have found their ranks swelled by families with unemployed or even working individuals who are victims of the recent economic downturn. While the plight of these newest members of the homeless population is likely to be temporary, the homeless substance abusers and mentally ill are likely to remain on the streets for long periods of time. It is estimated that 15 to 25 percent of the homeless are neither mentally ill nor dependent on alcohol or drugs.

Deinstitutionalization

deinstitutionalization
release of mental patients who pose no threat to others

Deinstitutionalization was a reform advanced by mental health care professionals and social welfare activists in the 1960s and 1970s to release chronic mental patients from state-run mental hospitals. It was widely recognized that aside from drugs, no psychiatric therapies have much success among the long-term mentally ill. Drug therapies can be administered on an outpatient basis; they usually do not require hospitalization. So it was argued that no one could be rightfully kept in a mental institution against his or her will; people who had committed no crimes and who posed no danger to others should be released. This argument was embraced by the Reagan administration, which saw deinstitutionalization as a way of shrinking the size of government and of saving money. The nation's mental hospitals were emptied of all but the most dangerous mental patients. The population of mental hospitals declined from about five hundred thousand in 1960 to about one hundred thousand in 1990.

Despite the commonly-held perception that the elderly are disproportionately impoverished, the reality is that children are the most likely population to live below the poverty line in the United States. Poor children, like those in this homeless family living in their car, might carry the burden of deprivation with them for their entire lifetimes.

Decriminalization

Vagrancy (homelessness) and public intoxication have been **decriminalized**. Involuntary confinement has been abolished for the mentally ill and for the substance abuser unless such a person is adjudged in court to be "a danger to himself or others." This means a person must commit a serious act of violence before the courts will intervene. For many homeless, this means the freedom to "die with their rights on." The homeless are victimized by cold, exposure, hunger, the availability of alcohol and illegal drugs, and violent street crimes perpetrated against them, in addition to the ravages of illness itself.

decriminalization
abolishing confinement for vagrancy or public intoxication of persons who pose no danger to others

Outside the Social Welfare System

Social welfare programs are frequently irrelevant to the plight of the chronic mentally ill persons and alcohol and drug abusers in the streets. Most are "uncooperative"; they are isolated from society; they have no family members, doctors, or counselors to turn to for help. The nation's vast social welfare system provides them little help. They may lose their Social Security, welfare, and disability checks because they have no permanent address. They cannot handle forms, appointments, or interviews; the welfare bureaucracy is intimidating. Welfare workers seldom provide the "aggressive care management" and mental health care that these people need.

CHAPTER SUMMARY

- The poor lack economic resources and are hence largely dependent on others for the things they need. Their lack of power derives from their dependency. But powerlessness is also an attitude, a feeling that no matter what one does it will have little effect on one's life. An attitude of powerlessness reinforces the condition of powerlessness, contributing to a sense of alienation.

- There are more than 43 million poor people (those below the official poverty level) in the United States, or over 14 percent of the population. The official poverty level is derived by calculating the minimum cash income required to maintain families of different sizes. This official definition of poverty emphasizes subsistence levels; it seeks to describe poverty objectively as the lack of enough income to acquire the minimum necessities of life.

- It is sometimes argued that the poor have a characteristic lifestyle, or culture of poverty, that assists them in adjusting to their world. Like other aspects of culture, it is passed on to future generations, setting in motion a self-perpetuating cycle of poverty.

- Today nearly one-third of the U.S. population receives some form of direct government benefit, including Social Security, Medicare or Medicaid, disability insurance, unemployment compensation, government employee retirement, veterans' benefits, food stamps, school lunches, job training, public housing, and cash public assistance payments.

KEY TERMS

alienation   a feeling of separation from society

block grant   funds provided by the federal government to states and municipalities for a specific use, such as education, transportation, or welfare

culture-of-poverty thesis   the idea that a lifestyle of poverty, alienation, and apathy is passed on from one generation to another

decriminalization   abolishing confinement for vagrancy or public intoxication of persons who pose no danger to others

deinstitutionalization   release of mental patients who pose no threat to others

entitlement   programs that include a guarantee of benefits to anyone who meets eligibility requirements set by law

homeless   persons living on street and in public places; persons accepting housing in public shelters

major public assistance in-kind programs food stamps, school lunches, Medicaid, public housing

official definition of poverty   government estimates each year of the minimum cash income required for families of various sizes to subsist

powerlessness   the inability to control the events that shape one's life

situational explanation thesis   poverty as a result of current social and economic conditions, or parental transmission of values and beliefs.

social insurance   compulsory savings for all with legal entitlement to benefits

the culture of poverty as present-orientedness the inability to plan or sacrifice for the future

TANF Temporary   Assistance for Needy Families (replaced AFDC)

ON THE WEB

EXPLORING POVERTY AND POWERLESSNESS

Visit the website for this textbook **www .cengagebrain.com** for text-specific information concerning the study of poverty and powerlessness. Many government agencies as well as private organizations maintain websites devoted to poverty and social welfare issues.

- **U.S. Department of Health and Human Services** The U.S. Department of Health and Human Services website (**www.dhhs .gov**) contains a wide variety of information on federal social welfare programs. The HHS site also includes a "health finder" gateway to health and human services information. In addition, the federal government's search engine for statistics on the Internet, Fedstats (**www .fedstats.gov**), provides an alphabetical index that includes many social welfare topics, including poverty, children, health care, and HIV/AIDS.

Try This: Go to **www.hhs.gov/safety/index .html** and read an overview of all six areas of prevention against sickness and disease. Out of these, which areas do you keep up with the best, and to which do you need to pay more attention?

- **Institute for Research on Poverty** The Institute for Research on Poverty at the University of Wisconsin is one of the nation's leading research centers focusing on the causes of poverty. Its website (**www.irp.wisc.edu**) provides up-to-date information on the characteristics of the nation's poverty population and changes over time in the poverty status of individuals and families.

Try This: Go to **www.irp.wisc.edu/research /inequality/inequalproj.htm** and read through the information found in the "Project on Inequality." What is the current outlook on health, education, and wealth inequality in our country, and what are ways in which our government is working to improve these situations?

REVIEW QUIZ

MULTIPLE CHOICE

1. A feeling of separation from society is called _____.
   a. anxiety
   b. depression
   c. alienation
   d. ennui

2. There are about _____ million poor people in the United States.
   a. 20
   b. 30
   c. 40
   d. 50

3. The _____ is derived by calculating the minimum cash income required to maintain families of different sizes.
   a. culture of poverty
   b. eligibility for Social Security benefits
   c. eligibility for Medicare benefits
   d. official definition of poverty

4. The idea that a lifestyle of poverty, alienation, and apathy is passed on from one generation is called _____.
   a. poverty orientation
   b. the generational effect
   c. the culture of poverty thesis
   d. the alienation generation thesis

5. One characteristic of the culture of poverty is _____.
   a. optimism
   b. present-orientedness
   c. planning for the future
   d. none of the above

6. The poor are disproportionately _____.
   a. female
   b. under age 18
   c. over age 65
   d. a and b

7. Major public assistance in-kind programs *do not* include _____.
   a. public housing
   b. Social Security
   c. Medicaid
   d. school lunches

8. Funds provided by the federal government to states and municipalities for a specific use, such as education, transportation, or welfare are called _____.
   a. social insurance programs
   b. block grants
   c. TANF
   d. public assistance

9. TANF funds _____.
   a. are guaranteed to unwed parents under age 18
   b. are guaranteed to children born to welfare recipients
   c. cannot be used for adults who have received welfare for more than five years
   d. a and b

10. The homeless include people living _____.
    a. on the streets
    b. in shelters
    c. in public places
    d. all of the above

FILL IN THE BLANK

11. The inability to control the events that shape one's life is called _____.

12. _____ objections to the definition of poverty include that many items considered "luxuries" are actually necessities.

13. _____ objections to the definition of poverty include that it does not include family assets.

14. Public assistance benefits are paid only to people who are _____.

15. The release of mental patients who pose no threat to others is called _____.

CHAPTER 12

Power, Violence, and Crime

Learning Objectives

After reading this chapter, students will be able to:

- Explain the main dilemma faced by a free society in protecting its citizens.
- Describe the sources of violence.
- List the types of violence the United States has seen throughout its history.
- Explain the requirements for effective deterrence of crime.

Power and Individual Freedom

For centuries people have wrestled with the question of balancing social power against individual freedom. How far can individual freedom be extended without undermining the stability of a society, threatening the safety of others, and risking anarchy? The English political philosopher Thomas Hobbes (1588–1679) believed that society must establish a powerful "Leviathan"—the state—in order to curb the savage instincts of human beings. Key to Hobbesian thought is the negative view of human nature—a nature that must be controlled by the state if anarchy is to be prevented. Thus, a powerful authority in society was needed to prevent people from attacking one another for personal gain—"war of every man against every man" in which "notions of right and wrong, justice and injustice, have no place." According to Hobbes, without law and order there is no real freedom. The fear of death and destruction permeates every act of life: "Every man is enemy to every man"; "Force and fraud are the two cardinal virtues"; and "The life of man [is] solitary, poor, nasty, brutish, and short." Freedom, then, is not the absence of law and order. On the contrary, law and order are required if there is to be any freedom in society at all.[1]

Violence in American History

Violence is not uncommon in American society. The nation itself was founded in armed revolution, and violence has been a source of power and a stimulus to social change ever since. Violence has been associated with most of the important movements in American history: the birth of the nation (revolutionary violence), the

Neville Elder/Sygma/Corbis

The terrorist attacks of September 11, 2001 marked a watershed in terms of violence in the United States. That day 2977 victims died as a result of the coordinated attacks of 19 terrorists.

freeing of the slaves and the preservation of the Union (Civil War violence), the westward expansion of the nation (Indian Wars), the establishment of law and order in frontier society (vigilante violence), the organization of the labor movement (labor–management violence), the civil rights movement (racial violence), and attempts to deal with the problems of cities (urban violence). In recent times, protection against violence in the form of terrorism and the response to terrorist violence, including the wars in Iraq and Afghanistan, have been the defining feature of domestic and foreign policy. The nature of violence is varied: History reveals that the patriot, humanitarian, pioneer, lawman, laborer, African American, and urban dweller have all used violence as a source of power. Despite pious pronouncements against it, Americans have frequently employed violence even in their most idealistic endeavors.

The Problem of Crime

In addition to the social and political violence that America has witnessed, there also has been violence in the form of crime. With criminal activity, criminals victimize individuals (and oftentimes society at large) by illegally exerting power over others, whether in the form of bodily harm or theft or destruction of property. Crime rates are the subject of a great deal of popular discussion. Very often they are employed to express the degree of social disorganization or even the effectiveness of law enforcement agencies. **Crime rates** are based on the Federal Bureau of Investigation's *Uniform Crime Reports*, but the FBI reports themselves are based on figures supplied by state and local police agencies.

crime rates
reported serious crimes per one hundred thousand people

The FBI has established a uniform classification of the number of serious crimes committed and reported to police per one hundred thousand people— murder and nonnegligent manslaughter, forcible rape, robbery, aggravated assault, burglary, larceny, and theft, including auto theft. These serious crimes are totaled and divided by the population in order to ascertain crime rates. These crimes, however, are only a small portion of all crimes (see Focus: "It's a Real Crime!").

We should be cautious in interpreting official crime rates. They are really a function of several factors: the willingness of victims to report crime to the police, the adequacy of the system for reporting and tabulating crime, and the amount of crime itself.

Changes in Crime Rates

The official FBI crime rate rose dramatically in the United States between 1960 and 1990. Increases occurred in both violent crime—murder, rape, robbery, and assault (Table 12-1)—and property crime—burglary, larceny, and theft. Certainly, some of the increase was a result of improved reporting. As more people insured their property, they filed more police reports in order to make insurance claims. The introduction of the 911 emergency phone number across the United States may also have increased reported crimes. The introduction of computers and sophisticated police data collection systems may also have contributed to the increases. But unquestionably crime itself also rose.

Since peaking in the early 1990s, however, crime rates have actually declined (Figure 12-1). Law enforcement officials attribute recent successes in crime fighting to police "crackdowns," more aggressive "community policing," and longer prison sentences for repeat offenders, including "three strikes you're out" laws. (All are discussed later in this chapter.) In support of this claim, these officials observe that the greatest reductions in crime have occurred in the nation's largest cities, especially those that have adopted tougher law enforcement practices,

TABLE 12-1 OFFENSES REPORTED TO POLICE PER ONE HUNDRED THOUSAND POPULATION

	1960	1970	1980	1985	1990	2000	2010
Violent Crimes	160	360	581	557	732	506	404
Murder	5	8	10	8	9	6	5
Forcible Rape	9	18	36	37	41	32	28
Robbery	60	172	244	209	257	145	119
Assault	85	162	291	303	424	324	252
Property Crimes	1,716	3,599	5,319	4,651	4,903	3,618	2,942

SOURCE: Federal Bureau of Investigation, *Uniform Crime Reports (annual) Crime in the United States 1991–2010*, http://www.fbi.gov/about-us/cjis/ucr/crime-in-the-u.s/2010/crime-in-the-u.s.-2010/tables/10tbl01.xls

FIGURE 12-1   VIOLENT CRIME RATES

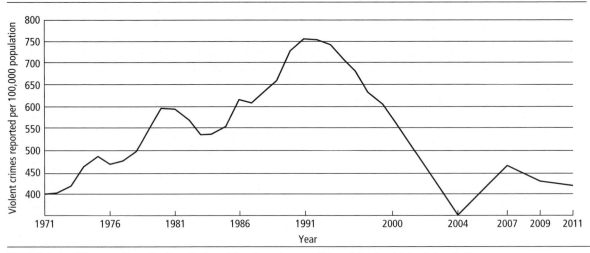

SOURCE: Federal Bureau of Investigation, Uniform Crime Reports, www.fbi.gov/about-us/cjis/ucr/crime-in-the-u.s.

such as New York City. However, the booming economy of the 1990s with low unemployment may also have contributed to the decline in crime (see Research This!). Though not shown in Figure 12-1, from 2000 through 2004, the crime rate dropped, but then began spiking higher, peaking in 2006. Since that year, the crime rate has again begun to drop. It is by no means certain that crime rates will not rise again in future years.

Victimization

How much crime is there in America today? We know that the FBI official crime rate understates the real amount of crime. Many crimes are not reported to the police and therefore cannot be counted in the official crime rate. In an effort to learn the real amount of crime in the nation, the U.S. Department of Justice regularly surveys a national sample of people, asking whether they have been the victim of a crime during the past year.[2] These surveys reveal that the **victimization rate** is many times greater than the official crime rate. The number of forcible rapes is three to five times greater than the number reported to police, the number of unreported burglaries is three times greater, and the number of robberies is over twice that of the reported rate. Only auto theft and murder statistics are reasonably accurate, indicating that most people call the police when their cars are stolen or when someone is murdered.

Why do people fail to report crime to the police? The most common reason interviewees give is the feeling that police cannot be effective in dealing with the crime. Other reasons include the feeling that the crime is "a private matter" or that the victim does not want to harm the offender. Fear of reprisal is mentioned

victimization rates
national survey responses to the question of whether one has been the victim of a crime in the past year

RESEARCH *THIS!*

The figure below shows people's responses over time to the question, "Is there any area near where you live—that is, within a mile—where you would be afraid to walk alone at night?"

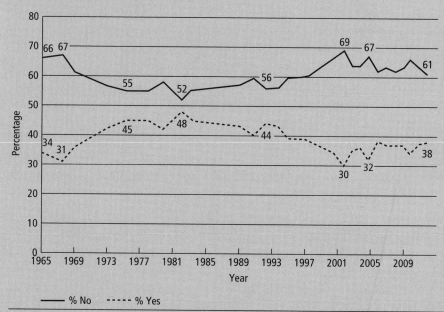

Is there any area near where you live—that is, within a mile—where you would be afraid to walk aloneat night?

SOURCE: Gallup Wellbeing Poll, www.gallup.com/poll/144272/nearly-americans-fear-walking-alone-night.aspx

YOUR ANALYSIS:

1. Describe the trend in general with people's feelings of security between 1965 and 2009. In general, does sense of security reflect the changes in national crime rates during this period?

2. During which period did people feel the most secure? What might explain this?

3. People's insecurity spiked in October, 2001. What might explain this sentiment?

much less frequently, usually in cases of assaults and family crimes. And while people are likely to report a murder, the prevalence of crimes perpetrated by people known to the victims can be seen in Figure 12-2. This figure shows that at least 44 percent of murder victims knew their murderer: in 14 percent of the cases, the murder was committed by a member of the victim's own family. In another 5 percent, a boyfriend or girlfriend was the perpetrator. Among the "other known" category, acquaintances were the most common perpetrators.

FOCUS

It's a Real Crime!

Crimes are often divided into two categories: felonies—crimes punishable by more than one year in prison—and misdemeanors—crimes punishable by less than one year. Most people who are convicted and incarcerated for a felony are sent to state prisons (or federal prison for federal felonies), but most people jailed for misdemeanors serve their sentences in city or county jails, which also hold people awaiting trial. All of the FBI uniform classified serious crimes are felonies; most other nonserious crimes are misdemeanors, although federal and most state laws define the sale and manufacturing of illegal drugs as felonies.

Serious Crimes

Serious crimes are used to calculate crime rates.

Violent Crimes

- **MURDER AND NONNEGLIGENT MANSLAUGHTER:** (a) murder and nonnegligent manslaughter (the willful killing of one human being by another); deaths caused by negligence, attempts to kill, assaults to kill, suicides, accidental deaths, and justifiable homicides are excluded; (b) manslaughter by negligence (the killing of another person through gross negligence; traffic fatalities are excluded)
- **FORCIBLE RAPE:** the penetration, no matter how slight, of the vagina or anus with any body part or object, or oral penetration by a sex organ of another person, without the consent of the victim; includes rapes by force and attempts to rape, but excludes statutory offenses (no force used and victim under age of consent)
- **ROBBERY:** the taking or attempting to take anything of value from the care, custody, or control of a person or persons by force or threat of force and/or by putting the victim in fear
- **AGGRAVATED ASSAULT:** an unlawful attack by one person upon another to inflict severe bodily injury; usually involves use of a weapon or other means likely to produce death or great bodily harm (simple assaults are excluded)

Property Crimes

- **BURGLARY:** unlawful entry, completed or attempted, of a structure to commit a felony or theft
- **LARCENY AND THEFT:** unlawful taking, completed or attempted, of property from another's possession that does not involve force, threat of force, or fraud; examples include thefts of bicycles or car accessories, shoplifting, pickpocketing

SOURCE: Federal Bureau of Investigation, *Crime in the United States, 2011,* www.fbi.gov/news/stories/2011/september/crime_091911/crime_091911

The Constitutional Rights of Defendants

Society needs the protection of police, but it is equally important in a free society to protect individuals *from* the power of the police. Arbitrary searches and arrests, imprisonment without trial, forced confessions, beatings and torture, secret trials, excessive punishments, and other human

- **MOTOR VEHICLE THEFT:** theft or attempted theft of self-propelled motor vehicle that runs on the surface and not on rails; excluded are thefts of boats, construction equipment, airplanes, and farming equipment
- **ARSON:** willful burning or attempt to burn a dwelling, public building, personal property, and so on

Other Crimes

- **SIMPLE ASSAULT:** assault and attempted assault involving no weapon and not resulting in serious injury
- **FORGERY AND COUNTERFEITING:** making, altering, uttering, or possessing, with intent to defraud, anything false in the semblance of that which is true
- **FRAUD:** fraudulent obtaining of money or property by false pretense; included are confidence games and bad checks
- **EMBEZZLEMENT:** misappropriation of money or property entrusted to one's care or control
- **STOLEN PROPERTY:** buying, receiving, and possessing stolen property, including attempts
- **VANDALISM:** willful destruction or defacement of public or private property without consent of the owner
- **WEAPONS:** carrying, possessing, and so on; all violations of regulations or statutes controlling the carrying, using, possessing, furnishing, and manufacturing of deadly weapons or silencers (attempts are included)
- **PROSTITUTION AND COMMERCIALIZED VICE:** sex offenses such as prostitution, keeping a bawdy house, or procuring, or transporting women for immoral purposes
- **SEX OFFENSES:** statutory rape and offenses against common decency, morals, and so on; excludes forcible rape and prostitution and commercial vice
- **DRUG ABUSE:** unlawful possession, sale, use, growing, and manufacturing of drugs
- **GAMBLING OFFENSES AGAINST THE FAMILY AND CHILDREN:** nonsupport, neglect, desertion, or abuse of family and children
- **DRIVING UNDER THE INFLUENCE, LIQUOR LAWS:** state/local liquor law violations, drunkenness and driving under the influence
- **DRUNKENNESS, DISORDERLY CONDUCT:** breach of the peace
- **VAGRANCY:** vagabonding, begging, loitering, and so on
- **ALL OTHER OFFENSES:** all violations of state/local laws, except as above and traffic offenses
- **CURFEW AND LOITERING LAWS:** persons under the age of 18 years old
- **RUNAWAYS:** persons under the age of 18 years old

rights violations are all too common throughout the world. The U.S. Constitution—especially the Fourth, Fifth, Sixth, and Eighth Amendments (Table 12-2)—limits the powers of police and protects the rights of accused persons.[3] It does this to protect not only the innocent but also all citizens from an all-powerful government.

FIGURE 12-2   RELATIONSHIP OF MURDER VICTIM TO OFFENDER

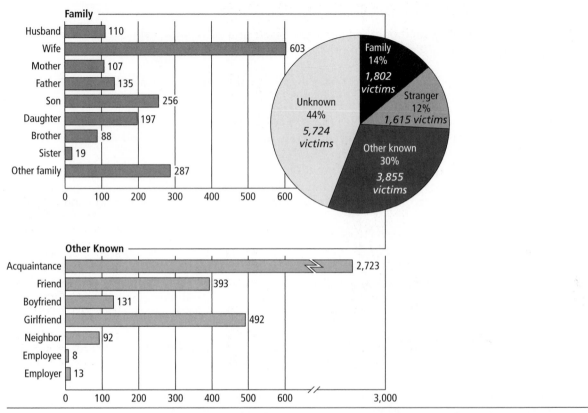

SOURCE: U.S. Department of Justice, Federal Bureau of Investigation, *Crime in the United States,* www.fbi.gov/about-us/cjis/ucr /ucr#ucr_cius

Guarantee of the Writ of Habeas Corpus

writ of habeas corpus
police may not hold a
defendant without
showing cause before a
judge

An ancient right in English common law is the right to obtain a **writ of habeas corpus**, a court order directing police who are holding a person in custody to bring the prisoner into court to explain the reasons for the confinement. Police must bring held persons before a judge as soon as possible or release them upon their written pledge to appear in court. If a judge finds that the prisoner is being unlawfully detained, or that there is not sufficient evidence that a crime has been committed or that the prisoner committed it, the judge orders the prisoner's immediate release.

Prohibition of Bills of Attainder and of Ex Post Facto Laws

bill of attainder
a legislative act that
inflicts punishment
without a trial

ex post facto law
making an act criminal
after it is committed or
retroactively increasing
punishment

A **bill of attainder** is a legislative act that inflicts punishment without a judicial trial. An **ex post facto law** is a retroactive criminal law that works to the detriment of the accused—for example, a law that makes an act a criminal one *after* the act is committed or a law that increases the punishment for

Spencer Grant/PhotoEdit

The Fourth Amendment protects individuals from unreasonable searches and seizures, but exceptions are made if the search is "incident to a lawful arrest," for the safety of police officers, for the preservation of evidence in danger of being immediately destroyed, or with the consent of the suspect.

a crime and applies it *retroactively*. Protection against bills of attainder and against ex post facto laws was, like the guarantee of habeas corpus, considered so fundamental to individual liberty that it was included in the original text of the Constitution.

Prohibition of "Unreasonable" Searches and Seizures

The Fourth Amendment protects individuals from **unreasonable search**–those without lawful warrant issued by a judge, by stating that "the right of the people to be secure in their persons, houses, papers, and effects, against **unreasonable searches and seizures** shall not be violated, and no warrants shall issue, but upon probable cause, supported by oath or affirmation, and particularly describing the place to be searched, and the persons or things to be seized." The requirement that the things to be seized must be described in the warrant is meant to prevent "fishing expeditions" into an individual's home and personal effects on the possibility that some evidence of unknown illegal activity might crop up. Exceptions to the requirement for a warrant are made if the search is "incident to a lawful arrest," for the safety of police officers, for the preservation of evidence in danger of being immediately destroyed, or with the consent of the suspect. Indeed, most police searches today take place without a warrant under one or another of these exceptions. A "lawful arrest" can be made by the police if they have "probable cause" to believe a person has committed a crime; "probable cause" has been very loosely defined by the courts.

unreasonable search
search without lawful warrant issued by a judge, unless "incident to a lawful arrest"

TABLE 12-2 CONSTITUTIONAL LIMITS ON POLICE POWERS

Criminal Justice Process	Individual Rights
Investigation by law enforcement officers Expectation that police act lawfully	Fourth Amendment: Protection against unreasonable searches and seizures Warranted searches for sworn "probable cause"; exceptions: consent searches, safety searches, car searches, and searches incident to a valid arrest; evidence "in plain view" may be seized Fifth Amendment: Protection against self-incrimination Miranda rights
Arrest Arrests based on warrants issued by judges and magistrates Arrests based on crimes committed in the presence of a law enforcement official Arrests for "probable cause"	Habeas Corpus Police holding a person in custody must bring the person before a judge with cause to believe that a crime was committed and that the prisoner committed it
Hearing and bail Preliminary hearing where prosecutor presents testimony that a crime was committed and probable cause for charging the accused	Eighth Amendment: No excessive bail Defendant considered innocent until proven guilty; release on bail and amount of bail depends on seriousness of crime, trustworthiness of defendant, and safety of community
Indictment Prosecutor, or a grand jury in federal cases, issues formal document naming the accused and specifying the charges	Fifth Amendment: Grand jury (federal) Federal prosecutors (but not necessarily state prosecutors) must convince a grand jury that a reasonable basis exists to believe that the defendant committed a crime and that he or she should be brought to trial
Arraignment Judge reads indictment to the accused and ensures that the accused understands charges and rights and has counsel Judge asks defendant to choose a plea: guilty, *nolo contendere* (no contest), or not guilty; if defendant pleads guilty or no contest, a trial is not necessary and defendant proceeds to sentencing	Sixth Amendment: Right to counsel Begins in investigation stage, when officials become "accusatory," extends throughout criminal justice process Free counsel for indigent defendants
Trial Impartial judge presides as prosecuting and defense attorneys present witnesses and evidence relevant to guilt or innocence of defendant and make arguments to the jury; jury deliberates in secret and issues a verdict	Sixth Amendment: Right to a fair, speedy and public trial Impartial jury Right to confront witnesses Right to compel favorable witnesses to testify Fourth Amendment: Exclusionary rule Illegally obtained evidence cannot be used against defendant
Sentencing If the defendant is found not guilty, the process ends; defendants who plead guilty or no contest and defendants found guilty by jury are sentenced by fine, imprisonment, or both by the judge	Eighth Amendment: Protection against cruel or unusual punishment
Appeal Defendants found guilty may appeal to higher courts for reversal of verdict or a new trial based on errors made anywhere in the process	Fifth Amendment: Protection against double jeopardy Government cannot try a defendant again for the same offense

freedom from self-incrimination

no physical or psychological force can be used to obtain a confession or incriminating evidence from a defendant

Freedom from Self-Incrimination

Although the Fifth Amendment establishes a number of procedural guarantees, including **freedom from self-incrimination**—the idea that no physical or psychological force can be used to obtain a confession or incriminating evidence from a defendant. Perhaps the most widely quoted clause of that amendment guarantees that no person "shall be compelled in any criminal case to be a witness against himself." The sentence "I refuse to answer that question on the ground that it might tend to incriminate me" is, today, a household expression. Freedom from self-incrimination has its origins in English resistance against torture and confession.

It now embodies the ideas that individuals should not be forced to contribute to their own prosecution and that the burden of proof of guilt is on the state. The constitutional protection against self-incrimination applies not only to accused persons in their own trials but also to witnesses testifying in any public proceedings, including criminal trials of other persons, civil suits, congressional hearings, or other investigations. The silence of an accused person cannot be interpreted as guilt; the burden of proving guilt rests with the prosecution.

Guarantee of a Fair Jury Trial

Trial by jury is guaranteed in both the original text of the Constitution and the Sixth Amendment: "In all criminal prosecutions, the accused shall enjoy the right to a speedy and public trial, by an impartial jury . . . and to be informed of the nature and cause of the accusation; to be confronted with the witnesses against him; to have compulsory process for obtaining witnesses in his favor. . . ." The requirement of a *speedy* trial protects the accused from long pretrial waits; but the accused may ask for postponements in order to prepare a defense. A *public* trial prevents secret proceedings, and *impartial* means that each juror must be able to judge the case objectively. Discrimination in the selection of the jury is forbidden. The guarantee of a fair trial can be violated if sensational pretrial publicity or an unruly courtroom hinders the jury from making an unbiased verdict. By tradition, a jury consisted of twelve persons, and the vote of the jurors had to be unanimous. But in *Apodaca v. Oregon*, the Supreme Court ruled that the Sixth Amendment requirement of a **twelve-person unanimous jury** applied only to federal courts, and that states are not required to mandate unanimous verdicts. Nonetheless, many states still require unanimity in most criminal cases (and in all cases where the death penalty is possible).

The **burden of proof**—that is, proof beyond a reasonable doubt—rests with the prosecution. It is up to the prosecution to convince a jury "beyond reasonable doubt" that the accused is guilty. Witnesses must appear in person against the accused. The accused or the counsel for the accused has the right to cross-examine those witnesses and may present witnesses on behalf of his or her own case. The accused may even obtain a "summons" to compel people to testify at the trial. If a guilty verdict is rendered, the defendant may appeal any errors in the trial to a higher court.

Protection against Double Jeopardy

The Fifth Amendment states: "Nor shall any person be subject for the same offense to be twice put in jeopardy of life or limb. . . ." Once a person has been tried for a particular crime and the trial has ended in a decision of not guilty, that person cannot be tried again for the same crime. However, this right of

twelve-person unanimous jury
not required in all cases; unanimity may not be required in some cases and six-person juries may also be acceptable

burden of proof
the requirement that the prosecution must prove guilt

double jeopardy
refers to a person being tried again for the same offense after being acquitted; prohibited by the Fifth Amendment

protection against **double jeopardy** does not prevent a new trial if the jury cannot agree on a verdict (a "hung jury") or if the verdict is reversed by an appeal to a higher court because of a procedural error. Moreover, an individual may be tried by federal and state courts on charges stemming from the same act. For example, National Football League star quarterback Michael Vick was indicted on federal charges for facilitating dog fighting at a home he owned in Virginia. While serving his 23-month federal prison sentence, Vick also faced state charges for dog fighting. Under a plea bargain, Vick pled guilty to one of the state charges and was given a suspended sentence. He then continued serving out his federal sentence in Leavenworth, Kansas, until his release in July 2009. Moreover, a verdict of guilt or innocence in a criminal trial does not prevent victims (plaintiffs) from suing the accused (defendants) for damages in a civil trial. For example, in 2008, financier Bernie Madoff pled guilty to eleven criminal charges stemming from his role in bilking billions of dollars from thousands of investors using a sophisticated Ponzi scheme. But Madoff also faced civil charges from those same investors, who sought not just to have the scam artist spend his life behind bars, but also to recoup some of their losses through the liquidation of his assets.

Protection against Excessive Bail and Cruel and Unusual Punishments

bail
money held by court to ensure that defendant will appear for trial

Arrested persons are considered innocent until tried and found guilty. They are entitled to go free prior to trial unless their freedom would unreasonably endanger society or unless there is reason to believe that they would not appear for trial. **Bail**, money that a defendant pays in order to guarantee their return to court to face the charges against them, does not always ensure that the accused will appear. Bail may be denied for major crimes, but most accused persons are entitled to be released on bail pending their trial. The Eighth Amendment states that bail must not be "excessive," although there are no fixed standards for determining what "excessive" is. It also prohibits "cruel and unusual punishments," but it does not define this phrase.

The Death Penalty

Opponents of the death penalty argue that it is "cruel and unusual punishment" in violation of the Eighth Amendment of the Constitution. They argue that it does not deter people from committing murder and that, as an irrevocable punishment, it does not allow for correction of injustice after an innocent person is put to death. In contrast, there is a strong sense of justice among many Americans that demands retribution for heinous crimes. Today, thirty-four states, the federal government, and the U.S. military authorize the use of the death penalty.

The U.S. Supreme Court has held that "the punishment of death does not invariably violate the Constitution." The Supreme Court first upheld the death penalty in 1976, recognizing that the writers of the Bill of Rights accepted death as a common sanction of crime.[4] The Court also recognized that more than half of the nation's state legislatures had reinstituted the death penalty since 1972. (In 1972 the Court had held that the death penalty when unfairly imposed, with some individuals receiving the death penalty for crimes for which many others were receiving lighter sentences, was unconstitutional.)[5] Moreover, said the Court, the social purposes of retribution and deterrence justify the use of the death penalty. This ultimate sanction is "an expression of society's moral outrage at particularly offensive conduct." The Court upheld the death penalty in states where the trial was a two-part proceeding, the second part of which provided the judge or jury with relevant information and standards for deciding whether to impose the death penalty. The Court approved the consideration of "aggravating and mitigating circumstances." The Court also required automatic review of all death sentences by state supreme courts to ensure that the sentences were not imposed under the influence of passion or prejudice, that aggravating factors were supported by the evidence, and that the sentences were not disproportionate to the crimes.

In 2006 the Supreme Court again upheld the death penalty in the case of *Kansas v. Marsh* by a five-to-four vote that a state court may require juries to sentence a defendant to death, even when there is an equal weight of mitigating circumstances and aggravating evidence. In this decision, the Court overturned a ruling made by the Kansas Supreme Court, which had declared the death penalty an unconstitutional violation of the Eighth Amendment's protection against cruel and unusual punishment. In the majority opinion, Justice Clarence Thomas noted, "Our precedents establish that a state enjoys a range of discretion in

AY-COLLECTION/SIPA/Newscom

Iran executed some 670 people last year in 2011, most of them for drug crimes that do not merit capital punishment under international law and more than 20 for offences against Islam. Only Iran, North Korea, and Yemen execute more people than the United States.

imposing the death penalty,"[6] thus concluding that a state may determine how mitigating circumstances, which work on the defendant's behalf, and aggravating circumstances, which work against the defendant, can be weighed. In his dissent, Justice David Souter wrote:

> a new body of fact must be accounted for in deciding what, in practical terms, the Eighth Amendment guarantees should tolerate, for the period starting in 1989 has seen repeated exonerations of convicts under death sentences, in numbers never imagined before the development of DNA tests. We cannot face up to these facts and still hold that the guarantee of morally justifiable sentencing is hollow enough to allow maximizing death sentences, by requiring them when juries fail to find the worst degree of culpability: when, by a State's own standards and a State's own characterization, the case for death is "doubtful."[7]

Today, there are over 3,200 prisoners nationwide on death row—that is, persons convicted and sentenced to death. Figure 12-3 shows that the number of people on death row grew significantly from 1980 through 2000, tapered off very slightly since 2002, and has held steady in the past several years. Approximately ten to twenty-five executions are actually carried out each year. (Figure 12-4 shows the extent to which the death penalty has been carried out in various states.) Civil rights groups have brought attention to the disproportionate extent the death penalty is used on blacks (see Figure 12-5 on page 370), which shows the sex and race of prisoners executed in the United States and their respective proportions of the population).

Concerns about the possibility of executing innocent persons have led to moratoriums on executions in some states. With the advances made in DNA testing in the past decade, the Innocence Project, a nonprofit legal clinic, has taken on death penalty cases in which post-conviction DNA can prove the convict's innocence. (See International Perspective: "The Death Penalty.")

FIGURE 12-3   DEATH ROW POPULATION, 1968-2012

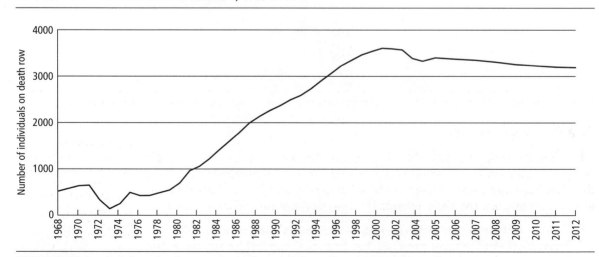

SOURCE: Death Penalty Information Center, www.deathpenaltyinfo.org/documents/FactSheet.pdf

FIGURE 12-4 MAP OF EXECUTIONS

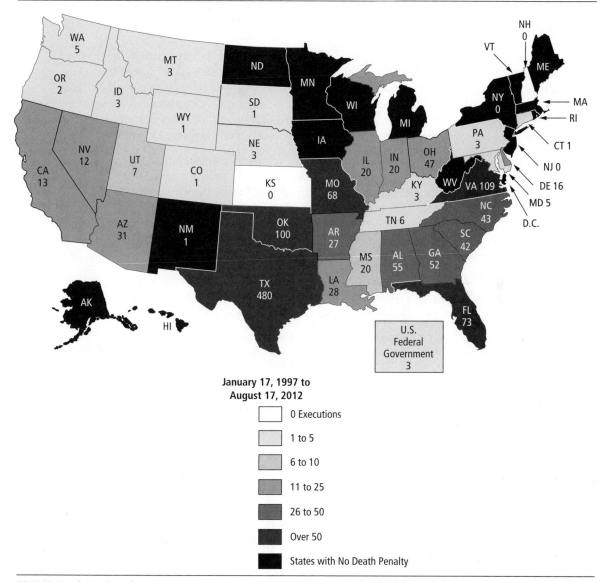

January 17, 1997 to
August 17, 2012

	0 Executions
	1 to 5
	6 to 10
	11 to 25
	26 to 50
	Over 50
	States with No Death Penalty

SOURCE: Death Penalty Information Center, www.deathpenaltyinfo.org/views-executions?order=exec_date&sort=desc

The Right to Counsel

The Sixth Amendment states "in all criminal prosecutions, the accused shall enjoy . . . the assistance of counsel for his defense." In a series of cases in the 1960s, the U.S. Supreme Court, under the leadership of Chief Justice Earl Warren, greatly strengthened the Sixth Amendment's guarantee of the **right to counsel**:

- *Gideon v. Wainwright* (1963)—Ruling that equal protection under the Fourteenth Amendment requires that free legal counsel be appointed for all indigent defendants in all criminal cases.

right to counsel
the right to an attorney
in all criminal cases right
to free counsel for
indigent defendants
counsel provided
at beginning of
investigation defendants
must be informed of
rights upon arrest

INTERNATIONAL PERSPECTIVE

The Death Penalty

The United States is the only industrialized Western democracy that executes its citizens as punishment for crimes committed (see the accompanying table). In nations where the death penalty is legal, an argument often heard in favor of the death penalty is that it deters crime. But surveys undertaken by the United Nations indicate that "it is not prudent to accept the hypothesis that capital punishment deters murder to a marginally greater extent than does the threat and application of the supposedly lesser punishment of life imprisonment."*

In 2010, at least 527 executions were carried out in 23 countries, excluding the thousands of executions that were believed to be carried out in China that year. Amnesty International, an organization that monitors executions around the world, decided not to publish minimum figures for the use of the death penalty in China, where such statistics are considered to be state secrets. Instead the organization challenged the Chinese government to publish figures for the number of people executed each year to confirm their claims that there has been a reduction in executions.

In 2010, at least 2,024 people were sentenced to die throughout the world. When excluding China, the United States ranks fourth, behind only Iran, North Korea, and Yemen in the number of confirmed executions it carried out:

COUNTRIES WITH THE MOST CONFIRMED EXECUTIONS IN 2010^

1. Iran (252+)	4. United States (46)
2. North Korea (60+)	5. Saudi Arabia (27+)
3. Yemen (53+)	

^ Excluding China, where thousands of executions are believed to have occurred.

Source: *Amnesty International: Death Sentences and Executions.* www.amnesty.org/en/library/asset/ACT50/001/2011/en/ea1b6b25-a62a-4074-927d-ba51e88df2e9/act500012011en.pdf

While several international human rights treaties—including the International Covenant on Civil and Political Rights, the American Convention on Human Rights, and the Convention on the Rights of the Child—prohibit death sentences for minors (under 18 years of age) who commit crimes, seven countries—China, the Democratic Republic of Congo, Iran, Nigeria, Pakistan, Saudi Arabia, and Yemen—execute individuals who were minors when they committed the crime for which they were sentenced to death. The U.S. Supreme Court ruled that the execution of

COUNTRIES WITH A DEATH PENALTY FOR ORDINARY CRIMES

AFGHANISTAN	GUINEA	QATAR
ANTIGUA AND BARBUDA	GUYANA	SAINT CHRISTOPHER & NEVIS
BAHAMAS	INDIA	SAINT LUCIA
BAHRAIN	INDONESIA	SAINT VINCENT & GRENADINES
BANGLADESH	IRAN	SAUDI ARABIA
BARBADOS	IRAQ	SIERRA LEONE
BELARUS	JAMAICA	SINGAPORE
BELIZE	JAPAN	SOMALIA
BOTSWANA	JORDAN	SUDAN
CAMEROON	KOREA (North)	SYRIA
CHAD	KUWAIT	TAIWAN
CHINA	LEBANON	THAILAND
COMOROS	LESOTHO	TRINIDAD AND TOBAGO
CONGO (Democratic Republic)	LIBYA	UGANDA
CUBA	MALAYSIA	UNITED ARAB EMIRATES
DOMINICA	MONGOLIA	UNITED STATES OF AMERICA
EGYPT	NIGERIA	VIETNAM
EQUATORIAL GUINEA	OMAN	YEMEN
ETHIOPIA	PAKISTAN	ZIMBABWE
GUATEMALA	PALESTINIAN AUTHORITY	

* Roger Hood, *The Death Penalty: A Worldwide Perspective*, 3rd ed. Oxford: Oxford University Press, 2002) 230.
SOURCE: Death Penalty Information Center, www.deathpenaltyinfo.org/death-penalty-international-perspective.

juveniles was unconstitutional in 2005, but between 1990 and the Court's ruling, the United States executed 19 people for crimes they committed as juveniles, some of whom were still juveniles when executed.

Opponents of the death penalty mainly cite humanitarian reasons, but concerns also have emerged about the execution of innocents. Since 1973 states have released more than 107 prisoners from death row after evidence of their innocence was presented to the courts. The problem of the potential execution of innocent convicts became so acute that in 2003, Illinois Governor George Ryan declared a moratorium on the implementation of the death penalty after 13 death row inmates were exonerated in that state. Currently more than 3,300 prisoners sit on death row in the United States.

(continued)

INTERNATIONAL PERSPECTIVE

INSTANCES OF THE DEATH PENALTY USED AGAINST CHILD OFFENDERS IN THE UNITED STATES

Name	Date of Execution	Place of Execution	Race	Age at Crime
UNITED STATES				
Charles Rumbaugh	9/11/85	Texas	White	17
J. Terry Roach	1/10/86	South Carolina	White	17
Jay Pinkerton	5/15/86	Texas	White	17
Dalton Prejean	5/18/90	Louisiana	Black	17
Johnny Garrett	2/11/92	Texas	White	17
Curtis Harris	7/1/93	Texas	Black	17
Frederick Lashley	7/28/93	Missouri	Black	17
Ruben Cantu	8/24/93	Texas	Latino	17
Chris Burger	12/7/93	Georgia	White	17
Joseph Cannon	4/22/98	Texas	White	17
Robert Carter	5/18/98	Texas	Black	17
Dwayne Allen Wright	10/14/98	Virginia	Black	17
Sean Sellers	2/4/99	Oklahoma	White	16
Douglas Christopher Thomas	1/10/00	Virginia	White	17
Steven Roach	1/13/00	Virginia	White	17
Glen McGinnis	1/25/00	Texas	Black	17
Shaka Sankofa (Gary Graham)	6/22/00	Texas	Black	17
Gerald Mitchell	10/22/01	Texas	Black	17
Napoleon Beazley	5/28/02	Texas	Black	17
T. J. Jones	8/8/02	Texas	Black	17
Toronto Patterson	8/28/02	Texas	Black	17
Scott Allen Hain	4/3/03	Oklahoma	White	17

- *Escobedo v. Illinois* (1964)—Ruling that a suspect is entitled to confer with counsel as soon as police investigation focuses on him or her, or once "the process shifts from investigatory to accusatory."
- *Miranda v. Arizona* (1966)—Ruling that police, before questioning a suspect, must inform the suspect of all his or her constitutional rights, including the right to counsel, appointed free of charge if necessary, and the right to

INSTANCES OF THE DEATH PENALTY USED AGAINST CHILD OFFENDERS INTERNATIONALLY

Country	Name of Prisoner	Year of Death	Crime (C), Sentence (S), or Execution (E)
CHINA			
	Zhao Lin	2003	16 (C), 18 (E)
DEMOCRATIC REPUBLIC OF CONGO			
	Kasongo	2000	14 (C/E)
IRAN			
	Kazeem Shirafkan	1990	17 (E)
	Male (name unknown)	1992	16 (E)
	Male (name unknown)	1992	17 (E)
	Male (name unknown)	1992	17 (E)
	Ebrahim Qorbanzadeh	1999	17 (E)
	Jasem Abrahimi	2000	17 (E)
	Mehrdad Youssefi	2001	16 (C)
	Mohammad Mohammadzadeh Mohammad A.	2004	17 (C), 21 (E)
	Alireza Mollasoltani	2010	15 (C), 17(E)
	H.B.	2011	17 (C), 17(E)
	A.N.	2011	17(C), 17 (E)
		2011	17 (C)
NIGERIA	Delara Derabi	2009	17(C)
	Chiebore Onuoha	1997	15 (C)
PAKISTAN	Name Unknown	1992	17 (E)
	Shamun Masih	1997	14 (C)
	Ali Sher	2001	13 (C)
SAUDI ARABIA			
	Sadeq Mal-Allah	1992	17 (S)
YEMEN			
	Nasser Munir Nasser al'Kirbi	1993	13 (E)

SOURCES: Amnesty International, "Indecent and Internationally Illegal: The Death Penalty Against Child Offenders," www.amnesty.org/en/library/info/AMR51/143/2002; Amnesty International, "Execution of Child Offenders – Updated Summary of Cases," www.amnesty.org/en/library/info/POL30/006/2004; The Death Penalty Information Center, and www.amnesty.org/en/news-and-updates/sharp-rise-public-executions-iran-executes-first-juvenile-offenders-2011-2011-04-27

remain silent (Figure 12-6 on page 370). Although the suspect may knowingly waive these rights, the police cannot question anyone who at any point asks for a lawyer or indicates "in any manner" that he or she does not wish to be questioned. If the police commit an error in these procedures, the accused goes free, regardless of the evidence of guilt.

FIGURE 12-5   EXECUTIONS BY RACE AND SEX, 2010

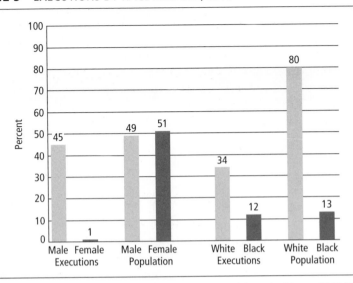

SOURCE: SOURCE: U.S. Bureau of the Census, Statistical Abstract of the United States, 2009 (Washington, DC: Government Printing Office, http://www.census.gov/compendia/statab/tables/09s0339.pdf).

The Exclusionary Rule

The exclusionary rule prevents illegally obtained evidence from being used in a criminal case. The rule, unique to the courts in the United States, was adopted by the U.S. Supreme Court in *Mapp v. Ohio* in 1961. Although illegally seized evidence may prove the guilt of the accused, it cannot be used in court, and the accused may go free because the police committed a procedural error. Many trial proceedings today are not concerned with the guilt or innocence of the

FIGURE 12-6   THE "MIRANDA CARD"

DEFENDANT	LOCATION

SPECIFIC WARNING REGARDING INTERROGATIONS

1. YOU HAVE THE RIGHT TO REMAIN SILENT.
2. ANYTHING YOU SAY CAN AND WILL BE USED AGAINST YOU IN A COURT OF LAW.
3. YOU HAVE THE RIGHT TO TALK TO A LAWYER AND HAVE HIM PRESENT WITH YOU WHILE YOU ARE BEING QUESTIONED.
4. IF YOU CANNOT AFFORD TO HIRE A LAWYER ONE WILL BE APPOINTED TO REPRESENT YOU BEFORE ANY QUESTIONING, IF YOU WISH ONE.

SIGNATURE OF DEFENDANT	DATE
WITNESS	TIME

☐ REFUSED SIGNATURE	SAN FRANCISCO POLICE DEPARTMENT	PR.9.1.4

© Cengage Learning

accused but instead center on possible procedural errors by police or prose-cutors. If the defendant's attorney can show that an error was committed, the defendant goes free, regardless of his or her guilt or innocence. Supreme Court Justice Felix Frankfurter wrote many years ago: "The history of liberty has largely been the history of procedural safeguards." These safeguards protect us all from the abuse of police powers. But Chief Justice Warren Burger attacked the exclusionary rule for "the high price it extracts from society—the release of countless guilty criminals."[8] Police and prosecutors must walk a fine line ensuring that proper procedure is used while protecting the public.

Plea Bargaining

Most convictions are obtained by guilty pleas. Indeed, about 90 percent of the criminal cases brought to trial are disposed of by guilty pleas before a judge, not trial by jury. **Plea bargaining**—in which the prosecution reduces the serious-ness of the charges, drops some but not all charges, or agrees to recommend lighter penalties in exchange for a guilty plea by the defendant—is very com-mon. Some critics of plea bargaining view it as another form of leniency in the criminal justice system that reduces the system's deterrent effects. Other critics view plea bargaining as a violation of the Constitution's protection against self-incrimination and guarantee of a fair jury trial. Prosecutors, they say, threaten defendants with serious charges and stiff penalties in order to force a guilty plea.

    The decision to plead guilty or go to jury trial rests with the defendant. A defen-dant may plead guilty and accept the certainty of conviction with whatever reduced charges the prosecutor offers, accept the prosecutor's pledge to recommend a lighter penalty, or both. Or the defendant may go to trial, confronting serious charges with stiffer penalties with the hope of being found innocent. However, the possibility of an innocent verdict in a jury trial is only one in six. This apparently strong record of conviction comes about because prosecutors have already dismissed charges in cases where the evidence is weak or illegally obtained. Thus, most defendants confront-ing strong cases against them decide to "cop a plea."

plea bargaining
criminal defendants agree to plead guilty and forgo a jury trial in exchange for reduced charges or lighter penalties

Crime and Drugs

It is difficult to estimate the various forms of drug use. According to the U.S. National Institute on Drug Abuse (NIDA), there are 12 to 14 million "problem drinkers," or about 6 percent of the population. There are an estimated 45 million cigarette smokers, or about 21 percent of the adult population (significantly less than the 45 percent of the population who smoked cigarettes in the 1940s and 1950s).[9] About 13 million people, or about 6 percent of the population, currently use illegal drugs, ranging from marijuana to cocaine and heroin. An estimated 11 million, or about 5 percent of the population, are current users of marijuana, although many more have smoked it at least once.[10] The medical evidence on the health effects of marijuana is mixed; conflicting reports have been issued about whether or not it is more dangerous than alcohol.[11] Recent referenda votes in 16 states plus the District of Columbia indicate that voters approve of the use of marijuana for therapeutic purposes, but the U.S. government still outlaws its sale.

It is difficult to estimate drug use, to measure whether it is rising or falling over time, or to assess the effectiveness of antidrug efforts. The NIDA annually surveys households in the United States, asking respondents whether they have used drugs in the past month, the past year, or ever in their lifetime. Past-month, or "current," use is the most widely cited NIDA statistic. Based on this survey evidence, overall drug use has declined over the last decade.

Drug Trafficking

Crime associated with drug trafficking is a serious national problem, whatever the health effects of various drugs. The world of drug trafficking is fraught with violence. Sellers rob and murder buyers and vice versa; neither can seek the protection of police or courts in their dealings with the other.

It is very difficult to estimate the total size of the drug market, but $30 to $40 billion per year is a common figure. This would suggest that the drug business is comparable in size to one of the ten largest U.S. industrial corporations. More important, perhaps, drugs produce huge profit margins: One kilogram of cocaine sold in Colombia may cost only $1,500; when sold in the United States, that kilogram may retail for $25,000. The price of smuggling a single, easily concealable kilogram may run to $15,000. These huge profits enable drug traffickers to corrupt police and government officials as well as private citizens in the United States and in other nations.

The War on Drugs

Federal antidrug policy can be divided into three categories: interdiction, enforcement, and education.

Interdiction

Efforts to seal U.S. borders against the importation of drugs have been frustrated by the sheer volume of smuggling. Each year increasingly larger drug shipments are intercepted by the U.S. Drug Enforcement Administration, the U.S. Customs Service, the Coast Guard, and state and local agencies. Yet, each year the volume of drugs entering the country seems to increase. Drug "busts" are considered just another cost of business to the traffickers. It is not likely that the use of U.S. military forces to augment other federal agencies can succeed in sealing our borders. American pressure against Latin American governments to destroy coca crops and assist in interdiction has already resulted in strained relationships. Our neighboring countries wonder why the U.S. government directs its efforts at the suppliers when the demand for drugs arises within the United States itself.

Enforcement

The federal Drug Enforcement Administration (DEA), together with the FBI and state and local law enforcement agencies, already devotes great effort to combating drugs; an estimated 40 percent of all arrests in the United States are drug related. Federal and state prisons now hold a larger percentage of the nation's population than ever before. Sentences have lengthened for drug trafficking, and prisons are overcrowded as a direct result of drug-related convictions. Drug testing in government and private employment is increasing, but unless it is random, it is not very useful, and some courts have prevented random testing of individuals without their consent.

Education

Efforts at educating the public about the dangers of drugs have inspired many public and private campaigns, from former First Lady Nancy Reagan's "Just Say No" to Jesse Jackson's "Up with Hope, Down with Dope," and police–community–school DARE programs. But it is difficult to evaluate the effects of these efforts. As a nation, the United States is both wealthy and free, two conditions that make it a perfect market for illicit drugs. The costs of truly effective enforcement—both in terms of dollar expenditures and, more important, in terms of lost individual liberty—may be more than our society wishes to pay.

An Economic Perspective on Crime

Crime is not only a major concern of citizens but also a topic of great interest to social scientists. Each of the social sciences brings a slightly different perspective to crime.

Economists tend to view crime as a product of people's rational calculations of the expected benefits and expected costs of criminal acts. They believe that the reason why the United States has so much crime is that crime *pays*; that is, its benefits outweigh its costs. The economic approach to criminal justice emphasizes **deterrence**—that is, convincing potential lawbreakers that the certainty and severity of punishment will impose costs on them far in excess of any benefit they might derive from criminal acts.

deterrence
making the certainty and severity of punishment so great as to inhibit potential criminals from committing crimes

Requirements for Deterrence

If law enforcement is to be a deterrent to crime, punishment must be *perceived* as (1) fairly certain, (2) swift enough to establish a link between the crime and its consequences, and (3) severe enough to outweigh the benefits of the crime. These criteria for an effective deterrent policy are ranked in the order of their probable importance. It is most important that punishment for crime is certain in the minds of potential criminals. The severity of the punishment is probably less important than its certainty or swiftness.

Questions about Deterrence

All types of crimes declined in the 1990s (see Table 12-1), though the pace of decline has slowed somewhat since 2002. It is not clear whether this decline is a product of the deterrent effect of current criminal justice policies in America or economic expansion with low unemployment that characterized the economy of much of the 1990s, or the fact that more wrongdoers are behind bars and therefore prevented from committing crimes outside prison walls. (See Controversies in Social Science: "Incarceration or Education?")

incarceration rate
the number of persons imprisoned per one hundred thousand population

The nation's **incarceration rate**—the number of people in prison per one hundred thousand people—has risen dramatically in the past decade. (Indeed, the incarceration rate nearly doubled from about 400 to 800 between 1990 and 2000.) Today it stands at 743, the highest in the world. [12] But does incarceration *deter* crime or simply *incapacitate* potential criminals?

If deterrence depends upon the *certainty* of punishment, then it is difficult to argue that deterrence is working. The likelihood of an individual's being jailed for a serious crime is less than one in a hundred. Many crimes are not even reported by the victim. Police are successful in clearing fewer than one in five reported crimes by arresting the offender. The judicial system released almost half of the persons arrested and charged; others are not prosecuted, handled as juveniles, found not guilty, or permitted to plead guilty to a lesser charge and released. Only about one-third of convicted felons are given prison sentences. Thus, the certainty of punishment for a crime in America is very low.

Finally, a great deal of crime may be "irrational"; that is, criminals do not stop to weigh benefits against potential costs before committing the criminal acts. Oftentimes, crimes are "crimes of passion" or "crimes of opportunity." Violent criminal behavior, perhaps more than property crime, often shows little sign of rational calculation.

A Psychological Perspective on Crime: The Antisocial Personality

Some crimes are committed by individuals suffering various personality disorders. These people are not "insane" (see Case Study: "The Insanity Defense"), but they exhibit long-standing patterns of maladaptive behavior—inappropriate ways of coping with stress, solving problems, and relating to others. Personality disorders may have their origin in either genetic or environmental factors.

The Antisocial Personality

antisocial personality
long-standing patterns of maladaptive behavior; lack of concern for others and no sense of guilt

Psychologists have identified an **antisocial personality** disorder that is often associated with criminal behavior. (Antisocial personalities are sometimes referred to as "psychopaths" or "sociopaths"; "pathology" is a disease leading to death.) Individuals with antisocial personalities have little sense of responsibility for their action, little concern for others, and little or no sense of morality. It can be said that they lack a conscience. They behave impulsively, they seek immediate gratification, and they cannot tolerate frustration.

The behavioral characteristics used to identify the antisocial personality are (1) a lack of empathy and concern for others and (2) a lack of shame or guilt or remorse for their own actions however harmful they may be. Antisocial personalities sometimes develop in children who first show signs of **attention deficit disorder (ADD)**, which is diagnosed when children have significant problems in maintaining attention and consistently display impulsive uncontrolled behavior. Their disruptive behavior may lead to rejection by teachers, playmates, and

attention deficit disorder (ADD)
difficulty maintaining attention; impulsive, uncontrolled behavior

CONTROVERSIES IN SOCIAL SCIENCE

Incarceration or Education?

Many people believe that the rate of crime in the United States has been reduced because the number of people incarcerated in jails or prisons has increased. But as the number of prisoners has increased, so too have the number of prisons, though many remain woefully overcrowded. Nonetheless, on average, it costs states $29,000 annually to house, feed, clothe, and keep an inmate in a state prison.

And although there is a great deal of variation among states (in California, for example, the annual cost is $44,563) in average per prisoner expenditures, the average cost in each state rivals the cost of tuition, room, and board at a college in that state. Nationally, in-state tuition (without room and board) at a four-year public college or university cost an average of $9,000 in 2011.

It is unrealistic to believe that states could send violent criminals to colleges or universities, and many convicts lack the necessary basic skills that are required for successful college work. Nonetheless, some argue that nonviolent first-time offenders often are corrupted by the state prison experience where they learn behaviors and skills from hardened criminals. These convicts then are disadvantaged when released from prison with their criminal record, thus increasing the chances that they will again commit crime, oftentimes more serious than their first offense.

And so the controversy is: Would some convicts benefit themselves and society more if they were sentenced to an education rather than a state prison?

even parents, thus leading to even more disruptive and aggressive behavior and eventually antisocial personality disorder.

Genetic Explanations

A genetic cause of antisocial personality disorder is revealed in studies of criminal behavior across generations and among identical twins. For example, the criminal records of adopted sons have been found to be more similar to the record of their biological fathers than their adoptive fathers. The criminal records of identical twins are much closer to each other than those of fraternal twins.

Environmental Influences

Not all children with genetic predisposition to antisocial personality disorder or to criminal behavior develop these characteristics. Parental conduct is a better predictor of the emergence of antisocial personality than genetics. Disruptive children who are unsupervised or poorly supervised are much more likely to develop a pattern of delinquent behavior than children of parents who are involved in their everyday life. Parents who closely monitor ADD and intervene consistently to overcome it can help children avoid the development of antisocial and criminal behaviors.

Genetic and environmental factors often combine to cause antisocial personality disorder. Maternal drug use, maternal exposure to toxic agents, and low birth weight are associated with childhood problems of irritability, impulsiveness, inattention, and slow learning. These children are difficult to care for and they are at risk for abuse and neglect. Both genetic and adverse home factors tend to contribute to aggressive behaviors in children, especially hitting.

Social and Cultural Perspectives on Crime

deviance
the failure to conform to social norms

Sociologists view crime as a form of **deviance**—the failure to conform to social norms. Deviance may range from the trivial (vulgar language) to the acute (serial murders). Not all deviance involves lawbreaking. Although norms may differ from one society to another, all societies have norms, and all societies impose some forms of punishment on those who violate norms. Not all sociologists who study deviance focus on crime (**criminology**), but those who do are generally referred to as criminologists.[13]

criminology
the scientific study of crime, criminals, and punishment

A sociological perspective on crime emphasizes its presumed "root causes"—poverty, unemployment, lack of opportunity, inequality, and discrimination. It shows how crime rates vary with gender, race, age, mobility, and other social characteristics of populations.

CASE STUDY

The Insanity Defense

In January 2010, Jared Loughner walked into a Safeway supermarket in Tucson, Arizona, where Rep. Gabrielle Giffords (D-AZ) was holding a "Congress on Your Corner" meeting with constituents. Loughner opened fire, shooting Giffords, the apparent target, in the head and killing six others. (Giffords survived but was severely injured.) Loughner pleaded not guilty to 49 charges and was forcibly medicated with psychotropic drugs at a Missouri prison in an effort to make him mentally competent to stand trial. After his arrest, evidence of his mental instability—including a suspension from a community college unless Loughner was able to obtain a mental health clearance—became apparent.

How should society deal with a mentally ill person who commits a crime? Should the mentally ill be held responsible for their actions in the same fashion as everyone else? Or should criminal law recognize that the mentally ill may not be able to control their conduct?

In an historic nineteenth-century case, a mentally ill Scotsman, Daniel M'Naghten, attempted to assassinate the English Prime Minister Robert Peel but instead shot his secretary. The trial judge was convinced by M'Naghten's senseless rambling and paranoid delusions that the defendant was insane, and he was sent to a mental hospital. But Queen Victoria was unsatisfied with the verdict; she asked the House of Lords to

On January 8, 2011, Rep. Gabrielle Giffords and eighteen other people were shot during a public meeting held in a supermarket parking lot near Tucson, Arizona. Jared Lee Loughner was arrested and charged with five separate offences. Loughner had been suspended by his college for disruptive behavior and was deemed to be mentally incompetent to stand trial.

review the decision. This resulted in the *M'Naghten Rules*—that a defendant may be found not guilty by reason of insanity if he did not know at the time what he was doing or did not know that what he was doing was wrong.

Later, American courts expanded on the M'Naghten Rules, holding that people are not responsible for a crime if, as a result of a mental disease or defect, they lack the capacity to appreciate the wrongfulness of their conduct or the ability to conform their conduct to the law. The word *appreciate* is considered a looser term than *know* in the original M'Naghten rule, implying that the defendant must have some understanding of the moral and legal consequences of his or her behavior.

Perhaps the most publicized successful insanity defense in American history was that of John Hinckley Jr. Accused in a Washington, DC, court of attempting to assassinate President Ronald Reagan in 1981, Hinckley was found not guilty by virtue of insanity. Many Americans were outraged by the verdict, and the insanity defense came under attack in Congress. Congress responded by enacting the Insanity Defense Reform Act of 1984, designed to make it more difficult to successfully employ the insanity defense.

The act stipulates that the defendant's mental disease or defect must be "severe" in order to avoid guilt. The intent is to exclude nonpsychotic disorders such as antisocial personality. The act also shifted the burden of proof of insanity to the defendant; the prosecution need not prove that the person was sane beyond a reasonable doubt. And the defendant must prove insanity with "clear and convincing evidence." Some states have adopted the use of the verdict "guilty but mentally ill." This verdict may be rendered when the jury decides that a mental disorder significantly impacted the judgment of the defendant at the time of the crime or his or her capacity to recognize reality. The verdict allows a judge to impose a sentence that may be served either in a mental hospital or in prison or both. The intent is to keep dangerous mentally ill people off the streets.

(continued)

Mental illness also intrudes into the criminal justice process early in the legal process when a judge declares that a defendant is not mentally competent to stand trial. After reviewing the psychological evidence, a judge may determine that a defendant is not competent to stand trial if he or she cannot understand the charges and cannot cooperate with a lawyer in preparing his or her defense. The judge's decision is based on the constitutional right to a fair trial; it is separate from the question of whether the defendant was insane at the time the crime was committed. The judge may drop criminal charges and commit the person to a psychiatric facility. Psychiatrists can later release the person after determining that he or she is no longer mentally incompetent.

Defendants have a better chance of convincing a judge that they are incompetent to stand trial than they have to convince a jury that they are not guilty by reason of insanity. Most juries hold individuals responsible for their criminal acts. Less than 1 percent of defendants charged with serious crimes are found not guilty by reason of insanity. Most defense attorneys consider the insanity defense a last resort.

Crime and Gender

Crime rates for women are much lower than those for men. Men account for about 80 percent of violent crime and 62 percent of property crime. [14] Sociologists offer a variety of explanations for this differential: Males are socialized to be active, assertive, and dominant—traits conducive to criminal behavior—whereas females are socialized to be more gentle and nurturing. Parents often impose a "double standard" of morality, monitoring their daughters' behavior more closely than their sons', providing more opportunities for males to commit crimes. Some research indicates that girls feel more strongly attached to families than boys and are more likely to value their parents' norms. If men's crime rates were as low as women's, crime in the United States would not be a major social problem.

Crime and Race

Crime disproportionately victimizes the poor and African Americans. A black male is almost eight times more likely to be murdered than a white male. The poor and black are also disproportionately represented among persons arrested and sentenced for crime. Blacks comprise 13 percent of the nation's population yet comprise 28 percent of all arrests for serious crimes, 47 percent of state prison inmates, 42 percent of prisoners under sentence of death, and 35 percent of all people executed.

There are a variety of sociological explanations of racial differences on crime statistics, all of them controversial. (Indeed, some social scientists and some texts avoid mentioning these statistics or discussing possible explanations for them.) The higher rate of father-absent households among African American families may result in less supervision and discipline of young males and fewer positive role models. Economic deprivation and conditions in inner-city neighborhoods where African Americans are concentrated are frequently cited as contributing to higher crime rates. Some research indicates that prejudice may factor into the disproportionately higher rate of black executions: One study indicated that stereotypically "black-looking" defendants are more likely to get the death penalty than their lighter-skinned African American counterparts.[15]

Age and Crime

Crime is closely related to age. Crime is primarily a young man's activity. Men between the ages of 16 and 34 years old commit three-quarters of the crimes in the nation. As people age, their likelihood of committing a crime drops significantly, and the elderly are the least likely group to commit crimes.

Sociologists cite a variety of factors influencing the "crime-prone" age group: Peer influences and the urge to assert independence are greatest among adolescents. Young men who have not yet acquired full-time jobs or gotten married or fathered children are less likely to have acquired a stake in conformity to social norms. Maturity usually brings greater control over one's compulsions. Risk-taking behavior becomes less attractive. Sociologists note that all other things being equal, an increase or decrease in the proportion of the population in the most crime-prone category of 16 to 25 years of age should result in increases and decreases in crime.

Subcultural Explanation

Crime is much more prevalent in urban areas. One explanation for the concentration of crime in the inner-city centers on the subculture of the streets.[16] A disproportionate number of female-headed households among poor black families inspire young males to seek masculine identities through peer-group associations in gangs. The gangs develop a subculture of "toughness," exaggerated masculinity, demands for respect, and danger and thrill seeking. These values lead young males to respond violently to remarks, gestures, and actions that most others would ignore. A reputation for violence brings respect, and symbols of violence, including guns, are marks of distinction. Arrest and imprisonment is sometimes regarded as a "coming of age." At the same time, these young males aspire to the wealth and material well-being of the larger culture. But economic opportunities are limited; drugs are a thriving business in the streets, and drug dealers provide role models. The gap between aspirations and opportunities creates the frustration that leads to crime.

But the problem with the criminal subculture thesis is that *most young males in the inner city do not turn to violence or crime.* While crime rates can be correlated with poverty, unemployment, age, and race, these conditions quite obviously do not cause crime, inasmuch as the majority of poor, unemployed, young, and black do *not* have criminal records. The overwhelming majority of children raised in single-parent households turn out to be law-abiding citizens. Sociological and cultural perspectives on crime, while helpful in identifying the factors associated with high crime rates and "deviant" behavior, fail to provide a policy remedy.[17]

CHAPTER SUMMARY

- In general, most types of crime have decreased in recent years. There are various explanations for this, including the high rate of incarceration.
- Constitutional protections guaranteed for criminal defendants include the writ of habeas corpus, prohibitions against bills of attainder, ex post facto laws, unreasonable searches and seizures, freedom from self-incrimination, guarantee of a fair jury trial, protection against double jeopardy, and protection against excessive bail and cruel and unusual punishment, though the death penalty is still used in the United States. Defendants also enjoy the right to counsel, and evidence collected must be obtained legally.

- Crime associated with the use and distribution of illegal drugs constitutes a large part of criminal activity in the United States. Interdiction, enforcement, and education are the primary components of federal anti-drug policy.
- Among the perspectives of social scientists on crime, economists oftentimes view crime as the result of a rational calculation, and stress deterrence as a means of combating crime.
- Psychological perspectives on crime include focus on the antisocial personality, genetic explanations, and environmental influences.
- Sociological and anthropological explorations on crime evaluate deviance and subculture as well as the demographic characteristics—including the age, race, and gender—of criminals.

KEY TERMS

antisocial personality long-standing patterns of maladaptive behavior; lack of concern for others and no sense of guilt

attention deficit disorder (ADD) difficulty maintaining attention; impulsive, uncontrolled behavior

bail money held by court to ensure that defendant will appear for trial

bill of attainder a legislative act that inflicts punishment without a trial

burden of proof the requirement that the prosecution must prove guilt

crime rates reported serious crimes per one hundred thousand people

criminology the scientific study of crime, criminals, and punishment

deterrence making the certainty and severity of punishment so great as to inhibit potential criminals from committing crimes

deviance the failure to conform to social norms

double jeopardy refers to a person being tried again for the same offense after being acquitted; prohibited by the Fifth Amendment

ex post facto law making an act criminal after it is committed or retroactively increasing punishment

freedom from self-incrimination no physical or psychological force can be used to obtain a confession or incriminating evidence from a defendant

incarceration rate the number of persons imprisoned per one hundred thousand population

plea bargaining criminal defendants agree to plead guilty and forgo a jury trial in exchange for reduced charges or lighter penalties

right to counsel the right to an attorney in all criminal cases right to free counsel for indigent defendants counsel provided at beginning of investigation defendants must be informed of rights upon arrest

twelve-person unanimous jury not required in all cases; unanimity may not be required in some cases and six-person juries may also be acceptable

unreasonable search search without lawful warrant issued by a judge, unless "incident to a lawful arrest"

victimization rates national survey responses to the question of whether one has been the victim of a crime in the past year

writ of habeas corpus police may not hold a defendant without showing cause before a judge

ON THE WEB

EXPLORING POWER, VIOLENCE, AND CRIME

The website for this textbook (**www.cengagebrain.com**) offers resources for exploring power, crime, and violence on the Internet. Other websites to check out are those of U.S. government agencies that compile extensive material on crime, drugs, courts, and prisons. All major crime-fighting agencies have their own websites, including the U.S. Department of Justice; the Federal Bureau of Investigation; the Office of Homeland Security; the Bureau of Alcohol, Tobacco and Firearms; and the Office of National Drug Control Policy. Visit **www.cengagebrain.com**.

The following are good websites to start with:

- **U.S. Bureau of Justice Statistics** Perhaps the most informative criminal justice website is that maintained by the Bureau of Justice Statistics (**www.ojp.usdoj.gov/bjs**). It includes data on characteristics of victims, criminal sentencing by courts, prison populations, and persons on probation and parole.

  Try this: Go to **bjs.ojp.usdoj.gov/fjsrc/tsec.cfm** start exploring Bureau of Justice Statistics by choosing "Mean prison or probation sentence, or fine amount, for defendants convicted" under "Select a statistic." Then input a year, and choose a title and section of the U.S. Code. You will then see the average sentence and number of people convicted of this crime. Compare years, and come up with a few theories that could explain the cause of the changing statistics.

- **FBI** The Federal Bureau of Investigation's website (**www.fbi.gov**) is frequently accessed for information on current topics in national crime fighting. The FBI's "Ten Most Wanted" page includes names and photos of fugitives. But perhaps its most important data are the *Uniform Crime Reports*, which provide up-to-date police reporting of various types of violent and property crimes.

  Try this: Go to **www.fbi.gov/about-us/investigate/what_we_investigate** and scan the varying roles of the FBI. Pick one category and examine in depth the role of the FBI in that particular area of crime, their history of crime-fighting within that area, and examples of ongoing or solved cases.

REVIEW QUIZ

MULTIPLE CHOICE

1. The FBI's classification of serious crimes *does not* include _____.
   a. criminal homicide
   b. forcible rape
   c. robbery
   d. vigilante violence

2. The principle that police may not hold a defendant without showing cause before a judge is known as _____.
   a. the Fifth Amendment right
   b. *habeas corpus*
   c. *carpe diem*
   d. Miranda rights

3. A legislative act that inflicts punishment without a trial is called _____.
   a. *habeas corpus*
   b. a bill of attainder
   c. an ex post facto law
   d. double jeopardy

4. Making an act criminal after it is committed or retroactively increasing punishment is called _____.
   a. *habeas corpus*
   b. a bill of attainder
   c. an ex post facto law
   d. double jeopardy

5. Money held by a court to ensure that a defendant will appear for trial is called _____.
   a. a bill of attainder
   b. court insurance
   c. bail
   d. *quid pro quo*

6. The right to counsel *does not* include _____.
   a. the right to an attorney in all criminal and civil cases
   b. the right to free counsel for indigent defendants
   c. that counsel must be provided at the beginning of an investigation
   d. that defendants must be informed of rights upon arrest

7. Aspects of the United States' antidrug policy *do not* include _____.
   a. acquiescence
   b. interdiction
   c. enforcement
   d. education

8. The idea of making the certainty and severity of punishment so great as to inhibit potential criminals from committing crimes is called _____.
   a. deterrence
   b. interdiction
   c. plea bargaining
   d. incarceration

9. Characteristics of a fair jury trial *do not* include _____.
   a. fairness
   b. speediness
   c. impartiality
   d. a jury of nine peers

10. The death penalty is disproportionately used on _____.
    a. women
    b. juveniles
    c. African Americans
    d. individuals with intellectual disabilities

FILL IN THE BLANK

11. The idea that law is required to protect individual freedom and governments are formed for collective self-protection was asserted by _____.

12. _____ are reported serious crimes per one hundred thousand people.

13. The Fifth Amendment guarantees protection against _____.

14. The burden of proof on the prosecution is _____.

15. Criminal defendants agreeing to plead guilty and forgo a jury trial in exchange for reduced charges or lighter penalties is called _____.

ANSWER KEY:

1. d; 2. b; 3. b; 4. c; 5. c; 6. a; 7. a; 8. a; 9. d; 10. c; 11. Thomas Hobbes; 12. Crime rates; 13. self-incrimination; 14. beyond a reasonable doubt; 15. plea bargaining.

CHAPTER 13

Power and the Global Community

Learning Objectives

After reading this chapter, students will be able to:

- Describe how poverty manifests itself in terms of hunger and disease.
- Understand recent trends regarding population growth and urbanization.
- Explain how poverty and population trends shape the exercise of power in the global community.

The Global Community

Globalization is an indisputable phenomenon of modern times. Globalization takes on many forms: increasing communication between individuals across the globe using cellular and Internet technologies, international tourism among individuals, growth in multinational corporations, the increasing presence of international nongovernmental organizations, increases in trade between nations, cooperation in international law enforcement, and the presence and increased influence of international media sources.

Throughout the world, the exercise of power necessarily takes place within a global context. Although power is exerted in families, in the workplace, and by governments, an important context in which power relations occur is the global community. Power is exercised by governments in relation to one another, as we will discuss in Chapter 14. But the global social, political, and economic context within which power relations occur is equally important. Comparatively speaking, people in different areas of the world have, in general, different levels of power at their disposal. The circumstances of one's birth play an important role in determining the structure of one's life. Whether an individual will have to compete with others for scarce resources, struggle to make a living, have access to adequate nutrition, health care, and educational opportunities, and enjoy personal freedoms and liberties are the result of the exercise of power by others and a factor in determining the extent of that individual's power. This chapter examines these issues—including modernization; the problems of poverty, hunger, and lack of personal freedom; the role of technology in increasing global connectedness; and the growing worldwide population—in an effort to examine the influences that shape individuals' exercise of power.

Globalization in Perspective

modernization theory
posits that the
industrialized nations
of the West play a
strategic role in
"developing" the
underdeveloped world

In analyzing globalization, two distinct theoretical ideas emerge regarding its nature. The first is **modernization theory** (sometimes called development theory), which posits that the industrialized nations of the West play a strategic role in "developing" the underdeveloped world. Modernization theory, which emerged after World War II, is based in ideas surrounding colonization. Modern nations, theorists assert—with industrialized economies, democratic systems of government, and modern culture and values—guide the way for less-developed countries (LDCs) to develop. In the 1950s, modernization theorists argued that mass electronic media would play an important role in demonstrating Western values that could then be adopted by those in the *second world* (then the communist nations) and the *third world* (LDCs). Today, modernization theorists argue that innovations in cellular technology, increases in international travel, and the Internet all contribute to better understanding of the merits of development and strategies for attaining it by underdeveloped nations.

Modernization theory was not (and is not) without its critics. Despite the obvious benefits of modernization—improved quality of life, greater life expectancy, increased political and cultural liberty, and improved economies both for individuals and nations—modernization spawned criticism. Specifically, scholars who developed **dependency theory** argued that the process of modernization came at a price: Modernization exploited both individuals within industrialized economies and LDCs on the whole. Dependency theorists argue that modernization occurs because of the toils of those exploited within the Western world and because of the exploitation of cheap labor and natural resources in the developing world.

dependency theory
argues that modern-
ization exploits both
individuals within indus-
trialized economies and
LDCs on the whole

Among the first social scientists to espouse dependency theory was Raul Prebisch, who analyzed the relationship between rich and poor nations. Prebisch argued that poor nations were being exploited by modernized nations, as his research indicated that poor nations became poorer when rich nations became richer. Prebisch's ideas were expanded upon by Andre Gunder Frank. Frank noted the similarities between dependency theory's ideas of modernized economies exploiting poorer ones and Marx's ideas of the capitalist class exploiting the labor of the working class (see Chapter 3, "Power and Ideology," for a more detailed explanation of Marx's ideas).

Other criticisms of modernization theory posit that it is ethnocentric in its worldview, idealizing the qualities of Western modern life over those of other cultures. One critic of dependency theory took issue with the duality of dependency. Sociologist Immanuel Wallerstein instead argued a **world systems theory**, asserting that the core wealthy nations of the world rely on a peripheral group of poorer countries in order to remain wealthy, but that some states act as both core and periphery in a world system economy.

world systems theory
asserts that the core
wealthy nations of the
world rely on a periph-
eral group of poorer
countries in order to
remain wealthy, but that
some states act as both
core and periphery in a
world system economy

The Global Problem of Poverty

Modernization theorists, dependency theorists, and world system theorists would disagree concerning the causes and nature of poverty. Modernization theorists would argue that poverty exists because LDCs have not yet developed, but poverty can be significantly reduced in those nations that follow the lead of the industrialized Western world and modernize. Dependency theorists would argue that poverty is the result of the bimodal nature of development that creates "haves" and "have-nots." World systems theorists would assert that poverty in peripheral nations is the result of their exploitation by core nations. Despite these differences, all would agree that poverty is the defining problem for most of the world's population.

From the problem of poverty emerges nearly all other social ills: disease, hunger, lack of opportunity, crime and violence, drug trafficking and use, prostitution, and on and on. As discussed in Chapter 11, poverty contributes to powerlessness. Extreme poverty is commonplace in the world, affecting 23 percent of the world's people. **Extreme income poverty**, defined as earning $1.25 per day or less, can be found in East Asia, Africa, and South America (see Focus: "The Least-Developed Countries"). Worldwide, the United Nations estimates that 421 million people in developing countries live in extreme poverty. The incidence of extreme poverty was significantly higher in African LDCs, where 59 percent of the population lives in extreme poverty. In sub-Saharan Africa, half of the employed workforce earns less than $1 per day.[1] The impact of this is clear: Each year, millions of children die preventable deaths because of a lack of potable water, housing, nutrition, vaccinations against common illnesses, or adequate medical care.

extreme income poverty earning less than $1.25 per day

Poverty is not just an issue in developing countries because extreme poverty exists in even the richest countries, including the United States. In industrialized societies, the conditions of the poorest people tend to be better than the poor in the developing world. But indicators of poverty, including poverty rates, unemployment rates, and income inequality statistics demonstrate the presence of a category of the poor in industrialized societies that appears to have been worsening in recent years. United Nations data indicate that most industrial countries have seen rising income inequalities, growing poverty rates, and increases in long-term unemployment.

In Chapter 11, we discussed the impact that poverty has on power in America. The dire implications concerning power among the world's poor should be evident when we compare the standards for poverty in the United States with the LDCs.

The Global Problems of Hunger and Malnourishment

The problems of hunger and malnutrition are directly related to the problem of poverty and contribute to individuals' powerlessness in a most basic way. Without proper nutrition, humans cannot function effectively. When individuals must focus on acquiring scarce food, they necessarily must forgo focusing on other areas that could maximize their potential, whether that is in the workforce, in political life, or in school. Individuals who suffer from undernourishment in the long term may suffer from stunted physical and mental development and are at increased risk for many diseases. When pregnant women face undernourishment, they place themselves and their babies at risk and increase the

FOCUS

The Least-Developed Countries

Those living in the least developed countries in the world comprise more than 880 million people (about 12 percent of world population), but account for less than 2 percent of world GDP. As discussed in Chapter 8, the per capita gross domestic product (GDP) in the United States is about $47,000. In nearly fifty countries, the GDP is $750 or less (see the accompanying table). But income as measured by the GDP is only one measure of development. The United Nations designates countries as the least-developed countries (LDCs) using several additional criteria. One is the availability of human resources (measured by a composite index called the Human Assets Index [HAI], which measures the availability of human assets including nutrition, health, education, and adult literacy, as shown in the accompanying figure). The HAI measures qualities like life expectancy at birth, per capita calorie intake, combined primary and secondary school enrollment, and adult literacy rates.

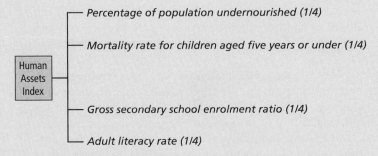

Numbers in parenthesis indicate the weight in the overall HAI.

The United Nations also uses another measure to determine LDC status. This measure is the Economic Vulnerability Index (EVI), which analyzes the stability of a nation's economy in determining whether that nation is economically vulnerable. The EVI consists of

- The instability of agricultural production.
- The instability of exports of goods and services.
- The economic importance of nontraditional activities (share of manufacturing and modern services in GDP).
- Merchandise export concentration.
- The handicap of economic smallness.
- Percentage of population displaced by natural disasters.

THE LEAST-DEVELOPED COUNTRIES IN THE WORLD (IN ALPHABETICAL ORDER)

Africa (33)

1	Angola		18	Madagascar
2	Benin		19	Malawi
3	Burkina Faso		20	Mali
4	Burundi		21	Mauritania
5	Central African Republic		22	Mozambique
6	Chad		23	Niger
7	Comoros		24	Rwanda
8	Democratic Republic of the Congo		25	São Tomé and Príncipe
9	Djibouti		26	Senegal
10	Equatorial Guinea		27	Sierra Leone
11	Eritrea		28	Somalia
12	Ethiopia		29	Sudan
13	Gambia		30	Togo
14	Guinea		31	Uganda
15	Guinea-Bissau		32	United Republic of Tanzania
16	Lesotho		33	Zambia
17	Liberia			

Asia (14)

1	Afghanistan		8	Nepal
2	Bangladesh		9	Samoa
3	Bhutan		10	Solomon Islands
4	Cambodia		11	Timor-Leste
5	Kiribati		12	Tuvalu
6	Lao People's Democratic Republic		13	Vanuatu
7	Myanmar		14	Yemen

Latin America and the Caribbean (1)

1	Haiti

SOURCE: www.unohrlls.org/en/ldc/25/

FIGURE 13-1   WORLDWIDE DISTRIBUTION OF UNDERNOURISHED PEOPLE

No Data   < 5%   5%–15%   15%–25%   25%–35%   >35%

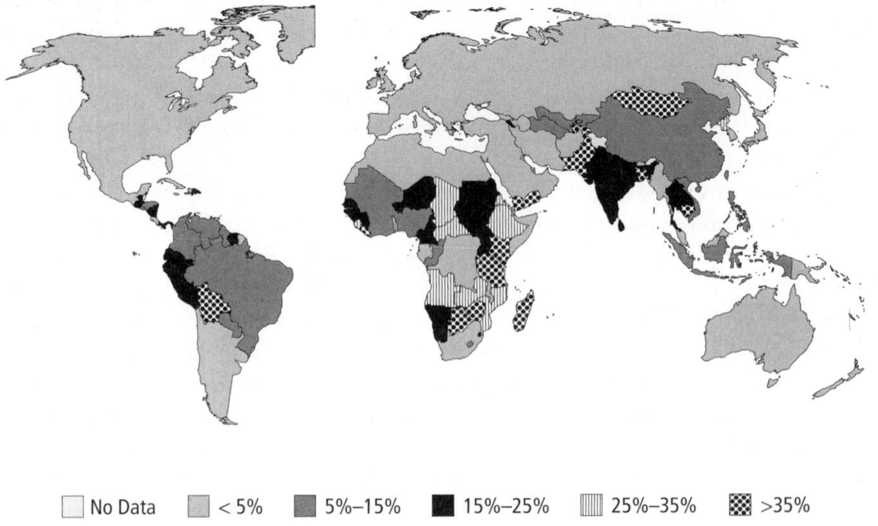

Source: The map can be accessed at the following URL: http://www.mdgmonitor.org/map.
cfm?goal=&indicator=&cd=© Copyright United Nations Development Programme, 2007. All Rights
Reserved. Reprinted by permission.

chances that their infant will be stillborn or suffer from birth defects or disease after birth.

The UN Food and Agriculture Organization estimates that more than one billion people are hungry, while another two billion are undernourished. An estimated 25,000 people a day die of hunger or hunger-related diseases, or about 10 million people per year.[2] Figure 13-1 shows the distribution of undernourished people throughout the world. Clearly, South Asia and the continent of Africa suffer the most from malnourishment. In fact, two-thirds of the world's hungry population lives in just seven countries in those areas: Bangladesh, China, the Democratic Republic of the Congo, Ethiopia, India, Indonesia, and Pakistan. Over 40 percent of the world's hungry live in China or India alone. Industrialized nations see comparatively little malnourishment. Yet remarkably, an estimated 10 million people in industrialized countries do suffer from inadequate nutrition.[3] This is in spite of the voluminous consumption of calories in the industrialized world—in many industrialized nations, daily caloric consumption exceeds 3,400 calories (on average, about 1,930 calories are required for adequate nutrition).

The problem of hunger has numerous causes, both natural and human-made. The most common cause of hunger is drought. In 2009, the global financial crisis meant that the price of food (including the cost of transporting it) increased, and those cost increases have made food less available to the world's poorest citizens. The lack of water, particularly in Africa, limits the crops that will grow. But in times where water is relatively plentiful, another threat to successful crops emerges: locusts. Such was the case in 2004 when favorable weather conditions caused locust infestation in many parts of Northern Africa. However, drought does not necessarily protect farmers from the crop-decimating bug: Desert locusts manage to survive in environments that kill other crop threats. Besides droughts and locusts causing crop failure, they also impact the availability of food in other ways. Both kill grazing grass, which limits the ability of herders to feed livestock. Disease also can cause food scarcity. Such was the case in 2012 in the Democratic Republic of the Congo (DRC) when a devastating livestock disease, peste des petits ruminants, killed over a hundred thousand goats and sheep, which threatened food security in that country and also threatened to spill-over into adjacent southern African nations. Other environmental situations such as floods, fires, monsoons, and frosts also can damage crops and make food scarce in a region. Such was the case with the 2004 tsunami in the Indian Ocean that killed nearly a quarter million people, displaced an estimated 1.5 million, and caused billions of dollars in property damage. The tsunami and other natural disasters impact the availability of food for several reasons. First, natural disasters destroy crops and food supplies (like livestock and fish). Second, disasters often interfere with fragile economies in the short term: the destruction of infrastructure—roads, bridges, and ports—means that foodstuffs cannot be transported to locations where they are needed. Finally, disasters often cause irrevocable long-term damage in LDCs where small farms, food-processing plants, and other businesses are less likely to have the resources to rebuild after a disaster.

Human-made situations—including war and instability, the political structure, and economic systems—can interfere with the marketing and distribution of food (see Focus: "Afghanistan"). Such is the case, for example, in the Sudan. Civil war in this African nation has meant an increase of more than two million undernourished people since 1995. War creates hunger in a number of ways: It makes food-producing activities, like farming and herding, more dangerous; people engaged in warfare do not have time to work to grow food; and war interferes with the distribution of food resources, oftentimes resulting in famine.

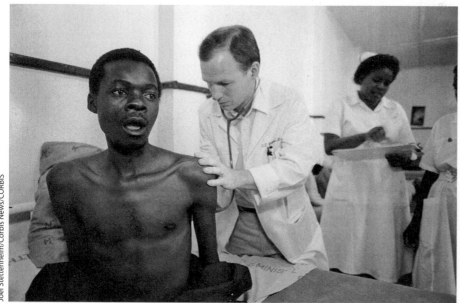

Joel Stettenheim/Corbis News/CORBIS

A doctor examines a patient in a Salvation Army HIV/AIDS hospital in Chikankata, Zambia. Nearly two-thirds of the world's population infected with HIV/AIDS lives in Africa.

One of the most surprising causes of hunger is the spread of HIV/AIDS.[4] In sub-Saharan Africa where malnutrition rose by 27 million during the 1990s, the United Nations is advocating a dual approach to preventing hunger and preventing the spread of HIV/AIDS. The rampant spread of HIV/AIDS has meant that 60 to 70 percent of farms have lost laborers due to the disease.[5] The lack of experienced farm workers has decimated agribusiness, resulting in food shortages. In addition to dealing with the issue of HIV/AIDS, the United Nations has prioritized international trade as one mechanism for dealing with the problem of hunger in the developing world.

Health and Health Care in the Global Community

One of the results of poverty and inadequate nutrition is poor health. Poverty causes health crises because the impoverished are less likely to have access to or be able to afford preventive health care, including vaccinations. They also are less likely to treat disease early, resulting in serious health risks and complications. Inadequate nutrition exacerbates this problem because the malnourished do not consume essential nutrients that help the body grow strong, help stave off disease, and help heal the body.

HIV/AIDS

Among the most preventable illnesses impacting the global community is HIV/AIDS. In our preceding discussion, we referenced the role HIV/AIDS plays in creating a food shortage in LDCs in the world. The impact of HIV/AIDS on the world's population, however, is not limited to its role in causing a shortage of labor and resultant food shortages.

Research indicates that when governments prioritize AIDS prevention, infection rates drop. Nonetheless, every day six thousand people throughout the world become newly infected with HIV, half of whom are between 15 and 24 years of age. Table 13-1 shows that AIDS is being disproportionately contracted in Africa, The top ten countries with the highest proportions of AIDS are African nations. Thirty-four million people live with AIDS, including 3.4 million children. In addition, 16 million children in the world are orphans because of AIDS. Since 1981, AIDS has caused an estimated 34 million deaths.

In the United States and other industrialized nations, it is possible to live a relatively normal and productive life with HIV, thanks to aggressive treatment using a complex combination of medications. But for most of the world, contracting the AIDS virus is a death sentence, with only a small proportion of the victims receiving treatment that could extend their lives and improve the quality of life.

Malaria

Every minute, a child in the world dies from malaria. This easily preventable and highly treatable disease infects about 216 million people each year. Of those, it kills 655,000, 90 percent of whom are African, and most of whom are children under age five.

TABLE 13-1 COUNTRIES WITH THE HIGHEST PERCENTAGE OF ADULTS LIVING WITH AIDS

	Country	Percent of adults 15–49 living with AIDS
1	Swaziland	26
2	Botswana	25
3	Lesotho	24
4	South Africa	18
5	Zimbabwe	14
6	Zambia	13
7	Namibia	13
8	Mozambique	12
9	Malawi	11
10	Uganda	6

SOURCE: https://www.cia.gov/library/publications/the-world-factbook/rankorder/2155rank.html

Malaria infection occurs through mosquito bites. A mosquito bites an infected person and then infects a healthy one by biting him or her. The parasites are introduced into the bloodstream where they travel to the liver, multiply, and destroy red blood cells. Typically, a week or so after becoming infected, the victim will have a high fever and sometimes other symptoms like lethargy, shivering, joint pain, headaches, nausea, vomiting, and diarrhea. If the illness is treated promptly, the chances of recovery are good, though even treated malaria may cause residual problems, particularly anemia, among children and pregnant women.

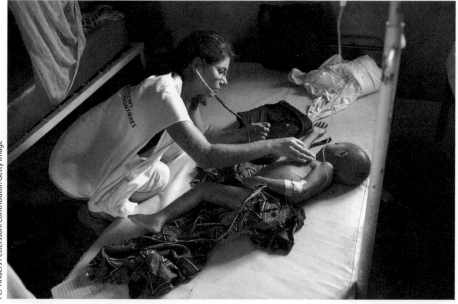

Per-Anders Pettersson/Contributor/Getty Image

A doctor from the international organization Doctors Without Borders examines a child in the Democratic Republic of the Congo, where war has created an enormous humanitarian crisis in which refugees face violence, malnourishment, and lack of adequate access to health care. As a result, millions of people, especially children, have died of preventable diseases such as malaria, measles, diarrhea, respiratory infections, and malnutrition.

FIGURE 13-2   WHERE MALARIA OCCURS

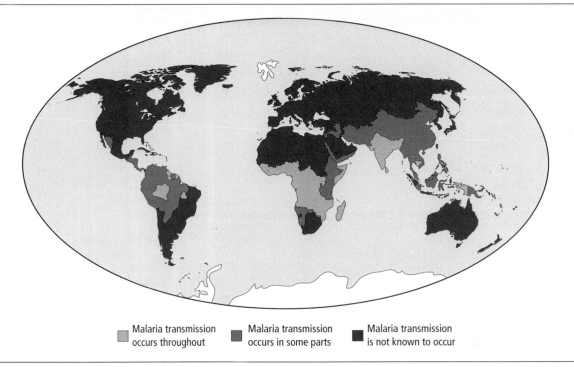

| | Malaria transmission occurs throughout | | Malaria transmission occurs in some parts | | Malaria transmission is not known to occur |

SOURCE: www.cdc.gov/malaria/malaria_worldwide/impact.html

As shown in Figure 13-2, malaria most commonly occurs in warm, humid climates. Tropical regions of Africa, Asia, and South America are the hardest hit by the disease. Lakes, ponds, and other pools of water constitute perfect breeding grounds for malaria-carrying mosquitoes. One of the most effective prevention techniques is relatively simple: sleeping under an insecticide-treated mosquito net. This technique is shown to reduce the number of infections by 25 percent. But for the world's poorest populations, this simple preventive tool is a luxury.

Currently, scientists are working on the creation of a vaccine that would inoculate children from malaria. In 2005, the Bill & Melinda Gates Foundation granted scientists a $107.6 million grant to further the development of an anti-malaria vaccine (see Focus: "A Cure for Poverty? The Gates Foundation" in Chapter 11). (In the time it took you to read this section, one child died of malaria.)

Rotavirus

Relatively few diseases cause the majority of deaths in children under age 5. One of the particularly lethal diseases is rotavirus, the most common cause of severe diarrheal disease in infants and young children worldwide. Rotavirus is typically caused by the consumption of fecal matter, often through contaminated water supplies. While children in the United States and other developed areas often develop rotavirus, treatment for dehydration (with uncontaminated water) is more readily available and so the disease is not typically lethal in the developed world.

Vaccines that prevent rotavirus exist, but problems of poverty oftentimes prevent their distribution to those in need. In particular, the fact that the vaccine needs to be refrigerated prevents many people in rural areas without access to electricity from getting the vaccine.

Still a Global Problem: Slavery

The Universal Declaration of Human Rights states: *No one shall be held in slavery or servitude: slavery and the slave trade shall be prohibited in all their forms.* When Americans think of slavery, they think of our nation's own historical experience with the institution of slavery: slave ships, plantation life, and the Civil War. But it surprises many that in the twenty-first century, slavery still exists. According to former UN Secretary General Kofi Annan,

> Nearly every day, there are shocking reports of men, women, and children who are exploited, denied their basic rights and their dignity, and deprived of a better future, through both ancient and modern forms of slavery.
>
> Slavery and trafficking, and related practices such as debt bondage, forced prostitution and forced labour, are violations of the most fundamental human rights: the right to life; the right to dignity and security; the right to just and favourable conditions of work; the right to health; and the right to equality.
>
> These are rights that we all possess—irrespective of our sex, our nationality, our social status, our occupation or any other characteristic.[6]

In modern times, slavery takes on a wide variety of forms: trafficking in women and children for prostitution, child labor, the use of children in armed conflicts, and debt bondage, among others. Victims of slavery are among the most powerless people in the world. They are fearful for their lives and are the least likely to report their abusers. They typically are impoverished and may be members of groups marginalized by society.

Trafficking in Humans for Sexual Exploitation

Women and children, particularly in Asia but also in countries of the former Soviet Union, are forced to be part of prostitution rings that operate in those countries as well as in Western democracies. In some countries, young women who respond to help-wanted ads for international work as nannies or domestic servants are essentially kidnapped and forced to work as prostitutes. The U.S. Department of State estimates that six hundred to eight hundred thousand people annually are trafficked across international borders worldwide, including an estimated fourteen thousand people trafficked into the United States.

The United Nations notes that the organized prostitution of both boys and girls in a number of countries is well documented and oftentimes is linked to international pedophilia and child pornography.[7] Among those who traffic in

Afghanistan

Afghanistan's birth can be traced to the end of the eighteenth century. From that time until it was declared a republic in 1973, Afghanistan was ruled by kings who confronted foreign invaders, power plays, and civil wars. Afghanistan's last monarch, King Zahir Shah, was himself the victim of a power play. His monarchy was overthrown in a coup led by his cousin, Muhammad Daud. In 1973 Daud declared Afghanistan a republic and declared himself president. Daud's rule lasted until a leftist military junta, the People's Democratic Party of Afghanistan (PDPA), overthrew and killed Daud in 1978. PDPA leader Noor Muhammad Taraki became president, but he faced insurrection by ethnic leaders and Islamic conservatives. Taraki, who had served as president for barely a year, was killed in 1979 and was replaced by another PDPA official, Hafizullah Amin. But the ethnic and religious insurrection by *mujaheddin* (guerrilla) rebels continued.

The Soviet Invasion

On December 25, 1979, Soviet troops invaded Afghanistan. Another PDPA leader, Babrak Karmal, known for his reformist views, became president. As president, Karmal tried to placate the *mujaheddin* rebels, but without much success. In the meantime, fighting between the rebels and the Soviet forces intensified. In the early 1980s, the United Nations estimated that about half of Afghanistan's population was displaced and about 1 million people had died in combat. The fighting also created an enormous refugee problem in the region, with 3 million refugees fleeing to Pakistan and another 1.5 million to Iran. The war also meant that the struggle toward development was essentially halted: Because of the bombing, the school system was decimated, industrialization was severely restricted, the economy crippled, and the agricultural structure destroyed due to damage done to irrigation projects.

The Soviet Retreat

In May 1986, Mohammad Najibullah became leader of PDPA, and he succeeded Karmal to the presidency in November 1987. In early 1988, the United Nations had successfully negotiated the Soviet withdrawal, and preparations began for the impending influx of refugees repatriating to Afghanistan.

Civil War

Nevertheless, ethnic and religious rebellion continued and by the early 1990s had intensified to the point that refugees poured out of Afghanistan and aid efforts were severely hampered. In 1992 the *mujaheddin* rebels seized Kabul, and Najibullah's PDPA government fell.

The Islamic State of Afghanistan

In 1992 leaders of the *mujaheddin* committed to the Peshawar Accord, which created the Islamic State in Afghanistan and formed a government under Sigbatullah Mojaddedi. The Peshawar

Accord called for Mojaddedi to lead the Transitional Council for two months and then turn power over to the Leadership Council, headed by Burhannudin Rabbani.

Rabbani was declared president of the Islamic State in Afghanistan in July 1992 and was to serve until October, but he would not relinquish power. Infighting between the parties crippled Kabul.

The Taliban

Joining in the fighting was the Taliban, who viewed the mujaheddin as corrupted. The Taliban fighters were composed primarily of sons, who had been raised in refugee camps in Pakistan, of mujaheddin. Many had been orphaned, either by civil war or during the Soviet invasion and occupation. By 1995 the Taliban had taken much of southern and western Afghanistan, and in September, Kabul fell to the Taliban. Rabbani fled to the north and joined an opposition alliance, the United Islamic Front for the Salvation of Afghanistan (also called the Northern Alliance). Fighting between the Taliban and the Northern Alliance continued.

Condemnations of the Taliban

International condemnations of the Taliban government centered on the Taliban's harboring terrorists, particularly after the coordinated 1998 terrorist attacks on U.S. embassies in Nairobi, Kenya, and Dar-es-Salaam, Tanzania. Other condemnation focused on the discriminatory and inhumane treatment of women and girls by the regime, widespread executions, the displacement of residents, the killing of two Afghan staff members of the UN's World Food Program, the murder of Iranian diplomats, and the increase in the cultivation, production, and trafficking of drugs.

In the late 1990s, according to the United Nations, "one quarter of all children born in Afghanistan died of preventable diseases before the age of five. Afghan women were nearly five times more likely to die in childbirth than in other developing countries. Typhoid and cholera epidemics were rampant and pneumonia and malaria had re-emerged as public health threats. The condition of women had deteriorated markedly, and only one in 20 girls received any kind of education."*

Post–September 11, 2001

With the implication of al Qaeda, whose terrorist training camps were based in Afghanistan, and Osama bin Laden, who was being harbored by the Taliban regime, as those who carried out the September 11 attacks on the United States, President George W. Bush sent U.S. forces to Afghanistan to support Northern Alliance efforts to overthrow the Taliban. By December 2001, they had succeeded and the Afghan Interim Authority, headed by Chairman Hamid Karzai, was established.

Rebuilding Afghanistan

According to the United Nations, international agencies have identified several projects that require attention in the rebuilding of Afghanistan, including the elimination of land mines, an education program, an irrigation project to increase food production, and a basic health-services package to reduce child and maternal mortality.

(continued)

FOCUS

The building of a democratic government in Afghanistan also was a priority. In 2003 a *Loya Jirga* (a "grand council" where elders meet to make decisions about the community) ratified a constitution that created an Islamic republic, with a three-branch government structure consisting of a president, a legislature, and a judicial branch, not unlike that of the United States. The constitution also created a system of checks and balances. In October 2004, Hamid Karzai was elected president after having served as the interim head of government after the fall of the Taliban in 2001. Karzai was credited with encouraging unification within the nation and strong leadership in foreign affairs, but critics charge that he has does little to combat the hold that Afghanistan local warlords have on the cultural, political, and economic life of the nation. Critics also point to Afghanistan's re-emergence as an exporter of poppy (from which heroin is derived).

In 2005, Afghanistan succeeded in holding free and fair popular elections for the Wolesi Jirga (People's House), the 249-seat lower house of parliament. Turnout averaged about 50 percent, with a diverse group elected, including former members of the Taliban and former mujaheddin. People of various ideologies and secularist and Islamic fundamentalists were elected. Although 25 percent of the seats were set aside for women, 28 percent were elected, exceeding their minimum quota by 3 percent. Ironically, the nation known for its deplorable treatment of women boasted one of the highest proportions of women in elected in government, far exceeding the proportion of women serving in the United States.

In 2009, Karzai again won reelection, with over 50 percent of the vote, but the man once lauded internationally as a courageous unifying force was now widely criticized for his close relationships with warlords and his association with political allies (including two of his vice presidential nominees) human rights organizations claimed had record of human rights abuses. These 2009 elections were also characterized by a host of other difficulties, including low rates of voter registration and turnout, election fraud, violence, and the urge of a boycott by the Taliban, all of which serve to delegitimize their outcome.[†] Against the backdrop of an escalation of military tensions between the United States and Taliban forces and warlords who protect them, the United States once again found itself precariously striving to balance its desire to maintain a positive, productive relationship with the government in Kabul, all the while having a vested interest in ensuring that the elections were free from fraud and abuse.

After Karzai's re-election, he faced pressure from the Obama administration to distance himself from the corrupt warlords, but Karzai recognized that he owed his election to some of the warlords who had supported him. He nominated several corrupt officials as cabinet ministers, though many were rejected by Parliament. Relations between the Obama administration and Karzai were cooler but warmed considerably after Obama visited Afghanistan in 2010 and after U.S. forces killed Osama bin Laden in May 2011. When Obama again visited Afghanistan in 2012, relations between the leaders appeared solid as Afghanistan prepared for the eventual withdrawal of U.S. and ally forces in 2014, and the turning over of security operations to the Afghani security forces.

---

[*] www.un.org/News/dh/latest/afghan/un-afghan-history.shtml.

[†] www.nytimes.com/2009/09/09/world/asia/09policy.html?_r=1&scp=10&sq=afghanistan%20election&st=cse.

Caroline Penn/CORBIS

In Volta, Ghana, girls are sometimes forced into sexual slavery to atone for the misdeeds of their male relatives. This *trokosi* ("slave of the gods") is a sexual slave and must work in the marketplace selling wares. The cord around her neck indicates her slave status.

children, the trafficker may be an acquaintance who convinces parents that their children will be better off. They may offer the promise of safety or mislead parents into believing that their child will be educated in a boarding school, taught a skill, or work as a companion to a rich child. Sometimes a trafficker or an accomplice will promise parents that the child will marry, but sometimes the trafficker simply abducts the child. That child may then wind up forced into prostitution.

Among adult victims of human trafficking, traffickers frequently rely on people's desire for a better life as a lure. Oftentimes traffickers advertise in the help-wanted sections of local newspapers, offering high-paying jobs as models, domestic servants, hotel maids, nannies, or shop clerks in Western nations. Once victims are out of their homeland, they may be raped and forced into prostitution. Frequently, traffickers will confiscate a victim's identification and travel permits (often forgeries), withhold food or shelter unless the victim complies, and use the threat of imprisonment by authorities or the threat of harm to the victim's family at home as a means of ensuring compliance.

Child Labor

Child labor is not typically thought of as a form of slavery, but the conditions under which children are forced to work constitute modern slavery. UNICEF makes a distinction between child work—economic activity that does not interfere with their health or development—and child labor. UNICEF defines child labor as economic activity by children under 12 years of age, economic activity by those aged 12 to 14 years old that is more than light work, or children who are enslaved, trafficked, prostituted, forced into illegal activities, or exposed to hazards.[8]

Forced child labor occurs in many parts of world, including Asia, Africa, and South America. Child laborers are in great demand because they work for very little and can be easily exploited by their employers. Work by children is particularly common in the agricultural sector , including in the production and harvesting of crops like rice and cotton, or in mining gold or coal. Child labor also occurs in industries including manufacturing of goods for import to industrialized democracies. In one recent scandal, human rights advocates revealed that nearly all soccer balls purchased in the United States and Europe, particularly those sold by Nike, were manufactured in plants in Pakistan that employed child laborers. Nike, which had subcontracted its manufacturing to another firm, frequently has been identified as a manufacturer that employs child labor, though this is done by subcontractors who manage the manufacturing process for Nike. Similarly, Nestlé faced criticism in 2012 because child labor in the Ivory Coast had produced some of the cocoa used in Nestlé' Cocoa.

Children also often work as domestic servants, frequently without pay because their employers charge them "room and board." These children also are at increased risk for physical and sexual abuse. Child domestics frequently are treated poorly, and their work interferes with their ability to thrive and acquire an education.

The United Nations also reports that in some countries, kidnapped children are held against their will in remote camps. They are chained at night and are forced to work building roads or in stone quarries during the day.[9]

Child Soldiers

Throughout the world, especially in the civil wars taking place in Africa, children are being forced into military service. Forcing children to serve as soldiers robs them of their childhood, endangers them, and often forces them to become murderers. Children serving as soldiers have been killed, disabled, tortured, held as prisoners of war, and psychologically ruined.[10] Often, child soldiers are conscripted under the threat that harm will come to their families if they do not serve. In other cases, the child's family is killed, and they are forced to serve with no other avenue of survival.

Debt Bondage

Debt bondage resembles traditional indentured servitude because the victim cannot leave his or her job until money, usually an outrageous sum, is repaid. Oftentimes debt bondage resembles the following scenario: A poor person who wants to immigrate to the United States or Europe pays a large down payment (often several years' wages collected from many family members) to a smuggler. The person is then smuggled (often in life-threatening fashion) into the country illegally where he or she is forced to work long days to pay off the debt. However, unscrupulous smugglers charge high interest rates and charge for room and board; the worker cannot repay the debt given the meager salary that he or she is collecting. Because the victim is in the country illegally and usually has limited command of the language, he or she has little recourse. In addition, the family back home has made enormous sacrifices to enable the worker to emigrate.

Reuters / Landov

In South Sudan, children are being forced into military service, like these Sudanese boy soldiers who are keeping watch outside a rebel military headquarters. Often, child soldiers are conscripted under the threat that harm will come to their families if they do not serve.

In debt bondage, the victim cannot leave the job until the debt is repaid. Sometimes this never occurs, and the victim's children inherit the debt. Debt bondage also occurs in agricultural societies where victims sharecrop on plots of land.

International Conventions

Although other forms of modern slavery exist, the preceding types are some of the most common ways in which victims are denied their most basic human rights and at their most powerless. To combat forms of modern slavery, there are several tools. Of course, when crimes take place in societies in which they are banned, some recourse is available, though we have already discussed the problems with reporting and prosecuting these offenses. Internationally, the U.N. Convention against Transnational Organized Crime contains two optional protocols, the "Protocol to Prevent, Suppress and Punish Trafficking in Persons, especially Women and Children," and the "Protocol against the Smuggling of Migrants by Land, Air and Sea," which nations can ratify. Of course, those nations in which slavery is most likely to be found are the least likely to ratify and implement the protocols.

Global Population Growth

The world's population is now approaching 7 billion people. The last seventy years of the twentieth century saw a true population explosion, a tripling of the earth's inhabitants from about 2 billion people in 1930. But the rate of population growth is forecast to slow down in the twenty-first century. By 2050 the world's population is expected to stabilize at around 9 billion people.

demography
the study of the population and population changes

    Demography is the study of the population and population changes—how births, death, and migration affect the number of people living in the countries of the world. Demographers theorize a three-stage model of world population growth. For many centuries, the global population grew very slowly. The world's population reflected both a high **fertility rate** (the number of births per one thousand women of childbearing age) and a high **mortality rate** (the number of deaths per one thousand people). Life expectancy was short—less than 40 years.

fertility rate
the number of births annually per one thousand women of childbearing age

    The Industrial Revolution, however, which began first in England and Western Europe and then extended to North America, drastically reduced the mortality rate, particularly the rate of infant deaths. For decades, even in the Western world, fertility rates remained high. The combination of high fertility rates and low mortality rates of course led to rapid population increases. Only in the last few decades has the fertility rate in the developed world declined, leading to a stabilization of the population.

mortality rate
the number of deaths annually per one thousand people

    Today, in less-developed areas of Africa, Asia, and Latin America—areas that are currently in the process of industrialization—high fertility and low mortality account for continued world population growth. But with economic development, fertility in these areas of the world is expected to decline, and the world's population is expected to stabilize around 9 billion people before the end of this century.[11] And among the poorest nations, evidence suggests that as infant and childhood mortality rates decline, so too does the fertility rate: In many societies, couples choose to have more children to ensure that some will live to care for them in their old age. As mortality rates improve, couples seeking to meet this need require fewer children.[12]

As late as the 1970s, some commentators predicted that the world's population growth would soon exhaust the world's natural resources, leading to global starvation, malnutrition, and disease. Reflecting the views of Thomas Malthus, who predicted in 1798 that populations everywhere would grow faster than agriculture's ability to feed them, these "neo-Malthusians" forecast widespread human misery and death in the twenty-first century. (In 1971 biologist Paul Ehrlich called earth a "dying planet" suffering from "overpopulation"; his book *The Population Explosion* inspired Earth Day.)

But just the opposite has occurred. Average life expectancy globally is now approaching 70 years. Infant death rates are declining everywhere, although they still remain unconscionably high in the LDCs of the world. The world's natural resources, especially food, are actually *cheaper* today than a century ago. This is clear evidence that improved productivity is increasing the supply of food and resources faster than the demands of a growing world population.[13]

Women worldwide women are having fewer children now than ever before. The United Nations estimates the current world fertility rate at 2.45 children per woman.[14] In developed regions, the fertility rate is estimated at 1.5, well below the replacement level fertility rate of 2.1 births per woman.[15] (The fertility rate for the United States is 2.0; however, the U.S. population continues to grow through immigration.) The fertility rate in the less-developed regions of the world is dropping rapidly, from an estimated 5.25 in 1970 to 4.52 today. China, with the world's largest population, made the greatest fertility rate reductions from 1970 to 2010—from an estimated 6.0 to 1.6. Nonetheless, population growth in the less-developed areas of the world will add more than two billion people by 2050 (see Table 13-2).

TABLE 13-2 GLOBAL POPULATION FORECASTS

Millions of People			
	1950	2000	2050
World	2,521	5,901	9,050
More-developed regions	813	1,182	1,245
Less-developed regions	1,709	4,719	7,805
Africa	221	749	1,784
Asia	1,402	3,585	5,340
Europe	547	729	654
South America	167	504	490
North America	172	305	738
Oceania (Australia, New Zealand, etc.)	13	30	45

SOURCE: U.S. Census Bureau, International Data Base, www.census.gov/ipc/www/ idbprint.html.

The Structure of Urban Life in the Global Community

About half of the world's population lives in urban areas. Urbanization is greatest in the developed world, where about 80 percent of people live in or near cities. Only about 40 percent of people of the less-developed world live in urban areas. However, urban growth is proceeding more rapidly in Asia, Africa, and Latin America than in Western Europe or the United States (see International Perspective: "Worldwide Urbanization"). Figure 13-3 shows the significant increases both in urbanization and in the size of urban areas since 1975. In 1975, three urban areas worldwide had populations over 10 million. Today, there are 21 such cities, and more than 5 percent of the world's population lives in them.

We look at urbanism because it is a trend that is increasing, and it changes power relations within societies. Increased urbanism can result in increased

FIGURE 13-3   INCREASES IN GLOBAL URBANIZATION, 1950–2010

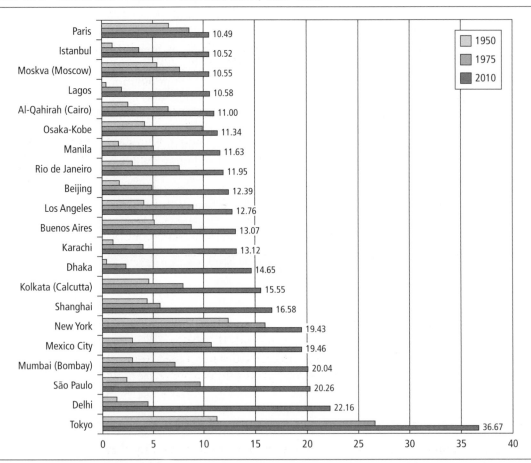

SOURCE: The Department of Health and Human Services, The Center for Disease Control and Prevention, The Impact of Malaria, a Leading Cause of Death Worldwide, http://www.cdc.gov/malaria/impact/index.htm.

economic opportunity, personal mobility, educational opportunity, and other conditions that can result in increases in personal power. However, moving away from rural societies also means forgoing traditional sources of power. In short, increased urbanization changes how people in many societies interact.

What is the impact of urbanization on the way people interact? To deal with this question, sociologists formulated a sociological definition of urbanism, one that would identify those characteristics most affecting social life. Sociologist Louis Wirth provided the classic definition of urbanism over fifty years ago: "For sociological purposes a city may be defined as a relatively large, dense, and permanent settlement of socially heterogeneous individuals."[16] Thus, according to Wirth, the distinguishing characteristics of urban life—a **sociological theory of urbanism**—includes *numbers*, *density*, and *heterogeneity*—large numbers of people, living closely together, who are different from one another.

sociological theory of urbanism
urbanism distinguished by numbers, density, and heterogeneity

Numbers and Heterogeneity

Large numbers of people involve a great range of individual variation. The modern economic system of a city is based on a highly specialized and complex division of labor. In early farm communities, a dozen occupations exhausted the job opportunities available to people. In a simple agricultural society, nearly everyone was a farmer or was closely connected to or dependent on farming.

The modern metropolis, however, has tens of thousands of different kinds of jobs. An industrial economy means highly specialized jobs, hence the **heterogeneity** of urban populations. Different jobs result in different levels of income, dress, and styles of living. People's jobs shape the way that they look at the world and their evaluations of social and political events. To acquire a job, one attains a certain level and type of education that also distinguishes one from those in other jobs with other educational requirements. Differences in educational level in turn produce a wide variety of differences in opinions, attitudes, and styles of living. Urban life concentrates people with all these different economic and occupational characteristics in a very few square miles.

heterogeneity
diversity in occupation, income, education; ethnic and racial diversity

Ethnic and Racial Diversity

Ethnic and racial diversities are also present in urban areas. In cities throughout the world, rural dwellers are drawn by the promise of jobs and a better way of life. Newcomers, even from the same nation, bring with them different needs, attitudes, and ways of life. The "melting pot" effect in cities may reduce some of the diversity over time, but the pot does not melt people immediately, and there always seem to be new arrivals.

Impersonal Relationships

Increasing the numbers of people in a community limits the possibility that each member of the community will know everyone else personally. Multiplying the number of persons with whom an individual comes into contact makes

INTERNATIONAL PERSPECTIVE

Worldwide Urbanization

Urbanization is occurring worldwide. Cities throughout the world offer greater opportunities than rural areas. It is estimated that the world's urban areas are growing at twice the rate of the world's population generally. Millions of people migrate from the countryside in search of economic opportunity, health care, education, and higher standards of living in the world's largest cities. However poor and unpleasant life may be in many LDC cities, these cities hold the promise of a better life for rural migrants. Many residents of these cities have no running water and lack sewage facilities. Mountains of garbage have become wretched shantytowns where the city's poor pick through waste to survive and build shacks from discarded materials. The problems of LDC cities make those of the largest U.S. cities seem minor by comparison.

Today, most of the largest cities in the world are found in less-developed societies (see the accompanying table and the figure "Worldwide Urban Populations"). Modernization brings urbanization, and as nations move from agricultural to industrial economies, their cities grow exponentially. Soon only one of the world's largest cities will be in the United States—New York. In the past fifty years, cities in less-developed nations have replaced Western cities in the list of the world's largest cities.

WORLDWIDE URBAN POPULATIONS

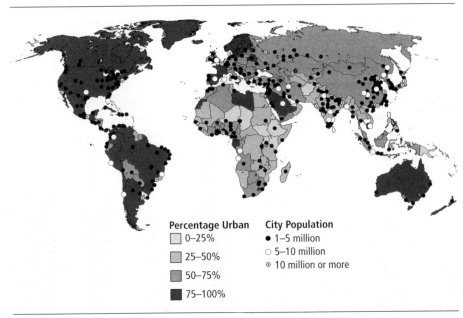

Percentage Urban
- ☐ 0–25%
- ☐ 25–50%
- ☐ 50–75%
- ■ 75–100%

City Population
- ● 1–5 million
- ○ 5–10 million
- ◉ 10 million or more

SOURCE: http://esa.un.org/unpd/wup/Maps/maps_urban_2011.htm

CHANGES IN THE DISTRIBUTION OF POPULATION

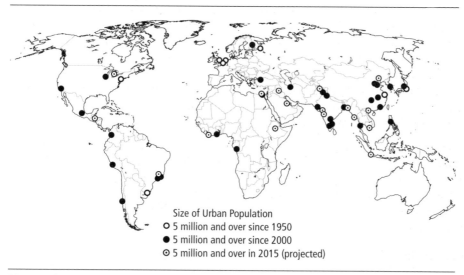

Size of Urban Population
○ 5 million and over since 1950
● 5 million and over since 2000
◉ 5 million and over in 2015 (projected)

SOURCE: The Washington Post, Behind the Numbers, http://voices.washingtonpost.com/behind-thenumbers/2008/11/ideological_shift_or_just_comp.html.

INCREASING GLOBAL URBANIZATION

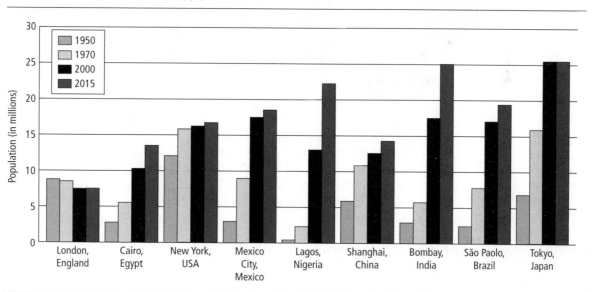

it impossible for that individual to know everyone very well. The result is a **segmentalization of human relationships**, in which an individual comes to know *many* people but only in highly *segmental, partial* roles. According to Wirth,

> The contacts of the city may indeed be face-to-face, but they are nevertheless impersonal, superficial, transitory, and segmental. The reserve, the indifference, and the blasé outlook that urbanites manifest in their relationships may thus be regarded as devices for immunizing themselves against the personal claims and expectations of others.[17]

Anomie

Large numbers mean a certain degree of freedom for the individual from the control of family groups, neighbors, churches, and other community groups. But urbanism also contributes to a sense of **anomie**—a sense of social isolation and a loss of the personal recognition, self-worth, and feeling of participation that come with living in a small, integrated society. The social contacts of urban dwellers are more anonymous than those of rural dwellers; they interact with persons who have little if any knowledge of their life histories.

Secondary Group Memberships

Rural life emphasized **primary group ties**—interactions within the extended family. Many sociologists believe that urban life emphasizes **secondary group ties**—interactions among members of age and interest groups rather than among families and neighbors. Urban life is said to center around voluntary associations and secondary group memberships—crowds, recreational groups, civic clubs, business groups, and professional and work groups. Sociologists believe that urban dwellers have a greater number of interpersonal contacts than rural dwellers and that urban dwellers are more likely to interact with people as occupants of specific social roles. In contrast, rural dwellers are more likely to interact with individuals as full personalities.

Social Control Mechanisms

Urban society also presents problems of social control. The anomie of urban life is believed to weaken social mores and social group controls. External controls through a series of formal institutions, laws, and organizations, such as the courts and the police, become more essential. Thus, **social control** in the cities depends in large degree on *formal mechanisms*. But laws generally express the minimum behavioral standard, and urban life involves a much wider range of behavior than rural life. Moreover, laws do not always succeed in establishing minimum standards of behavior; crime rates increase with increases in urbanism.

Mobility

Another characteristic of urban life is **mobility**, or ease of movement. Urban mobility is both **physical** (from one geographic area to another) and **social** (from one position of social status to another). Rural communities are more stable than urban communities in both respects. Traditionally, rural dwellers were more

---

segmental relationships
knowing many people, but only in their partial role

anomie
a sense of social isolation and loss of personal recognition and self-worth

primary group ties
interactions with family and neighborhood groups known personally

secondary group ties
interactions with interest or voluntary groups

social control
urban society based more on formal institutions than on social groups

physical mobility
movement from one location to another

social mobility
movement from one social status to another

likely to stay near the place of their birth. In contrast, urbanites frequently move from city to city or from one section of a city to another. Social mobility is also greater in the city because of the wider range of economic opportunities there. Moreover, urban dwellers are judged far less by their family backgrounds (which are unknown) than by their own appearances, occupational accomplishments, incomes, and lifestyles. Although mobility creates opportunities for individuals, it weakens the sense of community. City dwellers do not think of their city as a community to which they belong but rather as a place they happen to live—a geographic entity commanding little personal allegiance.

Political Conflict

Urban life presents a serious problem in political conflict management. Persons with different occupations, incomes, and educational levels are known to have different views on public issues. People at the bottom of the social ladder look at police—indeed, government authority in general—differently from the way those on higher rungs do. Persons who own their homes and those who do not own their homes regard taxation in different lights. Families with children and those without children have different ideas about school systems. And so it goes. Differences in the way that people make their living, in their income and educational levels, in the color of their skin, in the way that they worship, and in their style of living—all are at the roots of political life in the metropolis.

Summary of Sociological Theory of Urbanization

Thus, sociological theory provides us with a series of characteristics to look for in urban life:

- Large numbers of people
- Population density
- Social and economic heterogeneity
- Ethnic and racial diversity
- Numerous but superficial, segmental, utilitarian relationships
- Impersonality and anonymity
- Greater interaction in secondary groups
- Reliance on formal mechanisms of social control
- Physical and social mobility
- Greater potential for conflict

Not all these characteristics of urban life have been documented. Indeed, in highly industrialized and urbanized societies, it is sometimes difficult to discern any differences between rural and urban dwellers. Furthermore, urban dwellers display a great range and variation in lifestyle; some reflect the "typical" style described by sociological theory, and others do not. Many retain their commitment to the extended family, and many city neighborhoods are stable and socially cohesive communities. Despite the plausibility of the hypothesis that urban life leads to anonymity, impersonality, and segmentation in social relationships, it is hard to prove systematically that urban dwellers are becoming more impersonal or anonymous than are rural dwellers.

Technology's Increasing Role in Globalism

Increasingly, technology—particularly the Internet and portable cellular technology—is changing the global environment. As cellular technology becomes less expensive and more readily available, it is apparent that it is fostering development and communication in many societies that are "leap-frogging" over the traditional, costly wired communication system.

We are seeing technology's role in changing the global environment and how power is distributed throughout the world in several ways. Technology certainly has affected economic development (both in terms of production and as a medium of communication). Today, many nations' economies rely on the jobs provided in producing computers, tablets, and cell phones. And these technologies play an important role in shaping commerce within and between nations.

diaspora
the scattering of a people away from the ancestral homeland

Because of the increased ability to communicate, technology also is playing an important role in contributing to the **diaspora**, or the scattering of a people away from the ancestral homeland. Traditionally, immigration meant leaving one's family and way of live behind. Today, you might Facebook your mom in India, or Skype your cousin in Ethiopia. Technology has made increasing globalism possible, as migration no longer means prohibitively expensive communication.

Importantly, technology also is influences politics. From spawning the Arab Spring revolutions through Facebook and other social networking sites that succeeded in toppling dictatorial governments throughout the Middle East in the Spring of 2011 to its pivotal role in the 2012 U.S. presidential election, technology has changed how politics is done throughout the world. In changing how people mobilize, communicate with government officials, and how governments operate, technology has changed the distribution of power globally. While technology has proven important in the hands of the masses, like power, technology is not equally distributed, and the poorest people of the world are among the least likely to have access to this important, empowering tool.

CHAPTER SUMMARY

- Globalization is an indisputable phenomenon of modern times. Globalization takes on many forms: increasing communication between individuals across the globe using cellular and Internet technologies, international tourism among individuals, growth in multinational corporations, the increasing presence of international nongovernmental organizations, increases in trade between nations, cooperation in international law enforcement, and the presence and increased influence of international media sources.

- Modernization theory posits that the industrialized nations of the West play a strategic role in "developing" the underdeveloped world. Dependency theorists argue that modernization occurs because of the toils of those exploited within the Western world and because of the exploitation of cheap labor and natural resources in the developing world.

- From the problem of poverty emerges nearly all other social ills: disease, hunger, lack of opportunity, crime and violence, drug trafficking and use, prostitution, and on and on. Extreme poverty is commonplace in the world, affecting 23 percent of the world's people. Worldwide, the United Nations estimates that 421 million people in developing countries live in extreme poverty.

- The problems of hunger and malnutrition are directly related to the problem of poverty and contribute to individuals' powerlessness in a most basic way. The UN Food and Agriculture Organization estimates that there are more than one billion hungry people, while another two billion were undernourished.

- One of the results of poverty and inadequate nutrition is poor health. Poverty causes health crises because the impoverished are less likely to have access to or be able to afford preventive health care, including vaccinations. Among the deadliest diseases for the impoverished are HIV/AIDS, malaria, and rotavirus.

- In modern times, slavery takes on a wide variety of forms: trafficking in women and children for prostitution, child labor, the use of children in armed conflicts, and debt bondage, among others. Victims of slavery are among the most powerless people in the world.

- In less-developed areas of Africa, Asia, and Latin America—areas that are currently in the process of industrialization—high fertility and low mortality account for continued world population growth. But with economic development, fertility in these areas of the world is expected to decline, and the world's population is expected to stabilize around 9 billion people before the end of this century.

- Increasingly, technology—particularly the Internet and portable cellular technology—is changing the global environment. These changes are particularly apparent in the global economy, in communication, and in politics.

KEY TERMS

anomie   a sense of social isolation and loss of personal recognition and self-worth

demography   the study of the population and population changes

dependency theory   argues that modernization exploits both individuals within industrialized economies and LDCs on the whole

diaspora   the scattering of a people away from the ancestral homeland

extreme income poverty   earning less than $1.25 per day

fertility rate   the number of births annually per one thousand women of childbearing age

heterogeneity   diversity in occupation, income, education; ethnic and racial diversity

modernization theory   posits that the industrialized nations of the West play a strategic role in "developing" the underdeveloped world

mortality rate   the number of deaths annually per one thousand people

physical mobility   movement from one location to another

primary group ties   interactions with family and neighborhood groups known personally

secondary group ties   interactions with interest or voluntary groups

segmental relationships   knowing many people, but only in their partial roles

social control   urban society based more on formal institutions than on social groups

social mobility   movement from one social status to another

sociological theory of urbanism   urbanism distinguished by numbers, density, and heterogeneity

world systems theory   asserts that the core wealthy nations of the world rely on a peripheral group of poorer countries in order to remain wealthy, but that some states act as both core and periphery in a world system economy

ON THE WEB

EXPLORING POWER AND THE GLOBAL COMMUNITY

The website for this textbook (**www.cengagebrain.com**) offers resources for exploring power and the global community on the Internet. Further information can be found at the following websites:

• **United Nations** The best sources of information on the global community can be accessed through the official website of the United Nations (UN). The UN home page (**www.un.org**) contains links to "United Nations Member States," an alphabetical listing of all UN member nations with links to official national website of most nations. The UN's Department of Economic and Social Affairs provides access to extensive information pertaining to such things as the global environment, human settlement, population demographics, social development, human rights, and international trade.

Try This: Go to **www.un.org/en/globalissues/** and pick one of the subcategories for UN global issues from the side column. Discuss the issue and specific ways the UN is fighting to improve conditions.

• **UNICEF** The United Nations Children's Fund (**www.unicef.org**) provides specific country information, statistical data, and descriptive information about the special problems of the world's children, as well as opportunities for activism through its website.

Try This: Go to **www.unicef.org/infobycountry/index.html** to see the interactive map of areas where UNICEF is active. Click an area, and then a specific country, and identify what work UNICEF is doing for children in that corner of the world.

REVIEW QUIZ

MULTIPLE CHOICE

1. The theory that posits that the industrialized nations of the West play a strategic role in "developing" the underdeveloped world is _____ theory.
   a. modernization
   b. dependency
   c. co-dependency
   d. world systems

2. The theory that argues that modernization exploited both individuals within industrialized economies and LDCs on the whole is _____ theory.
   a. modernization
   b. dependency
   c. co-dependency
   d. world systems

3. Which of the following is a true statement about extreme income poverty?
   a. It is defined as earning less than $1.25 per day.
   b. It is found primarily in East Asia, Africa, and South America.
   c. It is defined as earning less than $5 per day.
   d. a and b

4. Hunger and malnourishment are caused by _____.
   a. locusts
   b. drought
   c. war
   d. all of the above

5. Since 1981, about _____ people have died of AIDS.
   a. 25,000
   b. 250,000
   c. 25 million
   d. 250 million

6. Which of the following is the most prevalent killer(s) of poor children under the age of 5?
   a. malaria
   b. rotavirus
   c. chicken pox
   d. a and b

7. The number of births annually per one thousand women of childbearing age is called the _____.
   a. mortality rate
   b. fertility rate
   c. reproduction rate
   d. per capita rate

8. Diversity in occupation, income, education, and ethnic and racial diversity is called _____.
   a. heterogeneity
   b. homogeneity
   c. demography
   d. genealogy

9. Interactions with family and neighborhood groups known personally are called _____.
   a. primary group ties
   b. secondary group ties
   c. segmental relationships
   d. homogeneity

10. Knowing many people, but only in their partial roles, is identified by the term _____.
    a. primary group ties
    b. secondary group ties
    c. segmental relationships
    d. heterogeneity

FILL IN THE BLANK

11. _____ is the study of the population and of population changes.

12. The number of deaths annually per one thousand people is called the _____.

13. A sense of social isolation and loss of personal recognition and self-worth is called _____.

14. Movement from one location to another is _____ mobility.

15. Movement from one social status to another is _____ mobility.

CHAPTER 14

Power among Nations

Learning Objectives

After reading this chapter, students will be able to:

- Explain the theories that have informed the exercise of power on the international level.
- Describe how the terror attacks of September 11, 2001, changed the foundations of American foreign policy.
- Understand the threats to global stability today.

International Politics

The distinguished political scientist Hans Morgenthau wrote:

> **International politics**, like all politics, is a struggle for power. Whatever the ultimate aims of international politics, power is always the immediate aim. Statesmen and peoples may ultimately seek freedom, security, prosperity, or power itself. They may define their goals in terms of a religious, philosophic, economic, or social ideal . . . But whenever they strive to realize their goal by means of international politics, they are striving for power.[1]

international politics
the worldwide struggle for power

In brief, we are reminded that the struggle for power is global—it involves all the nations and peoples of the world, whatever their goals or ideals.

National Sovereignty

About 200 independent nations are in the world today. Of these nations, 193 (as of 2012) are members of the United Nations. Yet all the nations of the world—whatever their size, location, culture, politics, economic system, or level of technological development—claim **sovereignty**. Sovereignty means formal, legal power over internal affairs; freedom from external intervention; and political and legal recognition by other nations. Sovereignty is a legal fiction, of course: Many nations have difficulty controlling their internal affairs; they are constantly meddling in one another's internal affairs and even trampling on one another's political and legal authority. Nonetheless, the struggle to achieve sovereignty is an important force in world politics.

sovereignty
legal power over internal affairs, freedom from external intervention, and legal recognition by other nations

Although sovereignty is highly valued by all nations, it creates an international system in which no authority—not even the United Nations—is given the power to make or enforce rules binding on all nations. There is no world government. Nations cooperate with one another only when it is in their own interests to do so. Nations can make treaties with one another, but no court exists to enforce the treaties, and they can be (and are) disregarded when it becomes advantageous for a nation to do so.

International Law

The series of customs and principles among nations known as **international law** helps guide relations among nations. But international "law" is also a fiction: No international "police force" enforces the law, and it is frequently broken or ignored. An International Court (at The Hague, the Netherlands) exists to decide conflicts according to international law, but nations do not have to submit to the authority of this court and can, if they wish, ignore its decisions. The United Nations has no real power to enforce its resolutions, unless one or more nations (acting in their own self-interest) decide to try to enforce a UN resolution with their own troops or contribute troops to a joint "UN force." But UN forces are really the forces of sovereign nations that have voluntarily decided to contribute troops to enforce a particular resolution.

international law
the series of customs and principles that helps to guide relations among nations; compliance with these norms is largely voluntary

Bringing Order to International Relations

The instability and insecurity of "the global game of power" have led to many attempts over the centuries to bring order to the international system.[2] Indeed, wars among nations have averaged one every two years, and if "civil wars" and "indirect aggressions" are counted, the rate of armed conflict is even greater.

The Balance-of-Power System: The Nineteenth Century

One method of trying to bring order to international relations is the balance-of-power system. The nineteenth century saw a deliberate attempt to stabilize international relations by creating a system of alliances among nations that was designed to balance the power of one group of nations against the power of another and thus discourage war. During this time, Great Britain, France, Russia, Germany, and Austria dominated the world scene. If the balance worked, war would be avoided, and peace would be ensured. For almost an entire century, from the end of the Napoleonic Wars (1815) to World War I (1914), the balance-of-power system appeared to be at least partially effective in Europe. However, an important defect in the balance-of-power system is that a small conflict between two nations that are members of separate alliances can draw all member nations of each alliance into the conflict.

This defect can result in the rapid expansion of a small conflict into a major war between separate alliances of nations. Essentially this is what happened in **World War I**, when a minor conflict in the Balkan nations resulted in a very destructive war between the *Allies* (England, France, Russia, and eventually the United States) and the *Central Powers* (Germany, Austria-Hungary, and Turkey) (see Focus: "Know Your Geography").

World War I
the Allies versus the Central Powers

FOCUS

Know Your Geography

In discussing international politics, American students are at a distinct disadvantage when compared with many of their international contemporaries. *National Geographic* has sponsored both international and U.S.-based studies that tested the ability of 18- to 24-year-olds to identify countries on a map of the world and geographic literacy—their understanding about "how people and places interact, where things come from, and where we're going." The international study indicated that the most geographically knowledgeable youth came from Sweden where, on average, those surveyed identified 79 percent of the countries correctly. The worst? The United States, where the average percentage correct was only 46 percent. Shockingly, 11 percent of the Americans surveyed could not even identify the United States on a map. More 18- to 24-year-old Americans knew where the original *CSI* television series was set than could identify Iraq on a map. Test your knowledge and see how you fare.

Respondents' Country and Average Percent Correct

Sweden	79	France	71	United Kingdom	54
Germany	77	Japan	62	Mexico	49
Italy	75	Canada	56	United States	46

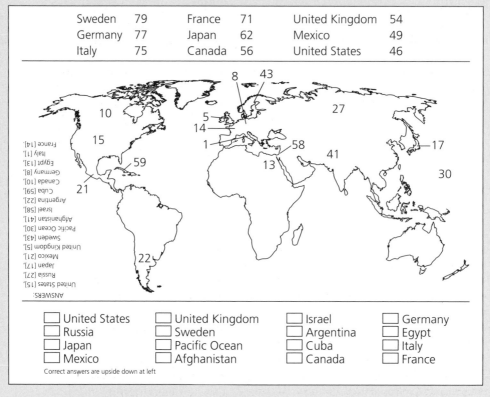

ANSWERS:
United States [15], Russia [27], Japan [17], Mexico [21], United Kingdom [5], Sweden [43], Pacific Ocean [30], Afghanistan [41], Israel [58], Argentina [22], Cuba [59], Canada [10], Germany [8], Egypt [13], Italy [1], France [14].

☐ United States   ☐ United Kingdom   ☐ Israel   ☐ Germany
☐ Russia   ☐ Sweden   ☐ Argentina   ☐ Egypt
☐ Japan   ☐ Pacific Ocean   ☐ Cuba   ☐ Italy
☐ Mexico   ☐ Afghanistan   ☐ Canada   ☐ France

Correct answers are upside down at left

SOURCE: *National Geographic* (www.nationalgeographic.com/geosurvey).

Indeed, World War I proved so destructive (10 million people were killed on the battlefields between 1914 and 1918) that a worldwide call resulted to replace the balance-of-power system with a new arrangement—"collective security."

Collective Security: The United Nations

Collective security originally meant that *all* nations would join together to guarantee one another's "territorial integrity and existing political independence" against "external aggression" by any nation.[3] This concept resulted in the formation of the League of Nations in 1919. However, opposition to international involvement was so great in the United States after World War I that after a lengthy debate in the Senate, the United States refused to join the League of Nations. More important, the League of Nations failed completely to deal with rising militarism in Germany, Japan, and Italy in the 1930s. During that decade, Japan invaded Manchuria, Italy invaded Ethiopia, and Germany invaded Czechoslovakia; the League of Nations failed to prevent any of these aggressions. Fascism in Germany and Italy and militarism in Japan went unchecked. **World War II** between the *Allies* (the United States, England, France, China, and the Soviet Union) and the *Axis Powers* (Germany, Italy, and Japan) was even more devastating than World War I: World War II cost more than 40 million lives, both civilian and military.

World War II
the Allies versus the Axis Powers

Yet even after World War II, the notion of collective security remained an ideal of the victorious Allied powers, especially the United States, Great Britain, the **USSR** (the Union of Soviet Socialist Republics, also called the Soviet Union, which was the fifteen "republics" including Russia that were under communist rule until 1991), France, and China. The Charter of the United Nations was signed in 1945. The new organization originally included fifty-one members. The United Nations provided for (1) a Security Council with eleven members, five of them being permanent members (the United States, the USSR, Britain, France, and China) and having the power to veto any action by the Security Council; (2) a General Assembly composed of all the member nations, each with a single vote; (3) a secretariat headed by a secretary-general with a staff at UN headquarters in New York; and (4) several special bodies to handle specialized affairs—for example, the Economic and Social Council, the Trusteeship Council, and the International Court at The Hague. Today, much of the original structure of the UN remains, though the Security Council has expanded to include fifteen members, with the five permanent members remaining part of the body (Russia assumed the seat held by the USSR when that nation dissolved), and ten other members rotating in.

USSR
Union of Soviet Socialist Republics (Soviet Union): fifteen "republics" including Russia; under communist rule 1917–1991; upon dissolution of the USSR in 1991, Russia assumed the USSR's UN seat

The Security Council has the "primary responsibility" for maintaining "international peace and security." For this reason the world's most powerful nations—the United States, Russia, Great Britain, France, and China—have permanent seats on the council and veto powers over all but procedural matters. (Germany and Japan, originally denied Security Council membership as defeated powers in World War II, are currently leading candidates for permanent Security Council seats.)

The General Assembly has authority over "any matter affecting the peace of the world," although it is supposed to defer to the Security Council if the council has already taken up a particular matter. No nation has a veto in the General Assembly; all UN member nations have one vote, regardless of size or power. Most resolutions can be passed by a majority vote.

Cold War
political, military, and ideological conflict between communist nations, led by the USSR, and the Western democracies, led by the United States, from 1945 to 1990

The United Nations proved largely ineffective during the long **Cold War** confrontation between the communist nations, led by the USSR, and the Western democracies, led by the United States. Many of the new nations admitted to the United Nations were headed by authoritarian regimes of one kind or another. The Western democracies were outnumbered in the General Assembly, and the USSR frequently used its veto to prevent action by the Security Council. Anti-Western and antidemocratic speeches became common in the General Assembly. The United Nations was overshadowed by the confrontation of the world's two **superpowers**: the United States and the USSR. Indeed, international conflicts throughout the world—in the Middle East, Africa, Latin America, Southeast Asia, and elsewhere—were usually influenced by some aspect of the superpower struggle.

superpowers
Cold War term referring to the United States and the USSR as the dominant world powers

The United Nations Today

The end of the Cold War resulted in increased prominence for the United Nations, particularly in its role as an international peacekeeper. Following the dissolution of the Soviet Union, Russia inherited the USSR's seat on the UN Security Council and has generally cooperated in UN efforts to bring stability to various regions in turmoil. During much of the 1990s, the United Nations passed numerous resolutions aimed at mandating the nation of Iraq, led by Saddam Hussein, to allow UN weapons inspectors to conduct searches. The searches were targeted at finding weapons of mass destruction. Iraq continually refused, leading to heightened tensions with both the UN and the United States. In 2003 President George W. Bush attempted to convince the United Nations to join the United States in taking military action to force Iraq to comply with the UN resolutions. But the UN Security Council rejected Bush's request, and the United States decided to undertake **unilateral action**, or to act alone, and invaded Iraq in March 2003. The U.S. forces were eventually joined by a bilateral coalition, including troops from Great Britain, the closest U.S. ally in the war.

unilateral action
action taken alone rather than as part of a coalition

The United Nations did not authorize the U.S.-led invasion of Iraq, but Hussein's government fell within a month of the U.S. military action, and in May 2003, President Bush declared that the U.S. mission in Iraq had been accomplished. But as months passed, insurgent violence continued as the number of dead—both U.S. soldiers and Iraqi civilians—increased. In August 2003 insurgents bombed the UN headquarters in Baghdad, and the organization pulled out of the country completely, returning the following year. The United Nations assisted in negotiating between various factions within the nations to draft the Iraqi constitution, but international opposition to the U.S. invasion has resulted in an unwillingness to commit UN peacekeeping forces in Iraq.

In recent times, the United Nations has chastised governments for violating UN resolutions. This has particularly been the case with North Korea, whose nuclear tests prompted a resolution from the UN Security Council condemning the tests and imposing additional financial restrictions on the nation while widening an arms embargo. Though China, a long-time ally of North Korea, has voted in favor of UN-imposed economic sanctions as punishment against the nuclear testing, the North Korean regime, now run by Kim Jong-un, who succeeded his father Kim Jong-il as North Korea's leader upon his death in 2012, remained defiant even when faced with condemnation by the Security Council. In many ways, the intractable situation in North Korea belies the stranglehold that rogue states like North Korea can put the Security Council in: the tools available to them—condemnation, inspections, and sanctions—can be and often are ignored by dictators intent on pursuing their own agenda.

Regional Security—NATO

General disappointment with the United Nations as vehicle for collective security gave rise as early as 1949 to a different approach: **regional security**. In response to aggressive Soviet moves in Europe, the United States and the democracies of Western Europe created the **North Atlantic Treaty Organization (NATO)**. In the NATO treaty, fifteen Western nations agreed that "an armed attack against one or more NATO nations . . . shall be considered an attack against them all." The United States made a specific commitment to defend Western Europe in the event of a Soviet attack. A joint NATO military command was established (with Dwight D. Eisenhower as its first commander) to coordinate the defense of Western Europe. After the formation of NATO, the Soviets made no further advances into Western Europe. The Soviets themselves, in response to NATO, drew up a comparable treaty among their own Eastern European satellite nations: the **Warsaw Pact**, a regional alliance between the Soviet Union, Poland, Hungary, Romania, Czechoslovakia, Bulgaria, and East Germany. Note that these regional security agreements—NATO and the Warsaw Pact—were more like the nineteenth-century balance-of-power alliances than like the true concept of *collective security*. The original notion of collective security envisioned agreement among *all* nations, whereas NATO and the Warsaw Pact were similar to the older systems of separate alliances.

The Warsaw Pact disintegrated following the dramatic collapse of the communist governments of Eastern Europe in 1989. Former Warsaw Pact nations—Poland, Hungary, Romania, Czechoslovakia, Bulgaria, and East Germany—threw out their ruling communist regimes and began negotiations leading to the withdrawal of Soviet troops from their territory. The Berlin Wall was smashed in 1989, and Germany was formally reunified in 1990, bringing together 61 million prosperous people of West Germany with 17 million less-affluent people of East Germany.

NATO Today

The reduced threat of attack on Western Europe raised several questions regarding the future of NATO and its role in the international arena.[4] Once an exclusive club of the original twelve signatory nations (Belgium, Canada, Denmark, France, Iceland, Italy, Luxembourg, the Netherlands, Norway, Portugal, the United Kingdom, and the United States), membership in NATO today has expanded to twenty-eight nations. Despite Russia's initial objections

regional security an attempt to bring order to international relations during the Cold War by creating regional alliances between a superpower and nations of a particular region

North Atlantic Treaty Organization (NATO) regional alliance of Western democracies to protect themselves against Soviet aggression

Warsaw Pact a regional alliance between the Soviet Union, Poland, Hungary, Romania, Czechoslovakia, Bulgaria, and East Germany to the expansion of NATO, NATO's enlargement policy has meant that NATO now includes many states that were once members of NATO's adversarial alliance, the Warsaw Pact. Today, former Eastern bloc states (including Albania, Bulgaria, Croatia, the Czech Republic, Estonia, Hungary, Latvia, Lithuania, Poland, Romania, Slovakia, and Slovenia) are all NATO members. In addition, Macedonia, Bosnia and Herzegovina, and Montenegro are in the process of becoming member states at this writing.

During the 1990s, NATO faced the question of whether or not ethnic conflicts in Eastern Europe, especially in the former Yugoslavia, were a threat to the security of Western Europe. The combination of security and humanitarian concerns drew NATO into the former Yugoslavian province of Bosnia in 1995 to assist in resolving conflict among Serbs, Croats, and Muslims. The United States provided about one-third of the NATO military forces deployed in Bosnia. NATO again acted militarily to halt ethnic conflict in Kosovo in 1999. NATO forces, including U.S. aircraft, bombed targets in both Kosovo and Serbia itself. Eventually, Serbian troops were withdrawn from Kosovo and replaced by NATO troops.

With the terror attacks on the United States on September 11, 2001, Article 5 (an attack on any member shall be considered to be an attack on all) of the NATO Charter was invoked for the first time in its history. NATO determined that the attacks were indeed eligible, and NATO forces began military operations in support of U.S. efforts, including participating in several operations in the Mediterranean Sea that sought to prevent the movement of terrorists. In 2003, NATO also took command of the International Security Assistance Force (ISAF) in Afghanistan. The ISAF has overseen the efforts to secure various areas of Afghanistan from the Taliban regime. NATO and the United Nations will also conduct an international peacekeeping mission in Afghanistan in 2014 when Afghan military will take over control of the nation's security forces.

NATO also has been involved in other efforts, specifically a training mission created in 2011 at the request of the Iraqi Interim Government. This mission enabled NATO forces to train Iraqi security forces. In 2009, in the wake of several episodes of piracy in the Gulf of Aden and the Indian Ocean, NATO deployed warships to prevent Somali pirates from seizing control of ships at sea. And in 2011 during the Libyan uprising that saw Libya's long-term dictator Muammar Gaddafi overthrown, NATO enforced a no-fly zone designed to protect civilians in that country. NATO also agreed to enforce an arms embargo in Libya, but lack of support from all NATO members led to an international incident in which the retiring U.S. Secretary of Defense, Robert Gates, publicly chastised some NATO members because only eight of the 28 member states had forces in combat operations. Gates complained of a two-tier system "between those willing and able to pay the price and bear the burdens of commitments, and those who enjoy the benefits of NATO membership but don't want to share the risks and the costs." Gates warned that "to avoid the very real possibility of collective military irrelevance, member nations must examine new approaches to boosting combat capabilities—in procurement, in training, in logistics, in sustainment." Otherwise, he said, NATO—organization spawned by the Cold War and striving for modern relevance—has a "dim and dismal" future.[5]

A Brief History of the Cold War

For forty-five years following the end of World War II, the United States and the Soviet Union confronted each other in a protracted political, military, and ideological struggle known as the Cold War.

Origins

During World War II, the United States and the Soviet Union joined forces to eliminate the Nazi threat to the world. The United States dismantled its military forces at the end of the war in 1945, but the USSR, under the brutal dictatorship of Joseph Stalin, used the powerful Red Army to install communist governments in the nations of Eastern Europe in violation of wartime agreements to allow free elections. Stalin also ignored pledges to cooperate in a unified allied occupation of Germany; Germany was divided and in 1948 Stalin tried unsuccessfully to oust the United States, Britain, and France from Berlin in a year-long "Berlin Blockade." Former British Prime Minister Winston Churchill warned the United States in a 1946 speech that the Soviets were dividing Europe with an "Iron Curtain." When Soviet-backed communist guerrilla forces threatened Greece and Turkey in 1948, President Harry Truman responded with a pledge to "support free people who are resisting attempted subjugation by armed minorities or by outside pressures," a policy that became known as the **Truman Doctrine**.

Truman Doctrine
foreign policy shaped by the goal of assisting in resistance against "outside pressures," usually in the form of communist movements

Containment

The threat of Soviet expansionism and communist world revolution caused the American government to assume world leadership on behalf of the preservation of democracy. The U.S. State Department's Russian expert, George F. Kennan, called for a policy of **containment**: "It is clear that the main element of any United States policy toward the Soviet Union must be that of a long-term, vigilant containment of Russian expansive tendencies."[6] To implement the containment policy, the United States first initiated the **Marshall Plan**, named for Secretary of State George C. Marshall, to rebuild the economies of the Western European nations. Marshall reasoned that *economically* weak nations were more susceptible to communist subversion and Soviet intimidation. The subsequent formation of NATO provided *military* support to contain the USSR.

containment
a policy of preventing the enemy from expanding its boundaries and/or influence; describes U.S. foreign policy vis-à-vis the USSR during the Cold War

Marshall Plan
a U.S. program to rebuild the nations of Western Europe in the aftermath of World War II in order to render them less susceptible to communist influence and/or takeover

The Korean War

The first military test of the containment policy came in June 1950 when communist North Korean armies invaded South Korea. President Truman believed (correctly) that the North Koreans were acting on behalf of their sponsor, the Soviet Union. The Soviets had already aided Chinese communists under the leadership of Mao Zedong in capturing control of mainland China in 1949. The United States quickly brought the Korean invasion issue to the Security Council. With the USSR boycotting this meeting because the Council had refused to seat the new communist delegation from China, the Council passed a resolution calling on member nations to send troops to repel the invasion.

America's conventional (nonnuclear) military forces had been largely dismantled after World War II. Moreover, President Truman insisted on keeping most of the nation's forces in Europe, fearing that the Korean invasion was a diversion to be followed by a Soviet invasion of Western Europe. But General Douglas MacArthur, in a brilliant amphibious landing at Inchon behind North Korean lines, destroyed a much larger enemy army, captured the North Korean capital, and moved northward toward the Chinese border. Then in December 1950, disaster struck American forces as a million-man Chinese army entered the conflict. Chinese troops surprised American forces, inflicting heavy casualties, trapping entire units, and forcing U.S. troops to beat a hasty retreat.

LATE OCTOBER

In October 1962, these intelligence photos showing Soviet missiles at Cuban bases touched off the thirteen-day Cuban missile crisis. The prospect of war seemed imminent; U.S. nuclear forces went on alert. Secretly, President Kennedy proposed withdrawing U.S. missiles from Turkey if the Soviets withdrew the Cuban missiles. They did, but Soviet leader Khrushchev's lost face in doing so.

General MacArthur urged retaliation against China, but Truman sought to keep the war "limited." When MacArthur publicly protested against political limits to military operations, Truman dismissed the popular general. The Korean War became a bloody stalemate.

Dwight Eisenhower was elected president in 1952 after he had promised to "go to Korea" to end the increasingly unpopular war. He also threatened to use nuclear weapons in the conflict, but eventually agreed to a settlement along the original border between North and South Korea. Communist expansion in Korea was "contained" but at a high price: The United States lost more than 38,000 people in the war.

Cuban Missile Crisis

The United States initially welcomed Fidel Castro's overthrow of the repressive Batista regime in Cuba in 1959, but when Castro allied his government with Moscow and invited Soviet military intervention into the Western Hemisphere, Washington sought his ouster. Under President Eisenhower, the CIA had planned a large "covert" operation—an invasion of Cuba by a brigade of Cuban exiles. Newly installed president John F. Kennedy approved the Bay of Pigs operation in early 1961, but when Castro's air force destroyed the makeshift invasion fleet offshore, Kennedy refused to provide U.S. Air Force support. The surviving Cubans were forced to surrender.

The young president was tested again in 1961 when the Russians erected the Berlin Wall, physically dividing that city. Despite heated rhetoric, Kennedy did nothing. Eventually the Wall would become a symbol of Soviet repression.

The most serious threat of nuclear holocaust during the entire Cold War, however, was the Cuban missile crisis.[7] In 1962 Soviet Premier Nikita Khrushchev sought to secretly install medium-range nuclear missiles in Cuba in an effort to give the USSR immediate nuclear capability against U.S. cities. In October 1962, intelligence photos showing Soviet missiles at Cuban bases touched off the thirteen-day Cuban missile crisis. President Kennedy publicly announced a naval blockade of Cuba, threatening to halt Soviet vessels at sea by force if necessary. The prospect of war appeared imminent; U.S. nuclear forces went on alert. Secretly, Kennedy proposed to withdraw U.S. nuclear missiles from Turkey in exchange for Soviet withdrawal of nuclear missiles from Cuba. Khrushchev's agreement to the deal appeared to the world as a backing down; Secretary of State Dean Rusk would boast: "We were eyeball to eyeball, and they blinked." Kennedy would be hailed for his statesmanship in the crisis; Khrushchev soon lost his job.

The Vietnam War

The involvement of the United States in Vietnam also grew out of the policy of "containment."[8] President Eisenhower had declined to intervene in the former French colony in 1954 when communist forces led by Ho Chi Minh defeated French forces at the battle of Dien Bien Phu. The resulting Geneva Accords of 1954 divided that country into North Vietnam, with a communist government, and South Vietnam, with a U.S.-backed government. When South Vietnamese communist (Vietcong) guerrilla forces threatened the South Vietnamese government in the early 1960s, President Kennedy sent a large force of advisers and counterinsurgency forces to assist in every aspect of training and support for the Army of the Republic of Vietnam (ARVN). In 1963 Kennedy was assassinated, and by 1964 units of the North Vietnamese Army (NVA) had begun to supplement the Vietcong guerrilla forces in the south. President Lyndon B. Johnson ordered U.S. combat troops into South Vietnam in February 1965 and authorized a gradual increase in air strikes against North Vietnam. Eventually over 500,000 American troops were committed to Vietnam; over 2.8 million served there before the **Paris Peace Agreement** was signed in 1973; 47,366 were killed in action. (A short history of the Vietnam War is presented in Chapter 6, Case Study: "The Vietnam War: A Political History.")

Paris Peace Agreement
treaty ending U.S. participation in the Vietnam War, 1973

The Vietnam Syndrome of the 1970s

A new isolationism permeated American foreign policy following defeat in Vietnam. The slogan "No More Vietnams" was used to oppose any U.S. military intervention, whether or not U.S. vital interests were at stake. Disillusionment replaced idealism. American leaders had exaggerated the importance of Vietnam; now Americans were unwilling to believe their leaders when they warned of other dangers. The USSR rapidly expanded its political and military presence in Asia, Africa, the Middle East, Central America, and the Caribbean in the late 1970s. The United States did little to respond to this wave of Soviet expansionism until the Soviet invasion of Afghanistan in 1979 when President Jimmy Carter authorized the largest covert action in CIA history—military support of the Afghan guerrilla forces fighting Soviet occupation. The Soviets suffered a heavy drain of human and economic resources during their nine-year war in Afghanistan, which some dubbed "Russia's Vietnam."

Rebuilding U.S. Defenses in the 1980s

A decision to rebuild U.S. military forces and reassert international leadership on behalf of democratic values gained widespread endorsement. In 1979 President Carter presented Congress with the first request for an increase in defense spending in more than a decade. The NATO nations jointly pledged to increase their defense efforts. British Prime Minister Margaret Thatcher, French President François Mitterrand, and German Chancellor Helmut Kohl all held fast against a "nuclear freeze" movement that would have locked in Soviet superiority in European-based nuclear weapons. When the Reagan administration arrived in Washington in 1981, the defense buildup had already begun.

the strategic defense initiative
Reagan's research program to develop a defense against ballistic missile attack; sometimes referred to as "Star Wars"

The Reagan defense buildup extended through 1985 with increases in defense spending, improvements in strategic nuclear weapons, and, perhaps more important, the rebuilding and re-equipping of U.S. conventional forces. President Reagan also announced a new **strategic defense initiative** (SDI), a research program to develop a defense against a ballistic missile attack, promptly labeled "Star Wars" by the media.

The American and NATO defense buildup of the 1980s, together with the promise of a new, expensive, and technologically sophisticated race for ballistic missile defense, forecast heavy additional strains on the weak economy of the Soviet Union. Thus, in 1985, when new Soviet President Mikhail Gorbachev came to power, the stage was set for an end to the Cold War.

Gorbachev and Reform

Gorbachev believed that economic progress in the Soviet Union required a reduction in that nation's heavy military expenditures and improved relations with the United States. He announced reductions in the size of the Soviet military and reached agreements with the United States on the reduction of nuclear forces. More important, in 1988 he announced that the Soviet Union would no longer use its military forces to keep communist governments in power in Eastern European nations. This stunning announcement (for which Gorbachev received the Nobel Peace Prize in 1990) encouraged opposition democratic forces in Poland (the Solidarity movement), Czechoslovakia, Hungary, Bulgaria, Romania, and East Germany to overthrow their communist governments in 1989. Gorbachev refused to intervene to halt the destruction of the Berlin Wall that same year, despite the pleas by the East German hard-line communist leader Eric Honnecker.

The Disintegration of the Soviet Union

Strong independence movements in the republics of the USSR emerged as the authority of the centralized Communist Party in Moscow waned. Lithuania, Estonia, and Latvia—nations that had been forcibly incorporated into the Soviet Union in 1939—led the way to independence in 1991. Soon all fifteen republics of the USSR declared their independence, and the Union of Soviet Socialist Republics officially ceased to exist after December 31, 1991. The red flag with its hammer and sickle was replaced with the flag of the Russian Republic. Boris Yeltsin became the first elected president in the history of Russia.

Russia after Communism

The transition from a centralized state-run economy to free markets turned out to be more painful for Russians than expected. Living standards for most people declined, alcoholism and death rates increased, and even average life spans shortened. President Boris Yeltsin was confronted by both extreme nationalists, who believed democracy weakened the power of Russia in the world, and the continuing efforts of communists to regain their lost power. Ethnic conflict and political separatism, especially in the largely Muslim province of Chechnya, has added to Russia's problems. In 2000 after prolonged fighting, Russian troops finally took control of most of the province. But corruption, embezzlement, graft, and organized crime continue to undermine democratic reforms. Ill health eventually forced Yeltsin to turn over power to Vladimir Putin, who won election as president of Russia in 2000 and re-election in 2004. Constitutionally prohibited from seeking reelection in 2008, Putin's hand-picked successor and former deputy chief of staff Dmitry Medvedev was elected president. Medvedev garnered over 71 percent of the vote, but independent international watchdog organizations, including Amnesty International, challenged whether those elections were conducted in a free and fair manner. These same claims again surfaced in 2012 when Putin reclaimed the presidency, winning 63 percent of the popular vote. Early in his tenure in 2012, Putin found himself at odds with the Obama administration who sought Putin's support in easing Syrian President

Bashar al-Assad out of power. Violence erupted in Syria during the Arab Spring protests of 2011 and continued as opponents of Assad continue to rebel against government forces. The U.S. and its western allies believed the only way to curb the violence was to remove the Syrian dictator, but Putin disagreed.

Despite these tensions, the United States has a vital continuing interest in promoting democracy and economic reform in Russia. Russia remains the only nuclear power capable of destroying the United States.[9]

The Control of Nuclear Arms

Nuclear weaponry made the Cold War infinitely more dangerous than any national confrontation in human history. The nuclear arsenals of the United States and the former USSR threatened a human holocaust. Yet, paradoxically, the very destructiveness of nuclear weapons caused leaders on both sides to exercise extreme caution in their relations with each other. Scores of wars, large and small, were fought by different nations during the Cold War years, yet American and Soviet troops never engaged in direct combat against each other.

In 1957 the USSR launched *Sputnik*, the first satellite developed by humans to orbit the earth. Americans were shocked to realize that the Soviets led in the space race. By the early 1960s, a new and very dangerous balance of nuclear terror had emerged. Both the United States and the Soviet Union possessed large arsenals of nuclear weapons and intercontinental ballistic missiles (ICBMs) capable of carrying these weapons through space to targets in each other's homeland.

SALT I

SALT I: 1972
the ABM treaty agreement and limits on the numbers of offensive missiles

Following the election of Richard Nixon as president in 1968, the United States, largely guided by former Harvard professor Henry Kissinger (national security adviser to the president and later secretary of state), began negotiations with the Soviet Union over nuclear arms. In 1972 the United States and the USSR concluded two and one-half years of Strategic Arms Limitation Talks (SALT) about limiting the nuclear arms race. The agreement, **SALT I**, consists of a treaty limiting antiballistic missiles (ABMs) and an agreement placing a numerical ceiling on offensive missiles. Under the offensive-arms agreement, each side was frozen at the total number of offensive missiles completed or under construction. Both sides could construct new missiles if they dismantled an equal number of older missiles. Each nation agreed not to interfere in the satellite intelligence-gathering activities of the other nation. Both nations pledged to continue efforts at further arms control—the SALT II talks.

SALT II

SALT II: 1979
agreement limiting all types of nuclear launchers as well as number of warheads on launchers

The United States and the Soviet Union signed the lengthy and complicated **SALT II** treaty in 1979. It set an overall limit on strategic nuclear launchers—ICBMs, SLBMs (submarine-launched ballistic missiles), bombers, and long-range cruise missiles—for each side. It also limited the number of missiles that could carry multiple independently targeted re-entry vehicles with nuclear warheads (MIRVs) and banned new types of ICBMs, with the exception of one new type of ICBM for each side. But the Soviets were allowed to keep 314 very heavy SS-18 missiles for which the United States had no equivalent. When the Soviet Union invaded Afghanistan, Carter withdrew the SALT II treaty from Senate consideration. However, Carter, and later Reagan, announced that the United States would abide by the provisions of the unratified SALT II treaty as long as the Soviet Union did so.

START

In negotiations with the Soviets, the Reagan administration pushed for reductions in missiles and warheads, not merely for limitations on future numbers and types of weapons as in previous SALT talks. To symbolize this new direction, President Reagan renamed the negotiations the **Strategic Arms Reduction Talks**, or **START**. The president emphasized that any new treaty must result in reductions of strategic arms to levels equal for both sides. The Soviets objected strongly to President Reagan's research efforts in the field of ballistic missile defense (SDI). In 1983 the Soviets walked out of the START talks and out of talks seeking to limit European nuclear weapons. But by 1985, after Reagan's re-election, the Soviets returned to the bargaining table at Geneva, Switzerland.

Strategic Arms Reduction Talks (START) renamed arms-control talks to emphasize reductions in strategic nuclear weapons

INF Treaty

The **Intermediate-Range Nuclear Forces (INF) Treaty** in 1987 was the first agreement between the superpowers that actually resulted in the destruction of nuclear weapons. It eliminated an entire class of nuclear weapons—missiles with an intermediate range, between three hundred and thirty-eight hundred miles. It was also the first treaty that resulted in equal levels (zero) of arms for the United States and the USSR. To reach an equal level, the Soviets were required to destroy more missiles and warheads than the United States. Finally, INF was the first treaty to provide for on-site inspection for verification. The proportion of each side's nuclear weapons covered by the INF Treaty was small, but this treaty set the pattern for future arms control agreements in its provisions for *reductions*, *equality*, and *verification*.

Intermediate-Range Nuclear Forces (INF) Treaty eliminated intermediate-range ballistic missiles

START I and II

The long-awaited agreement on long-range strategic nuclear weapons was finally signed in Moscow in 1991 by Presidents George H. W. Bush and Mikhail Gorbachev. The **START I Treaty** included a 30 percent reduction in the total number of deployed strategic nuclear delivery systems (ICBMs, SLBMs, and manned bombers) and a reduction of nearly 50 percent in the total number of strategic nuclear warheads to no more than six thousand.

The ink had not yet dried on the new treaty when Russia's first democratically elected president, Boris Yeltsin, agreed to even deeper cuts in nuclear weapons and, more important, to the eventual elimination of all land-based missiles with multiple (MIRV) warheads. The purpose of this historic agreement between Presidents Bush and Yeltsin in 1992, which was fully implemented in 2003, was to virtually eliminate the threat of a massive nuclear attack—a threat that had cast

START I Treaty reduced the total number of deployed strategic nuclear delivery systems by 30 percent and reduced the total number of strategic nuclear warheads by 50 percent.

FIGURE 14-1 STRATEGIC NUCLEAR ARMS AND START TREATIES

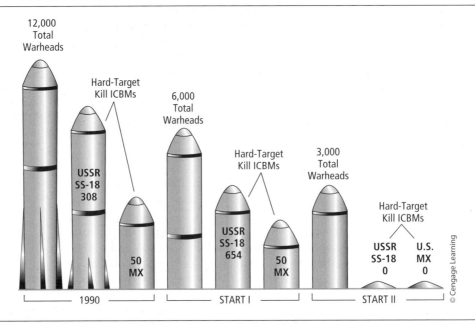

START II Treaty
reduced the number of
warheads to 3,000 for
each side and eliminated
all land-based missiles
with nuclear warheads
while providing on-site
verification

a menacing shadow over the world for decades. The **START II Treaty** includes
a reduction to three thousand nuclear warheads for each side, together with the
elimination of all "hard-target kill" land-based missiles with multiple warheads,
including Russia's huge SS-18 and the U.S. MX, and a provision for on-site verification of these reductions by teams of observers from both nations (Figure 14-1).

International Politics in a Post–September 11 World

On September 11, 2001, four planes hijacked by Islamic fundamentalist terrorists
crashed into the twin towers of the World Trade Center in New York City; into
the Pentagon in Washington, DC; and into a field in Pennsylvania, after passen-
gers aboard that plane fought the terrorists and prevented the plane from crashing into a fourth target. The nineteen terrorists were members of al Qaeda, a
terrorist network led by Osama bin Laden. Bin Laden and members of al Qaeda
apparently carried out the attacks in part because of their strong opposition to
the U.S. military's presence in Mecca, Islam's holiest city in Saudi Arabia. Since
that date, these incidents have defined and determined American foreign policy.

Huntington's Clash of Civilizations

clash of civilizations
a theory proposed by
Samuel P. Huntington
predicting that conflict
between modern, West-
ern democracies and
Islamic fundamentalist
nations will characterize
international relations in
the future

Political scientist Samuel P. Huntington has provided a context for the shape
of international relations in the future. Huntington asserts that "the **clash of
civilizations** will be the battle lines of the future," meaning that modern Western
democracies will continue to do battle with fundamentalist Islamic states.

Huntington's theory appears to be the basis of much of the foreign policy enacted by former President George W. Bush's administration.

In response to the attacks of September 11 and the implication of bin Laden and al Qaeda in the attacks, in late 2001 the United States attacked al Qaeda training camps in Afghanistan, which was being governed by a fundamentalist Islamic regime called the **Taliban**. The United States was joined by a coalition of allies, including anti-Taliban rebels from within Afghanistan. Within weeks of invading Afghanistan, the United States and its allies toppled the Taliban regime and worked to create an interim government in Afghanistan, though resistance from insurgent Taliban forces would keep the United States and its allies in Afghanistan through 2014.

Taliban
a fundamentalist Islamic regime that ruled Afghanistan from 1996 until 2001

Although the attack on Afghanistan certainly was intended to bring an end to Taliban rule, an additional goal of the invasion was to demonstrate the consequences for nations that support terrorism against the United States. The consequences were particularly apparent when President Obama ordered the execution of September 11 mastermind Osama bin Laden on May 2, 2011. Bin Laden, who had been in hiding for nearly a decade, was finally found by U.S. forces at a compound in Abbottabad, Pakistan, where he was killed by members of a U.S. Navy Seal team.

Staton R. Winter/The New York Times/Redux Pictures

Culture varies from place to place. In Turkey the juxtaposition of traditional Islamic culture contrasts with the overt sexuality commonplace in Western democracies. Do differences in culture necessarily mean conflict?

In addition to the Taliban, President George W. Bush also had set his sights on another foe: Iraq's Saddam Hussein. During his father's presidency, the United States had gone to war with Iraq over its invasion of Kuwait. In his 2003 State of the Union Address, Bush claimed that Iraq possessed weapons of mass destruction and was seeking to purchase the components of nuclear weapons, though no such weapons were ever found. The administration linked Hussein with al Qaeda.

In the spring of 2003, U.S. forces again invaded Iraq. It initially appeared that the United States had quickly succeeded in asserting its authority in toppling the Hussein regime, but as time wore on, resistance to the U.S. forces mounted. There were some successes in Iraq—notably the formation of a democratically elected government and formation of a constitution. But the insurgent opposition to U.S. involvement in Iraq fit Huntington's clash of civilizations model. And as the insurgency lingered, frustration in the United States grew as more lives were lost and more money was spent on an intractable conflict. Finally, U.S. forces withdrew from Iraq in December, 2011 leaving Iraqi security forces to deal with the rampant insurgent violence prevalent there.

President Obama's Change in Rhetoric

Though President Obama inherited a multi-front war from his predecessor, George W. Bush, and while he kept U.S. forces in Iraq and Afghanistan during portions of his presidency, the perspective of his foreign policy greatly differed from Bush's. Obama's rejection of the "clash of civilizations" thesis was perhaps best demonstrated in June 2009, when Obama travelled to Cairo, Egypt, to give what was touted as an address to the Muslim world. Reminding an international audience (the speech was broadcast on numerous Arab websites and television stations) of his own Muslim heritage (Obama's father was a Muslim), Obama sought to repair tattered and strained relations with Arab governments and individual followers of the Muslim faith:

> I have come here to seek a new beginning between the United States and Muslims around the world; one based upon mutual interest and mutual respect; and one based upon the truth that America and Islam are not exclusive, and need not be in competition. Instead, they overlap, and share common principles—principles of justice and progress; tolerance and the dignity of all human beings.

While the speech was met with skepticism by some in both the United States and in the international community, others regarded it as an important first step in repairing relationships between the Muslim and Arab worlds and the United States, though Obama himself noted the need for his words to be followed with action consistent with his vision.

The Continued Threat of Terrorism

In a post–September 11 world, the threat of terrorism creates two military requirements. The first is the ability to punish nations that sponsor terrorism and to dissuade other nations from continuing their support of terrorism. These types of operations are carried out by conventional military forces (see Research This!). A second requirement is the ability to take direct action

RESEARCH *THIS!*

The following are the results of various Gallup polls conducted over several years that gauge confidence in the U.S. military. Pollsters asked whether respondents had a great deal of confidence, quite a lot of confidence, some confidence, or very little confidence in the military.

Now I am going to read you a list of institutions in American society. Please tell me how much confidence you, yourself have in each one — a great deal, quite a lot, some, or very little?

The military

	Great deal %	Quite a lot %	Some %	Very little %	Great deal / Quite a lot %
2012	43	32	18	5	75
2011	47	31	16	3	78
2010	44	32	18	4	76
2009	45	37	12	5	82
2008	45	26	20	7	71
2007	39	30	21	8	69
2006	41	32	19	5	73
2005	42	32	18	7	74
2004	36	39	19	5	75
2003	48	34	14	4	82
2002	43	36	16	5	79
2001	32	34	24	6	66
2000	25	39	26	7	64
1999	34	34	26	6	68
1998	33	31	25	8	64
1997	30	30	27	10	60
1996	30	36	25	7	66
1995	33	31	27	7	64
1994	30	34	26	8	64
1993	32	35	23	8	67
1991	35	34	20	8	69
1991	52	33	11	3	85
1990	37	31	22	7	68
1989	31	32	26	9	63
1988	23	35	30	9	58
1987	24	37	28	9	61
1986	29	34	24	10	63

1985	24	37	28	8	61
1984	28	30	24	15	58
1983	23	30	29	12	53
1981	22	28	29	14	50
1979	25	29	29	14	54
1977	23	34	25	11	57
1975	27	31	25	11	58

(vol.) = Volunteered response*
Less than 0.5%

SOURCE: www.gallup.com/poll/1666/Military-National-Defense.aspx

YOUR ANALYSIS:

1. In general, what was the overall trend regarding confidence in the military before September 11, 2001?

2. How did September 11 impact people's confidence in the military?

3. In general, what has been the overall trend regarding confidence in the military since September 11, 2001?

against terrorists to capture or kill them or to free their hostages. These operations are carried out by highly trained, specially equipped special operations forces.

The Spread of Mass Terror Weapons

Since September 11, 2001, Americans have become more aware of the threat of mass terror weapons. The availability of the components of dangerous chemical and biological weapons—from research laboratories, government facilities, and industrial sites—and the innumerable ways in which they can be used to inflict harm—through food, water, and air—make defending against their use a difficult challenge for federal, state, and local government organizations.

The availability of nuclear weapons also is increasing (see Figure 14-2). In 2005 North Korea announced that it had achieved nuclear capacity, joining the so-called nuclear club of the United States, Russia, China, India, Pakistan, Britain, and France. In 2006 Iran asserted its right to enrich uranium (a key component of nuclear weapons) and rejected a freeze in its nuclear program (see Case Study: "Iran"), which remains a source of tension in relations between Iran and the United States.

CASE STUDY

Iran

We can trace today's tense and complex relations between the United States and Iran back to 1951. That year, the democratically elected prime minister of Iran, Mohammed Mossadegh, nationalized the country's oil reserves, meaning that the government took over ownership of reserves that had been held by private corporations.

Mossadegh's bold stroke set off a furious reaction by then-British Prime Minister Winston Churchill. Churchill and President Dwight Eisenhower, who was concerned about the increasing Soviet influence in Iran, agreed to enlist the Central Intelligence Agency in orchestrating a coup to depose Mossadegh in 1953.* The coup attempt eventually succeeded, and Mohammad Reza Pahlavi, Iran's monarch (Shah), was installed as prime minister Fazlollah Zahedi, the choice of Great Britain and the United States.

With continued British and U.S. support, the Shah modernized Iran's infrastructure. His autocratic rule, however, opened him to criticism by Ayatollah Ruhollah Khomeini, an influential Islamic Iranian cleric. Khomeini was exiled from the country but remained a vocal critic of both the Shah and the United States, which he characterized as "the Great Satan."

In early 1978, individuals from a broad coalition of Iranians—including students, Marxists, and pro-democracy activists—took to the streets protesting the Shah's oppressive government and calling for Khomeini's return. The demonstrations evolved into what became known as the Iranian Revolution and forced the Shah to flee Iran in January 1979. When a victorious Khomeini returned to Iran shortly after, many Iranians embraced the stern cleric. And although various groups had sought to depose the Shah, the Iranian people at large soon voted to make Iran an Islamic republic with Khomeini as its leader.

During the Iranian uprisings in 1979, students had seized control of the U.S. embassy in Tehran and taken its personnel as hostages. The students claimed that the diplomats were CIA agents plotting a coup against the Khomeini government, as indeed had occurred in 1953. During this time tensions between the United States and Iran were sky-high, and 52 Americans were held hostage for 444 days. Khomeini supported the students' actions. Part of the American response was to freeze more than $12 billion in Iranian assets in the United States. Although the United States later returned a sizeable portion of these assets, other parts remain frozen as the United States awaits the resolution of property disputes that arose out of the revolution. To the present day, this issue is a point of sharp contention between the two countries.

---

* www.nytimes.com/library/world/mideast/041600iran-cia-index.html

(continued)

Closely monitoring the bitter relations between the United States and its allies and Iran, Saddam Hussein, the president of neighboring Iraq, decided to exploit the ill will that Westerners felt for the Khomeini regime and the chaos that had accompanied the Iranian revolution. Hussein's Iraqi army invaded Iran in 1980, setting off the Iran–Iraq War. The United States backed Iraq in this six-year war, in which Hussein used chemical weapons against Iranian soldiers and civilians.

Over the next fifteen years, relations between the United States and Iran remained contentious. The United States denounced Iran's support of terrorist organizations and its pursuit of nuclear weapons. In 1995, the Clinton administration imposed economic sanctions on Iran. These sanctions were expanded with the passage of the Iran-Libya Sanctions Act of 1996, which penalized foreign corporations that invested in Iran's energy industry. This measure was a severe blow to the Iranian economy. In 1997, reformist Mohammad Khatami was elected president of Iran with a platform of strengthening democracy in Iran. Khatami made overtures to the United States, and for several years, the icy American–Iranian relations seemed to be thawing. When the terrorist attacks of September 11 occurred, young Iranians took to the streets in spontaneous demonstrations of support for the U.S. victims of the attacks.

That the good will had dissolved, however, was apparent when George W. Bush characterized Iran as part of an "Axis of Evil" in his 2002 State of the Union speech. Relations chilled primarily because of Iran's pursuit of nuclear weapons. Harsh rhetoric continued between the United States and Iran throughout the Bush administration, with Iranian president Mahmoud Ahmadinejad, widely perceived as anti-American, and President Bush trading barbs regularly.

During a June 2009 speech in Cairo, President Barack Obama seemed to try to end that cycle of criticism, pledging to engage Iran in respectful negotiations. But shortly after the speech, Ahmadinejad was elected to a second term, despite widespread protests by supporters of his more moderate opponent, including many students in Iran's capital city. Nonetheless, Ahmadinejad's reelection thwarted the optimism that a warmer relationship with Tehran would develop and that the nations would negotiate a deal to stop Iran's nuclear program. The hopes of achieving this outcome dissolved when Ahmadinejad, in a 2010 speech before the United Nations in New York City, proposed a conspiracy theory that the United States was behind the September 11 attack. Ahmadinejad's remarks prompted a massive walkout, and President Obama responded saying, "It was offensive. It was hateful. And particularly for him to make the statement here in Manhattan, just a little north of Ground Zero, where families lost their loved ones. People of all faiths, all ethnicities who see this as the seminal tragedy of this generation. For him to make a statement like that was inexcusable."^ In 2012, Ahmadinejad's regime continued to defy inspectors from the International Atomic Energy Agency, an arm of the United Nations, by refusing to allow inspection of sites that might be used to produce nuclear weapons, thus contributing to the anxious international speculation that Iran was seeking to build a nuclear weapon.

---

^ www.bbc.co.uk/news/world-us-canada-11407326

FIGURE 14-2 NUCLEAR POWERS IN THE WORLD

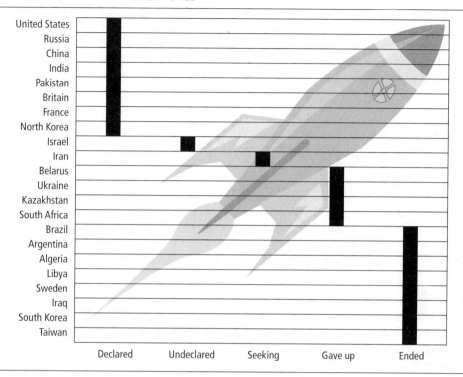

SOURCE: *Congressional Quarterly Weekly Report*, May 23, 1998, updated by author.

Unanticipated Threats

The United States anticipated very few of the dozens of crises that required the use of military force over the past decades. Few would have forecast that U.S. troops would be engaged in combat in Grenada in 1983, or Panama in 1989, or even the Persian Gulf in 1990–1991. General Colin Powell tried to convince the Congress that the real threat is the unknown, the uncertain. In a very real sense, the primary threat to our security is instability and being unprepared to handle a crisis or war that no one expected or predicted. But it is difficult to convince taxpayers or their elected representatives to prepare for the unknown.[10]

"International politics, like all politics, is a struggle for power." Fighting among peoples and societies has been a common occurrence throughout history. From time to time, nations have sought to provide greater order and stability to the international struggle for power. The advent of nuclear weapons made it imperative that nations seek a more stable world order through direct negotiations as well as collective security arrangements. The collapse of communism in Eastern Europe and the emergence of democracy in Russia reduced the threat of a nuclear holocaust. But regional conflicts continue to threaten world security. (See Controversies in Social Science: "When Should the United States Use Military Force?")

CONTROVERSIES IN SOCIAL SCIENCE

When Should the United States Use Military Force?

All modern presidents have acknowledged that the most agonizing decisions that they have made were to send U.S. military forces into combat. These decisions cost lives. The American people are willing to send their sons and daughters into danger—and even to see some of them wounded or killed—but *only* if a president convinces them that the outcome "is worth dying for." A recent Gallup poll indicated that 57 percent of Americans think that the United States should not attack another country unless that country has attacked the U.S. first.* So a president must be able to explain why American soldiers lost their lives and to justify their sacrifice. Often this must occur despite disagreement among the U.S. military, the diplomatic corps, and members of the president's administration.

Only to Protect Vital Interests?   The U.S. military learned many bitter lessons in its long, bloody experience in Vietnam. Among those lessons were these:

- The United States should commit its military forces only in support of vital national interests.
- If military forces are committed, they must have clearly defined military objectives—the destruction of enemy forces and/or the capture of enemy-held territory.
- Any commitment of U.S. forces must be of sufficient strength to ensure overwhelming and decisive victory with the fewest possible casualties.
- Before committing U.S. military forces, some reasonable assurances must be present that the effort has the support of the American people and their representatives in Congress.
- The commitment of U.S. military forces should be a last resort, after political, economic, and diplomatic efforts have proven ineffective.

These guidelines for the use of military force are widely supported within the U.S. military itself. Contrary to Hollywood stereotypes, military leaders are extremely reluctant to go to war when no vital interest of the United States is at stake, without any clear-cut military objectives, without the support of Congress or the American people, or without sufficient force to achieve speedy and decisive victory with minimum casualties. They are wary of seeing their troops placed in danger merely to advance diplomatic goals, to engage in "peacekeeping," to "stabilize governments," or to "show the flag." They are reluctant to undertake humanitarian missions while being shot at. They do not like to risk their soldiers' lives under "rules of engagement" that limit their ability to defend themselves.

To Support Important Political Objectives?   In contrast to military leaders, political leaders and diplomats often reflect the view that "war is a continuation of politics by other means"—a view commonly attributed to nineteenth-century German theorist of war Karl von Clausewitz. Military force may be used to protect interests that are important but not necessarily vital. Otherwise, the United States would be rendered largely impotent in world affairs. A diplomat's ability to achieve a satisfactory result often depends on the expressed or implied threat of military force. The distinguished international political theorist Hans Morgenthau wrote: "Since military strength is the obvious measure of a nation's power, its demonstration serves to impress others with that nation's power."

Currently American forces must be prepared to carry out a variety of missions in addition to the conduct of conventional war:

- Striking at terrorist targets to deter or retaliate
- Demonstrating U.S. resolve in crisis situations
- Demonstrating U.S. support for democratic governments
- Protecting U.S. citizens living abroad
- Peacemaking among warring factions or nations
- Peacekeeping where hostile factions or nations have accepted a peace agreement
- Providing humanitarian aid, often under warlike conditions

MAJOR DEPLOYMENT OF U.S. MILITARY FORCES SINCE WORLD WAR II

Year	Area	President
1950–1953	Korea	Truman
1958	Lebanon	Eisenhower
1961–1964	Vietnam	Kennedy
1962	Cuban waters	Kennedy
1965–1973	Vietnam	Johnson, Nixon
1965	Dominican Republic	Johnson
1970	Laos	Nixon
1970	Cambodia	Nixon
1975	Cambodia	Ford
1980	Iran	Carter
1982–1983	Lebanon	Reagan
1983	Grenada	Reagan
1989	Panama	G. H. W. Bush
1990–1991	Persian Gulf	G. H. W. Bush
1992–1993	Somalia	Bush, Clinton
1994–1995	Haiti	Clinton
1995–1996	Bosnia	Clinton
1999–2000	Kosovo	Clinton
2001–2014 (projected)	Afghanistan	G. W. Bush, Obama
2003–2011	Iraq	G. W. Bush, Obama

* www.gallup.com/poll/1666/Military-National-Defense.aspx.

In pursuit of such objectives, President George W. Bush sent troops into Afghanistan to eradicate al Qaeda training camps and end rule by the Islamic fundamentalist Taliban regime. In 2003 Bush cited Iraq's possession of weapons of mass destruction as the rationale for sending troops there. Opponents asserted that Bush's claims were false or exaggerated.

Other U.S. presidents have sent troops to Lebanon in 1982 to stabilize the government (Reagan), to Grenada in 1983 to rescue American medical students and restore democratic government (Reagan), to Panama in 1989 to oust drug-trafficking General Manuel Antonio Noriega from power and to protect U.S. citizens (Bush), to Somalia in 1992–1993 to provide emergency humanitarian aid (Bush and Clinton), to Haiti in 1994 to restore constitutional government (Clinton), and to Bosnia in 1995–1996 and Kosovo in 1999 for peacekeeping among warring ethnic factions (Clinton).

CHAPTER SUMMARY

- Although sovereignty is highly valued by all nations, it creates an international system in which no authority—not even the United Nations—is given the power to make or enforce rules binding on all nations. Nations cooperate with one another only when it is in their own interests to do so. Nations can make treaties with one another, but no court enforces the treaties, and they can be (and are) disregarded when it becomes advantageous for a nation to do so.

- The instability and insecurity of the international political arena have led to many attempts over the centuries to bring order to the international system. These systems of international order include the balance of power system, collective security, and regional security.

- For forty-five years following the end of World War II, the United States and the Soviet Union confronted each other in a protracted political,

military, and ideological struggle known as the Cold War.

- Nuclear weaponry made the Cold War infinitely more dangerous than any national confrontation in human history. Efforts to rein in a cataclysmic disaster prompted the negotiation and ratification of several nuclear weapons treaties, including SALT I and II, START I and II, and the INF Treaty.

- In a post-September 11 world, foreign policy initially was shaped by the clash of civilizations thesis that modern Western democracies will continue to do battle with fundamentalist Islamic states, embraced by former President George W. Bush's administration. President Barack Obama rejected the clash of civilizations thesis, calling instead for a more conciliatory approach with Islamic nations. Nonetheless, threats including terrorism and nuclear proliferation, and unanticipated threats, remain.

KEY TERMS

clash of civilizations   a theory proposed by Samuel P. Huntington predicting that conflict between modern, Western democracies and Islamic fundamentalist nations will characterize international relations in the future

Cold War   political, military, and ideological conflict between communist nations, led by the USSR, and the Western democracies, led by the United States, from 1945 to 1990

containment   a policy of preventing the enemy from expanding its boundaries and/or influence; describes U.S. foreign policy vis-à-vis the USSR during the Cold War

international politics   the worldwide struggle for power

international law   the series of customs and principles that helps to guide relations among nations; compliance with these norms is largely voluntary

Intermediate-Range Nuclear Forces (INF) Treaty   eliminated intermediate-range ballistic missiles

Marshall Plan   a U.S. program to rebuild the nations of Western Europe in the aftermath of World War II in order to render them less susceptible to communist influence and/or takeover

North Atlantic Treaty Organization (NATO) regional alliance of Western democracies to protect themselves against Soviet aggression

Paris Peace Agreement treaty ending U.S. participation in the Vietnam War, 1973

regional security an attempt to bring order to international relations during the Cold War by creating regional alliances between a superpower and nations of a particular region

sovereignty legal power over internal affairs, freedom from external intervention, and legal recognition by other nations

superpowers Cold War term referring to the United States and the USSR as the dominant world powers

SALT I: 1972 the ABM treaty agreement and limits on the numbers of offensive missiles

SALT II: 1979 agreement limiting all types of nuclear launchers as well as number of warheads on launchers

Strategic Arms Reduction Talks (START) renamed arms-control talks to emphasize reductions in strategic nuclear weapons

START I Treaty reduced the total number of deployed strategic nuclear delivery systems by 30 percent and reduced the total number of strategic nuclear warheads by 50 percent.

START II Treaty reduced the number of warheads to 3,000 for each side and eliminated all land-based missiles with nuclear warheads while providing on-site verification

Truman Doctrine foreign policy shaped by the goal of assisting in resistance against "outside pressures," usually in the form of communist movements

the strategic defense initiative Reagan's research program to develop a defense against ballistic missile attack; sometimes referred to as "Star Wars"

Taliban a fundamentalist Islamic regime that ruled Afghanistan from 1996 until 2001

unilateral action action taken alone rather than as part of a coalition

USSR Union of Soviet Socialist Republics (Soviet Union): fifteen "republics" including Russia; under communist rule 1917–19 91; upon dissolution of the USSR in 1991, Russia assumed the USSR's UN seat

Warsaw Pact a regional alliance between the Soviet Union, Poland, Hungary, Romania, Czechoslovakia, Bulgaria, and East Germany

World War I the Allies versus the Central Powers

World War II the Allies versus the Axis Powers

ON THE WEB

EXPLORING POWER AMONG NATIONS

Visit the website for this textbook (**www.cengagebrain.com**) for text-specific information concerning the study of power among nations.

The Internet offers a nearly limitless wealth of information on world affairs.

- **NATO** NATO forces undertake peacekeeping and crisis management missions in areas of conflict around the world. NATO on the

Internet (**www.nato.int**) provides researchers with information about the alliance's current activities and membership, the text of speeches by NATO officials, and the text of the original treaty signed in 1949.

Try This: Go to **www.natochannel.tv/** and pick one of the videos that highlight current world events. Identify the issue at hand and what NATO's role is in the process of maintaining peace or aiding a nation in need.

- **U.S. Department of Defense** The U.S. Department of Defense maintains a "Defenselink" site (**www.defenselink .mil**) that provides extensive information on national security affairs. It contains the latest Pentagon (Defense Department) news releases; public statements by defense officials; the Secretary of Defense's Annual Report to the President and Congress; facts on U.S. military forces, weapons, and deployments; as well as direct links to the websites maintained by the U.S. Army, Navy, Air Force, and Marine Corps.

  Try This: Go to **www.defense.gov /weekinphotos/weekinphotoslist.aspx** and click on one of the "Week in Photo" albums. After scanning the photos and reading through the captions, identify a handful of tasks the Department of Defense is behind all over the world in any given week.

- **Council on Foreign Relations** The Council on Foreign Relations is an influential private policy-planning organization in the United States that focuses on issues related to foreign policy. Its website (**www.cfr.org**) includes policy discussions and commentaries and summaries of articles appearing in the organization's journal, *Foreign Affairs*.

  Try This: Go to **www.cfr.org/publication /blogs.html?cid=otc-marketinguse-121510** and pick one of the blogs focusing on an area of the world where the Council on Foreign Relations is active. Read a number of the posts and familiarize yourself with the issues of that area and what's being done to combat them, and then discuss.

REVIEW QUIZ

MULTIPLE CHOICE

1. Legal power over internal affairs, freedom from external intervention, and legal recognition by other nations is called _____.
   a. authority
   b. representation
   c. sovereignty
   d. legitimacy

2. The idea that all nations would join together to guarantee one another's territory and independence against aggression by any other nation is a key tenet of the _____.
   a. balance of power system
   b. United Nations Charter
   c. collective security system
   d. Truman Doctrine

3. The political, military, and ideological conflict from 1945 to 1990 between communist nations (led by the USSR) and Western democracies (led by the United States) was called _____.
   a. World War I
   b. World War II
   c. the Cold War
   d. the Vietnam War

4. The attempt to bring order to international relations during the Cold War by creating regional alliances between a superpower and nations of a particular region was called _____.
   a. the balance of power system
   b. regional security
   c. the collective security system
   d. the Truman Doctrine

5. What was the regional alliance of Western democracies to protect themselves against Soviet aggression?
   a. the United Nations
   b. the League of Nations
   c. the Warsaw Pact
   d. NATO

6. What was the foreign policy shaped by the goal of assisting in resistance against "outside pressures," usually in the form of communist movements?
   a. the balance of power system
   b. the regional security system
   c. the collective security system
   d. the Truman Doctrine

7. What was the U.S. program to rebuild the nations of Western Europe in the aftermath of World War II in order to render them less susceptible to communist influence and/or takeover?
   a. the Marshall Plan
   b. the Kennan Theory
   c. the Kissinger Agenda
   d. the Truman Doctrine

8. The ABM treaty agreement and limits on the numbers of offensive missiles is called _____.
   a. SALT I
   b. SALT II
   c. START
   d. the INF Treaty

9. What was the treaty that provided for reduction to three thousand warheads for each side, elimination of all land-based missiles with nuclear warheads, and on-site verification?
   a. SALT I
   b. SALT II
   c. START
   d. the INF Treaty

10. What was President Reagan's research program to develop a defense against ballistic missile attack, sometimes referred to as "Star Wars"?
    a. START
    b. SALT
    c. the Iron Curtain
    d. the strategic defense initiative (SDI)

FILL IN THE BLANK

11. In _____ a minor conflict in the Balkan nations resulted in a very destructive war between the Allies (England, France, Russia, and eventually the United States) and the Central Powers (Germany, Austria-Hungary, and Turkey).

12. The _____ was created in 1945, and originally consisted of fifty-one members including a Security Council with eleven members.

13. Action taken alone rather than as part of a coalition is called _____.

14. A theory proposed by Samuel P. Huntington predicting that conflict between modern, Western democracies and Islamic fundamentalist nations will characterize international relations in the future is called the _____ thesis.

15. The fundamentalist Islamic regime that ruled Afghanistan from 1996 until 2001 is called the _____.

ANSWER KEY:
1. c; 2. c; 3. c; 4. b; 5. d; 6. d; 7. a; 8. b; 9. c; 10. d; 11. World War I; 12. United Nations; 13. unilateral action; 14. clash of civilizations; 15. Taliban.

Chapter 1

1. Bertrand Russell, *Power: A New Social Analysis.* (New York: W.W. Norton & Company, 1968), 11.
2. Harold Lasswell and Abraham Kaplan, *Power and Society* (New Haven, CT: Yale University Press, 1950), 219.
3. C. Wright Mills, *The Power Elite* (New York: Oxford University Press, 1956), 9.
4. Ibid., 10.
5. Russell, op. cit., p. 11.

Chapter 2

1. Chava Frankfort-Nachmias and David Nachmias, *Research Methods in the Social Sciences* (New York: St. Martin's Press, 1996).
2. Babbie Earl, *The Practice of Social Research*, 7th ed. (Belmont, CA: Wadsworth, 1997).
3. Barnard H. Russell, *Research Methods in Cultural Anthropology*, 3rd ed. (Walnut Creek, CA: Alta Mira Press, 2002), 324.
4. Laud Humphreys, *Tearoom Trade: Impersonal Sex in Public Places* (Chicago: Aldine, 1970).

Chapter 3

1. Leon P. Baradat, *Political Ideologies: Their Origin and Impact*, 6th ed. (Upper Saddle River, NJ: Prentice Hall, 2008).
2. Bernard Bailyn, *Ideological Origins of the American Revolution* (Cambridge, MA: Harvard University Press, 1967); Clinton Rossiter, *1787: The Grand Convention* (New York: Macmillan, 1966).
3. Richard Hofstadter, *The American Political Tradition* (New York: Knopf, 1948).

4. Milton Friedman, *Capitalism and Freedom* (Chicago: University of Chicago Press, 1963).
5. For an interesting assessment of liberal thought and why it remains important today, see Alan Wolfe, *The Future of Liberalism* (New York: Knopf, 2009).
6. See William F. Buckley and Charles R. Kesler, *Keeping the Tablets: Modern American Conservative Thought* (New York: Harper & Row, 1988).
7. David E. Campbell and Robert D. Putnam (August 16, 2011), "Crashing the Tea Party," *The New York Times*.
8. Thomas Hobbes, *Leviathan* (1651; New York: Oxford University Press, 1996), ch. 14.
9. See William Ebenstein and Edwin Fogelman, *Today's Isms: Socialism, Capitalism, Fascism, Communism, and Libertarianism*, 11th ed. (Upper Saddle River, NJ: Prentice Hall, 1999).

Chapter 4

1. See Marvin Harris, *Cannibals and Kings: The Origins of Cultures* (New York: Random House, 1977).
2. Barbara Miller, *Cultural Anthropology*, 6th ed. (Upper Saddle River, NJ: Pearson Education, 2012).
3. Ibid.
4. Clyde Kluckhohn and William Kelly, "The Concept of Culture," in *The Science of Man in the World Crisis*, ed. Ralph Linton (New York: Columbia University Press, 1945), 97.
5. See Gary Ferraro and Susan Andreatta, *Cultural Anthropology: An Applied Perspective*, 8th ed. (Belmont, CA: Cengage, 2010).
6. This approach was developed by Bronislaw Malinowski in *A Scientific Theory of Culture and*

Other Essays (Chapel Hill: University of North Carolina Press, 1944).

7. Elvin Hatch, "The Good Side of Relativism," *Journal of Anthropological Research* 53 (1997): 371–381.

8. See the argument presented by Thomas Sowell in "Cultural Diversity: A World View," *The American Enterprise* 2 (May/June 1991): 44–55.

9. Elizabeth M. Zechmeter, "In the Name of Culture: Cultural Relativism and the Abuse of the Individual," *Journal of Anthropological Research* 53 (1997): 319–347; see also Paul C. Rosenblatt, "Human Rights Violations Across Cultures," in *Research Frontiers in Anthropology*, ed. Carol R. Ember et al. (Upper Saddle River, NJ: Prentice Hall, 1998).

10. William W. Stephens, *The Family in Cross-Cultural Perspective* (New York: Holt, Rinehart & Winston, 1963).

11. UNICEF, 2005, *Early Marriage: A Harmful Traditional Practice*. http://www.unicef.org/publications/files/Early_Marriage_12.lo.pdf.

12. See William R. Jankowiak and Edward E. Fischer, "A Cross-Cultural Perspective on Romantic Love," *Ethnology* 31 (1992): 149–155.

13. U.S. Bureau of the Census, *Statistical Abstract of the United States 2009* (Washington, DC: Government Printing Office, 2009).

14. Erik Eckholm. "07 U.S. Births Break Baby Boom Record," *The New York Times*, March 18, 2009. http://www.nytimes.com/2009/03/19/health/19birth.html.

15. Centers for Disease Control and Prevention. http://www.cdc.gov/nchs/fastats/divorce.htm.

16. Carol R. Ember and Melvin Ember, *Cultural Anthropology*, 12th ed. (Englewood Cliffs, NJ: Prentice Hall, 2006), ch. 16.

17. Jonathan Glover and Martha G. Nussbaum, *Women, Culture and Development* (New York: Oxford University Press, 1999), 2.

18. Beatrice B. Whiting and Carolyn P. Edwards, "A Cross-Cultural Analysis of Sex Differences in the Behavior of Children Aged Three through Eleven," *Journal of Social Psychology* 91 (1973): 171–188; Eleanor E. Maccoby and Carol N. Jacklin, *The Psychology of Sex Differences* (Stanford, CA: Stanford University Press, 1974).

19. Marc H. Ross, "Female Political Participation: A Cross-Cultural Explanation," *American Anthropologist* 88 (1986): 841–858.

20. See Frank McGlynn and Arthur Tuden, *Anthropological Approaches in Political Behavior* (Pittsburgh: University of Pittsburgh Press, 1991).

Chapter 5

1. Melvin M. Tumin, *Social Stratification: The Forms and Functions of Social Inequality* (Englewood Cliffs, NJ: Prentice-Hall, 1985); see also Nelson Polsby, *Community Power and Political Theory*, 2nd ed. (New Haven, CT: Yale University Press, 1980); and John Myles and Adnan Turegon, "Comparative Studies in Class Structure," *Annual Review of Sociology* (New York: McGraw-Hill, 1994).

2. Gerhard Lenski, *Power and Privilege* (New York: McGraw-Hill, 1966); Jack Roach, Llewellyn Gross, and Orville R. Gursslin, *Social Stratification in the United States* (Englewood Cliffs, NJ: Prentice-Hall, 1969).

3. Richard Centers, *The Psychology of Social Classes* (Princeton, NJ: Princeton University Press, 1949).

4. Neil J. MacKinnon and Tom Langford, "The Meaning of Occupational Scores," *Sociological Quarterly* 35 (1994): 215–245.

5. Kingsley Davis and Wilbert Moore, "Some Principles of Stratification," *American Sociological Review* 10 (April 1945): 243.

6. See John J. Macionis, *Sociology*, 10th ed. (Upper Saddle River, NJ: Prentice Hall, 2005), ch. 9.

7. Edward N. Wolff, *Top Heavy: A Study of Increasing Inequality of Wealth in America* (New York: Twentieth Century Fund, 1995).

8. C. Wright Mills, "The Structure of Power in American Society," in *Power, Politics and People: The Collected Writings of C. Wright Mills*, ed. Irving L. Horowitz (New York: Oxford University Press, 1963), 24.

9. Nelson Polsby, "The Sociology of Community Power: A Reassessment" Social Forces 37 (March, 1959) pp. 232–236. Reprinted as P.S. 228 Bobbs Merrill Reprint Series in the Social Sciences.

10. Herbert Gans, *The Urban Villagers* (New York: Free Press, 1962), 246; see also Edward C. Banfield, *The Unheavenly City* (Boston: Little, Brown, 1968), ch. 3.

11. Karl Marx, *The Communist Manifesto*, ed. A. J. P. Taylor (New York: Penguin, 1967), 79.

Chapter 6

1. Henry Steele Commager, *The Study of History* (Columbus, OH: Merrill, 1965), 79.
2. Richard Hofstadter, *The American Political Tradition and the Men Who Made It* (New York: Vintage Books, 1956), viii.
3. Frederick Jackson Turner, "The West and American Ideals," in *The Frontier in American History* (New York: Holt, 1921).
4. Hofstadter, *The American Political Tradition*, 109.
5. Turner, "The West and American Ideals," 113.
6. C. Vann Woodward, *Reunion and Reaction* (Boston: Little, Brown, 1951).
7. *Plessy v. Ferguson*, 163 U.S. 537 (1896).
8. Henry Steele Commager, ed., *The Struggle for Racial Equality: A Documentary Record* (New York: Harper & Row, 1967), 19.
9. Hofstadter, *The American Political Tradition*, 323–324.

Chapter 7

1. Harold Lasswell, *Politics: Who Gets What, When and How* (New York: McGraw-Hill, 1936).
2. See Robert A. Dahl, *Democracy and Its Critics* (New Haven, CT: Yale University Press, 1989).
3. See Alan Wolfe, *The Future of Liberalism* (New York: Knopf, 2009).
4. Alexis de Tocqueville, *Democracy in America*, originally published in 1835 (New York: Mentor Books, 1956).
5. See Forrest McDonald, *Novus OrdoSeclorum* (Lawrence: University of Kansas Press, 1985).
6. Herbert J. Storing, ed., *The Anti-Federalist* (Chicago: University of Chicago Press, 1985).
7. *The Federalist Papers* were a series of essays by James Madison, Alexander Hamilton, and John Jay, written in 1787 and 1788 to explain and defend the new Constitution during the struggle over its ratification (*The Federalist*, Number 10, New York: Modern Library, 1937).
8. Samuel H. Beer, *To Make a Nation: The Rediscovery of American Federalism* (Cambridge, MA: Harvard University Press, 1993).
9. James Madison, *The Federalist*, Number 51.
10. See Daniel J. Elazar, *American Federalism: A View from the States* (New York: Crowell, 1966); Thomas R. Dye, *American Federalism: Competition among Governments* (Lexington, MA: Lexington Books, 1990); Paul Peterson, *The Price of Federalism* (Washington, DC: Brookings Institution, 1995).
11. *McCulloch v. Maryland*, 17 U.S. 316 (1819).
12. Theodore J. Lowi, *The Personal President* (Ithaca, NY: Cornell University Press, 1987).
13. Alexander L. George and Julliette L. George, *Presidential Personality and Performance* (Boulder, CO: Westview Press, 1998).
14. See Louis Fisher, *Presidential War Power* (Lawrence: University of Kansas Press, 1995).
15. Charles O. Jones, *The Presidency in a Separated System* (Washington, DC: Brookings Institution, 1994).
16. See Lawrence Baum, *The Supreme Court*, 6th ed. (Washington, DC: CQ Press, 1997).
17. Bernard Schwartz, *A History of the Supreme Court* (New York: Oxford University Press, 1995).
18. *West Virginia State Board of Education v. Barrett*, 319 U.S. 624 (1943).
19. See Margaret M. Conway, *Political Participation in the United States* (Washington, DC: CQ Press, 1991).
20. William H. Flanagan and Nancy H. Zingale, *Political Behavior of the American Electorate* (Washington, DC: CQ Press, 2005).
21. Marjorie Randon Hershey, *Party Politics in America*, 13th ed. (New York: Longman, 2000).
22. Herbert J. McClosky et al., "Issue Conflict and Consensus among Party Leaders and Followers," *American Political Science Review* 54 (June 1960): 595.

Chapter 8

1. See Daniel Yergen and Joseph Stanislaw, *The Commanding Heights: The Battle between Government and the Marketplace That Is Remaking the Modern World* (New York: Simon & Schuster, 1998).
2. However, see Robert Kuttner, *Everything for Sale: The Virtues and Limits of Markets* (New York: Knopf, 1997).
3. Karl E. Case, Ray C. Fair, and Sharon Oster. *Principles of Economics*, 9th ed. (Upper Saddle River, NJ: Prentice Hall, 2008), ch. 6.
4. Adam Smith, *An Inquiry into the Nature and Causes of the Wealth of Nations* (Methuen and Co., Ltd. 1904. Ed. Edwin Cannan), bk. II, ch. 3, para. 36.

5. http://www.faireconomy.org/press/2005/ResponsibleTaxPledgepr.html 3.

6. See U.S. Office of Management and Budget, *A Citizen's Guide to the Federal Budget* (Washington, DC: Government Printing Office, annual).

7. A. A. Berle Jr., *Power without Property* (New York: Harcourt Brace Jovanovich, 1959).

8. U.S. Bureau of the Census, *Statistical Abstract of the United States 2009–2010* (Washington, DC: Government Printing Office, 2009).

9. Michael Porter, *The Comparative Advantage of Nations* (New York: Free Press, 1991).

Chapter 9

1. For a full discussion, see David C. Myers. 2010. *Psychology*, 9th ed. (New York: Worth), ch. 3.

2. John C. Lochlin and Robert C. Nichols, *Heredity, Environment, and Personality* (Austin: University of Texas Press, 1976); and J. C. Lochlin and R. C. McCrae, "Heritabilities of Common Components of Personality," *Journal of Research in Personality* 32 (1998): 431–453.

3. Thomas J. Bouchard, Jr., David T. Lykken, Matthew McGue, Nancy L. Segal, and Auke Tellegen, "Sources of Human Psychological Differences: The Minnesota Study of Twins Reared Apart," *Science* 250 (1990): 223–228.

4. William Wright, *Born That Way: Genes, Behavior, Personality* (New York: Knopf, 1998).

5. Richard A. Lippa, 2002. *Gender, Nature, and Nurture* (Mahwah, NJ: Erlbaum, 2002).

6. Phoebe Dewing, Tao Shi, Steve Horvath, and Eric Vilain, "Sexuality Dimorphic Gene Expression in Mouse Brain Precedes Gonadal Differentiation," *Molecular Brain Research* 21 (2003): 82–90.

7. Carl Costantini and John R. Pehrson, "Histone MacroH2A1 Is Concentrated in the Inactive X Chromosome of Female Mammals," *Nature* 393 (1998): 599–601.

8. John Money, C. Weideking, P. A. Walker, and D. Gain, "Combined Antiandrogenic and Counseling Programs for Treatment for 46 XY and 47 XXY Sex Offenders," *Hormones, Behavior, and Psychopathology*, ed. E. Sacher (New York: Raven Press, 1976).

9. Julian Davidson, "Sexual Emotions, Hormones, and Behavior," *Advances* 6 (1989): 56–58.

10. See Myers, *Psychology*, ch. 11.

11. Albert Bandura, Dorothea Ross, and Sheila A. Ross, "Transmission of Aggression through Imitation of Aggressive Models," *Journal of Abnormal and Social Psychology* 63 (1961), 575–582.

12. T. W. Adorno et al., *The Authoritarian Personality* (New York: Harper, 1950).

13. Abraham H. Maslow, *The Farther Reaches of Human Nature* (New York: Viking Press, 1971), 43.

14. Rollo May, *Power and Innocence* (New York: Norton, 1972).

15. Ibid., 21.

16. Marvin E. Lickey and Barbara Gordon, *Medicine and Mental Illness* (New York: Freeman, 1991).

17. B. P. Dohrenwend et al., "Socioeconomic Status and Psychiatric Disorders," *Science* 255 (1992): 946–952.

Chapter 10

1. The classic essay on the impact of race on American society is Gunnar Myrdal, *An American Dilemma* (New York: HarperCollins, 1944). See also Andrew Hacker, *Two Nations: Black and White, Separate, Hostile, Unequal* (New York: Scribner, 1992).

2. *Brown v. Board of Education of Topeka, Kansas* 347 U.S. 483 (1954).

3. Kenneth B. Clark, *Dark Ghetto: Dilemmas of Social Power* (New York: Harper & Row, 1965), 75.

4. For arguments in support of affirmative action, see Barbara R. Bergman, *In Defense of Affirmative Action* (New York: Basic Books, 1996); and William G. Bowen and Derek Bok, *The Shape of the River* (Princeton, NJ: Princeton University Press, 1998). For arguments in opposition to affirmative action, see Nathan Glazer, *Affirmative Discrimination* (Cambridge, MA: Harvard University Press, 1987); and Stephen Thernstrom and Abigail Thernstrom, *America in Black and White* (New York: Simon & Schuster, 1997).

5. Rudolfo O. de la Garza et al., *Latino Voices: Mexican, Puerto Rican, and Cuban Perspectives on American Politics* (Boulder, CO: Westview, 1992).

6. See F. Chris Garcia, *Latinos in the Political System* (Notre Dame, IN: University of Notre Dame Press, 1988); Rodney Hero, *Latinos and the U.S.*

Political System (Philadelphia: Temple University Press, 1992).

7. Border Protection, Antiterrorism and Illegal Immigration Control Act, H.R. 4437 of 2006.

8. *Sale v. Haitian Centers Council* 125 L. Ed. 2nd 128 (1993).

9. American Security Council, *The Illegal Immigration Crisis* (Washington, DC: ASC, 1994).

10. Charles F. Wilkinson, *American Indians, Times and the Law* (New Haven, CT: Yale University Press, 1987).

11. See Carol R. Ember and Melvin Ember, *Anthropology*, 12th ed. (Upper Saddle River, NJ: Prentice Hall, 2006), ch. 16.

12. Martha C. Nussbaum and Jonathan Glover, *Women, Culture, and Development* (Oxford: Clarendon Press, 1995).

13. Lila Leibowitz, *Females, Males, Families: A Biological Approach* (Duxbury, MA: Duxbury Press, 1978).

14. Quoted in Jay M. Shafritz, *The HarperCollins Dictionary of American Politics* (New York: HarperCollins, 1992), 620.

15. Nancy E. McGlen, Karen O'Conner, Laura van Assendelft, and Wendy Gunther-Canada, *Women, Politics and American Society*, 4th ed. (New York: Longman, 2005).

16. Center for American Women and Politics, *Women in Elected Office Fact Sheet* (New Brunswick, NJ: Eagleton Institute of Politics, Rutgers, The State University of New Jersey). www.cawp.rutgers.edu/fast_facts/levels_of_office/Current_Numbers.php.

17. Kathleen A. Dolan, *Voting for Women: How the Public Evaluates Candidates* (Boulder, CO: Westview, 2004).

18. Barbara C. Burrell, "Women's and Men's Campaign for the U.S. House of Representatives, 1972–1982: A Finance Gap?" *American Politics Quarterly* 13 (1985): 251–272.

19. Richard L. Fox , "Gender, Political Ambition, and the Initial Decision to Run for Office," Center for American Women and Politics, Eagleton Institute of Politics, Rutgers, The State University of New Jersey, 2003. www.cawp.rutgers.edu/research/topics/documents/InitialDecisiontoRun.pdf.

20. Sue Thomas, *How Women Legislate* (New York: Oxford University Press, 1994).

21. *Harris v. McRae* 448 U.S. 297 (1980).

Chapter 11

1. Christopher Jenks and Paul E. Peterson, *The Urban Underclass* (Washington, DC: Brookings Institution, 1991).

2. William A. Kelso, *Poverty and the Underclass* (New York: New York University Press, 1994).

3. Edward C. Banfield, *The Unheavenly City* (Boston: Little, Brown, 1968), ch. 6.

4. Theda Skocpol, *Social Policy in the United States* (Princeton, NJ: Princeton University Press, 1995).

5. Robert C. Ellickson, "The Homelessness Muddle," *The Public Interest* (Spring 1990): 45–60.

6. Peter H. Rossi, *Down and Out in America* (Chicago: University of Chicago Press, 1989).

7. As reported in a survey of twenty-seven cities conducted by the U.S. Conference of Mayors. See *U.S. News & World Report*, January 15, 1990, 27–29.

Chapter 12

1. Thomas Hobbes, *Leviathan*, ed. Michael Oakeshott (New York: Crowell-Collier, 1962).

2. U.S. Department of Justice, *Criminal Victimization in the United States* (Washington, DC: Bureau of Justice Statistics, published annually).

3. See Akil Amar, *The Constitution and Criminal Procedures* (New Haven, CT: Yale University Press, 1997).

4. *Gregg v. Georgia* 428 U.S. 153 (1976).

5. *Furman v. Georgia* 408 U.S. 238 (1972).

6. *Kansas v. Marsh* 2006. (Docket No. 04-1170) 278 Kan. 520, 102 P. 3d 445.

7. Ibid.

8. Chief Justice Warren E. Burger, address on the State of the Federal Judiciary to the American Bar Association, August 10, 1970.

9. Centers for Disease Control and Prevention. *Tobacco Use in the United States.* www.cdc.gov/tobacco/data_statistics/fact_sheets/fast_facts/index.htm#use.

10. Substance Abuse and Mental Health Administration, *National Household Survey on Drug Abuse* (annual). www.oas.samhsa.gov/nhsda.htm.

11. Lynn Zimmer and John P. Morgan, *Marijuana Myths, Marijuana Facts* (New York: Lindesmith Center, 1997).

12. World Prison Brief 2010, International Centre for Prison Studies, *World Prison Brief*, King's

College London – School of Law, London, www.kcl.ac.uk/schools/law/research/icps.

13. See Frank Schmallenger, *Criminal Justice Today*, 10th ed. (Upper Saddle River, NJ: Prentice Hall, 2008).

14. FBI Uniform Crime Reports 2010. *Crime in the United States.* www.fbi.gov/about-us/cjis/ucr/crime-in-the-u.s/2010/crime-in-the-u.s.-2010/about-cius.

15. Jennifer L. Eberhardt, "Looking Deathworthy: Perceived Stereotypicality of Black Defendants Predicts Capital-Sentencing Outcomes," *Psychological Science* 17, no. 5 (2006): 383–386.

16. See Allen Liska and Steven Messner, *Perspectives on Crime and Deviance*, 3rd ed. (Upper Saddle River, NJ: Prentice Hall, 1999).

17. See James Q. Wilson, *Thinking about Crime*, rev. ed. (New York: Basic Books, 1983); James Q. Wilson and Richard J. Herrnstein, *Crime and Human Nature* (New York: Simon & Schuster, 1995).

Chapter 13

1. United Nations: End Poverty 2015. Millennium Development Goals. www.un.org/millenniumgoals/2008highlevel/pdf/newsroom/Goal%201%20FINAL.pdf.

2. MDG Monitor, Tracking the Millennium Goals: An initiative of the United Nations. www.mdgmonitor.org/browse_goal.cfm.

3. United Nations Food and Agriculture Organization (FAO), *The State of Food Insecurity in the World 2005* (SOFI 2005). www.fao.org/docrep/008/a0200e/a0200e00.htm.

4. The United Nations Food and Agriculture Organization (FAO), *The State of Food Insecurity in the World 2003* (SOFI 2003). www.fao.org/docrep/006/j0083e/j0083e00.htm.

5. SOFI 2005.

6. United Nations, press release SG/SM9039: *Secretary-General Kofi Annan, Message on the Occasion of the International Day for the Abolition of Slavery*, December 2, 2003. www.un.org/News/Press/docs/2003/sgsm9039.doc.

7. United Nations, Office of the High Commissioner for Human Rights, *Fact Sheet 14: Contemporary Forms of Slavery*. www.unhchr.ch/html/menu6/2fs14.htm.

8. United Nations, *UNICEF Fact Sheet: Child Labour*. www.unicef.org/protection/files/child_labour.pdf.

9. Ibid.

10. United Nations, *Special Concerns: Child Soldiers: An Affront to Humanity*. www.un.org/rights/concerns.htm (accessed November 27, 2006).

11. United Nations, *The State of the World Population 2000* (New York: United Nations, 2000).

12. www.gatesfoundation.org/annual-letter/Pages/2009-preventing-childhood-deaths.aspx.

13. See Gregg Easterbrook, *A Moment on the Earth: The Coming Age of Environmental Optimism* (New York: Penguin Books, 1995).

14. United Nations, Department of Economic and Social Affairs, Population Division, *World Fertility Report 2008*. www.un.org/esa/population/publications/wpp2006/WPP2006_Highlights_rev.pdf.

15. Ibid.

16. Louis Wirth, "Urbanism as a Way of Life," *American Journal of Sociology* 44 (July 1938).

17. Ibid., 24.

Chapter 14

1. Hans Morgenthau, *Politics among Nations* (New York: Knopf, 1960), 27.

2. See Glenn P. Hastedt, *American Foreign Policy: Past, Present, Future* (Upper Saddle River, NJ: Prentice Hall, 2000).

3. Terms used in Article X of the Covenant of the League of Nations.

4. Michael Mandelbaum, *The Dawn of Peace in Europe* (New York: Twentieth Century Fund, 1996).

5. Thom Shanker. "Defense Secretary Warns NATO of 'Dim' Future," *The New York Times*. June 10. 2011. www.nytimes.com/2011/06/11/world/europe/11gates.html.

6. George F. Kennan, writing under the pseudonym "X", "Sources of Soviet Conduct," *Foreign Affairs* (July 1947): 25.

7. Graham T. Allison, *Essence of Decision* (Boston: Little, Brown, 1971).

8. Robert S. McNamara, *In Retrospect: The Tragedy and Lessons of Vietnam* (New York: Time Books, 1995).

9. See Robert Service, *A History of Twentieth Century Russia* (Cambridge, MA: Harvard University Press, 1998).

10. Testimony of General Colin Powell, Committee on the Budget, U.S. Senate, February 3, 1992.

INDEX

A

Aboriginal Australians, culture of, 79–80
Abortion
  ideology on, 53
  rights to, 15, 194, 320–322
  Roe v. Wade on, 194, 320–321, 322
  sex ratio imbalance due to, 88–89, 129
  state restrictions on, 322, 323
Adams, Abigail, 315
Adams, John, 182
Adams, John Quincy, 182, 183, 190
Addiction disorders, 277. *See also* Substance abuse
  and trafficking
Affirmative action, 15, 53, 295–296,
  299–301, 316
Afghanistan
  Afghanistan War in, 70, 237, 352,
    395–396, 427, 435
  civil war in, 394
  commander-in-chief decisions impacting,
    186–187
  death penalty in, 367
  depression/mental illness in, 276
  establishment of, 394
  least-developed country status
    of, 387
  lifestyle in, 129
  mujaheddin in, 394–395
  NATO role in, 418
  rebuilding of, 395–396
  Soviet presence in, 394, 422, 425
  strife in, 394–396
  Taliban in, 395, 396, 427, 435
  terrorists based in, 395, 396, 427
Africa. *See also specific countries*
  child labor in, 398
  child soldiers in, 398, 399
  food and water scarcity in, 340–341, 388–389
  HIV/AIDS in, 88, 389–390, 391
  less-developed countries in, 128–129,
    385, 387
  malaria in, 390, 392
  marital age in, 87, 90
  political power in, 100
  population of, 401
  poverty in, 385
  urbanization of, 404–405
African Americans
  affirmative action for, 15, 53, 295–296,
    299–301
  civil rights movement of, 15,
    292–297, 352
  continuing inequalities for, 295–296
  crime involving, 378–379
  death penalty applied to, 364, 368,
    370, 379

desegregation of, 177, 193, 292, 293
education of, 113, 153–154, 193, 295, 301
emancipation of, 150, 290
genetic testing of, 258
income and wages of, 295
mental illness among, 275
political involvement of, 151, 154–155
poverty of, 295, 334–335, 337
racism against, 14, 15, 290–311 (*see also*
  Segregation; Slavery)
Reconstruction-era changes for, 150–155
segregation of, 150, 151–155, 177, 193,
  290–292, 293
slavery of, 144–145, 147–150, 151, 290
voting patterns/voter turnout of, 22–23, 25,
  200, 206
voting rights of, 150–151, 154
Age
  abortion relationship to, 322
  crime relationship to, 379
  marital, 87, 90, 92–93
  mental illness relative to, 275
  poverty relationship to, 334–335, 336–337
  voting patterns/voter turnout relative to,
    199, 206
Age of Reason, 44–45
Ahmadinejad, Mahmoud, 432
AIDS. *See* HIV/AIDS
Akan, chiefdom of, 100
Albania, NATO role in, 418
Alcohol abuse. *See* Substance abuse and
  trafficking
Aldrich, Nelson, 156
Algeria, nuclear weapons status of, 433
Alito, Samuel, 177, 195
Ally Financial, 242
al Qaeda, 395, 426, 427–428, 435
American Anthropological Association, 106
American Conservative Union, 68
American Convention on Human Rights, 366
American Enterprise Institute, 68
American Express Corp., 242
American Indian Movement, 311
American International Group (AIG), 244
American Psychiatric Association, 277
American Psychological Association, 281, 285
American Recovery and Reinvestment Act (2009),
  232, 235
Americans for Democratic Action, 68
American Sociological Association, 117, 136
Americans with Disabilities Act (1990),
  322, 324
Amin, Hafizullah, 394
Amnesty International, 366, 423
Anderson, John, 23
Angola
  least-developed country status of, 387

lifestyle in, 129
Annan, Kofi, 393
Anomie, urban, 406
Anthony, Susan B., 315
Anthropology
  archaeological, 11, 74, 83
  artifacts in, 74, 83
  beliefs in, 78, 80
  biological and physical, 11, 74–75
  components of culture studied in, 77–83
  cultural relativity in, 86
  definition of, 11
  economic influences studied in, 73–74, 78,
    84, 86, 87, 90, 91, 92–93, 95, 98, 99,
    101–103
  ethnographic studies in, 38–39
  examination of power in, 74–75
  familial authority and culture in, 12, 72–74,
    87–96, 99–100
  field research in, 37, 38–39
  functionalist perspective in, 83–84
  gender issues studied in, 78, 87, 88–89, 91,
    96–98
  idealist perspective in, 85–86
  Internet resources on, 106
  linguistic, 11, 75
  marriage studied in, 73, 80, 84, 87, 90–96
  materialist perspective in, 84–85
  nature of culture studied in, 83–86
  norms in, 78, 80, 81, 83
  origins of power in, 72–74
  political studies in, 97, 98, 99–101
  power and, 11–12, 72–104
  religion in, 78, 80–81, 82
  sanctions in, 72, 81, 83
  socio-cultural, 11, 75
  symbols in, 77–78
  values in, 78
  wars and warfare studied in, 73–74, 97, 98,
    100–101, 102
  ways of life studied in, 75–77
Anti-Federalists, 169
Antigua and Barbuda
  death penalty in, 367
  national debt of, 238
Anti-Semitism, 60–61
Antisocial personality disorder, 374–376
Antiwar protests, 159
Anxiety disorders, 279
Apodaca v. Oregon, 361
Approval ratings, presidential, 180, 182–185
Arab Spring/Jasmine Revolution, 2, 408, 424
Archaeology, 11, 74, 83
Argentina, nuclear weapons status of, 433
Art, culture expressed through, 80
Arthur, Chester A., 183
Artifacts, anthropological study of, 74, 83

Roosevelt, Theodore, 153, 182
Roots (Haley), 150
Roper Center for Public Opinion
 Research, 41
Rotavirus, 392–393
Royal Dutch Shell, 247
Rusk, Dean, 421
Russell, Bertrand, 4–5, 10
Russia. *See also* Soviet Union, former
 communism in, 62–64
 culture in, 82, 101
 immigrants from, 305
 nations in, 101
 nuclear weapons of, 430, 433
 post-communist, 423–424
 religion in, 82
 United Nations role of, 415, 416
 World War I role of, 413
Rwanda, least-developed country
 status of, 387
Ryan, George, 367

S

Saint Kitts and Nevis
 death penalty in, 367
 national debt of, 238
Saint Lucia
 death penalty in, 367
 national debt of, 238
Saint Vincent and the Grenadines
 death penalty in, 367
 national debt of, 238
Samoa, least-developed country
 status of, 387
Sampling errors, 33, 35
Samsung Electronics, 247
Sanctions
 anthropological study of, 72, 81, 83
 death penalty as, 362–365, 366–367,
  368–369, 370, 379
 Iran-Libya Sanctions Act on, 432
 nonviolent protests seeking, 296–297
 United Nations', 416–417
São Tomé and Principe, least-developed
 country status of, 387
Saudi Arabia
 culture in, 78, 89, 98, 102–103
 death penalty in, 366, 367, 369
 gender-based differences in, 98
 power in, political and government,
  102–103
 sex ratio imbalance in, 89
Scalia, Antonin, 177, 195
Scandals
 corporate, 244
 political, 160, 185
Schizophrenia, 278
Schools and education
 African Americans in, 113, 153–154, 193,
  295, 301
 Asian Americans in, 113, 303
 criminal reform via, 375
 drug education, 373
 Hispanic Americans in, 113, 302
 income relationship to, 112–113
 industrialized societies', 91–92
 institutional power of, 7
 legislation impacting, 179
 poverty impacting, 337
 Saudi Arabian, 103
 segregation in, 153, 154, 177,
  291–292, 293
 separation of church and state in, 53, 177
 social class relationship to, 112–113, 124
 sociological study of, 14, 112–113, 124

Scientific method
 case study using, 31–32, 39
 classic scientific research design in,
  27, 30–32
 data sources and collection in, 24,
  32–39, 41
 deductive and inductive reasoning in, 21–22
 definition of, 20
 explaining relationships in, 20–21
 fact determination in, 26–27
 field research in, 33, 37–39
 hypothesis development and testing in, 21,
  22–25, 39
 limitations of conducting research in, 29
 logical fallacies in, 29
 null hypothesis in, 30
 observable phenomena in, 25
 public attitudes in, 28
 research design constraints in, 29
 researcher attitudes in, 28–29
 researcher bias in, 28
 sampling errors in, 33, 35
 science, defined in, 20
 scientific attitude maintained in, 26
 social science studies using, 20–39
  (*see also* Research)
 survey research in, 32–37, 41 (*see also*
  Polling data)
 theory development in, 25–26
 universal *vs.* probabilistic statements in,
  26–27
 vocabulary of, 21
Second Amendment, 170
Segregation, 150, 151–155, 177, 193, 2
 90–292, 293
Self-actualization, 272–273
Self-awareness, 269, 272
Self-Determination and Education Assistance Act
 (1975), 311
Self-esteem, 273, 274
Senate. *See* Congress
Senegal
 food and water scarcity in, 340
 least-developed country status of, 387
Sensenbrenner, James, 305
September 11, 2001 terrorist attacks, 181, 230,
 281, 304, 395, 418, 426–427
Seventeenth Amendment, 172, 197
Seventh Amendment, 170
Seward, William H., 148
Sex, biological. *See also* Gender
 genetics determining, 257
 sex-based differences in power, 96–97,
  313–314
 sex ratio imbalance by, 88–89, 129
Sexism, 14, 15, 312–322. *See also* Gender
Sexual harassment, 318–320
Sexuality
 evolutionary psychology on mating
  and, 264
 gender differences in relation to,
  264, 314
 nature and nurture impacting, 257
 political sex scandals, 185
 slavery for sexual exploitation, 393,
  397–398
 women's movement influencing, 92–93
Sexual orientation. *See also* Gays and lesbians
 cultural beliefs on, 78
 fascist ideology on, 61
 inequality based on, 15, 324–325
Shah, Zahir, 394
Sierra Leone
 death penalty in, 367
 food and water scarcity in, 340
 least-developed country status of, 387

Singapore
 death penalty in, 367
 economy of, 65
 national debt of, 238
Sinopec Group, 247
Sitting Bull, Chief, 310
Sixth Amendment, 170, 357, 360, 361, 365
Skinner, B. F., 14
Slavery
 child labor in, 398
 child soldiers in, 398, 399
 Civil War involving, 147–150, 290
 Constitution on, 144–145, 148
 debt bondage as, 399–400
 Emancipation Proclamation on, 150, 290
 global problem of, 393, 397–400
 international conventions on, 400
 sexual exploitation in, 393, 397–398
 Supreme Court on, 148, 177
 Thirteenth Amendment abolishing, 144,
  151, 290
Slovakia
 NATO role of, 418
 women in workforce in, 94
Slovenia, NATO role of, 418
Smith, Adam, 45, 221–222
Smithsonian Institution, 163
SNCC (Student Nonviolent Coordinating
 Committee), 294
Social class
 American societal, 109–113, 117–124,
  131–133
 class consciousness, 127, 129–131
 class struggle and conflict, 57, 127–133
 communist ideology on, 57–58, 130–131
 conflict theory on, 114–115
 definition of, 109
 economics and income relationship to,
  14, 108–109, 110, 112–113, 117–121,
  122–124
 education relationship to, 112–113, 124
 employment relationship to, 110–112, 122,
  124, 126–127, 134
 functional theory on, 114
 less-developed countries', 128–129
 lifestyle determined by, 124–127,
  128–129, 133
 lower class as, 109–110, 127
 middle class as, 109–110, 122, 124, 126
 objective identification of, 112–113
 politics relationship to, 125, 126, 127, 133–134,
  199–200
 postmodernism on, 117
 power and, 14, 108–135
 race and ethnicity relationship to, 113
 reputational prestige impacting, 110–112
 self-classification by, 109–110
 social mobility among, 121–124, 133,
  406–407
 social stratification via, 14, 108–113
 sociology as study of, 14, 108–135, 403–407
 symbolic interaction theory on, 115–117
 upper class as, 109–110, 125–126, 133–134
 voter turnout relative to, 199–200
 working class as, 126–127
Social contracts, 45, 51, 167
Social Darwinism, 155
Socialism, 7, 50, 54, 58–59, 60
Socialization, 266, 269–270
Social learning theory, 261–262
Social mobility, 121–124, 133, 406–407
Social problems. *See also* each subtopic
 for details
 crime as, 14, 15–16, 352–380, 406
 globalization and global community
  relationship to, 14, 16, 383–409